MCTS: Microsoft Exchar Configuration Study Gui

Exam 70-236: TS: Microsoft Exchange Server 2007, Configuring

OBJECTIVE	CHAPTER
Installing and Configuring Microsoft Exchange Servers	
Prepare the infrastructure for Exchange installation.	2, 3
Prepare the servers for Exchange installation.	2
Install Exchange.	3, 4, 5, 10
Configure Exchange server roles.	4, 5
Configuring Recipients and Public Folders	
Configure recipients.	6
Configure mail-enabled groups.	6
Configure resource mailboxes.	6
Configure public folders.	6
Move mailboxes.	9
Implement bulk management of mail-enabled objects.	9
Configuring the Exchange Infrastructure	
Configure connectors.	4
Configure the antivirus and anti-spam system.	5
Configure transport rules and message compliance.	7
Configure policies.	7
Configure public folders.	8
Configure client connectivity.	8
Monitoring and Reporting	
Monitor mail queues.	9
Monitor system performance.	12
Perform message tracking.	9
Monitor client connectivity.	8

Sybex®
An Imprint of

OBJECTIVE	CHAPTER
Create server reports.	12
Create usage reports.	12
Configuring Disaster Recovery	
Configure backups.	11
Recover messaging data.	11
Recover server roles.	11
Configure high availability.	10

Exam objectives are subject to change at any time without prior notice and at Microsoft's sole discretion. Please visit Microsoft's website (`www.microsoft.com/learning`) for the most current listing of exam objectives.

Sybex®
An Imprint of
WILEY

MCTS
Microsoft® Exchange Server 2007 Configuration
Study Guide
(Exam 70-236)

Will Schmied
Kevin Miller

Wiley Publishing, Inc.

Acquisitions Editor: Jeff Kellum
Development Editor: Lisa Bishop
Technical Editor: Rodney Fournier
Production Editor: Eric Charbonneau
Copy Editor: Kim Wimpsett
Production Manager: Tim Tate
Vice President and Executive Group Publisher: Richard Swadley
Vice President and Executive Publisher: Joseph B. Wikert
Vice President and Publisher: Neil Edde
Media Project Supervisor: Laura Atkinson
Media Development Specialist: Kit Malone
Media Quality Assurance: Angela Deny
Book Designer: Judy Fung
Compositor: Craig Woods, Happenstance Type-O-Rama
Proofreader: Nancy Riddiough
Indexer: Ted Laux
Anniversary Logo Design: Richard Pacifico
Cover Designer: Ryan Sneed

Published by Wiley Publishing, Inc., Indianapolis, Indiana

Published simultaneously in Canada

ISBN: 978-0-470-06819-9

Library of Congress Cataloging-in-Publication Data is available from the publisher.

10 9 8 7 6 5 4 3 2 1

Dear Reader

Thank you for choosing *MCTS: Microsoft Exchange Server 2007 Configuration Study Guide (70-236)*. This book is part of a family of premium quality Sybex books, all written by outstanding authors who combine practical experience with a gift for teaching.

Sybex was founded in 1976. More than thirty years later, we're still committed to producing consistently exceptional books. With each of our titles we're working hard to set a new standard for the industry. From the paper we print on, to the authors we work with, our goal is to bring you the best books available.

I hope you see all that reflected in these pages. I'd be very interested to hear your comments and get your feedback on how we're doing. Feel free to let me know what you think about this or any other Sybex book by sending me an email at `nedde@wiley.com`, or if you think you've found a technical error in this book, please visit `http://sybex.custhelp.com`. Customer feedback is critical to our efforts at Sybex.

Best regards,

Neil Edde
Vice President and Publisher
Sybex, an Imprint of Wiley

To my wonderful and very understanding family: Thank you for your support on all those late nights and long weekends.
—Will Schmied

I would just like to thank my wife, Coraleigh, for her help and support in writing. It would not have been possible for me without her.
—Kevin Miller

Acknowledgments

I would like to thank all of the outstanding staff at Wiley Publishing, especially Lisa Brown, Jeff Kellum and Maureen Adams who brought this project to life. Thanks to contributing authors Russ Kaufman and Kevin Miller for the wonderful assistance in pulling together this project. Lastly, many thanks to Rodney Fournier, the hardest working Tech Editor I've had the pleasure to work with.

About the Authors

Will Schmied, BSET, MCITP, MCSE, MCTS, MCSA, CWNA, TICSA, Security+, Network+, A+, is a Senior Systems Administrator for a world renowned children's research hospital. As a freelance writer, Will has worked with many publishers, including Microsoft and Wiley. Will has also worked directly with Microsoft in the exam-development process on multiple occasions occasions and holds a Bachelor's degree in mechanical engineering technology from Old Dominion University, along with his various IT industry certifications. Before becoming a civilian, he served in the United States Navy for over 12 years in the nuclear power field.

Kevin Miller is an Exchange architect currently working for 3Sharp after leaving the Exchange team at Microsoft and the professional services consulting arm of Dell. Kevin has been involved with Exchange since the beginning, pre-Microsoft, when it was known as Network Courier. Before joining the Exchange team at Microsoft, Kevin was an Exchange MVP for a number of years and is still very involved in the Exchange communities. Kevin currently resides in Woodinville, Washington, with his wife Coraleigh and his son Trenton.

Contents at a Glance

Introduction		*xix*
Assessment Test		*xxxi*
Chapter 1	Exchange Server 2007 and Active Directory Review	1
Chapter 2	Preparing for the Exchange Server 2007 Installation	29
Chapter 3	Installing Exchange Server 2007	75
Chapter 4	Configuring Exchange Server Roles	123
Chapter 5	Configuring the Exchange Security Infrastructure	207
Chapter 6	Configuring and Managing Exchange Recipients	259
Chapter 7	Configuring Exchange Server Rules and Policies	341
Chapter 8	Configuring and Managing Client Connectivity and Public Folders	373
Chapter 9	Managing and Maintaining the Exchange Organization	435
Chapter 10	Creating, Managing Highly Available Exchange Server Solutions	475
Chapter 11	Disaster Recovery Operations for Exchange Server	535
Chapter 12	Monitoring and Reporting on the Exchange Server Infrastructure	577
Glossary		605
Index		*631*

Contents

Introduction *xix*

Assessment Test *xxxi*

Chapter 1 **Exchange Server 2007 and Active Directory Review** **1**

What's New in Exchange Server 2007? 2
What's No Longer Supported in Exchange Server 2007 4
Features That Have Been Removed or Replaced 5
Features That Have Been Deemphasized 6
Active Directory in Windows Server 2003 Review 6
Active Directory in Windows Server 2003 7
Active Directory and Exchange Server 2007 15
Summary 19
Exam Essentials 20
Review Questions 22
Answers to Review Questions 26

Chapter 2 **Preparing for the Exchange Server 2007 Installation29**

Exchange Server 2007 Editions and Licensing 30
Standard Edition Features 30
Additional Enterprise Edition Features 31
Exchange Server 2007 Compared to Previous Versions 31
Licensing Issues 32
Exchange Server 2007 Roles 34
Mailbox Server 34
Hub Transport Server 34
Client Access Server 35
Edge Transport Server 36
Unified Messaging Server 36
Preinstallation Server and Network Considerations 37
Verifying System Requirements 37
Verifying Windows Services and Components 45
Installing the Security Configuration Wizard 48
Verifying Name Resolution 48
Running Network and Domain Controller Diagnostics Tests 49
Configuring Storage for Exchange Server 2007 50
Preinstallation Modification of Active Directory 54
Verifying Domain and Forest Functional Levels 56
Preparing a Windows Active Directory Forest 57
Preparing the Root Windows Active Directory Domain 59

Preparing Other Windows Active Directory Domains 61
Modifying Existing Exchange Organizations to Support Migration 63
Summary 66
Exam Essentials 66
Review Questions 68
Answers to Review Questions 72

Chapter 3 Installing Exchange Server 2007 75

Choosing the Exchange Roles to Install 76
Installing Exchange Server 2007 77
Performing GUI-Based Installations 77
Performing Command-Line and Unattended Installations of Exchange Server 2007 87
Verifying the Installation of Exchange Server 2007 91
Securing Exchange Server 2007 with the Security Configuration Wizard 99
Configuring the Exchange Administrator Roles 109
Introducing the Exchange Server 2007 Administrative Roles 109
Configuring Administrative Roles 110
Summary 115
Exam Essentials 115
Review Questions 117
Answers to Review Questions 121

Chapter 4 Configuring Exchange Server Roles 123

Configuring the Mailbox Server 124
Understanding the Exchange Storage Structure 124
Configuring Storage Groups and Mailbox Databases 127
Configuring the Hub Transport Server 148
Understanding the Message Routing Process 149
Configuring Hub Transport 150
Configuring the Client Access Server 178
Understanding the Client Access Process 178
Configuring Client Access 179
Changing Roles and Removing Servers from the Exchange Organization 197
Adding and Removing Server Roles 198
Removing Exchange Servers from the Exchange Organization 198
Summary 198
Exam Essentials 199
Review Questions 200
Answers to Review Questions 204

Chapter 5 Configuring the Exchange Security Infrastructure 207

Configuring the Edge Transport Server 208
- Configuring and Managing EdgeSync 209
- Configuring and Managing Antispam Settings 217
- Using Edge Cloning 232

Configuring Microsoft Forefront Security for Exchange Server 234
- Installing Forefront Security for Exchange Server 235
- Configuring Forefront for Exchange Server 240

Summary 250
Exam Essentials 250
Review Questions 251
Answers to Review Questions 256

Chapter 6 Configuring and Managing Exchange Recipients 259

Configuring User Accounts and Mailboxes 261
- Mailbox-Enabled vs. Mail-Enabled 261
- Managing User Accounts and Mailboxes 261
- Modifying Mailbox-Enabled User Accounts 272
- Working with Deleted Mailboxes 283
- Managing Mail-Enabled User Accounts 287
- Managing Mail Users 290
- Configuring Send As Permissions 293

Configuring Mail-Enabled Groups 295
- Understanding Group Types and Scopes 295
- Managing Mail-Enabled Groups 297
- Modifying Distribution Groups 303
- Managing Dynamic Distribution Groups 309
- Modifying Dynamic Distribution Groups 312

Configuring Mail Contacts 314
- Creating Contacts with the Exchange Management Console 315
- Modifying Mail Contacts 319

Configuring Resource Mailboxes 321
- Creating Resource Mailboxes with the Exchange Management Console 322
- Creating Accounts and Mailboxes with the Exchange Management Shell 323
- Modifying Resource Mailboxes 324

Summary 328
Exam Essentials 329
Review Questions 330
Answers to Review Questions 338

Chapter 7 Configuring Exchange Server Rules and Policies 341

Configuring Message Compliance and Record Management 342
- Configuring Managed Folders 344
- Configuring Managed Content Settings 346
- Configuring Managed Folder Mailbox Policies 346
- Configuring the Managed Folder Assistant 350
- Configuring Rights Management Service (RMS) Exchange Agents 351
- Configuring Message Classifications 351

Configuring Transport Rules 354
- Configuring Email Address–Generation Policies 356
- Configuring Address Lists 359

Configuring Mobile Device Policies 361
Summary 364
Exam Essentials 364
Review Questions 365
Answers to Review Questions 370

Chapter 8 Configuring and Managing Client Connectivity and Public Folders 373

Managing Public Folders 374
- Creating the Public Folder Database 375
- Exploring the Public Folder Management Options 376
- Working with the Public Folder Hierarchy 389

Configuring Client Connectivity 403
- Using Autodiscover 403
- Supporting POP3 and IMAP4 Clients 410
- Configuring Windows Mobile Devices and ActiveSync 414

Summary 426
Exam Essentials 427
Review Questions 428
Answers to Review Questions 432

Chapter 9 Managing and Maintaining the Exchange Organization 435

Managing Mail Queues and Message Tracking 436
- Introducing the Exchange Queues 436
- Managing Exchange Queues and Queued Items 437
- Managing Message Tracking 448

Moving Mailboxes 453
- Using the Exchange Management Console 454
- Using the Exchange Management Shell 456

Performing Bulk Management 459
- Moving Mailboxes 459
- Creating Mailboxes 460

Populating Groups 463
Viewing Mailbox Sizes 464
Summary 466
Exam Essentials 467
Review Questions 468
Answers to Review Questions 473

Chapter 10 Creating, Managing Highly Available Exchange Server Solutions 475

Installing Server Clustering 478
Installing and Configuring Cluster Hardware 479
Hooking Up the Hardware 479
Installing and Configuring the Operating System 481
Configuring the Cluster Service 484
Installing and Configuring Network Load Balancing 489
Installing and Configuring the Network Load Balancing Driver 491
Using DNS Round-Robin 497
Configuring Local Continuous Replication 497
Preparing for Local Continuous Replication 499
Enabling Local Continuous Replication 500
Disabling Local Continuous Replication 502
Seeding a Local Continuous Replication Copy 503
Testing the Health of the Local Continuous Copy Process 505
Switching to the Copy Database 505
Configuring Single Copy Cluster 506
Meeting Basic Requirements for Single Copy Cluster 507
Installing SCC 508
Configuring Cluster Continuous Replication 512
Configuring Majority Node Set 513
File Share Witness 515
Introducing CCR 516
Installing CCR Cluster 519
Dealing with CCR Outages 521
Summary 525
Exam Essentials 525
Review Questions 527
Answers to Review Questions 532

Chapter 11 Disaster Recovery Operations for Exchange Server 535

What Is Disaster Recovery? 536
Avoiding Disasters and Reacting to Them 537
Avoiding Data Loss 538
Reacting to Disasters 539

Configuring Backups 541
Creating, Modifying, and Performing Backup Jobs 545
Monitoring and Validating Backup Jobs 547
Repairing a Damaged Exchange Database 548
Recovering Messaging Data 554
Recovering Messages with Deleted Items Retention 555
Recovering Deleted Mailboxes with Deleted Mailbox Retention 556
Recovering Mailbox Databases 559
Backing Up and Recovering Different Server Roles 562
Backing Up and Recovering a Client Access Server 563
Backing Up and Recovering a Hub Transport server 564
Backing Up and Recovering an Edge Transport server 565
Backing Up and Recovering a Mailbox Server 567
Summary 567
Exam Essentials 567
Review Questions 569
Answers to Review Questions 574

Chapter 12 Monitoring and Reporting on the Exchange Server Infrastructure 577

Monitoring System Performance 578
Monitoring Server Services 578
Monitoring Performance 583
Using the Exchange Performance Troubleshooter 586
Monitoring Hardware 589
Creating Server and Usage Reports 589
Creating Health Reports 589
Creating Availability Reports 592
Creating Database and Message Queue Reports 594
Creating Mailbox and User Usage Reports 596
Summary 600
Exam Essentials 600
Review Questions 601
Answers to Review Questions 603

Glossary 605

Index 631

Table of Exercises

Exercise	**2.1**	Installing Required Services and Components	45
Exercise	**2.2**	Installing the Security Configuration Wizard	48
Exercise	**2.3**	Verifying the Domain and Forest Functional Levels	56
Exercise	**2.4**	Running the /PrepareSchema Command	58
Exercise	**2.5**	Running the /PrepareAD Command	59
Exercise	**2.6**	Running the /PrepareDomain Command	62
Exercise	**2.7**	Running the /PrepareLegacyExchangePermissions Command	64
Exercise	**3.1**	Installing Exchange Server 2007 from the Graphical User Interface	78
Exercise	**3.2**	Performing Post-installation Configuration of Exchange Server 2007	84
Exercise	**3.3**	Installing the Security Configuration Wizard	99
Exercise	**3.4**	Using the Security Configuration Wizard to Configure Exchange Server security	101
Exercise	**3.5**	Adding Administrative Roles	111
Exercise	**4.1**	Creating a New Storage Group	128
Exercise	**4.2**	Changing Storage Group Paths	134
Exercise	**4.3**	Creating a New Mailbox Store	137
Exercise	**4.4**	Creating and Configuring the Postmaster Mailbox	154
Exercise	**4.5**	Creating a Remote Domain	157
Exercise	**4.6**	Creating an Accepted Domain	161
Exercise	**4.7**	Creating an SMTP Send Connector	164
Exercise	**4.8**	Creating an SMTP Receive Connector	170
Exercise	**4.9**	Configuring SharePoint and File Server Access	180
Exercise	**4.10**	Disabling SharePoint and File Server Integration with OWA	182
Exercise	**4.11**	Installing a Third-Party SSL Certificate	192
Exercise	**5.1**	Creating a New Edge Subscription	214
Exercise	**5.2**	Installing Forefront Security for Exchange Server	235
Exercise	**6.1**	Creating a New Mailbox-Enabled User	263
Exercise	**6.2**	Mailbox-Enabling an Existing User	266
Exercise	**6.3**	Creating a New User Account in Active Directory Users and Computers	270
Exercise	**6.4**	Connecting a Disconnected Mailbox	285
Exercise	**6.5**	Creating a New Mail-Enabled User	287
Exercise	**6.6**	Mail-Enabling an Existing User	288

Exercise 6.7 Configuring Send As Permissions on a Mailbox . . . 293
Exercise 6.8 Creating a New Distribution Group . . . 298
Exercise 6.9 Mail-Enabling an Existing Security Group. . . . 299
Exercise 6.10 Creating a New Group in Active Directory . . . 302
Exercise 6.11 Creating a New Distribution Group . . . 310
Exercise 6.12 Creating a New Mail Contact . . . 316
Exercise 6.13 Mail-Enabling an Existing Contact . . . 317
Exercise 6.14 Creating a New Contact in Active Directory Users and Computers . . 318
Exercise 6.15 Creating a New Resource Mailbox. . . . 322
Exercise 7.1 Creating a Managed Folder Using the Exchange Management Console . . . 345
Exercise 7.2 Creating a Managed Folder Using the Exchange Management Shell . 346
Exercise 7.3 Creating a Managed Content Setting Using the Exchange Management Console . . . 347
Exercise 7.4 Creating a Managed Content Setting Using the Exchange Management Shell . . . 348
Exercise 7.5 Creating a Managed Folder Mailbox Policy Using the Exchange Management Shell . . . 348
Exercise 7.6 Creating a Managed Folder Mailbox Policy Using the Exchange Management Shell . . . 349
Exercise 7.7 Applying a Managed Folder Mailbox Policy Using the Exchange Management Console . . . 349
Exercise 7.8 Applying a Managed Folder Mailbox Policy Using Exchange Management Shell . . . 349
Exercise 7.9 Scheduling the Managed Folder Assistant Using the Exchange Management Console . . . 350
Exercise 7.10 Scheduling the Managed Folder Assistant Using the Exchange Management Shell . . . 351
Exercise 7.11 Creating a New Transport Rule Using the Exchange Management Console . . . 355
Exercise 7.12 Creating a New Transport Rule Using the Exchange Management Shell . . . 356
Exercise 7.13 Creating a New Email Address Policy Using the Exchange Management Console . . . 358
Exercise 7.14 Creating a New Email Address Policy Using the Exchange Management Shell . . . 359
Exercise 7.15 Creating a New Address List Using the Exchange Management Console . . . 360

Exercise 7.16 Creating a New Address List Using the Exchange Management Shell . 361
Exercise 7.17 Creating an ActiveSync Mailbox Policy Using the Exchange Management Console 362
Exercise 7.18 Creating an ActiveSync Mailbox Policy Using the Exchange Management Shell 363
Exercise 8.1 Creating a New Public Folder Database 376
Exercise 8.2 Creating New Public Folders with Outlook 382
Exercise 8.3 Creating Public Folder Replicas. 394
Exercise 8.4 Installing an SSL Certificate 410
Exercise 8.5 Assigning an ActiveSync Policy to a User 419
Exercise 8.6 Configuring ActiveSync on a Mobile Device 420
Exercise 8.7 Wiping a Mobile Device 425
Exercise 9.1 Moving a Mailbox with the Exchange Management Console 454
Exercise 10.1 Installing and Configuring the Cluster Service 484
Exercise 10.2 Using the Exchange Management Console to Configure LCR for an Existing Storage Group 500
Exercise 10.3 Using the Exchange Management Shell (PowerShell) to Configure LCR for an Existing Storage Group 501
Exercise 10.4 Using the Exchange Management Console to Create a Storage Group and Enable It for LCR 501
Exercise 10.5 Using the Exchange Management Shell (PowerShell) to Create a Storage Group and Enable It for LCR. 502
Exercise 10.6 Using the Exchange Management Console to Disable LCR 502
Exercise 10.8 Seeding the LCR Database Using the Exchange Management Shell . 503
Exercise 10.7 Using the Exchange Management Shell to Disable LCR. 503
Exercise 10.9 Seeding the LCR Database Using the Exchange Management Console 504
Exercise 10.10 Testing Health of LCR Using Exchange Management Console 505
Exercise 10.11 Recovering from Corrupt Database to the Copy 506
Exercise 10.12 Installing SCC on Active Node and on Passive Node Computers Using the Exchange Management Shell 508
Exercise 10.13 Installing SCC on Active Node and on Passive Node Computers Using the Exchange Management Console 509
Exercise 10.14 Installing a Two-Node MNS Cluster 514
Exercise 10.15 Implementing File Share Witness 516
Exercise 10.16 Identifying Current Transport Dumpster Settings 517
Exercise 10.17 Setting Transport Dumpster Settings 518

Exercise 10.18 Installing a CCR Cluster . . . 519

Exercise 11.1 Backing Up the Exchange Server Mailbox Database with Windows Server Backup . . . 545

Exercise 11.2 Recovering Deleted Items in Outlook Web Access . . . 555

Exercise 11.3 Recovering Deleted Items in Outlook . . . 555

Exercise 11.4 Recovering a Deleted Mailbox Using the Exchange Management Console . . . 556

Exercise 11.5 Recovering a Deleted Mailbox Using the Exchange Management Shell . . . 558

Exercise 11.6 Recovering an Exchange Database . . . 561

Exercise 11.7 Backing Up an Edge Transport server . . . 566

Exercise 11.8 Restoring an Edge Transport server . . . 566

Exercise 12.1 Using the Exchange Performance Troubleshooter . . . 586

Exercise 12.2 Creating a Health Report . . . 590

Introduction

Microsoft has recently changed its certification program to contain three primary series: Technology, Professional, and Architect. The Technology series of certifications are intended to allow candidates to target specific technologies and are the basis for obtaining the Professional series and Architect series of certifications. The certifications contained within the Technology series consist of one to three exams, focus on a specific technology, and do not include job-role skills. By contrast, the Professional series of certifications focus on a job role and are not necessarily focused on a single technology but rather a comprehensive set of skills for performing the job role being tested. The Architect series of certifications offered by Microsoft are premier certifications that consist of passing a review board consisting of previously certified architects. To apply for the Architect series of certifications, you must have a minimum of 10 years of industry experience.

When obtaining a Technology series certification, you are recognized as a Microsoft Certified Technology Specialist (MCTS) on the specific technology or technologies on which you have been tested. The Professional series certifications include Microsoft Certified IT Professional (MCITP) and Microsoft Certified Professional Developer (MCPD). Passing the review board for an Architect series certification will allow you to become a Microsoft Certified Architect (MCA).

This book has been developed to give you the critical skills and knowledge you need to prepare for the 70-236 exam requirement for obtaining the MCTS: Configuring Exchange Server 2007.

The Microsoft Certified Professional Program

Since the inception of its certification program, Microsoft has certified more than two million people. As the computer network industry continues to increase in both size and complexity, this number is sure to grow—and the need for *proven* ability will also increase. Certifications can help companies verify the skills of prospective employees and contractors.

Microsoft has developed its Microsoft Certified Professional (MCP) program to give you credentials that verify your ability to work with Microsoft products effectively and professionally. Several levels of certification are available based on specific suites of exams. Microsoft has recently created a new generation of certification programs:

Microsoft Certified Technology Specialist (MCTS) The MCTS certification is considered the entry-level certification for the new generation of Microsoft certifications. The MCTS certification program targets specific technologies instead of specific job roles. You must take and pass one to three exams.

Microsoft Certified IT Professional (MCITP) The MCITP certification is a Professional series certification that tests network and systems administrators on job roles, rather than only on a specific technology. The MCITP generally consists of one to three exams, in addition to obtaining an MCTS-level certification.

Microsoft Certified Professional Developer (MCPD) The MCPD certification is a Professional series certification for application developers. Similar to the MCITP, the MCPD is focused on a job role rather than on a single technology. The MCPD generally consists of one to three exams, in addition to obtaining an MCTS-level certification.

Microsoft Certified Architect (MCA) The MCA certification is Microsoft's premier certification series. Obtaining the MCA requires a minimum of 10 years of experience and requires the candidate to pass a review board consisting of peer architects.

How Do You Become Certified on Exchange Server 2007?

Attaining a Microsoft certification has always been a challenge. In the past, students have been able to acquire detailed exam information—even most of the exam questions—from online "brain dumps" and third-party "cram" books or software products. For the new generation of exams, this is simply not the case.

Microsoft has taken strong steps to protect the security and integrity of its new certification tracks. Now prospective candidates must complete a course of study that develops detailed knowledge about a wide range of topics. It supplies them with the true skills needed, derived from working with the technology being tested.

The new generations of Microsoft certification programs are heavily weighted toward hands-on skills and experience. It is recommended that candidates have troubleshooting skills acquired through hands-on experience and working knowledge.

Fortunately, if you are willing to dedicate the time and effort to learn Exchange Server 2007, you can prepare yourself well for the exam by using the proper tools. By working through this book, you can successfully meet the exam requirements to pass the Configuring Exchange Server 2007 exam.

This book is part of a complete series of Microsoft certification study guides, published by Sybex, that together cover the new MCTS, MCITP, and MCPD exams, as well as the core MCSA and MCSE operating system requirements. Please visit the Sybex website at `www.sybex.com` for complete program and product details.

MCTS Exam Requirements

Candidates for MCTS certification on Exchange Server 2007 must pass one Exchange Server 2007 exam. Other MCTS certifications may require up to three exams. For a more detailed description of the Microsoft certification programs, including a list of all the exams, visit the Microsoft Learning Website at `www.microsoft.com/learning/mcp`.

The Configuring Exchange Server 2007 Exam

The Configuring Exchange Server 2007 exam covers concepts and skills related to installing, configuring, and managing Exchange Server 2007 in the enterprise. It emphasizes the following elements of Exchange Server 2007 support and administration:

- Installing and configuring Microsoft Exchange servers
- Configuring recipients and public folders
- Configuring the Exchange infrastructure

- Monitoring and reporting
- Configuring disaster recovery

This exam is quite specific regarding Exchange Server 2007 requirements and operational settings, and it can be particular about how administrative tasks are performed within the operating system. It also focuses on fundamental concepts of Exchange Server 2007 operation. Careful study of this book, along with hands-on experience, will help you prepare for this exam.

Microsoft provides exam objectives to give you a general overview of possible areas of coverage on the Microsoft exams. Keep in mind, however, that exam objectives are subject to change at any time without prior notice and at Microsoft's sole discretion. Please visit the Microsoft Learning website (`www.microsoft.com/learning`) for the most current listing of exam objectives.

Types of Exam Questions

In an effort to both refine the testing process and protect the quality of its certifications, Microsoft has focused its newer certification exams on real experience and hands-on proficiency. There is a greater emphasis on your past working environments and responsibilities and less emphasis on how well you can memorize. In fact, Microsoft says that certification candidates should have hands-on experience before attempting to pass any certification exams.

Microsoft will accomplish its goal of protecting the exams' integrity by regularly adding and removing exam questions, limiting the number of questions that any individual sees in a beta exam, limiting the number of questions delivered to an individual by using adaptive testing, and adding new exam elements.

Exam questions may be in a variety of formats: depending on which exam you take, you'll see multiple-choice questions, as well as select-and-place and prioritize-a-list questions. Simulations and case study–based formats are included as well. You may also find yourself taking what's called an *adaptive format exam*. Let's take a look at the types of exam questions and examine the adaptive testing technique, so you'll be prepared for all of the possibilities.

With the release of Windows 2000, Microsoft stopped providing a detailed score breakdown. This is mostly because of the various and complex question formats. Previously, each question focused on one objective. Recent exams, such as the Configuring Exchange Server 2007 exam, however, contain questions that may be tied to one or more objectives from one or more objective sets. Therefore, grading by objective is almost impossible. Also, Microsoft no longer offers a score. Now you will be told only whether you pass or fail.

Multiple-Choice Questions

Multiple-choice questions come in two main forms. One is a straightforward question followed by several possible answers, of which one or more is correct. The other type of multiple-choice question is more complex and based on a specific scenario. The scenario may focus on several areas or objectives.

Select-and-Place Questions

Select-and-place exam questions involve graphical elements that you must manipulate to successfully answer the question. For example, you might see a diagram of a computer network, as shown in the following graphic taken from the select-and-place demo downloaded from Microsoft's website.

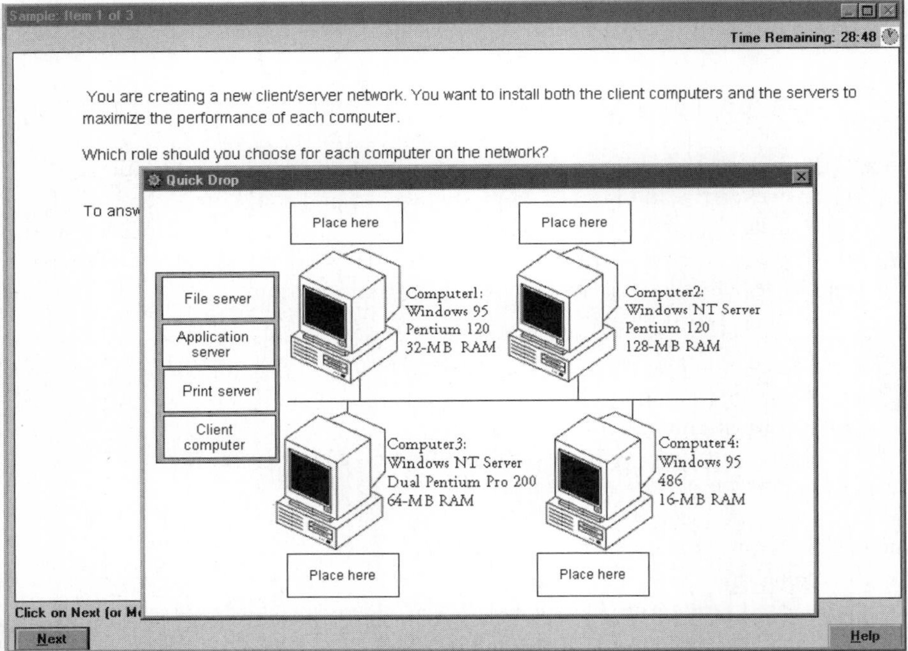

A typical diagram will show computers and other components next to boxes that contain the text *Place here*. The labels for the boxes represent various computer roles on a network, such as a print server and a file server. Based on information given for each computer, you are asked to select each label and place it in the correct box. You need to place *all* the labels correctly. No credit is given for the question if you correctly label only some of the boxes.

In another select-and-place problem, you might be asked to put a series of steps in order by dragging items from boxes on the left to boxes on the right and placing them in the correct order. One other type requires that you drag an item from the left and place it under an item in a column on the right.

For more information about the various exam question types, go to www.microsoft.com/learning/mcpexams/policies/innovations.asp.

Simulations

Simulations are the kinds of questions that most closely represent actual situations and test the skills you use while working with Microsoft software interfaces. These exam questions include a mock interface on which you are asked to perform certain actions according to a given scenario. The simulated interfaces look nearly identical to what you see in the actual product, as shown in this example.

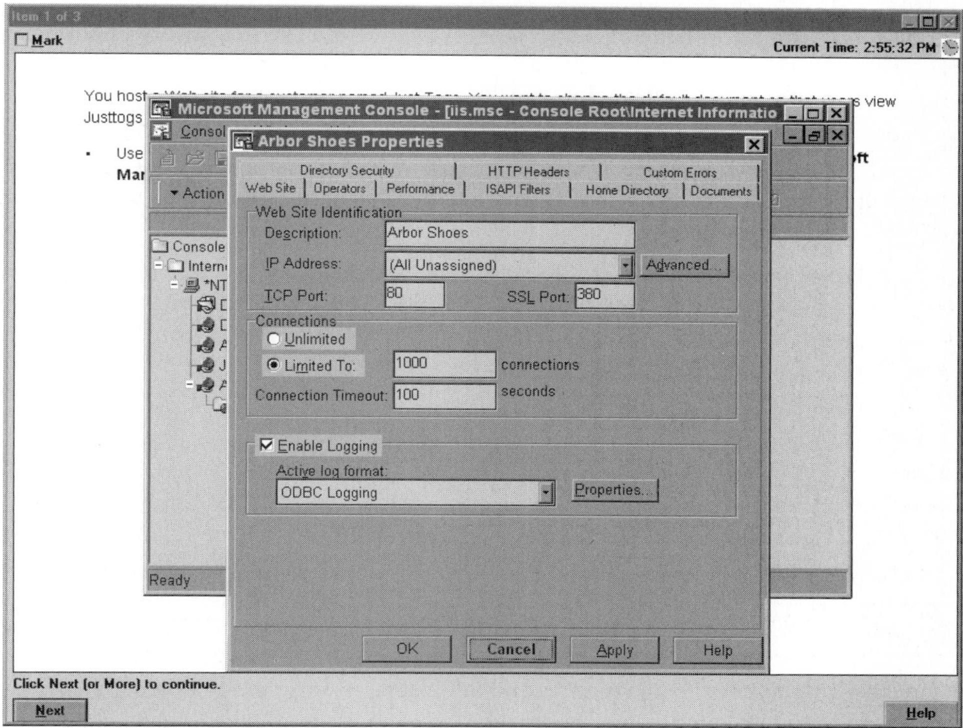

Because of the number of possible errors that can be made on simulations, be sure to consider the following recommendations from Microsoft:

- Do not change any simulation settings that don't pertain to the solution directly.
- When related information has not been provided, assume that the default settings are used.

- Make sure your entries are spelled correctly.
- Close all the simulation application windows after completing the set of tasks in the simulation.

Case Study–Based Questions

Case study–based questions first appeared in the MCSD program. These questions present a scenario with a range of requirements. Based on the information provided, you answer a series of multiple-choice and select-and-place questions. The interface for case study–based questions has a number of tabs, each of which contains information about the scenario. Currently, this type of question appears only in the Design exams.

Exam Question Development

Microsoft follows an exam-development process consisting of eight mandatory phases. The process takes an average of seven months and involves more than 150 specific steps. The exam development consists of the following phases:

Phase 1: Job Analysis Phase 1 is an analysis of all the tasks that make up a specific job function, based on tasks performed by people who are currently performing that job function. This phase also identifies the knowledge, skills, and abilities that relate specifically to the performance area to be certified.

Phase 2: Objective Domain Definition The results of the job analysis provide the framework used to develop objectives. The development of objectives involves translating the job-function tasks into a comprehensive set of more specific and measurable knowledge, skills, and abilities. The resulting list of objectives—the *objective domain*—is the basis for the development of both the certification exams and the training materials.

Phase 3: Blueprint Survey The final objective domain is transformed into a blueprint survey in which contributors are asked to rate each objective. These contributors may be past MCP candidates, appropriately skilled exam development volunteers, or Microsoft employees. Based on the contributors' input, the objectives are prioritized and weighted. The actual exam items are written according to the prioritized objectives. Contributors are queried about how they spend their time on the job. If a contributor doesn't spend an adequate amount of time actually performing the specified job function, his or her data is eliminated from the analysis. The blueprint survey phase helps determine which objectives to measure, as well as the appropriate number and types of items to include on the exam.

Phase 4: Item Development A pool of items is developed to measure the blueprinted objective domain. The number and types of items to be written are based on the results of the blueprint survey.

Phase 5: Alpha Review and Item Revision During this phase, a panel of technical and job-function experts reviews each item for technical accuracy and then answers each item, reaching a consensus on all technical issues. Once the items have been verified as technically accurate, they are edited to ensure that they are expressed in the clearest language possible.

Phase 6: Beta Exam The reviewed and edited items are collected into beta exams. Based on the responses of all beta participants, Microsoft performs a statistical analysis to verify the validity of the exam items and to determine which items will be used in the certification exam. Once the analysis has been completed, the items are distributed into multiple parallel forms, or *versions*, of the final certification exam.

Phase 7: Item Selection and Cut-Score Setting The results of the beta exams are analyzed to determine which items should be included in the certification exam based on many factors, including item difficulty and relevance. During this phase, a panel of job-function experts determines the *cut score* (minimum passing score) for the exams. The cut score differs from exam to exam because it is based on an item-by-item determination of the percentage of candidates who answered the item correctly and who would be expected to answer the item correctly.

Phase 8: Live Exam As the final phase, the exams are given to candidates. MCP exams are administered by Sylvan Prometric and Virtual University Enterprises (VUE).

Microsoft will regularly add and remove questions from the exams. This is called *item seeding*. It is part of the effort to make it more difficult for individuals to merely memorize exam questions that were passed along by previous test-takers.

Tips for Taking the Exchange Server 2007 Configuration Exam

Here are some general tips for achieving success on your certification exam:

- Arrive early at the exam center so you can relax and review your study materials. During this final review, you can look over tables and lists of exam-related information.
- Read the questions carefully. Don't be tempted to jump to an early conclusion. Make sure you know *exactly* what the question is asking.
- Answer all questions. If you are unsure about a question, then mark the question for review and come back to the question at a later time.
- On simulations, do not change settings that are not directly related to the question. Also, assume default settings if the question does not specify or imply which settings are used.
- For questions you're not sure about, use a process of elimination to get rid of the obviously incorrect answers first. This improves your odds of selecting the correct answer when you need to make an educated guess.
- Answer all questions.

Exam Registration

You may take the Microsoft exams at any of more than 1000 Authorized Prometric Testing Centers (APTCs) around the world. For the location of a testing center near you, call Prometric at 800-755-EXAM (755-3926). Outside the United States and Canada, contact your local Prometric registration center.

Find out the number of the exam you want to take, and then register with the Prometric registration center nearest to you. At this point, you will be asked for advance payment for the exam. The exams are $125 each and you must take them within one year of payment. You can schedule exams up to six weeks in advance or as late as one working day prior to the date of the exam. You can cancel or reschedule your exam if you contact the center at least two working days prior to the exam. Same-day registration is available in some locations, subject to space availability. Where same-day registration is available, you must register a minimum of two hours before test time..

You may also register for your exams online at www.prometric.com.

When you schedule the exam, you will be provided with instructions regarding appointment and cancellation procedures, ID requirements, and information about the testing center location. In addition, you will receive a registration and payment confirmation letter from Prometric.

Microsoft requires certification candidates to accept the terms of a Non-Disclosure Agreement before taking certification exams.

Is This Book for You?

If you want to acquire a solid foundation in Exchange Server 2007 and your goal is to prepare for the exam by learning how to use and manage the new operating system, this book is for you. You'll find clear explanations of the fundamental concepts you need to grasp and plenty of help to achieve the high level of professional competency you need to succeed in your chosen field.

If you want to become certified as an MCTS, this book is definitely for you. However, if you just want to attempt to pass the exam without really understanding Exchange Server 2007, this study guide is *not* for you. It is written for people who want to acquire hands-on skills and in-depth knowledge of Exchange Server 2007.

What's in the Book?

What makes a Sybex study guide the book of choice for hundreds of thousands of MCPs? We took into account not only what you need to know to pass the exam but also what you need to know to take what you've learned and apply it in the real world. Each book contains the following:

Objective-by-objective coverage of the topics you need to know Each chapter lists the objectives covered in that chapter.

The topics covered in this study guide map directly to Microsoft's official exam objectives. Each exam objective is covered completely.

Assessment test Directly following this introduction is an assessment test that you should take. It is designed to help you determine how much you already know about Exchange Server 2007. Each question is tied to a topic discussed in the book. Using the results of the assessment test, you can figure out the areas where you need to focus your study. Of course, we do recommend you read the entire book.

Exam essentials To highlight what you learn, you'll find a list of exam essentials at the end of each chapter. The "Exam Essentials" sections briefly highlight the topics that need your particular attention as you prepare for the exam.

Glossary Throughout each chapter, you will be introduced to important terms and concepts that you will need to know for the exam. These terms appear in italic within the chapters, and at the end of the book, a detailed glossary defines these terms, as well as other general terms you should know.

Review questions, complete with detailed explanations Each chapter is followed by a set of review questions that test what you learned in the chapter. The questions are written with the exam in mind, meaning they are designed to have the same look and feel as what you'll see on the exam. Question types are just like the exam, including multiple-choice questions, exhibits, and select-and-place questions.

Hands-on exercises In each chapter, you'll find exercises designed to give you the important hands-on experience that is critical for your exam preparation. The exercises support the topics of the chapter, and they walk you through the steps necessary to perform a particular function.

Real-world scenarios Because reading a book isn't enough for you to learn how to apply these topics in your everyday duties, we have provided real-world scenarios in special sidebars. These explain when and why a particular solution would make sense, in a working environment you'd actually encounter.

Interactive CD Every Sybex study guide comes with a CD complete with additional questions, flashcards for use with an interactive device, a Windows simulation program, and the book in electronic format. Details are in the following section.

What's on the CD?

With this new member of our best-selling Study Guide series, we are including quite an array of training resources. The CD offers numerous simulations, bonus exams, and flashcards to help you study for the exam. We have also included the complete contents of the study guide in electronic form. The CD's resources are described here:

The Sybex e-book for Exchange Server 2007 Many people like the convenience of being able to carry their whole study guide on a CD. They also like being able to search the text via computer to find specific information quickly and easily. For these reasons, we've supplied the entire contents of this study guide on the CD, in PDF. We've also included

Adobe Acrobat Reader, which provides the interface for the PDF contents as well as the search capabilities.

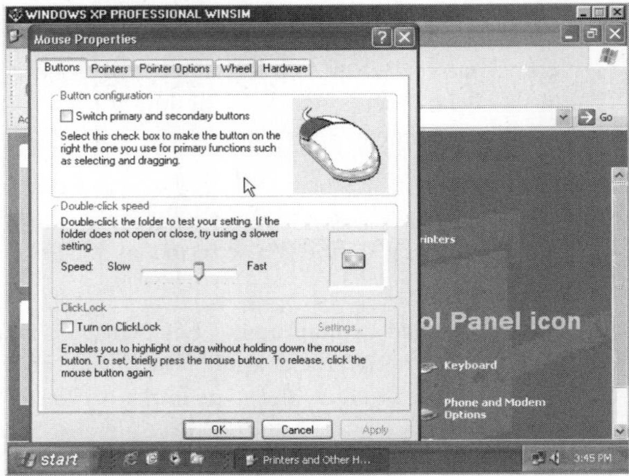

The Sybex test engine This is a collection of multiple-choice questions that will help you prepare for your exam. There are four sets of questions:

- Two bonus exams designed to simulate the actual live exam.
- All the questions from the study guide, presented in a test engine for your review. You can review questions by chapter or by objective, or you can take a random test.
- The assessment test.

Here is a sample screen from the Sybex test engine.

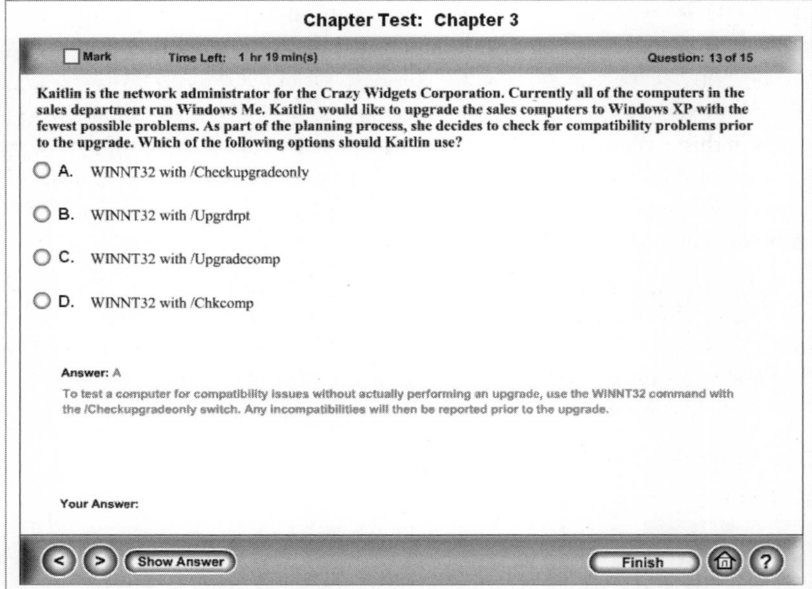

Sybex flashcards for PCs and handheld devices The "flashcard" style of question offers an effective way to quickly and efficiently test your understanding of the fundamental concepts covered in the exam. The Sybex flashcards set consists of 150 questions presented in a special engine developed specifically for this study guide. Here's what the Sybex flashcards interface looks like:

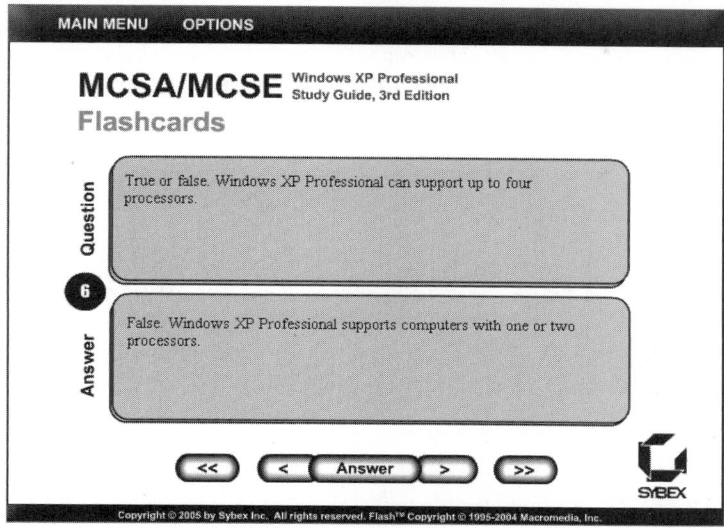

Because of the high demand for a product that will run on handheld devices, we have also developed, in conjunction with Land-J Technologies, a version of the flashcard questions that you can take with you on your Palm OS PDA (including the PalmPilot and Handspring's Visor).

Hardware and Software Requirements

You should verify that your computer meets the minimum requirements for installing Exchange Server 2007 as listed in Tables 2.2 through 2.6 in Chapter 2. We suggest that your computer meets or exceeds the recommended requirements for a more enjoyable experience.

The exercises in this book assume, in every chapter except Chapter 8, that you have performed a clean installation of Exchange Server 2007 into an empty forest. Chapter 8 assumes you have Exchange Server 2003 in your organization before installing Exchange Server 2007. Neither of these assumptions, if not met, should impact your ability to perform the exercises, though.

Contacts and Resources

To find out more about Microsoft Education and Certification materials and programs, to register with Prometric, or to obtain other useful certification information and additional study resources, check the following resources:

Microsoft Learning Home Page

`www.microsoft.com/learning`

This website provides information about the MCP program and exams. You can also order the latest Microsoft Roadmap to Education and Certification.

Microsoft TechNet Technical Information Network

`www.microsoft.com/technet`

800-344-2121

Use this website or phone number to contact support professionals and system administrators. Outside the United States and Canada, contact your local Microsoft subsidiary for information.

PalmPilot Training Product Development: Land-J

`www.land-j.com`

407-359-2217

Land-J Technologies is a consulting and programming business currently specializing in application development for the 3Com PalmPilot Personal Digital Assistant. Land-J developed the Palm version of the EdgeTests, which is included on the CD that accompanies this Study Guide.

Prometric

`www.prometric.com`

800-755-3936

Contact Prometric to register to take an MCP exam at any of more than 800 Prometric Testing Centers around the world.

MCP Magazine Online

`www.mcpmag.com`

Microsoft Certified Professional Magazine is a well-respected publication that focuses on Windows certification. This site hosts chats and discussion forums and tracks news related to the MCSE program. Some of the services cost a fee, but they are well worth it.

Windows & .NET Magazine

`www.windows2000mag.com`

You can subscribe to this magazine or read free articles at the website. The study resource provides general information on Windows 2000, XP, and .NET Server.

Assessment Test

1. Which Exchange Server 2007 server roles provide Outlook Web Access (OWA) functionality to clients?

   A. Mailbox

   B. Hub Transport

   C. Client Access

   D. Edge Transport

2. You are the Exchange administrator for a large network and are about to install the first Exchange server in the organization. Before you do that, however, you must prepare your forest. To which of the following groups must you belong in order to prepare the forest for an installation of Exchange Server 2007? (Choose all that apply.)

   A. Server Admins

   B. Domain Admins

   C. Schema Admins

   D. Enterprise Admins

3. What Exchange-related service is found only on mailbox servers?

   A. Microsoft Exchange EdgeSync

   B. Microsoft Exchange Active Directory Topology

   C. Microsoft Exchange Information Store

   D. Microsoft Exchange POP3

4. What is the function of the checkpoint file within each storage group?

   A. It stores the contents of the mailboxes in the storage group.

   B. It stores the contents of transactions that are not committed to the database.

   C. It stores configuration information about the mailbox databases.

   D. It contains information about which transaction logs have been committed to the database already.

5. What is the name of the Microsoft antivirus and antispam product that has been released for Exchange Server 2007?

   A. Client Security Suite

   B. Forefront Security for Exchange Server

   C. Microsoft Exchange Antivirus

   D. Windows Defender

6. Your company has hired an outside agency to provide accounting services. Many of your employees need to email messages to people in this agency using the Internet. You want to set it up so that the people in the agency appear in the Exchange global address list. What type of recipient object do you need to configure for each person in the outside agency?

   A. Mailbox

   B. Mail-enabled user

   C. Contact

   D. A mailbox with a foreign owner

7. Your manager comes to you and asks you to archive every email in every folder that is older than 60 days to your new archive solution. You don't think that this is the bright idea to do right now, so what arguments might you be able to use so you can put it off until off-hours?

   A. Processing this many messages will put a tremendous load on the server and might cause it to become unresponsive.

   B. You can't control the contents of every folder with MRM.

   C. FCC regulations say that you cannot archive all the emails and that some of them need to be maintained online for more than a year.

   D. Both A and B are correct.

8. You are taking a long-overdue vacation and want system notifications regarding public folders to be sent to one of your assistants while you are away. What permission would you assign the assistant on each of the folders?

   A. Folder Owner

   B. Folder Manager

   C. Folder Contact

   D. Folder Notification

9. Where are messages in routing held before they arrive at their final destination?

   A. A queue

   B. A transaction log

   C. A checkpoint file

   D. A storage group

10. Which type of clustering in Exchange Server 2007 has a single point of failure for its disk?

    A. Cluster continuous replication

    B. Network load balancing

    C. Volume shadow copy

    D. Single copy clustering

11. Why would you want to restore a database to a recovery storage group and not to the production storage group?
    - **A.** Because that is the only way you can restore a database in Exchange 2007.
    - **B.** So you don't overwrite the production database because you might want to recover data from it later.
    - **C.** The production database is not damaged. You are trying to recover a single mailbox, and this is the best way to do it.
    - **D.** You can't restore a database to a recovery storage group.
12. What Exchange tool can you use to quickly check performance statistics on your Exchange Server 2007 servers?
    - **A.** Exchange Performance Manager
    - **B.** Exchange Event Viewer
    - **C.** Exchange Server Performance Monitor
    - **D.** Exchange Performance Console
13. A hierarchical arrangement of one or more Windows Server 2003 domains that share a common namespace is referred to as a __________.
    - **A.** Windows Server 2003 site
    - **B.** domain site
    - **C.** domain tree
    - **D.** domain forest
14. What Exchange Server 2007 server role would you place in the DMZ of your company's network to accept and process SMTP messages?
    - **A.** Hub Transport
    - **B.** Unified Messaging
    - **C.** Client Access
    - **D.** Edge Transport
15. What utility will you need to use to configure security settings on your Exchange Server 2007 servers that are specific to their roles as Exchange servers?
    - **A.** Security Configuration Wizard
    - **B.** Exchange Security Wizard
    - **C.** Exchange Configuration Manager
    - **D.** Exchange Management Console
16. When a database is taken offline, the process is called what?
    - **A.** Mounting
    - **B.** Dismounting
    - **C.** Stopping
    - **D.** Suspending

17. What is responsible for updating recipient information in the Edge Transport servers' ADAM database?
   A. ADAMUpdate
   B. EdgeSync
   C. RecipientUpdate
   D. EdgeUpdate

18. From where can you create mailboxes in Exchange Server 2007? (Choose all that apply.)
   A. The Exchange Management Shell
   B. The Exchange Management Console
   C. The Active Directory Users and Computers console
   D. The Exchange System Manager

19. It is not a good idea to allow users to store email in PST files if you are implementing a MRM plan. Why?
   A. It takes more server resources for the server to attach to a workstation, mount the PST file, and then scan it for records that meet content settings.
   B. Users can turn off their computers, and if a server cannot connect to the user's computer, it cannot manage the records.
   C. PST files cannot be managed.
   D. Storing messages in a PST file breaks single instance storage.

20. A user named Mary is the owner of a public folder. Mary leaves your company, and the former administrator deletes her user account. As the current administrator, you now need to modify the client permissions on the public folder. What will you have to do?
   A. Create a new account with the same user information as the deleted account.
   B. Restore a backup tape of the server that was created before the user was deleted.
   C. Designate your account as the owner of the folder.
   D. Create a new public folder and move the contents of the old folder to it.

21. What tool can you use to determine the delivery status of a message sent from one user in your Exchange organization to another?
   A. Message tracking
   B. Exchange Best Practices Analyzer
   C. Microsoft Operations Manager
   D. Queue viewer

22. In a cluster, what kind of traffic is sent over the private network?
   A. Mailbox database access requests
   B. Heartbeat traffic
   C. Client access requests
   D. DNS query requests

23. If an Exchange 2007 Enterprise server can have 50 storage groups, how many recovery storage groups can it have?

 A. 49, because you are required to have one in production
 B. 1, because that's all you get
 C. 5, because this is based on the standard limit that applies to the Enterprise server too
 D. 50, because it's configurable with a registry key

24. What Exchange Management Shell cmdlet can you pipe input into to create CSV reports?

 A. `Export-CSV`
 B. `Create-CSV`
 C. `Make-CSV`
 D. `Import-CSV`

25. What administrative console is used to configure the link costs that Exchange Server 2007 uses when routing messages?

 A. Exchange System Manager
 B. Active Directory Users and Computers
 C. Active Directory Sites and Services
 D. Active Directory Domains and Trusts

Answers to Assessment Test

1. C. The Client Access server role provides all non-MAPI and RPC connectivity for clients, such as HTTP, POP3, and IMAP4. See Chapter 1 for more information.

2. C, D. To prepare the forest for Exchange installation; a user must belong to both the Schema Admins and Enterprise Admins global groups. The user must also belong to the local Administrators group on the computer on which the process is actually run. See Chapter 2 for more information.

3. C. Only the Microsoft Exchange Information Store service is found just on Mailbox servers. The other services listed are found on other server roles or multiple server roles. See Chapter 3 for more information.

4. D. The checkpoint file contains information about which transaction logs have been committed to the database and which transaction logs have not been committed to the database. There is one checkpoint file per storage group. See Chapter 4 for more information.

5. B. Forefront Security for Exchange Server, a product previously known as Antigen by Sybari, is now part of Microsoft through acquisition. See Chapter 5 for more information.

6. C. A contact (or mail-contact) holds the address of a non-Exchange mail recipient. Contacts are made visible in the global address list. See Chapter 6 for more information.

7. D. It would be better to establish custom managed folders, have users move mail into those folders, and then start to manage the default folders. Also, user-created folders are not manageable with MRM; only default and custom managed folders are manageable with MRM. See Chapter 7 for more information.

8. C. A person with the Folder Contact permissions can receive email notifications relating to a folder. Notifications include replication conflicts, folder design conflicts, and storage limit notifications. See Chapter 8 for more information.

9. A. A queue is a temporary staging location for those messages in transit that are between processing steps. There are multiple queues found on each Hub Transport server, and each one represents a set of messages to be processed in a specific way. See Chapter 9 for more information.

10. D. A single copy cluster is susceptible to a lost disk. See Chapter 10 for more information.

11. C. In the past you had to restore the database to an out-of-organization server, and then merge the mailbox out with `Exmerge` and deal with it. With the recovery storage group, you don't have to do this anymore. When you restore a database to a recovery storage group, the database is not linked to any mailboxes. If the mailbox is no longer in the dumpster, restoring from backup to the recovery storage group is the best way to get access to the mailbox. See Chapter 11 for more information.

12. C. Although the Performance console has always been available to you in Windows Server 2003, Exchange Server 2007 gives you a customized Performance console called the Exchange Server Performance Monitor that can be accessed from the Toolbox node of the Exchange Management Console. See Chapter 12 for more information.

13. C. A domain tree is a hierarchical arrangement of one or more Windows Active Directory domains that share a common namespace. Domain Name Service (DNS) domain names represent the tree structure. The first domain in a tree is called the *root domain*. See Chapter 1 for more information.

14. D. Of the new server roles in Exchange Server 2007, only the Edge Transport is designed to be placed in the DMZ, outside the Active Directory domain. See Chapter 2 for more information.

15. A. You will need to use the Security Configuration Wizard, a new addition in Windows Server 2003, to configure the security configuration on an Exchange Server 2007 server. See Chapter 3 for more information.

16. B. When you dismount a database, you take it offline and prevent clients from accessing it. See Chapter 4 for more information.

17. B. The EdgeSync process is responsible for updating the ADAM database on Edge Transport servers with configuration and recipient information. See Chapter 5 for more information.

18. A, B. In Exchange Server 2007, you can create mailboxes from the Exchange Management Shell or the Exchange Management Console. See Chapter 6 for more information.

19. C. MRM works only on folders that are stored in an Exchange database mounted on an Exchange server. See Chapter 7 for more information.

20. C. An administrator has the permission to change the owner of a folder. Once the administrator takes ownership of the folder, they can then perform administrative tasks, such as configuring client permissions. See Chapter 8 for more information.

21. A. You can search the message tracking logs to determine whether a message was delivered to a user's mailbox. See Chapter 9 for more information.

22. B. The private network of a cluster is used to pass heartbeat traffic, which is used to determine the status of the cluster nodes. See Chapter 10 for more information.

23. B. One is all you get per server. The recovery storage group should be mounted only when it is needed, so there was not much reason to have more than one. See Chapter 11 for more information.

24. A. You will use the `Export-CSV` cmdlet to take piped input and create CSV files. See Chapter 12 for more information.

25. C. The Hub Transport server, which is responsible for routing all messages in Exchange Server 2007, computes the lowest-cost route to the site containing the destination Mailbox server based on the site-link costs configured on site links between the sites. Sites (and site-link costs) are created and configured using the Active Directory Sites and Services tool. See Chapter 1 for more information.

Chapter 1

Exchange Server 2007 and Active Directory Review

Perhaps the most abused, and overused, phrase in information technology is "new and improved" or "new features that increase productivity" or something similar. With Exchange Server 2007, Microsoft really has every right to make those claims, and many more. Although Exchange Server is now more than 10 years old, it keeps growing and evolving, partly because of customer demands and partly because Microsoft continues to push messaging to places it has yet to go. When you get your Exchange Server 2007 environment deployed, you will have the most robust and feature-laden messaging platform available today at your disposal.

Since the primary goal of this book is to prepare you to pass the corresponding 70-236 exam, we'll spend most of our time together ensuring that you get the required knowledge and skills to help achieve that goal. Along the way, we might all learn a new thing or two and start to see just how many ways that Exchange Server 2007 can and will change the way Exchange administrators and Exchange users work.

We'll start this chapter by looking at what's new in Exchange Server 2007 as compared to previous versions. As part of that examination, we will cover what is no longer included in or supported by Exchange Server 2007. This will lead into later chapters in the book where you'll dig deeper into key concepts and core skills that will prove to be important in your day-to-day administration of Exchange Server 2007 and of course important to you on exam day.

We'll next briefly review Active Directory in Windows Server 2003. Active Directory has been a critical part of Exchange Server since Exchange 2000 Server was released. This importance grew in Exchange Server 2003, and now with the elimination of link-state routing groups (oops, there's the first removed feature for our discussion), Active Directory site-based routing is used for message transport within an organization. Of course, Active Directory is still critical for elements such as user accounts, groups, and global catalog servers.

This chapter provides you with a good conceptual background of the topics covered in the remainder of the book. Specifically, we will address the following issues:

- What is new and what has been removed in Exchange Server 2007
- Active Directory in Windows Server 2003 and its integration with Exchange Server 2007

What's New in Exchange Server 2007?

With any new release of an established product like Exchange Server, Microsoft includes new (and improved) features that benefit both the administrative side of the product and the end-user experience. We'll briefly highlight some of the key features that are new or improved in Exchange Server 2007 (although this list is certainly not all-inclusive):

- *Exchange Management Console*: The first, and most striking, change many administrators with Exchange experience will notice is that the familiar Exchange System Manager is gone and has been replaced with the completely redesigned Exchange Management Console (EMC). By examining the ways administrators worked and the tasks they needed to perform, Microsoft designed the EMC to be as intuitive and as workflow oriented as possible. The EMC also takes advantage of the improvements in the Microsoft Management Console 3.0. We will spend a good deal of our time together in this book working with the EMC.
- *Exchange Management Shell*: Another dramatic change from an administrative standpoint is the Exchange Management Shell, which is a new command-line shell and scripting environment for Exchange administrators. Any action that can be carried out in the EMC can be performed just as easily in the Exchange Management Shell, and many actions that an Exchange administrator will perform can be performed only from within the Exchange Management Shell. You'll see as you work with Exchange Server 2007 that almost every configuration action you perform in the EMC will present you with the corresponding Exchange Management Shell code that is actually being used to carry out the changes.
- *64-bit*: Exchange Server 2007 is the first messaging platform to fully utilize the benefits of 64-bit hardware and operating systems. In fact, Exchange Server 2007 is available for production use only in 64-bit versions. The amount of RAM available to be efficiently used in 64-bit environments is significantly higher than in 32-bit environments, thus allowing for more mailboxes and storage groups on a single Exchange server.
- *Active Directory (AD) site-based routing*: No longer do you need to plan, implement, and manage an Exchange-specific routing environment with routing groups. Exchange Server 2007 is AD site aware and will use the existing Active Directory sites configuration to perform routing and to select which Exchange servers it should directly communicate with. This change will allow a closer alignment of the physical network topology with the Exchange routing topology.
- *Server roles*: Gone are the days of every Exchange installation being the same as every other installation. Also gone are the days of a single check box being the determining factor in what role an Exchange server played. Exchange Server 2007 now allows you—in fact, it demands you—to deploy it in one or more of several available roles. The familiar back-end server of old is now referred to as a Mailbox server, although it can certainly still host public folders. The closest role to that of the old front-end server would be that of the Client Access server. You'll examine all the roles, uses, benefits, and limitations of Exchange Server in detail in Chapter 3, "Installing Exchange Server 2007" and in Chapter 4, "Configuring Exchange Server Roles."
- *Unified messaging*: Once a popular, complex, and costly third-party add-on for Exchange, unified messaging is now available within Exchange Server 2007 by deploying the Unified Messaging role and using Exchange Server 2007 Enterprise CALs. Unified messaging is outside the scope of the 70-236 exam, so we will not be discussing it in this book.

- *Highly available*: In the past, if you wanted highly available Exchange servers, you had two choices from Microsoft: active/passive clusters or active/active clusters. Both were certainly suitable but complex and costly—a reality that prevented many smaller organizations from providing a highly available Exchange solution. Additionally, many third-party applications promised various high-availability solutions for Exchange Server, many of which were very good products. Seeing the need to revamp the high-availability solutions offered in Exchange and wanting to take advantage of the Windows Server 2003 majority node set (MNS) clustering capability, Microsoft introduced two new high-availability solutions in Exchange Server 2007: local continuous replication (LCR) and cluster continuous replication (CCR). Clustering using active/passive nodes has been renamed to single copy clustering (SCC), while support for active/active clustering has been eliminated entirely. You will examine high availability for Exchange Server 2007 in Chapter 10, "Creating and Managing Highly Available Exchange Server Solutions."
- *Compliance and message management*: As email continues to grow and evolve as the number-one means of business-critical communication, the need to manage and enforce certain policies on email content and usage also grows. Exchange Server 2007 presents several novel, and quite useful, methods that allow organizations to control the growth of the messaging stores and also to monitor and control the usage of email, thus protecting the organization from legal or other troubles. You'll examine compliance and message management in Exchange Server 2007 in Chapter 7, "Configuring Exchange Server Rules and Policies."
- *Antivirus and antispam controls*: The Edge Transport role, one of the new Exchange Server 2007 server roles, is responsible for preventing spam messages from entering your Exchange organization. The intelligent message filter (IMF) has been removed from the Exchange servers that host mailboxes and public folders or that handle client access requests and has been moved into the Edge Transport role, which is designed to operate in a DMZ network if desired. Additionally, Sybari's Antigen antivirus product is now a Microsoft product known as Forefront Security for Exchange Server. Forefront is a complete Exchange-aware antivirus application that can be used on the Edge Transport server as a network edge scanner and also on the Hub Transport server to scan messages traversing your internal network. You'll examine antivirus and antispam issues in more detail in Chapter 5, "Configuring the Exchange Security Infrastructure."

What's No Longer Supported in Exchange Server 2007

In any new release of a software product, discontinued or deemphasized features are inevitable. Such is the case with Exchange Server 2007, although some of the items you'll examine here might be a surprise to experienced Exchange administrators. The items that follow in no way represent every change that has occurred in Exchange Server 2007, but they do represent some of the more interesting ones.

Features That Have Been Removed or Replaced

The following key features and functionality have been removed from Exchange Server 2007:

- *Routing groups*: Link-state routing is no longer used in Exchange Server 2007 and has been replaced by Active Directory site-based routing. This places further importance on the proper planning and design of the Active Directory forest that Exchange Server 2007 will be installed into, but it reduces the overall amount of planning and administration required to maintain an Exchange organization. Now all routing (both AD and Exchange) is controlled and configured from a single location—the Active Directory Sites and Services console—thus providing consistent, predictable results that can be controlled as your physical network dictates. You'll examine Active Directory more as it relates to the installation of Exchange Server 2007 in Chapter 2, "Preparing for the Exchange Server 2007 Installation."
- *Administrative groups*: Administrative groups, which were previously used in Exchange Server to control administrative access to groups of servers, have been replaced by the Exchange Server 2007 split permissions model that emphasizes using universal security groups. We'll cover administrative roles more in Chapter 3.
- *Exchange management via Active Directory Users and Computers*: Management of all recipient objects (discussed more in Chapter 6, "Configuring and Managing Exchange Recipients") is now performed via the Exchange Management Console. Management of Exchange recipients has been integrated in the Active Directory Users and Computers (ADUC) console in the previous two versions of Exchange Server, but Exchange administrators who've worked with Exchange Server 5.5 will recall this method of management very well.
- *Streaming database*: The streaming database (`*.stm`), first introduced in Exchange 2000 Server, has been removed in Exchange Server 2007.
- *Recipient Update Service*: The Recipient Update Service (RUS) has been removed from Exchange Server 2007 and has been replaced with two Exchange Management Shell cmdlets. These cmdlets can be scheduled, however, to provide a similar function that the RUS provided. You will examine email address generation more in Chapter 7.
- *Exchange 5.5 interaction*: Exchange Server 2007 does not interoperate with the Active Directory Connector (ADC) or Site Replication Service (SRS) as in the previous two versions of Exchange. As a result, you can no longer directly migrate from Exchange Server 5.5 to Exchange Server 2007. We'll discuss migration briefly in Chapter 2.
- *NNTP*: This has been removed completely. You'll need to use Exchange Server 2003 or Exchange 2000 Server to provide this protocol to clients.
- *X.400 message transfer agent*: This has been removed completely. You'll need to use Exchange Server 2003 or Exchange 2000 Server if your organization needs this message transfer agent protocol.
- *Novell GroupWise connector*: This has been removed completely. You'll need to use Exchange Server 2003 or Exchange 2000 Server to provide this connector.
- *Louts Notes connector*: This is no longer available, but Microsoft has provided migration and coexistence tools for Exchange Server 2007.

- *Active/active clustering*: This is no longer supported. You'll need to implement either an active/passive SCC model or consider using the new high-availability features provided by CCR. You'll spend all of Chapter 10 looking at highly available Exchange Server 2007 implementations.
- *IMAP4 access to public folders*: You'll need to retain Exchange Server 2003 or Exchange 2000 Server to provide IMAP4 access to public folders to clients.
- *Exchange WebDAV extensions*: Exchange WebDAV has been replaced by the Exchange Web Services.

Features That Have Been Deemphasized

The following key features and functionality have been deemphasized in Exchange Server 2007:

- *Public folders*: Public folders are no longer required in a clean installation of Exchange Server 2007. In previous versions of Exchange Server, public folders contained critical system data such as the Offline Address Book (OAB) and free/busy calendaring data. This is no longer the case, because no system data is stored in public folders in Exchange Server 2007. Public folders, however, are still supported in Exchange Server 2007, although Microsoft recommends moving to SharePoint Portal Server or another similar product for those items that previously used public folders. It's expected that public folders (which were initially advertised as not being supported in Exchange Server 2007) will not be supported in the next release of Exchange Server. We'll cover public folders in Exchange Server 2007 in Chapter 8, "Configuring and Managing Client Connectivity and Public Folders."
- *Exchange Server 2003 virus scanning API (VSAPI)*: Although Exchange Server 2007 still supports the VSAPI, its role is being deemphasized because Microsoft has started to integrate antiviral controls at the transport layer. We'll cover antiviral controls in Exchange Server 2007 in Chapter 5.
- *Exchange streaming backup API*: The Exchange Server 2007 database structure has changed, eliminating the streaming database (`*.stm`). As a result, this backup API is no longer required.

You can look at the entire list of new and removed features in Exchange Server 2007 by visiting the TechNet website at `http://technet.microsoft.com/en-us/library/aa996018.aspx`.

Active Directory in Windows Server 2003 Review

Active Directory is one of the most important components of Windows Server 2003 networking. Although a full discussion of Active Directory is outside the scope of this book, the nature of Exchange Server 2003's tight integration with Active Directory warrants a brief discussion of the technology and an examination of how it affects the Exchange environment.

Active Directory in Windows Server 2003

To understand Active Directory, it is first necessary to understand what a directory is. Put simply, a *directory* contains a hierarchy that stores information about objects in a system.

A directory service is the service that manages the directory and makes it available to users on the network. Active Directory stores information about objects on a Windows Server 2003 network and makes this information easy for administrators and users to find and use. Active Directory uses a structured data store as the basis for a hierarchical organization of directory information.

You can use Active Directory to design a directory structure tailored to your organization's administrative needs. For example, you can scale Active Directory from a single computer to a single network or to many networks. Active Directory can include every object, server, and domain in a network.

What makes Active Directory so powerful, and so scalable, is that it separates the logical structure of the Windows Server 2003 domain hierarchy from the physical structure of the network.

Logical Components

In Exchange 5.5 Server and prior versions, resources were organized separately in Windows and Exchange. Now, the organization you set up in Windows Server 2003 and the organization you set up in Exchange Server 2007 are the same. In Active Directory, the domain hierarchy is organized using a number of constructs to make administration simpler and more logical. These logical constructs, which are described in the following sections, allow you to define and group resources so that they can be located and administered by name rather than by physical location.

Objects

An *object* is the basic unit in Active Directory. It is a distinct named set of attributes that represents something concrete, such as a user, printer, computer, or application. *Attributes* are the characteristics of the object; for example, a computer is an object, and its attributes include its name and location, among other things. A user is also an object. In Exchange, a user's attributes include the user's first name, last name, and email address. User attributes also include Exchange-related features, such as whether the object can receive email, the formatting of email it receives, and the location where it can receive email.

Organizational Units

An *organizational unit* (OU) is a container in which you can place objects such as user accounts, groups, computers, printers, applications, file shares, and other organizational units. You can use organizational units to hold groups of objects, such as users and printers, and you can assign specific permissions to them. An organizational unit cannot contain objects from other domains and is the smallest unit to which you can assign or delegate administrative authority. Organizational units are provided strictly for administrative purposes and convenience. They are transparent to the end user but can be extremely useful to an administrator when segmenting users and computers within an organization.

You can use organizational units to create containers within a domain that represent the hierarchical, logical structures within your organization. This enables you to manage how accounts and resources are configured and used.

You can also use organizational units to create departmental or geographical boundaries. In addition, you can use them to delegate administrative authority over particular tasks to particular users. For instance, you can create an OU for all your printers and then assign full control over the printers to your printer administrator.

Domains

A *domain* is a group of computers and other resources that are part of a network and share a common directory database. A domain is organized in levels and is administered as a unit with common rules and procedures. All objects and organizational units exist within a domain.

You create a domain by installing the first domain controller inside it. A domain controller is simply a Windows Server 2003 computer that has Active Directory enabled on it. Once a server has been installed, you can use the Active Directory Wizard to install Active Directory. To install Active Directory on the first server on a network, that server must have access to a server running the *Domain Name Service* (DNS). If it does not, you'll be given the chance to install and configure DNS during Active Directory installation.

A domain can exist in one of four possible domain functional levels as outlined in the following list:

- *Windows 2000 mixed*: The default domain functional level all new domain controllers are installed in allows for Windows NT 4.0 backup domain controllers (BDCs), Windows 2000 Server domain controllers, and Windows Server 2003 domain controllers. Local and global groups are supported, but universal groups are not. Global catalog servers are supported.
- *Windows 2000 native*: The minimum domain functional level at which universal groups become available, along with several other Active Directory features, allows for Windows 2000 Server and Windows Server 2003 domain controllers only.
- *Windows Server 2003 interim*: This supports only Windows NT 4.0 and Windows Server 2003 domain controllers. The domains in a forest are raised to this functional level; the forest level has been increased to interim.
- *Windows Server 2003*: The highest domain functional level available, this provides all new features and functionality and allows for only Windows Server 2003 domain controllers.

The mixed mode and native mode you might have been used to when using Windows 2000 Server have been replaced by the domain and forest functional levels in Windows Server 2003. Note, however, that the Windows 2000 mixed mode is similar to the Windows 2000 mixed functional level and that the Windows 2000 native mode is similar to the Windows Server 2003 functional level.

The move from a lower functional level to a higher one is irreversible, so take care to ensure that all older (Windows NT 4.0 or Windows 2000 Server) domain controllers have been retired or upgraded before changing the functional level.

Domain Trees

A *domain tree* is a hierarchical arrangement of one or more Windows Active Directory domains that share a common namespace. DNS domain names represent the tree structure. The first domain in a tree is called the *root domain*. For example, a company named Wiley Publishing (that has the Internet domain name wileypublishing.com) might use the root domain wileypublishing.com in its primary domain tree. Additional domains in the tree under the root domain are called *child domains*. For example, the domain sales.wileypublishing.com would be a child domain of the wileypublishing.com domain. Figure 1.1 shows an example of a domain tree.

FIGURE 1.1 A domain tree is a hierarchical grouping of one or more domains.

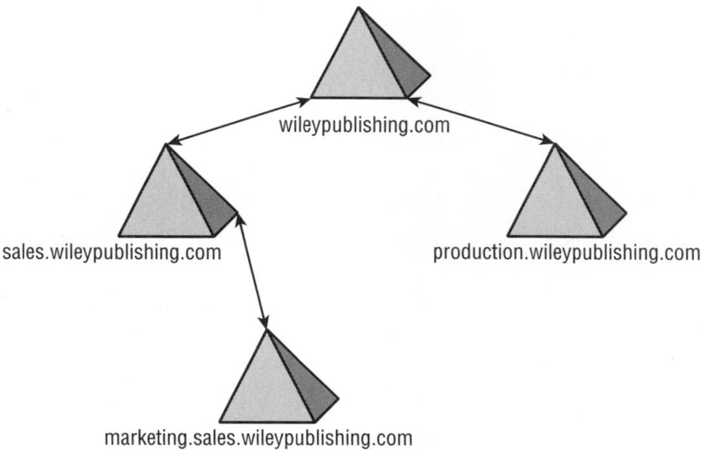

Domains establish trust relationships with one another that allow objects in a trusted domain to access resources in a trusting domain. Windows Server 2003 and Active Directory support transitive, two-way trusts between domains. When a child domain is created, a trust relationship is automatically configured between that child domain and the parent domain. This trust is two-way, meaning that resource access requests can flow from either domain to the other. The trust is also transitive, meaning that any domains trusted by one domain are automatically trusted by the other domain. For example, in Figure 1.1, consider the three domains named wileypublishing.com, sales.wileypublishing.com, and marketing.sales.wileypublishing.com. When sales.wileypublishing.com was created as a child domain of wileypublishing.com, a two-way trust was formed between the two. When marketing.sales.wileypublishing.com was created as a child of sales.wileypublishing.com, another trust was formed between those two domains. Though no explicit trust relationship was ever defined directly between the marketing.sales.wileypublishing.com and wileypublishing.com domains, the two domains trust each other anyway because of the transitive nature of trust relationships.

Domain Forests

A *domain forest* is a group of one or more domain trees that do not form a contiguous namespace but might share a common schema and global catalog. There is always at least one forest on the network, and it is created when the first Active Directory–enabled computer (domain controller) on a network is installed. This first domain in a forest is called the *forest root domain* and is special because it is really the basis for naming the entire forest. It cannot be removed from the forest without removing the entire forest. Finally, no other domain can ever be created above the forest root domain in the forest domain hierarchy. Figure 1.2 shows an example of a domain forest with multiple domain trees.

FIGURE 1.2 A domain forest consists of one or more domain trees.

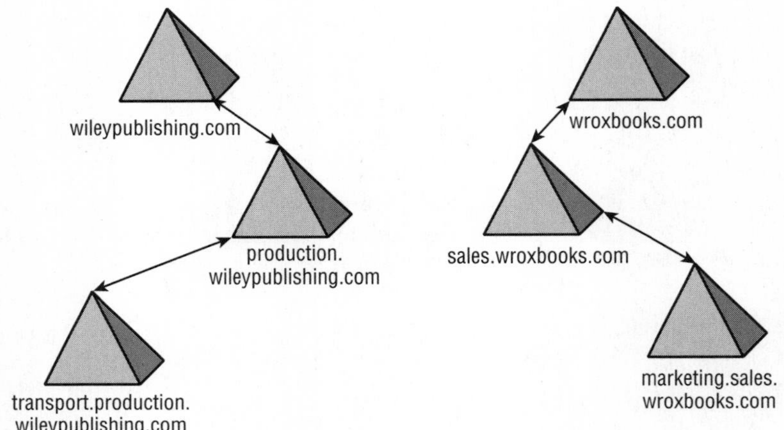

A forest is the outermost boundary of Active Directory; the directory cannot be larger than the forest. You can create multiple forests and then create trust relationships between specific domains in those forests; this would let you grant access to resources and accounts that are outside a particular forest. However, an Exchange organization cannot span multiple forests.

Physical Components

The physical side of Active Directory is primarily represented by domain controllers and sites. These enable organizations to optimize replication traffic across their networks and to assist client workstations in finding the closest domain controller to validate logon credentials.

Domain Controllers

Every domain must have at least one *domain controller*, a computer running Windows Server 2003 that validates user network access and manages Active Directory. To create a domain controller, all you have to do is install Active Directory on a Windows Server 2003 computer. During this process, you have the option of creating a new domain or joining an existing domain. If you create a new domain, you also have the option of creating or joining an existing domain tree or forest. A domain controller stores a complete copy of all Active Directory information for that domain, manages changes to that information, and replicates those changes to other domain controllers in the same domain. Schema and infrastructure configuration information are replicated between all domain controllers in a forest.

In previous versions of Windows, a distinction was drawn between primary and backup domain controllers. In Windows Server 2003 and Windows 2000 Server, all domain controllers are considered peers, and each holds a complete copy of Active Directory.

Global Catalog

In a single-domain environment, users can rely on Active Directory for the domain to provide all of the necessary information about the resources on the network. In a multidomain environment, however, users often need to access resources outside their domain—resources that might be more difficult to find. For this, a *global catalog* holds information about all objects in a forest. The global catalog enables users and applications to find objects in an Active Directory domain tree if the user or application knows one or more attributes of the target object.

Through the replication process, Active Directory automatically generates the contents of the global catalog from the domain controllers in the directory. The global catalog holds a partial replica of Active Directory. Even though every object is listed in the global catalog, only a limited set of attributes for those objects is replicated in it. The attributes listed for each object in the global catalog are defined in the schema. A base set of attributes is replicated to the global catalog, but you can specify additional attributes to meet the needs of your organization.

By default, the entire forest has only one global catalog, and that is the first domain controller installed in the first domain of the first tree. All others must be configured manually. We recommend adding a second global catalog for backup and load balancing. Furthermore, each domain should have at least one global catalog to provide for more efficient Active Directory searches and network logons.

Windows Server 2003 Sites

A Windows Server 2003 site is a group of computers that exist on one or more IP subnets. Computers within a site should be connected by a fast, reliable network connection. Using *Windows sites* helps maximize network efficiency and provide fault tolerance. DNS also uses Windows sites to help clients find the closest domain controller to validate logon credentials.

Exchange Server 2007 makes extensive use of Active Directory information on global catalog servers. For efficient communication, Exchange Server 2007 requires direct access to a global catalog server in your LAN.

Sites are created and configured using the Active Directory Sites and Services tool. No direct relationship exists between Windows domains and sites, so a single domain can span multiple sites, and a single site can span multiple domains.

Schema

A *schema* represents the structure of a database system—the tables and fields in that database and how the tables and fields are related to one another. The Active Directory information is also represented by a schema. All objects that can be stored in Active Directory are defined in the schema.

Installing Active Directory on the first domain controller in a network creates a schema that contains definitions of commonly used objects and attributes. The schema also defines objects and attributes that Active Directory uses internally. When Exchange Server 2007 is installed, Exchange setup extends the schema to support information that Exchange needs. Updates to the schema require replication of the schema across the forest and also to all domain controllers in the forest. For more information about how Exchange updates the schema, see Chapter 2.

Active Directory Partitions, Masters, and Replication

The information contained within Active Directory as a whole is not all contained in a single location, or partition in this case. Actually, five different Active Directory partitions contain different pieces of information about the Active Directory forest and domains. Because each partition type contains different information, the domain controllers that each partition type is replicated to within the forest are also different. We'll briefly cover these directory partitions in the following sections.

Domain Partition

The domain partition contains all the objects that you as an administrator are used to working with on a daily basis. These objects include items such as user accounts, computer accounts, and groups. The contents of the domain partition thus are specific to each individual domain within a forest and therefore are replicated only to the domain controllers in that specific domain.

Configuration Partition

The configuration partition contains all the configuration information about the forest, including information about Active Directory and AD-integrated applications such as Exchange Server. As such, the configuration partition is replicated to every domain controller in the entire forest. Applications benefit from storing their configuration data in the configuration partition because no additional work or configuration is needed to ensure that configuration information is available forest-wide.

Schema Partition

The schema partition, true to its name, is the housing location for the information that defines what objects exist within that Active Directory forest. Each object also has multiple attributes that can be configured, and thus they are also defined in the schema. The schema partition, being so critical to Active Directory, is also replicated to every domain controller in the forest. Unlike other data in Active Directory, only one copy of the schema partition is writable—that is to say that only one domain controller can make changes to the schema. That special domain controller is known as the *schema master*. We'll discuss the "roles" that domain controllers hold, including that of the schema master, later in this chapter.

Application Partition

Application partitions are new in Windows Server 2003 and are for holding data that is specific to an application. By default, no application partitions are created in a fresh installation of Windows Server 2003 Active Directory; however, usually some are created to house the information that makes up Active Directory–integrated DNS zones. Application partitions are not limited to being replicated to only a single domain or the entire forest—replication can occur with any domain controller in the forest, spanning multiple domains.

Global Catalog Partition

The global catalog partition is a special type of Active Directory partition that is replicated to configured domain controllers across the entire forest. Unlike other AD partitions, you cannot directly enter information into the global catalog partition; instead, information is placed into it based on the contents of each domain.

Active Directory Masters

Within each Active Directory forest, five unique "roles"—or more properly, *operations masters*—exist that reside on certain domain controllers. Active Directory uses a multimaster replication system, which means that all domain controllers are equal. Well, mostly equal. Certain tasks do not lend themselves well to having multiple domain controllers performing them (especially at the same time), so the operations master roles exist. Active Directory has five operations master roles, and initially all five exist on the first domain controller that is installed in a new forest. You can, and should, move roles around as additional domain controllers are joined to the forest and as subsequent domains are created within the forest.

The operations master roles in Active Directory are as follows:

- *Domain naming master*: The domain naming master role exists only one time within the entire forest. The domain controller that holds this role is responsible for creating new domains in the forest and also for removing domains from the forest. These tasks cannot normally be performed if the domain controller holding this role is unavailable.
- *Schema master*: The schema master role also exists only once within the forest. As we discussed briefly, any changes that need to be made to the schema of the forest must be made on the schema master. Once the changes are made on the domain controller holding this role, they are then replicated to the rest of the domain controllers in the forest. A failure of the schema master will prevent only schema modifications from being made in that forest. Exchange Server 2007, specifically, requires schema modifications and thus will fail to install if the schema master cannot be contacted.
- *Infrastructure master*: The infrastructure master role exists once in every domain in the forest and is responsible for updating changes made to user account names and group

memberships. The domain controller holding this role in the domain maintains the up-to-date copy of this information as it is changed and then replicates it to the other domain controllers in the domain.

- *PDC emulator master*: The primary domain controller (PDC) emulator master role also exists once in each domain in the forest. The PDC emulator master is required to provide backward interoperability with Windows NT 4.0 backup domain controllers (BDCs). In a mixed environment, the PDC emulator master processes all password changes in the domain. Additionally, failed authentication attempts are forwarded to the PDC emulator to be retried, accounting for changes that might have occurred to the password. The PDC emulator master also typically functions as the Network Time Protocol (NTP) source for the domain and is usually configured to take time input from a trusted internal (that is, atomic clock, satellite clock) or external NTP time source.
- *RID master*: The RID master role also exists once in every domain in the forest and is responsible for issuing blocks of relative identifiers (RIDs) to other domain controllers in the domain. This block of RIDs is known as the *RID pool*. When a domain controller runs low on RIDs in its RID pool, it makes a request to the RID master for another block of RIDs for its usage. Each object that exists within a domain has a unique security identifier (SID). This SID is composed of two parts: a domain RID (common throughout the domain) and a unique RID from the RID pool. These are combined to create a globally unique (within the forest) SID for that object. When the pool of RIDs has been exhausted on a domain controller, it will be unable to create new objects in the domain. Exchange Server 2007 creates several security principals during its installation and thus requires the usage of some RIDs from the RID pool of a domain controller.

Replication

Although we've mentioned replication in Active Directory several times now, we have not yet properly discussed it. We'll remedy that situation now before moving into the next section of this chapter.

Replication is the process by which all domain controllers in a domain or forest pass changes to other domain controllers and thus update their copies of the specific Active Directory partitions they hold as they themselves receive replication updates from other domain controllers. Because changes occur almost constantly across multiple domain controllers within a forest, the replication used for Active Directory is referred to as *loosely consistent*, meaning that not every domain controller in the forest with a certain partition will have the same information at any time. However, over time, *convergence* occurs as all domain controllers receive and pass replication updates and the partitions that they hold become closer to matching exactly. In a production environment, complete convergence is almost impossible to achieve, but that rarely poses a problem. Administrators with the appropriate permissions can always manually trigger replication to be performed between domain controllers, so important changes can be forced to replicate if normal replication schedules are not appropriate at the time, which is typically only a problem when dealing with *intersite replication*.

Given that Active Directory uses sites to map the Active Directory network to that of the physical network, replication thus occurs differently between sites (intersite replication) than it does between domain controllers in the same site (intrasite replication). Intersite replication is designed to have the minimum possible impact on the typically slower wide area network (WAN) links that commonly separate the physical locations that Active Directory sites represent. As such, the replication traffic is highly compressed and also occurs on a schedule that is configured on the *site link* object that is created to logically connect two Active Directory sites. Thus, changes made on a domain controller in Site A will not be sent to a domain controller in Site B until the next scheduled replication time based on the replication interval and allowable replication times that were configured. Conversely, intrasite replication occurs almost immediately after a change has been to some bit of Active Directory information. The domain controller that the change is made on will wait 15 seconds (to account for any additional changes) and then will begin replicating its changes to the other domain controllers within that site. After replication has occurred with the first replication partner that domain controller has, it will wait three seconds and then commence replication with its next replication partner, and so forth, until the original domain controller has replicated with all replication partners within that site.

Replication latency occurs when a change made on one domain controller has not been replicated to another domain controller, either in the same site or in a different site. Obviously, the replication latency within a site should always be much lower than that between sites, but should replication problems arise between domain controllers, latency can even begin to exist within a site. On the surface, replication latency is not completely desirable, but it must be dealt with accordingly when using a distributed multimaster replication environment like Active Directory uses. Faster, higher-quality (or cheaper) WAN links will lend themselves to configuration replication to occur more frequently than slower, less reliable (or more expensive) WAN links will. The price to be paid for lower replication latency, in an Active Directory environment that is otherwise healthy and functioning properly, is the cost of pushing more data over these typically congested and high-cost WAN links. You, or the administrator who is ultimately responsible for managing Active Directory across your organization, will have to determine what is best to meet your specific needs.

To learn more about Active Directory, start by checking out the Windows Server 2003 product documentation. It provides an overview of the technology and illustrates many of the benefits of using Active Directory. If you are interested in going beyond the basics, take a look at *Active Directory for Microsoft Windows Server 2003 Technical Reference*, by Mike Mulcare and Stan Reimer (Microsoft Press, 2003).

Active Directory and Exchange Server 2007

In versions of Exchange Server prior to Exchange 2000 Server, Exchange maintained a directory of its own through a service known as the Directory Service. On each Exchange server, the Directory Service maintained a copy of the directory in a database file on the Exchange server and took care of replicating changes in the directory to other Exchange servers. In Exchange Server 2007, the Exchange Directory Service has been removed altogether. Exchange is now totally reliant on Active Directory to provide its directory services.

This new reliance causes a shift in the way that the Exchange directory is maintained. The "Forests" section examines the effects that boundaries of a forest place on Exchange. Then the "Domain Name Service" section looks at the interaction of DNS in an Exchange organization. Finally, the "Directory Replication" section looks at the differences in directory replication now that Exchange no longer handles the directory information or uses the Active Directory Connector to exchange data with previous versions of Exchange Server.

Forests

By default, the global catalog shows objects only within a single Windows Server 2003 forest, so an Exchange organization must be within the boundaries of a forest. This is different from earlier versions of Windows NT and Exchange 5.5. In previous versions, an Exchange organization could span domains that did not trust one another because Exchange 5.5 did not rely so much on the underlying security structure of Windows NT. With Active Directory and Exchange Server 2007, the security structure is integrated, which means a single Exchange organization cannot span multiple forests but can span multiple domains within a single forest.

Domain Name Service (DNS)

In previous versions of Windows NT, the *Windows Internet Name Service* (WINS) was the primary provider of name resolution within an organization because it provided dynamic publishing and full names to network address mapping. DNS was really required only for those organizations that needed Internet connectivity, though it was usually a recommended practice to use DNS with earlier versions of Exchange Server as well. Windows Server 2003 relies almost exclusively on DNS because it provides maximum interoperability with Internet technologies. For Exchange Server 2007 to function, a DNS service must be running in your organization. Outlook Web Access, SMTP connectivity, and Internet connectivity all rely on DNS.

Active Directory is often called a *namespace*, which is similar to the directory service in earlier versions of Exchange and means any bounded area in which a given name can be resolved. The DNS name creates a namespace for a tree or forest, such as wileypublishing.com. All child domains of wileypublishing.com, such as sales.wileypublishing.com, share the root namespace. In Exchange Server 2007, Active Directory forms a namespace in which the name of an object in the directory can be resolved to the object. All domains that have a common root domain form a *contiguous namespace*. This means the domain name of a child domain is the child domain name appended to the name of the parent domain.

In Windows Server 2003 domains using DNS, a domain name such as hsv.widgets.com does not affect the email addresses for Exchange users created in that domain. Although a user's logon name might be user@sales.wileypublishing.com, you control how email addresses are generated using email address generation policies in the Exchange Management Console.

Directory Replication

In versions of Exchange Server prior to Exchange 2000 Server, the directory was part of Exchange, and Exchange Server handled replication of that directory. When attributes of directory objects changed, the entire object was replicated throughout the organization.

Now, all directory functions have been passed to Active Directory, which replicates at the attribute level instead of the object level. This means if a change is made to an attribute, only that attribute (and not the entire object) is replicated to other domain controllers in the domain, resulting in less network traffic and more efficient use of server resources.

The removal of the Exchange Directory Service first occurred with the release of Exchange 2000 Server.

Active Directory Partitions

Although you've examined briefly already how Exchange Server 2007 uses the different Active Directory partitions, you'll dig a bit deeper in this section. Recall that there can be only one Exchange Server organization within an entire forest. This limitation is imposed because of the storage of Exchange information in the Active Directory partitions of that forest, which are not replicated between forests. Specific examples of how Exchange Server 2007 uses these Active Directory partitions include the following:

- The configuration partition stores all configuration information about the Exchange organization. This information includes items such as recipient policies, address lists, and Exchange settings. The configuration partition is replicated to every domain controller in the forest; therefore, this critical Exchange configuration information is available to every domain user no matter in which domain their user account is located.
- The domain partition stores information about the basic blocks of Exchange Server: its recipient objects. Recipient objects include users, contacts, and groups that have email addresses configured on them. We'll go into great depth about configuring and managing recipients in Chapter 6.
- The schema partition is modified by the Exchange Server 2007 setup routine to add attributes to existing objects, such as users and groups. Additionally, the schema is extended to include Exchange Server–specific objects that are required for Exchange Server to function properly. We'll cover modifying the schema to support the installation of Exchange Server 2007 in Chapter 2.
- The global catalog partition received many new items of information as a result of the installation of Exchange Server 2007 in a forest. Exchange uses the global catalog to generate address lists for usage by Exchange recipients, and Exchange Server also uses it to locate a recipient to aid in the delivery of mail items to that recipient. Exchange Server automatically generates the global address list (GAL) from all recipients listed in the global catalog.

Message Flow

In previous versions of Exchange Server, a complex link-state routing algorithm was used to route messages between geographically separated Exchange Servers. Exchange used routing groups that were connected with routing group connectors to perform this routing. With the elimination of routing groups and link-state routing in Exchange Server 2007, all Exchange message routing is performed by Hub Transport servers using the Active Directory sites and site links that service Active Directory itself. As such, message routing (both within the same site and across site links) is significantly less complex in Exchange Server 2007.

We will cover all the Exchange Server 2007 roles, including the Hub Transport role, in Chapter 3.

Within each Active Directory site that contains a Mailbox server (or Unified Messaging server), you must have at least one Hub Transport server. The Hub Transport server is responsible for routing all messages within a site and between connected sites. Even a message that is sent from a recipient on Server A to another recipient on Server A must first cross through a Hub Transport server for delivery—a big change in message routing from Exchange Server 2003. When messages must be routed between sites, the Hub Transport server in the originating site determines the best route available at that time to the destination server and routes the message accordingly.

Message routing between sites occurs as detailed here:

1. The sending user submits the message to his or her mailbox on the Mailbox server.
2. The Mailbox server notifies a Hub Transport server in its Active Directory site that it has a message awaiting pickup.
3. A Hub Transport server in the same Active Directory site as the originating Mailbox server picks up (retrieves) the message from the Mailbox server.
4. The Hub Transport server performs a query against Active Directory to determine what Mailbox server the recipient of the message is on.
5. The Hub Transport server then computes the lowest-cost route to the site containing the destination Mailbox server based on the site link costs configured on site links between the sites.
6. The Hub Transport server in the originating Active Directory site then sends the message along the lower-cost route it has computed.
7. If multiple Active Directory sites must be crossed, the message is delivered to a Hub Transport server along the path and then passed along to a Hub Transport server in the destination site.
8. If there are no operating Hub Transport servers in the destination site, the message will be queued on a Hub Transport server in the site closest to the one where the destination Mailbox server resides. The message will not be delivered until a Hub Transport server in the destination site is available to deliver it.
9. When the message reaches the Hub Transport in the destination site, that Hub Transport server assumes responsibility to deliver the message, and the message is sent to the appropriate destination Mailbox server.

Real World Scenario

Planning the Active Directory Deployment

If you are lucky enough to be planning a completely new Active Directory deployment for your organization, then you can be certain to place domain controllers and global catalog servers in locations that make sense for how your organization is organized and how it operates. When planning how and where to locate these key servers in your Active Directory environment, there is no absolute answer that works for all scenarios. The saying "the more, the better" is not necessarily true, especially if replication over slow WAN links becomes too much for those links to handle. Conversely, saying "less is more" is almost always untrue when it comes to implementing a solid Active Directory infrastructure. Remember, this will be the foundation of your entire network, so you should take the time you need to get it right the first time.

These are a few general guidelines you should keep in mind as you're working in different scenarios:

- Every domain in the Active Directory forest must have at least two domain controllers. This is for both client load balancing and disaster recovery in case one domain controller should happen to fail.
- You should place additional domain controllers in domains as organizational structures (such as physical location or client groupings) dictate.
- You should be aware that additional domain controllers will cause additional replication traffic, which can be problematic for intersite replication across slow WAN links.
- Every Active Directory site must have at least one domain controller and one domain controller configured as a global catalog if Exchange recipients are in that site.
- If a site has multiple domain controllers, consider using Bridgehead servers for Active Directory replication.

Summary

The better you understand how the Exchange system works, the better you'll be able to plan a viable network and troubleshoot that network when problems occur. This chapter examined three basic aspects of Exchange Server 2003 architecture: how Exchange is integrated with Active Directory, how information is stored on an Exchange server, and how messages flow within an Exchange organization.

At the top of the Active Directory hierarchy is the domain forest, which represents the outside boundary that any Exchange organization can reach. A domain tree is a hierarchical arrangement of domains that share a common namespace. The first domain in a tree is the root domain. Domains added under this are child domains. Within the domain tree, domains establish trust relationships with one another that allow objects in a trusted domain to access resources in a trusting domain. A domain is a group of computers and other resources that are part of a network and share a common directory database. Each domain contains at least one domain controller. Multiple domain controllers per domain can be used for load balancing and fault tolerance.

When Exchange is installed, many objects, such as users, are enhanced with Exchange-related features. A global catalog holds information about all the objects in a forest. Objects can be grouped into organizational units that allow administrators to effectively manage large groups of similar objects at the same time.

Within Active Directory, five partitions store certain pieces of the total information that makes up Active Directory. These partitions are the domain partition, configuration partition, schema partition, global catalog partition, and application partition(s). There can be multiple application partitions within the forest and domains.

Although Active Directory uses multimaster replication, there are five specific roles that only one domain controller in a forest or domain can hold at any one time. The five roles are the domain naming master (one per forest), schema master (one per forest), infrastructure master (one per domain), PDC emulator master (one per domain) and RID master (one per domain). The failure of a domain controller holding each role will cause different effects on the forest and domain. Exchange Server 2007 must contact the domain controller holding the schema master role during setup to modify and extend the schema.

Active Directory is loosely consistent, meaning that not every domain controller in the forest with a certain partition will have the same information at any time. However, over time, convergence occurs as all domain controllers receive and pass replication updates and the partitions that they hold become closer to matching exactly. In a production environment, complete convergence is almost impossible to achieve, but that rarely poses a problem.

Intersite replication is designed to have the minimum possible impact on the typically slower WAN links that commonly separate the physical locations that Active Directory sites represent. As such, the replication traffic is highly compressed and also occurs on a schedule that is configured on the site link object that is created to logically connect two Active Directory sites. Conversely, intrasite replication occurs almost immediately after a change to some bit of Active Directory information has taken place. The domain controller that the change is made on will wait 15 seconds (to account for any additional changes) and then will begin replicating its changes to the other domain controllers within that site.

Exam Essentials

Understand Active Directory. Although this book is not trying to prepare you for an exam related to Active Directory design, support, or administration, it is absolutely imperative that you understand how Active Directory is designed and how it functions. With Exchange being completely Active Directory–integrated and aware, all administrative functions related to users and mailboxes are tied into Active Directory. To that end, ensure that you have a good understanding of both the logical and physical structure of Active Directory. In addition, you should understand the various domain functional levels that are available in Windows Server 2003 and how they will impact your overall network.

Understand basic message routing. It is helpful, both in preparing for this exam and in the day-to-day administration of Exchange Server 2003, to understand how messages are routed within the same site and between different sites. All messages are routed through the Hub Transport server, even if the originating and destination recipients reside on the same Mailbox server.

Review Questions

1. You are currently running in the Windows 2000 mixed domain functional level and are considering making the switch to the Windows 2000 native domain functional level. Which of the following would be valid concerns to take into account before making the switch? (Choose all that apply.)

   A. The switch is irreversible.

   B. If you later decide to switch to the Windows 2000 mixed domain functional level, all object configuration will be lost.

   C. Exchange Server 5.5 cannot be run in a Windows 2000 native domain functional-level environment.

   D. You must upgrade or retire all Windows NT 4.0 domain controllers.

2. Which of the following statements is true of domains in a single-domain tree?

   A. Domains are not configured with trust relationships by default.

   B. Domains are automatically configured with one-way trust relationships flowing from parent domains to child domains.

   C. Domains are automatically configured with two-way nontransitive trusts.

   D. Domains are automatically configured with two-way transitive trusts.

3. By default, how long will a Windows Server 2003 domain controller wait to initiate replication to its replication partners in the same Active Directory site after a change is made on it?

   A. 3 seconds

   B. 3 minutes

   C. 15 seconds

   D. 15 minutes

4. A hierarchical arrangement of one or more Windows Server 2003 domains that share a common namespace is referred to as a __________.

   A. Windows Server 2003 site

   B. domain site

   C. domain tree

   D. domain forest

5. You have just installed the first Windows Server 2003 server on your network and want to make it a domain controller. How would you do this?

   A. The first Windows Server 2003 server is automatically made a domain controller.

   B. Install Active Directory on the computer.

   C. Install DNS on the computer.

   D. Install the schema on the computer.

6. Which of the following statements about an organizational unit is true?
   - **A.** An organizational unit cannot contain objects from other domains.
   - **B.** An organizational unit can contain objects only from other trusted domains.
   - **C.** An organizational unit can contain objects only from other domains in the same domain tree.
   - **D.** An organizational unit can contain objects only from other domains in the same domain forest.

7. What service is the primary provider of name resolution on a Windows Server 2003 network?
   - **A.** X.400
   - **B.** DNS
   - **C.** WINS
   - **D.** SMTP

8. Messages in Exchange Server 2007 are routed by which server?
   - **A.** The global catalog server
   - **B.** The infrastructure master server
   - **C.** The Hub Transport server
   - **D.** The Mailbox server

9. If Exchange Server 2007 fails to contact a certain operations master role holder during installation, the installation process will fail. Which operations master role is this?
   - **A.** Infrastructure master
   - **B.** Schema master
   - **C.** RID master
   - **D.** Domain naming master

10. Message routing between Exchange Server 2007 Mailbox servers uses what method to determine the best route?
    - **A.** Link-state algorithms
    - **B.** Site link costs
    - **C.** Packet latency
    - **D.** Open shortest path first routing

11. Of the following features available in Exchange Server 2003, which are no longer supported in Exchange Server 2007? (Choose two answers.)
    - **A.** Public folders
    - **B.** The streaming database
    - **C.** Command-line management
    - **D.** Integration with Exchange Server 5.5

12. User account objects are found in which Active Directory partition?
    A. Configuration
    B. Global catalog
    C. Schema
    D. Domain

13. What impact does the failure of the domain controller holding the schema master role have on the normal operations of Active Directory?
    A. Active Directory will cease to function properly until the schema master role has been brought back online.
    B. Active Directory will continue to function normally except that schema modifications cannot be processed until the schema master role has been brought back online.
    C. Active Directory will continue to function normally except that intrasite replication will fail until the schema master role has been brought back online.
    D. Active Directory will continue to function normally except that down-level Windows NT 4.0 BDCs will not be able to interact with the domain they are part of.

14. To use universal groups in your Active Directory domain, what minimum domain functional level must you be running at?
    A. Windows Server 2003
    B. Windows 2000 mixed
    C. Windows Server 2003 interim
    D. Windows 2000 native

15. Which of the following is the smallest object that other Active Directory objects can be placed within and have authority delegated over them?
    A. Organizational unit
    B. Forest
    C. Domain
    D. Site

16. Which domain controllers in an Active Directory environment maintain a copy of the configuration partition?
    A. Certain domain controllers in all domains
    B. All domain controllers in a single domain
    C. All domain controllers in the forest
    D. Certain domain controllers in the forest

17. *Intersite replication* refers to which of the following?
    A. Replication between domain controllers in the same Active Directory site
    B. Replication between domain controllers in different domains
    C. Replication between domain controllers in different forests
    D. Replication between domain controllers in different Active Directory sites

18. Which Active Directory partition is used to create the Exchange address lists?
    - A. Configuration
    - B. Global catalog
    - C. Schema
    - D. Domain

19. If the Hub Transport server in the destination site is unavailable, where will a message in routing be queued up temporarily?
    - A. On the Hub Transport server in the source site
    - B. On the Mailbox server in the destination site
    - C. On the Hub Transport server in the destination site
    - D. On the Hub Transport server in the site nearest to the destination site

20. What administrative console is used to configure the link costs that Exchange Server 2007 uses when routing messages?
    - A. Exchange System Manager
    - B. Active Directory Users and Computers
    - C. Active Directory Sites and Services
    - D. Active Directory Domains and Trusts

Answers to Review Questions

1. A, D. The switch to the Windows 2000 native domain functional level is a one-time, one-way switch and is irreversible. Once you have switched to the Windows 2000 native domain functional level, you will no longer be able to have Windows NT 4.0 domain controllers within the organization.

2. D. Windows Server 2003 (along with Windows 2000 Server) and Active Directory support transitive two-way trusts between domains. When a child domain is created, a trust relationship is automatically configured between that child domain and the parent domain. This trust is two-way, meaning that resource access requests can flow from either domain to the other.

3. C. The domain controller that the change is made on will wait 15 seconds (to account for any additional changes) and then will begin replicating its changes to the other domain controllers within that site. After replication has occurred with the first replication partner that domain controller has, it will wait three seconds and then commence replication with its next replication partner, and so forth, until the original domain controller has replicated with all replication partners within that site.

4. C. A domain tree is a hierarchical arrangement of one or more Windows Active Directory domains that share a common namespace. Domain Name Service (DNS) domain names represent the tree structure. The first domain in a tree is called the *root domain*.

5. B. To create a domain controller, all you have to do is install the Active Directory service on it. During this process, you have the option of creating a new domain or joining an existing domain. If you create a new domain, you also have the option of creating or joining an existing domain tree or forest.

6. A. An organizational unit is a container in which you can place objects such as user accounts, groups, computers, printers, applications, file shares, and other organizational units. An organizational unit cannot contain objects from other domains and is the smallest unit to which you can assign or delegate administrative authority. Organizational units are provided strictly for administrative purposes and convenience.

7. B. DNS is the primary provider of name resolution for Windows Server 2003–based networks. In fact, the Windows Server 2003 domain structure is based on DNS structure, and Active Directory requires that DNS be used.

8. C. All messages in Exchange Server 2007 are routed to their destination mailbox by the Hub Transport server, even if the message is sent between recipients on the same Exchange Mailbox server.

9. B. Any changes that need to be made to the schema of the forest must be made on the schema master. Exchange Server 2007 requires schema modifications and thus will fail to install if the schema master cannot be contacted.

10. B. The Hub Transport server, which is responsible for message routing in Exchange Server 2007, computes the lowest cost route to the site containing the destination Mailbox server based on the site link costs configured on site links between the sites.

11. B, D. The streaming database (`*.stm`), first introduced in Exchange 2000 Server, has been removed in Exchange Server 2007. Several other enhancements have been made to storage in Exchange Server 2007. Exchange Server 2007 does not interoperate with the Active Directory Connector (ADC) or Site Replication Service (SRS) as in the previous two versions of Exchange. As a result, you can no longer directly migrate from Exchange Server 5.5 to Exchange Server 2007.

12. D. The domain partition contains all of the objects that you as an administrator are used to working with on a daily basis. These objects include user accounts, computer accounts, and groups. The contents of the domain partition thus are specific to each individual domain within a forest and therefore are replicated to the domain controllers in that specific domain only.

13. B. A failure of the schema master will prevent only schema modifications from being made in that forest.

14. D. The Windows 2000 native domain functional level is the minimum domain functional level at which universal groups become available, along with several other Active Directory features; it allows for Windows 2000 Server and Windows Server 2003 domain controllers only.

15. A. The organizational unit (OU) is a container in which you can place objects such as user accounts, groups, computers, printers, applications, file shares, and other organizational units. An organizational unit cannot contain objects from other domains and is the smallest unit to which you can assign or delegate administrative authority.

16. C. The configuration partition contains all the configuration information about the forest, including information about Active Directory and AD-integrated applications such as Exchange Server. As such, the configuration partition is replicated to every domain controller in the entire forest.

17. D. Intersite replication occurs between domain controllers in different Active Directory sites. Intrasite replication occurs between domain controllers in the same Active Directory site. Sites can span domains, and domains can span sites; thus, no direct relationship must exist between the two. Forests do not replicate.

18. B. Exchange uses a global catalog to generate address lists for usage by Exchange recipients and also uses it to locate a recipient to aid in delivering mail items to that recipient. The global address list (GAL) is automatically generated by Exchange Server from all recipients listed in the global catalog.

19. D. If there are no operating Hub Transport servers in the destination site, the message will be queued on a Hub Transport server in the site closest to the one where the destination Mailbox server resides. The message will not be delivered until a Hub Transport server in the destination site is available to deliver it.

20. C. The Hub Transport server, which is responsible for routing all messages in Exchange Server 2007, computes the lowest-cost route to the site containing the destination Mailbox server based on the site link costs configured on site links between the sites. Sites (and site link costs) are created and configured using the Active Directory Sites and Services tool.

Chapter 2

Preparing for the Exchange Server 2007 Installation

MICROSOFT EXAM OBJECTIVES COVERED IN THIS CHAPTER

✓ **Installing and Configuring Microsoft Exchange Servers**

- Prepare the infrastructure for Exchange installation.
- Prepare the servers for Exchange installation.

Because Exchange Server 2007 is a Microsoft Windows Server 2003 application, the installation process is pretty straightforward. However, you still need to address some issues in a careful manner. In this chapter, you will learn the necessary steps to prepare for installing Microsoft Exchange Server 2007. The main subjects of this chapter are as follows:

- Exchange Server 2007 editions and licensing
- Exchange Server 2007 roles
- Preinstallation server and network considerations
- Preinstallation modification of Active Directory
- Modification of existing Exchange organizations to support migration

Exchange Server 2007 Editions and Licensing

Microsoft Exchange Server 2007 is available in two editions: a *Standard Edition*, which is simply called Exchange Server 2007, and an *Enterprise Edition*. The main difference between them is the advanced features supported in the Enterprise Edition. However, it's important to reiterate that both versions of Exchange Server 2007 are 64-bit applications, meaning that they must be installed on a 64-bit version of Windows Server 2003 and on hardware that provides 64-bit support.

Standard Edition Features

The Standard Edition includes the following features:

- Basic messaging functionality
- Role-based server installation
- Support for volume shadow copy
- Usage of the recovery storage group
- Support for Outlook Anywhere (replaces HTTP over RPC) and Outlook Web Access
- No limit on database size (new in Exchange Server 2007)
- Maximum of five storage groups per mailbox server
- Maximum of five databases per mailbox server
- Support of local continuous replication

Additional Enterprise Edition Features

The Enterprise Edition includes all the features of the Standard Edition and adds the following:

- Allows up to 50 storage groups per mailbox server
- Allows up to 50 databases per mailbox server
- Supports all clustering models: single copy clusters, local continuous replication, and cluster continuous replication

Exchange Server 2007 Compared to Previous Versions

To allow you to see just how much different Exchange Server 2007 is from the versions that came before it, Table 2.1 compares a small subset of features across each version of Exchange Server from 2000 to 2007.

TABLE 2.1 Exchange Server 2007 Compared to Previous Versions

Key Feature	Exchange Server 2007	Exchange Server 2003	Exchange 2000 Server
Virus scanning API	Available	Available	Available
Exchange Server intelligent message filter (IMF)	Available	Available	Not available
Distribution groups restricted to only authenticated senders	Available	Available	Not available
Attachment stripping	Available	Not available	Not available
Open proxy detection (prevents DoS) and spam	Available	Not available	Not available
OWA traffic SSL protected by default	Available	Not available; must be manually configured	Not available; must be manually configured
Journaling	Available	Available	Available
Per-user journaling	Available	Not available	Not available
Message retention and expiration policies	Available	Not available	Not available
Hub Transport rules	Available	Not available	Not available
Active/passive clustering	Available	Available	Available

TABLE 2.1 Exchange Server 2007 Compared to Previous Versions *(continued)*

Key Feature	Exchange Server 2007	Exchange Server 2003	Exchange 2000 Server
Active/active clustering	Not available	Available	Not available
Continuous replication	Available	Not available	Not available
Recover a database to any Exchange server	Available	Not available	Not available
Recovery storage groups	Available	Available	Not available
Outlook Web Access	Available	Available	Available
Forms-based authentication	Not available	Available	Not available
Different out-of-office messages for internal and external senders	Available	Not available	Not available
Outlook Mobile Access	Not available	Available	Not available
Over-the-air search of mailbox from wireless device	Available	Not available	Not available
Voicemail delivery to mailbox	Available	Not available	Not available
Fax delivery to mailbox	Available	Not available	Not available
Outlook Voice Access	Available	Not available	Not available

Obviously, this is just a small sampling of the overall feature set of each version of Exchange, but it does give a quick glimpse into some of the newer features that help make Exchange Server 2007 stand out from its predecessors. You can get a complete review of the feature set of each version of Exchange by visiting the following page on the Microsoft website: `www.microsoft.com/exchange/evaluation/features/ex_compare.mspx`.

Licensing Issues

Licensing issues relate to matters of legality (specifically, the number of servers Exchange can be installed on and the number of clients that can access a server). Three main licenses pertain to the various Microsoft Exchange product packages:

- Server license
- Client access license (CAL)
- Client license

Server License

The basic *server license* provides the legal right to install and operate Microsoft Exchange Server 2007 on a single-server machine. In addition, you can install the Exchange Management Console (the primary utility used to administer an Exchange Server 2007 organization) on additional machines without additional licenses.

Since licensing policies can change over time, always check the latest policy to ensure your compliance. You can find the licensing policies for Exchange Server 2007 at `www.microsoft.com/exchange/howtobuy/enterprise.asp`.

Client Access License

A *client access license (CAL)* gives a user the legal right to access an Exchange server. An organization designates the number of CALs it needs when a Microsoft Exchange server is purchased. Each CAL provides one user with the legal right to access the Exchange server. Any client software that has the ability to be a client to Microsoft Exchange Server is legally required to have a CAL purchased for it. Microsoft Exchange Server 2007 uses either the per-user or per-device licensing mode, which means that each user or device accessing the server must possess a valid CAL.

Client access licenses are *not* included in any version of Microsoft Windows or Microsoft Office. For example, the version of Office Outlook 2007 that comes with Microsoft Office 2007 requires, by law, that a separate CAL be purchased before accessing an Exchange server.

New with Exchange Server 2007, however, is the designation of two types of CALs. What previously would have been the only type of CAL is now referred to as the Exchange Server Standard CAL. The Standard CAL provides licenses for Exchange Server 2007 functionality such as email, calendaring, and remote access via Outlook Web Access (OWA). The new Exchange Server Enterprise CAL is required to access the advanced features of Exchange Server 2007 such as Forefront Security for Exchange Server (antivirus and antispam), unified messaging, and other desirable features such as compliance controls, managed folders, and per-user journaling. Enterprise CALs are added to existing standard CALs to make all functionality available.

Client License

In addition to having a CAL, each piece of client software must also be licensed for use on the client computer. This means each piece of client software, such as Office Outlook 2007, needs its own license to be legally installed on the client computer plus a CAL to legally connect to an Exchange server.

Exchange Server 2007 Roles

As you learned in Chapter 1, "Exchange Server 2007 and Active Directory Review," Exchange Server 2007 no longer uses the familiar front-end and back-end names to designate a server's primary function. Exchange Server 2007, in a move toward modular computing (and thus increased functionality and security), offers five distinctly different server roles for deployment. Some, such as the Hub Transport and Mailbox server roles, are absolutely mandatory. Others, such as the Client Access and Edge Transport, will vary in usage from organization to organization. The Unified Messaging server role, while one of the most exciting changes in Exchange Server 2007, will be utilized less frequently in most organizations because they won't have a compatible phone system or a desire to move to unified messaging from their current voicemail and fax solutions.

Mailbox Server

The Mailbox server is the first of two required Exchange Server 2007 roles you'll examine here. As its name implies, the primary function of the Mailbox server role is to provide users' with mailboxes that can be accessed directly from the Outlook client. The Mailbox server also contains the databases that hold public folders if you are still using them in your organization, so, as a point of comparison, the Mailbox server is most like the back-end server from previous versions of Exchange.

As noted previously, the Mailbox server can hold up to 50 storage groups per server with a total of 50 databases (stores) per server. Each storage group has its own set of transaction logs, so single-database storage groups do have a place in just about any size of organization from a disaster recovery and business continuity perspective.

The Mailbox server role is also where high availability for mailboxes and public folders comes from. Mailbox servers in Exchange Server 2007 can be clustered using either single-copy clusters (the traditional active/passive clustering provided in previous versions of Exchange) or cluster continuous replication (CCR). Additionally, smaller organizations will find significant value in the new local continuous replication (LCR) functionality offered by Mailbox servers.

Unlike previous versions of Exchange Server, messages are not actually routed between mailboxes by Mailbox servers in Exchange Server 2007. All message routing, even between mailboxes on the same Mailbox server, is now the responsibility of the Hub Transport server, which we'll cover next. Because of the nature of the data contained on Mailbox servers, they do not need to be directly accessible from the Internet. Additionally, Mailbox servers must be members of Active Directory domains that have been prepared for the installation of Exchange Server 2007, and they must have fast, reliable connectivity to global catalog servers and domain controllers.

Hub Transport Server

The Hub Transport server is the second mandatory Exchange Server 2007 role that must be deployed. The primary function of the Hub Transport server is to route messages for delivery within the Exchange organization. By moving message routing to another server (other than the Mailbox server), many new and needed features and functions become available. As an example, while messages are being routed through the Hub Transport server, they can have transport rules and filtering policies applied to them that determine where they'll wind up, such as being delivered to a compliance mailbox in addition to the recipient's mailbox, or what they'll look like, such as stamping a disclaimer on every outbound message.

Along with the responsibility for message routing, all message categorization that used to occur on the originating Mailbox server in previous versions of Exchange is now performed on the Hub Transport server. Hub Transport servers are thus a critical part of your healthy and functioning Exchange Server 2007 organization. Although Hub Transport servers cannot be clustered for high availability, multiple Hub Transport servers can (and should) be placed in each Active Directory site. In this arrangement, all Hub Transport servers essentially become equal and function as a team.

Another key role that Hub Transport servers fill is providing antivirus and antispam controls inside your internal network. Although it's intended that the primary means to root out virus-infected messages and spam messages will be the Edge Transport server (or some other hardware or software third-party device), the Hub Transport server allows you to put internal controls in place to prevent virus-laden (or even spam-like) messages from being sent between internal recipients or to external recipients. As well, the extra layer of antivirus and antispam controls is part of the in-depth defense strategy that places many layers of protection around your most critical data.

Hub Transport servers must be members of Active Directory domains and must have fast, reliable connectivity to Mailbox servers and either Edge Transport servers or the SMTP gateway in use at your organization. There must also be at least one Hub Transport server in every Active Directory site that contains a Mailbox server or Unified Messaging server—if not, no messages will ever be sent from or to these servers in that site.

Client Access Server

As mentioned in the discussion of the Mailbox server role, Outlook clients can connect directly to the Mailbox server to access mailboxes and public folders. Other non-MAPI clients, such as POP3, IMAP4, mobile, and web-based clients must connect to the Mailbox servers via a Client Access server. In this way, the Client Access server is most like the front-end servers utilized in previous versions of Exchange Server. All requests from these non-MAPI clients are received by the Client Access server and then forwarded to the applicable Mailbox server for action.

In addition to providing non-MAPI client access to the Exchange databases, the Client Access server also provides other features such as Outlook Autodiscover, which allows an Outlook 2007 client to automatically configure a user's profile without the need to enter information as with previous versions of Outlook. Although a Client Access server is not required as an absolute rule, most organizations should plan to have at least one Client Access server per Active Directory site that contains a Mailbox server. With the prolific usage of Outlook Web Access and Windows-powered mobile devices, it's a good bet that not every client in an organization will be a MAPI one.

Client Access servers also need to be members of Active Directory domains and should typically be located on the internal portion of your organization's network. If the Client Access server must be accessible from the Internet, it should be presented to the Internet via some sort of application-layer firewall to secure connections to and from the Client Access server and the Internet.

Edge Transport Server

The Edge Transport server, an optional role, is an entirely new dedicated role in Exchange Server 2007. Designed to be deployed in the DMZ of your network, the Edge Transport server is used to provide a secure SMTP gateway for all messages entering or leaving your Exchange organization. As such, the Edge Transport server is responsible for antivirus and antispam controls, as well as protecting the recipient data held within Active Directory.

When an inbound message is received by the Edge Transport server, it scans it for viral and spam qualities and then takes the appropriate (as configured) actions if it determines that the message is one or both of these items. Normal, clean messages are delivered to a Hub Transport server for policy and compliance enforcement, as well as delivery to the final recipients.

Unlike all other Exchange Server 2007 roles, the Edge Transport role cannot be deployed with any other role—it must be deployed by itself on a completely separate server. This is done to further increase Exchange security and the overall security of the internal network. The Edge Transport server, because of its specialized role, is not intended to be a member of the Active Directory domain. This change from the front-end servers in previous versions of Exchange Server should be a welcome one to many network and messaging administrators who fought with getting a front-end server (that was a member of the Active Directory) domain working correctly and securely in the DMZ previously.

Since recipient information is needed for proper message acceptance and routing, the Edge Transport server uses a specialized instance of Active Directory Application Mode (ADAM) to store its configuration and recipient information. The Edge Transport server then initiates one-way replication from Active Directory to the ADAM instance to keep it up-to-date.

Because of its specialized role, the Edge Transport server requires two-way SMTP access only through the external firewall. This is a radical departure from previous versions of Exchange Server and will increase the security of that server dramatically. Only two-way SMTP and one-way (from the inside) Active Directory synchronization traffic is required through the internal firewall.

Unified Messaging Server

The last of the Exchange Server 2007 server roles is also the most radically different from any previous version of Exchange Server. Seeing the increasing integration with Exchange Server by third-party voice and fax messaging companies, Microsoft raised the bar and built that functionality, and much more, into Exchange Server 2007.

The Unified Messaging server role provides the following functionality to an Exchange Server 2007 organization:

- Fax reception and delivery to Exchange mailboxes
- Voice call answering and delivery of recorded voicemail file to Exchange mailboxes

- Voicemail access via a phone connection
- Message read back via a phone connection, including replying to the message or forwarding it to another recipient
- Calendar access via a phone connection, including meeting request acceptance
- Out-of-office messages in voicemail via a phone connection

Unified Messaging servers are intended to be deployed only in the internal network and must be deployed in sites that contain at least one Hub Transport server. Additionally, the Unified Messaging server must have reliable, high-speed connectivity to the Mailbox servers, domain controllers, and global catalog servers in the organization. An IP PBX or VoIP gateway device is required to tie the Unified Messaging server to the phone system.

The Unified Messaging server role is outside the scope of the 70-236 exam; therefore, we will not be discussing it any detail throughout the rest of the text.

Preinstallation Server and Network Considerations

You must address several important issues before installing Exchange Server. Having the correct information and making the right decisions about these issues will go a long way toward ensuring a successful installation. The following preinstallation issues are covered in the following sections:

- Verifying system requirements
- Verifying Windows services and components
- Installing the Security Configuration Wizard
- Verifying name resolution
- Running network and domain controller diagnostics tests
- Configuring storage for Exchange Server 2007

Verifying System Requirements

We'll now list the minimum requirements for the computer system upon which Exchange is to be installed. These minimums are valid when you install only the core components. Using additional Exchange components, and depending on your particular performance demands, could require more resources than the following minimum requirements.

Hardware Requirements

Table 2.2 details the minimum recommended hardware requirements for installing Exchange.

TABLE 2.2 Exchange Server 2007 Hardware Requirements

Item	Minimum Requirements
CPU	Must be an x64 64-bit architecture server system that provides support for the Intel EM64T or AMD64 platform. The Intel Itanium IA64 platform is not supported; 32-bit x86 systems are not supported except in a management station role. See Table 2.3 for specifics on the number of CPU cores recommended.
Operating system	Windows Server 2003 SP1 x64 or Windows Server 2003 R2 x64, Standard or Enterprise versions. The management tools can be installed on a 32-bit Windows Server 2003 or Windows XP SP2 computer.
Memory	Minimum of 2GB RAM; see Table 2.4 for specifics on the amount of RAM recommended for each server role.
Hard disk space	Minimum of 200MB on the server's system drive. Minimum of 1.2GB on the server drive where the Exchange executables will be installed.
Optical drive	A DVD drive, local or network accessible, is required.

The Microsoft Exchange Server software comes on a DVD, a first for Exchange Server. If the machine intended to be the Exchange server has no DVD drive, the administrator can copy the necessary files from the DVD to a shared hard disk or share a DVD drive on another computer.

Table 2.3 details the recommended processor specifications for installing Exchange. Unlike previous versions of Exchange Server, it's not really easy to give blanket specifications for processors in Exchange Server 2007. What each server will need depends not only on the role of the server but also on the size of the organization. The values in Table 2.3 are guidelines that Microsoft has provided.

TABLE 2.3 Exchange Server 2007 Processor Recommendations

Server Role	Minimum CPU	Recommended CPU	Recommended Maximum CPU
Edge Transport	1 CPU core	2 CPU cores	4 CPU cores
Hub Transport	1 CPU core	4 CPU cores	4 CPU cores

TABLE 2.3 Exchange Server 2007 Processor Recommendations *(continued)*

Server Role	Minimum CPU	Recommended CPU	Recommended Maximum CPU
Client Access	1 CPU core	4 CPU cores	4 CPU cores
Mailbox	1 CPU core	4 CPU cores	8 CPU cores
Unified Messaging	1 CPU core	4 CPU cores	4 CPU cores
Multiple roles	1 CPU core	4 CPU cores	4 CPU cores

You'll notice in Table 2.3 that we've referred to CPU cores instead of CPUs. With dual-core CPUs currently shipping in servers and quad-core CPUs expected to be shipping before the end of 2007, it's becoming easier and easier to pack a large amount of processing power into size-efficient rack mount servers.

Table 2.4 details the minimum recommended memory specifications for installing Exchange. As with the CPU recommendations given previously in Table 2.3, memory specifications are not easily nailed down to exact values. Table 2.4 presents guidelines that Microsoft has established, but you'll see a bit later how you can get some more exact numbers that work in your specific organization.

TABLE 2.4 Exchange Server 2007 Memory Recommendations

Server Role	Minimum RAM	Recommended RAM	Recommended Maximum RAM
Edge Transport	2GB	Not less than 1GB per CPU core; 2GB minimum	16GB
Hub Transport	2GB	Not less than 1GB per CPU core; 2GB minimum	16GB
Client Access	2GB	Not less than 1GB per CPU core; 2GB minimum	8GB
Mailbox	2GB, but depends on number of storage groups	2GB plus 2MB–5MB per mailbox on the server	32GB

TABLE 2.4 Exchange Server 2007 Memory Recommendations *(continued)*

Server Role	Minimum RAM	Recommended RAM	Recommended Maximum RAM
Unified Messaging	2GB	Not less than 1GB per CPU core; 2GB minimum	4GB
Multiple roles	2GB, but depends on number of storage groups	4GB plus 2MB–5MB per mailbox on the server	8GB

As noted in Table 2.4, the minimum recommended memory for a Mailbox server depends on the number of storage groups that the Mailbox server is hosting. Table 2.5 outlines the recommendations for memory based on the number of storage groups.

TABLE 2.5 Exchange Server 2007 Memory Recommendation vs. Storage Groups

Number of Storage Groups	Minimum Memory
1–4	2GB
5–8	2GB
9–12	6GB
13–16	8GB
17–20	10GB
21–24	12GB
25–28	14GB
29–32	16GB
33–36	18GB
37–40	20GB
41–44	22GB
45–48	24GB
49–50	26GB

Additionally, the recommended memory for a Mailbox server is specified as a value (as given in Table 2.5) plus 2MB–5MB per user with a mailbox on the Mailbox server. Users are broken into four basic groups based on the number of messages they send and receive in an average day. Table 2.6 outlines these profiles and the corresponding amount of RAM to be allocated per user.

TABLE 2.6 Exchange Server 2007 Memory Recommendations vs. User Behavior

User Type	Messages Sent/Received per Day (50KB Each)	RAM per Mailbox
Light	5 sent/20 received	2MB per mailbox
Average	10 sent/40 received	3.5MB per mailbox
Heavy	20 sent/80 received	5MB per mailbox
Very heavy	30 sent/120 received	No value specified

Oddly enough, Microsoft defined the "very heavy" user type but did not provide any recommendations for the amount of RAM to plan for per mailbox of that category. At a minimum, it would be best to plan for at least 5MB of RAM for each mailbox that falls into that category.

So, as you can see, determining the amount of memory or even the number of CPU cores you need to plan for in your Exchange Server 2007 servers can be a challenging task. Planning for storage availability is no easier. It's not that Microsoft wanted to make it difficult to get good, solid numbers for planning and building Exchange servers—it's really just that the final answer depends in large part on the size of your organization and also how users interact with Exchange. In an effort to try to take a lot of the confusion out of the process (and also to help ensure you get the best possible result), the Exchange team has created the helpful Exchange 2007 Mailbox Server Role Storage Requirements Calculator, a Microsoft Excel file that you can use to plan all aspects of a Mailbox server, including storage, memory, and CPU. You can download the file from the team's blog, You Had Me At EHLO, at the following location: `http://msexchangeteam.com/archive/2007/01/15/432207.aspx`.

The calculator takes into account many parts of the Exchange organization, including the number of mailboxes, types of users, clustering model (if any) in use, and the day-to-day operational and administrative tasks. Figure 2.1 presents some sample output of the calculator for an organization that wants to place 2,000 mailboxes on a server in a CCR model. In that case, two Mailbox servers would need to be configured, as the calculator recommends.

FIGURE 2.1 Sample output from the Exchange 2007 Mailbox Server Role Storage Requirements Calculator

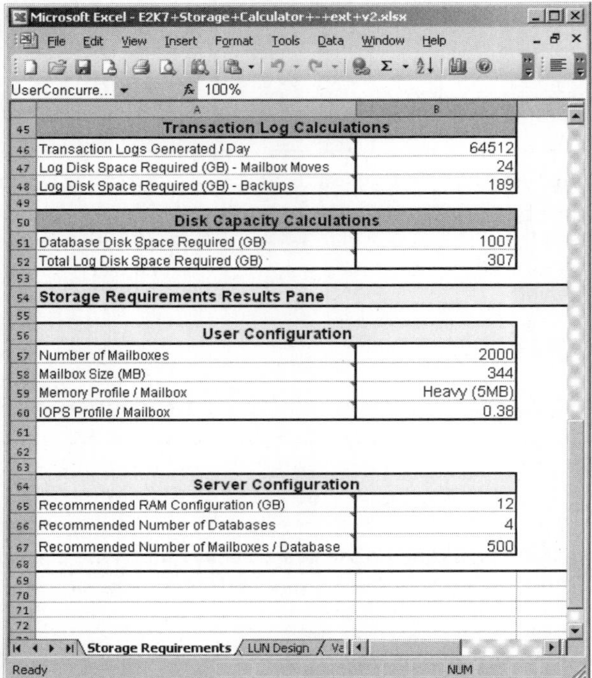

	A	B
45	**Transaction Log Calculations**	
46	Transaction Logs Generated / Day	64512
47	Log Disk Space Required (GB) - Mailbox Moves	24
48	Log Disk Space Required (GB) - Backups	189
49		
50	**Disk Capacity Calculations**	
51	Database Disk Space Required (GB)	1007
52	Total Log Disk Space Required (GB)	307
53		
54	**Storage Requirements Results Pane**	
55		
56	**User Configuration**	
57	Number of Mailboxes	2000
58	Mailbox Size (MB)	344
59	Memory Profile / Mailbox	Heavy (5MB)
60	IOPS Profile / Mailbox	0.38
61		
62		
63		
64	**Server Configuration**	
65	Recommended RAM Configuration (GB)	12
66	Recommended Number of Databases	4
67	Recommended Number of Mailboxes / Database	500

Directory Services and Network Requirements

To successfully install Exchange Server 2007 in your organization, you'll need to ensure that the following directory services requirements are met first:

- The schema master role must be held by a domain controller that is running Windows Server 2003 SP1 or higher.
- At least one global catalog server must exist in each Active Directory site where you plan to install any Exchange Server 2007 role. These global catalog servers must also be running Windows Server 2003 SP1 or higher.
- For non-English domain controllers, you must install a hotfix if you will be using OWA in your organization. The hotfix is discussed in Microsoft Knowledge Base article 919166.
- In each domain that will have Exchange recipients or Exchange Server roles installed, the domain functional level must be at the Windows 2000 Server native mode or higher.
- A functional Domain Name System (DNS) implementation must be in place in your Active Directory forest and domains.

- Any existing Exchange 2000 Server, Exchange Server 2003, or mixed Exchange 2000 Server/Exchange Server 2003 organizations must be running in native mode.
- No Exchange Server 5.5 organizations should exist within your Active Directory forest.
- Active Directory has been prepared at the forest level and within each domain that will have Exchange recipients or Exchange Servers installed. We'll discuss this process later in this chapter in the "Preparing Active Directory" section.

As with previous versions of Exchange Server, Microsoft is currently recommending that there be a 4:1 ratio (minimum) of Exchange Server processor cores to global catalog server processor cores. This recommendation assumes that all processor cores are of similar speed and architecture.

Software Requirements

Exchange Server 2007 can be installed only on a 64-bit version of Windows Server 2003 SP1 (Standard or Enterprise Edition) or Windows Server 2003 R2 (Standard or Enterprise Edition). The Exchange management tools can be installed on 64-bit Windows XP Professional or Windows Server 2003 or on 32-bit Windows XP Professional SP2 using the 32-bit Exchange Server 2007 media.

The other general software requirements you must meet to install any Exchange Server 2007 server role are as follows:

- Microsoft .NET Framework 2.0
- Windows PowerShell 1.0
- Microsoft Management Console (MMC) 3.0
- Windows Installer 3.1 for 32-bit computers that will have the Exchange management tools installed

You must meet additional software requirements depending on the specific server role being installed.

Edge Transport

For servers that will have the Edge Transport role installed, ADAM must be installed on the server using all default options. Additionally, the following requirements apply to Edge Transport servers:

- Must not be a member of an Active Directory domain
- Must have a DNS suffix configured
- Must be able to successfully perform name resolution of Hub Transport servers from the Edge Transport server
- Must be able to successfully perform name resolution of Edge Transport servers from the Hub Transport server

Hub Transport

For servers that will have the Hub Transport role installed, there are no software requirements, but the servers must be able to successfully perform name resolution of Edge Transport servers from the Hub Transport server.

Client Access

For servers that will have the Client Access role stalled, the following software requirements apply:

- Internet Information Services (IIS) 6.0
- World Wide Web (WWW) publishing component
- ASP.NET 2.0
- Remote Procedure Call (RPC) over Hypertext Transfer Protocol (HTTP) Proxy Windows networking component

Mailbox

For servers that will have the Mailbox role installed, the following software requirements apply:

- Internet Information Services (IIS) 6.0.
- World Wide Web (WWW) publishing component.
- Network COM+ access is enabled.
- Windows Server 2003 x64 hotfix 904639 and 918980.
- The Simple Mail Transfer Protocol (SMTP) and Network News Transfer Protocol (NNTP) must not be installed.

Unified Messaging

For servers that will have the Unified Messaging role installed, the following software requirements apply:

- Microsoft Speech service (Exchange will install this if needed).
- Windows Media Encoder.
- Windows Media Audio Voice codec.
- Microsoft Core XML Services (MSXML) 6.0.
- The Simple Mail Transfer Protocol (SMTP) and Network News Transfer Protocol (NNTP) must not be installed.

Requirements for Previous Versions of Exchange

Many organizations will not be installing Exchange Server 2007 in a completely new forest; thus, coexistence with previous versions of Exchange is likely. If you will be installing Exchange Server 2007 into an Exchange organization that contains Exchange Server 2003 or earlier versions of Exchange, you'll need to keep the following requirements in mind:

- Exchange Server 2007 cannot be installed in an Exchange organization that contains Exchange Server 5.5. You must migrate all mailboxes and public folders to Exchange Server 2003 or Exchange 2000 Server first in this scenario.

- All Exchange Server 2003 servers must have, at a minimum, Exchange Server 2003 SP2 installed.
- All Exchange 2000 Server servers must have, at a minimum, Exchange 2000 Server SP3 installed.
- All Exchange 2000 Server servers must also have the most current post-SP3 update rollup installed as well. See MSKB 870540 to obtain the most current post-SP3 update rollup for Exchange 2000 Server.

Client Access Requirements

The last requirements that you'll need to ensure are met are those for client access to Exchange Server 2007. Microsoft has stipulated that only Outlook 2007, Outlook 2003, and Outlook XP (2002) are supported for access to mailboxes and public folders on Exchange Server 2007. Older versions might work but have not been tested, and Microsoft doesn't support them.

OWA obviously requires a web browser to function on the client end, although only Internet Explorer can provide Integrated Windows authentication in a supported configuration. In general, you'll get the best OWA experience using Internet Explorer 6 or higher on a Windows computer or the corresponding versions for other operating system platforms.

Mobile devices can also access Exchange Server 2007, but the only supported types are the following: Windows Mobile 2003 Second Edition; Windows Mobile 5.0, Windows Mobile 5.0 with Messaging and Security Feature Pack (MSFP); and devices that are compatible with Exchange ActiveSync, such as Palm OS–powered devices.

Verifying Windows Services and Components

Microsoft has made the Exchange Server 2007 setup process easier and more error proof than ever before. As part of this improved setup process, you are prompted to verify and install, as necessary, those key services that are required to support the installation of Exchange Server 2007. Before you can install Exchange Server 2007 on a server, however, you must install the required services and components discussed previously. As practice, you'll install and verify the correct services and components for a Mailbox server in Exercise 2.1.

The steps to verify Windows services, perform network diagnostics, and run /PrepareSchema and /PrepareDomain are all part of the regular installation sequence for a new Exchange Server 2007 organization.

EXERCISE 2.1

Installing Required Services and Components

1. Open the Add or Remove Programs applet, located in the Control Panel.
2. Click the Add/Remove Windows Components button.

EXERCISE 2.1 *(continued)*

3. In the Windows Components dialog box, select the Application Server option, and click the Details button.

4. In the Application Server dialog box, shown here, select the Enable Network COM+ Access option.

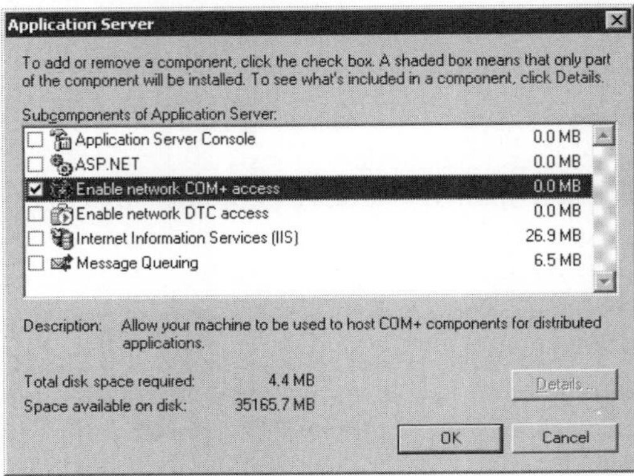

5. Select the Internet Information Services (IIS) option, and click the Details button.

6. In the Internet Information Services (IIS) dialog box, shown here, select the World Wide Web Service option. The Common Files and Internet Information Services Manager options will be selected also.

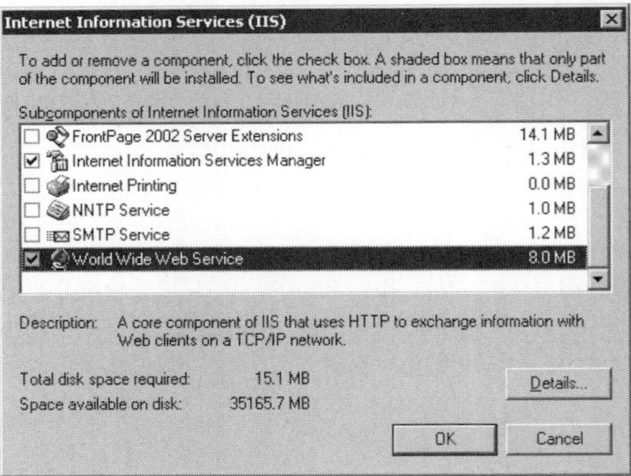

7. Click OK to close the Internet Information Services (IIS) dialog box.

8. Click OK to close the Application Server dialog box.

EXERCISE 2.1 *(continued)*

9. Back in the Windows Components dialog box, scroll down, and select the Microsoft .NET Framework 2.0 option, as shown here.

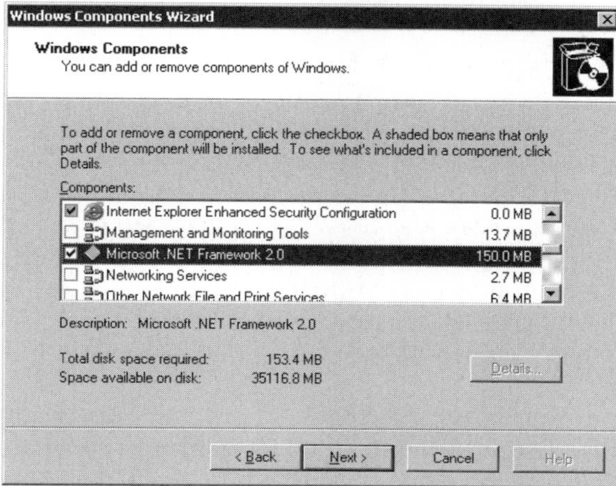

10. Click Next to continue.
11. Click Finish when prompted.
12. Download the Windows PowerShell 1.0 (KB 926139) and the Microsoft Management Console (MMC) 3.0 (KB 907265) installers from the Microsoft website.
13. Start the installation of the PowerShell by double-clicking the downloaded file.
14. When prompted, click Next to dismiss the opening page of the installation wizard.
15. Accept the EULA, and click Next again to continue.
16. Install the MMC 3.0 package using the same steps as the PowerShell package.
17. Download and install the hotfixes for Windows Server 2003 x64 in KB 904639 and KB 918980.
18. Install the Windows Server 2003 SP1 Support Tools package from the Windows CD-ROM. The installer is located in the `X:\SUPPORT\TOOLS` folder.

You can download the Microsoft .NET Framework 2.0 installer from the Microsoft website if you don't see it in your list of components available to install.

You can verify that services are running by opening the Services console located in the Administrative Tools folder.

Installing the Security Configuration Wizard

The Security Configuration Wizard (SCW) is an advanced role-based security configuration management and hardening tool available in Windows Server 2003 SP1 and Windows Server 2003 R2. By default, the SCW is not installed on your Windows Server 2003 computer, but you can easily install it as outlined in Exercise 2.2. Exchange Server 2007 provides extensions that can be imported into the Security Configuration Wizard to increase the role-based security of your Exchange Server 2007 servers. Although you cannot utilize this functionality until after one or more Exchange Server 2007 roles are installed on the server, you can install the SCW ahead of time. Exercise 2.2 will show how to install the Security Configuration Wizard.

Using the Security Configuration Wizard is an optional step that Microsoft highly recommends. We will return to the SCW in Chapter 3, "Installing Exchange Server 2007," after we show how to install some Exchange Server 2007 roles on your server.

EXERCISE 2.2

Installing the Security Configuration Wizard

1. Open the Add or Remove Programs applet, located in the Control Panel.
2. Click the Add/Remove Windows Components button.
3. Select the Security Configuration Wizard option, and then click OK.
4. Back in the Windows Components dialog box, click Next to continue.
5. Click Finish when prompted.

Verifying Name Resolution

It should go without saying that functional name resolution within an Active Directory forest is absolutely critical. Because Exchange Server 2007 extends the existing foundation provided by Active Directory, functional name resolution is thus absolutely required for the proper operation of the Exchange organization. In short, you're not likely going to be at the stage of deploying Exchange Server 2007 if your name resolution isn't functioning at that time.

All Exchange Server 2007 servers must be able to resolve names and IP addresses for all other Exchange Server 2007 servers, all domain controllers, and all global catalog servers. For organizations using the Edge Transport role in the DMZ, this also means that all Edge Transport servers must be able to contact all Hub Transport servers inside the protected internal network, and vice versa. To that end, functional name resolution becomes more than just an issue of making sure that you've done your job within Active Directory; it is also a task that the network administrator in charge of configuring and maintaining your organizational firewalls and external DNS must be involved in.

You can perform quick network resolution testing using the `nslookup` command from an Exchange Server 2007 server. Figure 2.2 shows how the `nslookup` command has been used to resolve both internal and external names.

FIGURE 2.2 Using `nslookup` to verify functional name resolution within the network

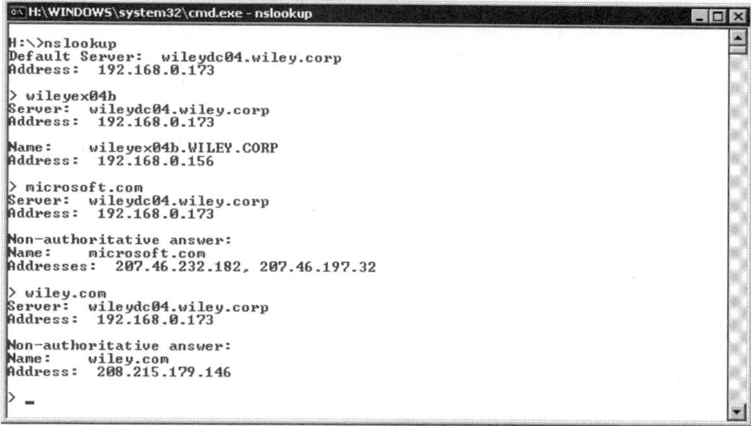

Running Network and Domain Controller Diagnostics Tests

If you've installed the Windows Support Tools as discussed previously in Exercise 2.1, then you'll have the `dcdiag` and `netdiag` diagnostics tools available to you. In Exchange Server 2003, these tools were linked in the setup preparation tasks and recommended to be run. You should run these commands manually before even getting to the setup process of the first Exchange Server 2007 server.

The `dcdiag` command performs the following types of checks (among others):

- *Connectivity*: Verifies proper DNS records and LDAP/RPC connectivity
- *Replications*: Checks for replication errors
- *NetLogons*: Verifies that the proper permissions exist to allow for replication
- *RIDManager*: Verifies that the RID master is accessible and functional

- *KCCEvent*: Verifies that the Knowledge Consistency Checker (KCC) is functional and error free
- *Topology*: Verifies that an accurate and functional replication topology has been generated by the KCC
- *DNS*: Verifies proper operation and health of DNS services

Figure 2.3 presents some sample output from the `dcdiag` command.

FIGURE 2.3 Using the `dcdiag` command to verify domain functionality

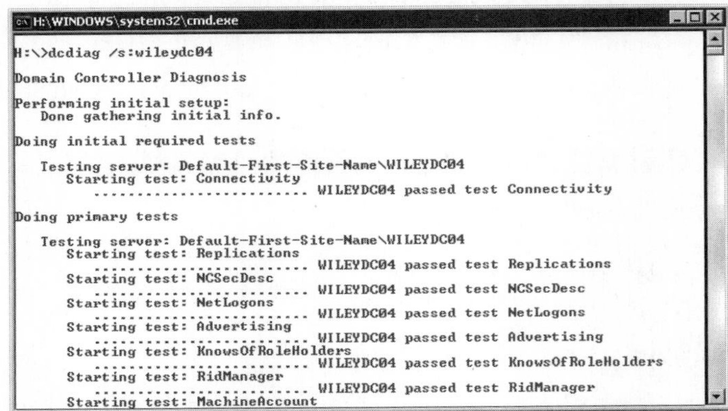

The `netdiag` command performs the following types of checks (among others):

- Checks for IPConfig on each network adapter
- Checks for automatic private IP addressing (APIPA) on each network adapter
- Checks the domain membership of the server
- Checks the default gateway of the server
- Performs domain controller discovery
- Performs LDAP testing
- Performs Kerberos testing

Figure 2.4 presents some sample output from the `netdiag` command.

You should resolve any issues noted with either test before installing and configuring Exchange Server 2007.

You can get more information about the tests performed, usage of, and corrective actions to perform as a result of the `dcdiag` and `netdiag` tools by searching the Microsoft website for *Windows Support Tools*.

Configuring Storage for Exchange Server 2007

Planning for and configuring storage for Exchange Server 2007 is an immensely large topic, one that could fill an entire book this size. To that end, we're not going to cover every possible scenario or every technology available. We will, however, touch on some of the basic concepts in this area including storage technologies, volume (or LUN) configuration and design, and redundant array of inexpensive disks (RAID) levels.

FIGURE 2.4 Using the `netdiag` command to verify network functionality

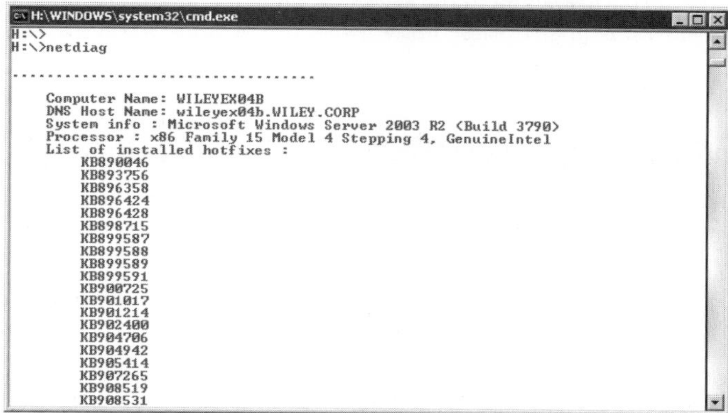

Storage Technologies

Storage technologies, like Exchange Server, continue to grow and evolve over time. When planning for storage for Exchange Server 2007, you can opt to use four acceptable storage technologies. The correct choice will depend on the needs of your organization and the expense you are prepared to bear.

- *Fibre Channel*: Still the most expensive and most reliable and robust storage solution on the market, Fibre Channel–attached SCSI drives are the best choice for almost any size of organization. With backbone network speeds that range as high as 4Gbit/sec now, Fibre Channel storage area networks provide many exciting and business-relevant solutions that make placing Exchange databases on them ideal. Many vendors, with the largest being EMC, HP, and IBM, have Fibre Channel solutions. Fibre Channel–attached SCSI disks come in 10,000 and 15,000 RPM speeds, although most new installations will use 15,000 RPM exclusively.
- *Serial-attached SCSI (SAS)*: SAS disks are the next step down from Fibre Channel–attached SCSI disk systems. SAS disks can be found both as internal components of most new Intel-based servers and as external disk array cabinets that can be easily attached to the Exchange server. Many SAS arrays have throughput as high as 3Gbit/sec, surpassing many older Fibre Channel systems, as well as SATA drives and older SCSI drives. One drawback of SAS drives is that they are currently limited to 10,000 RPM in speed, which might not be fast enough for larger organizations that need both high capacity and high input/output.
- *Serial ATA (SATA)*: Serial ATA is a new serial interface for standard ATA/IDE disk drives. These drives are typically found in workstation computers, not server-class computers. SATA disks are almost always slower than SAS or SCSI disks, with speeds of typically either 5,400 or 7,200 RPM. The upsides to SATA drives are their rather large size and their exceptionally low price. However, with the low mean time between failure

(MTBF) of SATA disks and their slow speed, SATA drives are not a solid choice for anything but the smallest Exchange Server 2007 implementation.

- *Internet SCSI (iSCSI)*: iSCSI is the single network-based storage method that Microsoft supports for Exchange Server 2007. iSCSI connects SCSI disks to servers using standard Ethernet cabling and dedicated Ethernet adapters in servers. Although most new Ethernet adapters have TCP/IP offload engines (TOE) on them to support iSCSI usage, you won't want to deploy iSCSI using the same network adapters in use for normal network traffic because of the amount of traffic going to and from the storage network. Treat iSCSI as you would Fibre Channel–attached storage systems, and place two to four Ethernet ports in each server dedicated to the iSCSI storage network. iSCSI is somewhat mature now, at several years of age, but is still far behind traditional Fibre Channel SAN systems in many regards. However, iSCSI is typically less expensive than Fibre Channel.

Other than iSCSI, no other network-attached storage transports are supported in Exchange Server 2007.

Volume (LUN) Configuration and Design

In Exchange Server 2003, the basic recommendation was to create a volume (or LUN) for each storage group's databases and another for its transaction logs. As such, you'd typically have two volumes per storage group. The same basic recommendation holds true in Exchange Server 2007. However, Microsoft now recommends that only one database be created per storage group for better backup, transactions, and high availability. Thus, a single Exchange Server 2003 storage group that contained five databases (such as four mailbox stores and a public folder store) occupied only two volumes in the recommended configuration. In Exchange Server 2007, five databases (stores) would now occupy five times as many volumes, or a total of ten volumes since the guidance is to place only one database per storage group. The reasoning behind this change is simple: Exchange disk I/O is mostly random access, and storage systems benefit greatly when a set of disks (a volume) is performing a single task at a time. In short, you cannot read and write at the same time on a single volume, and you cannot read two different places at the same time or write two difference places at the same time. By isolating a single database on a single volume and placing its transaction logs on a separate single volume, you maximize disk I/O.

The catch, of course, to this approach is that if you had 50 storage groups configured on your mailbox server, each with two volumes assigned, you'd need 100 drive letters just for Exchange—far in excess of the 23 drive letters typically available on a server. The solution to that problem is to use NTFS file system mount points. In this way, you can present (for example) three databases to Exchange Server, as outlined here:

- Database1, stored in `e:\database1`, where database1 is an actual directory on that volume, volume1
- Database2, stored in `e:\database2`, where database2 is a mount point from volume2
- Database3, stored in `e:\database3`, where database3 is a mount point from volume3

Of course, you must carefully consider many other considerations and scenarios when designing an Exchange Server 2007 deployment for anything beyond a few databases. There is a large amount of documentation around storage considerations in Exchange Server 2007 on the Microsoft TechNet website. Also, the Exchange 2007 Mailbox Server Role Storage Requirements Calculator discussed previously in the "Hardware Requirements" section of this chapter can help you make educated decisions about how much storage you'll need and how it should be configured on your storage subsystems.

RAID Levels

Regardless of how you configure your volumes (LUNs), you're likely not going to allocate a single disk drive to a single volume. This is because you need to prevent data loss in the event of drive failure and because you likely won't have the right sized disks to allocate just one for a volume to Exchange Server 2007. As such, you'll likely pool several disks together using a RAID solution that is controlled by a battery-backed RAID controller. Several types of RAID are available, and many vendors have further modified the basic types of RAID with their own proprietary types.

The most common RAID types in usage today are as follows:

- *RAID-10*: RAID-10 arrays are actually a combination of two other RAID types, RAID-0 and RAID-1. In RAID-10, data is striped across multiple disks (RAID-0) and then mirrored (RAID-1) to another set of striped (RAID-0) disks. Since data is written to all disks simultaneously in the striped set and no striping is done for parity information, the data throughput of a RAID-10 set is very good. A single disk failure in a RAID-10 array does not impact write performance because the other member of the mirror set is still intact. Read performance is moderately impacted because reads are able to be performed against only a single mirror in the set. The RAID-10 array can sustain the loss of disks only from a single mirror in the array; should disks be lost from both mirrors in the array, the array will need to be completely rebuilt from restored data.
- *RAID-5*: RAID-5 arrays take a group of disks and write parity information to them for all data that is written. As an example, if you take five 70GB disks and create a RAID-5 array, approximately 70GB will be taken for parity data and the remaining 280GB of space will be available for data. Since parity information is written each time data is written to the array, disk I/O increases dramatically. A single disk failure will not prevent the RAID-5 array from functioning, but it will slow down both reads and writes because data must be reconstructed using the parity information. If a second disk fails before the RAID-5 array has been completely rebuilt, the data is lost, and the array will need to be completely rebuilt from restored data.
- *RAID-6*: RAID-6 arrays (also called RAID-5E by IBM) take the RAID-5 concept a single drive further and allocate two drives for parity information; thus, in the example, using five 70GB disks to create a RAID-6 array, there would be approximately 140GB of parity space and 210GB for data. RAID-6 is exceptionally useful with larger arrays that can have long rebuild times that range from many hours to several days because of the size of the array and the ongoing disk I/O.

Of course, the real trick to the whole RAID situation is figuring out what type of RAID array to construct for your Exchange data. Transaction logs, by their very nature of being critical to Exchange and of needing fast sequential read/write access, should always be placed on RAID-10 (or RAID-1) arrays if possible. These arrays should be controlled by battery-backed controllers to prevent data loss. The recommendation in the past has been to put the databases for Exchange on RAID-5 or RAID-6 arrays; however, the times are changing, and RAID-10 is gaining popularity and support now as the preferred storage for the databases as well.

Preinstallation Modification of Active Directory

Because of Exchange Server 2007's involvement with Active Directory, its installation involves a number of Windows Active Directory user and group security accounts. Some of the more pertinent groups are as follows:

Schema Admins
: Members of this group have the rights and permissions necessary to modify the schema of Active Directory. To run the setup with the /PrepareSchema or /PrepareAD option, which modifies the schema for Exchange Server 2007 and is described later in this chapter, you must belong to the Schema Admins group, the Enterprise Admins group, and the local Administrators group on the computer on which you actually run the command.

Enterprise Admins
: Members of this group have the rights and permissions necessary to administer any domain in a forest. To run setup with the /PrepareSchema, /PrepareLegacyExchangePermissions, /PrepareDomain, or /PrepareAD option, you must be a member of the Enterprise Admins group and the local Administrators group on the computer running the tool.

Domain Admins
: Members of this group have the rights and permissions necessary to administer any computer or resource in a domain. You must be a member of this group in order to run setup with the /PrepareDomain option that prepares each domain for Exchange Server 2007 installation.

Administrators
: Members of this local group are given the rights necessary to administer a local computer and install software on it. To install Exchange Server 2007 on a Windows Server 2003 computer, you must be a member of this group. This level of privileges is needed because, during installation, services will be started and files will be copied to the `\<winnt_root>\SYSTEM32` directory.

The installation of Exchange Server 2007 will also create several new security groups:

Exchange Organization Administrators	Members of this group have full access to all Exchange Server properties throughout the Exchange organization. By default, the administrative account that is used to install Exchange Server 2007 is placed into this group.
Exchange Recipient Administrators	Members of this group have the required permissions to modify any Exchange-related property on all Exchange recipients. By default, the Exchange Organization Administrators group is placed into this group.
Exchange Server Administrators (*servername*)	Members of this group have access to the specified Exchange Server configuration data in Active Directory and also have administrative access to the Exchange Server. By default, this group contains no members.
Exchange Servers	Members of this group are the computer accounts for all Exchange servers. This security group provides Exchange servers with the permissions necessary to access one another and perform necessary Exchange functions.
Exchange View-Only Administrators (*servername*)	Members of this group have view-only access permissions to all Exchange Server properties and recipient objects in the Exchange organization. By default, the Exchange Recipient Administrators and Exchange Server Administrators (*servername*) are members of this group.
Exchange2003Interop	This group is created and utilized only during an upgrade scenario from Exchange Server 2003. This group provides authentication for connections made between Exchange Server 2007 Hub Transport servers and Exchange Server 2003 Bridgehead servers.

Before installing the first Exchange server in an organization, you might need to prepare the forest and each domain into which Exchange will be installed. For these tasks, you will use three commands available within the Exchange Server 2007 `setup.exe` command: */PrepareSchema, /PrepareAD,* and */PrepareDomain.*

/PrepareSchema must be run once in a forest and should be run on the domain controller that is configured with the schema master role, although this is not a requirement. It extends the Active Directory schema with the objects necessary to run Exchange Server 2007. The /PrepareAD command must also be run within the domain root of the forest and is used to create the global Exchange objects and configuration. If the schema has not yet been extended, the /PrepareAD command will accomplish that. Additionally, the /PrepareAD command accomplishes the tasks performed by the /PrepareDomain command in the domain root. The /PrepareDomain must be run in each domain to identify the domain's address list server and to create special domain accounts that Exchange needs in order to run properly.

In previous versions of Exchange Server, you had to run the ForestPrep and DomainPrep commands. In Exchange Server 2007, these commands have been removed and replaced with other options, allowing greater flexibility in how Exchange Server 2007 is deployed.

Though this seems like a complicated installation routine, it does provide a significant advantage. Many networks separate the administrative responsibilities of domain management, schema management, and Exchange management. For example, one group might be in charge of administering the schema and the primary domains of the forest, another might be in charge of managing the child domains, and still another group might be in charge of managing Exchange.

These additional setup tools provide the ability for separate administrators to perform their necessary part of the Exchange installation and simplify the Exchange deployment. For example, the group in charge of managing the schema will have the permissions required to run the /PrepareSchema command to extend the schema. Domain administrators will have the permissions required to use the /PrepareDomain command that modifies domains. To run the /PrepareAD command, the administrator will need both Schema Admins and Enterprise Admins permissions because this command is all encompassing. Once these tasks are completed, Exchange administrators can install and manage Exchange without receiving permissions for the other preparation tasks.

If a single administrator or group runs the network and has all the appropriate permissions (or if there is only one domain in your forest), this simplifies the installation of Exchange. If the account with which you install the first Exchange server belongs to the Schema Admins, Enterprise Admins, and Administrators groups for the local computer, you do not need to manually run /PrepareAD, /PrepareSchema, or /PrepareDomain since you will run them during the regular Exchange setup process.

Verifying Domain and Forest Functional Levels

Before you can move on to the actual preparation of the Active Directory forest and domains for the installation of Exchange Server 2007, you must ensure that they are at the Windows 2000 native functional level or higher. Exercise 2.3 outlines the steps to verify and/or raise the domain and forest functional levels of your Active Directory environment.

EXERCISE 2.3

Verifying the Domain and Forest Functional Levels

1. In the root domain of the Active Directory forest, log into a domain controller with Domain Admins credentials.
2. Open the Active Directory Users and Computers console.

EXERCISE 2.3 *(continued)*

3. Right-click the domain name in the console, and select Raise Domain Functional Level. The dialog box shown here opens.

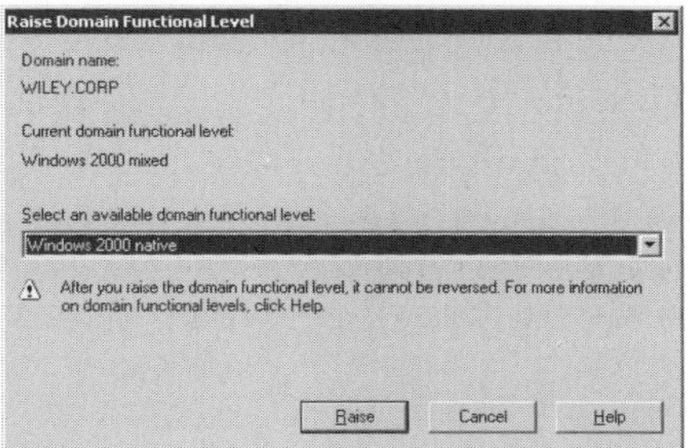

4. If the domain functional level is less than Windows 2000 native, select either Windows 2000 Native or (ideally if there are no Windows 2000 domain controllers) Windows Server 2003 Level, and click the Raise button.

5. When prompted to make the change, click OK. Note that this is a one-way change that cannot be undone.

6. Repeat the steps for every other domain in the forest.

7. To change or verify the forest functional level, open the Active Directory Domains and Trusts console while logged into a root domain controller with Enterprise Admins credentials.

8. In the console, right-click the root of the Active Directory Domains and Trusts node, and select Raise Forest Functional Level. The dialog box shown here opens.

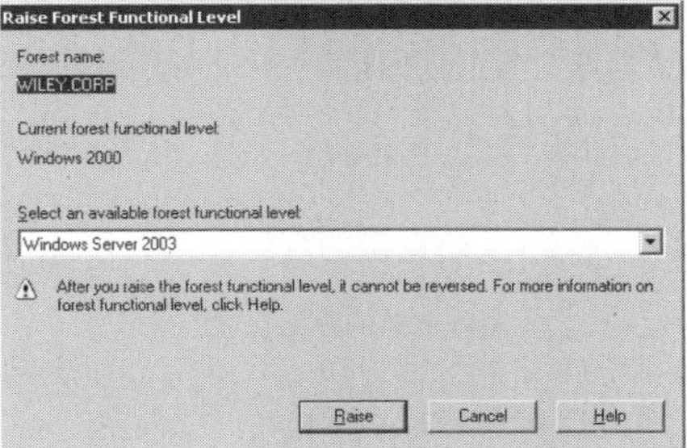

9. Raise the forest functional level to at least the Windows 2000 Native option, and click the Raise button. You'll be prompted to accept the change here as well.

Preparing a Windows Active Directory Forest

To run the /PrepareSchema command, you must belong to the Schema Admins and Enterprise Admins security groups. In addition, you must belong to the local Administrators group on the server on which Exchange will be installed. If you are not a member of these groups, the appropriate administrator will have to run the /PrepareSchema command before you can install Exchange Server 2007.

When the /Prepare Schema command is run, it performs only one task: it extends the Active Directory schema with Exchange-related information.

Exercise 2.4 outlines the steps for running the /PrepareSchema command in a forest that does not have a previous version of Exchange running. We'll discuss the process to prepare a forest and domain for Exchange Server 2007 to coexist with Exchange Server 2003 or Exchange 2000 Server later in this chapter.

WARNING

Do not run the /PrepareSchema command as your first preinstallation step if you have an existing legacy Exchange Server 2003 or Exchange 2000 Server organization. You must run the /PrepareLegacyExchangePermissions command first. See the "Modifying Existing Exchange Organizations to Support Migration" section later in this chapter for more discussion about this scenario.

EXERCISE 2.4

Running the /PrepareSchema Command

1. Insert the Microsoft Exchange Server 2007 DVD into the server's DVD-ROM drive. If the server does not have a DVD-ROM drive, you can copy the files to a network location and then proceed using that location.

2. Open a command interpreter window by selecting Start ➢ Run, entering **CMD**, and pressing Enter.

3. In the command interpreter window, enter the following command: ***X*:\setup /prepareschema**, where *X* represents the location of the Exchange Server 2007 setup files, local or remote. Press Enter to start the schema preparation process, as shown here.

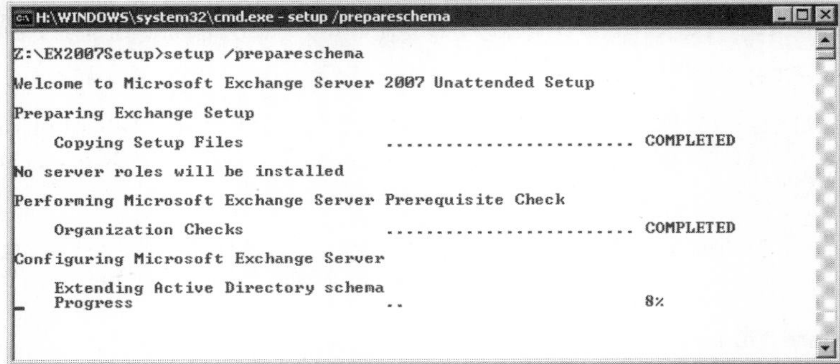
H:\WINDOWS\system32\cmd.exe - setup /prepareschema
Z:\EX2007Setup>setup /prepareschema
Welcome to Microsoft Exchange Server 2007 Unattended Setup
Preparing Exchange Setup
Copying Setup Files .... COMPLETED
No server roles will be installed
Performing Microsoft Exchange Server Prerequisite Check
Organization Checks .... COMPLETED
Configuring Microsoft Exchange Server
Extending Active Directory schema
Progress .. 8%

4. If setup finds any errors, they will be displayed, and the /PrepareSchema process will fail. You will need to rerun the command after you have corrected the noted errors.

You can run the /PrepareSchema portion of setup while installing the first Exchange Server 2007 computer. This situation is typically encountered only in smaller organizations where only one domain exists within the Active Directory forest.

Preparing the Root Windows Active Directory Domain

Once the forest has been prepared by extending the schema with the /PrepareSchema command, the next step you'll need to perform to ready the forest for an installation of Exchange Server 2007 is to prepare the root-level domain in the forest and create the Exchange global objects in Active Directory. You accomplish this process by issuing the /PrepareAD command, which will also prepare the root domain with the /PrepareDomain command.

When the /PrepareSchema command is run, it performs several tasks:

- If the forest contains no existing versions of Exchange Server, /PrepareAD prompts you for an Exchange organization name and then creates the organization object in the Active Directory. The organization is at the top of the Exchange hierarchy. This case-sensitive field can be up to 64 characters in length. The organization name is associated with every object in the Exchange directory, such as mailboxes, public folders, and distribution lists. The organization name cannot be modified after installation.
- It creates the universal security groups that were discussed previously in this chapter in the "Preinstallation Modification of Active Directory" section.

Exercise 2.5 outlines the steps for running the /PrepareAD command.

EXERCISE 2.5

Running the /PrepareAD Command

1. Insert the Microsoft Exchange Server 2007 DVD into the server's DVD-ROM drive. If the server does not have a DVD-ROM drive, you can copy the files to a network location and then proceed using that location.

2. Open a command interpreter window by selecting Start ➢ Run, entering **CMD**, and pressing Enter.

EXERCISE 2.5 *(continued)*

3. In the command interpreter window, enter the following command: ***X*:\setup /preparead /organizationname:*NAME***, where *X* represents the location of the Exchange Server 2007 setup files, local or remote, and *NAME* represents the name you want the Exchange organization to have. In this example, we'll call the new organization WILEY. Press Enter to start the root domain preparation process, as shown here.

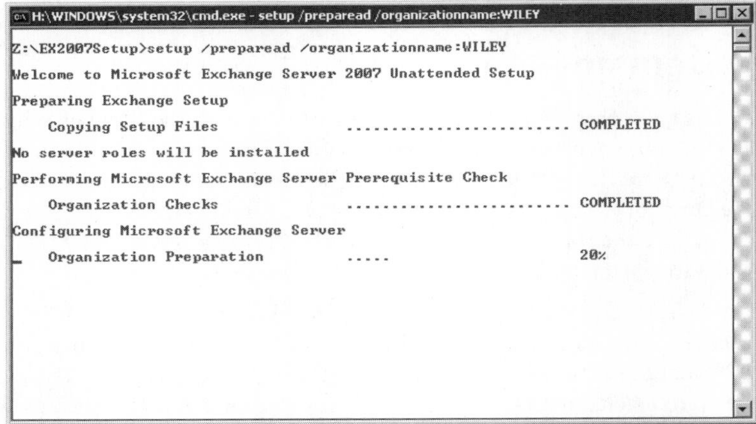
H:\WINDOWS\system32\cmd.exe - setup /preparead /organizationname:WILEY
Z:\EX2007Setup>setup /preparead /organizationname:WILEY
Welcome to Microsoft Exchange Server 2007 Unattended Setup
Preparing Exchange Setup
Copying Setup Files .... COMPLETED
No server roles will be installed
Performing Microsoft Exchange Server Prerequisite Check
Organization Checks .... COMPLETED
Configuring Microsoft Exchange Server
Organization Preparation 20%

4. If setup finds any errors, they will be displayed, and the /PrepareAD process will fail. You will need to rerun the command after you have corrected the noted errors.

TIP

You can run the /PrepareAD portion of setup while installing the first Exchange Server 2007 computer. This situation is typically encountered only in smaller organizations where only one domain exists within the Active Directory forest.

After the /PrepareAD command has been completed and replication has occurred between domain controllers, you can check two places to quickly identify changes that have been made within Active Directory. The Active Directory Users and Computers console will contain a new organizational unit named Microsoft Exchange Security Groups, as shown in Figure 2.5, which will contain the universal security groups discussed previously.

As shown in Figure 2.6, the Active Directory Sites and Services console (Services node) displays the Exchange organization that was created and several configuration items for it. To enable the Services node, you will need to click the Active Directory Sites and Services root node and then select View ➢ Show Service Node.

FIGURE 2.5 Viewing changes in Active Directory Users and Computers after running the /PrepareAD command

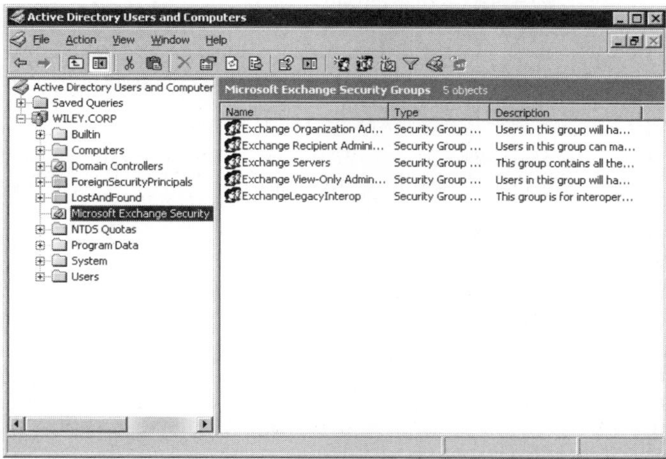

FIGURE 2.6 Viewing changes in Active Directory Sites and Services after running the /PrepareAD command

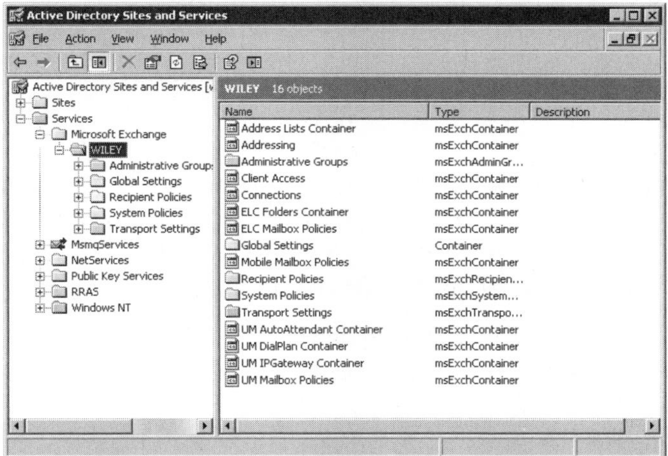

Preparing Other Windows Active Directory Domains

Once you have prepared the Windows Active Directory forest using /PrepareSchema and created the Exchange organization and global objects using the /PrepareAD command, you must also prepare each additional domain in the forest that will run Exchange Server 2007 using the /PrepareDomain command. You must run the /PrepareDomain command in each domain that will contain Exchange Server 2007 servers or recipient objects or that has users or groups that will manage Exchange Server 2007 computers.

To run the /PrepareDomain command, you must be a member of the Domain Admins group for that domain and the Administrators group on the local computer where you will be running DomainPrep. DomainPrep performs the following tasks:

- Configures the required permissions on the domain container for the Exchange Servers group, Exchange Organization Administrators group, Authenticated Users group, and Exchange Recipient Administrators group.
- Creates a new container named Microsoft Exchange System Objects and sets permissions on the container for the Exchange Servers group, Exchange Organization Administrators group, and the Authenticated Users group.
- Creates a domain global group in the domain called Exchange Install Domain Servers. This group is then added to the Exchange Servers universal security group in the root domain.

Exercise 2.6 outlines the steps for running the /PrepareDomain command.

EXERCISE 2.6

Running the /PrepareDomain Command

1. Insert the Microsoft Exchange Server 2007 DVD into the server's DVD-ROM drive. If the server does not have a DVD-ROM drive, you can copy the files to a network location and then proceed using that location.

2. Open a command interpreter window by selecting Start ➢ Run, entering **CMD** and pressing Enter.

3. In the command interpreter window, enter the following command: ***X*:\setup /prepare-domain**, where *X* represents the location of the Exchange Server 2007 setup files, local or remote. Press Enter to start the root domain preparation process, as shown here.

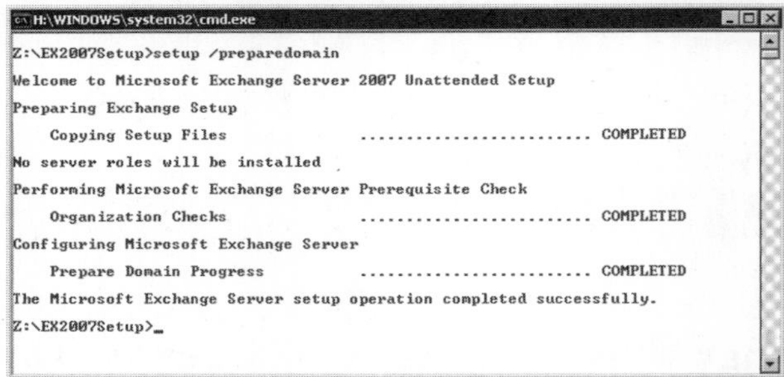
H:\WINDOWS\system32\cmd.exe
Z:\EX2007Setup>setup /preparedomain
Welcome to Microsoft Exchange Server 2007 Unattended Setup
Preparing Exchange Setup
Copying Setup Files .... COMPLETED
No server roles will be installed
Performing Microsoft Exchange Server Prerequisite Check
Organization Checks .... COMPLETED
Configuring Microsoft Exchange Server
Prepare Domain Progress .... COMPLETED
The Microsoft Exchange Server setup operation completed successfully.
Z:\EX2007Setup>_

4. If setup finds any errors, they will be displayed, and the /PrepareDomain process will fail. You will need to rerun the command after you're corrected the noted errors.

You can run the /PrepareDomain portion of setup while installing the first Exchange Server 2007 computer. This situation is typically encountered only in smaller organizations where only one domain exists within the Active Directory forest.

As shown in Figure 2.7, the Microsoft Exchange System Objects container now exists, although it cannot be clicked and opened like other containers or organizational units. You will need to select View ➢ Advanced Features to enable viewing of advanced objects such as the Microsoft Exchange System Objects container within Active Directory Users and Computers.

FIGURE 2.7 Viewing changes in Active Directory Users and Computers after running the /PrepareDomain command

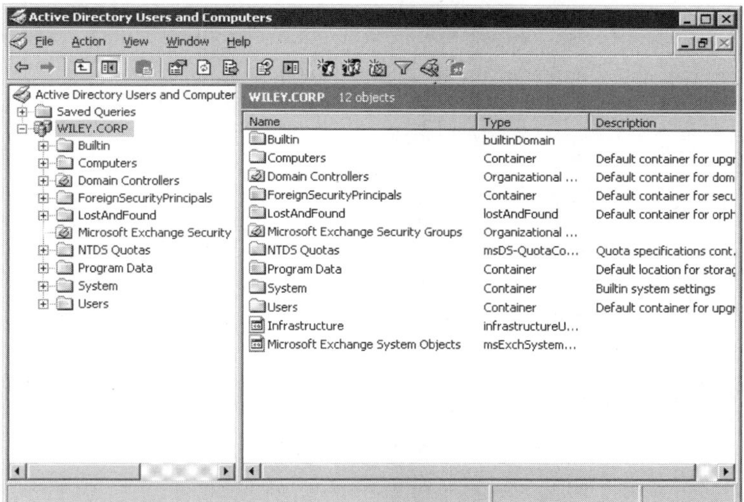

Modifying Existing Exchange Organizations to Support Migration

If you will be installing Exchange Server 2007 into an existing Exchange Server 2003 or Exchange 2000 Server organization, you must make additional configuration changes to Active Directory and the legacy Exchange organization. The /PrepareLegacyExchangePermissions command must be run in every domain in which the Exchange Server 2003 or Exchange 2000 Server DomainPrep has been previously run to ensure that the legacy Recipient Update Service (RUS) continues to operate correctly on the older Exchange servers. The RUS is required in legacy Exchange Server 2003 and Exchange 2000 Server environments to update some attributes on a recipient such as the proxy address and the email address. If you've ever created a new mailbox-enabled user before in an Exchange Server 2003 or Exchange 2000 Server organization and had to wait a few minutes for an email address to be stamped on it, then you were waiting on RUS to fire.

In these older Exchange environments, the RUS runs in the context of the local server account for the Exchange server on which it is running. Each Exchange server's computer account is a member of the Exchange Enterprise Servers security group, which is created during the DomainPrep process. The attributes that RUS needs to be able to modify and update are grouped together into a property set, and DomainPrep grants the Exchange Enterprise Servers security group the required permissions to modify the attributes in question. Since Exchange Server 2007 no longer uses this legacy Exchange Enterprise Servers security group, a solution is needed to allow RUS to continue to operate properly.

As outlined at the beginning of this section of the chapter, Exchange Server 2007 now uses a universal security group named Exchange Recipient Administrators. The members of this group have the required permissions to manage the email-related attributes of all recipients. The legacy Exchange Enterprise Servers security group does not access, by default, to the property set that is created to allow the Exchange Recipient Administrators group access to these email-related attributes. To that end, when the schema modification is performed as part of the preinstallation of Exchange Server 2007, RUS will no longer have permission to manage recipients' email attributes and stops functioning entirely. The workaround to this problem is to run the setup /PrepareLegacyExchangePermissions command before any other setup steps when integrating Exchange Server 2007 with legacy Exchange organizations.

Exercise 2.7 outlines the steps for running the /PrepareLegacyExchangePermissions command. You will need to be a member of the Domain Admins group and the Exchange Organization Administrators groups in each domain in which this command is run. To run the command as shown in Exercise 2.7, which runs against all domains in the forest, you will need to be a member of the Enterprise Admins group as well.

EXERCISE 2.7

Running the /PrepareLegacyExchangePermissions Command

1. Insert the Microsoft Exchange Server 2007 DVD into the server's DVD-ROM drive. If the server does not have a DVD-ROM drive, you can copy the files to a network location and then proceed using that location.

2. Open a command interpreter window by selecting Start ➢ Run, entering **CMD**, and pressing Enter.

3. In the command interpreter window, enter the following command: ***X*:\setup /preparelegacyexchangepermissions**, where *X* represents the location of the Exchange Server 2007 setup files, local or remote. Press Enter to start the root domain preparation process.

4. If setup finds any errors, they will be displayed, and the /PrepareLegacyExchangePermissions process will fail. You will need to rerun the command after you've corrected the noted errors.

Real World Scenario

Deploying Exchange Server 2007 in a Large Organization

You are the lead network administrator for a large manufacturing corporation that has 45 geographical locations within North America. In the past, your company has never had a real company-wide network that spanned all locations and linked all users and resources together. You have just completed installing a new Windows Server 2003 Active Directory network that provides one unified network to all users and all locations within your organization.

Your network consists of a single Active Directory forest and five domains under the root domain named canada.manufacturing.com, mexico.manufacturing.com, west.manufacturing.com, central.manufacturing.com, and east.manufacturing.com.

The root domain of manufacturing.com contains no user accounts or member servers. You have two assistant administrators for each of the five child domains that have the Domain Admins permissions for their applicable child domain. Only your user account has the Enterprise Admins and Schema Admins permissions configured. As well, only your user account has the Domain Admins permissions for the root domain. You have local administrative access on the servers in the root domain, and your assistant administrators have local administrative access on all computers and servers in their child domain. Your office is located within the east.manufacturing.com child domain.

To facilitate the process of installing Exchange Server 2007 on six Windows Server 2003 computers in each child domain, you have provided network shares in each child domain that contain the installation source files. As well, you have run the /PrepareSchema portion of the Exchange setup program to extend the Active Directory Schema to support the installation of Exchange Server 2007. After the /PrepareSchema command has been run, you will next need to run the /PrepareAD command and specify the Exchange organization name.

Once you've completed these tasks, you should run the /PrepareDomain command for the root domain and the east.manufacturing.com child domain. You can then start to install Exchange Server 2007 servers in the east.manufacturing.com child domain if desired. As well, your assistant administrators might begin to install the remaining Exchange Server 2007 servers using the installation source files located on their local network shares. As you can see, the Exchange installation process can be quite lengthy and complicated in a large network environment; however, careful planning and execution can lead to first-time success. In reality, this process can actually be simpler than the ForestPrep and DomainPrep process of Exchange Server 2003 that required you to delegate permissions from within the Exchange System Manager before the assistant administrators could start installing Exchange servers.

Summary

Before you ever start to install the first Exchange Server 2007 server, many items need your time and consideration. Taking the time to properly prepare your organization for the introduction of Exchange Server 2007 will yield positive results, regardless of whether this is an upgrade/coexistence scenario with legacy versions of Exchange or whether it's a completely new installation of Exchange Server 2007.

One of the most important phases of an installation is preinstallation. Before starting the actual installation, you must make sure that the minimum requirements for Exchange are met. You must obtain the proper licenses to ensure compliance with legal issues. Because Exchange utilizes user accounts from Active Directory, Exchange Server 2007 is tightly integrated with Active Directory. Before Exchange can be installed, you will need to ensure that the required Windows services and components are installed and running. To avoid problems during the setup process, you should use the `dcdiag` and `netdiag` tools to test your network's connectivity. Finally, you must prepare the Active Directory forest and domains by running the appropriate commands.

Exam Essentials

Understand preinstallation *setup.exe* options. If you're working in single-domain forest, you might never need to work with the /PrepareSchema, /PrepareAD, and /PrepareDomain commands. Even if this is the case, you should still learn what these powerful setup commands do and what permissions are required to use them. Consider the example of a very large, geographically dispersed network where multiple administrators at various levels work together to manage and maintain the network—in this situation, these commands are invaluable tools that can assist in getting Exchange Server 2007 installed by splitting the installation tasks up according to domain group permissions that have been assigned.

Remember which groups interact with Exchange. Several different security groups interact with Exchange before, during, and after the installation of Exchange is complete. You should keep in mind the basic functions and responsibilities of each of these groups.

Know the limitations of coexisting with older versions of Exchange. There is no direct upgrade path for Exchange Server 2007 as there was with Exchange Server 2003. As such, you'll likely be coexisting with older versions of Exchange for a while if they exist in your organization. If you will be installing Exchange Server 2007 into an Exchange organization that contains Exchange Server 2003 or earlier versions of Exchange, you'll need to keep the following requirements in mind:

- Exchange Server 2007 cannot be installed in an Exchange organization that contains Exchange Server 5.5. You must migrate all mailboxes and public folders to Exchange Server 2003 or Exchange 2000 Server first in this scenario.

- All Exchange Server 2003 servers must have, at a minimum, Exchange Server 2003 SP2 installed.
- All Exchange 2000 Server servers must have, at a minimum, Exchange 2000 Server SP3 installed.
- All Exchange 2000 Server servers must also have the most current post-SP3 update rollup installed as well. See MSKB 870540 to obtain the most current post-SP3 update rollup for Exchange 2000 Server.

Remember the requirements to install Exchange Server 2007. Exchange Server 2007 can be installed only on a Windows Server 2003 x64 SP1 or R2 computer. All domain controllers and global catalog servers that the Exchange Server 2007 computer will communicate with must be at least Windows Server 2003 SP1, and the domain and forest functional levels must be at the Windows 2000 native functional level or higher. The hardware and software requirements detailed previously in this chapter must also be met to successfully install and operate an Exchange Server 2007 organization.

Review Questions

1. One of your company's locations contains an Exchange server with 25 users, each using Microsoft Outlook. You have purchased 25 client access licenses (CALs). The company hires 10 new employees who will connect to the site remotely using Outlook Web Access. How many additional CALs must you purchase?

   A. 0

   B. 2

   C. 5

   D. 6

   E. 10

   F. 12

2. You are the Exchange administrator for a large network. You do not have the appropriate permissions to update the Active Directory schema on your network, so you must get another administrator to do this before you can install Exchange Server 2007. To which of the following groups must that person belong in order to run the /PrepareSchema utility? (Choose all that apply.)

   A. Server Admins

   B. Domain Admins

   C. Schema Admins

   D. Enterprise Admins

3. You will have two Exchange Server 2007 computers that provide all messaging access for your 250 network users. If all 250 of your users connect to the Exchange server using Office Outlook 2007 and Outlook Web Access, how many CALs do you need to have?

   A. 1

   B. 2

   C. 250

   D. 500

4. Your company is running a messaging system that consists of four Exchange 2000 Servers running on Windows 2000 Advanced Server. Which of the following steps must you take to migrate to Exchange Server 2007? (Choose all that apply.)

   A. Upgrade all servers to Exchange 2000 Server Service Pack 3.

   B. Upgrade all servers to Exchange 2000 Server Service Pack 2.

   C. Install Windows Server 2003 on all servers.

   D. Update the legacy permissions for the RUS.

5. In a large organization with thousands of Exchange mailboxes, what storage technology provides the highest performance, although it costs the most to implement?

   A. iSCSI

   B. SAS

   C. SATA

   D. Fibre Channel

6. Exchange Server 2007 breaks from the standard client access license (CAL) model and uses two different CALs that provide different functionality to Exchange clients. What functionalities are available only when using the Enterprise CAL? (Choose all that apply.)
   A. Managed folders
   B. Calendaring
   C. Antivirus controls
   D. Outlook Web Access (OWA)
   E. Outlook usage

7. Your network consists of a single Active Directory forest with three domains: one root domain and two child domains. If Exchange Server is to be installed in only one of the two child domains and not at all in the root domain, how many times must you run the /PrepareSchema command?
   A. None
   B. One time
   C. Two times
   D. Three times

8. What software components must be installed on any server that will have any Exchange Server 2007 role installed? (Choose all that apply.)
   A. Microsoft .NET Framework 2.0
   B. Security Configuration Wizard
   C. Windows PowerShell 1.0
   D. Windows Installer 3.1
   E. Microsoft Management Console (MMC) 3.0
   F. Simple Mail Transfer Protocol (SMTP)

9. Your network consists of a single Active Directory forest with three domains: one root domain and two child domains. If Exchange Server is to be installed in only one of the two child domains and not at all in the root domain, how many times (minimum) must you run the /PrepareDomain tool?
   A. None
   B. One time
   C. Two times
   D. Three times

10. Which of the following Exchange Server 2007 created universal security groups would not be present in a fresh installation of Exchange Server 2007?
   A. Exchange Organization Administrators
   B. Exchange Server Administrators (*servername*)
   C. Exchange Recipient Administrators
   D. Exchange2003Interop
   E. Exchange View-Only Administrators (*servername*)

11. Your Windows Active Directory forest consists of a single domain tree. That tree consists of a single root-level domain and four child domains of that root domain. You are about to prepare the root-level domain for an Exchange Server 2007 installation. After you've prepared the forest schema, what other command must you next run in the root-level domain?

    A. `setup /PrepareDomain`

    B. `setup /PrepareAD`

    C. `setup /DomainPrep`

    D. `setup /PrepareLegacyExchangePermissions`

12. Which of the following storage technologies is the only network protocol storage technology approved for usage with Exchange Server 2007?

    A. iSCSI

    B. SAS

    C. SATA

    D. Fibre Channel

13. What listed component is required to support the installation of the Mailbox server role on an Exchange Server 2007 server?

    A. Microsoft Core XML Services (MSXML) 6.0

    B. ASP.NET 2.0

    C. Active Directory Application Mode (ADAM)

    D. Network COM+ access

14. What type of RAID array is recommended for holding the Exchange transaction logs?

    A. RAID-5

    B. RAID-6

    C. RAID-10

    D. RAID-0

15. Exchange Server 2007 uses the concept of role-based server installation, allowing each "role" to be installed separate from the others. What two roles are mandatory in a new Exchange Server 2007 installation?

    A. Edge Transport

    B. Mailbox

    C. Client Access

    D. Unified Messaging

    E. Hub Transport

16. What Exchange Server 2007 server role do the Edge Transport servers communicate with to ensure proper mail flow and delivery?

    A. Hub Transport

    B. Unified Messaging

    C. Client Access

    D. Mailbox

17. When running the setup /PrepareAD command, what extra information is required for an installation of Exchange Server 2007 into an organization with no previous Exchange installations?

    A. `/CleanInstall`

    B. `/OrganizationName:`*`NAME`*

    C. `/CreateOrganization`

    D. `/NewOrganization`

18. If you are installing Exchange Server 2007 into a forest that has never had an Exchange organization before and the forest contains only a single domain, which of the following commands must be issued before starting the actual installation of Exchange Server 2007?

    A. `setup /PrepareSchema`

    B. `setup /PrepareAD`

    C. `setup /PrepareDomain`

    D. All of the listed commands

    E. None of the listed commands

19. Exchange Server 2007 supports which of the following types of clustering? (Choose all that apply.)

    A. Active/active

    B. Active/passive

    C. Cluster continuous replication

    D. Partial cluster replication

20. Which of the following Exchange Server 2007–created universal security groups have full access to all Exchange Server properties throughout the Exchange organization?

    A. Exchange Organization Administrators

    B. Exchange Server Administrators (*servername*)

    C. Exchange Recipient Administrators

    D. Exchange2003Interop

    E. Exchange View-Only Administrators (*servername*)

Answers to Review Questions

1. E. Every user who connects to the Exchange server will need a CAL, no matter what method (Outlook, Outlook Web Access, and so on) is used to connect.

2. C, D. To run the /PrepareSchema utility, a user must belong to both the Schema Admins and Enterprise Admins global groups. The user must also belong to the local Administrators group on the computer on which the utility is actually run.

3. C. Exchange Server 2007 is licensed in the per-user or per-device mode, meaning that each client (user or device) that accesses the server must have a valid CAL. Since you have a total of 250 clients, you need to have 250 CALs for your organization, even if the clients access the Exchange server in more than one way, such as Outlook or Outlook Web Access.

4. A, D. To migrate Exchange 2000 Server computers to Exchange Server 2007 computers, the Exchange organization must be operating in Exchange native mode. In addition, all Exchange 2000 Server installations must be updated with Exchange 2000 Server Service3. Additionally, the /PrepareLegacyExchangePermissions setup command will need to be run to ensure that the RUS continues to operate after the Active Directory schema is updated for Exchange Server 2007.

5. D. Fibre Channel is still the most expensive and most reliable and robust storage solution on the market. Fibre Channel–attached SCSI drives are the best choice for almost any size organization. With backbone network speeds as fast as 4Gbit/sec now, Fibre Channel storage area networks provide many exciting and business-relevant solutions that make placing Exchange databases on them ideal. Many vendors, with the largest being EMC, HP, and IBM, have Fibre Channel solutions. Fibre Channel–attached SCSI disks come in 10,000 and 15,000 RPM speeds, although most new installations will use 15,000 RPM exclusively.

6. A, C. The standard CAL provides licensed Exchange Server 2007 functionality such as email, calendaring, and remote access via OWA. The new Exchange Server Enterprise CAL is required to access the advanced features of Exchange Server 2007 such as Forefront Security for Exchange Server (antivirus and antispam), unified messaging, and other desirable features such as compliance controls, managed folders, and per-user journaling. Enterprise CALs are added to existing Standard CALs to make all functionality available.

7. B. You must run the /PrepareSchema command one time, and one time only, for each Active Directory forest that will have Exchange Server 2007 installed into it.

8. A, C, E. Any server that will have any Exchange Server 2007 role installed on it must have, at a minimum, the following software installed:

   - Microsoft .NET Framework 2.0
   - Windows PowerShell 1.0
   - Microsoft Management Console (MMC) 3.0

   Additional software requirements must be met depending on the specific server role being installed.

9. C. Once the Windows Active Directory forest is prepared using the /PrepareSchema command, each domain in the forest that will run Exchange Server 2007 must also be prepared using the /PrepareDomain command. In addition, the forest root domain and each domain that will contain Exchange Server 2007 mailbox-enabled objects or that has users or groups that will manage Exchange Server 2007 computers must have the /PrepareDomain command run in it.

10. D. The Exchange2003Interop security group is created and utilized only during an upgrade scenario from Exchange Server 2003. This group provides authentication for connections made between Exchange Server 2007 Hub Transport servers and Exchange Server 2003 Bridgehead servers.

11. B. In the root-level domain, you will need to use only the /PrepareAD command after the /PrepareSchema command has been run. The /PrepareAD command includes the functionality of the /PrepareDomain command. The /PrepareDomain command would then be used in each other domain in which Exchange will be installed.

12. A. Internet SCSI (iSCSI) is the single network-based storage method that Microsoft supports for Exchange Server 2007. iSCSI connects SCSI disks to servers using standard Ethernet cabling and dedicated Ethernet adapters in servers. Although most new Ethernet adapters have TCP/IP offload engines (TOE) on them to support iSCSI usage, you will not want to deploy iSCSI using the same network adapters in use for normal network traffic. Treat iSCSI as you would Fibre Channel–attached storage systems, and place two to four Ethernet ports in each server dedicated to the iSCSI storage network. iSCSI is somewhat mature now, at several years of age, but is still far behind traditional Fibre Channel SAN systems in many regards. iSCSI, however, is typically less expensive than Fibre Channel.

13. D. For servers that will have the Mailbox role installed, the following software requirements apply:

- Internet Information Services (IIS) 6.0.
- World Wide Web (WWW) publishing component.
- Network COM+ access is enabled.
- Windows Server 2003 x64 hotfix 904639 and 918980.
- The Simple Mail Transfer Protocol (SMTP) and Network News Transfer Protocol (NNTP) must not be installed.

14. C. Transaction logs, by their very nature of being critical to Exchange and needing fast sequential read/write access, should always be placed on RAID-10 (or RAID-1) arrays if at all possible. These arrays should be controlled by battery-backed controllers to prevent data loss.

15. B, E. The Hub Transport and Mailbox roles are mandatory in all Exchange Server 2007 installations. The Client Access role will be used in nearly every Exchange Server 2007 implementation, although usage of the Edge Transport and Unified Messaging roles will vary by organizational needs and comfort.

16. A. When an inbound message is received by the Edge Transport Server, it scans the message for viral and spam qualities and then takes the appropriate (as configured) actions if it determines that the message is one or both of these items. Normal, clean messages are delivered to a Hub Transport server for policy and compliance enforcement, as well as delivery to the final recipients. All message routing and delivery is accomplished by the Hub Transport servers in Exchange Server 2007.

17. B. When Exchange Server 2007 is being installed and no legacy Exchange organizations exist, you will need to specify the Exchange organization name by running the following command: `setup /PrepareAD /OrganizationName:`*`NAME`*, where *NAME* is the name you want to call the Exchange organization.

18. E. If there is only one domain in your forest, the installation of Exchange is simplified. If the account with which you install the first Exchange server belongs to the Schema Admins, Enterprise Admins, and Administrators groups for the local computer, you do not need to manually run /PrepareAD, /PrepareSchema or /PrepareDomain since you will run them during the regular Exchange setup process.

19. B, C. Exchange Server 2007 supports two types of true clustering: single-instance clusters (also referred to as *active/passive clusters*) and cluster continuous replication. Active/active clusters, which were supported by Exchange Server 2003 and Exchange 2000 Server, are no longer supported in Exchange Server 2007. Exchange Server 2007 also provides another high-availability solution known as *local continuous replication* that creates a second (standby) copy of the databases.

20. A. The members of the Exchange Organization Administrators group have full access to all Exchange Server properties throughout the Exchange organization. By default, the administrative account that is used to install Exchange Server 2007 is placed into this group.

Installing Exchange Server 2007

MICROSOFT EXAM OBJECTIVES COVERED IN THIS CHAPTER:

✓ **Installing and Configuring Microsoft Exchange Servers**

- Install Exchange.

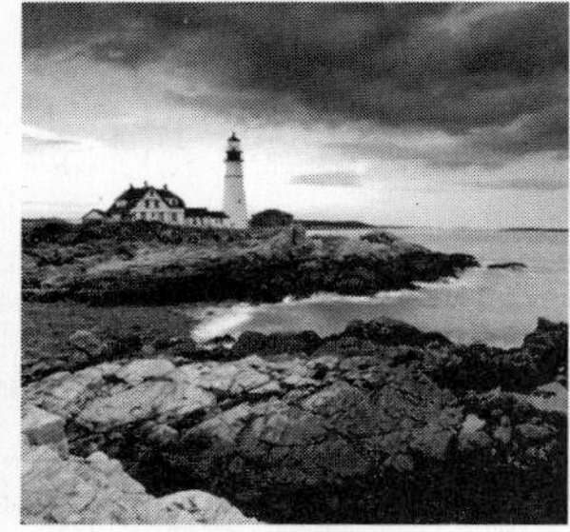

Now that you've completed the pre-installation verification and configuration, you're ready install Exchange Server 2007 server roles. Exchange Server 2007 provides plenty of flexibility in how you can install it, and you'll spend time in this chapter looking at the three methods you can use to install Exchange Server 2007. After you've done that, you'll spend some time examining the various Exchange Administrator roles available and configuring and assigning them as appropriate.

The main subjects of this chapter are as follows:

- Choosing the appropriate role or roles to be installed
- Performing graphical user interface installations
- Performing unattended installations
- Performing command-line installations
- Configuring the Exchange Administrator roles

Choosing the Exchange Roles to Install

Before you actually start to install your new Exchange Server 2007 servers, you should take some time to plan what roles you'll be installing, how many of each role you'll be installing, and, most important, where within your Active Directory forest you'll be installing the servers. Recall, as we discussed previously in Chapter 2, "Preparing for the Exchange Server 2007 Installation," that certain requirements and limitations govern how you can install each Exchange Server 2007 server role. As a quick summary, consider the following points:

- Edge Transport servers must not be members of any Active Directory domain.
- Edge Transport servers should be installed in the portion of your network that is exposed to the Internet, such as the DMZ.
- The Edge Transport server role cannot be installed in combination with any other Exchange Server 2007 server role.
- Each Active Directory site that is to contain a Mailbox server or Unified Messaging server must have at least one Hub Transport server.
- The Hub Transport server is a required server role.
- Hub Transport servers cannot be clustered or use network load balancing.
- The Mailbox server role is no longer responsible for message routing.

- At least one Mailbox server must be installed before you can install a Unified Messaging server.
- The Client Access server role is required for any type of client access other than Outlook MAPI access.
- A Client Access server is required to enable Outlook 2007 Autodiscover.
- Client Access servers must be part of an Active Directory domain and should never be directly exposed to the Internet.
- The Hub Transport, Mailbox, and Client Access server roles will be installed by default on the first Exchange Server 2007 server.

In almost every installation of Exchange Server 2007, you will be using two or more Exchange servers. Perhaps one server will be a Client Access and Mailbox server and the other will be a Hub Transport server. Or maybe two Mailbox servers are installed in a cluster continuous replication model, and two additional servers are installed with the Client Access and Hub Transport roles. Perhaps in the DMZ, there might also be two Edge Transport servers installed for message routing and hygiene controls. The bottom line is that there is no specific number of Exchange Server 2007 servers that you must have as a rule—rather your organization's size, locations, and needs will determine how many you need, where you place them, and what roles you install.

Installing Exchange Server 2007

As briefly discussed in Chapter 2, Exchange Server 2007 gives you several ways to install the product. Most installations will likely be standard graphical user interface (GUI) installations, so you'll examine that method first. However, when you have many Exchange Server 2007 installations to perform or you want to do something besides watch the installation take place, you can perform an unattended installation of Exchange. As you also saw previously in Chapter 1, "Exchange Server 2007 and Active Directory Review," you can perform the installation steps from the command line, which you'll examine here as well. Of course, before you start any of the installation methods we'll be discussing in this chapter, make sure you meet all of the requirements outlined in Chapter 1.

Performing GUI-Based Installations

The most common installation method for Exchange Server 2007 will likely be the standard GUI-based method. This method is especially well suited for smaller organizations that might be installing only a few Exchange Server 2007 servers or for administrators who are not as comfortable or familiar with the other installation methods available. Exercise 3.1 outlines the process to install the first Exchange Server 2007 server into an organization.

For the purposes of Exercise 3.1, we're not going to prepare the Active Directory forest or domain. This type of installation is well suited for the single-domain forests common in smaller organizations. You'll utilize the Active Directory preparation discussed in Chapter 1 later when we cover command-line-based installation methods.

EXERCISE 3.1

Installing Exchange Server 2007 from the Graphical User Interface

1. Insert the Exchange Server 2007 DVD into your server's DVD drive, or browse to the network location that holds the Exchange Server 2007 setup files. The DVD should autostart.
2. If the DVD does not autostart or you have a network-based installation, double-click the `setup.exe` file to launch the Exchange Server 2007 installer.
3. If prompted with a security warning when running `setup.exe`, as shown here, click Run to allow the setup program to run.

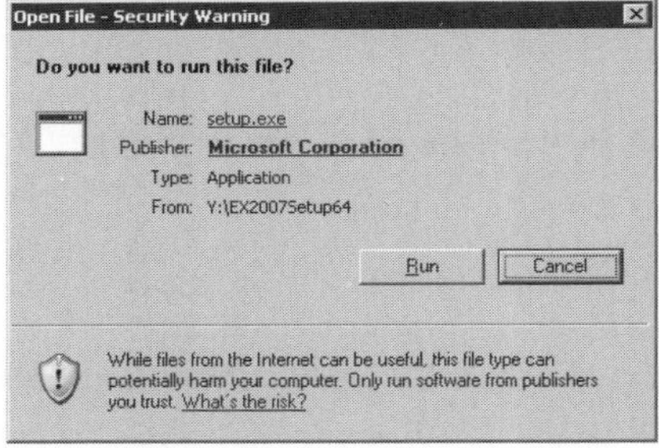

4. If you have installed all the required prerequisites, you will be able to click Step 4. If not, you'll need to click the steps before that and install the required software, as shown here.

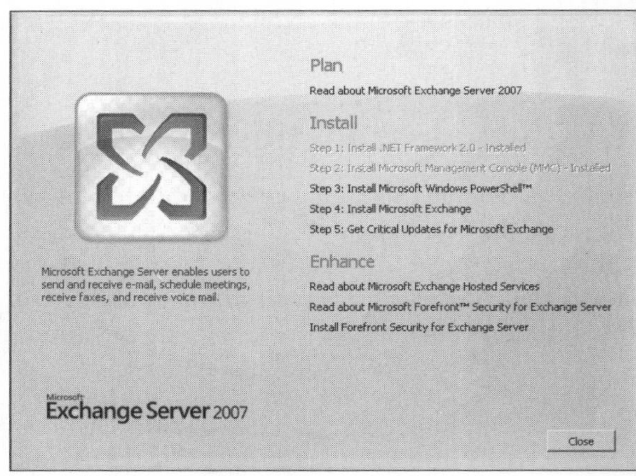

EXERCISE 3.1 *(continued)*

5. The Copying Files dialog box might briefly appear. After a short wait, the Exchange Server 2007 Setup dialog box appears, as shown here. Click Next to continue.

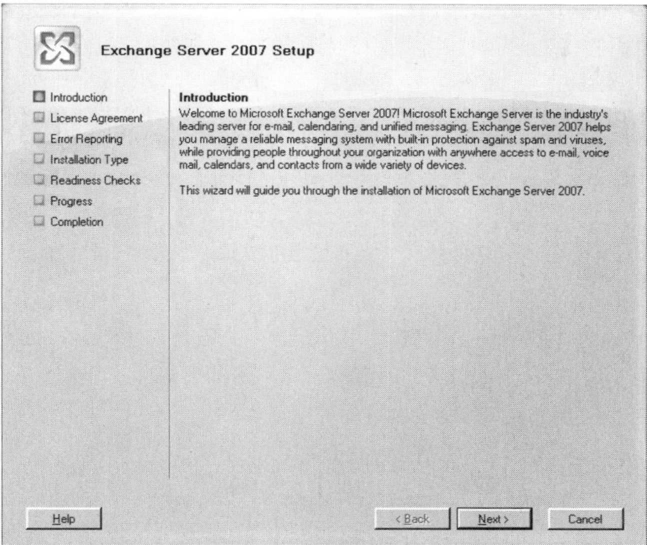

6. In the License Agreement dialog box, accept the terms of the licensing agreement, and then click Next to continue.

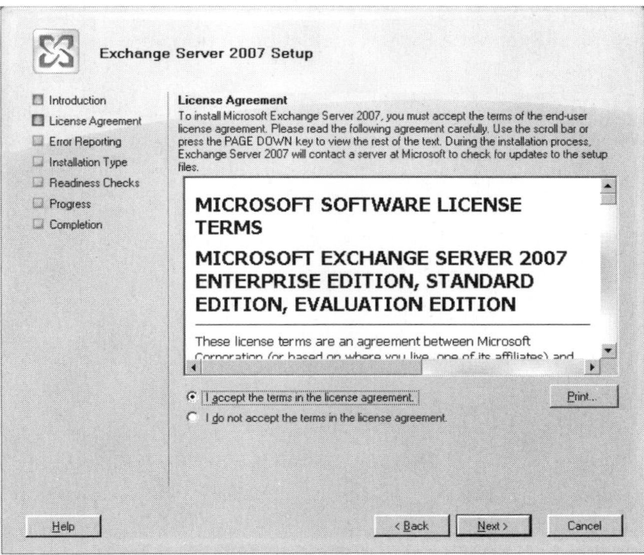

EXERCISE 3.1 *(continued)*

7. In the Error Reporting dialog box, you will need to select whether you want to report errors in the operation of Exchange Server 2007 to Microsoft. After making your choice, click Next to continue.

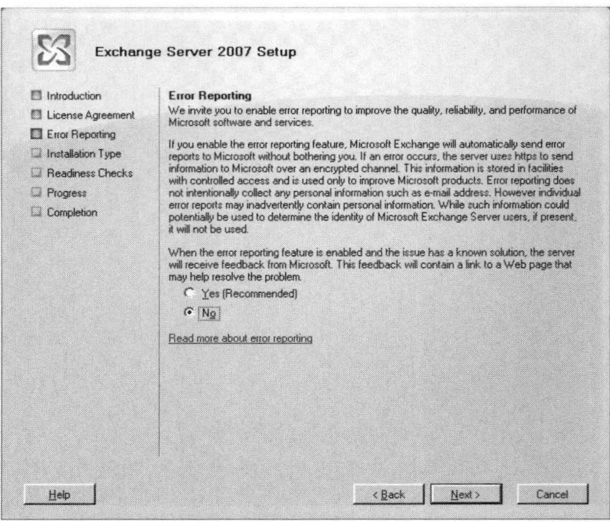

8. In the Installation Type dialog box, you will need to determine what server roles you will want to install. Since this is the first Exchange Server 2007 server you're installing, you must install at least the Hub Transport and Mailbox roles. For the purposes of this exercise, select the Typical Exchange Sever Installation option, and click Next.

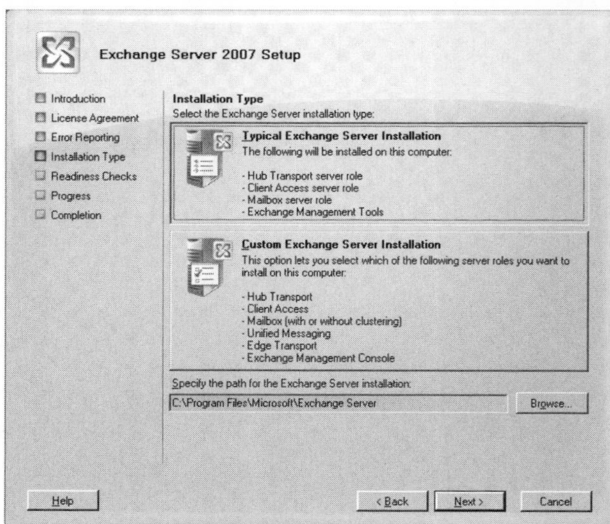

EXERCISE 3.1 *(continued)*

9. In this exercise, no forest or domain preparation has been done previously; thus, in the Exchange Organization dialog box, setup asks you for the Exchange organization name that will be used. Specify your organization name, and click Next to continue.

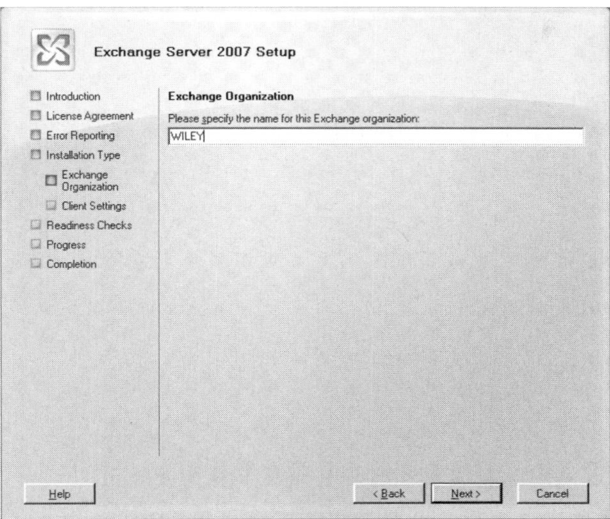

10. In the Client Settings dialog box, Exchange Setup asks whether you will be using older versions of the Outlook client or any Entourage (for Macintosh) clients to access the server. The answer to this question determines whether public folders are created during installation. Select Yes (to create the public folders), and then click Next to continue.

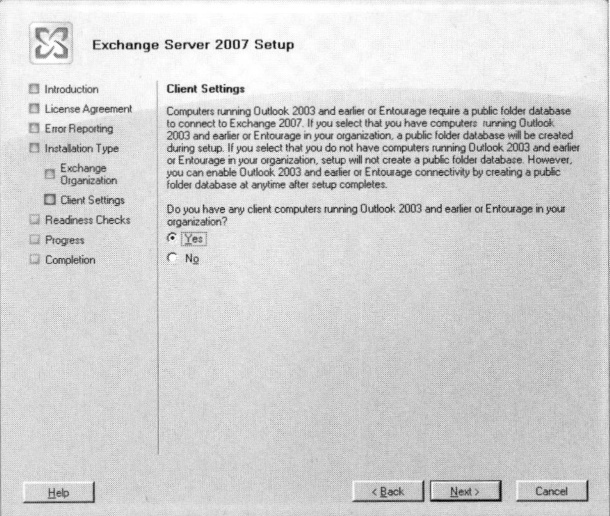

EXERCISE 3.1 *(continued)*

11. If the Readiness Checks dialog box notes any failures, address these items before continuing. Once you have no failure items here, click Install to continue.

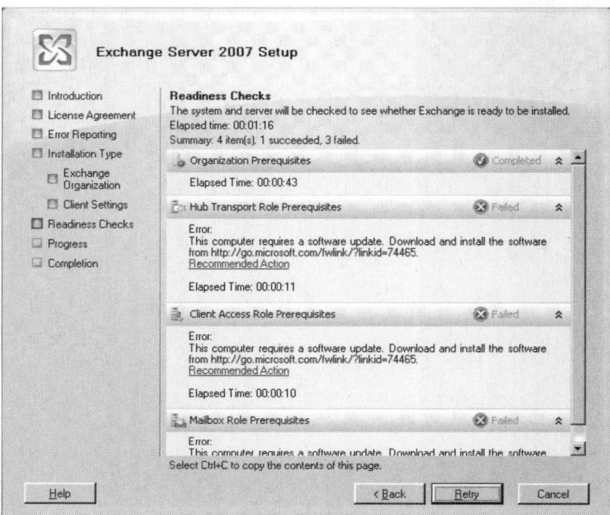

12. The installation process now starts, as shown here. Notice how the setup routine configures the forest schema since you did not perform that process manually.

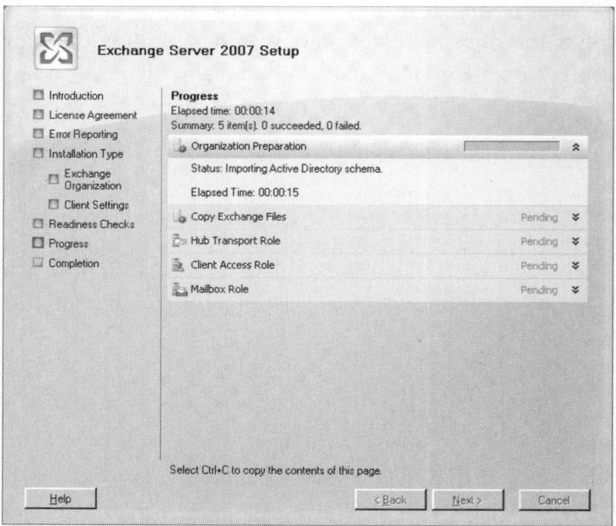

EXERCISE 3.1 *(continued)*

13. After you've installed Exchange Server 2007 on your server, you need to perform some final steps. Select Finalize Installation Using the Exchange Management Console, and click Finish.

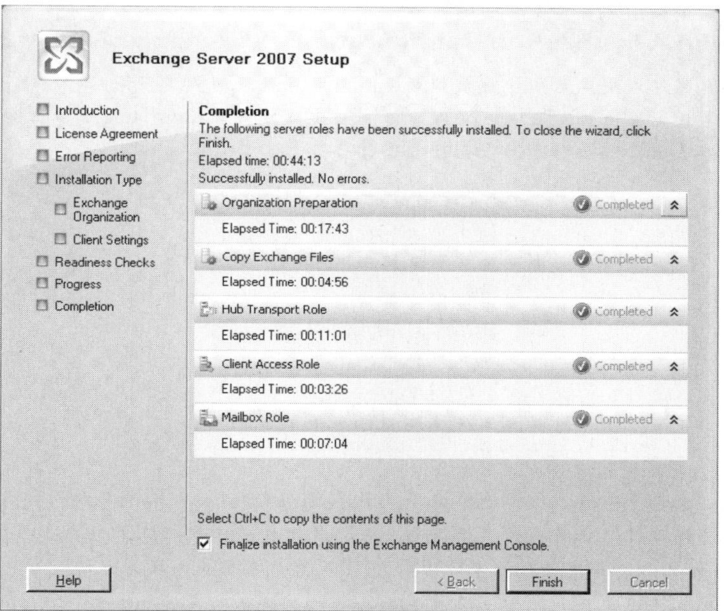

The Exchange organization name cannot contain any of the following special characters: ~ (tilde), ` (grave accent), ! (exclamation point), @ (at sign), # (number sign), $ (dollar sign), % (percent sign), ^ (caret), & (ampersand), * (asterisk), () (parentheses), _ (underscore), + (plus sign), = (equal sign), {} (braces), [] (brackets), | (vertical bar), \ (backslash), : (colon), ; (semicolon), " (quotation mark), ' (apostrophe), <> (angle brackets), , (comma), . (period), ? (question mark), / (slash mark), and whitespace at the beginning or end.

If you are performing this exercise on the same server as the ones you performed the exercises in Chapter 2 on, you won't be asked for the Exchange organization name.

With Exchange Server 2007 now installed on your server, we'll move onto the post-installation configuration steps you need to perform to complete the installation process. Exercise 3.2 will examine some of these tasks. You can perform the rest of the tasks at your convenience.

EXERCISE 3.2

Performing Post-installation Configuration of Exchange Server 2007

1. As soon as the Exchange Management Console loads, you'll be prompted to license the server that Exchange Server 2007 was installed on, as shown here, by entering in the product key. Click OK to acknowledge the licensing prompt.

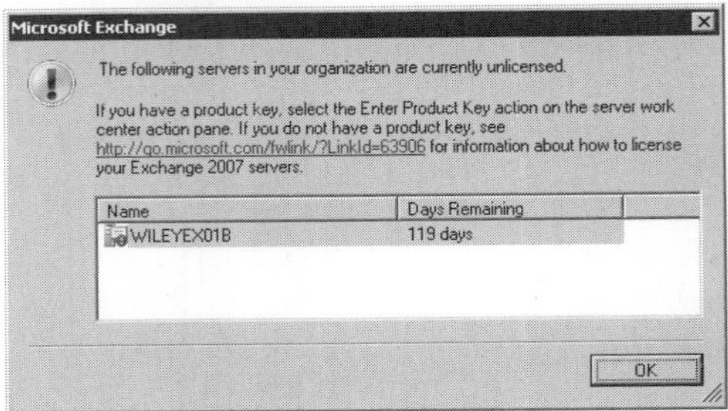

2. The middle pane of the newly redesigned Exchange Management Console, as shown here, displays all of the configuration steps Exchange Server 2007 recommends or requires that you perform after installation has been completed.

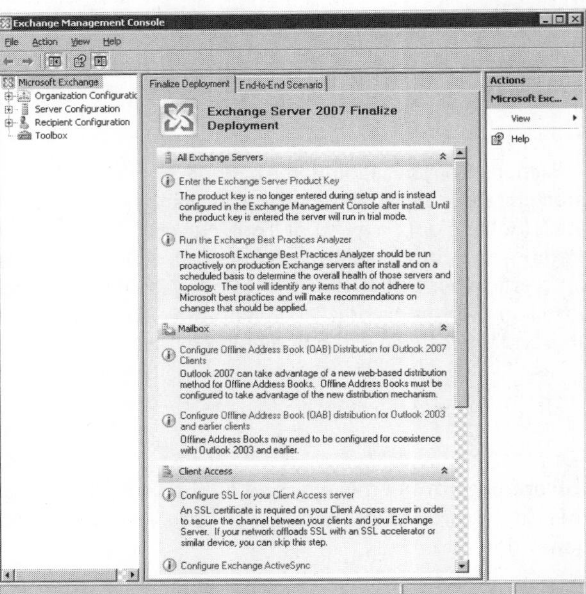

EXERCISE 3.2 *(continued)*

3. To properly license the Exchange server, click the Enter the Exchange Server Product Key link. A new pop-up dialog box tells you how to configure the server with the product key.

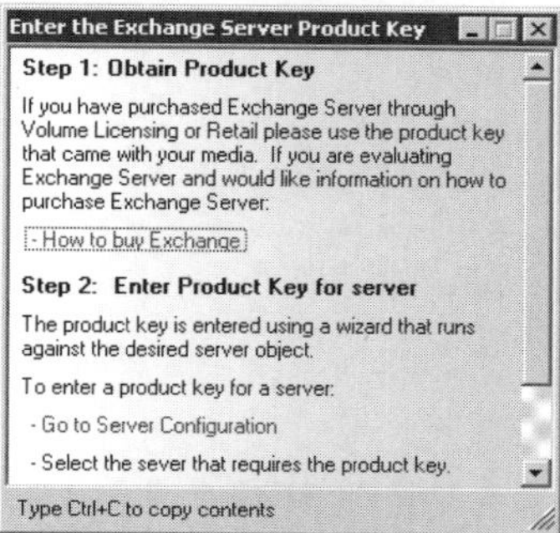

4. Click the Server Configuration node in the left pane of the Exchange Management Console. Select the server to be licensed, as shown here, and then click the Enter Product Key link on the right side of the Exchange Management Console.

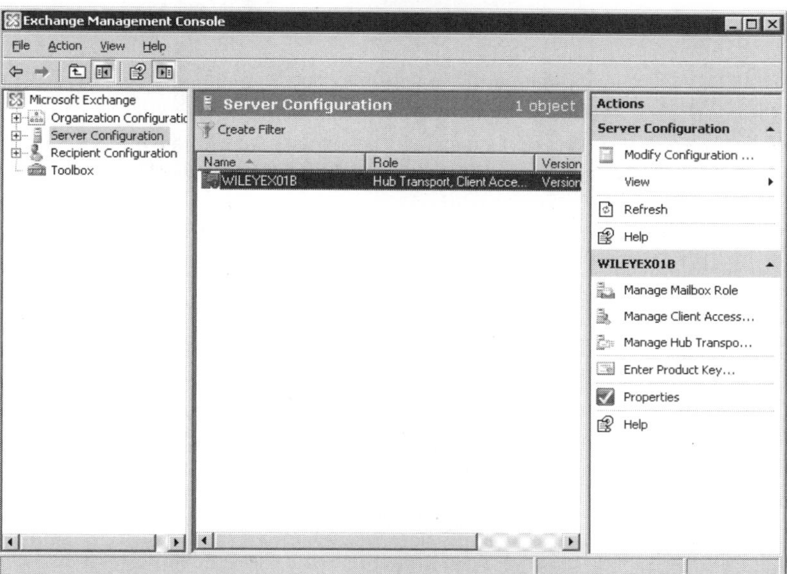

EXERCISE 3.2 *(continued)*

5. Enter your product key in the Enter Product Key dialog box, as shown here, and then click Enter.

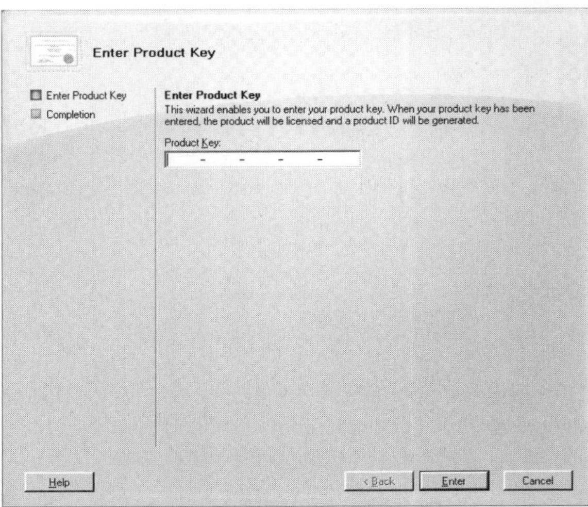

6. The product key will be validated, and the server's licensing status will be updated as indicated. Note the PowerShell code that is displayed. This illustrates how you can license a server from the command line or via a script. Click Finish to complete the licensing process.

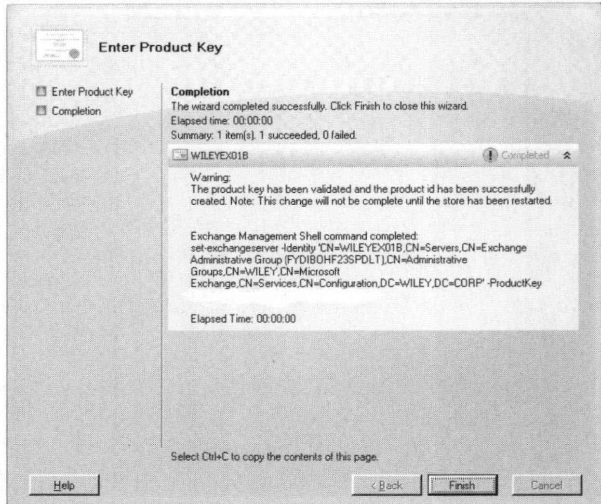

EXERCISE 3.2 *(continued)*

7. You can return to the list of post-installation configuration tasks to be performed by clicking the Microsoft Exchange node at the root of the left display tree. Other common tasks to perform now include running the Exchange Best Practices Analyzer (ExBPA), configuring Offline Address Books (OABs), configuring the SMTP domains that will accept mail, and configuring the postmaster mailbox for the organization.

8. As a last step, check for critical updates that need to be installed after the installation of Exchange Server 2007 by visiting `http://update.microsoft.com/microsoftupdate/` or by clicking the Step 5 link in the Exchange setup splash page shown previously.

You will examine each of the remaining post-installation configuration steps in Chapter 4, "Configuring Exchange Server Roles," and in Chapter 12, "Monitoring and Reporting on the Exchange Server Infrastructure."

Performing Command-Line and Unattended Installations of Exchange Server 2007

As with nearly every Exchange Server 2007 task, you can perform the installation of Exchange Server 2007 from the command line fairly easily. The basic syntax of the `setup.com` command when used from the command line is as follows:

```
Setup.com /mode:<setup mode> /roles:<server roles to install> [/
OrganizationName:<name for the new Exchange organization>] [/TargetDir:<target
directory>] [/UpdatesDir:<directory from which to install updates>] [/
DomainController <FQDN of domain controller>] [/DoNotStartTransport] [/
EnableLegacyOutlook] [/LegacyRoutingServer] [/AddUmLanguagePack:<UM language
pack name>] [/RemoveUmLanguagePack:<UM language pack name>] [/
NewProvisionedServer] [/RemoveProvisionedServer] [/ForeignForestFQDN] [/
ServerAdmin <user or group>] [/NewCms] [/RemoveCms] [/RecoverCms] [/
CMSName:<name>] [/CMSIPAddress:<IP address>] [/CMSSharedStorage] [/
CMSDataPath:<CMS data path>] [/AnswerFile <filename>] [/EnableErrorReporting]
[/NoSelfSignedCertificates] [/AdamLdapPort <port>] [/AdamSslPort <port>]
```

The number of options presented can be overwhelming, but you can examine each of the options available in Table 3.1.

TABLE 3.1 Exchange Server 2007 *Setup.exe* Options

Option	Explanation
/mode:<setup mode>	Tells setup what mode of installation to perform. The default selection, if no mode is specified, is `Install`, and the following choices are available: `Install`, `Upgrade`, `Uninstall`, and `RecoverServer`. The Upgrade option upgrades only a prerelease version of Exchange Server 2007 on the server and cannot be used to upgrade a previous version of Exchange to Exchange Server 2007. The `RecoverServer` mode is used for Exchange Server recovery operations, which we'll discuss in Chapter 11, "Disaster Recovery Operations for Exchange Server."
/roles:<server roles to install>	Specifies what server roles will be installed, in a command-separated listing: `CA` or `ClientAccess`, `HT` or `HubTransport`, `MB` or `Mailbox`, `ET` or `EdgeTransport`, `UM` or `UnifiedMessaging`, and `MT` or `ManagementTools`. If a server role is specified, you do not need to specify the `MT` option because the Exchange management tools will automatically be installed at that time. Also, remember that at least one Hub Transport server in every Active Directory site must contain a Mailbox server and the Edge Transport server cannot be installed on a domain member server.
/OrganizationName:<name for the new Exchange organization>	Specifies the Exchange organization name. This is required only for the first installation being performed in the organization.
/TargetDir:<target directory>	Specifies the location where Exchange Server 2007 will be installed on the server. The default location is `%programfiles%\Microsoft\Exchange Server`.
/UpdatesDir:<directory from which to install updates>	Specifies the location from which updates will be installed.
/DomainController <FQDN of domain controller>	Specifies the domain controller to be used to read and write to Active Directory.
/DoNotStartTransport	Specifies that the Microsoft Exchange Transport service will not start when setup completes. Use this option if you need to perform additional configuration before the Edge Transport or Hub Transport server accepts messages, such as when configuring antispam agents or transport rules.

TABLE 3.1 Exchange Server 2007 *Setup.exe* Options *(continued)*

Option	Explanation
/EnableLegacyOutlook	Specifies that older versions of the Outlook client will be used in your organization. This option causes setup to create a public folder database on the Mailbox server. Public folders are optional if all clients are Outlook 2007. Omitting this option will prevent setup from creating a public folder database. This option can be used only on the first Mailbox server installed in the Exchange organization.
/LegacyRoutingServer	Specifies the legacy Exchange Server 2003 or Exchange 2000 Server Bridgehead server that has a routing group connector created for coexistence between Exchange 2007 and either Exchange 2003 or Exchange 2000.
/AddUmLanguagePack <UM language pack name>	Specifies which unified messaging language pack to install.
/RemoveUm LanguagePack:<UM language pack name>	Specifies which unified messaging language pack to remove.
/NewProvisionedServer	Creates a server placeholder object in Active Directory so you can delegate the setup of a server. Grants a user permissions on this placeholder server object so the user can install Exchange Server 2007 on the server later.
/RemoveProvisionedServer	Removes a previously created server placeholder object, provided Exchange Server 2007 has not already been installed on the server.
/ForeignForestFQDN	Specifies a user in another Active Directory forest who can administer Exchange Server 2007.
/ServerAdmin <user or group>	Grants permission to a user account or group in Active Directory on a provisioned server object. This option must be used with the /NewProvisionedServer option.
/NewCms	Creates a new clustered Exchange 2007 Mailbox server. This option must be used with the /CMSName and the /CMSIPAddress options.
/RemoveCms	Removes an Exchange 2007 clustered Mailbox server. Must be used with the /CMSName option.
/RecoverCms	Specifies recovery of an Exchange 2007 clustered Mailbox server. This option must be used with the /CMSName option.

TABLE 3.1 Exchange Server 2007 *Setup.exe* Options *(continued)*

Option	Explanation
/CMSName	Specifies the name of the Exchange clustered Mailbox server.
/CMSIPAddress	Specifies the IP address of the Exchange clustered Mailbox server.
/CMSSharedStorage	Specifies that the cluster node will use shared storage. By default, the cluster node will not use shared storage.
/CMSDataPath	Specifies the path for shared disks.
/AnswerFile, or /a <filename>	Specifies an answer file that contains advanced options for setup. You can specify these options in the answer file: /EnableErrorReporting, /NoSelfSignedCertificates, /AdamLdapPort, and /AdamSslPort.
/EnableErrorReporting	Enables error reporting.
/NoSelfSignedCertificates	Specifies that setup should not create self-signed certificates in the case where no other valid certificate is found for Secure Sockets Layer (SSL) or Transport Layer Security (TLS) sessions. You can use this option only if you are installing the Client Access or Unified Messaging roles.
/AdamLdapPort <port>	Specifies which LDAP port the ADAM instance should use. This option is used only when installing the Edge Transport role.
/AdamSslPort <port>	Specifies which DAP SSL port the ADAM instance should use. This option is used only when installing the Edge Transport role.

So, a typical command-line installation might use an entry like the following:

```
Setup.com /mode:Install /roles:HT, CA, MB
/DomainController wileydc01.wiley.corp
```

If this were the first server in the organization to be installed, you might use the following entry:

```
Setup.com /mode:Install /roles:HT, CA, MB
/DomainController wileydc01.wiley.corp
/OrganizationName:WILEY /EnableLegacyOutlook
```

If you wanted to prevent the Microsoft Exchange Transport service from starting so you could perform additional configuration on the Hub Transport server, you might use the following entry:

```
Setup.com /mode:Install /roles:HT, CA, MB
/DomainController wileydc01.wiley.corp
/DoNotStartTransport
```

Figure 3.1 illustrates the installation of a new server in an existing Exchange organization.

FIGURE 3.1 Performing the command-line installation process for Exchange Server 2007

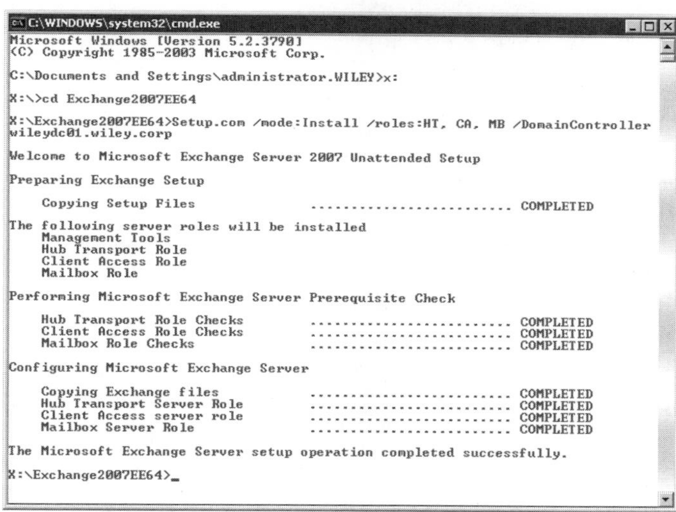

Verifying the Installation of Exchange Server 2007

After you complete the installation process on each Exchange Server 2007 computer in your organization, take some time to ensure that the installation process was completed successfully. If any errors are encountered during installation, the setup routine will alert you. You should review applicable setup logs, services, folder structures, and other items to ensure the success of the installation.

PowerShell

You can verify the list of installed server roles on the Exchange Server 2007 server by using the `Get-ExchangeServer` *servername* cmdlet from the Exchange Management Shell. Select Start ➢ Programs ➢ Microsoft Exchange Server 2007 ➢ Microsoft Command Shell to open the command shell, as shown in Figure 3.2. If you use the cmdlet without specifying a server, all installed servers and their roles are returned.

FIGURE 3.2 Verifying the installation of an Exchange Server 2007 server with PowerShell

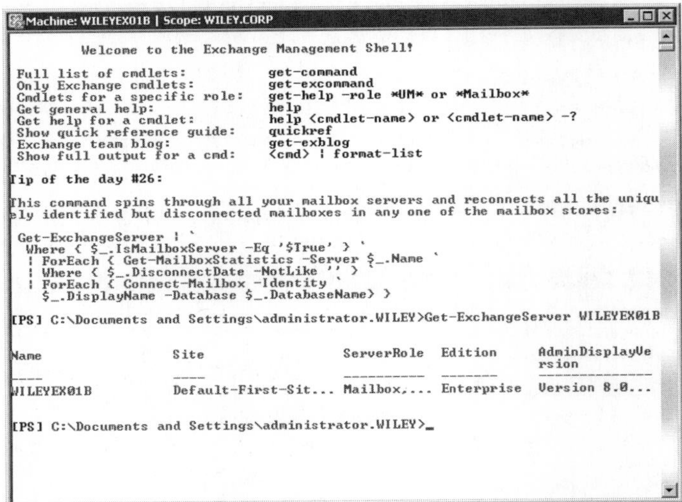

Event Viewer

The Exchange Server 2007 setup process writes several logs to the Application log. You should examine these log entries to ensure that no warning or error events were logged that relate to the setup of Exchange Server 2007. Figure 3.3 illustrates a sample Application log event entry indicating the successful installation of the Mailbox server role.

FIGURE 3.3 Verifying the installation of an Exchange Server 2007 server with the Application log

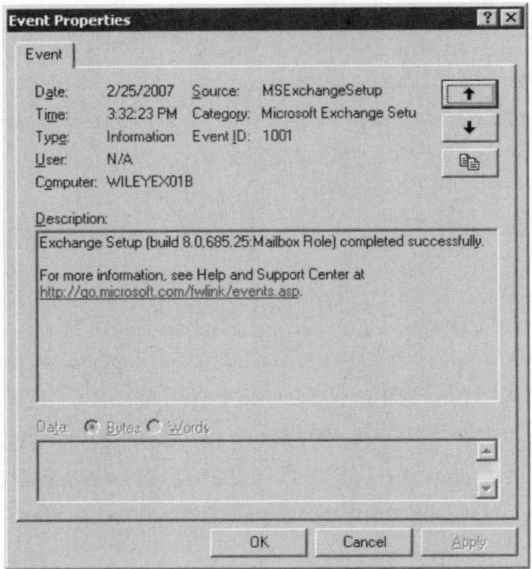

Setup Log Files

As with previous versions of Exchange, Exchange Server 2007 creates a setup log that can be reviewed for errors or for the successful completion of the setup process. The following logs will be created during setup:

- `C:\ExchangeSetupLogs\ExchangeSetup.log`: This log file tracks every task performed as part of the setup process and contains information about the status of all checks performed, installation steps carried out, and changes made to the system. Figure 3.4 provides a sample of the information found in this log file.
- `C:\ExchangeSetupLogs\ExchangeSetup.msilog`: This log file contains information about unpacking the installation code from the installer MSI file. Figure 3.5 provides a sample of the information contained in this log file.

If you installed Windows to a volume letter other than C, substitute that letter in the previous paths to locate the Exchange setup logs.

FIGURE 3.4 Examining the `ExchangeSetup.log` log file

ExchangeSetup.log - Notepad

File Edit Format View Help

```
[2/25/2007 2:05:35 PM] [0] ***********************************************
[2/25/2007 2:05:35 PM] [0] Starting Microsoft Exchange 2007 Setup
[2/25/2007 2:05:35 PM] [0] ***********************************************
[2/25/2007 2:05:35 PM] [0] Setup version: 8.0.685.25.
[2/25/2007 2:05:35 PM] [0] Logged on user: WILEY\administrator.
[2/25/2007 2:05:35 PM] [0] Command Line Parameter Name='mode',
Value='Install'.
[2/25/2007 2:05:35 PM] [0] Command Line Parameter Name='sourcedir',
Value='X:\Exchange2007EE64'.
[2/25/2007 2:05:35 PM] [0] Command Line Parameter Name='fromsetup',
Value=''.
[2/25/2007 2:05:35 PM] [0] ExSetupUI was started with the following
command: '-mode:install -sourcedir:X:\Exchange2007EE64 /FromSetup'.
[2/25/2007 2:05:43 PM] [0] Setup is choosing the domain controller to use
[2/25/2007 2:05:44 PM] [0] Setup is choosing a local domain controller...
[2/25/2007 2:05:48 PM] [0] Setup has chosen the local domain controller
WILEYDC01.WILEY.CORP for initial queries
[2/25/2007 2:05:48 PM] [0] PrepareAD has either not been run or has not
replicated to the domain controller used by Setup. Setup will attempt to
use the Schema Master domain controller WILEYDC01.WILEY.CORP
[2/25/2007 2:05:48 PM] [0] The schema master domain controller is available
[2/25/2007 2:05:48 PM] [0] The schema master domain controller is in the
local domain; setup will use WILEYDC01.WILEY.CORP
[2/25/2007 2:05:48 PM] [0] Setup is choosing a global catalog...
[2/25/2007 2:05:48 PM] [0] Setup has chosen the global catalog server
WILEYDC01.WILEY.CORP.
[2/25/2007 2:05:48 PM] [0] Setup will use the domain controller
'WILEYDC01.WILEY.CORP'.
[2/25/2007 2:05:48 PM] [0] Setup will use the global catalog
'WILEYDC01.WILEY.CORP'.
[2/25/2007 2:05:48 PM] [0] No Exchange configuration container was found
for the organization. Message: 'Could not find the Exchange Configuration
Container.'.
[2/25/2007 2:05:48 PM] [0] The following roles are unpacked:
[2/25/2007 2:05:48 PM] [0] The following roles are installed:
[2/25/2007 2:05:48 PM] [0] The local server does not have any Exchange
files installed.
[2/25/2007 2:05:48 PM] [0] Setup will use the path 'X:\Exchange2007EE64'
```

These log files are quite extensive and contain a large quantity of information. The best way to start looking for any issues is to search each log file for the string "error." If the "error" string is found, then you can read the text at that point in the log file to determine the specific error. You can search within most applications, including Notepad, by pressing F3 to open the Find/Search dialog box.

FIGURE 3.5 Examining the ExchangeSetup.msilog log file

```
ExchangeSetup.msilog - Notepad
File Edit Format View Help
=== Verbose logging started: 2/25/2007  15:05:59  Build type: SHIP UNICODE
3.01.4000.2435  Calling process:
C:\WINDOWS\Temp\ExchangeSetup\ExSetupUI.exe ===
MSI (c) (14:64) [15:05:59:114]: Resetting cached policy values
MSI (c) (14:64) [15:05:59:114]: Machine policy value 'Debug' is 0
MSI (c) (14:64) [15:05:59:114]: ******* RunEngine:
           ******* Product: X:\Exchange2007EE64\exchangeserver.msi
           ******* Action:
           ******* CommandLine: **********
MSI (c) (14:64) [15:05:59:114]: Client-side and UI is none or basic:
Running entire install on the server.
MSI (c) (14:64) [15:05:59:114]: Grabbed execution mutex.
MSI (c) (14:64) [15:05:59:129]: Cloaking enabled.
MSI (c) (14:64) [15:05:59:129]: Attempting to enable all disabled
priveleges before calling Install on Server
MSI (c) (14:64) [15:05:59:129]: Incrementing counter to disable shutdown.
Counter after increment: 0
MSI (s) (6C:30) [15:05:59:161]: Grabbed execution mutex.
MSI (s) (6C:E4) [15:05:59:161]: Resetting cached policy values
MSI (s) (6C:E4) [15:05:59:161]: Machine policy value 'Debug' is 0
MSI (s) (6C:E4) [15:05:59:161]: ******* RunEngine:
           ******* Product: X:\Exchange2007EE64\exchangeserver.msi
           ******* Action:
           ******* CommandLine: **********
MSI (s) (6C:E4) [15:05:59:161]: Incrementing counter to disable shutdown.
Counter after increment: 0
MSI (s) (6C:E4) [15:05:59:161]: Machine policy value 'DisableUserInstalls'
is 0
MSI (s) (6C:E4) [15:05:59:192]: File will have security applied from
OpCode.
MSI (s) (6C:E4) [15:06:01:114]: Decrementing counter to disable shutdown.
If counter >= 0, shutdown will be denied.  Counter after decrement: -1
MSI (s) (6C:E4) [15:06:01:114]: SOFTWARE RESTRICTION POLICY: Verifying
package --> 'X:\Exchange2007EE64\exchangeserver.msi' against software
restriction policy
MSI (s) (6C:E4) [15:06:01:114]: SOFTWARE RESTRICTION POLICY:
X:\Exchange2007EE64\exchangeserver.msi has a digital signature
MSI (s) (6C:E4) [15:06:01:364]: SOFTWARE RESTRICTION POLICY:
```

Additionally, you can use the Exchange Management Shell script `Get-SetupLog.ps1` to parse the setup logs looking for errors. To use the `Get-SetupLog.ps1` script, start the Exchange Management Shell and change directories to the location of the Exchange Server scripts, typically `c:\Program Files\Microsoft\Exchange\Scripts` if Exchange Server 2007 was installed on volume C of the server. After changing to the Scripts directory, enter the following command, as shown in Figure 3.6: `Get-SetupLog c:\exchangesetuplogs\exchangesetup.log -error -tree`. Any errors should be brought quickly to your attention. As you can see in Figure 3.6, an error was encountered during an installation attempt because the domain and forest were not at the correct functional levels. The setup logs are cumulative from all installation attempts, so you delete them if an installation attempt is abandoned to correct errors.

Active Directory

As discussed in Chapter 2, several changes are made to the forest and domain level during an installation of Exchange Server 2007. The easiest change to look for is the existence of the Exchange-related universal security groups, as shown in Figure 3.7.

You can also view an advanced change made to Active Directory by opening the Active Directory Sites and Services console. Click the Active Directory Sites and Services node at the root of the left pane, and then select View ➢ Show Services Node to enable the display of the Services node in the tree on the left side. Expand the Services node, and you'll see an entry named Microsoft Exchange. If you click that entry in the left pane, you'll see pertinent information displayed on the right side of the window, as shown in Figure 3.8. The amount of information displayed depends on the specific Exchange organization and whether legacy Exchange servers exist.

FIGURE 3.6 Searching the ExchangeSetup.log log file with PowerShell

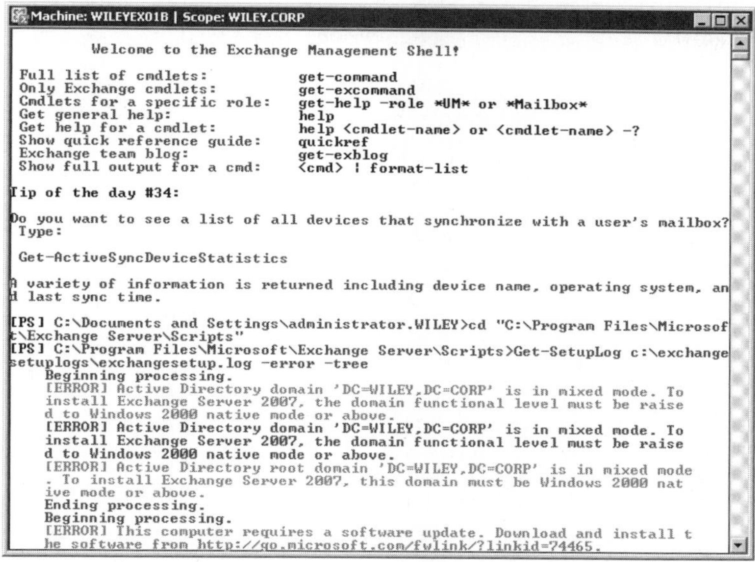

FIGURE 3.7 Viewing the Exchange universal security groups

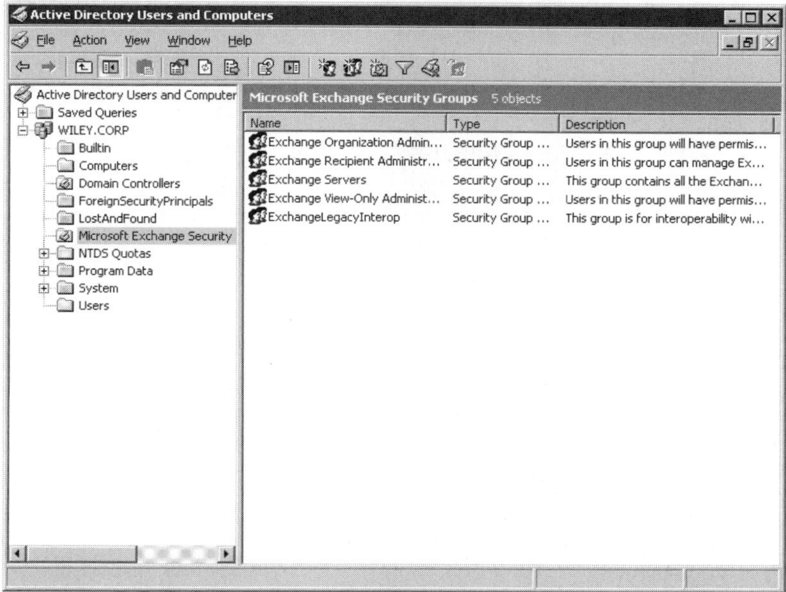

FIGURE 3.8 Viewing the Exchange services node

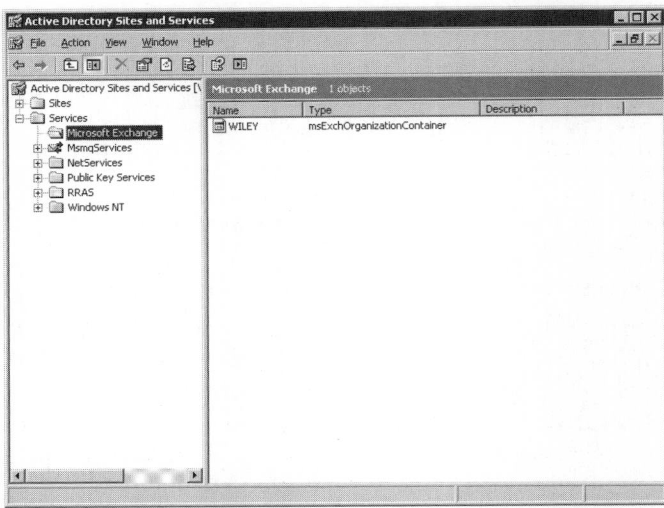

Installation Folder Structure

You can also examine the contents of the installation folder to determine whether all Exchange setup steps have completed properly. In the default installation, Exchange Server 2007 is installed to `C:\Program Files\Microsoft\Exchange Server`, as shown in Figure 3.9; however, you can modify this during setup.

FIGURE 3.9 Viewing the Exchange installation folder

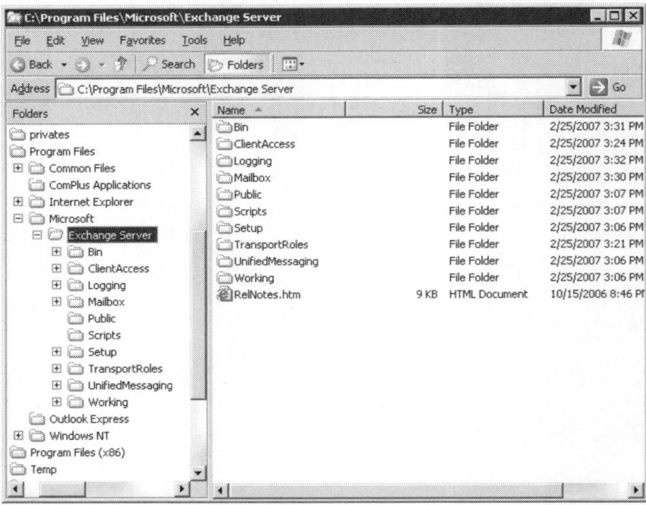

The following folders will be available in this location following the successful installation of Exchange Server 2007:

- `\bin`: Contains all of the executable applications and related files used by Exchange Server 2007. This is created during the installation of any server role.
- `\ClientAccess`: Contains the configuration files needed by the Client Access server role and thus is created only during the installation of a Client Access server. Inside this folder are the following Client Access role-related folders: Autodiscover, Exchweb, Owa, PopImap, and Sync.
- `\ExchangeOAB`: Contains the offline address book data. This folder is found only on the Client Access server role.
- `\Logging`: Contains log files for Exchange Server 2007 and is found on all server roles.
- `\Mailbox`: Contains the schema files, DLL files, database log files, and transaction log files for the mailbox and public folder databases that are created during setup. This folder is found only on the Mailbox server role and contains the following subfolders: Addresses, First Storage Group, MDB Temp, OAB, and Schema. If public folders were installed with the Mailbox server, the Second Storage Group subfolder will also be present here.
- `\Public`: Contains XML files and drivers that are needed for address lookup and header processing during transport operations. This folder is found only on the Hub Transport and Edge Transport server roles.
- `\Scripts`: Contains prewritten Exchange Management Shell scripts that can be used to automate management tasks. This folder is found on all server roles.
- `\Setup`: Contains the subfolders Data and Perf, which contain XML and data files that are used during the configuration of Exchange Server 2007. This folder is found on all server roles.
- `\TransportRoles`: Contains the subfolders Agents, Data, Logs, Pickup, Replay, and Shared. The Pickup and Replay folders are used in certain mail-flow situations. The Logs folder contains all data logged by Hub Transport and Edge Transport servers. The Agents folder contains any binary files that are associated with a transfer agent. The Shared folder contains any agent configuration files, and the Data folder contains the IP filtering database if in use. This folder is found only on the Hub Transport and Edge Transport server roles.
- `\UnifiedMessaging`: Contains several subfolders that hold the configuration and setup files for unified messaging operations and speech recognition. The following subfolders are located here: AdministrativeTools, Badvoicemail, Common, Config, Doc, Grammars, Logs, Prompts, Speech, Voicemail, and WebService. This folder is found on Unified Messaging servers.

Exchange Services

The installation of Exchange Server 2007 creates and configures many services on the server. Figure 3.10 illustrates the services you'll see based on the default installations performed earlier in this chapter, and Table 3.2 outlines the services created for all server roles.

FIGURE 3.10 Viewing Exchange services

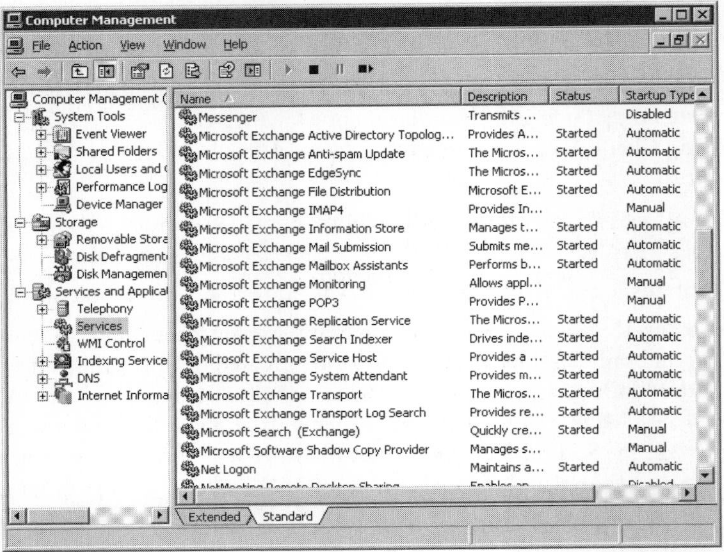

TABLE 3.2 Exchange Server 2007 Services

Service	Server Role Where Found
Microsoft Exchange Active Directory Topology	Mailbox, Client Access, Hub Transport, Unified Messaging
Microsoft Exchange ADAM	Edge Transport
Microsoft Exchange Credential Service	Edge Transport
Microsoft Exchange EdgeSync	Hub Transport
Microsoft Exchange File Distribution Service	Client Access, Unified Messaging
Microsoft Exchange Anti-spam Update	Hub Transport, Hub Transport
Microsoft Exchange IMAP4	Client Access
Microsoft Exchange Information Store	Mailbox
Microsoft Exchange Mail Submission Service	Mailbox
Microsoft Exchange Mailbox Assistants	Mailbox

TABLE 3.2 Exchange Server 2007 Services *(continued)*

Service	Server Role Where Found
Microsoft Exchange Monitoring	Mailbox, Client Access, Hub Transport, Unified Messaging, Edge Transport
Microsoft Exchange POP3	Client Access
Microsoft Exchange Replication Service	Mailbox
Microsoft Exchange Search Indexer	Mailbox
Microsoft Exchange Service Host	Mailbox, Client Access
Microsoft Exchange Speech Engine	Unified Messaging
Microsoft Exchange System Attendant	Mailbox
Microsoft Exchange Transport	Hub Transport, Edge Transport
Microsoft Exchange Transport Log Search	Mailbox, Hub Transport, Edge Transport
Microsoft Exchange Unified Messaging	Unified Messaging
Microsoft Search (Exchange Server)	Mailbox

Securing Exchange Server 2007 with the Security Configuration Wizard

As discussed in Chapter 2, you should run the Security Configuration Wizard shortly after installing any Exchange Server 2007 role on your servers. If you haven't already installed the Security Configuration Wizard on your server, you should do follow the steps outlined in Exercise 3.3.

EXERCISE 3.3

Installing the Security Configuration Wizard

1. Open the Add or Remove Programs applet, located in the Control Panel.
2. Click the Add/Remove Windows Components button.
3. Select the Security Configuration Wizard option, and then click OK.
4. Back in the Windows Components dialog box, click Next to continue.
5. Click Finish when prompted.

To perform any of the Security Configuration Wizard–related tasks, you will need to be logged into the Exchange Server 2007 server with an account that has at least the Exchange Server Administrator role and is a member of the local Administrators group on that server. For Edge Transport servers, you'll just need to use an account that is a local administrator on that server. By default, if you're using the same account you installed Exchange Server 2007 with, you'll be OK.

Once you have gotten the Security Configuration Wizard installation, you'll next need to register the Exchange Server 2007 server role extensions for the Security Configuration Wizard—in effect, extending the ability of the Security Configuration Wizard to intelligently help you secure your Exchange Server 2007 server. To register the extensions, enter the following command from the command line:

```
scwcmd register
/kbname:Ex2007KB /kbfile:"%programfiles%\
Microsoft\Exchange Server\scripts\Exchange2007.xml"
```

If you're performing the process on an Edge Transport server, use the following command instead:

```
scwcmd register
/kbname:Ex2007EdgeKB /kbfile:"%programfiles%\
Microsoft\Exchange Server\scripts\Exchange2007Edge.xml"
```

Figure 3.11 illustrates the process for the server you installed in Exercise 3.1.

FIGURE 3.11 Registering the Exchange server role extensions for the Security Configuration Wizard

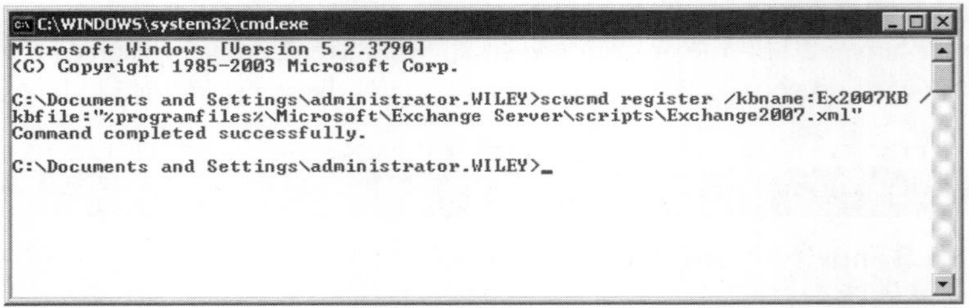

After the extensions for the Exchange Server 2007 server roles are registered, you can then use the Security Configuration Wizard to secure the Exchange server, as detailed in Exercise 3.4.

EXERCISE 3.4

Using the Security Configuration Wizard to Configure Exchange Server security

1. Select Start ➢ Programs ➢ Administrative Tools ➢ Security Configuration Wizard.
2. Click Next to dismiss the welcome page of the Security Configuration Wizard.
3. On the Configuration Action page, shown here, select the Create a New Security Policy option, and then click Next.

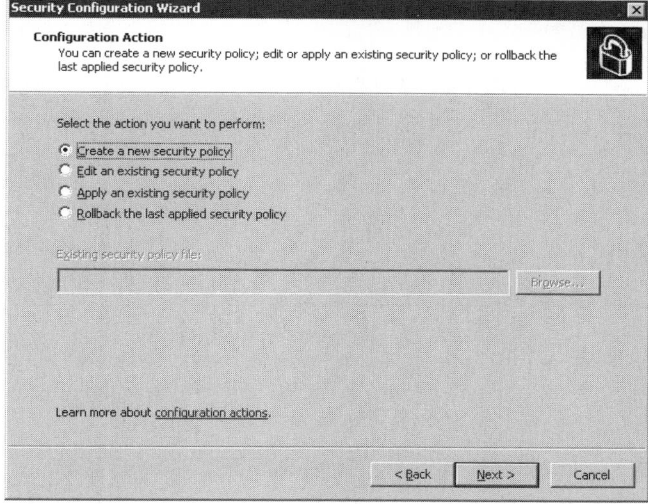

4. On the Select Server page, verify that the correct server name appears or enter the server name or IP address, and click Next to continue.
5. When the progress bar has completed on the Processing Security Configuration Database page, click Next to continue.
6. On the Role-Based Service Configuration page, take the time to read the notice given, and then click Next to continue.

EXERCISE 3.4 ***(continued)***

7. On the Select Server Roles page, shown here, verify that the Exchange Server 2007 roles you have installed on the server are selected. You'll also notice several other pertinent items depending on the server's configuration, such as Web Server, Middle-Tier Application Server, and so on. Click Next to continue.

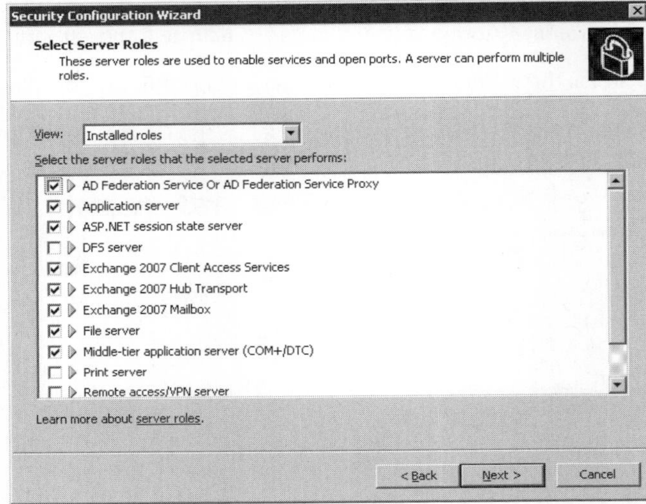

8. On the Select Client Features page, shown here, you need to select each client feature that is required on the Exchange server. Typically the default selections are correct, and no changes should be made. Click Next to continue.

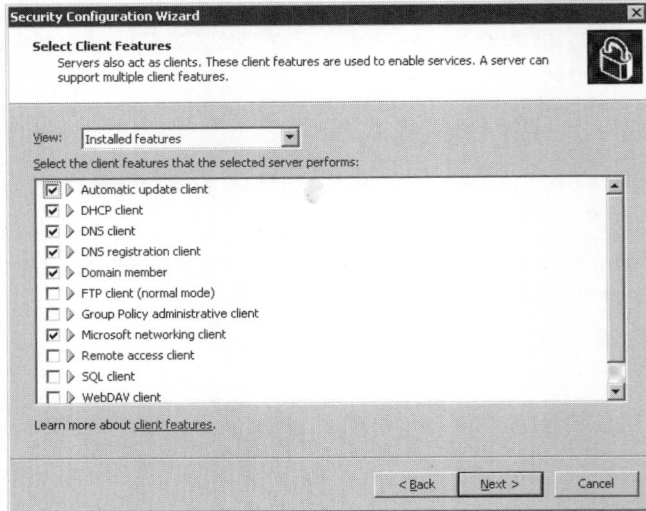

EXERCISE 3.4 *(continued)*

9. On the Select Administration and Other Options page, shown here, you will need to select each administration feature that is required on your Exchange server. The default selections are typically correct, and no changes should be made in most cases. Click Next to continue.

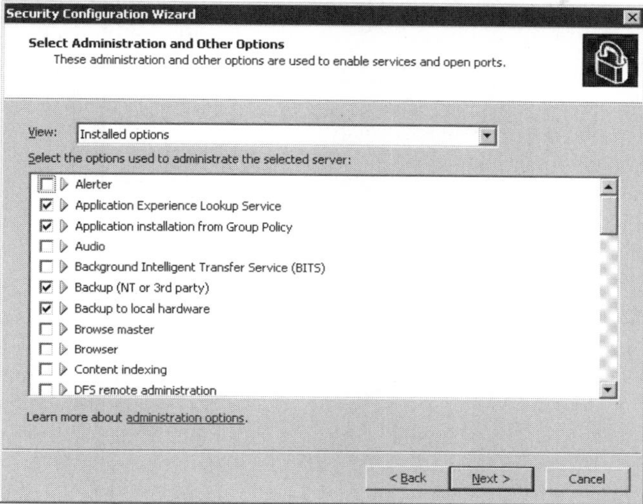

10. On the Select Additional Services page, shown here, you will have the opportunity to select additional services that are required to be enabled on the Exchange server. This is commonly where you'll see antivirus settings and other third-party application services. Click Next to continue.

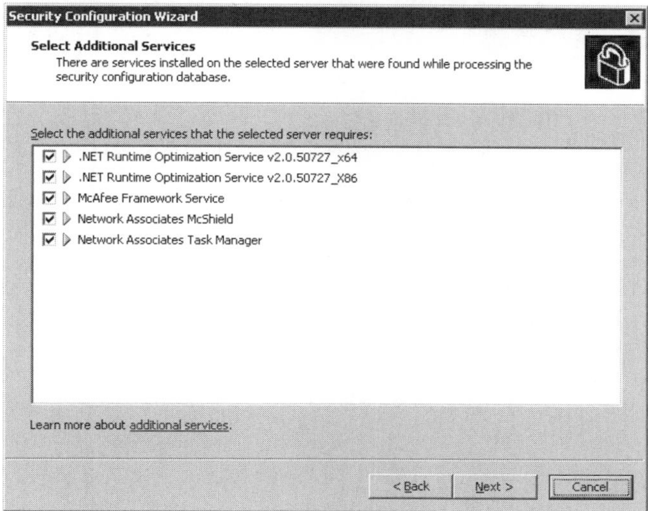

EXERCISE 3.4 *(continued)*

11. On the Handling Unspecified Services page, shown here, you will need to select the action that is performed when a service not currently installed on the local server is found. The default option of Do Not Change the Startup Mode of the Service is recommended in most cases, although selecting to automatically disable new services is a significantly more secure configuration. For this exercise, leave the default selection, and click Next to continue.

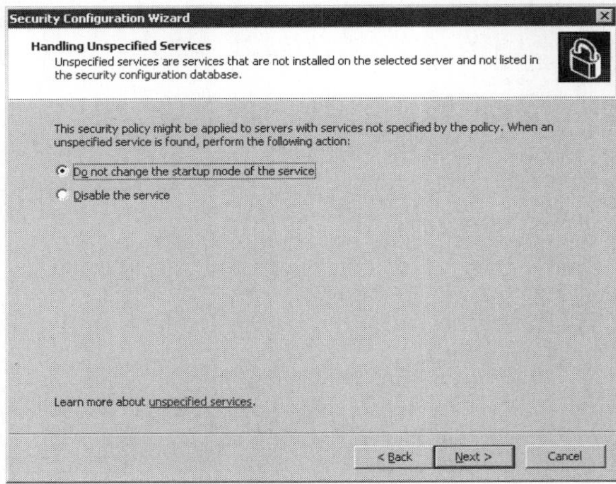

12. On the Confirm Service Changes page, shown here, you will be able to review the changes the new Security Configuration Wizard policy will make to the current service configuration. After reviewing the changes, click Next to continue.

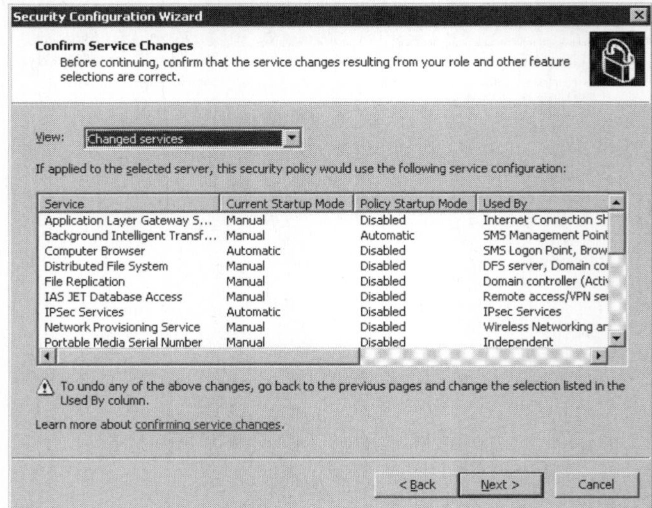

EXERCISE 3.4 *(continued)*

13. Now the Security Configuration Wizard moves into the next phase, network security. On the Network Security page, shown here, ensure that Skip This Section is not selected, and then click Next to continue.

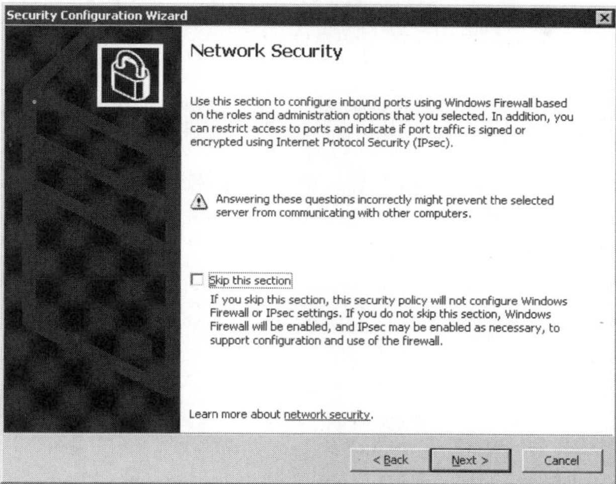

14. On the Open Ports and Approve Applications page, shown here, you will have a chance to verify and add open ports on the Exchange server. If you were running the Security Configuration Wizard on Edge Transport servers, you'd need to add open ports for LDAP communication between ADAM and Active Directory on TCP ports 50389 and 50636. In this exercise, the currently configured ports are acceptable. Click Next to continue.

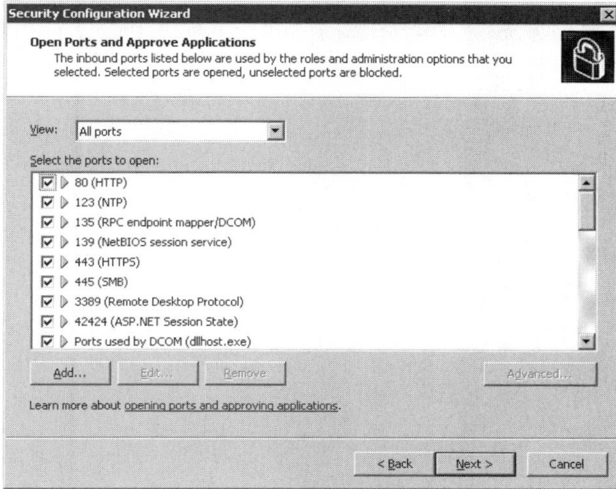

EXERCISE 3.4 *(continued)*

15. On the Confirm Port Configuration page, shown here, you'll get a summary of the open and approved ports on the server. After verifying that everything is acceptable, click Next to continue.

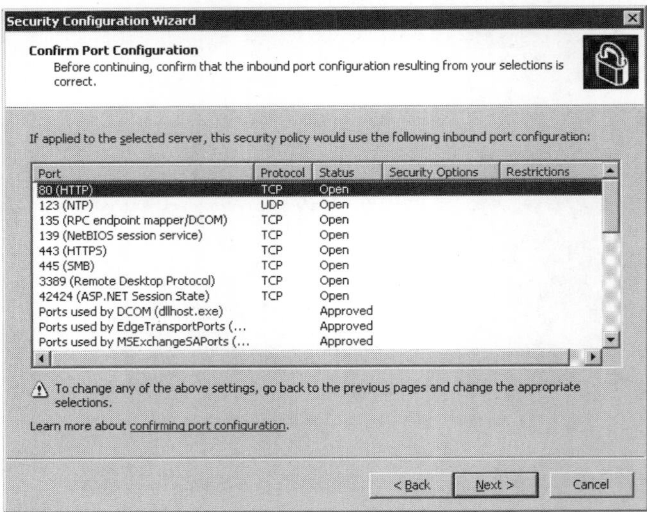

16. You don't need to use the Security Configuration Wizard to configure any additional settings for the Exchange Server 2007 server roles. On the Registry Settings page, shown here, select the Skip This Section check box, and then click Next to continue.

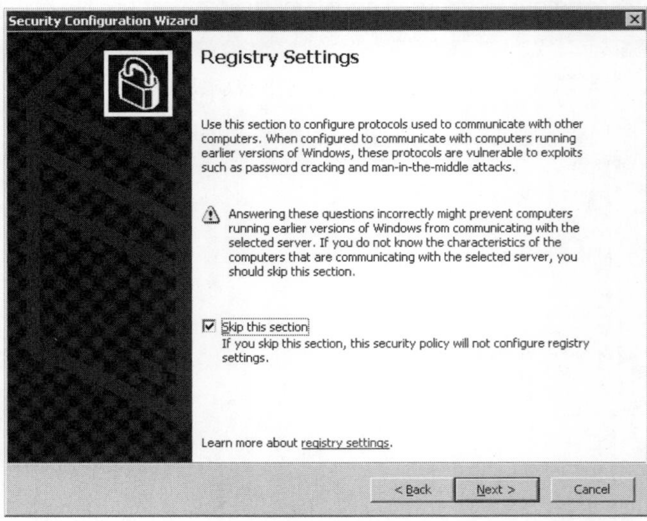

EXERCISE 3.4 *(continued)*

17. On the Audit Policy page and the Internet Information Services (IIS) page, ensure that the Skip This Section check box is selected, and then click Next to continue.

18. On the Save Security Policy page, click Next to continue.

19. On the Security Policy File Name page, shown here, you will need to enter a filename for the security policy and an optional description. Click Next to save the policy.

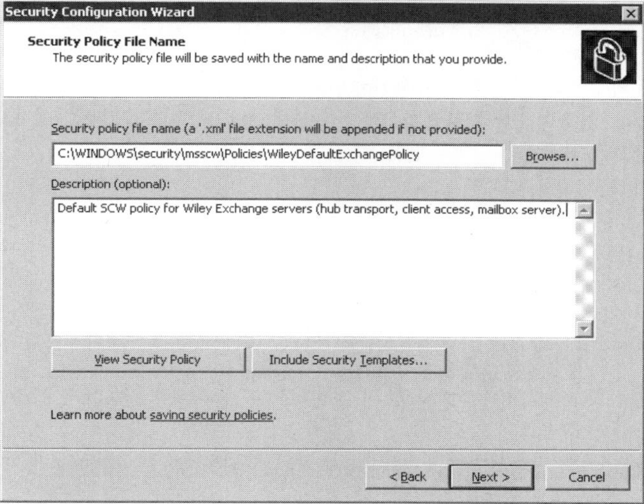

20. If prompted that a reboot of the server, as shown here, is needed, click OK to acknowledge the warning.

EXERCISE 3.4 *(continued)*

21. On the Apply Security Policy page, shown here, select the Apply Now option, and then click Next to continue.

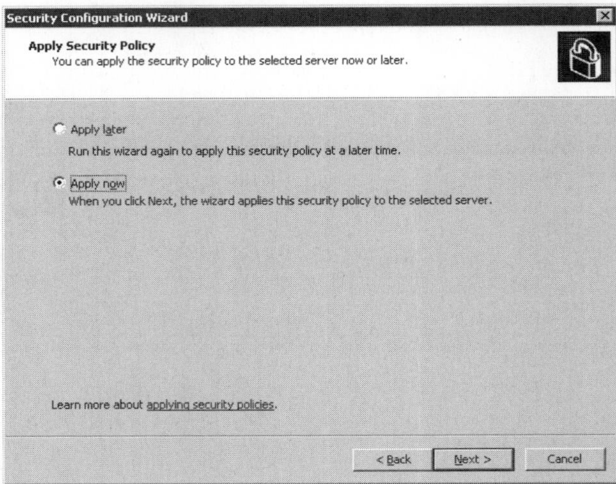

22. The policy might take some time to be applied, as shown here. When it has been applied, click Next to continue.

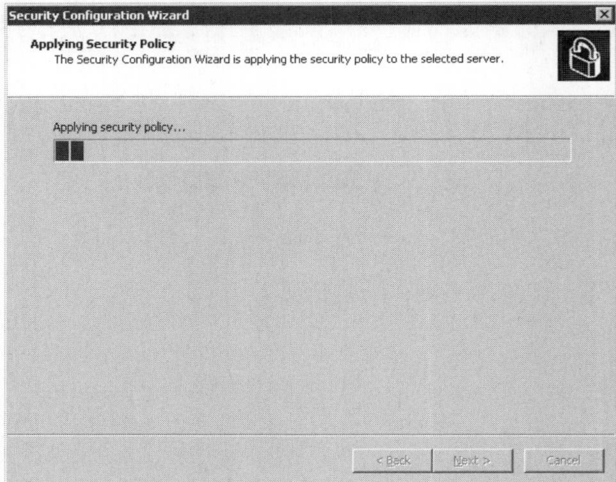

23. When prompted, click Finish to complete the Security Configuration Wizard.

24. Restart the server if you were previously informed that it was necessary to apply the configured policy.

Configuring the Exchange Administrator Roles

In Exchange Server 2003, there was little real separation in permissions between administrators responsible for Active Directory and administrators responsible for Exchange. For changes to be made to messaging-specific properties on a group or user account, the administrator had to be (at a minimum) an Account Operator. By the same token, that administrator could actually manage any account in the domain—certainly not a good separation of administrative responsibilities.

In Exchange Server 2007, the assignment of administrative permissions can be grouped into three scenarios:

- One administrator (or a group of administrators) has the ability to perform administrative tasks for both Active Directory and Exchange Server 2007.
- Different administrators (or groups of administrators) have the ability to perform specific tasks related to Active Directory and Exchange Server 2007.
- All Exchange Server 2007 tasks can be completed isolated from Active Directory by installing Exchange into an Exchange resource forest, although this scenario will less likely be utilized in many organizations.

Recall that in Chapter 2 we introduced the concept of a property set. A *property set* is simply a means of grouping together many different Active Directory attributes and then controlling permissions on that group of attributes using a single access control entry (ACE) as opposed to configuring the ACE on each individual property. Exchange Server 2007 uses the property sets model and creates a property set known as email information that is used to control permissions entries on all Exchange-related attributes. Through that model, the Exchange Server 2007 administrative roles become much more defined and separated from Active Directory administrative roles than in previous versions of Exchange Server.

Introducing the Exchange Server 2007 Administrative Roles

To allow for better separation of administrative duties with Exchange Server 2007, the following roles are implemented, and the appropriate security groups are created during the setup of Exchange:

- *Exchange Organization Administrators role*: The members of the Exchange Organization Administrators security group have the highest level of permissions over Exchange-related items within the Exchange organization. This gives members of this group the ability to perform tasks that impact the entire organization, such as creating, modifying, or deleting connectors; creating, modifying, or removing server policies; and changing any global configuration option. Additionally, this group is a member of the Exchange Recipient Administrators group and inherits all the permissions and rights granted to that group.

- *Exchange Recipient Administrators role*: The members of the Exchange Recipient Administrators security group have the needed permissions to enable them to modify any Exchange-related property on any Active Directory user, group, public folder contact, or dynamic distribution list. The members of this group also have the ability to manage Client Access mailbox settings and Unified Messaging mailbox settings as applicable to the organization. Additionally, this group is a member of the Exchange View-Only Administrators group and inherits all permissions and rights granted to that group.
- *Exchange View-Only Administrators role*: The members of the Exchange View-Only Administrators security group have read-only access to the Exchange organization and read-only access on all Exchange recipients.
- *Exchange Server Administrators role*: The last role available, and the only one that doesn't have a security group created for it during the /ADPrep phase of setup, allows access to the local server's Exchange configuration data. Users configured with this role have the permissions needed to administer a certain server but cannot make any changes that would globally impact the Exchange organization as a whole.

By default, no Exchange Server Administrators are configured, so you will need to do that on your own, as detailed in the next section, if you intend to use that role. As you'll see, you must manually add the selected user or group to the local Administrators group on the Exchange servers in question after you configure the Exchange Server Administrator role within Exchange.

Configuring Administrative Roles

You can configure administrative roles, like most everything else in Exchange Server 2007, from either the Exchange Management Shell or the Exchange Management Console. In Figure 3.12, you can see the administrative role configuration for our Exchange organization in the default (post-installation) state. Notice there is one entry for each of the first three roles we discussed previously.

FIGURE 3.12 Examining configured administrative roles with the Exchange Management Console

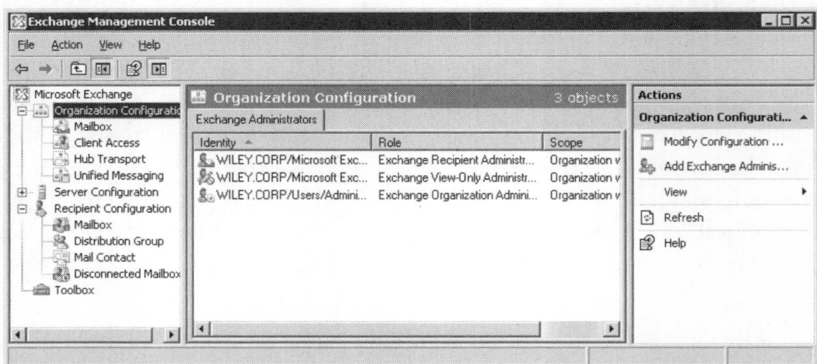

Conversely, you can perform the same task using PowerShell by using the following command in the Exchange Management Shell: `Get-ExchangeAdministrator`. Figure 3.13 shows the results of this action.

FIGURE 3.13 Examining configured administrative roles with the Exchange Management Shell

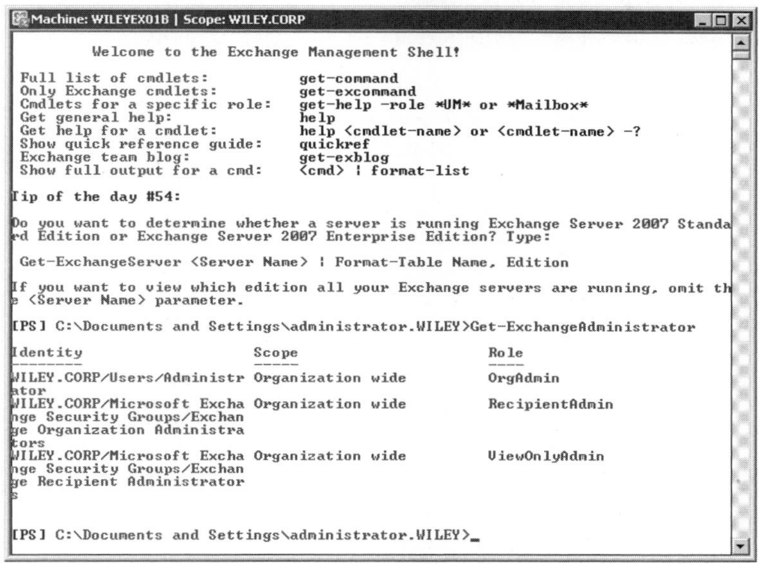

To add an administrative role to a user, follow the steps detailed in Exercise 3.5.

EXERCISE 3.5

Adding Administrative Roles

1. Open the Exchange Management Console by selecting Start ➢ Programs ➢ Microsoft Exchange Server 2007 ➢ Exchange Management Console.

2. Click the Organization Configuration node, as shown previously in Figure 3.12.

EXERCISE 3.5 *(continued)*

3. In the action pane, on the right side of the window, click the Add Exchange Administrator link. The Add Exchange Administrator Wizard opens, as shown here.

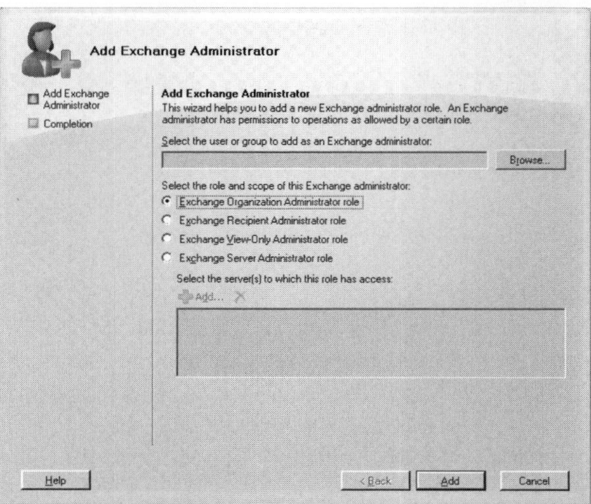

4. Click the Browse button to locate the user or group account to which you want to add the Exchange administrative role.

5. Select the appropriate role you want for the selected user or group account. If you are configuring the Exchange Server Administrator role, you will need to select the specific Exchange Servers for the user or group configuration. When you're done, you might have something similar to that shown here.

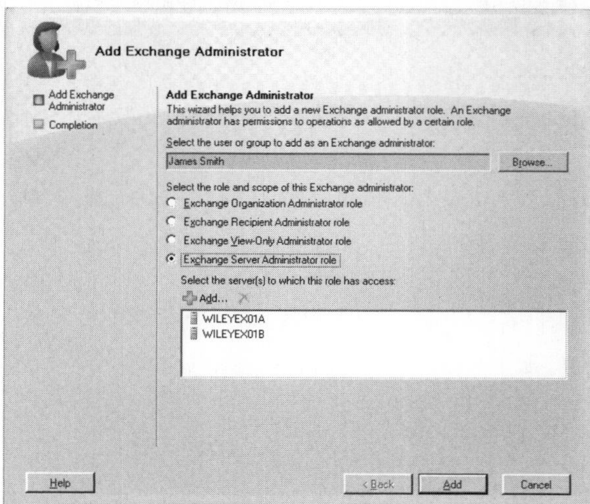

EXERCISE 3.5 *(continued)*

6. Click Add to create the administrative role configuration.

7. If you've configured the Exchange Server Administrator role, you might see results similar to those shown here. Check for any errors, and be sure to note any additional steps you need to complete. When you're done, click Finish to complete the process.

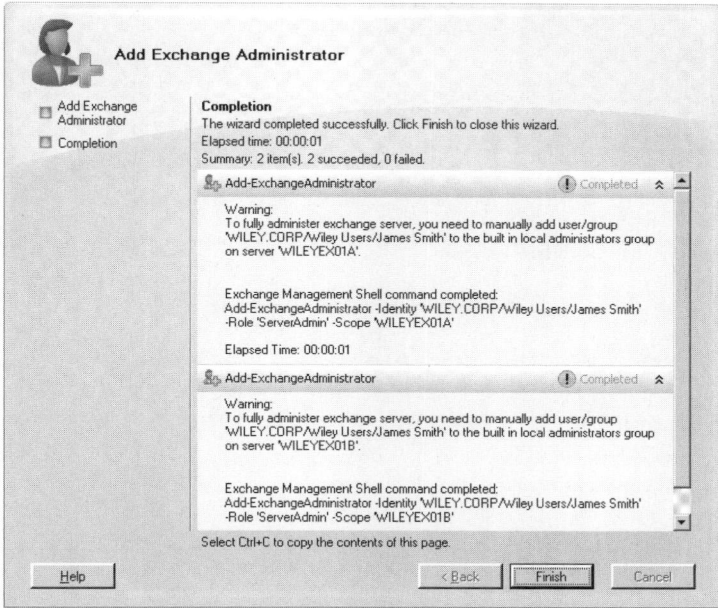

To configure an administrative role using the Exchange Management Shell, you would enter the following command: `Add-ExchangeAdministrator -Role` *Role* `-Identity` *Domain\User*. For example, to add Emily West in the Wiley domain as an Exchange Organization Administrator, your entry would look like this: `Add-ExchangeAdministrator -Role OrgAdmin -Identity Wiley\ewest`, as shown in Figure 3.14.

To remove a user or group that has been configured with an Exchange administrative role, you can simply select the user or group name in the list shown in Figure 3.12 and then click the Remove link in the right pane of the Exchange Management Console window. When prompted, if you are sure you want to remove the user or group, click Yes. You will next be presented with a summary of the operation that was completed. Click OK, and you have just removed that user or group. You can perform the same task from the Exchange Management Shell using the following command: `Remove-ExchangeAdministrator -Role` *Role* `-Identity` *Domain\User*.

FIGURE 3.14 Configuring Exchange administrator roles using the Exchange Management Shell

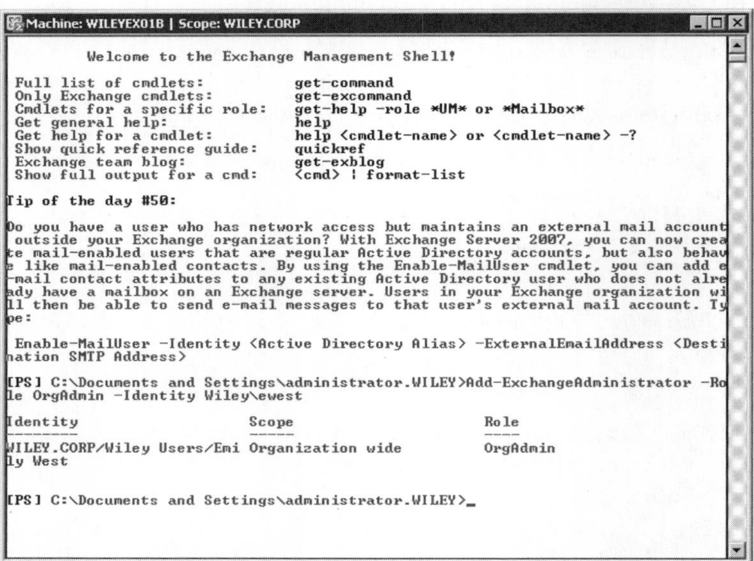

Real World Scenario

Take Command!

One of the most profound, and in my opinion, best features of Exchange Server 2007 is the wealth of command-line and PowerShell options you have at your disposal. You can now install, configure, administer, and manage an Exchange Server 2007 organization completely from the command line…what a change! In fact, some less commonly performed tasks within Exchange Server 2007 can be performed *only* using the Exchange Management Shell—how's that for a twist?

Of course, to get the most from the power and flexibility that the Exchange Management Shell offers you, you will need to learn about PowerShell scripting and start to build your own administrative tool set of scripts and cmdlets. The Exchange setup process will help get you started, because it copies several dozen prewritten PowerShell scripts during the setup process to the Scripts directory, which is found on a default installation at `C:\Program Files\Microsoft\Exchange Server\Scripts`.

Beyond that start, you'll want to spend some time learning about PowerShell and how it is used specifically within Exchange Server 2007. You can find a wealth of information about PowerShell at the following locations:

- `http://www.microsoft.com/technet/scriptcenter/hubs/msh.mspx`
- `http://blogs.msdn.com/PowerShell/`
- `http://channel9.msdn.com/wiki/default.aspx/Channel9.WindowsPowerShellWiki`
- `http://www.microsoft.com/windowsserver2003/technologies/management/powershell/default.mspx`

You'll likely also want to consider using a professionally written scripting application, moving up a few notches from Notepad. One of our favorites is PrimalScript from SAPIEN Technologies. You can find more information about that product at its website, located at `http://www.primalscript.com/`.

Regardless of how you proceed, you should learn how to maximize the power and control that PowerShell in the Exchange Management Shell gives you—you won't be disappointed with the results and the time you saved!

Summary

Although installing Exchange Server 2007 is fairly straightforward, you must complete many important tasks successfully beforehand to ensure that the actual installation process will be successful. Planning and analyzing the desired Exchange organization ensures that the correct number of servers and the proper roles are installed where needed. It's just as important to know how to install an Exchange server as it is to know how to plan for the installation of an Exchange server—one cannot create success without the other.

Exam Essentials

Keep your roles straight. Exchange Server 2007, for the first time ever, actually has specific roles defined that allow you to configure and install only the Exchange components and services you need on each individual server. Remember, not all roles are intended to be installed together, and the Edge Transport role must be installed on a server that is not part of the Active Directory forest. Know which roles are required and which ones are optional and how each role interacts with the others.

Know the Exchange Management Shell. As you've seen, just about every task performed in Exchange Server 2007 can be performed from both the Exchange Management Console and the Exchange Management Shell. Be sure you understand how to perform basic tasks from the shell. There are actually some more advanced, less frequently performed tasks that can be performed *only* from the Exchange Management Shell!

Trust but verify. After you complete the installation of Exchange Server 2007 on each server, take some time to verify that the installation completed successfully by examining the setup logs for errors and verifying that the correct services are installed and running. You can also examine the directory structure created during Exchange setup, check for the Exchange universal security groups in Active Directory, and examine the Event Viewer for indications of how setup really went.

Review Questions

1. Your Exchange Server 2007 plans call for one Edge Transport server and one Mailbox server. What other server role must you install at a minimum?

   A. The Client Access server role

   B. A second Mailbox server role for redundancy

   C. The Unified Messaging role

   D. The Hub Transport role

2. Your organization plans to use the Outlook MAPI client, Outlook Web Access, and the Entourage IMAP4 client for Macintosh in your environment. Which optional Exchange Server 2007 server role must you install in this scenario?

   A. Mailbox server

   B. Hub Transport

   C. Edge Transport

   D. Client Access

   E. Unified Messaging

3. When entering the Exchange organization name, which of the following characters would be considered valid? (Choose all that apply.)

   A. The underscore, _

   B. The dash, -

   C. The slash, /

   D. The letters a–z and A–Z

   E. The backslash, \

4. Which of the following must you perform after an Exchange Server 2007 has been installed?

   A. License the server.

   B. Join the server to the Active Directory domain.

   C. Configure a static IP address for the server.

   D. Install the Forefront antivirus application.

5. What command-line setup option must you use to enable access for Outlook 2003 clients to the Mailbox server?

   A. /LegacyRoutingServer

   B. /EnableLegacyOutlook

   C. /EnableErrorReporting

   D. /AllowOutlook

6. When using a command-line installation method in a single domain forest with no existing Exchange organization, what would be the required command to use if only a single Exchange Server 2007 server will be used? There will be only Outlook 2007 clients in the organization, and Outlook 2007 Autodiscover is required to be available.

   A. `setup /mode:Install /roles:HT, MB /OrganizationName:`*name*

   B. `setup /mode:Install /roles:HT, CA, MB`

   C. `setup /mode:Install /roles:HT, CA, MB /OrganizationName:`*name*

   D. `setup /mode:Install /OrganizationName:`*name*

7. Your Active Directory forest contains only a single domain. Which of the following actions must you complete manually before starting a GUI-based installation of the first Exchange Server 2007 server in the domain?

   A. `setup /prepareschema`

   B. `setup /prepareAD`

   C. `setup /preparedomain`

   D. None of these actions

8. You have just completed the installation of several Exchange Server 2007 servers and roles in your organization. What PowerShell cmdlet can you use to quickly determine the status of all servers and their roles in the Exchange organization?

   A. `Get-ExchangeServer`

   B. `View-ExchangeServer` *orgname*

   C. `Get-ExchangeRoles` *orgname*

   D. `Get-ExchangeServer` *servername*

9. You have just completed installing several Exchange Server 2007 servers and roles in your organization. Where will you find a text log on each server that details every task performed during the installation of Exchange on that server? Assume the default installation path was used.

   A. `C:\ExchangeSetupLogs\ExchangeSetup.msilog`

   B. `C:\Program Files\Microsoft\Exchange Server\Setup\ExchangeSetup.log`

   C. `C:\ExchangeSetupLogs\ExchangeSetup.log`

   D. `C:\Program Files\Microsoft\Exchange Server\ExchangeSetup.log`

10. You have just completed installing several Exchange Server 2007 servers and roles in your organization. What Exchange Management Shell PowerShell script can you use to quickly search through the text setup log looking for errors?

    A. `Get-ExchangeServer`

    B. `Get-SetupLog`

    C. `View-SetupLog`

    D. `View-ExchangeServer`

    E. `View-ErrorLog`

11. You've just completed installing a new Exchange Server 2007 server that contains the Hub Transport and Mailbox roles. When looking at the list of running Exchange services, which of the following would indicate that a problem occurred during the installation if it were not listed? (Choose all that apply.)

    A. Microsoft Exchange IMAP4

    B. Microsoft Exchange Speech Engine

    C. Microsoft Exchange Information Store

    D. Microsoft Exchange System Attendant

    E. Microsoft Exchange Anti-spam Update

    F. Microsoft Exchange Credential Service

12. You are planning the security permissions and rights assignments for your recently installed Exchange Server 2007 organization. What administrative role should you assign to administrative user accounts that should be able to modify messaging-related properties on other users and groups but perform no other tasks?

    A. Exchange Server Administrators role

    B. Exchange Recipient Administrators role

    C. Exchange Organization Administrators role

    D. Exchange View-Only Administrators role

    E. Exchange Messaging Configuration Administrators role

13. What PowerShell cmdlet can you use to configure administrative roles?

    A. `Set-ExchangeAdministrator -Role` *Role* `-Identity` *Domain\User*

    B. `Configure-ExchangeAdministrator -Role` *Role* `-Identity` *Domain\User*

    C. `Change-ExchangeAdministrator -Role` *Role* `-Identity` *Domain\User*

    D. `Add-ExchangeAdministrator -Role` *Role* `-Identity` *Domain\User*

14. Exchange Server 2007 creates several universal security groups during the setup process. When looking for these groups in the Active Directory Users and Computers console, where will they be found?

    A. The Builtin container

    B. The Users container

    C. The Microsoft Exchange Security Groups organizational unit

    D. The Microsoft Exchange Security Groups container

    E. The system container

15. Your Exchange Server 2007 plans call for a single server that has the Mailbox server role, the Client Access role, the Hub Transport role, and the Edge Transport role. Which of these roles cannot be installed on this server as planned?

    A. Mailbox server

    B. Client Access

    C. Edge Transport

    D. Hub Transport

16. When using the command line to install Exchange Server 2007, which modes of setup are available for Exchange Server 2007? (Choose all that apply.)

    A. RecoverServer

    B. Uninstall

    C. RemoveServer

    D. Upgrade

    E. Install

    F. RemoveOrg

17. When using the command line to install Exchange Server 2007, what option must you specify to ensure that the Exchange Management Console and Exchange Management Shell are installed along with the Mailbox server role?

    A. `/role: MB`

    B. `/role: MB, MT`

    C. `/role: MB /tools: yes`

    D. `/role: MB, MT /localtools: yes`

18. When using the command line to install Exchange Server 2007, which of the following options are required only when installing the Edge Transport role? (Choose all that apply.)

    A. /AdamLdapPort *port*

    B. /CMSName *name*

    C. /NewCMS

    D. /AdamSslPort *port*

    E. /TargetDir: *installation directory*

    F. /mode: Install

19. Your organization plans to use the Outlook 2007 MAPI client, Outlook 2003 MAPI client, Outlook Web Access, and the Entourage IMAP4 client for Macintosh in your environment for email access. What must you install during the installation of the first Mailbox server in your Exchange organization?

    A. The Client Access server role

    B. Public folders

    C. The Forefront antivirus application

    D. Error reporting

20. Your Active Directory forest contains an empty root domain and nine child domains below the root domain. There will be six Exchange Server 2007 Mailbox servers installed in six of the child domains, one in each domain. What minimum number of Hub Transport servers must you have in your organization?

    A. Ten, one per domain

    B. Six, one per domain containing a Mailbox server

    C. Nine, one per child domain

    D. One in the root domain

Answers to Review Questions

1. D. You must have a Hub Transport server role installed before you install any other Exchange Server 2007 server role. You can install the Hub Transport server role on the same server as the Mailbox server role and the Client Access server role if desired, although only the Mailbox server role can be clustered.

2. D. A Client Access server is required to be installed in an Exchange Server 2007 organization where any non-MAPI clients will be used to access the Mailbox server. Of the clients and access methods listed, only Outlook is a MAPI client.

3. B, D. The Exchange organization name cannot contain any of the following special characters: ~ (tilde), ` (grave accent), ! (exclamation point), @ (at sign), # (number sign), $ (dollar sign), % (percent sign), ^ (caret), & (ampersand), * (asterisk), () (parentheses), _ (underscore), + (plus sign), = (equal sign), {} (braces), [] (brackets), | (vertical bar), \ (backslash), : (colon), ; (semicolon), " (quotation mark), ' (apostrophe), <> (angle brackets), , (comma), . (period), ? (question mark), / (slash mark), or whitespace at the beginning or end.

4. A. Legally, you are required to license the server after completing the installation. You need to configure a static IP for the server and join the server to the domain before installing Exchange Server 2007, except in the installation of the Edge Transport role, which must not be part of the domain. Forefront, or any other antivirus application, should be installed as soon as possible, but it is not required.

5. B. Using the `/EnableLegacyOutlook` option when performing a command-line installation of the Mailbox server role specified that public folders are to be installed, thus allowing access from Outlook clients older than Outlook 2007 and the Entourage Macintosh client.

6. C. In this scenario, you'll need to use (at a minimum) the following command to perform the installation: `setup /mode:Install /roles:HT, CA, MB /OrganizationName:`*name*. Optionally, you can also specify the domain controller to be used for Active Directory reads and writes by using this command instead: `Setup.com /mode:Install /roles:HT, CA, MB /DomainController` *DC FQDN* `/OrganizationName:`*name*.

7. D. In the scenario where the forest contains only a single domain, there is no requirement to extend the schema or perform any other manual preinstallation tasks that were previously discussed in Chapter 2. You can simply start the installation process, either via the GUI or from the command line, and setup will perform all required configuration steps during the installation of Exchange Server 2007.

8. A. You can verify the list of installed server roles on a single Exchange Server 2007 server by using the `Get-ExchangeServer` *servername* cmdlet from the Exchange Management Shell. If you use the cmdlet without specifying a server, all installed servers and their roles are returned.

9. C. The `ExchangeSetup.log` log file located at `C:\ExchangeSetupLogs\` tracks every task that is performed as part of the setup process and contains information about the status of all checks performed, installation steps carried out, and changes made to the system.

10. B. The `Get-SetupLog` *logpath* `-error -tree` script will parse the setup logs for any errors and return them to the screen for viewing.

11. C, D, E. The Microsoft Exchange Information Store service and the Microsoft Exchange System Attendant should be found only on servers; thus, their absence indicates a problem. The Microsoft Exchange Anti-spam Update should be found on Hub Transport servers (and Edge Transport servers); thus, its absence indicates a problem. The other services would not be found on a server configured only with the Hub Transport and Mailbox server roles.

12. B. Accounts granted the Exchange Recipient Administrators role have the needed permissions to enable them to modify any Exchange-related property on any Active Directory user, group, public folder contact, or dynamic distribution list. The members of this group also have the ability to manage Client Access mailbox settings and Unified Messaging mailbox settings as applicable to the organization. Additionally, this group is a member of the Exchange View-Only Administrators group and inherits all permissions and rights granted to that group.

13. D. You will use the `Add-ExchangeAdministrator -Role` *Role* `-Identity` *Domain\User* cmdlet to add administrative roles. You can use the `Remove-ExchangeAdministrator -Role` *Role* `-Identity` *Domain\User* cmdlet to remove administrative roles.

14. C. The Exchange universal security groups you will see are created in the Microsoft Exchange Security Groups organizational unit.

15. C. The Edge Transport server role must not be installed on a server that is part of an Active Directory domain and cannot be installed on an Exchange Server 2007 server that has any other role installed on it.

16. A, B, D, E. When using the command-line `setup.com` command, you must specify one of the following four modes: Install, Upgrade, Uninstall, RecoverServer.

17. A. The management tools are installed automatically when any server role is installed on the server; therefore, you do not need to specify any additional options other than those required to install the Mailbox server role on the server.

18. A, D. Since the Edge Transport server is not part of the Active Directory domain, it must have some means to determine what are and are not valid recipients in the forest. The Edge Transport server uses a specially configured ADAM instance on the Edge Transport server to store this recipient information; thus, you must specify which ports will be used by ADAM for secure and insecure LDAP communication through the firewall into the internal network.

19. B. Although you will need a Client Access server in this scenario, the question asked what you will need to install during the installation of the Mailbox server role. During the installation of the Mailbox server role, you will be asked whether you have legacy Outlook (pre–Outlook 2007) or Macintosh Entourage clients connecting to your Mailbox server. If the answer is yes, then you must install public folders on that server.

20. B. You must have at least one Hub Transport server in every Active Directory domain that contains a Mailbox or Unified Messaging server. Having more Hub Transport servers, such as two per domain, is even better.

Configuring Exchange Server Roles

MICROSOFT EXAM OBJECTIVES COVERED IN THIS CHAPTER:

✓ **Installing and Configuring Microsoft Exchange Servers**

- Install Exchange.
- Configure Exchange server roles.

✓ **Configuring the Exchange Infrastructure**

- Configure connectors.

With the basic task of installing your first Exchange Server 2007 server behind you, you're now off to the bread and butter of installing an Exchange organization: configuring the server roles.

The main subjects of this chapter are as follows:

- Configuring the Mailbox server role
- Configuring the Hub Transport server role
- Configuring the Client Access server role
- Changing server roles and removing servers from the Exchange organization

Configuring the Mailbox Server

The Mailbox server role is almost always going to be one of the first Exchange Server 2007 roles you'll be installing in your organization, whether it's on the same server as the Hub Transport server (and possibly the Client Access server) or on a dedicated server. Perhaps your Mailbox servers will be in a highly available configuration (as discussed in Chapter 10, "Creating and Managing Highly Available Exchange Server Solutions"), or maybe your organization is smaller and a single Exchange server is all you need. Whatever the case may be, the Mailbox server will require some configuration and management actions before it is ready to perform its function in your organization.

Understanding the Exchange Storage Structure

Before we get to some of the configuration and management tasks you might perform on your Mailbox server, we'll discuss the Exchange storage structure and provide some important fundamentals that we'll build on later in this chapter and throughout the remainder of the book.

Exchange Databases

Mailbox servers contain databases, whether mailbox databases or public folder databases. Within these databases reside all the messages and other content items that exist within the emails and public folder items of the organization. Each database in Exchange Server 2007 consists of a single *rich-text (EDB)* file. In Exchange Server 2003 and Exchange 2000 Server, two separate files actually made up a single database, but that has changed for Exchange Server 2007. By default, Exchange Server 2007 creates the first database for you in a default storage group (we'll discuss storage groups in the next section of this chapter). You can find the default `Mailbox Database.edb` file, by default, in the `C:\Program Files\Microsoft\Exchange Server\Mailbox\First Storage Group` directory, as shown in Figure 4.1.

FIGURE 4.1 The default mailbox database

C:\Program Files\Microsoft\Exchange Server\Mailbox\First Storage Group

File Edit View Favorites Tools Help

Back Search Folders

Address C:\Program Files\Microsoft\Exchange Server\Mailbox\First Storage Group Go

Name	Size	Type	Date Modified	Attributes
CatalogData-353c6034-ecdb-...		File Folder	2/25/2007 7:29 PM	
E00.chk	8 KB	Recovered File Frag...	3/19/2007 5:44 PM	A
E00.log	1,024 KB	Text Document	3/19/2007 5:43 PM	A
E000000000A.log	1,024 KB	Text Document	2/25/2007 9:16 PM	A
E000000000B.log	1,024 KB	Text Document	2/25/2007 9:19 PM	A
E000000000C.log	1,024 KB	Text Document	2/25/2007 9:19 PM	A
E000000000D.log	1,024 KB	Text Document	3/3/2007 9:21 AM	A
E000000000E.log	1,024 KB	Text Document	3/4/2007 1:11 AM	A
E000000000F.log	1,024 KB	Text Document	3/4/2007 1:11 AM	A
E00res00001.jrs	1,024 KB	JRS File	2/25/2007 7:28 PM	A
E00res00002.jrs	1,024 KB	JRS File	2/25/2007 7:28 PM	A
E00tmp.log	0 KB	Text Document	3/19/2007 5:43 PM	A
E0000000001.log	1,024 KB	Text Document	2/25/2007 7:28 PM	A
E0000000002.log	1,024 KB	Text Document	2/25/2007 7:29 PM	A
E0000000003.log	1,024 KB	Text Document	2/25/2007 7:30 PM	A
E0000000004.log	1,024 KB	Text Document	2/25/2007 7:45 PM	A
E0000000005.log	1,024 KB	Text Document	2/25/2007 8:00 PM	A
E0000000006.log	1,024 KB	Text Document	2/25/2007 8:15 PM	A
E0000000007.log	1,024 KB	Text Document	2/25/2007 8:30 PM	A
E0000000008.log	1,024 KB	Text Document	2/25/2007 8:46 PM	A
E0000000009.log	1,024 KB	Text Document	2/25/2007 9:01 PM	A
E0000000010.log	1,024 KB	Text Document	3/19/2007 5:43 PM	A
Mailbox Database.edb	4,112 KB	EDB File	3/19/2007 5:43 PM	A
tmp.edb	2,064 KB	EDB File	3/19/2007 5:43 PM	A

If during the installation of the Exchange Mailbox server role you opted to create a public folder database, it would be created by default at `C:\Program Files\Microsoft\Exchange Server\Mailbox\Second Storage Group` and be named `Public Folder Database.edb`.

Storage Groups and Related Files

Exchange Server 2007 provides support for multiple databases and *storage groups* on a single server. As outlined earlier in Chapter 2, "Preparing for the Exchange Server 2007 Installation," Exchange Server 2007 Enterprise Edition allows up to 50 databases and 50 storage groups. Exchange Server 2007 Standard Edition allows for up to five databases and five storage groups. Although you can still create multiple databases per storage group, you can clearly see the model that Microsoft is promoting in a single database per storage group.

Each storage group is represented by a single instance of the *Extensible Storage Engine (ESE)* and shares a single set of transaction log files. Whenever a transaction occurs on an Exchange server, the responsible service first records the transaction in a *transaction log*. Using transaction logs allows for faster completion of the transaction than if the service had to immediately commit the transaction to a database, because the transaction log structure is much simpler than the database structure. Data is written to these log files sequentially as transactions occur. Regular database maintenance routines commit changes in the logs to the actual databases later, when system processes are idle. Consequently, the most current state of an Exchange service is represented by the EDB file plus the current log files.

The *checkpoint files* are used to keep track of transactions that are committed to the database from a transaction log. Using checkpoint files ensures that transactions cannot be committed to a database more than once. Checkpoint files are named `Exx.chk` and reside in the same directories as their log files and databases, although you can change this. Those transaction logs that have been committed to the database are cleared during a database backup (we discuss this further in Chapter 11, "Disaster Recovery Operations for Exchange Server"). You can see the checkpoint file, log files, and other storage group files in Figure 4.1.

Using multiple databases and storage groups allows you to plan your organization's data storage by classifying various types of data or assigning separate databases to more important users.

The function of each type of file shown in Figure 4.1 is as follows:

- `Exx.chk`: The checkpoint file is named with the log file prefix, such as E00 for the first storage group, E01 for the second storage group, and so on. The check file determines which logs have been committed to the Exchange database and which transaction logs still remain to be committed.
- `Exx.log`: This file is the current (actively being written to) transaction log in use by that storage group. When this log is full, at 1,024KB, it will be renamed to the next sequential number for the storage group. A new `Exx.log` file will then be created, and transactions will be written to it until it is full. In previous versions of Exchange, these log files were 5 MB in size.
- `Exxhhhhhhhh.log`: These are older transaction log files and are named with the log prefix, such as E01, followed by an eight-character hexadecimal number, so you would have `E0100000001.log` as the first log file for the second storage group on the server. Hexadecimal uses the numbers 1 through 0 and the letters *A* through *F* in its numbering system. These files will always be 1,024KB in size.
- `Exxres00001.jrs` and `Exxres00002.jrs`: These two files are reserve transaction log files and serve only as emergency storage if the volume the logs are located on becomes full. When the volume that the transaction logs are located on becomes full, the current transactions being processed are written to disk, and the databases in the storage group(s) on that volume are dismounted. By having two reserved transaction logs, Exchange can ensure that no transactions are lost during this process. These files will always be 1,024KB in size.
- `Tmp.edb`: This file is a temporary workspace for processing active transactions. This file is typically only a few megabytes in size and will be deleted automatically when all databases in the storage group are dismounted or the server's Microsoft Exchange Information Store process has stopped.
- `Exxtmp.log`: This file serves as the transaction log file for the `Tmp.edb` workspace. This file will never be larger than 1,024KB in size.
- `name.edb`: This file is the actual rich-text database file. In Figure 4.1, it was named Mailbox Database (which is a default name), but you will likely see different names in your organization over time for each mailbox and public folder database file.

All of the file locations discussed and shown in Figure 4.1 are the defaults provided by the Exchange setup process. As with any database, however, you will want to have transaction logs and actual database files on different physical volumes if possible. Transactions that occur within Exchange Server 2007 are always first written to the transaction logs and then read and written into the actual database file at a later time depending on the current load being placed on the server. Transaction log access is typically sequential, whereas database access is almost always random. By placing each storage group's transaction logs on one physical volume and the databases for that storage group on another physical volume, you'll increase speed, performance, reliability, and recoverability of that storage group as a whole. With the emphasis in Exchange Server 2007 on one database per storage group, you should effectively be planning for two different physical volumes per server for each storage group on that server.

Configuring Storage Groups and Mailbox Databases

Now that you have a basic understanding of how the Exchange storage structure is designed, let's examine some common storage group tasks and database-related tasks that you'll be performing on Mailbox servers.

In this chapter, you'll be examining mailbox databases. We discuss public folders in Chapter 8, "Configuring and Managing Client Connectivity and Public Folders."

Using Storage Groups

Since storage groups are basically containers that hold stores, they are fairly simple to create, and there is not much to manage about them other than a few simple details. The following sections describe how to create, configure, and manage storage groups.

Creating a Storage Group

By default, a single storage group is created on each server and is named First Storage Group. Since every storage group is created on and associated with a single server, you will always find storage groups listed on the Database Management tab of the Mailbox server view in the Exchange Management Console, as shown in Figure 4.2.

FIGURE 4.2 Storage groups always belong to a specific server.

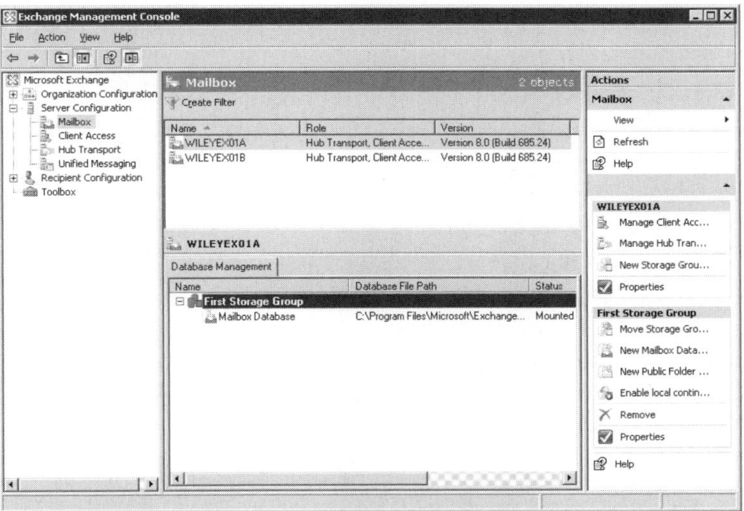

Exercise 4.1 outlines the steps for creating a new storage group.

EXERCISE 4.1

Creating a New Storage Group

1. Click Start ➢ Programs ➢ Microsoft Exchange Server 2007, and then select Exchange Management Console.
2. Expand the Microsoft Exchange root object, expand the Server Configuration folder, and then click the server for which you want to add a storage group.
3. In the Actions pane on the right for that Mailbox server, click the New Storage Group link, as shown here.

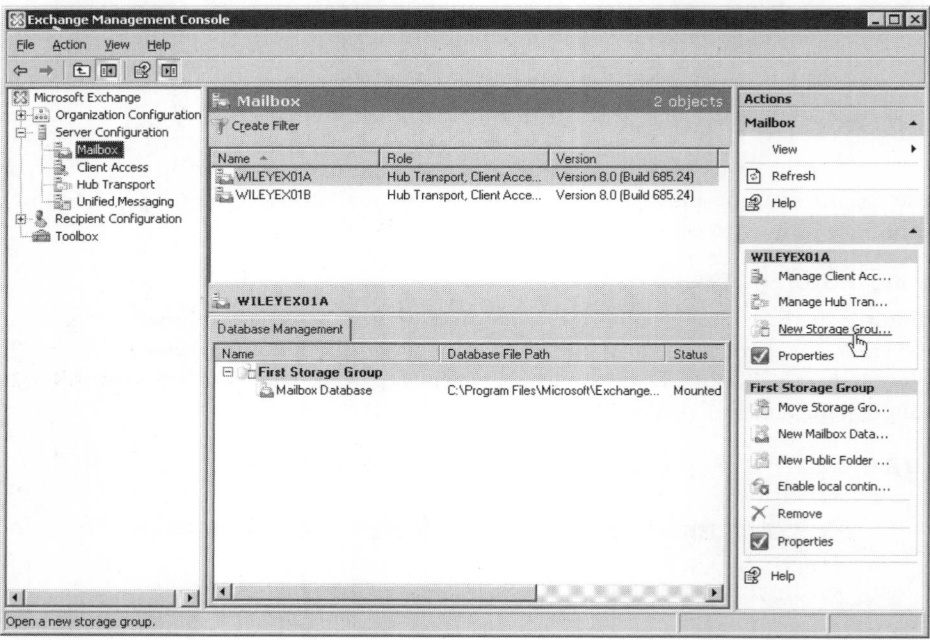

EXERCISE 4.1 *(continued)*

4. The New Storage Group Wizard opens, as shown here.

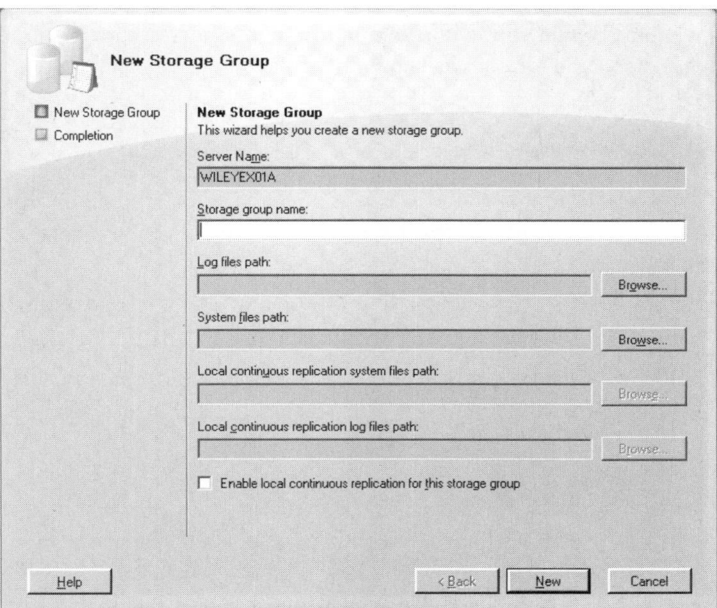

5. Provide a name for the storage group, and then use the Browse buttons to locate the path for the log files and system files associated with the storage group:

   - The transaction log location is the directory in which the transaction log file for the storage group resides. By default, a location is created for the log file based on the name you give the storage group. You can change this location while creating the storage group or any time after creation.

   - The system path location is where any temporary database files (named `TMP.EDB`) and checkpoint files (named `EDB.CHK`) are stored. You can change this location during or after creation.

EXERCISE 4.1 *(continued)*

6. By default, Exchange will place both the log files and the system files in the same location. If you'll be configuring local continuous replication, configure those options as well. Click the New button when you're done configuring options to create the storage group. The results are displayed for you, as shown here.

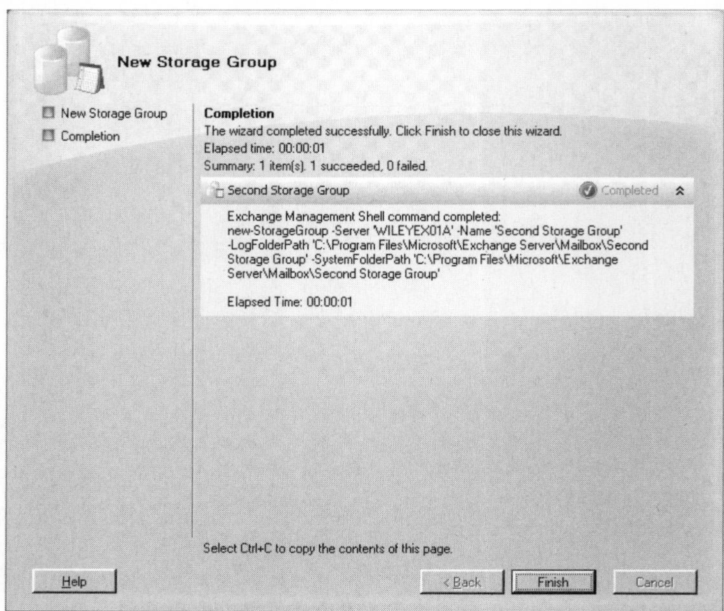

7. Click Finish to close the wizard and complete the storage group creation process.

Notice how the Exchange Management Console tries to always show you the corresponding Exchange Management Shell code you'd need to perform the same task. In most cases, you can copy and paste the code displayed into Notepad, edit it accordingly, and use it to perform the same task again—and that's exactly what you're going to do here by creating the Third Storage Group on your server. Be sure to create the folder itself first using Windows Explorer to house the files and then run the PowerShell script that looks like this from the Exchange Management Shell:

```
new-StorageGroup -Server 'WILEYEX01A' -Name 'Third Storage Group'
-LogFolderPath
'C:\Program Files\Microsoft\Exchange Server\Mailbox\Third Storage Group'
-SystemFolderPath
'C:\Program Files\Microsoft\Exchange Server\Mailbox\Third Storage Group'
```

You'll find the Exchange Management Shell shortcut in the same folder as the Exchange Management Console. Click Start ➢ Programs ➢ Microsoft Exchange Server 2007 to get there.

Figure 4.3 shows the results of the action.

FIGURE 4.3 Creating a new storage group from the Exchange Management Shell

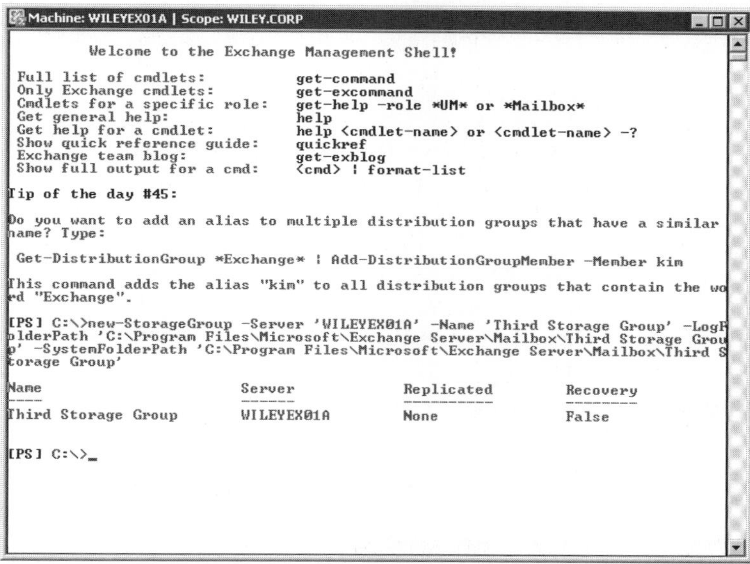

Look at the Exchange Management Console, shown in Figure 4.4; you can now see the Second Storage Group and the Third Storage Group we just created, although they do not yet have any databases in them. We'll get to that task shortly.

Configuring Storage Group Properties

Only one property page is available for storage groups in Exchange Server 2007. You can open the storage group properties by right-clicking a storage group from the view shown in Figure 4.4 and selecting Properties from the context menu. Alternatively, you can click the Properties link under the storage group options in the Actions pane on the right of the Exchange Management Console. In the storage group's Properties dialog box, shown in Figure 4.5, you're given the option to change the storage group name or to enable or disable circular logging. This is quite a far cry from Exchange Server 2003, which allowed you to change storage group paths from this dialog box as well.

FIGURE 4.4 Viewing the newly created storage groups

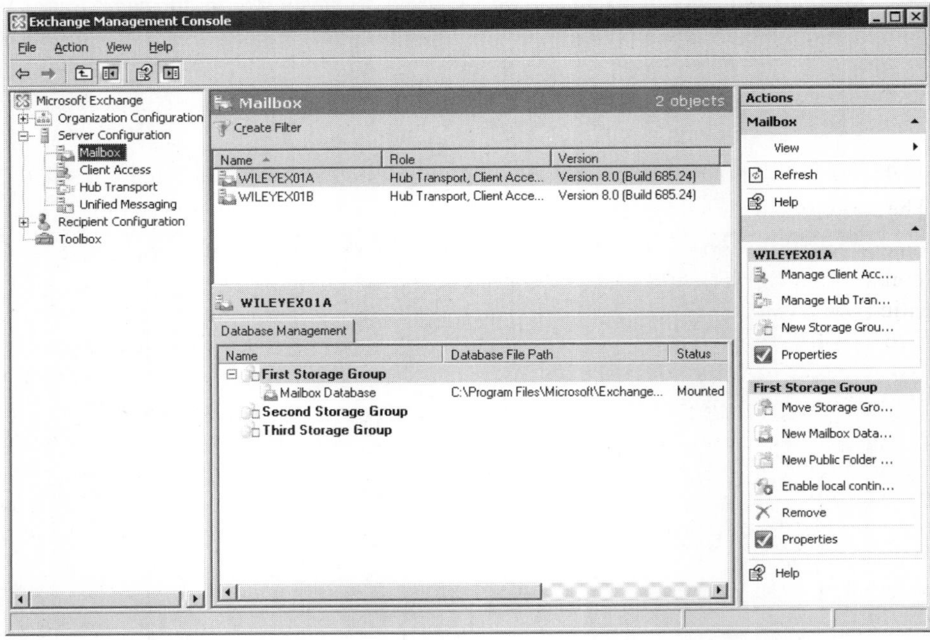

FIGURE 4.5 Configuring storage group properties

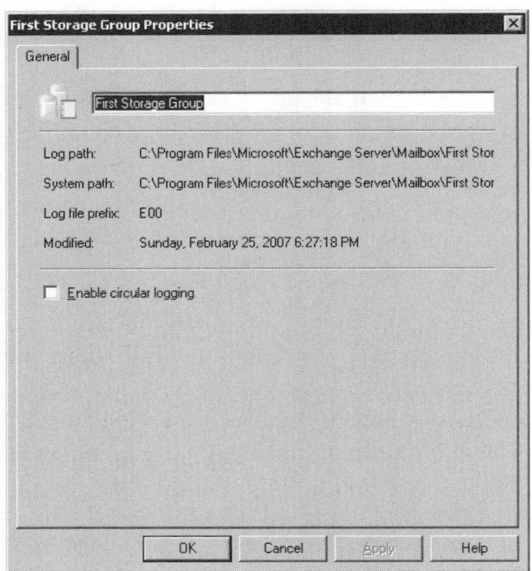

The following information is displayed for you in the storage group's Properties dialog box:

- The storage group name
- The transaction log location
- The system path location
- The log file prefix, which is chosen by the system and cannot be altered. It designates the prefix, such as E00 or E01, attached to the log file for the group
- The date and time the storage group properties were last modified
- The status of circular logging for the storage group, which you can opt to enable or disable.

You can configure transaction log files for each storage group to recycle themselves to prevent constant accumulation on the hard disk. This process is called *circular logging*. Instead of continually creating new log files and storing the old ones, the database engine "circles back" to the oldest log file that has been fully committed and overwrites that file. Circular logging minimizes the number of transaction log files on the disk at any given time. The downside is that these logs cannot be used to re-create a database because the logs do not have a complete set of data. They have only the data not yet committed. Another disadvantage of circular logging is that it does not permit a differential or incremental backup of the databases.

Circular logging is disabled by default and can be enabled or disabled as discussed previously. Table 4.1 summaries and compares what happens when circular logging is enabled and disabled.

TABLE 4.1 Circular Logging Enabled vs. Disabled

Circular Logging Enabled	Circular Logging Disabled (the Default)
Transaction log files are recycled.	Old transaction log files are stored.
The re-creation of a database is not permitted.	The re-creation of a database is permitted.
Differential or incremental backups are not permitted.	Differential and incremental backups are permitted.
A full or incremental backup will not delete old transaction log files.	A full or incremental backup automatically deletes old transaction log files.

As mentioned earlier, circular logging enables Exchange to conserve disk space by maintaining a fixed number of transaction logs and overwriting those logs as needed. Without circular logging, Exchange creates new log files when old ones fill up. Circular logging is disabled by default, and it is generally recommended that you leave it disabled except possibly for storage groups that contain only public folder databases with noncritical data—if such a thing exists anymore.

Beyond the configuration choices you have in the storage group's Properties dialog box, you might also need at some point to change the log file and/or system file paths associated with the storage group. Although you can no longer perform these tasks from the Properties dialog box, Exchange Server 2007 still has you covered.

Exercise 4.2 outlines the steps for changing the storage group paths.

EXERCISE 4.2

Changing Storage Group Paths

1. Click Start ➤ Programs ➤ Microsoft Exchange Server 2007, and then select Exchange Management Console.

2. Expand the Microsoft Exchange root object, expand the Server Configuration folder, and then click the server that contains the storage group with the path you want to change.

3. Click the storage group whose path you want to change; in this example, select the First Storage Group.

4. To change either or both of these paths, simply click the Move Storage Group Path link under the storage group options in the Actions pane on the right of the Exchange Management Console. Alternatively, you can right-click the storage group and select the Move Storage Group Path menu item from the context menu that appears. Either way, the Move Storage Group Path Wizard opens, as shown here.

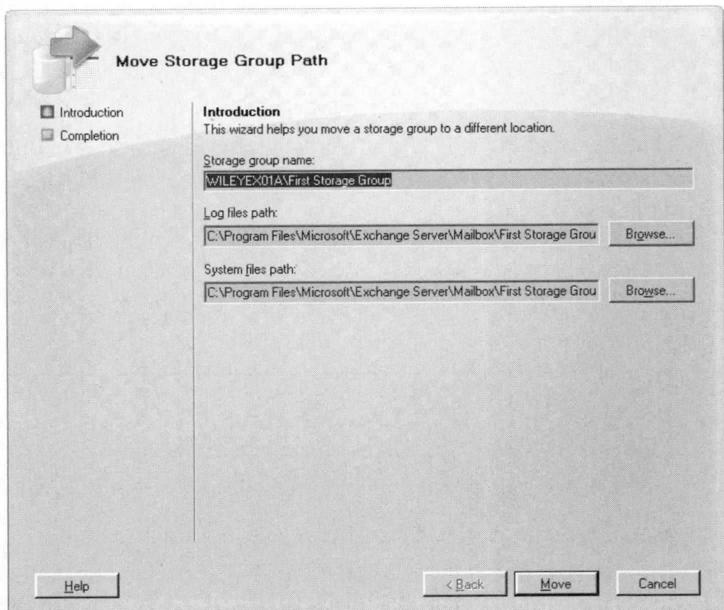

EXERCISE 4.2 *(continued)*

5. The process to change the paths is the same as when you created the storage group in Exercise 4.1. Note that this time the system file path will *not* automatically follow whatever you select for the log file path, so you will need to change both paths manually if you're looking to move both to the same location. When you've configured the desired paths, click the Move button to commit the changes. If the storage group contains any databases, you'll be prompted to allow the dismounting of the databases, as shown here. Click Yes to continue.

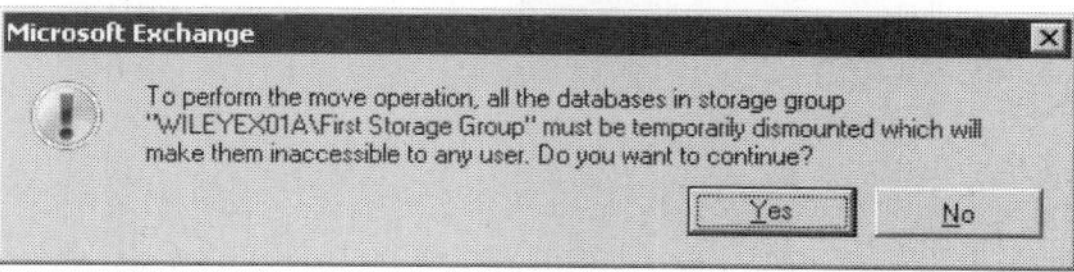

6. As always, Exchange Server 2007 will display a summary page requiring you to click Finish to close the wizard. Again, notice that the code displayed was the code actually used to perform the change.

Remember, all you're actually changing here by altering the storage group paths are the locations of the transaction log files and the location of the system files associated with the storage group. The actual database files associated with the storage groups have their locations configured with the database properties, which will be discussed later in this chapter. As a net result of making the changes discussed here, your default `Mailbox Database.edb` file will remain in its default location of `C:\Program Files\Microsoft\Exchange Server\Mailbox\First Storage Group`, while the transaction logs and system files will be moved to the new location of `C:\Program Files\Microsoft\Exchange Server\Mailbox\First Storage Group NEW` (see Exercise 4.2). Of course, when working on a production system, you would not typically just move the logs and system files to a different location on the same volume; you'd move them to a completely separate physical volume attached to the server.

To change the storage group paths from the Exchange Management Shell, you would just need to copy and paste the code and edit it accordingly. As you did when you created a new storage group with PowerShell previously, make sure you create the appropriate folder(s) with Windows Explorer before running your code, which might look something like this:

```
move-StorageGroupPath -Identity 'WILEYEX01A\Second Storage Group'
-LogFolderPath
'C:\Program Files\Microsoft\Exchange Server\Mailbox\Second Storage Group NEW'
-SystemFolderPath
'C:\Program Files\Microsoft\Exchange Server\Mailbox\Second Storage Group NEW'
```

Figure 4.6 shows the results of the action.

FIGURE 4.6 Changing storage group paths from the Exchange Management Shell

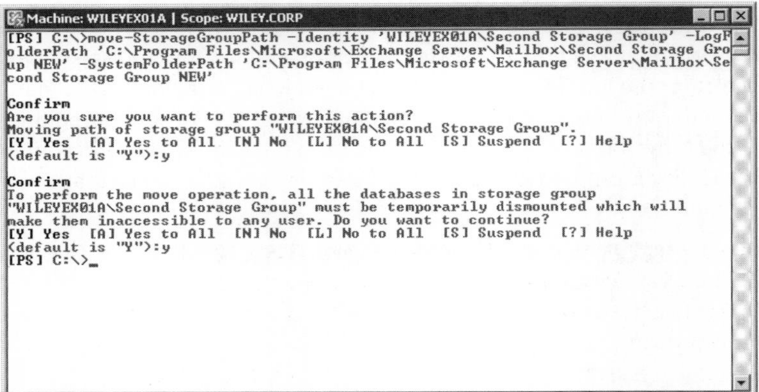

You'll need to actually have files in the source paths before you can use this command to change the storage group paths. In other words, if your storage group is empty and has no databases, this command won't work. The Exchange Management Shell will inform you of this and present the alternative command to make a configuration-only change, which updates only the configuration information in Active Directory but does not move any files associated with the storage group.

Using Databases

The default storage group, named First Storage Group, is created during Exchange installation. A single database is also created within that storage group: a mailbox database named `Mailbox Database.edb`.

You can create up to four additional new databases in the First Storage Group, although the best practice is to limit databases to one per storage group and to create additional storage groups for any additional databases. Recall that the limitation of Exchange Server 2007 is 50 databases total and 50 storage groups total. The process for creating a mailbox database and a public folder database is functionally identical and, for the most part, so is the configuration of the two different types of databases. In the sections that follow, we'll cover creating, configuring, and managing a new mailbox database. When configuring a public folder database, many of the properties you will configure and much of the management are identical. Some differences in the configuration, such as the replication of public folders, are discussed in Chapter 8.

Creating a Database

Creating a new database is a straightforward process. Exercise 4.3 outlines the steps for creating a new mailbox database.

EXERCISE 4.3

Creating a New Mailbox Store

1. Click Start ➢ Programs ➢ Microsoft Exchange Server 2007, and then select Exchange Management Console.

2. Expand the Microsoft Exchange root object, expand the Server Configuration folder, and then click the server that contains the storage group in which you want to create a new database.

3. Right-click the storage group object in which you want to create the database, and select the New Mailbox Database option from the context menu. This opens the New Mailbox Database Wizard, as shown here. Alternatively, you can click the New Mailbox Database link under the storage group options in the Actions pane on the right of the Exchange Management Console.

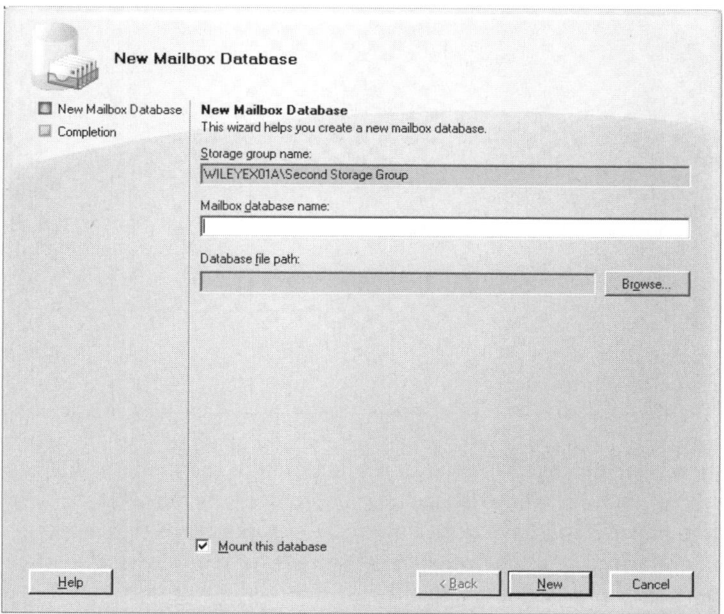

4. Type a name for the new mailbox database, and select the database file path by clicking the Browse button. Remember, the database should be on a different physical volume than its storage group's transaction logs if possible. To ensure the database is available for immediate use, leave the Mount This Database option checked. Click New to complete the database creation process.

EXERCISE 4.3 *(continued)*

5. As usual, Exchange displays a summary page showing the success or failure of the actions you instructed it to perform. Notice this time, however, there were two different actions performed: creating the database and mounting the database.

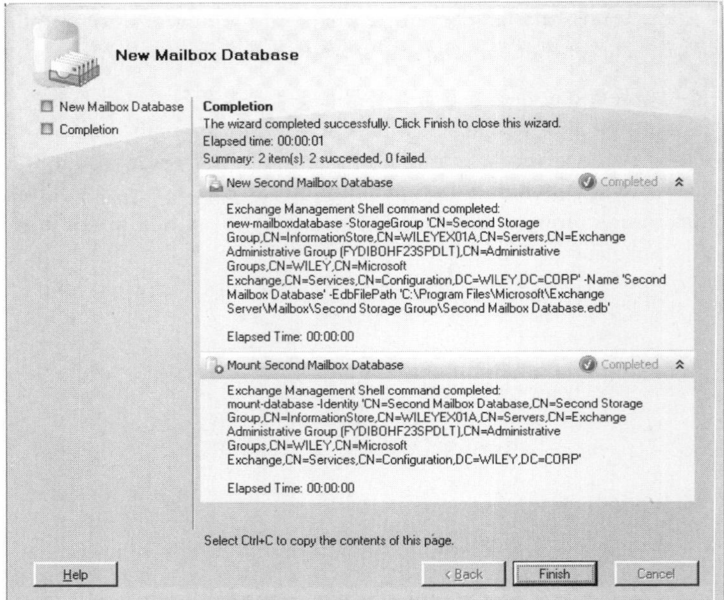

6. Click Finish to close the wizard.

To perform the same process from the Exchange Management Shell, you'll need to ensure the database path exists by creating the appropriate folder with Windows Explorer. Additionally, you'll need to ensure you have both PowerShell scripts correctly written to both create and mount the database. Your code might look similar to the following. Notice how almost all of the text pertains to making an Active Directory configuration.

```
new-mailboxdatabase -StorageGroup
'CN=Third Storage Group,CN=InformationStore,CN=WILEYEX01A,CN=Servers,
CN=Exchange Administrative Group (FYDIBOHF23SPDLT),CN=Administrative Groups,
CN=WILEY,CN=Microsoft Exchange,CN=Services,CN=Configuration,DC=WILEY,DC=CORP'
-Name 'Third Mailbox Database' -EdbFilePath
'C:\Program Files\Microsoft\Exchange Server\Mailbox\
Third Storage Group\Third Mailbox Database.edb'
mount-database -Identity
```

```
'CN=Third Mailbox Database,CN=Third Storage Group,CN=InformationStore,
CN=WILEYEX01A,CN=Servers,CN=Exchange Administrative Group (FYDIBOHF23SPDLT),
CN=Administrative Groups,CN=WILEY,CN=Microsoft Exchange,CN=Services,
CN=Configuration,DC=WILEY,DC=CORP'
```

Figure 4.7 shows the results of the action.

Looking at the Exchange Management Console, shown in Figure 4.8, you can see that now you have three storage groups, each of which has a mailbox database within it.

FIGURE 4.7 Creating a new mailbox database from the Exchange Management Shell

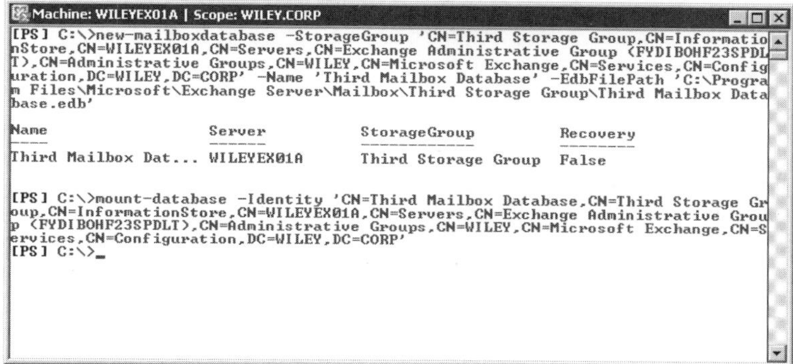

FIGURE 4.8 Examining the results of the mailbox database creation process

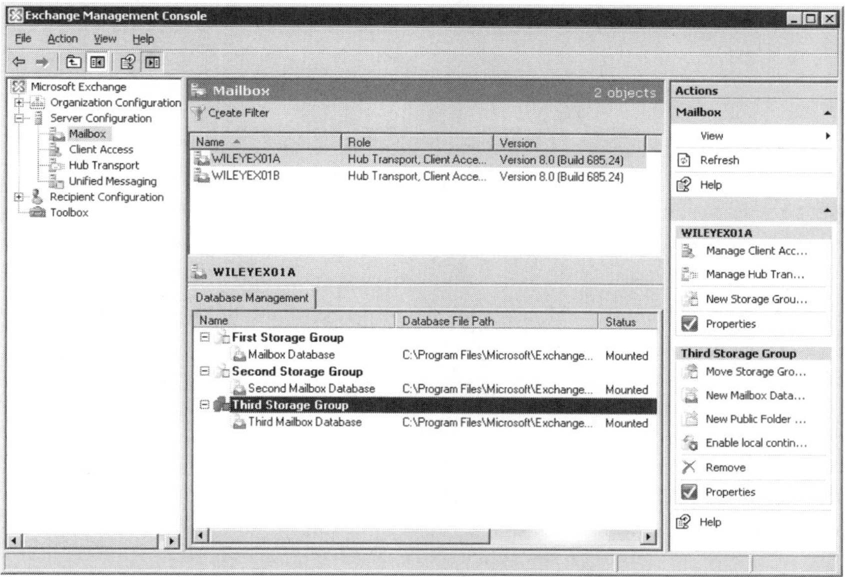

Configuring Database Properties

You use three property pages to configure a mailbox database. Unlike previous versions of Exchange, you cannot configure any of these properties until after you've created the mailbox database. To access the mailbox database properties, either you can right-click the mailbox database of concern and select Properties from the context menu or you can click the Properties link under the mailbox database options in the Actions pane on the right of the Exchange Management Console. Either way, the Properties dialog box shown in Figure 4.9 opens for you.

FIGURE 4.9 General properties of a mailbox store

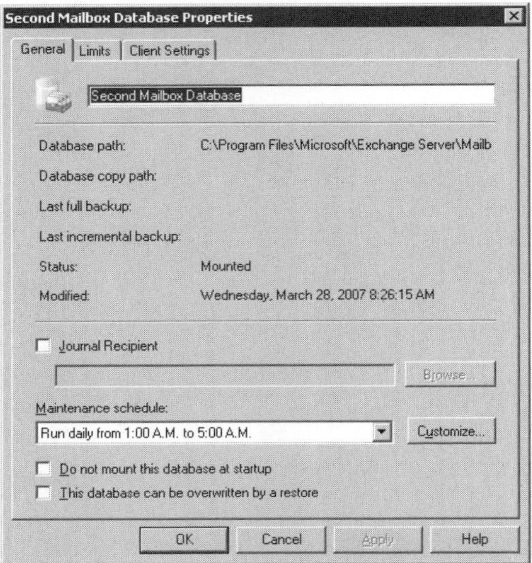

GENERAL

You use a mailbox database's General tab, shown in Figure 4.9, to configure the following properties:

- Naming the database during its creation. As with storage groups, you can change the name of a database after creation as well.
- Selecting the destination mailbox to which messages will be journaled. Depending on your needs and the type of CAL your organization is using (standard vs. enterprise), you will be able to journal all communications for an entire mailbox database (standard) or, to get more granular, perhaps journal only those messages for certain users on a mailbox database that are sent to recipients outside the organization.

Journaling is outside the scope of exam 70-236 but is covered in detail on exam 70-237. You can get more information about that exam by visiting `www.microsoft.com/learning/exams/70-237.mspx`.

- Choosing the times at which you want the automatic database maintenance routines to run. Select from several preset values using the drop-down list, or click Customize to open a calendar-style interface.
- Deciding whether to mount the store when the Exchange server starts (if it doesn't, you'll have to do it manually).
- Deciding whether the store can be overwritten during a restore from backup. Check out Chapter 11 for more about backup and recovery.

The following properties are only for display on the General tag of the Properties dialog box and cannot be changed:

- The database path
- The database copy path, if local continuous replication is in use
- The date and time of the last full backup
- The date and time of the last incremental backup
- The status of the database
- The date and time the database was last modified

LIMITS

You use the Limits tab, shown in Figure 4.10, to configure limits values that are applied to all mailboxes within the mailbox database. Values set at this level are automatically applied to all mailboxes, but you can manually configure individual mailboxes as well, thereby overriding these limits.

FIGURE 4.10 Limits properties of a mailbox store

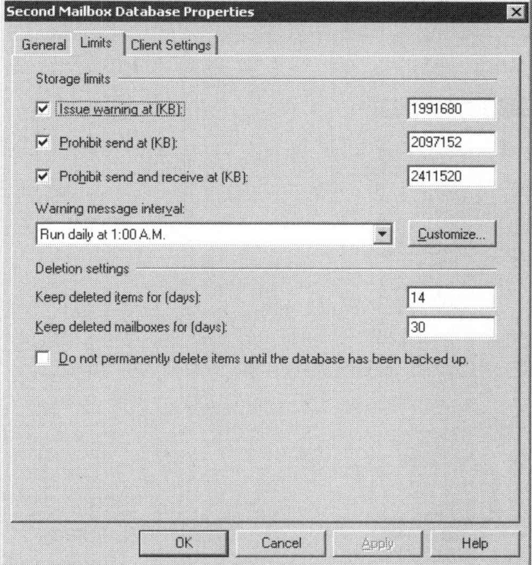

This tab lets you set configure settings in two areas: storage limits and deletion settings. Storage Limits refer to the limits (in kilobytes) placed on the size to which mailboxes in the store can grow and to what happens when that limit is exceeded. By default rather large limits are set, so you'll likely want to change them soon after creating the mailbox database. You can set limits for when to issue a warning, when to prohibit sending, and when to prohibit sending and receiving. You can also configure the interval when the Information Store checks these values and issues warnings.

Deletion Settings refer to how long (measured in days) deleted items in a mailbox and deleted mailboxes are retained on a server after a user or administrator deletes them. You can also configure the store to keep deleted items and mailboxes until the store has been backed up, regardless of the actual values entered.

CLIENT SETTINGS

You use the Client Settings tab, shown in Figure 4.11, to configure settings that are applied to the client sessions of users who have mailboxes in the mailbox store. You can configure the following here:

- *Default public store*: Every Exchange user must have a default public store that is used for public folder access. This does not limit access to only the chosen public store but rather provides an entry point—the first place the client will look for public folder content. Click the Browse button to open a list of available public stores from which to choose. We discuss public folders in Chapter 8.
- *Offline address list*: The Offline Address Book field specifies the default offline address list that users of this mailbox store will download when synchronizing the offline address list on their client. Like the public folder setting, this is simply a default value and does not prevent other available offline address lists from being used. We discuss offline address lists in Chapter 7, "Configuring Exchange Server Rules and Policies."

FIGURE 4.11 Client access properties of a mailbox store

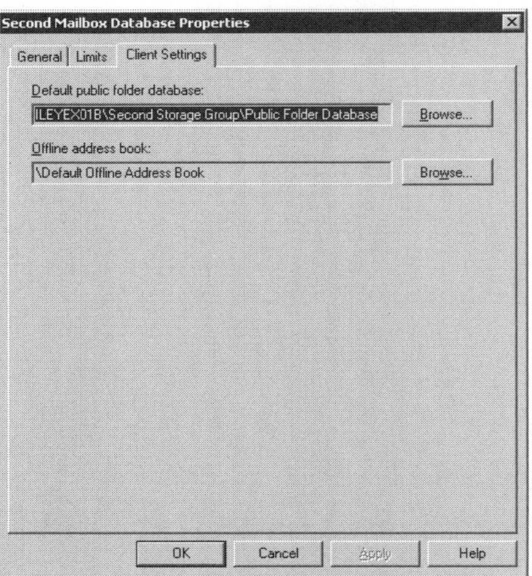

Managing Stores and Storage Groups

Once they are created and properly configured, both storage groups and stores require proper management to keep everything running smoothly. Much of this management is covered elsewhere in this book:

- Backing up and restoring (Chapter 11)
- Managing public folders and replication (Chapter 8)
- Managing individual users and their mailboxes (Chapter 6, "Configuring and Managing Exchange Recipients")
- Tracking messages and monitoring the status of message flow (Chapter 9, "Managing and Maintaining the Exchange Organization")
- Configuring client access to the store data (Chapter 8)

Viewing and Managing Mailbox Information

Unlike Exchange Server 2003, Exchange Server 2007 does not group mailboxes under their mailbox databases by default. You can still get a listing of just those mailboxes that are physically in a specific mailbox database, but you'll have to work a little bit to get there. When you look at Exchange Server 2007 mailboxes, which we'll cover in great detail in the next chapter, you'll see the default view of all mailboxes, as shown in Figure 4.12.

FIGURE 4.12 Viewing Exchange mailboxes

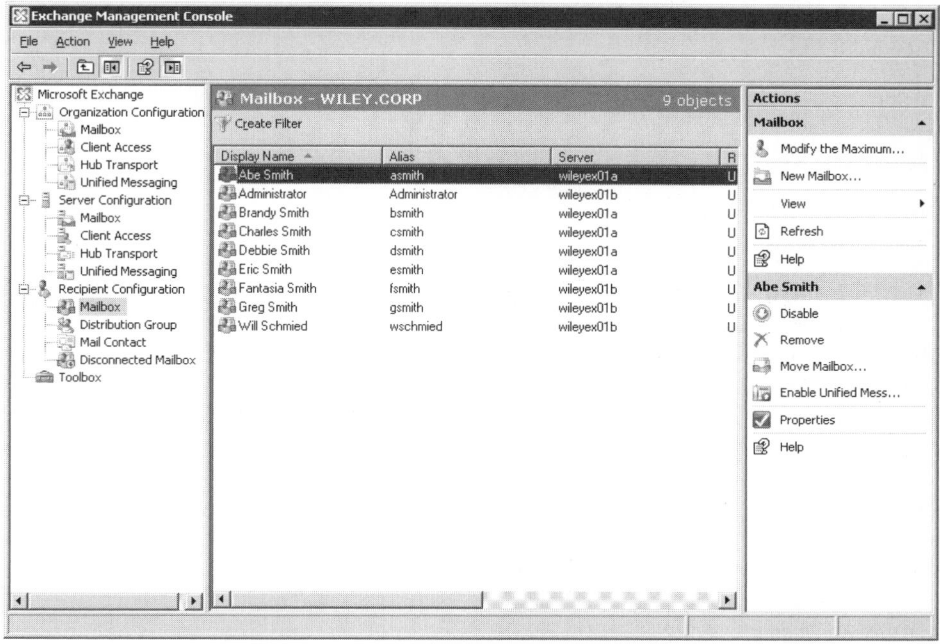

If you want to see just those mailboxes located within a specific mailbox store on a Mailbox server as a whole, you'll need to create a filter. To create the filter, click the Create Filter button that appears above the mailbox listing, and then select the desired filter items. For example, to filter the display to just those mailboxes in a specific mailbox database, you'd select the Database and Equals options and then browse to and select the database whose mailboxes you're interested in seeing. When you have the filter configured, be sure to click the Apply Filter button. Figure 4.13 displays a sample filtered output; compare this to the listing shown in Figure 4.12.

FIGURE 4.13 Using display filters to display mailboxes in a specific mailbox database

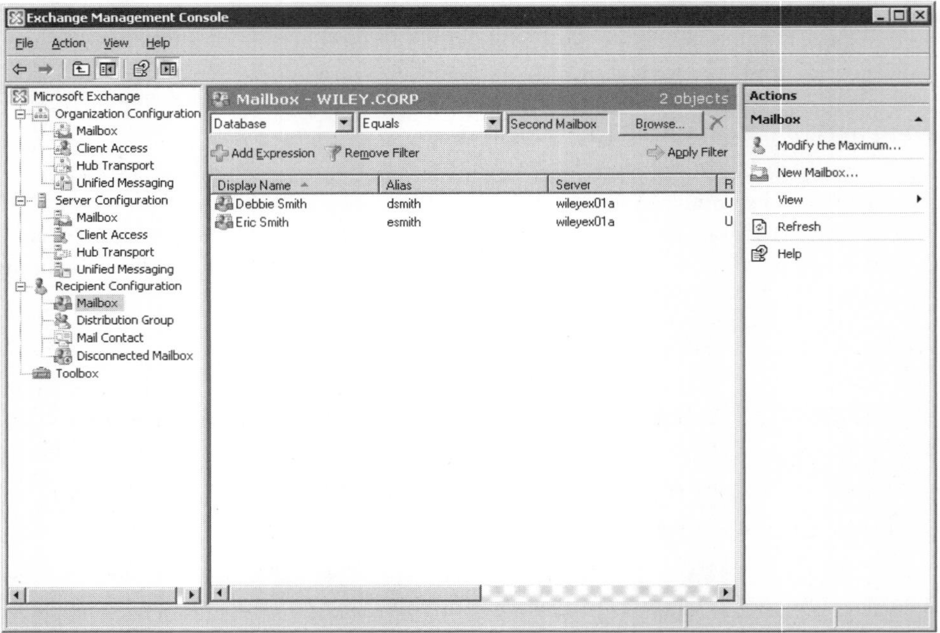

If you've worked with previous versions of Exchange, you'll notice that some information you're used to seeing at this point is not available in this view. For example, you can't see login information about the last date and time a user accessed the mailbox, you can't see information about the client that was used to perform that login, and (perhaps most important) you can't see information about how large the mailbox is within the mailbox database. Perhaps some of these missing items will be accounted for when Exchange Server 2007 Service Pack 1 (SP1) is made available in late 2007.

Another radical change from previous versions of Exchange Server is that now you once again actually perform recipient management from within the Exchange management tools instead of through Active Directory Users and Computers. Double-clicking a mailbox in a list will open the Properties dialog box for that mailbox, as shown in Figure 4.14. This might be what you were accustomed to seeing in Active Directory Users and Computers, but now it definitely has a messaging feature focus.

FIGURE 4.14 Viewing a mailbox object

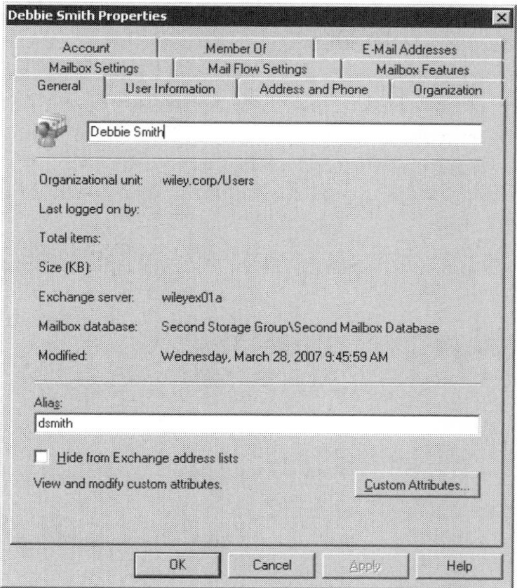

Since managing mailboxes and all mail-related settings is now done within the Exchange management tools, you'll be able only to delete a mailbox from the Exchange management tools. We discuss all the available configuration and management options for mailboxes in Chapter 6.

Mounting and Dismounting Databases

One of the great advantages of having multiple databases is that you can take individual databases down for maintenance without affecting other databases on the server. Taking a database offline is referred to as *dismounting*; bringing it back online is referred to as *mounting*. To mount or dismount a database, simply right-click the database, and choose the appropriate option from the context menu. Alternatively, you can click the appropriate link under the database options in the Actions pane on the right of the Exchange Management Console.

To perform these tasks from the Exchange Management Shell, you'll need to use a PowerShell script that looks similar to this for dismounting:

```
dismount-database -Identity
'CN=Third Mailbox Database,CN=Third Storage Group,CN=InformationStore,
CN=WILEYEX01A,CN=Servers,CN=Exchange Administrative Group (FYDIBOHF23SPDLT),
CN=Administrative Groups,CN=WILEY,CN=Microsoft Exchange,CN=Services,
CN=Configuration,DC=WILEY,DC=CORP'
```

For mounting, your PowerShell will be similar to this:

```
mount-database -Identity
'CN=Third Mailbox Database,CN=Third Storage Group,CN=InformationStore,
CN=WILEYEX01A,CN=Servers,CN=Exchange Administrative Group (FYDIBOHF23SPDLT),
CN=Administrative Groups,CN=WILEY,CN=Microsoft Exchange,CN=Services,
CN=Configuration,DC=WILEY,DC=CORP'
```

Figure 4.15 shows the results of these actions.

FIGURE 4.15 Dismounting and mounting databases from the Exchange Management Shell

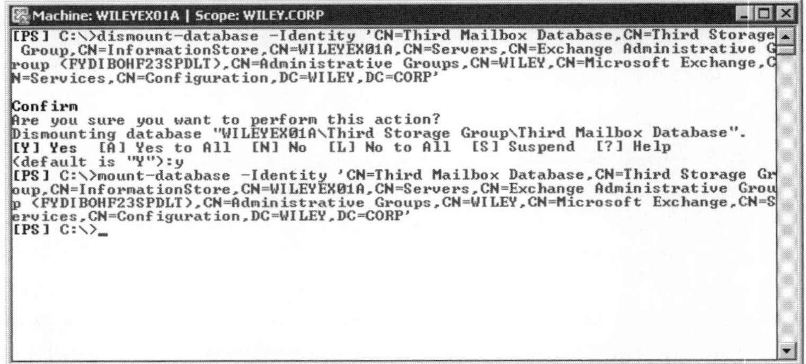

Deleting Mailbox Databases

To delete a mailbox database, just right-click it, and choose Remove from the context menu. Alternatively, you can click the Remove link under the database options in the Actions pane on the right of the Exchange Management Console. Before you can delete a mailbox database, you must either delete or move all mailboxes within that database. Exchange will not let you delete a database that contains mailboxes.

To remove a mailbox database using PowerShell from the Exchange Management Shell, you'll execute a script similar to this one:

```
remove-mailboxdatabase -Identity
'CN=Third Mailbox Database,CN=Third Storage Group,
CN=InformationStore,CN=WILEYEX01A,CN=Servers,
CN=Exchange Administrative Group (FYDIBOHF23SPDLT),CN=Administrative Groups,
CN=WILEY,CN=Microsoft Exchange,CN=Services,CN=Configuration,DC=WILEY,DC=CORP'
```

Figure 4.16 shows the results of this action.

FIGURE 4.16 Deleting a mailbox database from the Exchange Management Shell

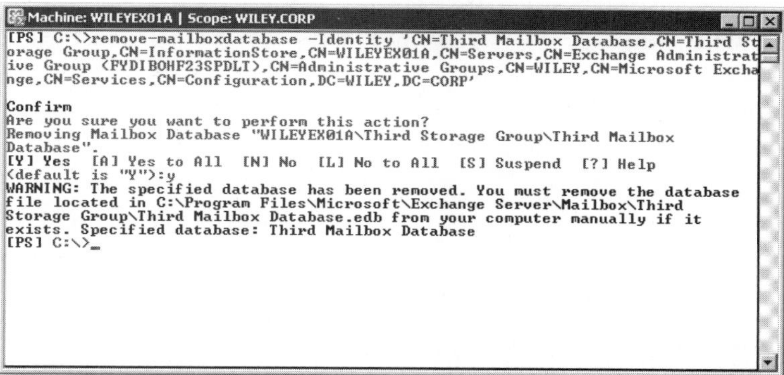

```
Machine: WILEYEX01A | Scope: WILEY.CORP
[PS] C:\>remove-mailboxdatabase -Identity 'CN=Third Mailbox Database,CN=Third St
orage Group,CN=InformationStore,CN=WILEYEX01A,CN=Servers,CN=Exchange Administrat
ive Group (FYDIBOHF23SPDLT),CN=Administrative Groups,CN=WILEY,CN=Microsoft Excha
nge,CN=Services,CN=Configuration,DC=WILEY,DC=CORP'

Confirm
Are you sure you want to perform this action?
Removing Mailbox Database "WILEYEX01A\Third Storage Group\Third Mailbox
Database".
[Y] Yes  [A] Yes to All  [N] No  [L] No to All  [S] Suspend  [?] Help
(default is "Y"):y
WARNING: The specified database has been removed. You must remove the database
file located in C:\Program Files\Microsoft\Exchange Server\Mailbox\Third
Storage Group\Third Mailbox Database.edb from your computer manually if it
exists. Specified database: Third Mailbox Database
[PS] C:\>_
```

Regardless of which method you use to delete a mailbox database, you'll need to manually remove the database file and some other related files from the storage location. You'll be informed of this requirement regardless of which deletion process you use.

Deleting a Storage Group

You can delete any storage group by right-clicking it and choosing Remove from the context menu. Alternatively, you can click the Remove link under the storage group options in the Actions pane on the right of the Exchange Management Console. However, the storage group must not have any stores associated with it. This means you must first remove all stores in the storage group before you can delete the group. To remove a storage group using PowerShell from the Exchange Management Shell, you'll execute a script similar to this one:

```
remove-StorageGroup -Identity 'WILEYEX01A\Third Storage Group'
```

Figure 4.17 shows the results of this action.

FIGURE 4.17 Deleting a storage group from the Exchange Management Shell

```
Machine: WILEYEX01A | Scope: WILEY.CORP
[PS] C:\>remove-StorageGroup -Identity 'WILEYEX01A\Third Storage Group'

Confirm
Are you sure you want to perform this action?
Removing Storage Group "WILEYEX01A\Third Storage Group".
[Y] Yes  [A] Yes to All  [N] No  [L] No to All  [S] Suspend  [?] Help
(default is "Y"):y
WARNING: The specified storage group has been removed. You must remove the log
file located in C:\Program Files\Microsoft\Exchange Server\Mailbox\Third
Storage Group from your computer manually if it exists. Specified storage
group: WILEYEX01A\Third Storage Group.
[PS] C:\>_
```

Regardless of which method you use to delete a storage group, you'll need to manually remove the folders previously used by the storage group. You'll be informed of this requirement no matter which deletion process you use.

Using Databases and Storage Groups

Many theories abound on how you should configure your Exchange organization's storage groups and databases. We'll examine some cold hard facts here and then let you determine the best solution for your organization's needs.

A storage group, regardless of how many databases are in it, uses only one set of transaction logs. This is a good thing until you need to configure circular logging for any reason. Circular logging is configured at the storage group level and thus applies equally to all databases inside that storage group. This can become a large problem if that storage group contains critical email databases. In reality, is there such a thing anymore as a noncritical email database? For databases on which you will configure circular logging, consider creating a storage group just to hold the databases on which you will configure circular logging.

When performing backups of the Exchange organization, you should be aware that you can configure backups only at the storage group level. Thus, you have the option to back up only an entire storage group and its databases, not individual databases within the storage group. However, when performing a restoration, you can opt to restore only specific databases within the storage group. Storage groups are backed up as a whole, and this can impact the length of time required to perform your backups, especially when performing full (normal) backups. We cover Exchange backup and restoration more in Chapter 11.

The combination of storage groups and databases that you ultimately configure will depend on the needs of your network. However, with the limitation of 50 databases in 50 storage groups in Exchange Server 2007, it really doesn't make sense to design your Exchange implementation in any other way than with one database per storage group. When we examine highly available solutions in Chapter 10, this design will make even more sense.

Configuring the Hub Transport Server

The Hub Transport server role also will always be one of the first Exchange Server 2007 roles you'll install in your organization, whether it's on the same server as the Mailbox server role (and possibly the Client Access server) or on a dedicated server. Perhaps your Hub Transport servers will be highly available by virtue of more than one per Active Directory site being installed, or maybe your organization is smaller and a single Exchange server is all you need.

Whatever the case, the Hub Transport server will require that you perform some configuration and management actions before it is ready to perform its function in your organization.

Understanding the Message Routing Process

In previous versions of Exchange Server, a complex link-state routing algorithm was used to route messages between geographically separated Exchange Servers. Exchange used routing groups that were connected with routing group connectors to perform this routing. With the elimination of routing groups and link-state routing in Exchange Server 2007, all Exchange message routing is performed by Hub Transport servers using the Active Directory sites and site links that service Active Directory. As such, message routing (both within the same site and across site links) is significantly less complex in Exchange Server 2007.

Within each Active Directory site that contains a Mailbox server (or Unified Messaging server), you must have at least one Hub Transport server. The Hub Transport server is responsible for routing all messages within a site and between connected sites. Even a message that is sent from a recipient on Server A to another recipient on Server A must first cross through a Hub Transport server for delivery—a big change in message routing from Exchange Server 2003. When messages must be routed between sites, the Hub Transport server in the originating site determines the best route available at that time to the destination server and routes the message accordingly.

Message routing within a single Active Directory site occurs as detailed here:

1. The sending user submits the message to his or her mailbox on the Mailbox server that contains his or her mailbox. Using the Outlook client, the message is submitted via MAPI and written directly into the sending user's Outbox.
2. The Microsoft Exchange Mail Submission service, running on the Mailbox server of the sender, detects a message in a user's mailbox Outbox and randomly selects an available Hub Transport server in that Active Directory site.
3. The sending Mailbox server then submits a new message notification to the Exchange store driver on the Hub Transport server, which causes the Hub Transport server to retrieve the queued message from the user's Outbox on the Mailbox server via MAPI.
4. The store driver on the Hub Transport server then submits the message to the categorizer queue on the Hub Transport server for the categorizer to process. The categorizer moves a copy of the message from the user's Outbox to the Sent Items folder within the sending mailbox.
5. The Hub Transport server also performs any additional modifications on the message that the configuration of the Exchange organization requires. Such modifications might include stamping a disclaimer, blocking delivery of the message, or stripping undesirable attachments from the message.
6. The Hub Transport server then places a copy of the message into a local delivery queue, where the store driver running on the Hub Transport server delivers the message using an Exchange Data Objects connection to the Mailbox server where the recipient resides.

Configuring Hub Transport

Now that you've got a basic understanding of how the Exchange message routing process works, let's examine some common hub transport configuration tasks that you'll be performing on Hub Transport servers. We discuss more advanced configuration of the hub transport, such as managed folders and transport rules, in Chapter 7. To start the hub transport configuration, you'll need to locate the Hub Transport servers within the Exchange Management Console, as shown in Figure 4.18.

Configuring Server Settings

You use four property pages used to configure a Hub Transport server. To access the Hub Transport server properties, either you can right-click the Hub Transport server of concern and select Properties from the context menu or you can click the Properties link under the server options in the Actions pane on the right of the Exchange Management Console. Either way, the Properties dialog box shown in Figure 4.19 opens for you.

FIGURE 4.18 Viewing the Hub Transport servers

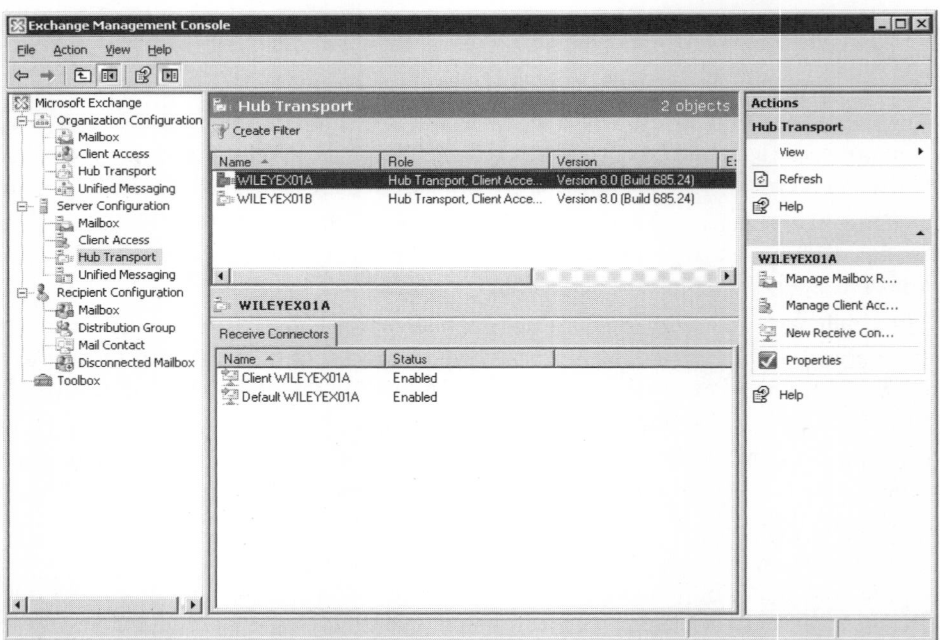

FIGURE 4.19 The General tab of the Hub Transport server's Properties dialog box

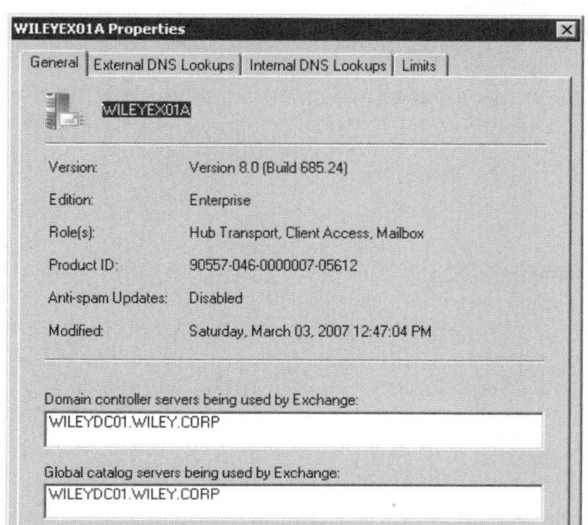

General

A Hub Transport server's General tab, shown in Figure 4.19, contains only one directly configurable option but displays information about many other items. The lone directly configurable option is whether to enable error reporting to Microsoft for this server.

You'll be able to view information about the following items on the General tab:

- The version and edition of Exchange installed on the server
- The roles installed on the Exchange server
- The product ID of the installed version of Exchange
- The status of antispam updates on the server
- The last time the Exchange configuration on the server was modified
- The domain controllers and global catalog servers in use by Exchange

External DNS Lookups

The External DNS Lookups tab, shown in Figure 4.20, allows you to configure how some send connectors perform DNS lookups. You can opt either to use the DNS server settings configured on all adapters (or just one adapter installed in the server) or to manually enter the DNS servers to be used for external DNS lookups. Typically you'll configure the Hub Transport server to use the same DNS servers as configured on the installed network adapters or some other internal DNS server. These internal DNS servers are typically configured to be able to forward unresolved queries to external DNS servers as needed.

Internal DNS Lookups

The External DNS Lookups tab, shown in Figure 4.21, allows you to configure how DNS lookups are performed internally to the organization. You can opt either to use the DNS server settings configured on all adapters (or just one adapter installed in the server) or to manually enter the DNS servers to be used for internal DNS lookups.

FIGURE 4.20 The External DNS Lookups tab of the Hub Transport server's Properties dialog box

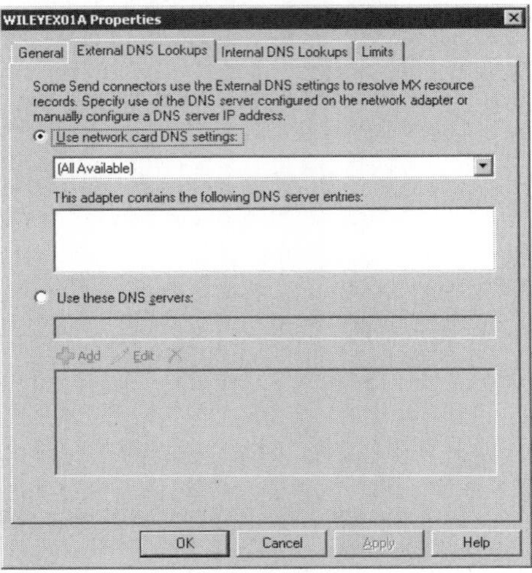

FIGURE 4.21 The Internal DNS Lookups tab of the Hub Transport server's Properties dialog box

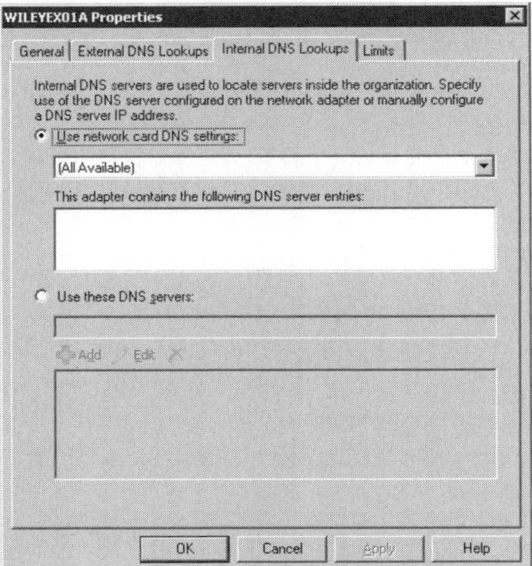

Limits

The Limits tab, shown in Figure 4.22, allows you to configure how the Hub Transport server attempts to deliver messages. The following options are available to configure:

- *Outbound Connection Failure Retry Interval (Minutes)*: Specifies the retry interval for subsequent connection attempts to a remote server where earlier connection attempts have failed. The default value is 10 minutes and is not recommended to be changed without guidance from Microsoft Product Support Services (PSS).
- *Transient Failure Retry Interval (Seconds)*: Specifies the retry interval between each connection attempt. The default value is 300 seconds (5 minutes).
- *Transient Failure Retry Attempts*: Specifies the maximum number of retry attempts the Hub Transport server should perform to immediately make a connection when it experiences a connection failure with a remote server. The default value is 6, and a setting of 0 forces the Hub Transport server not to attempt to immediately reconnect to the remote server.
- *Maximum Time Since Submission (Days)*: Specifies the timeout duration for messages. If a message is still in the queue to be delivered longer than this setting, the message is returned to the sender as undeliverable. The default setting is 2 days.
- *Notify Sender When Message Is Delayed More Than (Hours)*: Specifies when the sender of a message should be notified that a message has not yet been delivered. The default value is 4 hours.
- *Maximum Concurrent Outbound Connections*: Specifies the maximum number of outgoing connections that can be open at one time on the server. When the configured connection is reached, the server will open new connections until the current connections are closed. The default value is 1000.
- *Maximum Concurrent Outbound Connections per Domain*: Specifies how many connections should be allowed to a specific domain. The default value is 20.

FIGURE 4.22 The Limits tab of the Hub Transport server's Properties dialog box

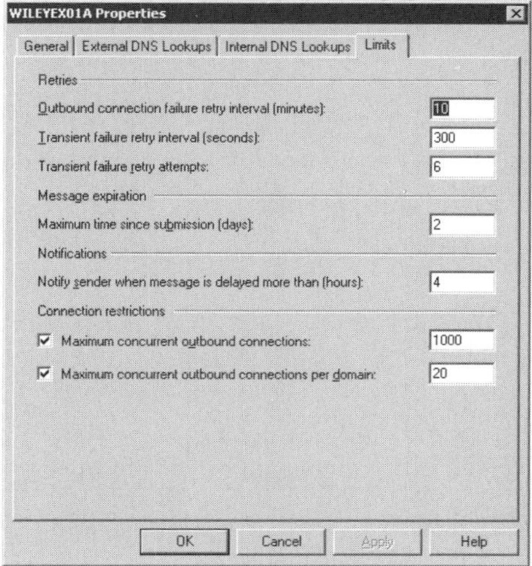

Configuring the Postmaster Mailbox

As we briefly discussed earlier in Chapter 3, "Installing Exchange Server 2007," there is no postmaster mailbox created by default when you install an Exchange Server 2007 organization. This is one of the most important mailboxes your Exchange organization will have, and you should create one as soon as possible after installing the Hub Transport server role on a server. The postmaster mailbox is required in every messaging infrastructure per RFC 2822 and receives nondelivery reports and delivery status notifications. These reports and notifications will be useful to you over time as you troubleshoot and respond to reports of message delivery problems within your Exchange organization.

Many organizations will opt to add just the postmaster alias to an existing mailbox user, such as the default built-in Administrator, but it's almost always better to create and configure a separate mailbox user account just for this purpose. To create and configure the postmaster mailbox, we'll jump ahead just a bit and look at creating and configuring mailbox users from within the Exchange Management Console, a topic covered fully later in Chapter 6. Exercise 4.4 outlines the steps for creating and configuring the postmaster mailbox.

EXERCISE 4.4

Creating and Configuring the Postmaster Mailbox

1. Click Start ➢ Programs ➢ Microsoft Exchange Server 2007, and then select Exchange Management Console.

2. Expand the Microsoft Exchange root object, expand the Recipient Configuration folder, and then click the Mailbox node, as shown here.

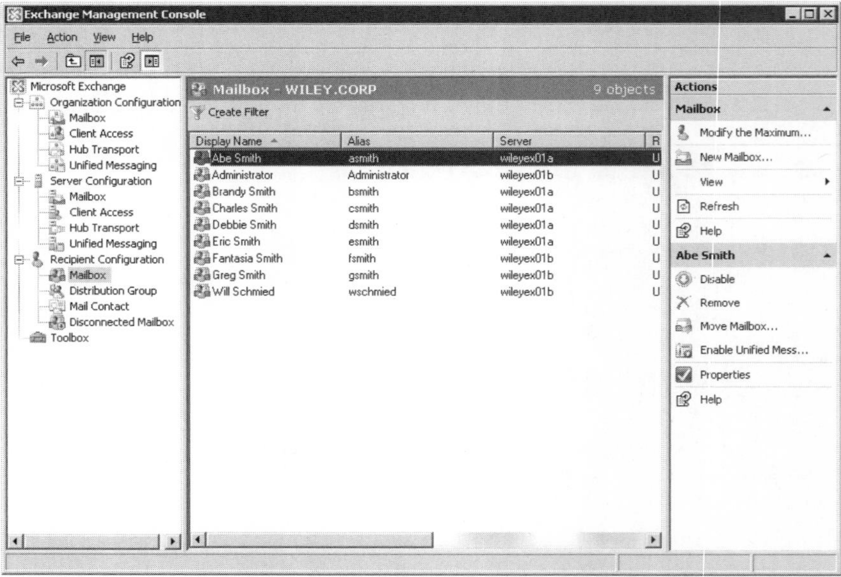

EXERCISE 4.4 *(continued)*

3. On the right of the Exchange Management Console, click the New Mailbox link under the Mailbox group. The New Mailbox Wizard appears, as shown here.

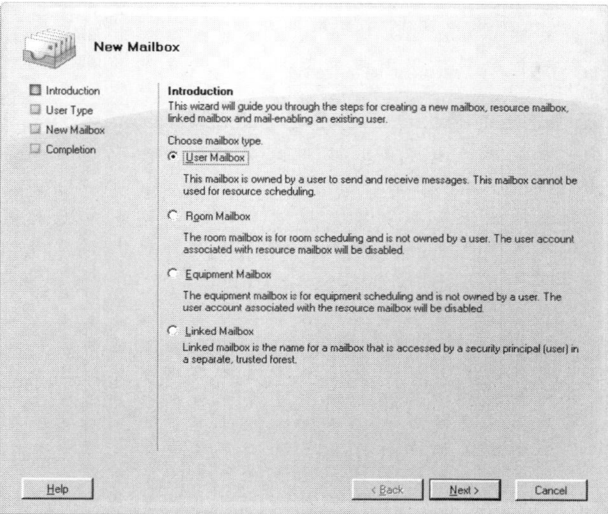

4. On the Introduction page, select User Mailbox, and click Next.
5. On the User Type page, select New User, and click Next.
6. On the User Information page, configure a new user, as shown here, that is appropriate for your environment. Click Next to continue.

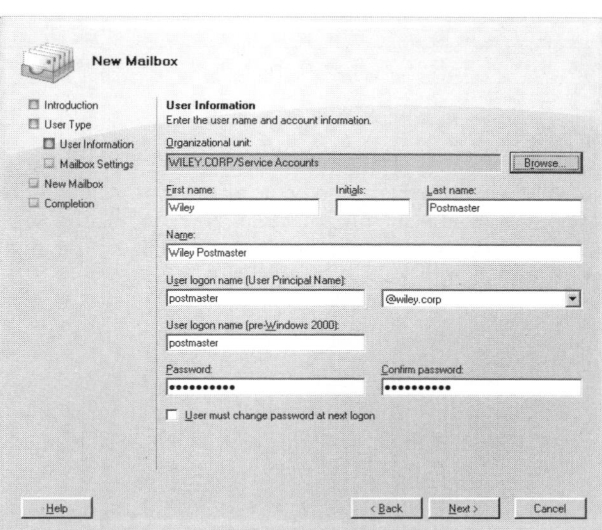

EXERCISE 4.4 *(continued)*

7. On the Mailbox Settings page, select the Mailbox server, storage group, and mailbox database that will contain the mailbox. Click Next to continue.

8. On the summary page, review the configuration, and click New to create the mailbox.

9. Click Finish to complete and close the wizard.

10. Now that the postmaster account and mailbox have been created, you will need to configure that mailbox as the postmaster address for the Exchange organization. You can do this via the Exchange Management Shell using the following command: `Set-TransportServer` *servername* `-ExternalPostmasterAddress` *postmaster e-mail address*. So, for our example organization, the actual command might look like this: `Set-TransportServer WILEYEX01A -ExternalPostmasterAddress postmaster@wiley.corp`. The result of this command is shown here.

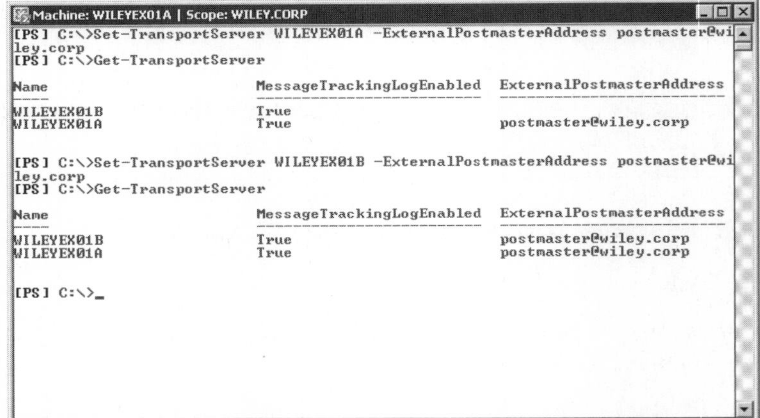

You will need to perform the postmaster configuration once for every Hub Transport server in the organization. You can use the `Get-TransportServer` command to view the configuration and make sure that all Hub Transport servers have been correctly configured.

Configuring Domains

You can configure, and thus control to some extent, domains from which Exchange Server 2007 is allowed to accept and send mail. To configure which email domains mail is allowed to be sent to, or to control how email is sent to a specific domain, you will need to create and configure remote domains. To configure which email domains inbound messages will be accepted for, you will need to create and configure accepted domains.

Remote Domains

A *remote domain* is always outside your Exchange organization. You can create and configure remote domains to control mail flow more exactly, such as specifying how delivery reports are handled and which character sets to used. Exercise 4.5 outlines the steps for creating a remote domain.

EXERCISE 4.5

Creating a Remote Domain

1. Click Start ➢ Programs ➢ Microsoft Exchange Server 2007, and then select Exchange Management Console.

2. Expand the Microsoft Exchange root object, expand the Organization Configuration folder, and then click the Hub Transport node, as shown here.

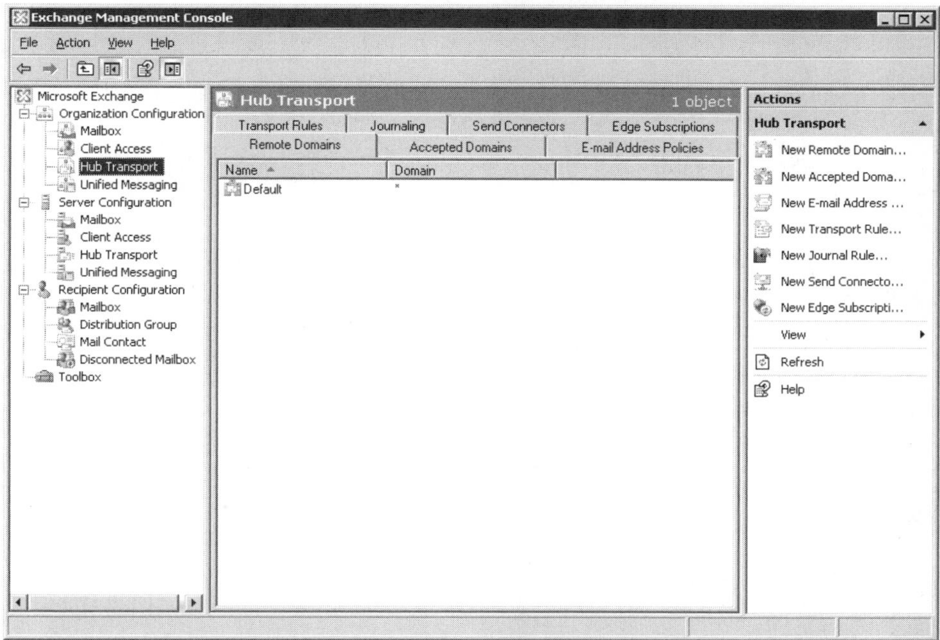

EXERCISE 4.5 *(continued)*

3. Click the New Remote Domain link under the hub transport options in the Actions pane on the right of the Exchange Management Console. The New Remote Domain Wizard opens, as shown here.

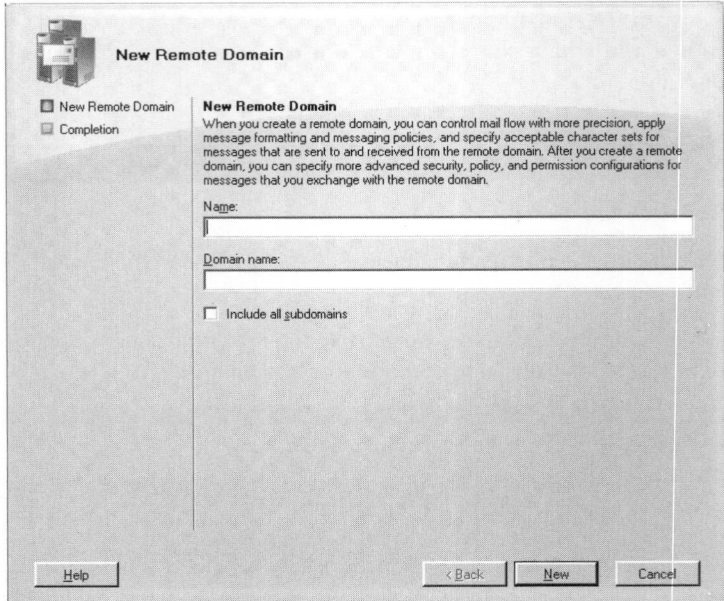

4. Enter a descriptive name and an SMTP domain name. You may want to check the Include All Subdomains box to allow global configuration for this SMTP domain. Click the New button to proceed.

5. As usual, you will be presented with a summary of what Exchange did and also given the chance to copy the actual PowerShell code used to perform the configuration. Click Finish to close the wizard.

You can create a remote domain from the Exchange Management Shell by using the following command to create a remote domain, including all subdomains, for the Cliffs Notes SMTP domain:

```
new-RemoteDomain -Name 'Cliffs Notes' -DomainName '*.cliffsnotes.com'
```

Figure 4.23 shows the results of this configuration action.

FIGURE 4.23 Creating a remote domain from the Exchange Management Shell

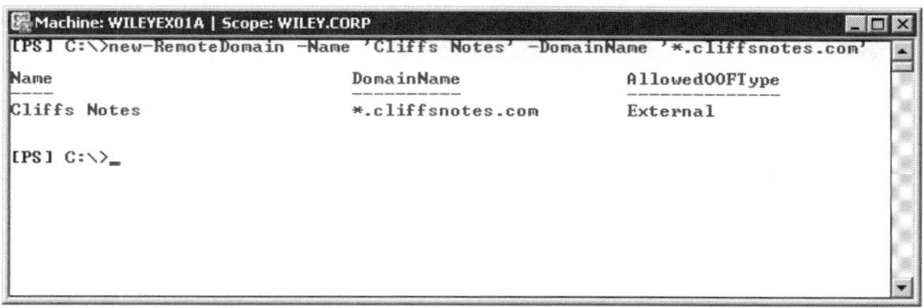

The SMTP domain name field is limited to 256 characters in length.

You can see the results of your remote domain creation efforts by looking at the Exchange Management Console, as shown in Figure 4.24.

FIGURE 4.24 Viewing remote domains in the Exchange Management Console

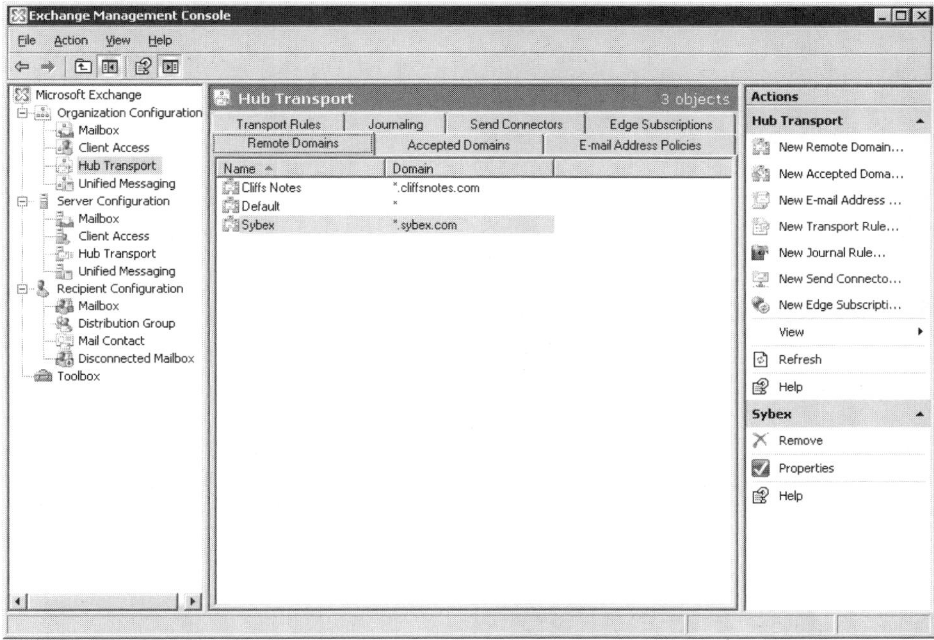

Regardless of how you create the remote domain object, two configuration tabs are available for you to configure afterward. You can open the remote domain's Properties dialog box by right-clicking the remote domain and selecting Properties from the context menu or by clicking the Properties link under the remote domain options in Actions pane on the right of the Exchange Management Console.

The remote domain's Properties dialog box opens to the General tab, as shown in Figure 4.25. From the General tab, you can rename the remote domain object and configure how out-of-office (OOF) messages should be handled when senders from the remote SMTP domain send messages to an internal user who has OOF configured on his mailbox. The default setting is to allow external messages only.

The Message Format tab of the remote domain's Properties, shown in Figure 4.26, allows you to configure several options that control how the messages sent to the remote domain are handled. You can enable or disable processes such as delivery and nondelivery reports, configure rich-text settings, and even configure a character set to be used for messages to the remote domain. These settings give you much more flexibility than in previous versions of Exchange as to which messages should leave your Exchange organization and also what they should look like.

Accepted Domains

An *accepted domain* may or may not be within your Exchange organization or Active Directory forest, but it's almost certain to be a domain with which you have an administrative relationship, such as a partner domain or a domain within another Active Directory forest in your company or organization.

Accepted domains are used to specify for which SMTP domains the Exchange server organization will accept and/or route messages. By default, the first accepted domain is created for you when the Exchange organization is created. You can create and configure additional accepted domains as needed or just make changes to the default accepted domain that was created automatically. Exercise 4.6 outlines the steps for creating an accepted domain.

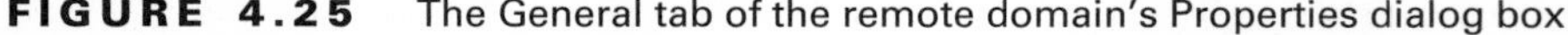

FIGURE 4.25 The General tab of the remote domain's Properties dialog box

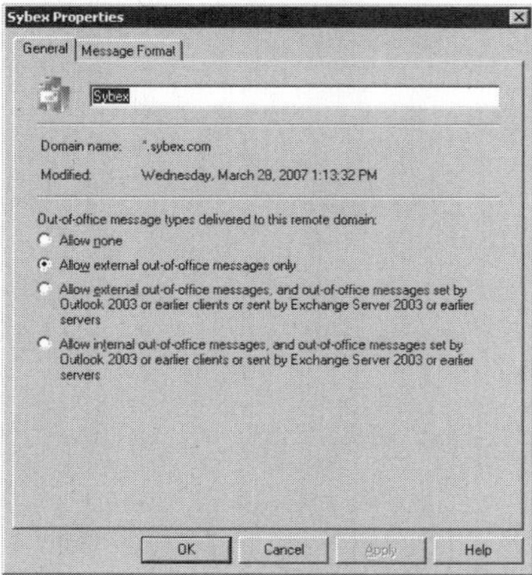

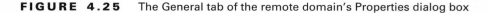

FIGURE 4.26 The Message Format tab of the remote domain's Properties dialog box

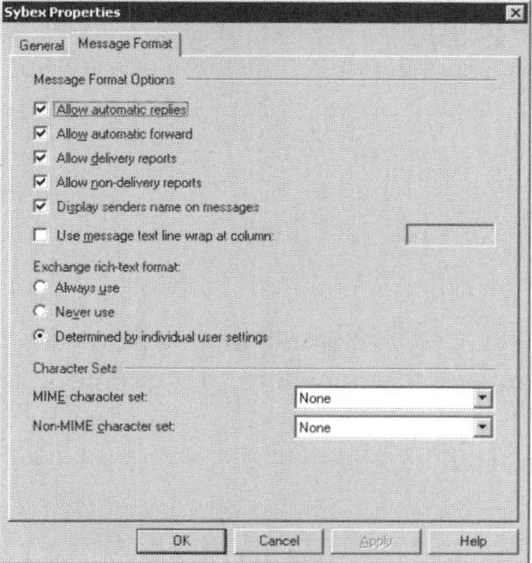

EXERCISE 4.6

Creating an Accepted Domain

1. Click Start ➢ Programs ➢ Microsoft Exchange Server 2007, and then select Exchange Management Console.
2. Expand the Microsoft Exchange root object, expand the Organization Configuration folder, and then click the Hub Transport node.
3. Click the New Accepted Domain link under the hub transport options in the Actions pane on the right of the Exchange Management Console. The New Accepted Domain Wizard opens, as shown here.

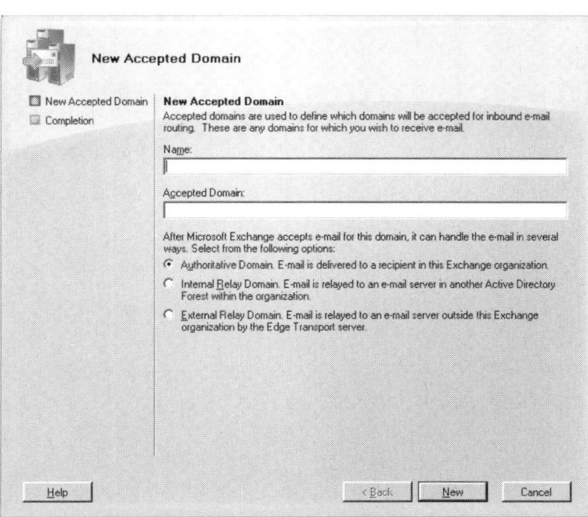

EXERCISE 4.6 *(continued)*

4. Enter a descriptive name and an SMTP domain name. You will also need to select how Exchange should route the messages that are received to this SMTP domain. For organizations that have multiple external domain names but only a single Exchange organization, leave the default first option selected. If you have multiple Active Directory forests in your organization and they each have mail systems other than this Exchange organization, select the second option. If you are routing mail to a server outside your organization, then you may want to select the third option. Click New once you've made your selection.

5. As usual, you will be presented with a summary of what Exchange did and also given the chance to copy the actual PowerShell code used to perform the configuration. Click Finish to close the wizard.

You can create an accepted domain from the Exchange Management Shell by using the following command to create an accepted domain for the Wrox SMTP domain:

```
new-AcceptedDomain -Name 'Wrox' -DomainName 'wrox.com'
-DomainType 'Authoritative'
```

Figure 4.27 shows the results of this configuration action.

Regardless of how you go about creating the accepted domain object, there is just one configuration tab available for you to configure afterward. You can open the accepted domain's Properties dialog box either by right-clicking the accepted domain and selecting Properties from the context menu or by clicking the Properties link under the accepted domain options in the Actions pane on the right of the Exchange Management Console.

On the General tab of the accepted domain's Properties dialog box, shown in Figure 4.28, you'll have the opportunity to change the friendly name of the accepted domain object and to change the type of accepted domain it is, as outlined previously in Exercise 4.6.

FIGURE 4.27 Creating an accepted domain from the Exchange Management Shell

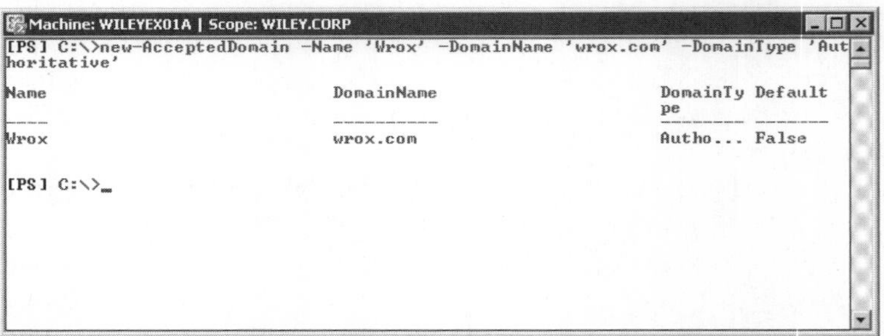

FIGURE 4.28 The General tab of the accepted domain's Properties dialog box

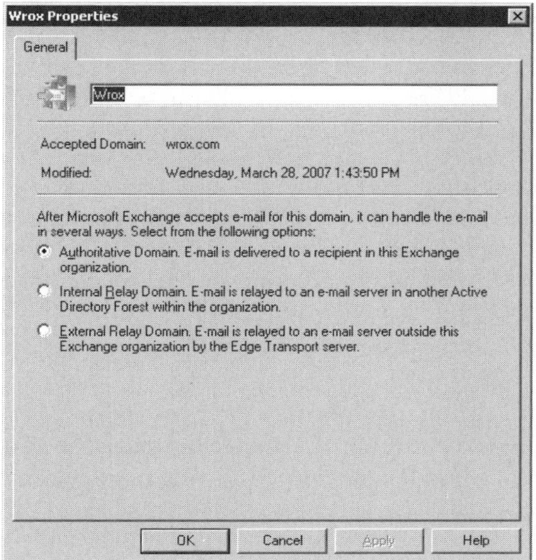

Once you configure accepted domains, you'll want to configure address policies. We cover address policies in Chapter 7.

Configuring SMTP Connectors

Two types of SMTP connectors exist in Exchange Server 2007: send connectors and receive connectors. Hub Transport servers use connectors to send and receive mail amongst themselves and also to transfer mail to and from Edge Transport servers or another SMTP device responsible for the routing of SMTP traffic in the organization's external network. Hub Transport servers use invisible send connectors that are automatically configured according to the Active Directory site topology to send messages internally amongst themselves. However, no default configuration is in place to ensure end-to-end mail from outside the organization to inside, and vice versa. You will need to create and configure the appropriate SMTP connectors to make this happen.

How you go about making these SMTP connectors, however, will depend on the installation and configuration of your Exchange organization. If you are in the recommended configuration that has Edge Transport servers in the DMZ, you'll need to use the Edge Subscription service to subscribe an Edge Transport server to an Active Directory site, thus allowing replication of recipient and configuration data into an Active Directory Application Mode (ADAM) instance on the Edge Transport server. When you complete the subscription process for an Edge Transport server to an Active Directory site, the following default SMTP connectors are created by the Microsoft Exchange EdgeSync service:

- An implicit send connector from the Hub Transport servers to the Edge Transport server
- A send connector from the Edge Transport server to the Hub Transport servers in the Active Directory site to which the Edge Transport server was subscribed
- A wildcard (*) send connector from the Edge Transport server to the Internet

These SMTP connectors allow full end-to-end SMTP message routing in and out of the Exchange organization; thus, having the Edge Transport servers correctly configured with the Edge Subscription service is the easiest way to create all of your default SMTP connectors. After the defaults are created, you can always create additional connectors and make additional configurations if needed.

However, if you are not using Edge Transport servers, either because you are routing mail directly to your Hub Transport servers from the Internet or because you have some other SMTP device performing SMTP routing in your external network, you will need to manually configure at least one SMTP send connector for your Exchange organization. This SMTP send connector should be a wildcard (*) SMTP connector, allowing mail delivery to all SMTP domains.

Configuring SMTP Send Connectors

For the purposes of this chapter and the specific discussion about Hub Transport servers, we'll assume your Exchange organization is one without an Edge Transport server. In that scenario, either mail flow is handled by some other SMTP device in your external network (the DMZ) or, in the worst possible case, SMTP traffic is directed straight to the Hub Transport server from the Internet. Either way, you need an SMTP send connector to get mail messages out of the Exchange organization and on their way to their final recipients.

We'll examine Edge Transport servers and the Edge Subscription process in detail in Chapter 5, "Configuring the Exchange Security Infrastructure."

Exercise 4.7 outlines the steps for creating an SMTP send connector.

EXERCISE 4.7

Creating an SMTP Send Connector

1. Click Start ➢ Programs ➢ Microsoft Exchange Server 2007, and then select Exchange Management Console.
2. Expand the Microsoft Exchange root object, expand the Organization Configuration folder, and then click the Hub Transport node.

EXERCISE 4.7 *(continued)*

3. Click the New Send Connector link under the hub transport options in the Actions pane on the right of the Exchange Management Console. The New SMTP Send Connector Wizard opens, as shown here.

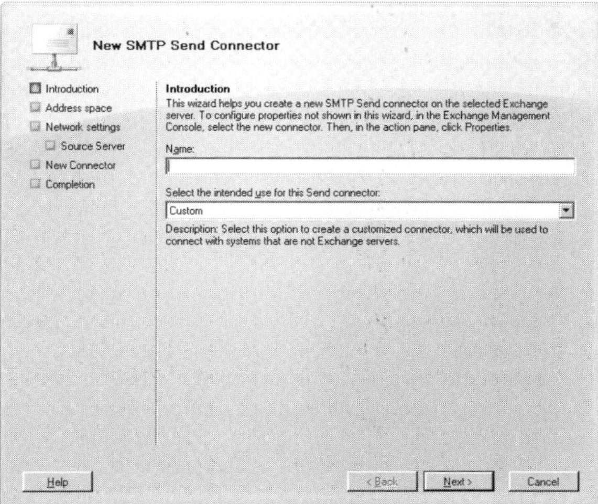

4. Provide a descriptive name for the send connector, such as **Internet SMTP Connector**, and then select the Internet option from the drop-down menu. Click Next to continue to the Address Space page.

5. On the Address Space page, configure the default wildcard address of * by clicking the Add button and entering an asterisk (*) in the Add Address Space dialog box. Click OK to close the dialog box and return to the Address Space page. Click Next to continue to the Network Settings page shown here.

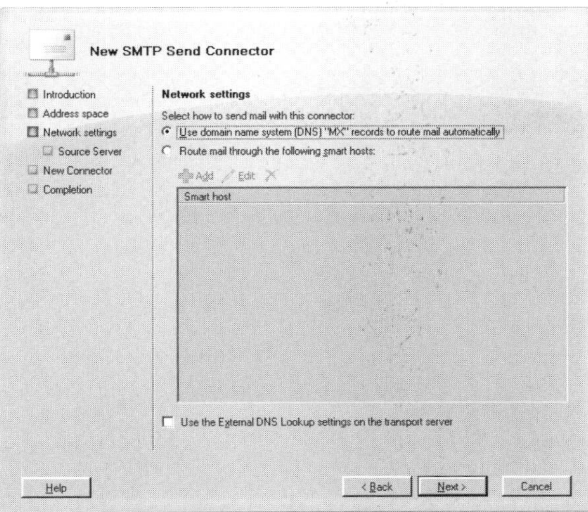

EXERCISE 4.7 *(continued)*

6. On the Network Settings page, you will need either to allow the connector to use DNS MX records to route mail or to configure a smart host to route the mail. A smart host would be any SMTP device in your external network that can perform DNS queries and route SMTP traffic accordingly. Many organizations have existing appliance devices or third-party applications that provide this function; thus, they won't be using an Edge Transport server. When you've made your selections, click Next to continue to the Source Server page.
7. On the Source Server page, you will be able to select which servers will be allowed to send SMTP messages through the send connector. Be careful not to select any server that you previously selected as a smart host on the Network Settings page. Add any other Exchange servers that should be allowed to send SMTP messages directly to the Internet (the fewer, the better for security's sake) or to your smart host. Then, click Next to continue.
8. You'll be presented with a summary page allowing you to review your configuration. Click New to create the send connector.
9. As usual, you will be presented with a summary of what Exchange did and also given the chance to copy the actual PowerShell code used to perform the configuration. Click Finish to close the wizard.

You can also create a send connector from the Exchange Management Shell by using a command similar to this one:

```
new-SendConnector -Name 'Internet SMTP Connector (WILEYEX01B)'
-Usage 'Internet' -AddressSpaces 'smtp:*;1' -DNSRoutingEnabled $true
-UseExternalDNSServersEnabled $false -SourceTransportServers 'WILEYEX01B'
```

Figure 4.29 shows the results of this configuration action.

FIGURE 4.29 Creating a send connector from the Exchange Management Shell

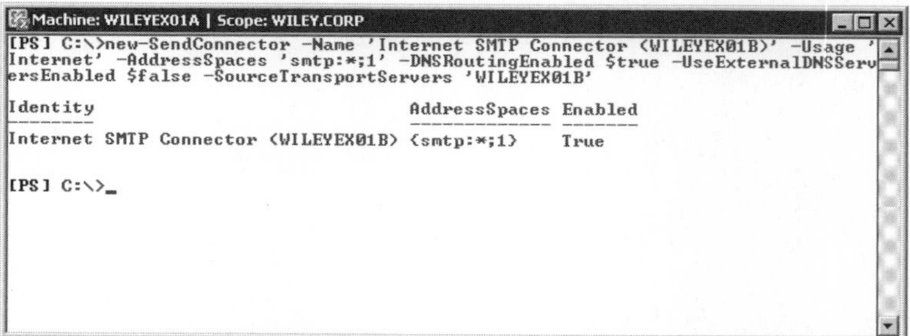

Regardless of how you create the send connector, four configuration tabs are available for you to configure afterward. You can open the send connector's Properties dialog box either by right-clicking the send connector and selecting Properties from the context menu or by clicking the Properties link under the send connector options in the Actions pane on the right of the Exchange Management Console.

GENERAL

On the General tab of the send connector's Properties dialog box, shown in Figure 4.30, you'll have the opportunity to change the friendly name of the send connector as well as to specify the protocol logging level and the fully qualified domain name (FQDN) that the send connector will return in reply to the HELO or EHLO queries. The logging level options are pretty simple: either none (logging off) or verbose (logging on). If no FQDN entry is made on the General tab, the connector will return the FQDN of the authoritative SMTP domain in the Exchange organization to which the Hub Transport server belongs.

ADDRESS SPACE

On the Address Space tab of the send connector's Properties dialog box, shown in Figure 4.31, you'll be able to change, add, or delete the address spaces that are covered by this send connector.

FIGURE 4.30 The General tab of the send connector's Properties dialog box

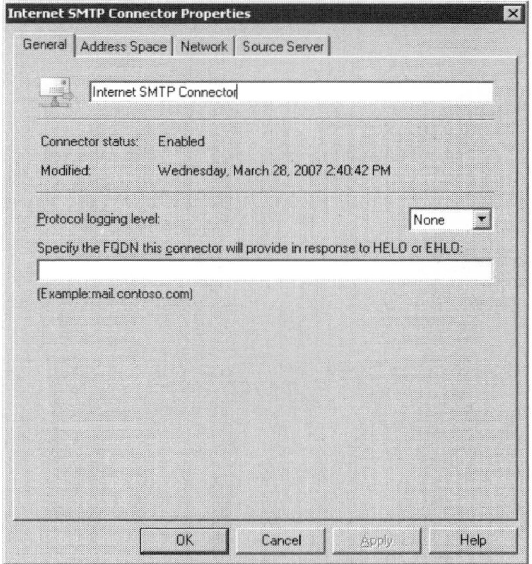

NETWORK

On the Network tab of the send connector's Properties dialog box, shown in Figure 4.32, you have several options to change the network configuration of the send connector. The only option that is not directly available during the creation process of the send connector is the Enable Domain Security (Mutual Auth TLS) option. This is actually the same as selecting the Partner option where previously we selected the Internet option in Exercise 4.7. This option will allow you to configure a send connector to a specific partner's SMTP address space and to attempt to make a connection with TLS security for all messages going out of that connector.

FIGURE 4.31 The Address Space tab of the send connector's Properties dialog box

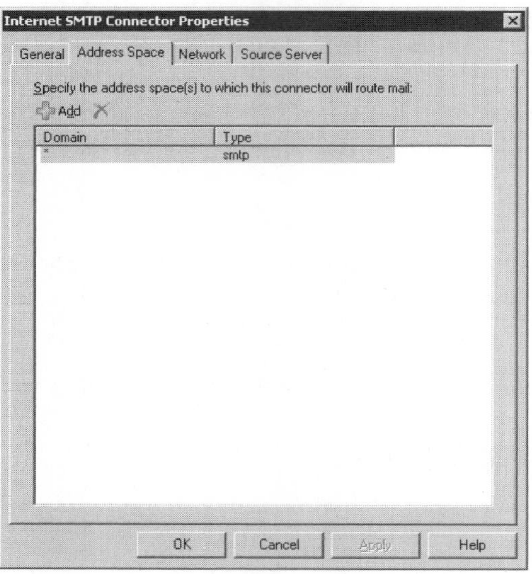

FIGURE 4.32 The Network tab of the send connector's Properties dialog box

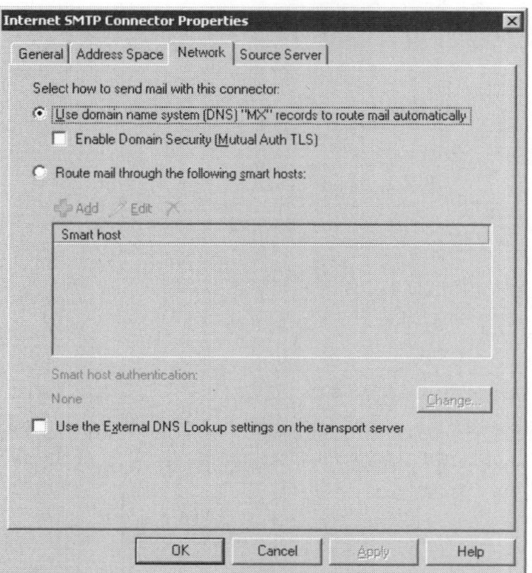

Of course, it's not as easy as checking a box to enable TLS security to a partner address space—it never is. You'll need to perform several other tasks that are outside the scope of this exam if you're interested in using Domain Security. They include the following: import the TLS certificate into your Edge Transport servers, import the TLS certificate into your Edge Transport servers, configure inbound domain and outbound domain security, and test mail flow and verify TLS protection is in place.

SOURCE SERVER

The Source Server tab of the send connector's Properties dialog box, shown in Figure 4.33, provides no new configuration options but does allow you to change, add, or delete the source servers that should be allowed to send SMTP messages across this send connector.

FIGURE 4.33 The Source Server tab of the send connector's Properties dialog box

Configuring SMTP Receive Connectors

By default, the Exchange installation process creates two default SMTP receive connectors on each Hub Transport server:

- The default SMTP receive connector, Client *servername*, accepts mail on TCP port 587, which is the default port for receiving messages from all non-MAPI clients for SMTP relay. The connector accepts mail on all installed network adapters in the Hub Transport server by default and also accepts the inbound messages from all IP addresses on the network by default and will accept mail from any client.

- The default SMTP receive connector, Client *servername*, accepts mail on TCP port 25, which is the default port for receiving messages from SMTP clients. The connector accepts mail on all installed network adapters in the Hub Transport server by default and also accepts the inbound messages from all IP addresses on the network by default, but only from Exchange servers. Additionally, this connector will not accept anonymous submissions.

The default SMTP receive connectors are visible for each Hub Transport server in the Exchange organization by examining the Server Configuration ➤ Hub Transport node of the Exchange Management Console, as shown in Figure 4.34.

FIGURE 4.34 The default SMTP receive connectors viewed in the Exchange Management Console

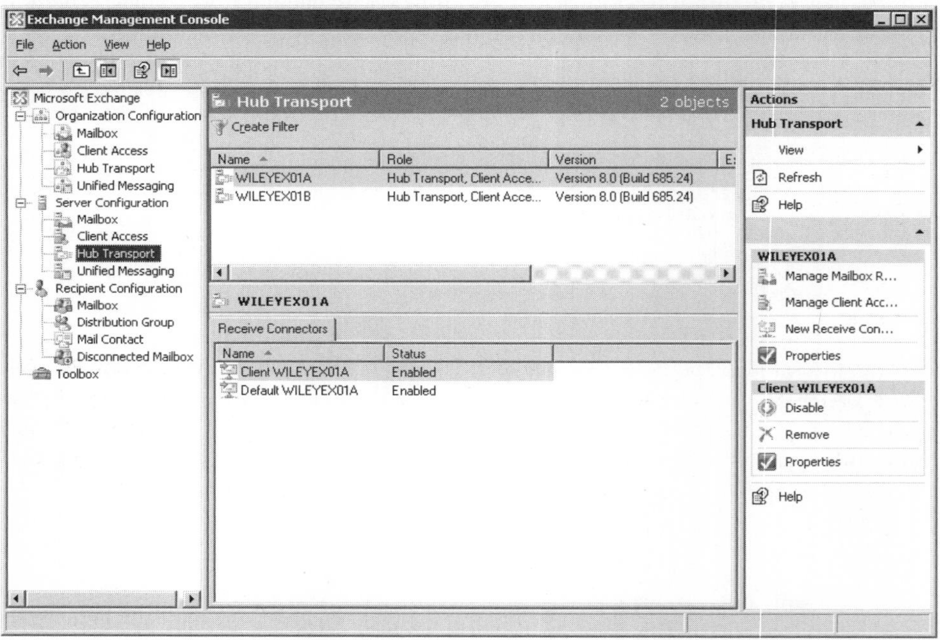

Exercise 4.8 outlines the steps for creating an SMTP receive connector.

EXERCISE 4.8

Creating an SMTP Receive Connector

1. Click Start ➤ Programs ➤ Microsoft Exchange Server 2007, and then select Exchange Management Console.

2. Expand the Microsoft Exchange root object, expand the Server Configuration folder, and then click the Hub Transport node.

EXERCISE 4.8 *(continued)*

3. Select the server to configure the receive connector on, and then click the New Receive Connector link under the server options in the Actions pane on the right of the Exchange Management Console. The New SMTP Receive Connector Wizard opens, as shown here.

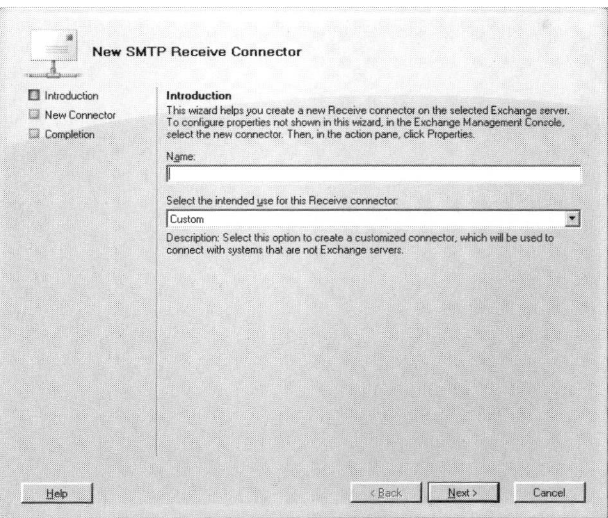

4. Provide a descriptive name for the receive connector, such as **Monitoring System Receive SMTP Connector**, and then select the appropriate option from the drop-down menu. In this example, select the Custom option to create a receive connector for receiving SMTP messages from an internal server monitoring application. Click Next to continue to the Local Network Settings page, as shown here.

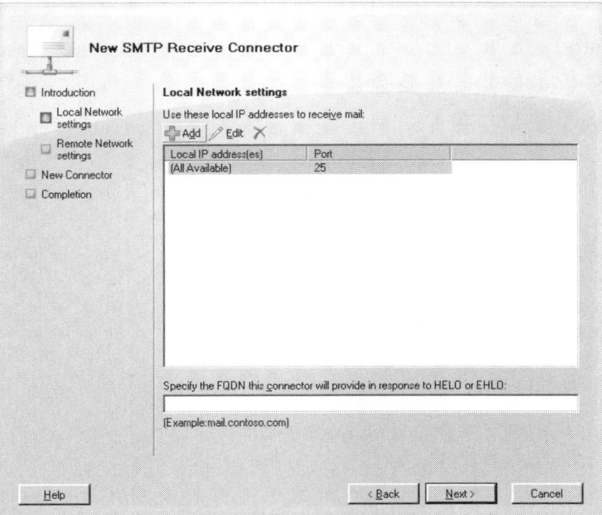

EXERCISE 4.8 *(continued)*

5. On the Local Network Settings page, configure the IP addresses and TCP ports on which the receive connector should accept inbound messages. The default of (All Available) on port 25 will be suitable in most cases. Click Next to continue to the Remote Network Settings page, as shown here.

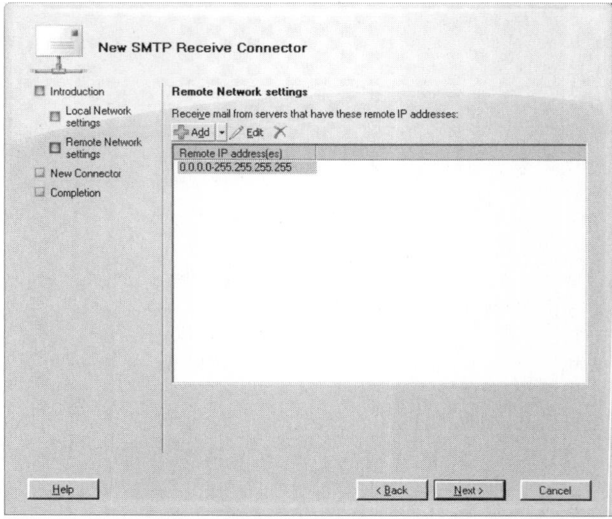

6. On the Remote Networks Settings page, you can leave the default selection of all IP addresses or edit the listing to specify just those servers you want to allow inbound mail from using this receive connector. In the example of an internal server monitoring application, you might want to configure this list to just include the IP addresses of the server hosting that monitoring application. Click Next to continue.

7. You'll be presented with a summary page allowing you to review your configuration. Click New to create the send connector.

8. As usual, you will be presented with a summary of what Exchange did and also given the chance to copy the actual PowerShell code used to perform the configuration. Click Finish to close the wizard.

You can also create a receive connector from the Exchange Management Shell by using a command similar to this one, which creates a custom receive connector that accepts messages only from an internal pager server:

```
new-ReceiveConnector -Name 'Pager System Receive SMTP Connector'
-Usage 'Custom' -Bindings '0.0.0.0:25'
-RemoteIPRanges '192.168.0.242-192.168.0.242' -Server 'WILEYEX01A'
```

Figure 4.35 shows the results of this configuration action.

FIGURE 4.35 Creating a receive connector from the Exchange Management Shell

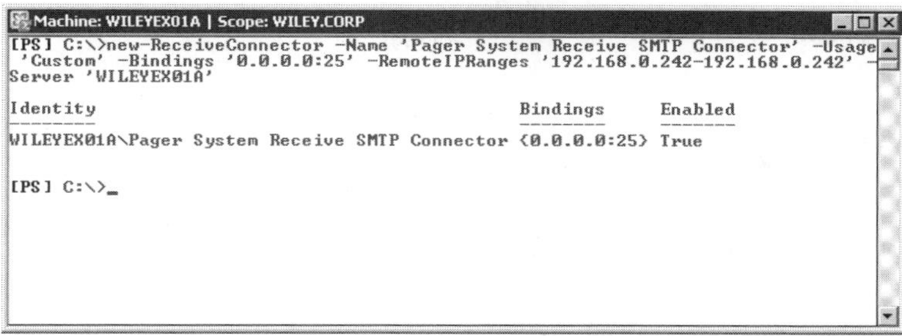

Regardless of how you create the receive connector, four configuration tabs are available for you to configure afterward. You can open the receive connector Properties dialog box either by right-clicking the receive connector and selecting Properties from the context menu or by clicking the Properties link under the receive connector options in the Actions pane on the right of the Exchange Management Console.

GENERAL

On the General tab of the receive connector's Properties dialog box, shown in Figure 4.36, you'll have the opportunity to change the friendly name of the receive connector as well as specify the protocol logging level and the fully qualified domain name (FQDN) that the receive connector will return in reply to the HELO or EHLO queries. The logging level options are pretty simple: either none (logging off) or verbose (logging on).

FIGURE 4.36 The General tab of the receive connector's Properties dialog box

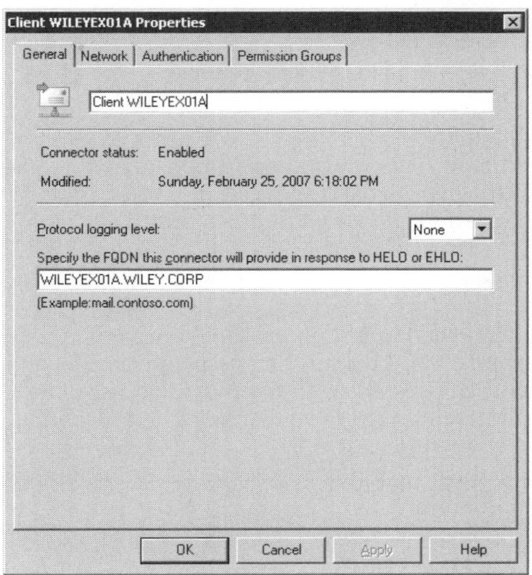

NETWORK

On the Network tab of the receive connector's Properties dialog box, shown in Figure 4.37, you can change the local IP addresses and ports the connector will receive SMTP messages on as well as the remote IP addresses that are allowed to send messages through the receive connector.

The combination of the local IP address, local TCP port, and remote IP address range must be unique and cannot be duplicated by any other receive connector on *that specific* Hub Transport server. You can, however, create the same receive connector on multiple Hub Transport servers.

AUTHENTICATION

On the Authentication tab of the receive connector's Properties dialog box, shown in Figure 4.38, you can configure the authentication method to be used on the receive connector. Table 4.2 describes each method available.

TABLE 4.2 Receive Connector Authentication Methods

Authentication Type	Description
None selected	No authentication configured.
Transport Layer Security (TLS)	Configures the server to advertise STARTTLS when connection attempts are made to remote systems. TLS requires that a server certificate be installed.
Basic Authentication	Uses standard authentication, which transmits credentials in clear text.
Exchange Server	Uses an Exchange authentication method, such as TLS or Kerberos through TLS.
Integrated Authentication	Uses Integrated Windows authentication, which includes NTLM (NT LAN Manager) and Kerberos. This is a good solution if both sides of the connection are Windows-based systems.
Externally Secured	Used when the other end of the connection is secured by some other external means, such as use of a private network or Internet Protocol Security (IPSec). Configuring this option tells Exchange that the connection is secured, even though the Exchange server cannot actually verify this fact. You must also select the Exchange server's permissions group on the Permissions Group tab when using this method.

FIGURE 4.37 The Network tab of the receive connector's Properties dialog box

Client WILEYEX01A Properties

General | Network | Authentication | Permission Groups

Use these local IP addresses to receive mail:

Add | Edit

Local IP address(es)	Port
(All Available)	587

Receive mail from remote servers that have these IP addresses:

Add | Edit

Remote IP address(es)
0.0.0.0-255.255.255.255

OK | Cancel | Apply | Help

FIGURE 4.38 The Authentication tab of the receive connector's Properties dialog box

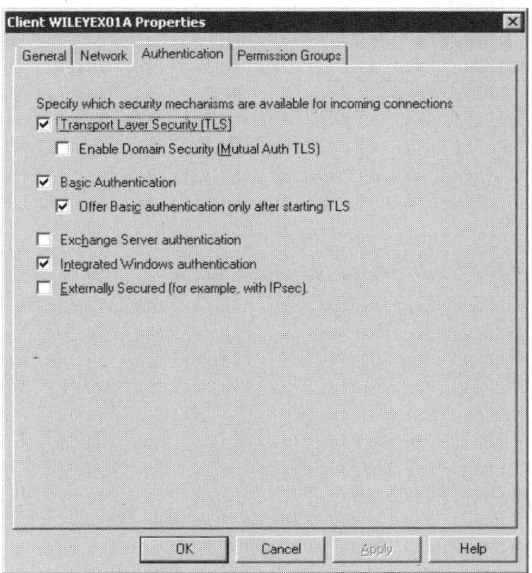

PERMISSION GROUPS

On the Permission Groups tab of the receive connector's Properties dialog box, shown in Figure 4.39, you can select the permissions groups associated with this receive connector. Permissions groups are predefined sets of permissions that are granted to well-known security principals such as users, computers, and security groups. A permissions group defines the permissions that are then assigned to security principals. Table 4.3 outlines the permissions groups, the corresponding security principals, and the specific Exchange permissions allowed to each.

FIGURE 4.39 The Permission Groups tab of the receive connector's Properties dialog box

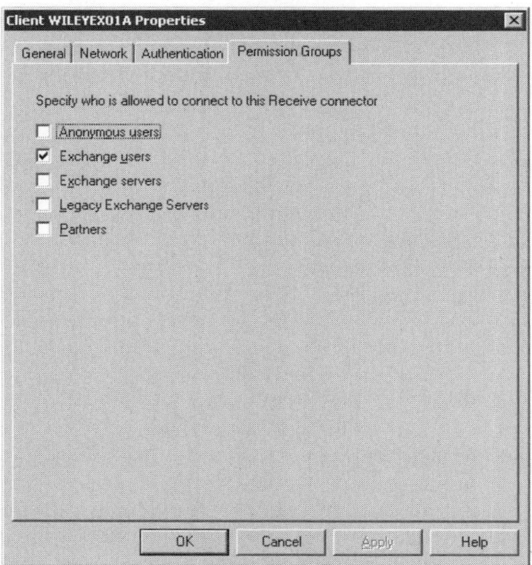

TABLE 4.3 Receive Connector Permissions Groups

Permission Group	Member Security Principals	Exchange Permissions Granted
Anonymous users	Anonymous user account	Ms-Exch-SMTP-Submit Ms-Exch-SMTP-Accept-Any-Sender Ms-Exch-SMTP-Accept-Authoritative-Domain-Sender Ms-Exch-Accept-Headers-Routing
Exchange users	Authenticated user accounts	Ms-Exch-SMTP-Submit Ms-Exch-SMTP-Accept-Any-Recipient Ms-Exch-Bypass-Anti-Spam Ms-Exch-Accept-Headers-Routing

TABLE 4.3 Receive Connector Permissions Groups *(continued)*

Permission Group	Member Security Principals	Exchange Permissions Granted
Exchange servers	Hub Transport servers Edge Transport servers Exchange Servers security group (on the Hub Transport server only) Externally Secured servers	Ms-Exch-SMTP-Submit Ms-Exch-SMTP-Accept-Any-Sender Ms-Exch-SMTP-Accept-Any-Recipient Ms-Exch-Accept-Authoritative-Domain-Sender Ms-Exch-Bypass-Anti-Spam Ms-Exch-SMTP-Accept-Authentication-Flag Ms-Exch-Bypass-Message-Size-Limit Ms-Exch-Accept-Headers-Routing Ms-Exch-Accept-Exch50 Ms-Exch-Accept-Headers-Organization (Externally Secured servers only) Ms-Exch-Accept-Headers-Forest (Not granted to Externally Secured servers)
Legacy Exchange servers	Exchange Legacy Interop security group	Ms-Exch-SMTP-Submit Ms-Exch-SMTP-Accept-Any-Sender Ms-Exch-SMTP-Accept-Any-Recipient Ms-Exch-Accept-Authoritative-Domain-Sender Ms-Exch-Bypass-Anti-Spam Ms-Exch-SMTP-Accept-Authentication-Flag Ms-Exch-Bypass-Message-Size-Limit Ms-Exch-Accept-Headers-Routing Ms-Exch-Accept-Exch50
Partners	Partner Server account	Ms-Exch-SMTP-Submit Ms-Exch-Accept-Headers-Routing

In the example where we created a receive connector to receive messages from our server monitoring application or internal pager server, we didn't select any permissions groups during the creation process. As such, the receive connector should receive messages from any source. If the messages are being submitted using a known service account, you could consider configuring the Exchange Users option to secure the receive connector somewhat. By comparison, the default receive connectors do have permissions groups configured on them. The Client *servername* receive connector is configured with only the Exchange users permissions group as being allowed to send messages through it. The Default *servername* connector is configured to allow the Exchange users, Exchange server, and legacy Exchange servers permissions groups to send messages through it.

Deleting SMTP Connectors

The process of deleting SMTP connectors is much simpler than the creation and configuration process for the SMTP connector. Just select the send or receive SMTP connector in the Exchange Management Console, right-click it, and select Remove from the context menu. Alternatively, you can click the Remove link under the connector options in the Actions pane on the right of the Exchange Management Console.

If you're not certain you will no longer need the SMTP connector but don't want it to be available for use, you can opt instead to disable it using the same process as earlier, but select Disable instead of Remove.

Configuring the Client Access Server

The Client Access server role will also almost always be present in any Exchange organization, especially given the prevalence of Outlook Web Access and Windows Mobile devices using ActiveSync now. Like Mailbox servers, Client Access servers can be configured for high availability, but not through clustering. Client Access servers can be, and should be, made highly available using network load balancing. Whatever your exact organization design calls for, the Client Access server will require that you perform some configuration and management actions before it is ready to perform its function in your organization.

Understanding the Client Access Process

If you have only Outlook MAPI clients, you don't actually need Client Access servers in your Exchange organization. Of course, even if you have only Outlook MAPI clients (meaning you're not even using Outlook Web Access), the Client Access server does provide some other nice functions, such as Outlook Autodiscover and the Availability service, that you'll want in place. Before we get into the configuration of the Client Access server, let's first examine how the Client Access server assists those non-MAPI client sessions in accessing a mailbox.

The Client Access server must be part of the Active Directory domain; thus, it needs to be inside the firewall and not directly exposed to the DMZ or the Internet. You need to open only the specific client access ports of concern to the Client Access server from outside the organization.

The following are some common non-MAPI client types you are likely to encounter:

- Outlook Web Access (OWA)
- Outlook Anywhere (replaces HTTP over RPC in Exchange Server 2003)
- Exchange ActiveSync (for Windows Mobile or third-party ActiveSync-compatible devices)
- POP3 or IMAP4 client applications

The Client Access server should also exist in every Active Directory site where a Mailbox server resides for best performance and reliability. Unlike the Hub Transport server, this is not an absolute requirement, however.

When a non-MAPI client needs to access a mailbox stored on an Exchange Server 2007 Mailbox server, the following basic steps occur:

1. The non-MAPI client contacts the Client Access server using whichever client access protocol is used, such as POP3 or HTTP.
2. The Client Access server connects to a domain controller using Kerberos to attempt to authenticate the user. The Internet Information Services (IIS) component on the Client Access server performs this authentication.
3. If the authentication was successful, the Client Access server next performs an LDAP query to an available global catalog server to locate the Mailbox server that houses the requested mailbox.
4. The Client Access server next connects to the required Mailbox server using MAPI over RPC. Messages can now be read from the mailbox or submitted to the database for routing. For all client protocols except POP3 and IMAP4, submitted messages are routed as discussed previously in the "Understanding the Message Routing Process" section earlier in this chapter. For POP3 and IMAP4 clients, submitted messages are sent directly to an SMTP server, which would be either a Hub Transport server accessible from the Internet or an Edge Transport server.

All communications between the Client Access server and the Mailbox server occur using only MAPI over RPC. This is a major change from previous versions of Exchange, where the front-end Exchange server would contact the back-end Exchange server using whichever protocol the client itself was using.

Configuring Client Access

Now that we've briefly examined the client access process, let's discuss the configuration of the more common Client Access server configuration and management items you'll need to perform. You'll examine Outlook Web Access, Outlook Anywhere, mobile device management, basic client security, and a few more advanced client access options. Additionally, you'll look at some other Client Access server configuration options in Chapter 7 and Chapter 8.

Configuring and Managing Outlook Web Access

Outlook Web Access (OWA) in Exchange Server 2007 is, in a word, great. The interface almost exactly mimics that of Outlook 2007, and it works "out of the box" after an installation of the Client Access server. If you do no other configuration, your users could (and likely would) use OWA as it is—but there are some configuration options that will customize and enhance the OWA experience for your users.

Configuring OWA for SharePoint and File Server Access

With the release of Exchange Server 2007, the original plan was to completely eliminate public folders and move that data into Microsoft Office SharePoint Server (MOSS). Well, that didn't exactly happen as Microsoft originally envisioned it because public folder support did ship with Exchange Server 2007 (although the folders are no longer required to be used but are now completely optional). As a result, the original version of OWA in Exchange Server 2007 does not provide any support for public folder access (a problem that will be corrected with the release of Service Pack 1 in late 2007). Since the original plan called for customers to move all data into SharePoint, the Exchange development team ensured that there would be some integration between OWA and SharePoint in Exchange Server 2007.

By default, SharePoint and file server access are enabled in OWA, but they are not likely configured the way you will need them for your organization's environment. For example, you might want to allow access to some servers but block access to the other servers on your network. Or maybe it's the opposite—you want to allow access from OWA to every server on your network except a select few. Whatever your needs may be, Exchange Server 2007 has the tools you need to create your configuration. Exercise 4.9 outlines the steps for configuring allowed and blocked SharePoint and file servers for OWA access.

EXERCISE 4.9

Configuring SharePoint and File Server Access

1. Click Start ➢ Programs ➢ Microsoft Exchange Server 2007, and then select Exchange Management Console.
2. Expand the Microsoft Exchange root object, expand the Server Configuration folder, and then click the Client Access node.
3. Select the server to configure in the top half of the middle pane, and then select the owa (Default Web Site) item, as shown here.

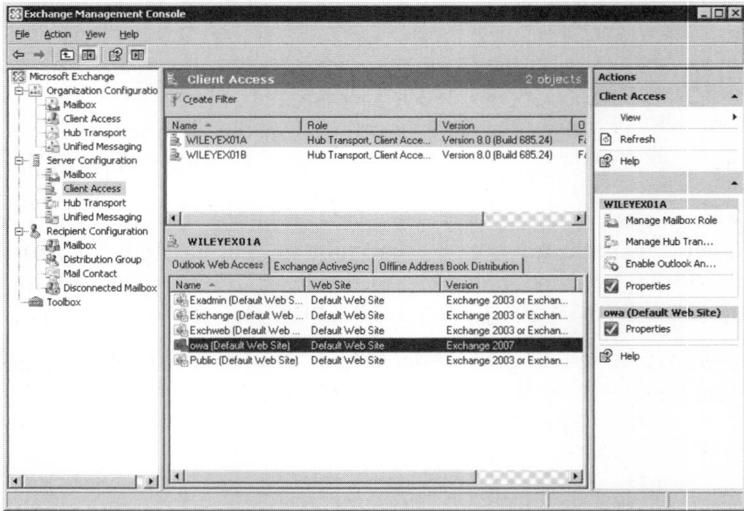

EXERCISE 4.9 *(continued)*

4. Open the OWA website properties by right-clicking the virtual directory and selecting Properties from the context menu. Alternatively, you can click the Properties link under the owa (Default Web Site) options in the Actions pane on the right of the Exchange Management Console. The owa (Default Web Site) Properties dialog box opens to the General tab.

5. Select the Remote File Servers tab, as shown here.

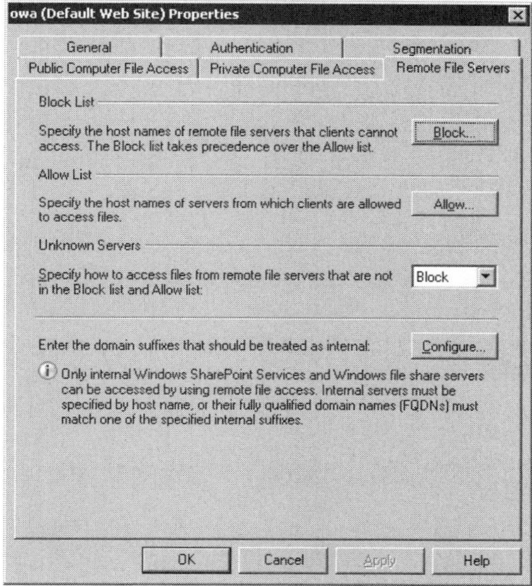

6. To block specific SharePoint or file servers from being accessed from OWA, click the Block button to open the Block List dialog box. Add, edit, or delete servers from the list as needed, and then click OK to return to the Remote File Servers tab.

7. To explicitly allow specific SharePoint or file servers to be accessed from OWA, click the Allow button to open the Allow List dialog box. Add, edit, or delete servers from the list as needed, and then click OK to return to the Remote File Servers tab.

8. For the Unknown Servers option, most organizations will likely leave the default selection of Block in place, thus allowing access only to those servers configured on the Allow list.

9. If you have multiple DNS suffixes in your organization, you can control or prevent access to certain suffixes by omitting them from the internal DNS suffix list. By default, no entries are configured here, allowing access to any internal server.

10. When you are finished making your configuration, click OK to save the changes, and close the owa (Default Web Site) Properties dialog box.

By default, all computers accessing OWA (both public and private) can access SharePoint and file servers that you configured in Exercise 4.9. Exercise 4.10 outlines the steps for disabling and enabling SharePoint and file server access for OWA clients.

EXERCISE 4.10

Disabling SharePoint and File Server Integration with OWA

1. Click Start ➢ Programs ➢ Microsoft Exchange Server 2007, and then select Exchange Management Console.
2. Expand the Microsoft Exchange root object, expand the Server Configuration folder, and then click the Client Access node.
3. Select the server to configure in the top half of the middle pane, and then select the owa (Default Web Site) item.
4. Open the OWA website properties by right-clicking the virtual directory and selecting Properties from the context menu. Alternatively, you can click the Properties link under the owa (Default Web Site) options in the Actions pane on the right of the Exchange Management Console. The owa (Default Web Site) Properties dialog box opens to the General tab.
5. Select the Public Computer File Access tab, as shown here.

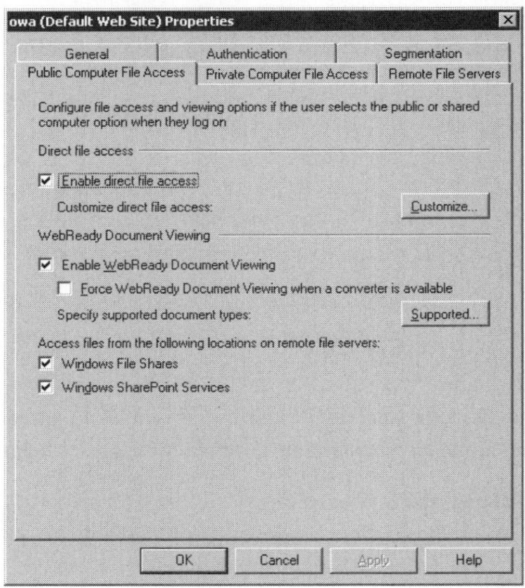

6. To disable access to file shares or SharePoint servers from public computers (determined by the user's selections on the OWA login page), remove the check from the appropriate option.

EXERCISE 4.10 *(continued)*

7. On the Private Computer File Access tab, shown here, you have the same options to disable access to file shares or SharePoint servers from private computers (determined by the user's selections on the OWA login page).

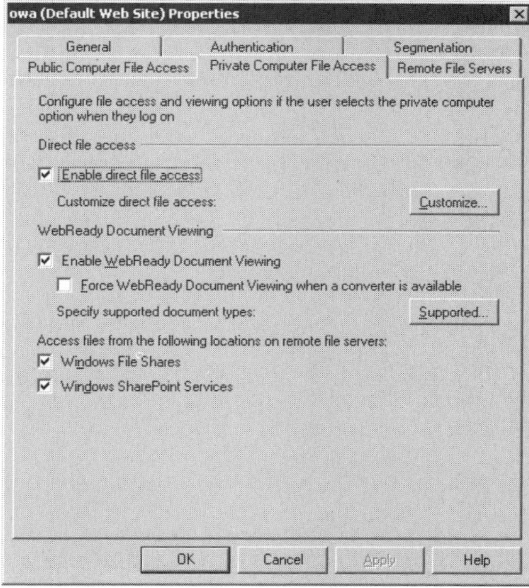

8. When you are done creating your configuration, click OK to save the changes, and close the owa (Default Web Site) Properties dialog box.

Unfortunately, there is no means to make certain file or SharePoint servers are available to OWA when the users log in. Users can, however, create and manage their own Favorites list of servers that they commonly access. To actually access a file server or SharePoint server from within OWA, click the Documents button at the bottom of the OWA screen, as shown in Figure 4.40.

From the Documents page that loads, as shown in Figure 4.41, click the Open Location link to open a dialog box that allows you to enter a UNC path to a server or a server such as \\myservera\salesdocs. As you can also see in Figure 4.41, the user has configured a favorite place that he can quickly access again later by clicking it in the Favorites list.

Configuring Other OWA Options

Several other OWA-related options are available to configure on the owa (Default Web Site) virtual directory. Next, you'll briefly examine these items.

GENERAL

On the General tab of the owa (Default Web Site) Properties dialog box, shown in Figure 4.42, the only real configuration you perform is changing the default value of the internal OWA URL and providing an external OWA URL.

FIGURE 4.40 The OWA interface

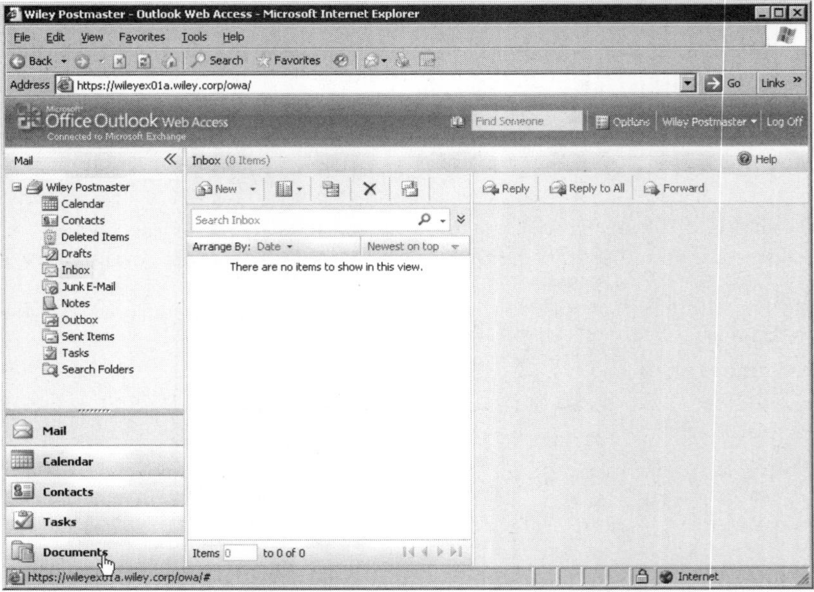

FIGURE 4.41 Working with file and SharePoint servers in OWA

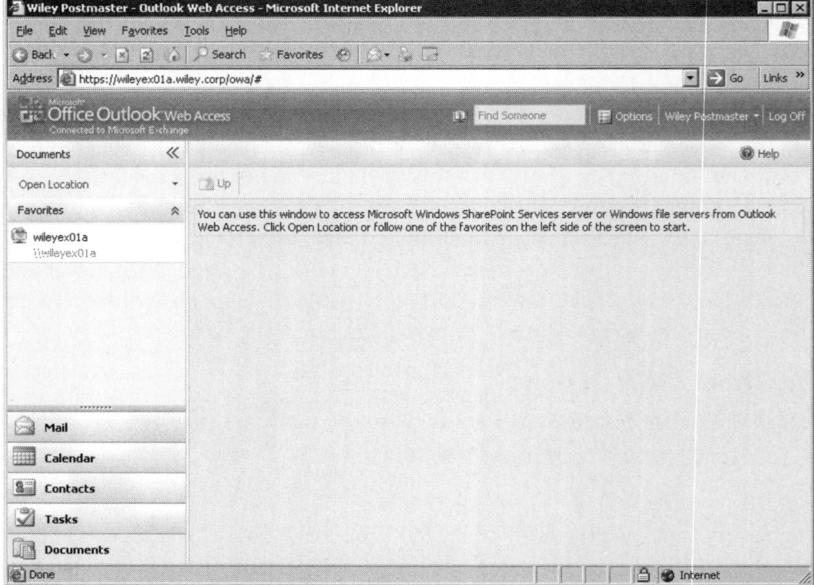

AUTHENTICATION

On the Authentication tab of the owa (Default Web Site) Properties dialog box, shown in Figure 4.43, you can change the authentication method used by the OWA website if you desire. By default, OWA in Exchange Server 2007 is configured for forms-based authentication using a self-issued SSL certificate. Replacing this certificate with one issued by a trusted third-party certificate authority such as Thawte or VeriSign should be a top priority when it comes to configuring OWA. You'll configure the SSL certificate, however, via the IIS console, which we will discuss later in this chapter.

By default, the forms-based authentication is configured to use the domain\username format for OWA login. You can change this if desired to either UPN based (user@company.corp) or username based. If you select this method, you will need to select the default logon domain, of which only one can be selected.

SEGMENTATION

On the Segmentation tab of the owa (Default Web Site) Properties dialog box, shown in Figure 4.44, you have perhaps some of the best changes to OWA in Exchange Server 2007. These segmentation options allow you to configure globally (for that Client Access server) what OWA options will and will not be available. Previously there was no easy way to configure these options in OWA—certainly no easy way within the standard Exchange management tools.

FIGURE 4.42 The General tab of the owa (Default Web Site) Properties dialog box

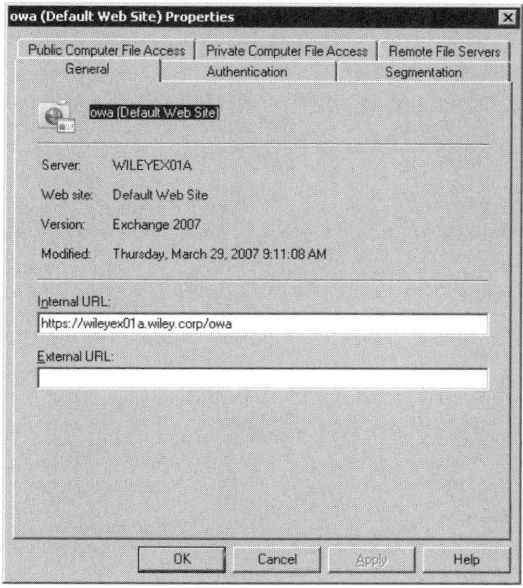

FIGURE 4.43 The Authentication tab of the owa (Default Web Site) Properties dialog box

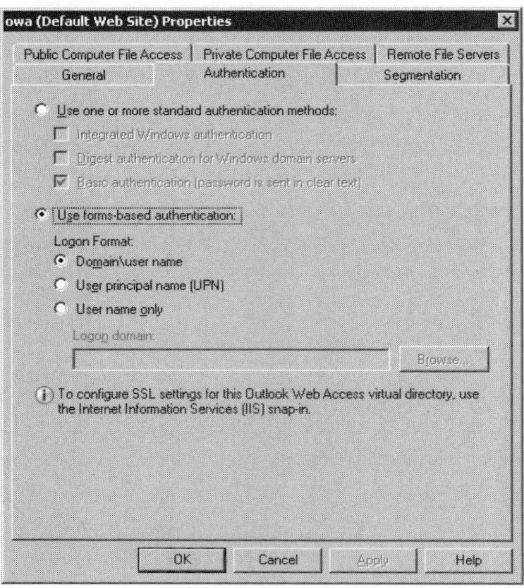

FIGURE 4.44 The Segmentation tab of the owa (Default Web Site) Properties dialog box

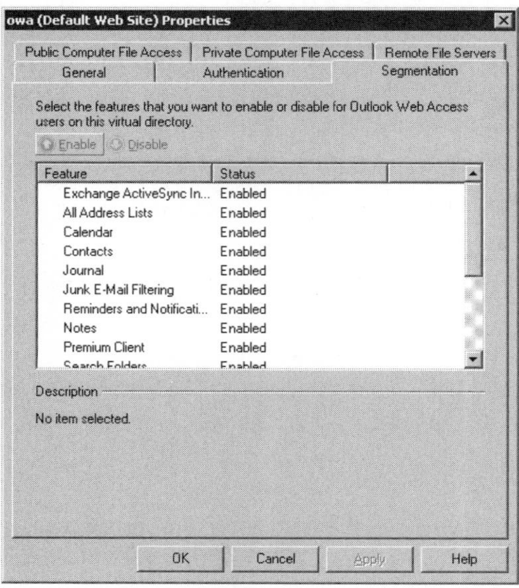

The following OWA options can be disabled or enabled from the Segmentation tab:

- *Exchange ActiveSync Integration*: If disabled, it hides the Mobile Devices option in OWA.
- *All Address Lists*: When disabled, only the global address list (GAL) is available.
- *Calendar*: If disabled, it hides the user's Calendar folder in OWA. The Calendar folder is still available in Outlook sessions.
- *Contacts*: If disabled, it hides the user's Contacts folder in OWA. The Contacts folder is still available in Outlook sessions.
- *Journal*: If disabled, it hides the user's Journal folder in OWA. The Journal folder is still available in Outlook sessions.
- *Junk E-mail Filtering*: When disabled, users are not able to control or change junk mail settings from OWA. These settings are still available to be changed from Outlook, and any settings in place will work but cannot be changed.
- *Reminders and Notifications*: When disabled, users will not get reminders and notifications. Reminders and notifications are not available in OWA Light, which is a scaled version of OWA that was referred to as Basic in the version of OWA provided by Exchange Server 2003.
- *Notes*: If disabled, it hides the user's Notes folder in OWA. The Notes folder is still available in Outlook sessions. Notes are read-only in OWA.
- *Premium Client*: When disabled, it allows only OWA Light to be used.
- *Search Folders*: When disabled, search folders are not available to the user in OWA.
- *E-mail Signature*: When disabled, OWA users cannot manage message signatures.
- *Spelling Checker*: When disabled, spell checking is not available to OWA users. Spell checking is not available in OWA Light.
- *Tasks*: If disabled, it hides the user's Tasks folder in OWA. The Tasks folder is still available in Outlook sessions.
- *Theme Selection*: When disabled, theme selection is not available to OWA users. Theme selection checking is not available in OWA Light.
- *Unified Messaging Integration*: When disabled, OWA users cannot manage their unified messaging settings.
- *Change Password*: If disabled, it hides the Change Password option in OWA.

By default, every option is enabled.

PUBLIC COMPUTER FILE ACCESS

On the Public Computer File Access tab of the owa (Default Web Site) Properties dialog box, shown in Figure 4.45, you have options to control how different file types are handled when accessed via OWA or from file or SharePoint servers. The settings you make on this tab are applied to OWA sessions that come from "public" computers and are configured by the user from the OWA login page.

In the Direct File Access area, you can opt to enable or disable direct file access. Direct file access determines which file types can be opened directly within OWA, which file types can never be opened within OWA, and which file types must be saved first and then opened from the local computer's hard drive. By default, direct file access is enabled, and you'll almost certainly want to leave that setting in place. You may, however, want to customize the allow, block, and force save configurations by clicking the Customize button to open the Direct File Access Settings dialog box shown in Figure 4.46.

FIGURE 4.45 The Public Computer File Access tab of the owa (Default Web Site) Properties dialog box

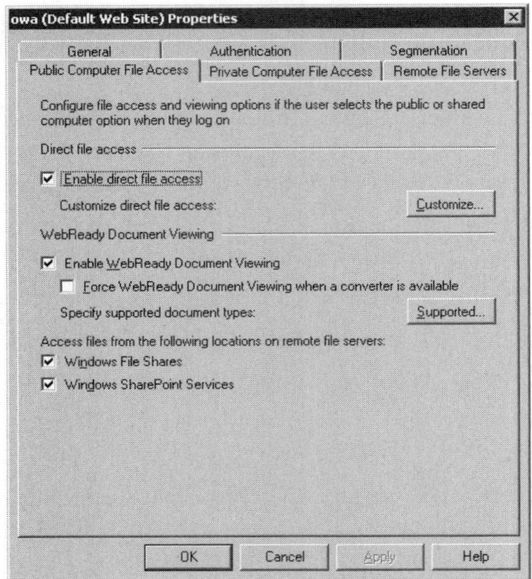

FIGURE 4.46 The Direct File Access Settings dialog box

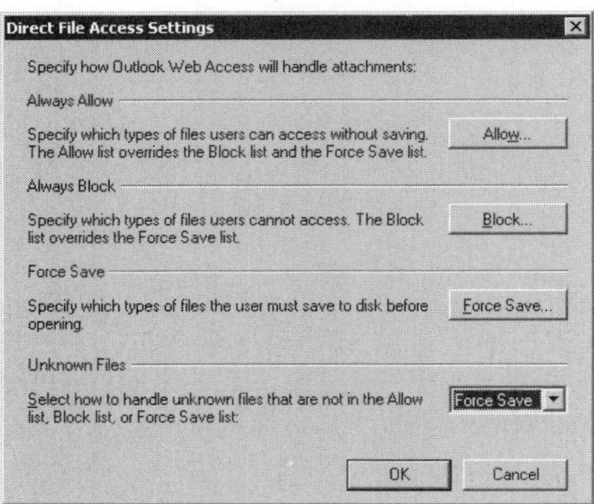

From the Direct File Access Settings dialog box, you can see which file types are always allowed to be opened within OWA, which file types are never allowed to be opened within OWA, which file types must be saved first before they can be opened, and what to do when a file type that hasn't been otherwise accounted for is encountered. Exchange provides many default entries in each section, but take some time to look through them to make sure they make sense for your organization. When you're finished, click the OK button to save your changes and close the Direct File Access Settings dialog box.

Certain file types, such as Microsoft Word documents and Adobe Acrobat PDF documents, can be converted to HTML easily. These file types are known as WebReady file types. You can configure OWA to display these file types as HTML documents, thus allowing access to them even on computers that may not have the original applications they were created in installed—this can be a great benefit for computers in public places such as web cafes and public libraries. You can opt to force WebReady display if you like, but it is not enabled by default. Clicking the Supported button opens the WebReady Document Viewing Settings dialog box, as shown in Figure 4.47. From here you can change the default settings that Exchange provides.

FIGURE 4.47 The WebReady Document Viewing Settings dialog box

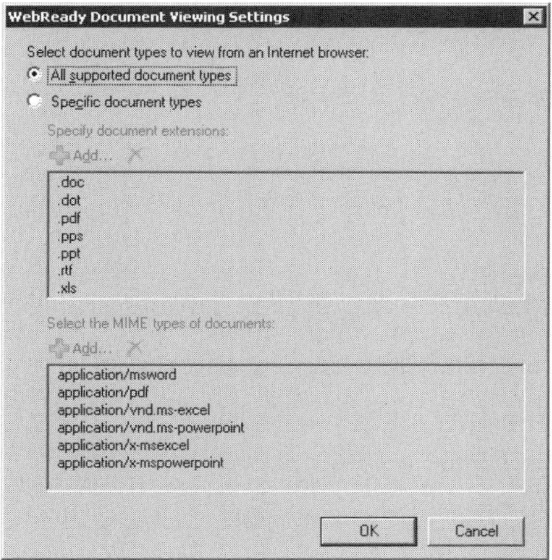

The other options on the Public Computer File Access tab of the owa (Default Web Site) Properties dialog box pertain to file server and SharePoint server access via OWA, which we've already discussed.

PRIVATE COMPUTER FILE ACCESS

On the Private Computer File Access tab of the owa (Default Web Site) Properties dialog box, you have the same settings as those on the Public Computer File Access tab. The only difference is that these settings will be applied to OWA sessions that originate from "private" computers as selected by the user on the OWA login page.

REMOTE FILE SERVERS

On the Private Computer File Access tab of the owa (Default Web Site) Properties dialog box, you have options to configure remote file and SharePoint servers for OWA clients to access. We examined these settings previously in this section.

Configuring and Managing Outlook Anywhere

Outlook Anywhere is the replacement for HTTP over RPC in Exchange Server 2003, and it allows mailbox owners to work outside their network with their Outlook clients without needing to establish a VPN or another remote connection method. In a pure Exchange Server 2007 organization, Outlook Anywhere is fairly simple to configure and maintain. In organizations that still have mailboxes on Exchange Server 2003 servers, the configuration and management are more complex but can still be done.

By default, Outlook Anywhere is not enabled on any Client Access server after installing the Client Access server role. You can enable Outlook Anywhere for a Client Access server by selecting the Client Access server in the Exchange Management Console (Microsoft Exchange ➤ Server Configuration ➤ Client Access) and clicking the Enable Outlook Anywhere link under the server options in the Actions pane on the right of the Exchange Management Console. The Enable Outlook Anywhere Wizard opens, as shown in Figure 4.48. Select your hostname, authentication, and SSL options, and then click Enable to complete the enablement process.

FIGURE 4.48 The Enable Outlook Anywhere Wizard

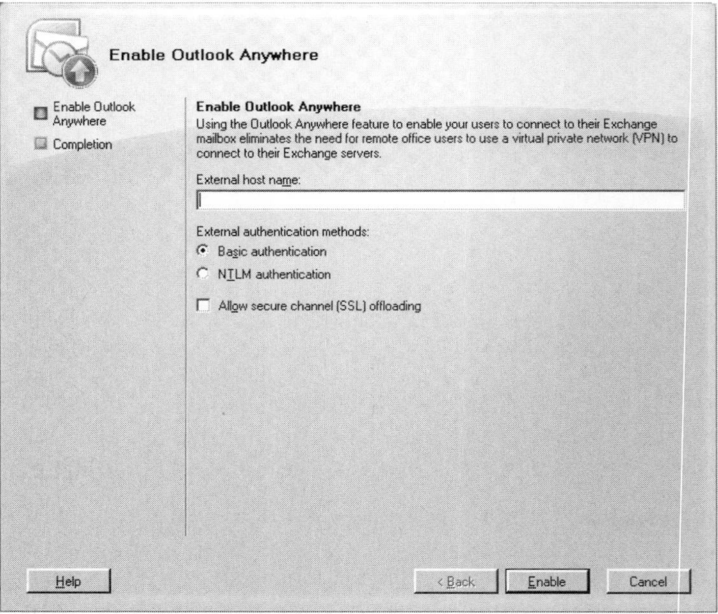

After the wizard completes, you can change the options you've configured by using the appropriate PowerShell command or by opening the Properties dialog box of the Client Access server. You can open the Client Access server's Properties dialog box by selecting the server, right-clicking, and selecting Properties from the context menu or by clicking the Properties link under the server options in the Actions pane on the right of the Exchange Management Console. The General tab of the Client Access server Properties dialog box doesn't contain any settings you can edit, but the Outlook Anywhere tab, shown in Figure 4.49, will allow you to make changes to the configuration you entered for Outlook Anywhere.

FIGURE 4.49 Changing Outlook Anywhere options

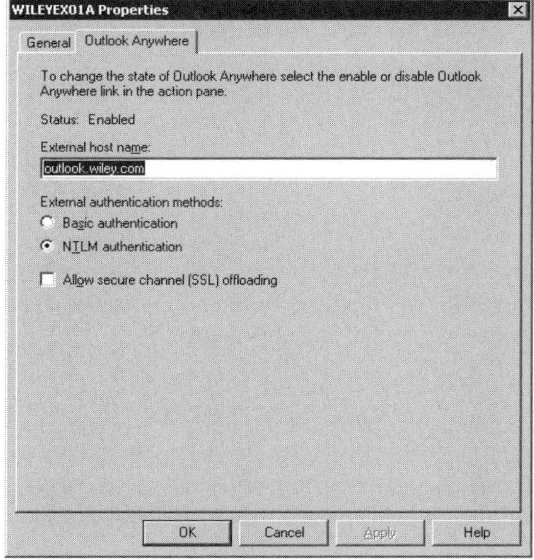

You will need to perform other configuration items, however, to completely implement Outlook Anywhere. These items are beyond the scope of this discussion, but you can get more information from the TechNet website by visiting `http://technet.microsoft.com/en-us/library/bb123889.aspx`.

Configuring SSL for the Client Access Server Virtual Directories

As discussed previously, Exchange Server 2007 actually issues its own self-signed SSL certificate for the Client Access server to use on all IIS virtual directories. This is good and bad. It's good because your clients can begin using OWA on Exchange Server 2007 with forms-based security the moment the installation of the Client Access server is complete. It's bad because your clients will receive, and continue to receive, certificate errors when they access OWA because there is no verification chain to follow to verify the validity of the certificate they're being given. Error feedback from Internet Explorer, like that shown in Figure 4.50, will likely confuse your users.

FIGURE 4.50 OWA certificate errors from the user's perspective

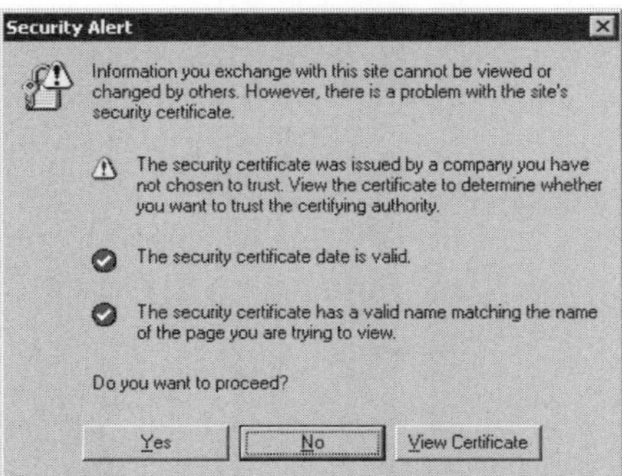

You can, and should, replace the default self-signed SSL certificate as soon as possible with one from a trusted third-party certificate authority such as Thawte or VeriSign. Exercise 4.11 details the process to request and subsequently install the certificate.

During this process, you will be changing the behavior of the Client Access server in regard to OWA access. It's recommended that you perform the SSL certificate replacement as soon as possible after installing the Client Access server and before you make it available to users for OWA usage.

EXERCISE 4.11

Installing a Third-Party SSL Certificate

1. Click Start ➢ Programs ➢ Administrative Tools, and then select Internet Information Services (IIS) Manager.

2. Expand the Internet Information Services root node, the *servername* node, and the Web Sites node.

EXERCISE 4.11 (continued)

3. Right-click the Default Web Site node, and select Properties from the context menu to open the Default Web Site Properties dialog box, as shown here.

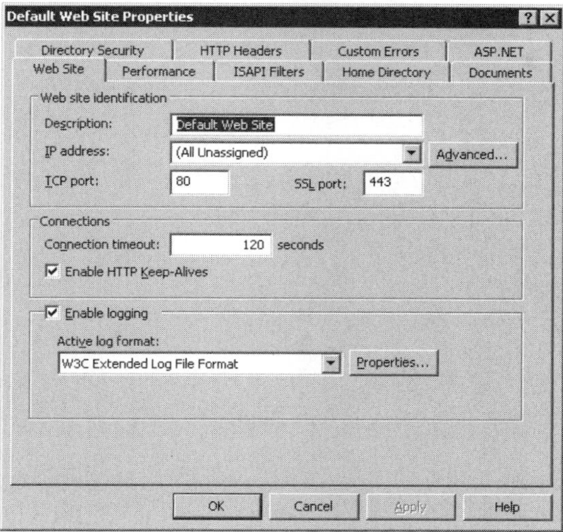

4. Select the Directory security tab, as shown here.

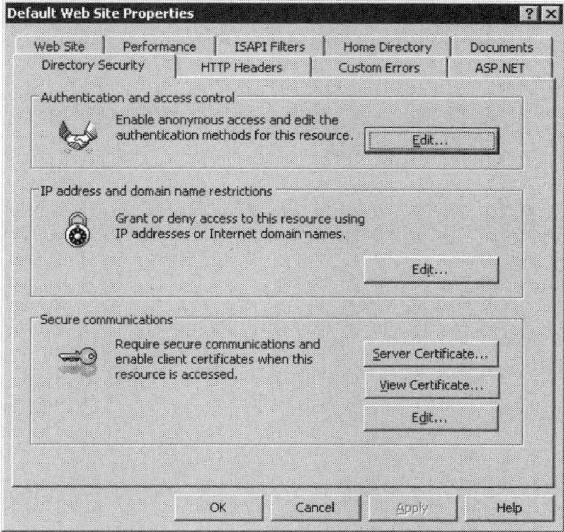

EXERCISE 4.11 *(continued)*

5. Remove the existing self-signed certificate from the Client Access server. To start this process, click the Server Certificate button to open the Web Server Certificate Wizard. Click Next to dismiss the first page of the wizard, and then you'll see the Modify the Current Certificate Assignment page, as shown here.

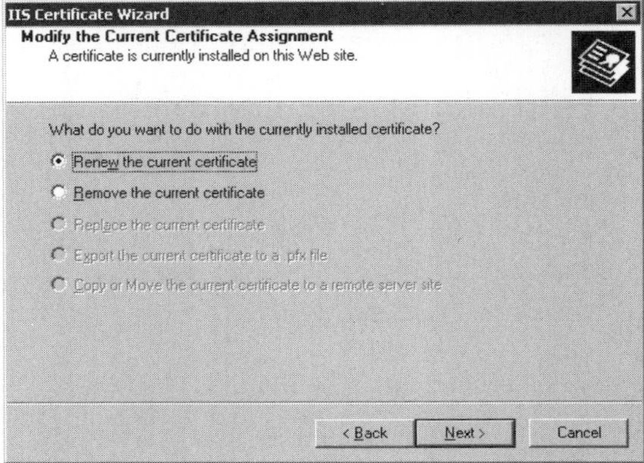

6. Select the Remove the current certificate option, and complete the remaining steps of the wizard to remove the self-signed certificate.

7. To start the process of requesting a third-party certificate, click the Server Certificate button again. Click Next to dismiss the first page of the wizard, and then you'll see the Server Certificate page, as shown here.

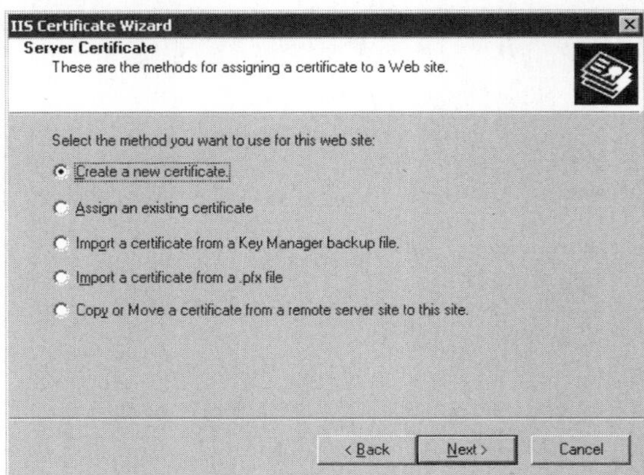

EXERCISE 4.11 *(continued)*

8. On the Server Certificate page, select the Create a New Certificate option, and click Next to continue to the Delayed or Immediate Request page, as shown here.

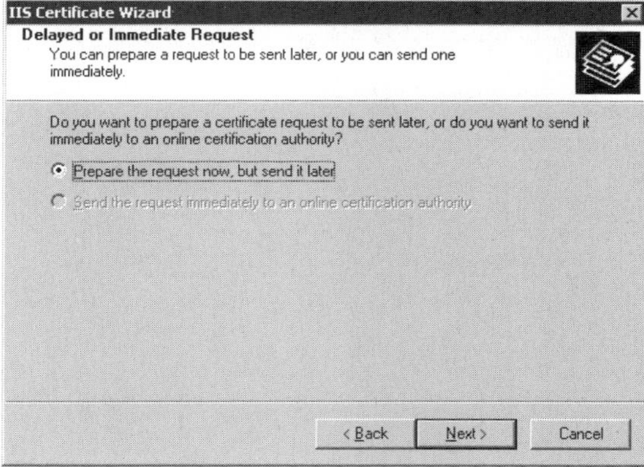

9. On the Delayed or Immediate Request page, select the option to create the request now and send it later, and click Next to continue to the Name and Security Settings page

10. On the Name and Security Settings page, enter a friendly name, and select the key length. It is usually best to just use the external OWA URL as the friendly name for simplicity. Click Next to continue to the Organization Information page, as shown here.

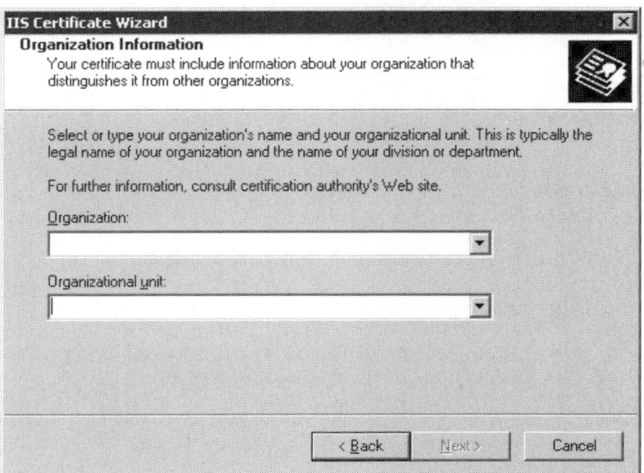

EXERCISE 4.11 *(continued)*

11. On the Organization Information page, enter the name of your company or organization and the organizational unit. Typically, a two-letter country code will be adequate here. Click Next to continue to the Your Site's Common Name page, as shown here.

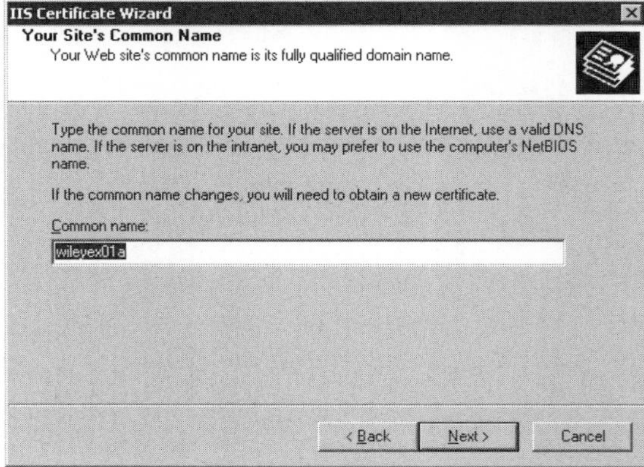

12. The Your Site's Common Name page is the most important part of the entire certificate request process. Many things will cause your request to be rejected by the issuing authority, but entering the wrong external URL on this page will render the certificate useless. Enter the external OWA URL, such as **owa.mycompany.com**, that clients will use to access OWA, and click Next to continue to the Geographical Information page, as shown here.

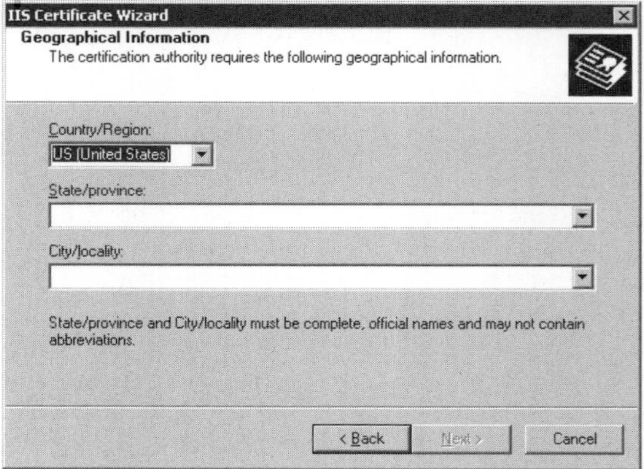

13. On the Geographical Information page, select your country, and provide the complete (not abbreviated) state/province and city/locality information the page requests. Click Next to continue to the Certificate Request File Name page.

EXERCISE 4.11 *(continued)*

14. On the Certificate Request File Name page, enter the location and filename to use when saving the request, and click Next to continue the Request File Summary page.

15. On the Request File Summary page, verify that all the details are correct, and click Next to create the request file.

16. Click Finish to close the wizard. You now have a certificate request file that can be submitted to your certificate authority of choice. Once you submit the request and pay the required fees, the certificate authority will send you a block of text or a text file that contains the actual certificate.

17. To import the certificate, return to the Directory Security tab once again, and click the Server Certification button one more time. Click Next to dismiss the opening page of the wizard and go to the Pending Certificate Request page, as shown here.

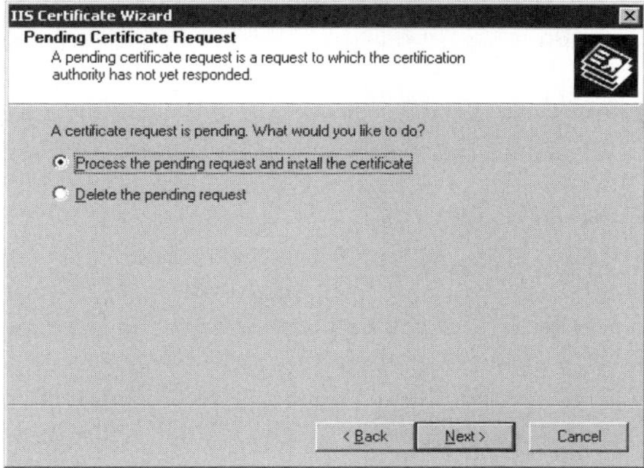

18. On the Pending Certificate Request page, select the Process the Pending Request option, and click Next to process the text block you received from the certificate authority. If you made a mistake and the certificate authority rejects the certificate request, you can delete the pending request and then restart the process.

Changing Roles and Removing Servers from the Exchange Organization

As your company or organization changes over time, your Exchange messaging needs are likely to change as well. Perhaps your company will implement a Voice over IP (VoIP) solution to replace an aging PBX system and you'll be asked to implement unified messaging. More commonly, the size of the company will change and thus will require more or fewer Exchange servers to be available. Sometimes servers need to be retired (and replaced) and thus removed from the Exchange organization. Whatever your situation, you're likely to need to change installed server roles or remove Exchange servers from the Exchange organization at some point.

Adding and Removing Server Roles

To add more server roles to an existing Exchange server, you need to make sure the server can support those roles and that the prerequisite software and conditions have been met on the server. For example, you can't add any other roles to a clustered Mailbox server, and you can't install the Edge Transport server with any other roles. Once you are ready to add the role, you can use either the Exchange setup GUI in "change" mode, which can be accessed from the Add/Remove Programs applet in the Control Panel, or the Exchange command-line setup process as detailed previously in Chapter 3, selecting just the roles in which you're interested.

To remove server roles already installed on an Exchange server, you can use the GUI in "change" mode or the command line as well. To remove the Client Access server role from a server, you might use a command that looks like this from the command line:

```
Setup.com /mode:Uninstall /role:CA
```

Removing Exchange Servers from the Exchange Organization

If you want to completely remove an Exchange server from the Exchange organization, you can also perform this task from the Exchange setup GUI or from the command line. From the command line, be sure to specify all the server's installed roles. If you use the setup GUI from the Add/Remove Programs applet of the Control Panel, select Remove as the mode and not Change.

Summary

We've covered a lot of ground in this chapter, and all of it focused on the basic configuration and management of the three most common and critical Exchange Server 2007 roles: Mailbox, Hub Transport, and Client Access. Every organization that deploys Exchange Server 2007 will have Hub Transport and Mailbox servers. Virtually every organization that deploys Exchange Server 2007 will also use Client Access servers—there is really no reason not to do so. The one role covered on the exam that we didn't examine in this chapter is the Edge Transport role. We'll discuss the Edge Transport role in the next chapter when we examine external security configuration and management for Exchange.

Exam Essentials

Understand the difference between a storage group and a database. Storage groups contain databases, plain and simple. In Exchange Server 2007 Enterprise Edition, you can have up to 50 storage groups and 50 databases. That one-to-one relationship leads you to design Exchange with one database per storage group. Recall that some items are configured at the storage group level, while others are configured at the database level. A storage group, regardless of how many databases it contains, uses only one set of transaction logs.

Understand the structure of the Exchange storage group and its files. The Exchange Server 2007 database structure is a fairly simple one, although it has many files that comprise the entire database. Be sure to know each file type and its function in the overall operation of the storage group.

Learn the PowerShell commands. Almost every configuration or management action you perform from the Exchange Management Console will present you with the PowerShell code that was used to perform the action. Take advantage of this information and learn how to use the Exchange Management Shell to your advantage. Some of these commands are likely to make an appearance on your exam as well.

Know where to go to get the job done. Many times on the exam you are asked what configuration is needed to produce the required results. The Exchange Management Console has been completely redesigned to make it easier to navigate and to get to tasks, but that doesn't mean it won't be difficult to remember this later. Take the time as you review the material in this book to think about what types of configuration and management tasks you find yourself performing in each major node of the Exchange Management Console.

Review Questions

1. You have just installed a new drive on your Exchange server and want to move the transaction logs for one of your storage groups to that drive. Where would you go to do this?

   A. Click the Move Storage Group Path link under the storage group options in the Actions pane on the right of the Exchange Management Console.

   B. Click the Change Transaction Logs Location link under the storage group options in the Actions pane on the right of the Exchange Management Console.

   C. Open the storage group's Properties dialog box, and change the path of the transaction logs from the General tab.

   D. You cannot do this. Once a transaction log is created, it cannot be moved.

2. Which of the following files is used to keep track of the information in a transaction log that has already been committed to the database?

   A. `EDB.LOG`

   B. `CHECK.LOG`

   C. `EDB.CHK`

   D. `RES1.LOG`

3. One of your Exchange servers has unexpectedly shut down its Information Store service. You check the Event Log and discover that the disk containing the log files for the Information Store has run out of space. What has happened to any transactions that were outstanding when the problem occurred?

   A. The transactions are stored in memory and must be committed before shutting down the computer.

   B. The transactions are written to reserve logs and will be committed when the IS comes back online.

   C. Circular logging is turned on, and the oldest committed transaction log is overwritten.

   D. The transactions are lost.

4. By default, what type of authentication mechanism does Outlook Web Access use on an Exchange Server 2007 Client Access server?

   A. Integrated Windows authentication

   B. Forms-based authentication with a self-signed SSL certificate

   C. Forms-based authentication with a third-party SSL certificate

   D. Digest authentication

5. What PowerShell command or commands would you use to create a new mailbox database that is immediately available for use? (Choose all that apply.)

   A. `new-database`

   B. `start-database`

   C. `mount-database`

   D. `new-mailboxdatabase`

   E. `create-mailboxdatabase`

   F. `install-mailboxdatabase`

6. When a remote POP3 client has a session with a Client Access server and sends a message to be delivered, which server could receive the message for delivery? (Choose two.)

   A. A Mailbox server

   B. A Client Access server

   C. A Unified Messaging server

   D. A Hub Transport server

   E. An Edge Transport server

7. Which of the following PowerShell commands is the correct one to use if you want to move only the transaction logs for the Second Storage Group on a server named SERVERA to a folder named Second Storage Group Logs?

   A. `move-StorageGroupPath -Identity 'SERVERA\Second Storage Group' -LogFolderPath 'L:\Program Files\Microsoft\Exchange Server\Mailbox\Second Storage Group Logs' -SystemFolderPath 'L:\Program Files\Microsoft\Exchange Server\Mailbox\Second Storage Group Logs'`

   B. `move-StorageGroupPath -Identity 'Second Storage Group' -LogFolderPath 'L:\Program Files\Microsoft\Exchange Server\Mailbox\Second Storage Group Logs'`

   C. `move-StorageGroupPath -Identity 'SERVERA\Second Storage Group' -SystemFolderPath 'L:\Program Files\Microsoft\Exchange Server\Mailbox\Second Storage Group Logs'`

   D. `move-StorageGroupPath -Identity 'SERVERA\Second Storage Group' -LogFolderPath 'L:\Program Files\Microsoft\Exchange Server\Mailbox\Second Storage Group Logs'`

8. What option do you need to change on a client access to increase the length of time a delayed message is attempted for delivery?

   A. Outbound Connection Failure Retry Interval (Minutes)

   B. Maximum Time Since Submission (Days)

   C. Transient Failure Retry Interval (Seconds)

   D. Transient Failure Retry Attempts

9. What purpose does it serve for you to configure additional accepted domains on the Hub Transport server?

   A. There is no need to configure additional accepted domains on the Hub Transport server.

   B. Configuring them allows you to send messages to these SMTP domains securely.

   C. Configuring them allows you to accept and route messages for these SMTP domains correctly.

   D. Configuring them allows you to enable journaling for messages received for these SMTP domains.

10. When a new transaction log is created in a storage group that contains a single mailbox database, how large is that transaction log initially?

    A. 0KB.

    B. 5,120KB.

    C. 1,024KB.

    D. The size is not fixed.

11. Where can you find the files for the First Storage Group immediately after the Mailbox server is first installed on a server?

    A. `C:\Program Files\Microsoft\Exchange\Mailbox\First Storage Group`

    B. `C:\Program Files\Microsoft\ExchSvr\First Storage Group`

    C. `C:\Program Files\Microsoft\Exchange Server\First Storage Group`

    D. `C:\Program Files\Microsoft\Exchange Server\Mailbox\First Storage Group`

12. You've recently completed the installation of a new Client Access server, and you now have users running Outlook Web Access on it. You've gotten a few complaints about users being unable to open any file or SharePoint servers from their OWA sessions. What are the most likely reasons for this problem? (Choose two.)

    A. The users do not have the proper credentials to access the locations.

    B. You did not configure any Allowed file or SharePoint servers for that OWA virtual directory.

    C. You configured the servers the users want to access as Blocked on that OWA virtual directory.

    D. You did not enable remote file and SharePoint server access on that OWA virtual directory.

    E. You did not change the default setting for Unknown Servers on that OWA virtual directory.

13. Your organization is not sure it needs to deploy a Client Access server in its new Exchange Server 2007 organization. Prior to having Exchange, all email was hosted by a third party and accessed using a variety of methods. Which of the following access methods would require that you have a Client Access server installed? (Choose all that apply.)

    A. Outlook 2007

    B. IMAP4 clients

    C. Outlook Web Access

    D. POP3 clients

    E. Outlook 2003

    F. Windows Mobile devices using ActiveSync

14. You want to configure a Postmaster mailbox for your new Exchange Server 2007 organization. Which of the following PowerShell commands must you use to perform the configuration for a server named SERVERA?

    A. `Set-TransportServer SERVERA -ExternalPostmasterAddress postmaster@mycompany.com`

    B. `Put-TransportServer SERVERA -ExternalPostmasterAddress postmaster@mycompany.com`

    C. `Set-OrganizationPostmaster SERVERA -ExternalPostmasterAddress postmaster@mycompany.com`

    D. `Set-TransportServer SERVERA -PostmasterAddress postmaster@mycompany.com`

15. You have decided to use circular logging on a storage group that contains a single mailbox database with noncritical mailboxes. Which types of backups will you be able to perform on this storage group once circular logging is configured? (Choose all that apply.)

    A. Differential

    B. Incremental

    C. Normal

    D. Shadow

16. Your company does not want to send out-of-office messages to several SMTP domains outside the company. What can you create and configure in Exchange Server 2007 to allow this type of control?

    A. Accepted domains

    B. SMTP send connectors

    C. SMTP receive connectors

    D. Remote domains

17. Your company wants to exchange messages securely with an external partner company. What can you create and configure in Exchange Server 2007 to allow this type of control?

    A. Accepted domains

    B. SMTP send connectors

    C. SMTP receive connectors

    D. Remote domains

18. Your Exchange Server 2007 organization consists of four servers: ServerA is a Mailbox server, ServerB is a Client Access server, ServerC is a Hub Transport server, and ServerD is a Mailbox server. When a user with a mailbox on ServerA sends a message from Outlook to a user on ServerD, which servers are involved in the message transfer process?

    A. ServerA and ServerD only

    B. ServerA, ServerB, and ServerD only

    C. ServerA and ServerC only

    D. ServerA, ServerC, and ServerD only

    E. ServerA, ServerB, ServerC, and ServerD

19. What problem is caused by the SSL certificate that Exchange uses by default for Outlook Web Access?

    A. It cannot be validated against a trusted root; thus, users will receive warning messages.

    B. It does not provide true SSL security and should be used only for testing forms-based authentication.

    C. It expires 30 days after the Client Access server role is installed, thus rendering OWA inaccessible after that time.

    D. It is valid only in North America, so clients in other locations will not be able to use OWA on that server.

20. By default, two SMTP receive connectors are configured during the installation of a Hub Transport server. What TCP ports are they listening on? (Choose two.)

    A. 25

    B. 3268

    C. 389

    D. 587

    E. 110

    F. 443

Answers to Review Questions

1. A. To change the transaction log path or the system file path for a storage group, simply click the Move Storage Group Path link under the storage group options in the Actions pane on the right of the Exchange Management Console. Alternatively, you can right-click the storage group and select the Move Storage Group Path menu item from the context menu that appears. Either way, the Move Storage Group Path Wizard opens and allows you choose the new path for either or both items.

2. C. As transactions in transaction log files are committed to the database files, a checkpoint file (`EDB.CHK`) is updated. The checkpoint file keeps track of which transactions in the sequential list still need to be committed to a database by maintaining a pointer to the last information that was committed. This tells the engine that everything after that point still needs to be committed to a database.

3. B. Exchange creates two reserve log files (`Exxres00001.jrs` and `Exxres00002.jrs`) for each database. They are used if the system runs out of disk space. If that happens, Exchange shuts down the database service, logs an event to the Event Log, and writes any outstanding transaction information into these reserve log files. These two files reserve an area of disk space that can be used after the rest of the disk space is used.

4. B. By default, Outlook Web Access in Exchange Server 2007 uses forms-based authentication with a self-signed SSL certificate. You should procure and install a trusted third-party SSL certificate as soon as possible after installing a Client Access server.

5. C, D. You will need to use the `new-mailboxdatabase` command to create the new mailbox database and the `mount-database` command to mount the database, thus making it available for usage.

6. D, E. For POP3 and IMAP4 clients, submitted messages are sent directly to an SMTP server, which would be either a Hub Transport server accessible from the Internet or an Edge Transport server.

7. D. The PowerShell command `move-StorageGroupPath -Identity 'SERVERA\Second Storage Group' -LogFolderPath 'L:\Program Files\Microsoft\Exchange Server\Mailbox\Second Storage Group Logs'` is the only one that will move the transaction logs for the Second Storage Group correctly without moving any other files.

8. B. The Maximum Time Since Submission (Days) option specifies the timeout duration for messages. If a message is still in the queue to be delivered longer than this setting, the message is returned to the sender as undeliverable. The default setting is 2 days, but can be set to any value from 1 to 90 days.

9. C. Accepted domains are used to specify for which SMTP domains the Exchange Server organization will accept and/or route messages. Most commonly an organization will have multiple SMTP domains if it accepts mail for multiple subsidiary companies or if it has multiple public domain names in use, such as microsoft.com and xbox.com.

10. C. The transaction logs used by Exchange Server 2007 are named `Exxhhhhhhhh.log`, which is the log prefix (such as E01) followed by an eight-character hexadecimal number, so you would have `E0100000001.log` as the first log file for the Second Storage Group on the server. Hexadecimal uses the numbers 1 through 0 and the letters A through F in its numbering system. These files will always be 1,024KB in size.

11. D. By default, Exchange creates the storage groups on the system root, where Windows is installed. So, on a typical server, the location would be `C:\Program Files\Microsoft\Exchange Server\Mailbox\First Storage Group`. You should move the transaction logs/system files and databases to their own separate physical volumes as soon as possible—definitely before putting the server into production use.

12. B, E. By default, there are no file or SharePoint servers configured in the Allow or Block lists on the OWA virtual directory. As well, the default behavior is to block all unknown servers, so you have a situation where no file or SharePoint servers can be accessed by users on that OWA server.

13. B, C, D, F. All non-MAPI clients require the Client Access server in order to access mailboxes on an Exchange Server 2007 Mailbox server. Only Outlook MAPI over RPC can directly access the Mailbox server without needing a Client Access server.

14. A. You will need to use the `Set-TransportServer SERVERA -ExternalPostmasterAddress postmaster@mycompany.com` command to configure the postmaster address on SERVERA.

15. C. When you use circular logging, you must perform full (or normal) backups, because the transaction logs will not be available if you need to recover the database, so incremental or differential backups are not suitable.

16. D. You need to create remote domain objects for the external SMTP namespaces that you do not want out-of-office messages to be sent to.

17. B. You need to create and configure and SMTP a send connector that uses the Enable Domain Security (Mutual Auth TLS) option. Additional configuration will also be required beyond the creation of the SMTP send connector.

18. D. All messages go through the Hub Transport server for delivery, so the message would go from the user's Outbox on ServerA, go through the Hub Transport on ServerC, and be delivered to the Inbox of the user's mailbox on ServerD.

19. A. The SSL certificate that OWA uses by default after the installation of the Client Access server role is self-issued and self-signed, and thus it has no validation chain that leads up to a trusted root authority. Users connecting to the OWA site will receive a warning of such, which will ultimately lead to confusion. You should replace this certificate as soon as possible, preferably before putting the Client Access server into production.

20. A, D. The Client *servername* connector accepts messages on port 587, and the Default *servername* connector accepts messages on port 25.

Configuring the Exchange Security Infrastructure

MICROSOFT EXAM OBJECTIVES COVERED IN THIS CHAPTER:

✓ **Installing and Configuring Microsoft Exchange Servers**

- Install Exchange.
- Configure Exchange server roles.

✓ **Configuring the Exchange Infrastructure**

- Configure the antivirus and anti-spam system.

In this chapter we'll show how to install the last server role discussed in this book, the Edge Transport server. Additionally, we'll explain how to install and configure Microsoft Forefront Security for Exchange Server to manage virus and spam issues within your Exchange organization. The main subjects of this chapter are as follows:

- Configuring the Edge Transport server
- Configuring Microsoft Forefront Security for Exchange Server

Configuring the Edge Transport Server

The Edge Transport server is one of the server roles introduced in Exchange Server 2007 that really never had a place in previous versions of Exchange Server. Many organizations used various solutions in the DMZ network to route and scan inbound and outbound Simple Mail Transfer Protocol (SMTP) mail, such as SMTP gateways and various third-party appliance and software-based applications. With the introduction of Exchange Server 2007, you have a choice to make: you can either continue to use the existing routing and scanning implementation you already have or implement one or more Edge Transport servers for your Exchange organization. Either choice is acceptable and will work as long as you ensure the proper configuration is completed.

For our purposes here, we'll assume that an Edge Transport server is desired in your Exchange organization; thus, we'll show how to install, configure, and manage one. Installing the Edge Transport server is really no different from the previous installations discussed in Chapter 3, "Installing Exchange Server 2007." With that fact in mind, we'll jump right into the configuration and management tasks associated with a freshly installed Edge Transport server, as shown in Figure 5.1.

For the installation of the Edge Transport role to be successfully completed, you'll need to install the following components before starting the installation: .NET Framework 2.0, PowerShell 1.0, Microsoft Management Console (MMC) 3.0, and Active Directory Application Mode (ADAM) with Service Pack 1. Additionally, setup may prompt you to download and install some other updates if not done already. Lastly, you will need to configure a fully qualified domain name for your Edge Transport servers, which is not typically done with servers located in the DMZ. Exchange will refuse to install the Edge Transport role if these prerequisite items are not in place.

FIGURE 5.1 The Edge Transport role viewed from the Exchange Management Console

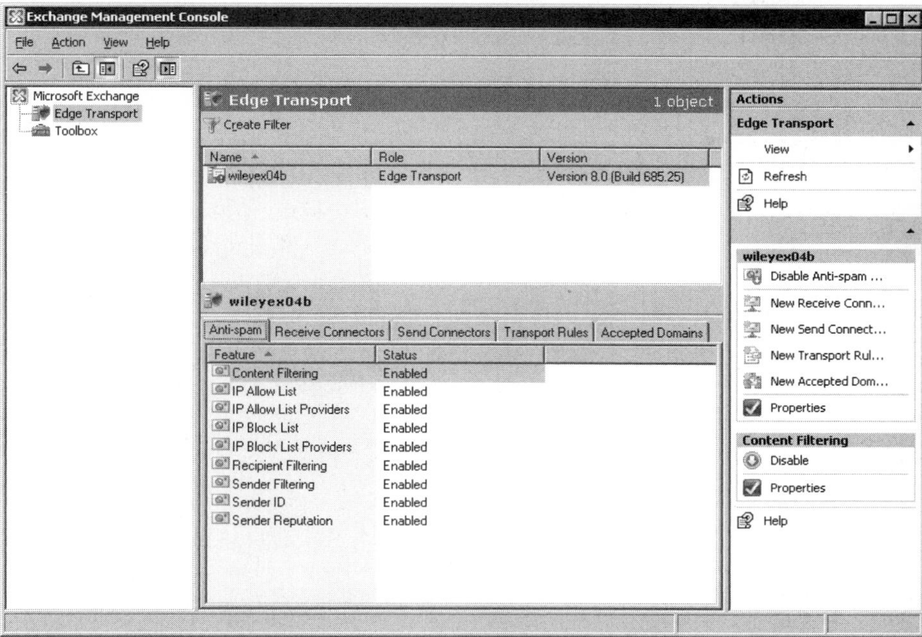

Configuring and Managing EdgeSync

The primary role of the Edge Transport server is to route inbound and outbound SMTP messages, checking them for spam and virus characteristics. Sometime after Exchange Server 2003 was released, Microsoft decided that running antispam and antiviral software on the same servers that housed mailbox and public folder databases was not necessarily the best design, and thus the role-based implementation of Exchange Server 2007 was born. The Edge Transport server now assumes these roles in organizations where no other third-party software or hardware solution is in place. Some benefits realized through the use of the Edge Transport server (or similar solution) include the following:

- Reduces load on Mailbox servers because of filtering out unwanted messages, such as those containing spam or viruses
- Adds extra layer(s) of protection to the Exchange servers located on the internal network
- Prevents Internet connections directly to the Exchange servers located on the internal network

The first step you'll need to take to start realizing these benefits in your Exchange organization is to configure the EdgeSync service between your Edge Transport servers and your Hub Transport servers. By configuring EdgeSync, you'll enable the ADAM instance installed on the Edge Transport server to contain all the pertinent information needed to start filtering both inbound and outbound SMTP traffic. The following information is replicated to the ADAM database on the Edge Transport server once EdgeSync has been configured:

- A listing of all internal accepted domains
- A listing of all remote domains
- Any configured message classifications
- Information about internal send connectors that have been configured
- A listing of all valid internal SMTP addresses for the domain, which includes mailbox-enabled users, mail users, mail contacts, mail-enabled groups, and mail-enabled public folders.
- The list of safe and blocked sender lists that have been configured for each of these users

The Edge Transport server is a powerful weapon against undesirable SMTP traffic entering your Exchange organization because of the information it has in the ADAM database plus the antispam and antivirus capabilities it provides. Even if you already have a third-party solution in place in your DMZ that provides some of these features, there might be business justification for placing an Edge Transport server (or multiple Edge Transport servers) in the DMZ between the Exchange organization and the third-party solution so you can take advantage of the Edge Transport server's benefits.

The basic process to enable EdgeSync includes the following steps:

1. Ensure the required ports on the Internet to DMZ and DMZ to internal network firewalls are configured.
2. Ensure that accepted domains for which your Exchange organization will handle mail are configured on a Hub Transport server. Refer to Chapter 4, "Configuring Exchange Server Roles," for a refresher if needed.
3. Ensure that DNS name resolution is functional between the Edge Transport servers in the DMZ and the Hub Transport servers on the internal network.
4. Define all internal Hub Transport servers so that Sender ID does not reject messages from them.
5. Create the edge subscription file on an Edge Transport server.
6. Copy the edge subscription file to a Hub Transport server.
7. Use the New Edge Subscription Wizard on the Hub Transport server to complete the process.

We will examine some of the pertinent steps in the following sections.

Firewall Ports Required for EdgeSync

Table 5.1 details the required port configuration that needs to be in place (at a minimum) to allow your Edge Transport servers to function correctly in the DMZ.

TABLE 5.1 Edge Transport Firewall Ports

Firewall Location	Rule	Description
Internet: DMZ	Allow port 25 to and from all Internet hosts to and from the Edge Transport servers.	Port 25 is used for SMTP.

TABLE 5.1 Edge Transport Firewall Ports *(continued)*

Firewall Location	Rule	Description
Internet: DMZ	Allow port 53 to all Internet hosts from the Edge Transport servers.	Port 53 is required for DNS resolution, which is required to properly route outbound SMTP messages to Internet hosts.
Internal: DMZ	Allow port 25 to and from specified Hub Transport servers to and from specified Edge Transport servers.	Port 25 is used for SMTP.
DMZ: Internal	Allow port 50636 from specified Hub Transport servers to specified Edge Transport servers.	Port 50636 is used for Secure Lightweight Directory Access Protocol (LDAP) replication between Hub Transport servers and the ADAM database located on the Edge Transport servers.
Internal: DMZ	Allow port 3389 from the internal network to the specified Edge Transport servers.	Port 3389 is used for Remote Desktop Protocol (RDP) connections for managing servers remotely.
Internal: DMZ	Allow port 53 from the internal network to the specified Edge Transport servers.	Port 53 is required for DNS resolution, which is required to properly route outbound SMTP messages to Internet hosts.

Defining Internal SMTP Servers

Before you can enable EdgeSync, you need to define the list of internal SMTP servers (Hub Transport servers) that exist in your Exchange organization. This is required so that Sender ID on the Edge Transport server knows which servers are internal to your organization and so that connection filters know they should not reject connections from these internal SMTP servers. This required configuration is one of those tasks that you cannot perform from the Exchange Management Console, so you'll need to use the `Set-TransportConfig` cmdlet from the Exchange Management Shell. If your Hub Transport servers had IP addresses of 192.168.0.150 and 192.168.0.151, then the command to enter would look like this:

```
Set-TransportConfig -InternalSMTPServers 192.168.0.150,192.168.0.151
```

You need to perform this step from a Hub Transport server, not from an Edge Transport server. Once EdgeSync is enabled, most information related to routing messages will be overwritten on the Edge Transport server. This is also the reason why you wouldn't create send and receive connectors or accepted domains on the Edge Transport server.

As you can see in Figure 5.2, there is no feedback provided to let you know that you've done anything right or wrong, but given that PowerShell is very good about alerting you to syntax errors, you can rest assured you've probably gotten the task accomplished.

FIGURE 5.2 Setting the list of internal SMTP servers

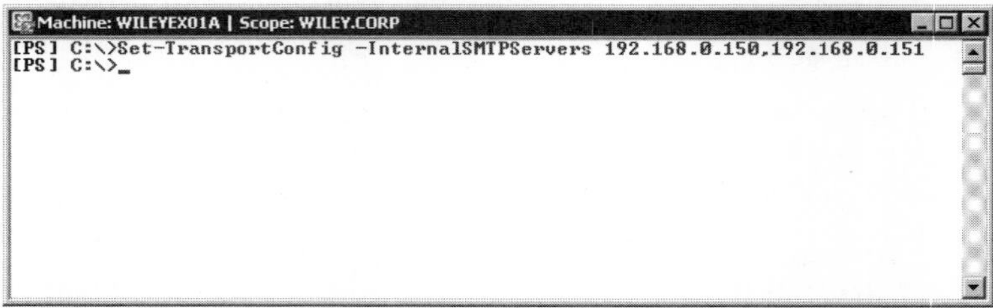

Creating the Edge Subscription File

To create the edge subscription file, you will need to move back to the Edge Transport server and once again use an Exchange Management Shell cmdlet, `New-EdgeSubscription`, to create the file. If you wanted to save the file to the F drive, your entry might look like this:

```
New-EdgeSubscription -FileName "F:\EdgeSubscription.xml"
```

As you can see in Figure 5.3, you are presented with a list of items to consider before completing the edge subscription file creation process. Note the tasks that are disabled if you continue; you'll be performing them from the Hub Transport server only after EdgeSync is enabled.

FIGURE 5.3 Creating the edge subscription file

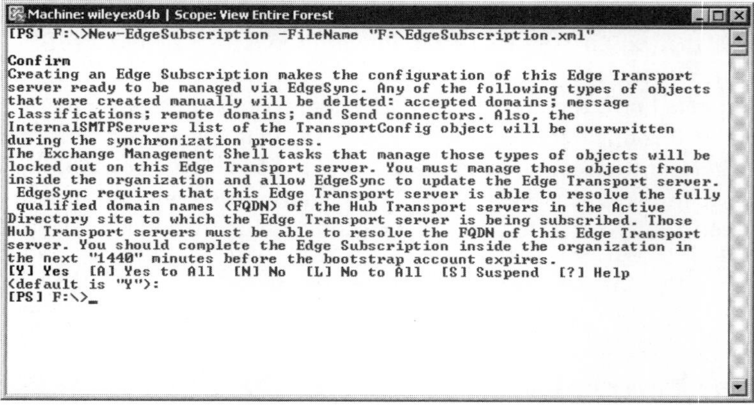

The full text presented to you to read is duplicated here for clarity because it is important to understand the implications of the decision to move forward with creating the edge subscription file.

```
Confirm
Creating an Edge Subscription makes the configuration of this Edge
Transport server ready to be managed via EdgeSync. Any of the following
types of objects that were created manually will be deleted: accepted
domains; message classifications; remote domains; and Send connectors.
 Also, the InternalSMTPServers list of the TransportConfig object will
be overwritten during the synchronization process.
The Exchange Management Shell tasks that manage those types of objects
will be locked out on this Edge Transport server. You must manage those
objects from inside the organization and allow EdgeSync to update the
Edge Transport server.  EdgeSync requires that this Edge Transport
server is able to resolve the fully  qualified domain names (FQDN) of
the Hub Transport servers in the Active Directory site to which the
Edge Transport server is being subscribed. Those Hub Transport servers
must be able to resolve the FQDN of this Edge Transport server. You
should complete the Edge Subscription inside the organization in the
next "1440" minutes before the bootstrap account expires.

[Y] Yes  [A] Yes to All  [N] No  [L] No to All  [S] Suspend  [?] Help
(default is "Y"):
```

If you open the resulting XML file in Notepad, you can see what is inside it, as shown in Figure 5.4. Notice the file contains both the short and fully qualified domain names of the Edge Transport server; the Hub Transport servers must be able to resolve this name via DNS queries.

FIGURE 5.4 Viewing the edge subscription file

EdgeSubscription.xml - Notepad

File Edit Format View Help


```
<?xml version="1.0"?>
<EdgeSubscriptionData xmlns:xsi="http://www.w3.org/2001/XMLSchema-instance"
xmlns:xsd="http://www.w3.org/2001/XMLSchema">
  <EdgeServerName>WILEYEX04B</EdgeServerName>
  <EdgeServerFQDN>wileyex04b.wiley.corp</EdgeServerFQDN>

<EdgeCertificateBlob>CwAAAAEAAAAmAAAATQBpAGMAcgBvAHMAbwBmAHQAIABFAHgAYwBoAGEAbgBnAGUAAAADAAAAAQAAA
BQAAACvt8ReBoxr3rUK36BUr2gvP268egIAAAABAAAAbAAAABwAAAAAAAAADAAAACAAAAAAAAAAAAAAAAEAAAA5ADcAYgBmADQ
ANgA2ADEALQA4ADAAMQBlAC0ANAA3ADkAYQAtADkAYgBkAGMALQAzAGEAZQA2ADgAMQBlADYANgA1ADUANgAAAAAAAAAAABQAA
AABAAAAFAAAADroZigkvT/rp50QC7AEJrS61JcmIAAAAAEAAAAbAwAAMIIDFzCCAf+gAwIBAgIQ+FFRZVBkF5ZPKc0EecpW/zA
NBgkqhkiG9w0BAQUFADAVMRMwEQYDVQQDEwp3aWxleWV4MDRiMB4XDTA3MDQyOTE2MDUzOFoXDTA4MDQyOTE2MDUzOFowFTETM
BEGA1UEAxMKd2lsZXlleDA0YjCCASIwDQYJKoZIhvcNAQEBBQADggEPADCCAQoCggEBAOSaj6qGIG0EENKX+xSGo/GEAW5AEgp
Kshr7yv1xv7GkX2ylC4yA7rbe6YVRC2KA/TsahTvB5vG4UwS5iSlH3p5JAxHl+1UCdSmEVY5xz+BcTOBkSeNaYksqDbsqT7e7l
+V7fmHoC1LjmF0xbenHPLSQgNXMYNc+fqIeDPhgXAE4fitPznFNrW36RG4fSdpAFJlPZlk4EDh2RoJh/kKp5XVT/rnB0KLoPW5
jZma+oQocAAI89oUx1FQ6WqRtrSNjfKd2tvNmIW8nEzLGBDqEBiXo2kmbKNbCPUamYHAjKvAQP4kvj/V42YbPf1YXjI5IEL4Sn
/ezR7SO3zRO2l0tMMUCAwEAAaNjMGEwDgYDVR0PAQH/BAQDAgWgMCwGA1UdEQQlMCOCCndpbGV5ZXgwNGKCFXdpbGV5ZXgwNGI
ud2lsZXkuY29ycDATBgNVHSUEDDAKBggrBgEFBQcDATAMBgNVHRMBAf8EAjAAMA0GCSqGSIb3DQEBBQUAA4IBAQCibgeWMij9W
tpcMs8HtoDnvplRq+uaRB/Ky/r3mo8fWkFxqSlPelCFCkYEDhJgbR6UbA6UWqHIA5paSEY52njLSmIIl/BYIzTyRFw6wgew6ke
KpGpnLTRTofFRujxDVbw6XhA+cVuX/87SPxyd/PsHWuo72an+UOL/PT8KJ4IHPDXXDTAd9pI7ed/WSxIioHFRdstEFOuqvzaow
C7Mz3lto3vxbTCTq0Lptn8wi43jJY0vcSBq0heAIormRsSYjQj0AU7GcCgF9xdb2ZgkF2npYxJ+8gIYxa3+4T30RAp6ejEJZ5T
rtKFKtV9Cug/2h7ouTWrm6bFo62HEFhCmovr+</EdgeCertificateBlob>

<ESRAUsername>CN=ESRA.WILEYEX04B,CN=Services,CN=Configuration,CN={67E9AD9B-2D4C-4E33-BAEA-28295AE4
9B99}</ESRAUsername>
  <ESRAPassword>TgZhD+1zKfo=)5ZbXhmL</ESRAPassword>
  <EffectiveDate>633134724031670675</EffectiveDate>
  <Duration>864000000000</Duration>
  <AdamSslPort>50636</AdamSslPort>
  <ServerType>□□□□□□□□□□□□□□□□□□□□□□□□□□□□□□□</ServerType>
  <ProductID />
  <VersionNumber>1912636077</VersionNumber>
</EdgeSubscriptionData>
```

Finishing the EdgeSync Process

Once you've gotten the edge subscription file created, you will need to copy it somehow to the Hub Transport server on which you'll be completing the EdgeSync process. With that task completed, you're ready to complete the EdgeSync process by running the New Edge Subscription Wizard, as detailed in Exercise 5.1.

EXERCISE 5.1

Creating a New Edge Subscription

1. Click Start ➤ Programs ➤ Microsoft Exchange Server 2007, and then select Exchange Management Console.
2. Expand the Microsoft Exchange root object, expand the Organization Configuration folder, and then click the Hub Transport node.
3. In the Actions pane on the right, click the New Edge Subscription link. The New Edge Subscription Wizard opens, as shown here.

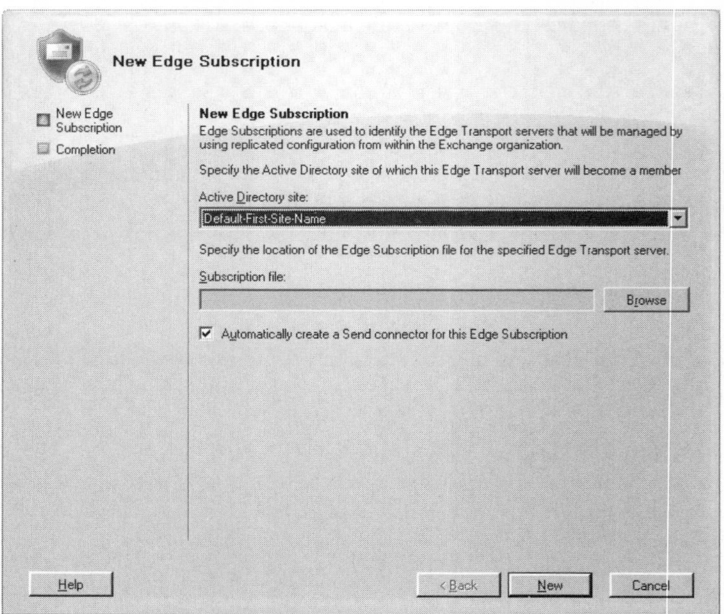

4. Select the Active Directory site that the edge subscription pertains to from the drop-down list provided, and then use the Browse button to locate the XML file you created previously. You should typically leave the default selection to create a send connector for this subscription checked. Click New when you're ready to proceed.

EXERCISE 5.1 *(continued)*

5. After a few seconds, the completion details will be presented. Note that once again you are informed that the Hub Transport servers must be able to resolve the name of the Edge Transport server in order for EdgeSync to work correctly.

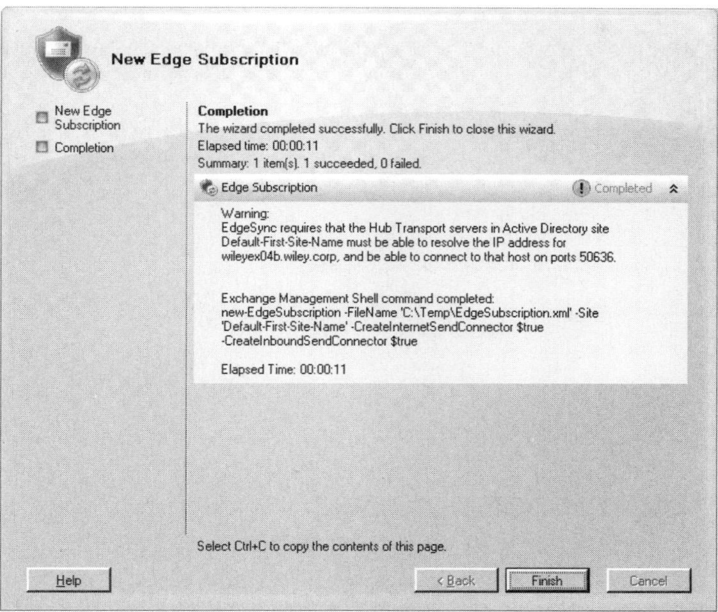

The corresponding Exchange Management Shell cmdlet you could have used to complete the EdgeSync process is `New-EdgeSubscription`. Assuming the filename was as we created it previously and the file was located in `C:\Temp`, your code might look like this:

```
New-EdgeSubscription -FileName 'C:\Temp\EdgeSubscription.xml'
-Site 'Default-First-Site-Name' -CreateInternetSendConnector $true
-CreateInboundSendConnector $true
```

After the wizard has completed, the edge synchronization process should start and begin to synchronize configuration data every hour. Recipient information will be synchronized every four hours. Should you need to force synchronization to occur at some other time, you can use the `Start-EdgeSynchronization` cmdlet.

You can verify that edge synchronization is occurring properly by viewing the Application log on the Hub Transport server looking for log entries from the MSExchange EdgeSync source. Figure 5.5 illustrates a successful configuration synchronization event, and Figure 5.6 illustrates a successful recipient configuration.

FIGURE 5.5 Viewing a successful configuration synchronization event log entry

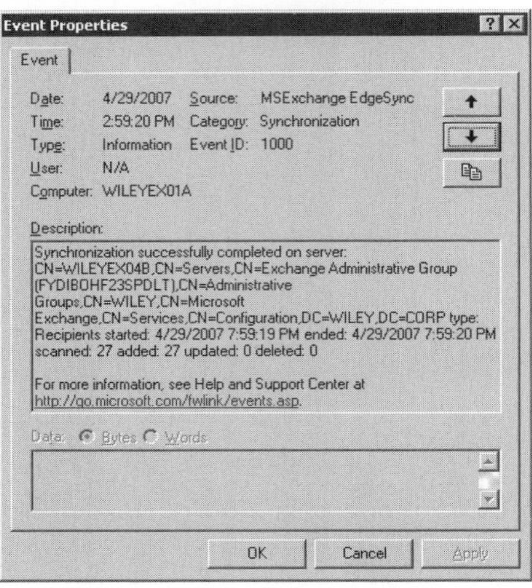

FIGURE 5.6 Viewing a successful recipient synchronization event log entry

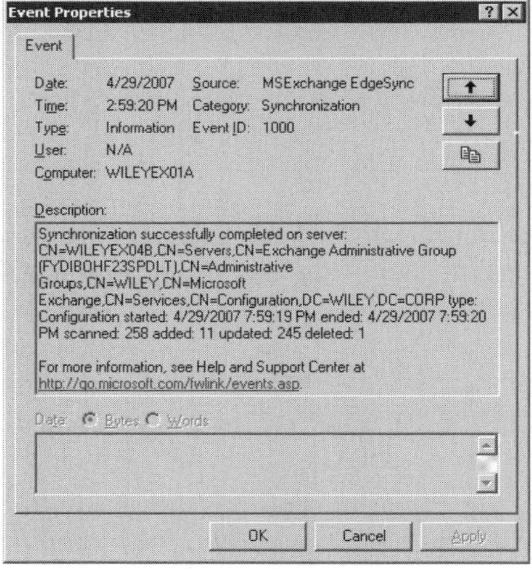

If you look closely at the Description field on both event log entries, you'll notice that the times in the Exchange logs are actually GMT times! Just keep that small (and not entirely trivial) fact in mind should you happen to be troubleshooting EdgeSync.

Moving back to the Edge Transport server, you can verify synchronization has occurred by examining the accepted domains that are configured on the server, as shown in Figure 5.7. Note that these are the same accepted domains configured on the Hub Transport servers in Chapter 4, "Configuring Exchange Server Roles."

FIGURE 5.7 Viewing the list of accepted domains on the Edge Transport server

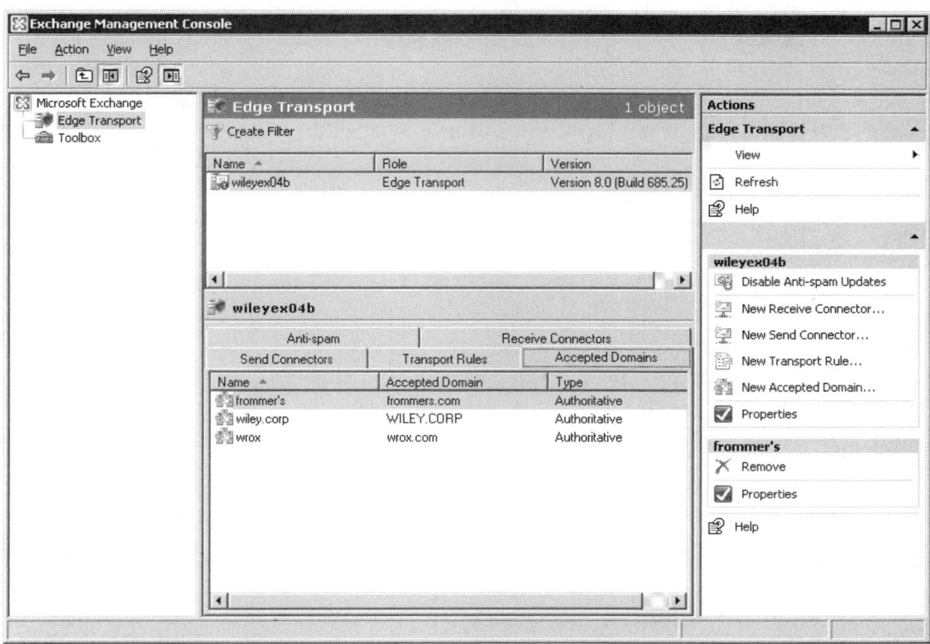

Configuring and Managing Antispam Settings

Exchange Server 2007 builds upon the success of the intelligent message filter (IMF) introduced in Exchange Server 2003 and provides some fairly robust antispam capabilities on the Edge Transport server. You will, of course, need to take the time to configure and implement these antispam tools to meet your needs, but they are there "out of the box" and won't cost you anything additional to use.

The Edge Transport server has several antispam and antivirus options that you can configure to protect your internal network and also to prevent outbound messages from leaving that are classified as spam or virus-laden. In the next sections, we'll examine the following items:

- Content filtering
- IP allow lists
- IP block lists
- Recipient filtering
- Sender filtering
- Sender ID
- Sender reputation
- Attachment filtering

Content Filtering

Content filtering in Exchange Server 2007 really is the second generation of the IMF that was introduced in Exchange Server 2003. The content filter works by examining the content of each message passing through the Edge Transport server based on keyword analysis, message size, and several other factors. When the analysis has been completed, the message is then assigned a spam confidence level (SCL) value from 0 to 9. A value of 0 means the message has been determined to almost certainly not be spam, whereas a value of 9 means the message has been determined to almost certainly be spam. In all reality, the majority of the messages coming into your network will fall somewhere in between these high and low values, and thus you have a series of configurable options that will determine what happens to these messages.

To configure the Content Filtering options, select the Content Filtering item from the Anti-spam tab of the hub transport options, as shown previously in Figure 5.1. You can either right-click the Content Filtering item and select Properties from the context menu or click the Properties link in the Actions pane on the right for the Content Filtering item. Either way, the Content Filtering Properties dialog box opens to the General tab, as shown in Figure 5.8. The General tab provides no configurable options but does provide information about the status of content filtering and the last modification date.

Custom Words

The Custom Words tab, shown in Figure 5.9, allows you to enter a list of words that will modify the default behavior of the content filter. In the top area of this tab, you can enter words that will never be blocked, such as those that might otherwise typically be blocked by the content filter. The bottom half of the tab allows you to enter words that will always be blocked, except if they are also contained in the "always allowed" list.

FIGURE 5.8 The General tab of the Content Filtering Properties dialog box

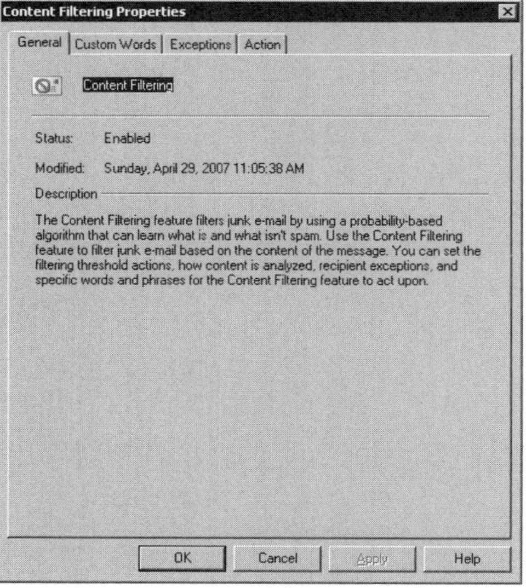

Exceptions

The Exceptions tab, shown in Figure 5.10, allows you to enter a list of email addresses that should always receive messages even if those messages would have ordinarily been blocked by the content filter. You might want to enter a generic spam email address here to collect these messages, such as spamcollection@mycompany.com. As well, there will likely be one or more users who want to opt completely out of the content filter, so you'll need to enter their email addresses here.

FIGURE 5.9 The Custom Words tab of the Content Filtering Properties dialog box

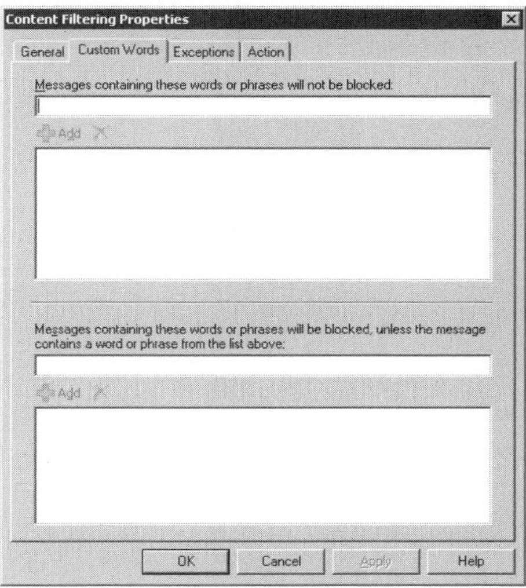

FIGURE 5.10 The Exceptions tab of the Content Filtering Properties dialog box

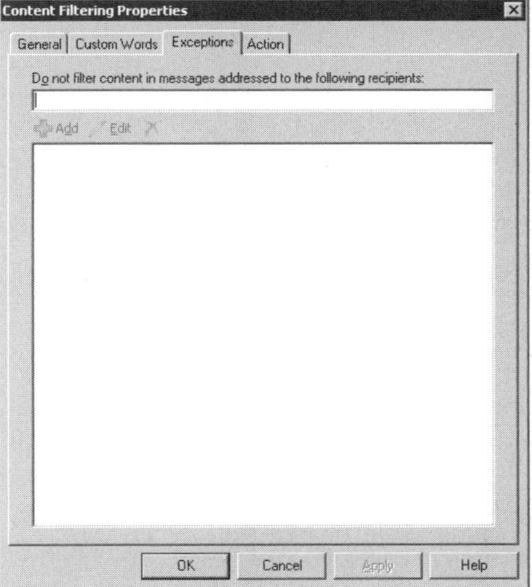

Action

The Action tab, shown in Figure 5.11, allows you to configure what the content filter will do when a message has been classified at a certain SCL. You have three options: delete the message (with no nondelivery report [NDR]), reject the message (with an NDR), or quarantine the message to an internal mailbox. By default, only message rejection is enabled, and it has an SCL value of 7. You will want to configure these options to suit your organization's needs and tolerance of spam.

FIGURE 5.11 The Action tab of the Content Filtering Properties dialog box

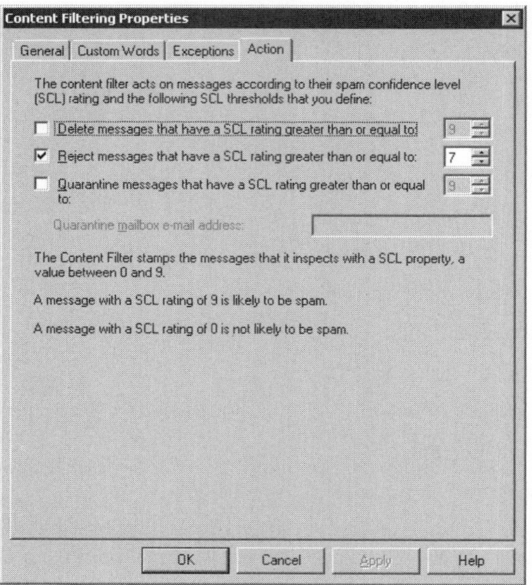

IP Allow Lists

Sometimes you'll find it easier to just configure one or more IP addresses that are always allowed to send messages without being treated as spam, as long as you know those senders are authentic. A common implementation of this might be to configure the IP addresses of business partners, thereby allowing their messages to always be delivered even if they trigger an SCL rating as they pass through the Edge Transport server.

You can manually configure IP addresses to be allowed by opening the Properties dialog box for the IP Allow List item. On the Allowed Addresses tab, shown in Figure 5.12, you'll be able to add IP addresses that are to be allowed or to remove existing entries if they should no longer be allowed to send with the content filter taking action.

If you've subscribed to an external service that maintains a verified list of "safe" IP addresses that are known to not send spam, you can configure the IP Allow List Providers item to allow the Edge Transport server to do lookups against that provider upon the receipt of inbound messages. On the Providers tab of the IP Allow List Providers Properties dialog box, shown in Figure 5.13, you can add or remove providers. You can disable or enable providers on the list at any time and change the order as well. You should always put the best or faster providers highest on the list because Exchange will stop querying other providers once it has matched the IP address of the sending system against an allow list provider's list.

FIGURE 5.12 The Allowed Addresses tab of the IP Allow List Properties dialog box

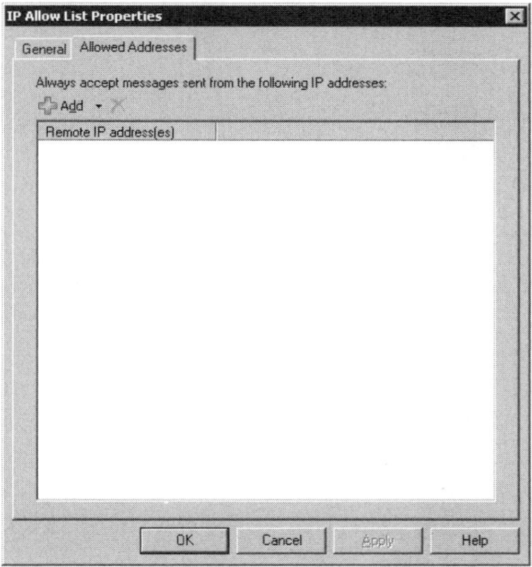

FIGURE 5.13 The Providers tab of the IP Allow List Providers Properties dialog box

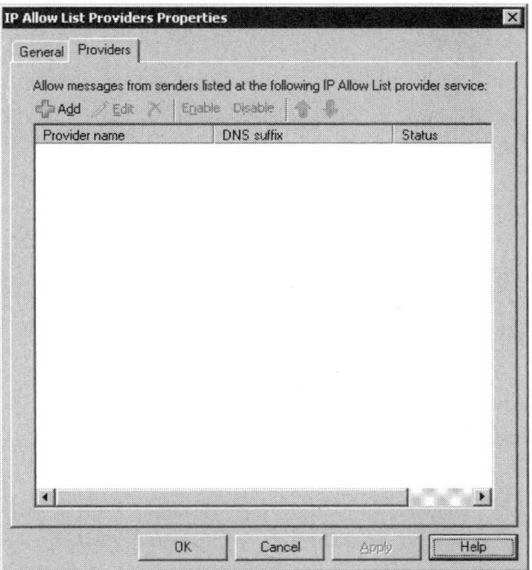

IP Block Lists

Configuring IP addresses to be blocked works the same way as for configuring an IP address to be allowed. You can either enter addresses manually from the Blocked Address tab of the IP Block List Properties dialog box, shown in Figure 5.14, or configure one or more external services to provide this information to you.

FIGURE 5.14 The Blocked Addresses tab of the IP Block List Properties dialog box

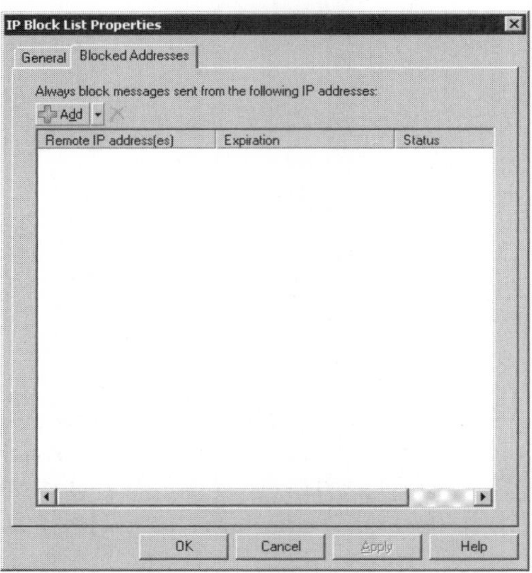

Configuring the IP block list providers options will almost immediately cause a difference in the amount of spam your users receive, so treat this area with the importance it deserves. On the Providers tab of the IP Block List Providers Properties dialog box, shown in Figure 5.15, you can configure one or more providers that the Edge Transport server should consult with to determine whether the sending IP address of a received message is a known spammer. Just as with the IP Allow List Providers item, you can add or remove providers as you want, as well as disable, enable, or reorder the providers in the list. Using the best or fastest provider here, as your experience dictates, will provide the best results since the Edge Transport server will stop looking to see whether the IP address belongs to a known spammer once it finds a match.

Some of the more popular block list providers include the following, although you can use any provider you trust:

- Spamhaus, `www.spamhaus.org`
- Spamcop, `www.spamcop.net`
- ABUSEAT CBL, `http://cbl.abuseat.org`
- SORBS, `www.sorbs.net`

FIGURE 5.15 The Providers tab of the IP Block List Providers Properties dialog box

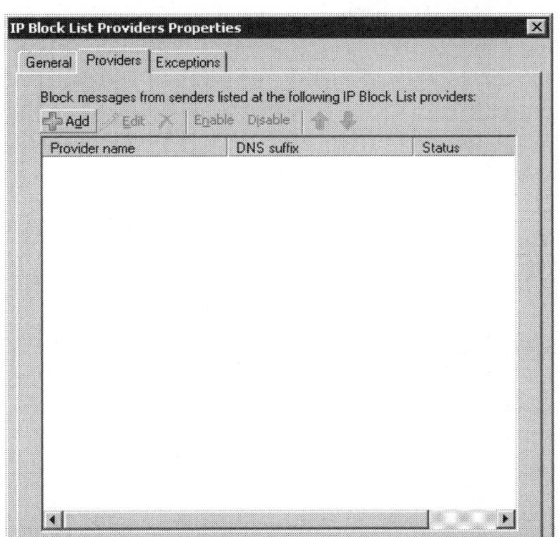

Because sometimes you or your users will want or need to get every message sent to them, regardless of its SCL rating, you can configure a list of email addresses on the Exceptions tab of the IP Block List Providers Properties dialog box, shown in Figure 5.16, that will always get messages addressed to them.

FIGURE 5.16 The Exceptions tab of the IP Block List Providers Properties dialog box

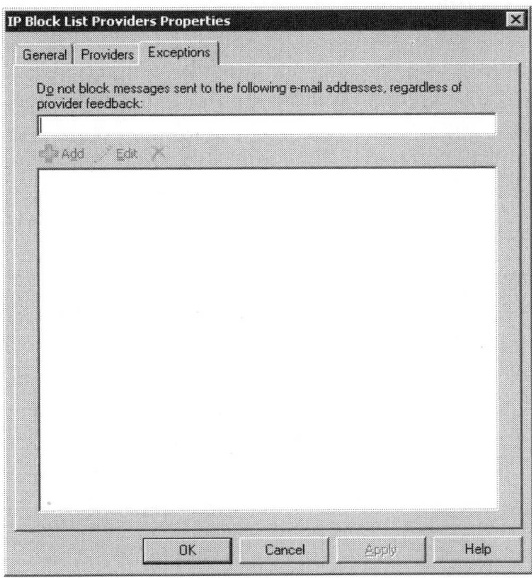

Recipient Filtering

Another powerful spam reduction tool you have available by default in Exchange Server 2007 is recipient filtering. Considering how much email is misaddressed and eventually winds up in the Postmaster mailbox, using recipient filtering to block inbound messages to recipients who don't exist in the global address list (GAL) is a powerful tool. The Blocked Recipients tab of the Recipient Filtering Properties dialog box, shown in Figure 5.17, allows you to block messages sent to recipients of your choosing and/or those not in the GAL. Take the time to at least enable the GAL-based filtering, and you'll save your organization a lot of spam that might otherwise be delivered.

FIGURE 5.17 The Blocked Recipients tab of the Recipient Filtering Properties dialog box

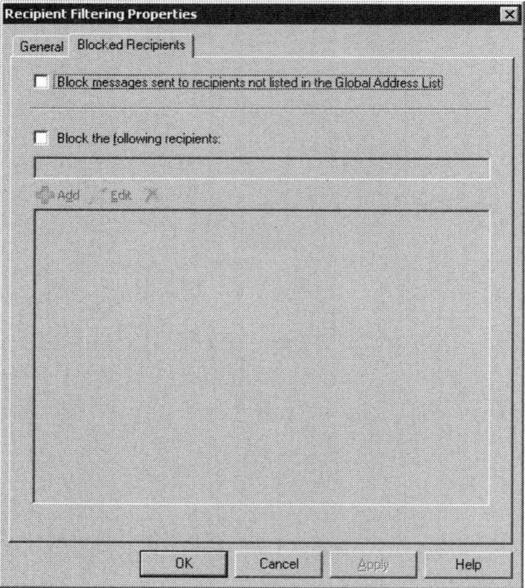

You can use the option to block additional recipients in situations where you might have some internal email addresses that should never receive mail from the Internet. Typical scenarios for this include compliance reporting, spam and virus reporting, and mail-enabled public folders used for workflow applications.

Sender Filtering

Another powerful, and easy to configure, tool you have to control spam delivered to your users' mailboxes is the Sender Filtering options. Sometimes using an IP block list provider isn't good enough if you need to block certain senders. This can happen when a new IP address starts sending you mail that isn't in the block list provider's database yet but is obviously sending you spam. Alternatively, you might need to block messages from IP addresses that are not sending spam but are otherwise sending messages that your organization has deemed it does not want to receive, such as job offers sent to employees from competing businesses in the area. You can add a list of sender IP addresses to block from the Blocked Senders tab of the Sender Filtering Properties dialog box, as shown in Figure 5.18. Note the option at the bottom of the dialog box to block messages from blank senders, a common tactic used by spammers.

On the Action tab, shown in Figure 5.19, you can configure the desired action to occur if the IP address of the sending system is found in the Blocked Senders listing. Either you can block the message entirely, which is the default setting, or you can opt to continue processing the message but add to the SCL rating of the message because the sender is a blocked sender. Most organizations will likely opt to block the message entirely.

FIGURE 5.18 The Blocked Senders tab of the Sender Filtering Properties dialog box

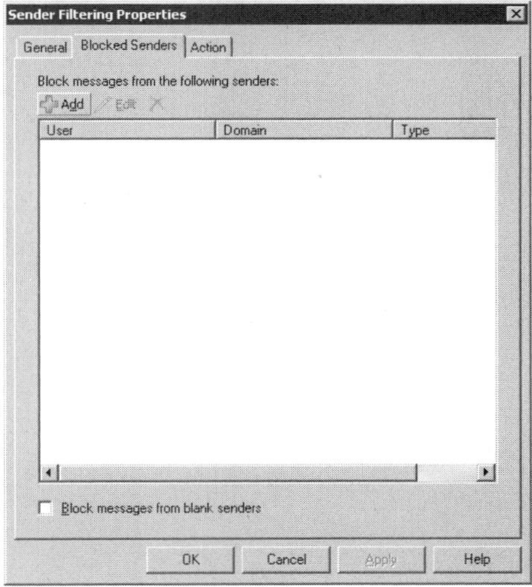

FIGURE 5.19 The Action tab of the Sender Filtering Properties dialog box

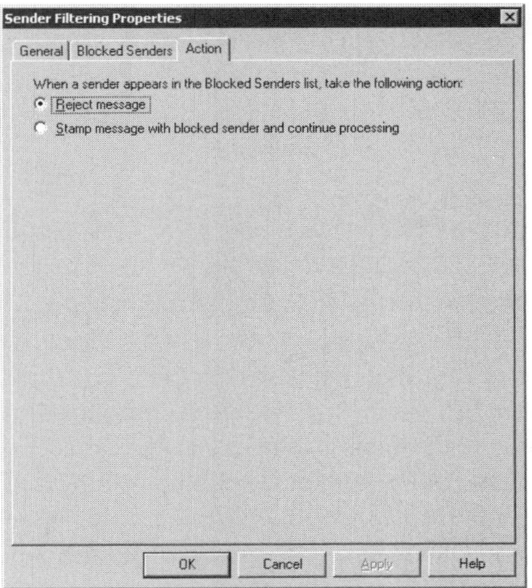

Sender ID

Sender ID is a relatively new method being used to fight both spam and phishing email messages. As such, it is not to be counted on 100 percent of the time to be accurate and up-to-date. Many sending systems are not participating in Sender ID yet, even though they are legitimate and valid senders; thus, you should not use Sender ID as an absolute just yet. To that end, the default configuration is to simply note the Sender ID status in the message headers for SCL evaluation and pass the message along for further analysis. You can configure the action that the Edge Transport server should take when a Sender ID check fails on an inbound message from the Actions tab of the Sender ID Properties dialog box, as shown in Figure 5.20.

FIGURE 5.20 The Action tab of the Sender ID Properties dialog box

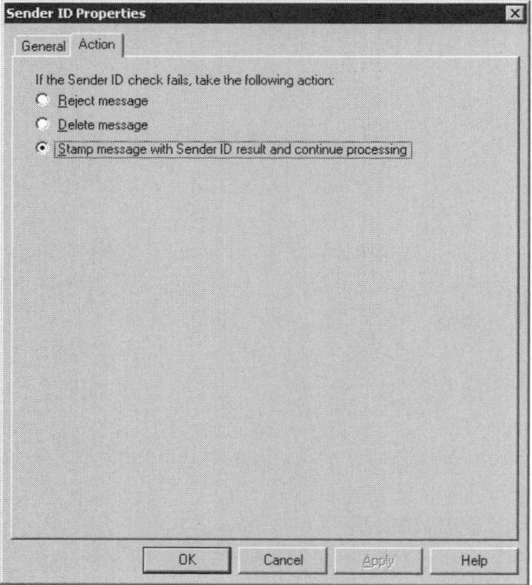

Sender Reputation

The Sender Reputation item is a dynamic method Exchange Server 2007 uses to add (and subsequently remove) sending IP addresses to the IP block list depending on their recent behavior patterns. If a certain IP address does not otherwise appear in any IP block list but has sent a large amount of spam as classified by your Edge Transport servers, then it can be dynamically added to the IP block list for a certain amount of time. Assuming that the IP address does not continue to send spam messages above your SCL ratings, it will be automatically removed from the IP block list after this period of time. Because of its dynamic nature, sender reputation can be both a powerful tool and a complex one to use. You could end up putting an IP address on the block list that you did not want to end up there, although if the rest of the settings are working correctly (per your organization's needs) than any IP address that the Sender Reputation item adds to the block list is almost certainly there for a good reason.

By default, the Edge Transport server is configured to detect open ports and relays on sending systems. The Sender Confidence tab of the Sender Reputation Properties dialog box, shown in Figure 5.21, allows you to turn off this option, although there is no reason why you would ordinarily do this.

FIGURE 5.21 The Sender Confidence tab of the Sender Reputation Properties dialog box

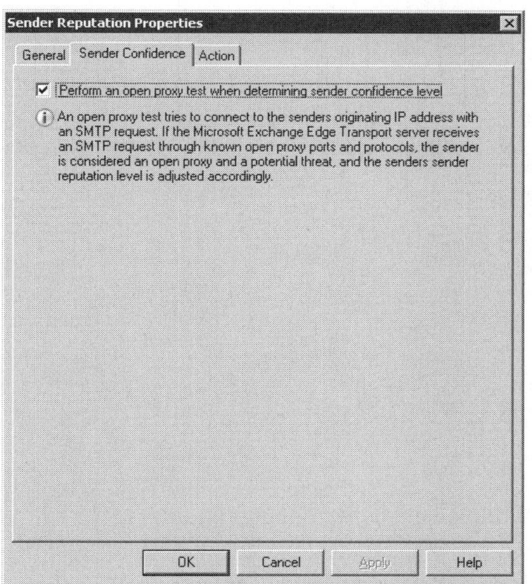

The Action tab, shown in Figure 5.22, allows you to configure the sender reputation level (SRL) value that will result in the sender being added to the IP block list for the number of hours configured. A setting of 0 on the slider indicates that the sender is almost certainly not a spammer, with a less than 1 percent probability of being a spam source. Conversely, a setting of 9 on the slider indicates that sender is almost certainly a spammer, with a greater than 99 percent probability of being a spam source. The default setting is a SRL of 7, which most organizations will find acceptable. If anything, you will most likely move the slider up to a setting of 8 to decrease the chances of inadvertently adding an acceptable sender to the IP block list.

Attachment Filtering

The last antispam agent we'll examine here is the attachment filtering agent. Unlike the previous items we've covered, no Exchange Management Console configuration is available for attachment filtering, so warm up your Exchange Management Shell! By default, the attachment filtering agent is enabled on a newly installed Edge Transport server, but you can check to be sure by issuing the `Get-TransportAgent` cmdlet from the Exchange Management Shell, as shown in Figure 5.23.

FIGURE 5.22 The Action tab of the Sender Reputation Properties dialog box

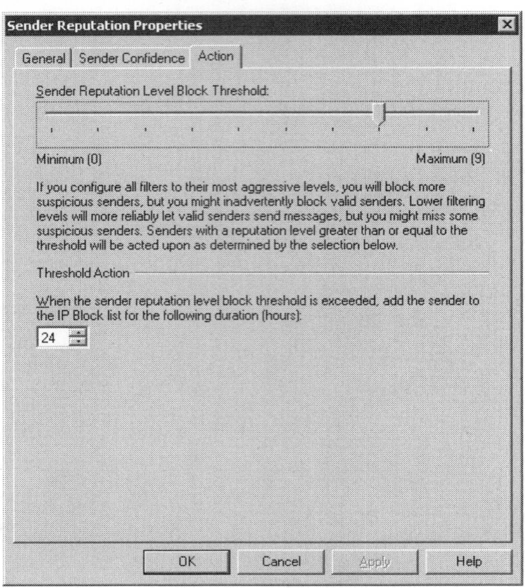

FIGURE 5.23 Checking the status of antispam transport agents

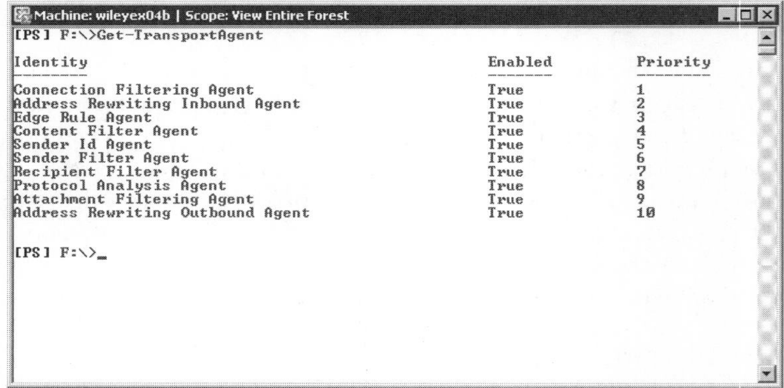

To see the default configuration of the attachment filtering agent, you will need to use the `Get-AttachmentFilterListConfig` cmdlet. This should return the following result on a newly installed Edge Transport server:

```
Name                 : Transport Settings
RejectResponse       : Message rejected due to unacceptable attachments
```

```
AdminMessage         : This attachment was removed.
Action               : Strip
ExceptionConnectors  : {}
AttachmentNames      : {ContentType:application/x-msdownload,
ContentType:message/partial, ContentType:text/scriptlet,
ContentType:application/prg, ContentType:application/msaccess,
ContentType:text/javascript, ContentType:application/x-javascript,
ContentType:application/javascript, ContentType:x-internet-signup,
ContentType:application/hta, FileName:*.xnk, FileName:*.wsh,
FileName:*.wsf, FileName:*.wsc, FileName:*.vbs, FileName:*.vbe...}

AdminDisplayName     :
ExchangeVersion      : 0.1 (8.0.535.0)
DistinguishedName    : CN=Transport Settings,
CN=First Organization,CN=MicrosoftExchange,CN=Services,CN=Configuration,
CN={67E9AD9B-2D4C-4E33-BAEA-28295AE49B99}
Identity             : Transport Settings
Guid                 : 07e65d0f-206b-45ee-9d7e-cd935eed2aaa
ObjectCategory       : CN=ms-Exch-Transport-Settings,
CN=Schema,CN=Configuration,CN={67E9AD9B-2D4C-4E33-BAEA-28295AE49B99}
ObjectClass          : {top, container, msExchTransportSettings}
WhenChanged          : 4/29/2007 2:28:17 PM
WhenCreated          : 4/29/2007 11:03:48 AM
OriginatingServer    : localhost
IsValid              : True
```

As you can see, a few file types such as Access databases, JavaScript files, and VBScript files are going to be stripped from messages by default. You will likely want to add and/or remove file types of your own. To add new file types to the attachment filtering agent, you will need to use the `Add-AttachmentFilterEntry` cmdlet. If you wanted to add all attachments with the file extension of `.pdf`, you would use a command like this:

```
Add-AttachmentFilterEntry -name *.pdf -type FileName
```

If you wanted to use a MIME type value to block attachments, you would use the following command to strip all MPEG audio/video files:

```
Add-AttachmentFilterEntry -name audio/mpeg -type ContentType
```

You can get a listing of all registered MIME types by visiting the following website: `http://www.iana.org/assignments/media-types/`.

You can see the results of the commands in Figure 5.24.

FIGURE 5.24 Adding file types to the Attachment Filter Agent

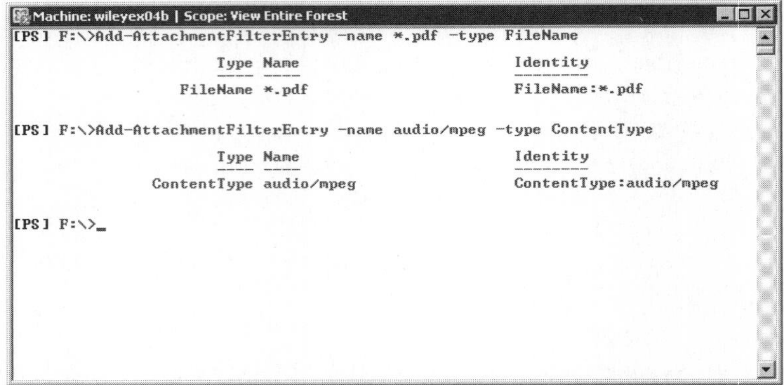
```
[PS] F:\>Add-AttachmentFilterEntry -name *.pdf -type FileName

                 Type Name                           Identity
                 ---- ----                           --------
             FileName *.pdf                          FileName:*.pdf

[PS] F:\>Add-AttachmentFilterEntry -name audio/mpeg -type ContentType

                 Type Name                           Identity
                 ---- ----                           --------
          ContentType audio/mpeg                     ContentType:audio/mpeg

[PS] F:\>_
```

Conversely, you can remove a file type from the Attachment Filter Agent by using the `Remove-AttachmentFilterEntry` cmdlet. If you wanted to remove the previously added entry for MPEG files, you command would look like this:

```
Remove-AttachmentFilterEntry -Identity contenttype:audio/mpeg
```

You'll be prompted to confirm your intention, however, as shown in Figure 5.25, when you remove an entry from the list.

If you want an easier way to view the full and current list of file types that are covered by the Attachment Filter Agent, you can use the `Get-AttachmentFilterEntry` cmdlet, as shown in Figure 5.26. The information provided here is much easier to read than that provided by the `Get-AttachmentFilterListConfig` cmdlet you saw earlier.

FIGURE 5.25 Removing file types from the Attachment Filter Agent

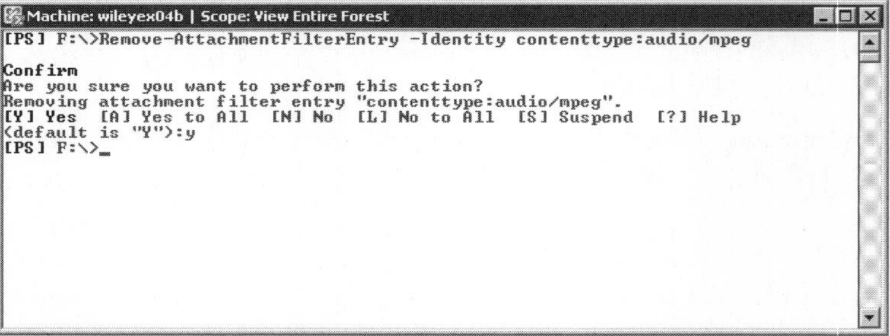
```
[PS] F:\>Remove-AttachmentFilterEntry -Identity contenttype:audio/mpeg

Confirm
Are you sure you want to perform this action?
Removing attachment filter entry "contenttype:audio/mpeg".
[Y] Yes  [A] Yes to All  [N] No  [L] No to All  [S] Suspend  [?] Help
(default is "Y"):y
[PS] F:\>_
```

FIGURE 5.26 Viewing file types configured for the Attachment Filter Agent

```
Machine: wileyex04b | Scope: View Entire Forest
[PS] F:\>Get-AttachmentFilterEntry

           Type Name                            Identity
           ---- ----                            --------
       FileName *.pdf                           FileName:*.pdf
    ContentType application/x-msdownload        ContentType:applicatio...
    ContentType message/partial                 ContentType:message/pa...
    ContentType text/scriptlet                  ContentType:text/scrip...
    ContentType application/prg                 ContentType:applicatio...
    ContentType application/msaccess            ContentType:applicatio...
    ContentType text/javascript                 ContentType:text/javas...
    ContentType application/x-javascript        ContentType:applicatio...
    ContentType application/javascript          ContentType:applicatio...
    ContentType x-internet-signup               ContentType:x-internet...
    ContentType application/hta                 ContentType:applicatio...
       FileName *.xnk                           FileName:*.xnk
       FileName *.wsh                           FileName:*.wsh
       FileName *.wsf                           FileName:*.wsf
       FileName *.wsc                           FileName:*.wsc
       FileName *.vbs                           FileName:*.vbs
       FileName *.vbe                           FileName:*.vbe
       FileName *.vb                            FileName:*.vb
       FileName *.url                           FileName:*.url
       FileName *.shs                           FileName:*.shs
       FileName *.shb                           FileName:*.shb
       FileName *.sct                           FileName:*.sct
       FileName *.scr                           FileName:*.scr
       FileName *.scf                           FileName:*.scf
       FileName *.reg                           FileName:*.reg
       FileName *.prg                           FileName:*.prg
       FileName *.prf                           FileName:*.prf
       FileName *.pif                           FileName:*.pif
       FileName *.pcd                           FileName:*.pcd
       FileName *.ops                           FileName:*.ops
       FileName *.mst                           FileName:*.mst
       FileName *.msp                           FileName:*.msp
       FileName *.msi                           FileName:*.msi
       FileName *.psc2                          FileName:*.psc2
       FileName *.psc1                          FileName:*.psc1
       FileName *.ps2xml                        FileName:*.ps2xml
```

If you want to change the default behavior or message when attachment stripping occurs, you will need to use the `Set-AttachmentFilterListConfig` cmdlet, which has the following syntax:

```
Set-AttachmentFilterListConfig [-Action <Reject | Strip | SilentDelete>]
[-AdminMessage <String>] [-DomainController <Fqdn>]
[-ExceptionConnectors <MultiValuedProperty>]
[-Instance <AttachmentFilteringConfig>] [-RejectResponse <String>]
```

You can set the `Action` behavior to one of the following options:

- `Reject`, which issues an NDR to the sender and prevents the message and attachment from passing
- `Strip`, which removes the attachment but allows the message to pass through with text indicating an attachment was stripped
- `SilentDelete`, which deletes the message and sends no NDR to the sender

The `AdminMessage` value specifies the contents of a text file that will be attached to messages to replace a stripped attachment. The default value is "This attachment was removed." However, you might want to customize it to include a contact email address or phone number for the help desk in your organization so that a recipient can get more information about attachment filtering policies. The `RejectResponse` value specifies the message body of NDR messages sent to senders whose attachments have been rejected. The default value of "Message rejected due to unacceptable attachments" is fairly useful, but you might want to also customize it with an externally available contact phone number or email address if a sender needs help determining what attachment types are allowed through your email system. The `RejectResponse` value has a limit of 240 characters, so be sure to check your text before changing the value. You can configure connectors that the Attachment Filter Agent should not function on by using the `ExceptionConnectors` value.

The following example command will change the default `Action` behavior to `Reject` and will change the `RejectResponse` value to be more informative:

```
Set-AttachmentFilterListConfig -Action Reject
-RejectResponse "Your message and attachment(s) have not been delivered
to the intended recipient.  Please contact the Wiley Publishing Help
Desk at 1-877-555-1234 for more information."
```

Figure 5.27 shows the changes and the verification of the changes using the `Get-AttachmentFilterListConfig` cmdlet.

FIGURE 5.27 Modifying the Attachment Filter Agent behavior

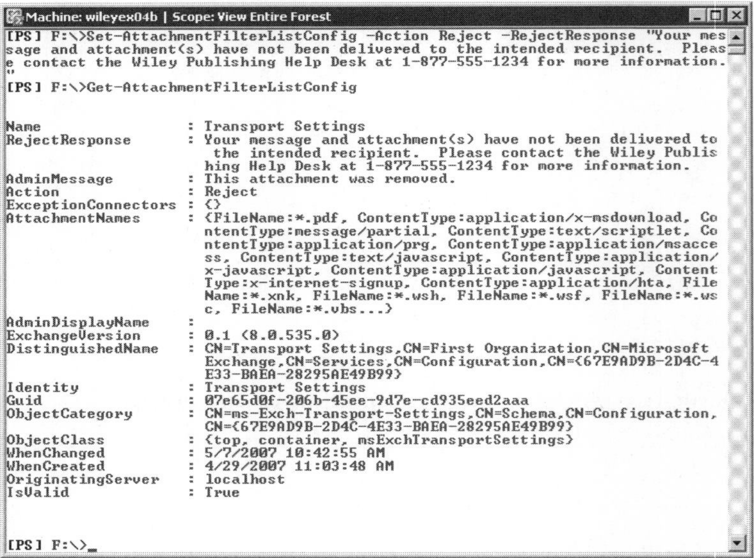

Using Edge Cloning

For all the power and flexibility that Edge Transport servers offer you, you need to be aware of one glaring limitation: Edge Transport servers don't replicate or otherwise transfer their configuration amongst themselves the same way the other Exchange Server 2007 roles do. To that end, if you will have multiple Edge Transport servers in your organization (which is a highly recommended configuration), you will need to transfer that configuration manually each time you make a change.

The process of edge cloning is not required when your Edge Transport servers have been subscribed to Hub Transport servers, as discussed earlier in the "Configuring and Managing EdgeSync" section of this chapter. Edge cloning is required only for stand-alone Edge Transport servers.

To export the configuration from an Edge Transport server that you've already configured, you will need to use the `ExportEdgeConfig` PowerShell script from the Exchange Management Shell. Your command to perform the export would look like this if you were exporting to the F drive on your server:

```
ExportEdgeConfig -CloneConfigData:"F:\CloneConfigData.xml"
```

Figure 5.28 shows how to use the command from the Exchange Management Shell, and Figure 5.29 shows a sample XML file resulting from the export.

FIGURE 5.28 Performing the Edge Transport server export process

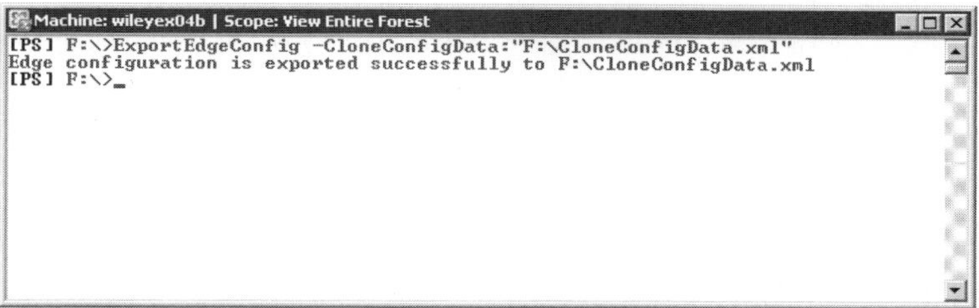

FIGURE 5.29 Examining the XML export output file

CloneConfigData.xml - Notepad

File Edit Format View Help


```
<?xml version="1.0" encoding="utf-8"?>
<ExportedEdgeConfiguration>
  <TransportServer>
    <AntispamAgentsEnabled>True</AntispamAgentsEnabled>
    <AntispamUpdatesEnabled>True</AntispamUpdatesEnabled>
    <ConnectivityLogEnabled>False</ConnectivityLogEnabled>
    <ConnectivityLogMaxAge>30.00:00:00</ConnectivityLogMaxAge>
    <ConnectivityLogMaxDirectorySize>250MB</ConnectivityLogMaxDirectorySize>
    <ConnectivityLogMaxFileSize>10MB</ConnectivityLogMaxFileSize>
    <ConnectivityLogPath>F:\Program Files\Microsoft\Exchange
Server\TransportRoles\Logs\Connectivity</ConnectivityLogPath>
    <ContentConversionTracingEnabled>False</ContentConversionTracingEnabled>
    <DelayNotificationTimeout>04:00:00</DelayNotificationTimeout>
    <DistinguishedName>CN=wileyex04b,CN=Servers,CN=Exchange Administrative Group
(FYDIBOHF23SPDLT),CN=Administrative Groups,CN=First Organization,CN=Microsoft
Exchange,CN=Services,CN=Configuration,CN={67E9AD9B-2D4C-4E33-BAEA-28295AE49B99}</DistinguishedName
>
    <ExchangeVersion>0.1 (8.0.535.0)</ExchangeVersion>
    <ExternalDelayDsnEnabled>True</ExternalDelayDsnEnabled>
    <ExternalDNSAdapterEnabled>True</ExternalDNSAdapterEnabled>
    <ExternalDNSAdapterGuid>00000000-0000-0000-0000-000000000000</ExternalDNSAdapterGuid>
    <ExternalDNSProtocolOption>Any</ExternalDNSProtocolOption>
    <ExternalDNSServers>$null</ExternalDNSServers>
    <ExternalDsnDefaultLanguage>en-US</ExternalDsnDefaultLanguage>
    <ExternalDsnLanguageDetectionEnabled>True</ExternalDsnLanguageDetectionEnabled>
    <ExternalDsnMaxMessageAttachSize>10MB</ExternalDsnMaxMessageAttachSize>
    <ExternalDsnReportingAuthority>wiley.corp</ExternalDsnReportingAuthority>
    <ExternalDsnSendHtml>True</ExternalDsnSendHtml>
    <ExternalIPAddress>$null</ExternalIPAddress>
    <ExternalPostmasterAddress>$null</ExternalPostmasterAddress>
    <Guid>9db4ce3a-3884-415b-bdd4-1f11ac159ea1</Guid>
    <Identity>wileyex04b</Identity>
    <InternalDelayDsnEnabled>True</InternalDelayDsnEnabled>
```

To import the XML file, you will need to use the `ImportEdgeConfig` PowerShell script from the Exchange Management Shell. This process, however, is a two-step one. The first step involves creating an answer file that contains the server settings specific to the Edge Transport server on which the import is being performed. The command you would use for this process will look similar to the following. Note that the `-IsImport` variable is set to `$false` during this step, which is what allows for the creation of the answer file without actually importing the XML configuration file.

```
ImportEdgeConfig -CloneConfigData:"F:\CloneConfigData.xml" -IsImport $false
-CloneConfigAnswer:"F:\CloneConfigAnswer.xml"
```

Figure 5.30 shows how to use the command from the Exchange Management Shell.

FIGURE 5.30 Creating the import answer file for edge cloning

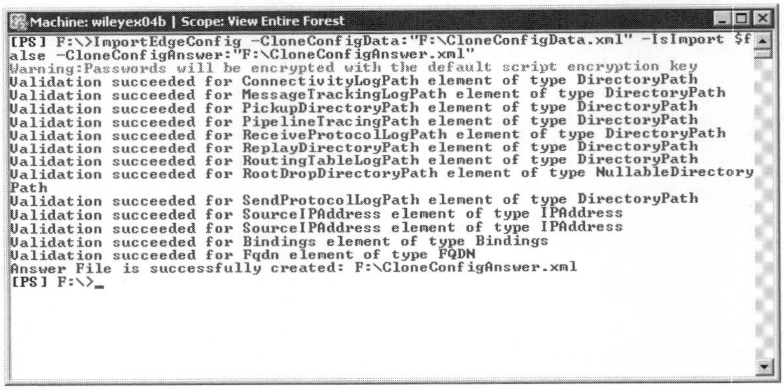

Once the answer file has been created, you can import the XML configuration file by using the following command:

```
ImportEdgeConfig -CloneConfigData:"F:\CloneConfigData.xml" -IsImport $true
-CloneConfigAnswer:"F:\CloneConfigAnswer.xml"
```

Configuring Microsoft Forefront Security for Exchange Server

Although the built-in antispam functionality of Exchange Server 2007 is pretty good, odds are that you'll want to use an additional antispam and/or antivirus product on your Edge Transport servers. The obvious choice for this Microsoft's own Forefront Security for Exchange Server, a product previously known as Antigen by Sybari but now part of Microsoft through acquisition.

Installing Forefront Security for Exchange Server

The installation process for Forefront is fairly straightforward and can be initiated from one of two places: either by using the Exchange Server DVD from which you installed Exchange Server or by using a separate Forefront for Exchange Server CD. In Exercise 5.2, we'll show how to install via the Exchange Server DVD for simplicity.

You can find and download the Forefront Security for Exchange Server user's guide at the following location: `http://www.microsoft.com/technet/antigen/2006/gettingstarted/exchange-userguide/default.mspx?mfr=true`.

EXERCISE 5.2

Installing Forefront Security for Exchange Server

1. Open Windows Explorer or My Computer on the server containing the Exchange Server 2007 DVD and navigate to the Forefront directory on the DVD.
2. Double-click the `Setup.exe` item to start the installation process. Click Next to dismiss the opening page of the installation wizard.
3. On the License Agreement page, click Yes to accept the EULA after reading and/or printing it. You will not be able to continue with the installation without clicking Yes.
4. On the Customer Information page, shown here, enter the pertinent information, and click Next to continue to the Installation Location page.

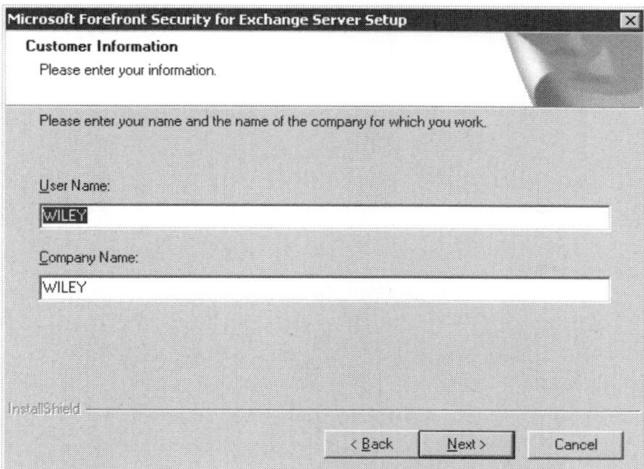

EXERCISE 5.2 *(continued)*

5. On the Installation Location page, shown here, select the Local Installation option to install the relevant Forefront product on the local Edge Transport Exchange server. Click Next to continue to the Installation Type page.

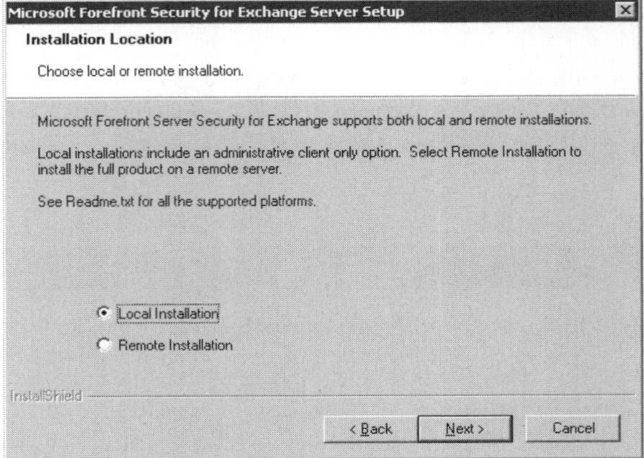

6. On the Installation Type page, shown here, select Full Install to install the relevant Forefront application files and the administrative console on the Edge Transport server. Click Next to continue to the Quarantine Security Settings page.

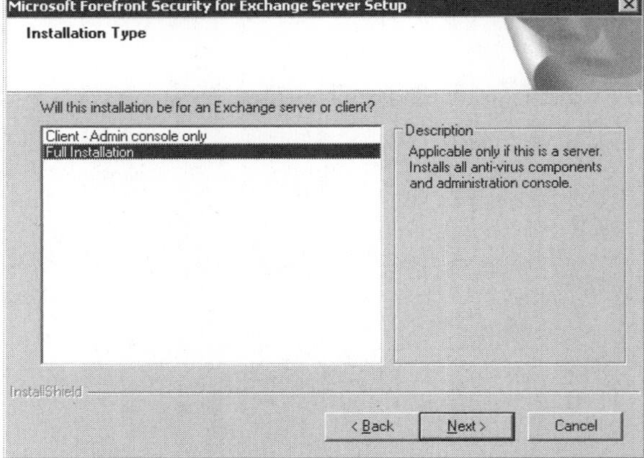

EXERCISE 5.2 *(continued)*

7. On the Quarantine Security Settings page, shown here, you will need to select how you want messages in the quarantine to be handled when you attempt to manually deliver them. You have the following two options:

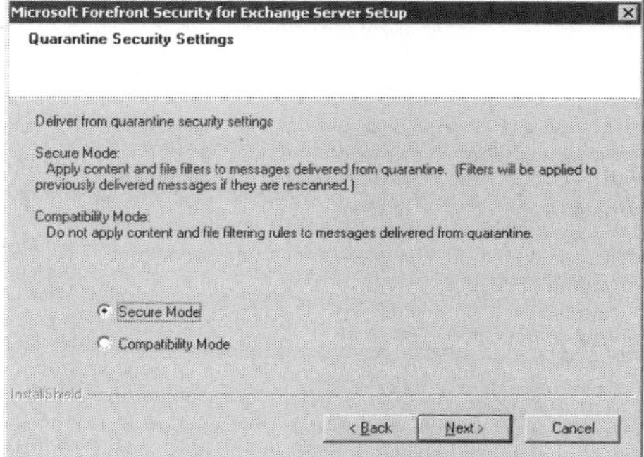

- *Secure Mode*: The default setting causes all messages and their attachments that are delivered from the quarantine to be scanned again at that time for viruses and spam filter matches. This setting will often result in items not being deliverable from the quarantine.
- *Compatibility Mode*: This option will allow messages and attachments to be delivered from the quarantine without being scanned for spam filter matches. Virus scanning always occurs, however, on messages and attachments that are delivered from the quarantine.

8. For the purposes of this installation, select the Compatibility Mode option, and then click Next to continue to the Engines page.

9. On the Engines page, shown here, you can either accept the engines that Forefront has randomly configured or choose your own scan engines up to a maximum of five, including the always-selected Microsoft Antimalware Engine. You can select fewer than five engines, but you cannot select more than five engines. Click Next to continue to the Engine Updates Required page.

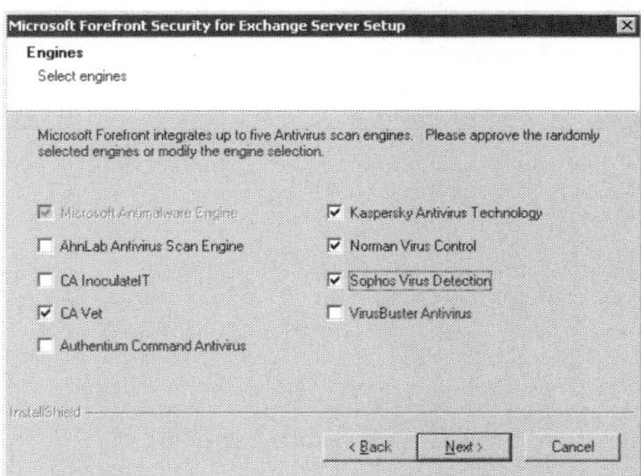

EXERCISE 5.2 *(continued)*

10. On the Engine Updates Required page, shown here, you will be notified that the scan engines you've selected will need to be updated at the completion of the Forefront installation. Click Next to continue to the Enable Anti-Spam Updates page.

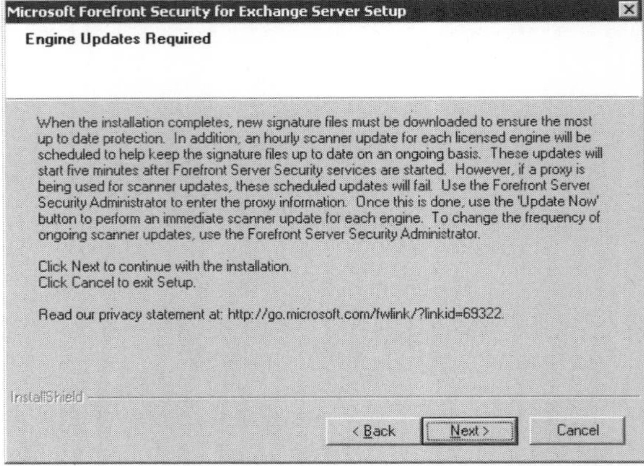

11. On the Enable Anti-Spam Updates page, shown here, you will have the option to enable antispam updates to occur automatically via Microsoft Update. Leave this option selected, and click Next to continue to the Choose Destination Location page.

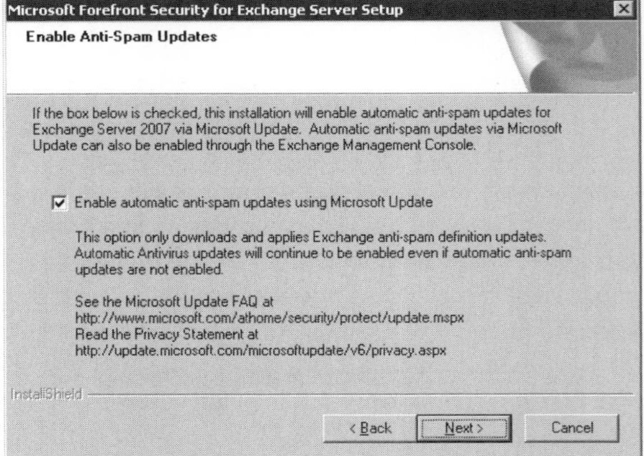

EXERCISE 5.2 *(continued)*

12. On the Choose Destination Location page, shown here, you will be able to change the install location for the Forefront files. In most cases, you should just leave the default selection. Click Next to continue to the Select Program Folder page.

13. On the Select Program Folder page, you have the option to change the name of the folder created on the Start menu from its default value. Leave the default selection intact, and click Next to continue to the Start Copying Files page.

14. On the Start Copying Files page, you will have a chance to review your settings. Click Next to allow Forefront to start installing onto your Edge Transport server.

15. After some time, the Restart Exchange Transport Service page, shown here, will appear. Click Next to allow the Exchange Transport Service to be restarted. You must restart this service to allow the Forefront installation to complete.

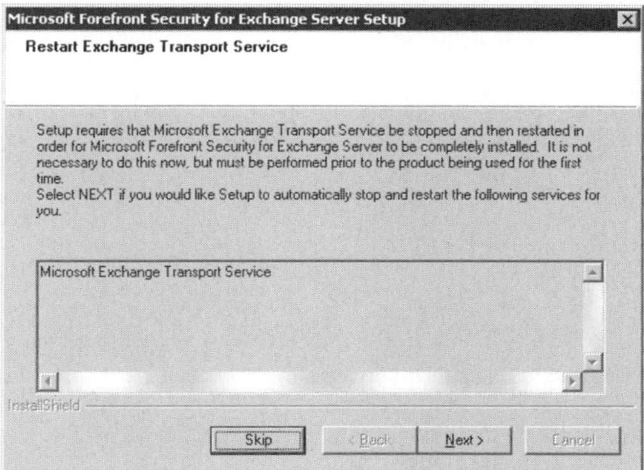

16. When the service has been restarted, click Next to continue.

17. When the installation has completed, click the Finish button to close the wizard.

Now that the installation is completed, you can move on to configuring Forefront.

Configuring Forefront for Exchange Server

Administrators familiar with Sybari's Antigen product for Exchange Server 2003 will have little trouble adjusting to the new version, Microsoft Forefront Security for Exchange Server. For those administrators who've never worked with Antigen or Forefront, the adjustment can be a bit overwhelming at first. Fortunately, all tasks within Forefront are organized into one of four areas of the Forefront administrative console. We'll examine each area of the administrative console in the following sections of this chapter.

Settings

The default view of the Forefront administrative console is of the settings area, as shown in Figure 5.31. The Settings area is divided into five smaller areas of administration:

- Scan Job
- Antivirus
- Scanner Updates
- Templates
- General Options

FIGURE 5.31 The Forefront administrative console

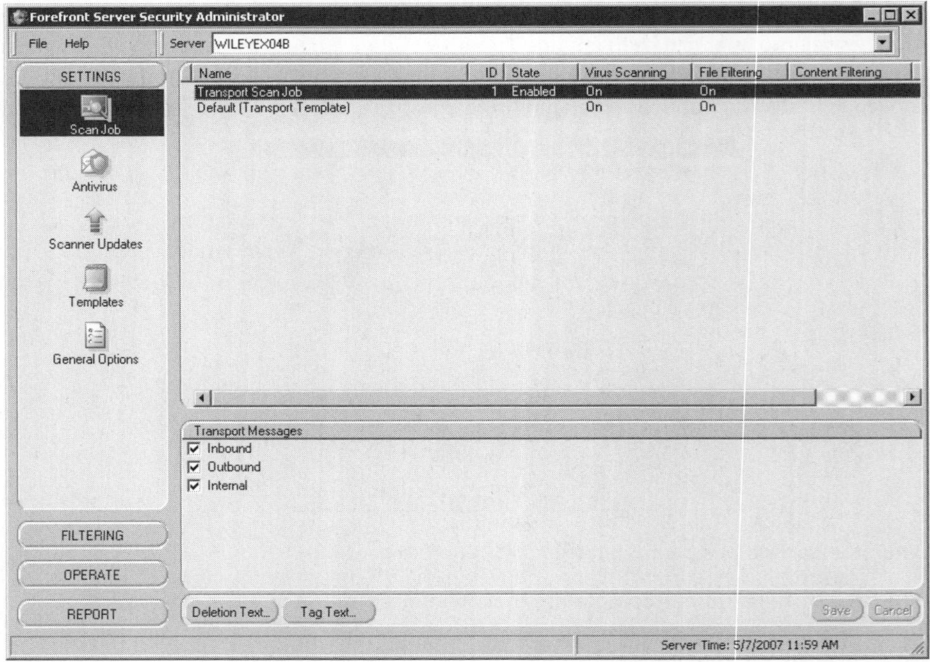

The entire Forefront system revolves around using templates. By default, the installation of Forefront on an Edge Transport server uses one scan job and one template: the Transport Scan Job (which is enabled by default with a priority setting of 1) and the Default Transport Template. The Transport Scan Job uses the Default Transport Template for its settings. In older installations of Antigen, there would typically be many more templates depending on the number of storage groups on the server.

For the purposes of this exam, we'll cover only the antivirus portion of the Forefront Security for Exchange Server product, which is actually a smaller portion of the overall functionality. Most of the spam-filtering tasks to manage and maintain a Forefront installation are beyond the scope of the exam and require a significant investment in time or training to understand and perform correctly. Also, we'll cover the default Transport Scan Job only.

Scan Job

The configuration options in the Scan Job section are pretty simple; the job is on for any combination of inbound messages, outbound messages, or internal-only messages. The Internal messages option has little consequence on an Edge Transport server, but the Inbound and Outbound options do. In addition to configuring which messages the template will apply to, you can also change the deletion text or tag text by clicking the appropriate buttons at the bottom of the console.

Clicking the Deletion Text button opens the File Deletion Text dialog box, as shown in Figure 5.32. From here you can change the default text from its current value if desired. This text is used to create a replacement file when an infected file is deleted from a message. You might customize this text with information about how to contact the help desk for assistance.

```
Microsoft Forefront Security for Exchange Server removed a file since
 it was found to be infected.
File name: "%File%"
Virus name: "%Virus%"
```

Clicking the Tag Text button opens the Tag Text dialog box, as shown in Figure 5.33. From here you can configure options to tag the subject line or MIME header of a message when a filter action has been set to Identify: Tag Message.

FIGURE 5.32 Changing the deletion text for viruses in messages

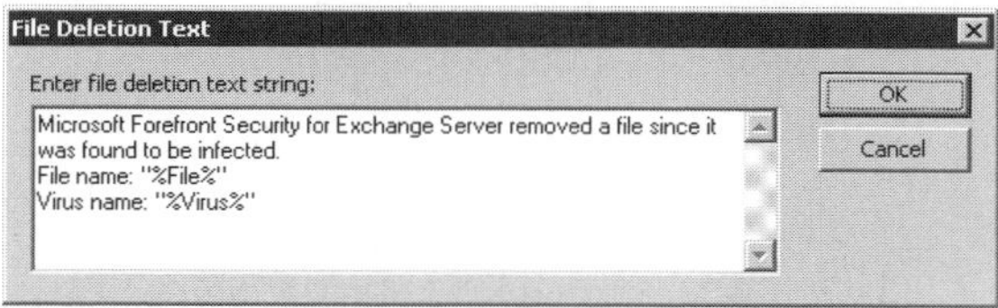

FIGURE 5.33 Changing the tag text for messages

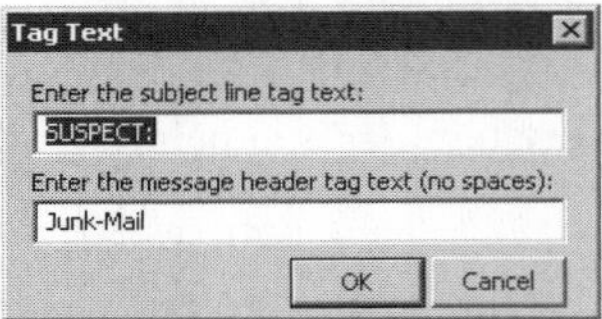

Antivirus

In the Antivirus area, shown in Figure 5.34, you can configure how the template or job scans messages, including which scan engines to use, how the engines should be used, and what action to perform when a virus is found.

To change the scan engines in use by a template, select the template in the top section of the administrative console, and then change the scan engines by deselecting or selecting scan engines in the bottom portion of the console. Recall that you can have a maximum of five scan engines configured at any one time.

FIGURE 5.34 The Antivirus area of the administrative console

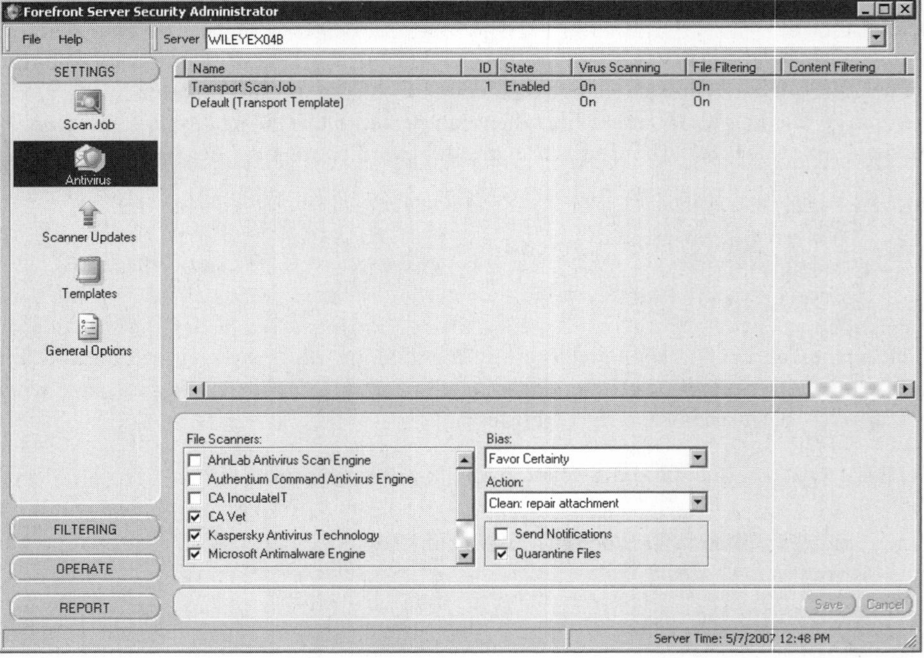

The Bias setting determines how many scan engines will be used on each attachment when checking for infected items. The following options are available:

- *Maximum Performance*: Each item is scanned using only one of the selected scan engines. This option provides the fastest performance but offers the least protection.
- *Favor Performance*: Each item is randomly scanned with either one of the selected scan engines or half of the selected scan engines. This option provides slightly better protection and slightly lower performance.
- *Neutral*: Each item is scanned with at least half of the selected scan engines.
- *Favor Certainty*: Each item is randomly scanned with either all of the selected scan engines or at least half of the selected scan engines. This is the default option.
- *Maximum Certainty*: Each item is scanned with all the selected scan items. This option provides the best protection but will result in the slowest performance.

You can configure the action to be performed by Forefront when a virus is detected from the following options:

- *Skip: Detect Only*: This option configures Forefront to only detect and report on infected files. No attempt to clean or delete the infected files is made. You should not ordinarily use this option on any production installation of Forefront because of the significant decrease in functionality when selected.
- *Clean: Repair Document*: The default action of Forefront is to attempt to clean the virus from the infected file. If the cleaning action is successful, the previously infected attachment will be replaced with a clean version. Should the cleaning attempt fail, the attachment is deleted from the message and replaced with a text file indicating the action taken. The message body remains in place, and the message is delivered to the recipient in this state.
- *Delete*: The infected attachment is deleted from the message without any attempt being made to clean it first. A text file is then attached to the message indicating an infected attachment was deleted by Forefront. The message is then delivered to the recipient.

In addition, you can select to have notifications generated as a result of infected files. We'll discuss the configuration of notifications later in the "Report" section. The option to save messages and their infected attachments to the quarantine is enabled by default and should not ordinarily be turned off. Leaving this option on will allow you to review the quarantine and attempt message delivery at a later time.

Scanner Updates

The Scanner Updates area, shown in Figure 5.35, is possibly the first place you'll actually want to come to after a new installation of Forefront. As indicated in the installation process, the scan engines need to be updated to the most current definitions available to provide the best level of protection.

FIGURE 5.35 The Scanner Updates area of the administrative console

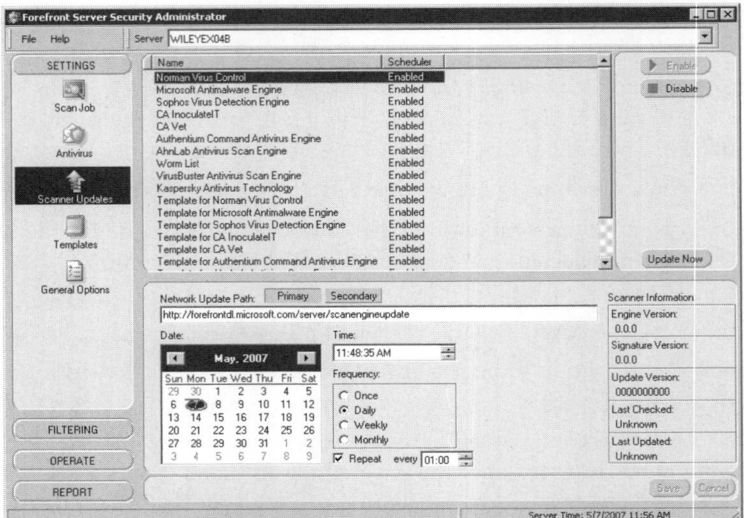

The options you have in this area are fairly straightforward. To manage a particular scan engine, select it from the list in the center part of the administrative console. On the right side of the console, you have options to enable, disable, or update the selected engine. To get your engines up-to-date, you should select each one displayed and click the Update Now button. You can monitor the status of the update process in the bottom of the administrative console, as shown in Figure 5.36. In addition, once the update has been applied, the version information will be updated appropriately in the bottom right side of the administrative console, as shown in Figure 5.37.

FIGURE 5.36 Updating scan engines

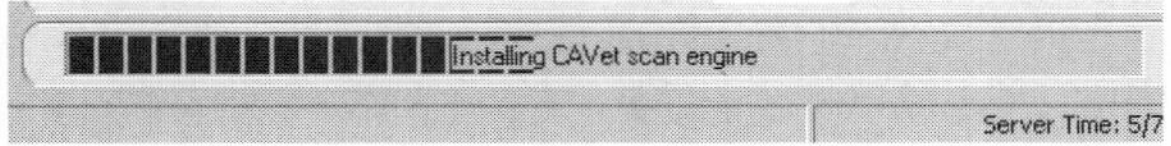

FIGURE 5.37 Viewing scan engine version information

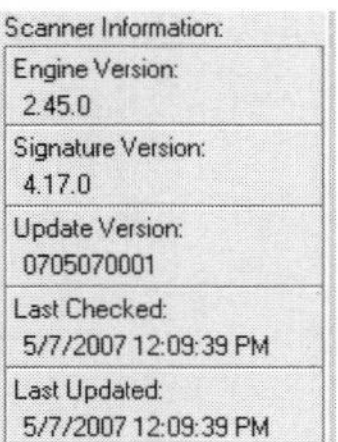

In the bottom middle section of the Scanner Updates area, you can configure a custom update schedule for each engine as well as a secondary download location should the primary location be unavailable. By default, each engine is configured to check for updates hourly, with each engine separated from the previous engine by a five-minute interval. Templates that are shown in this location are also configured to automatically check for updates hourly, in five minutes intervals from each other. You cannot manually check for template updates, though, as you can with scan engine updates.

General Options

The General Options area, shown in Figure 5.38, allows you to configure many other settings that control how Forefront works. Here you can find items such as email notifications on service startup, event logging, and update notification, among many others.

FIGURE 5.38 The General Options area of the administrative console

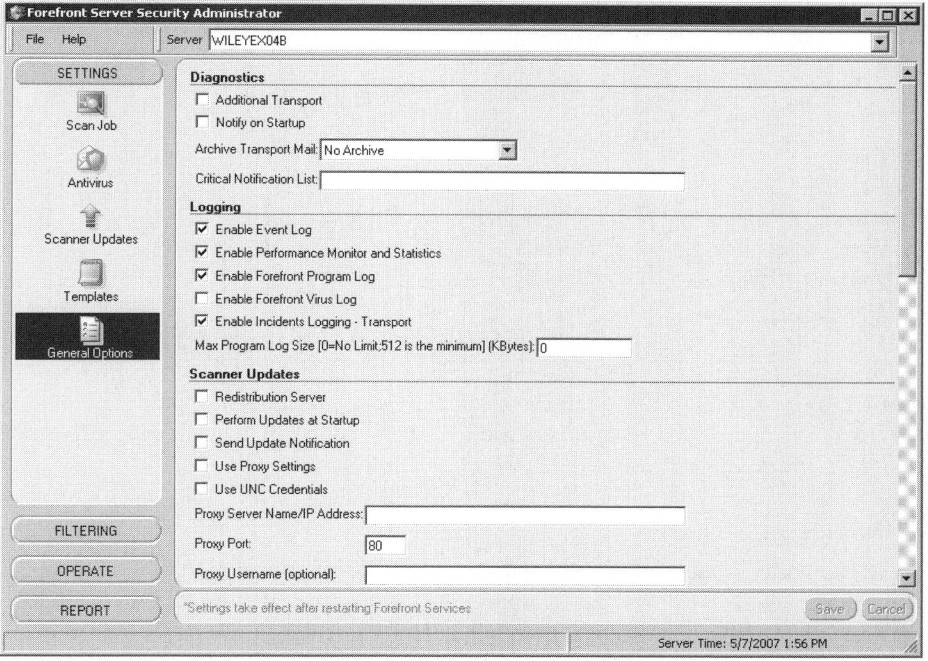

We will not be discussing the Filtering area of the Forefront Security for Exchange Server administrative console here.

Operate

The Operate area of the Forefront administrative console allows you to manage configured jobs. By default, the only area available within the Operate area is the Run Job area, as shown in Figure 5.39.

FIGURE 5.39 The Run Job area of the administrative console

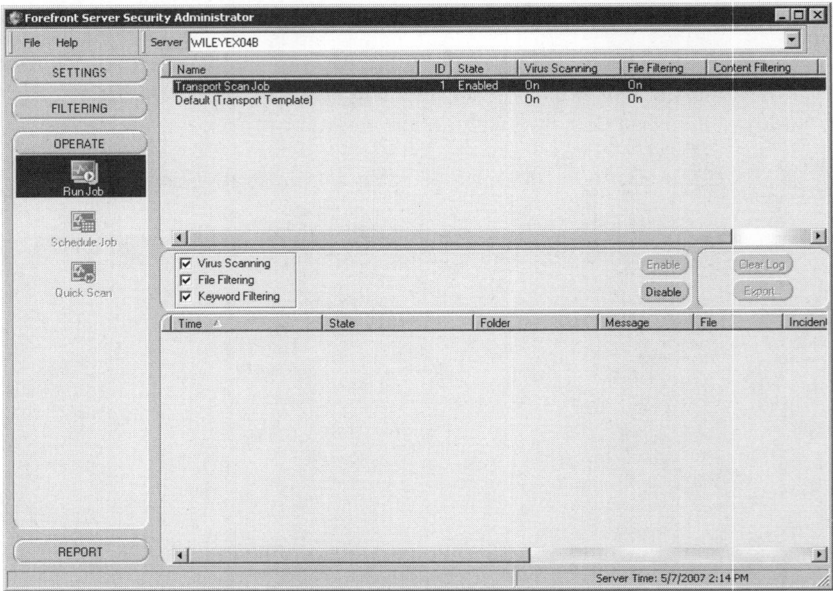

From here, you can disable or enable a job or change the particular areas that a job covers such as virus scanning, keyword filtering, and file filtering. Be sure to click Save after making any changes or click Cancel to cancel any changes without saving them.

Report

As with any antivirus application, Forefront has a quarantine area that you'll want to examine and manage periodically. You can find the quarantine as well as other important items in the Report area of the administrative console, as shown in Figure 5.40, which shows the Notification area.

Notification

In the Notification area, shown in Figure 5.40, you have the ability to configure options associated with various notifications that can be enabled or disabled for various events that might occur with Forefront. For each notification, you can also configure the following email-related fields:

- The To address(es) to send notifications to
- The CC address(es) to send notifications to

- The BCC address(es) to send notifications to
- The Subject text of the notification
- The Body text of the notification

FIGURE 5.40 The Notification area of the administrative console

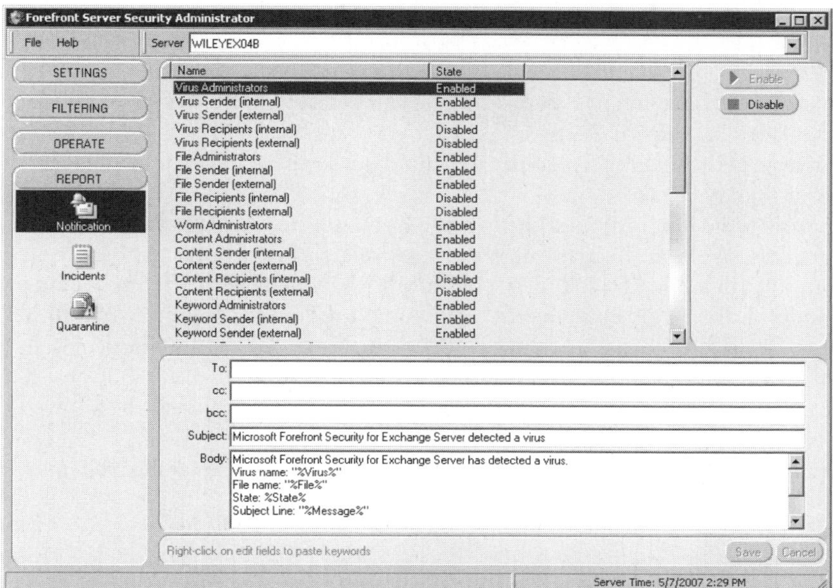

As they pertain to viruses, the following notifications are available to configure:

- *Virus Administrators*: Sends alert messages to administrators for all viruses detected on the server. Typically these alerts will be sent to a distribution group containing the mailboxes of all messaging administrators.
- *Virus Sender (internal)*: Sends alert messages to the sender of the message, if the sender is located in your Exchange organization, when a virus has been detected in a message they have sent. The body text of this notification might be customized with information about how to get help with the virus problem.
- *Virus Sender (external)*: Sends alert messages to the sender of the message if the sender is not located in your Exchange organization.
- *Virus Recipients (internal)*: Sends alert messages to the recipient of the message, if the recipient is located in your Exchange organization, that the message contained an infected attachment. The body text of this notification might be customized with information about how to contact the help desk for further assistance.
- *Virus Recipients (external)*: Sends alert messages to the recipient of the message if the recipient is not located in your Exchange organization.

Incidents

The Incidents area, shown in Figure 5.41, lists virus detections or filter operations for the server. The incidents are logged into the Incidents database, `Incidents.mdb`, and stored indefinitely by default. You will likely want to enable the automatic purging of incidents to occur every 30 days or so to keep the size of the database from growing too large. You can also filter the view for items between specific dates and export the information to a text file for archiving or later viewing.

Quarantine

The Quarantine area, shown in Figure 5.42, lists all detected files. A copy of the detected file is placed here before a clean, delete, or skip action occurs within Forefront. Over time, the number of items in the Quarantine folder will build up, so you might want to enable automatic purging after 30 days or so.

Depending on the Quarantine security option you selected while installing Forefront, you will be able to release items from the quarantine by selecting them and clicking the Deliver button without filter matching occurring (Compatibility Mode) or with filter matching occurring (Secure Mode). Either way, all items that attempted for delivery from the quarantine will always be rescanned for viruses. Should you not be able to deliver a message and its attachment from the quarantine, you can save the attachment using the Save As button—a task you will likely find yourself performing often for files that wouldn't ordinarily be allowed through but higher level users will want anyway.

You can also filter the view of the quarantine or export a list of quarantine items as desired.

FIGURE 5.41 The Incidents area of the administrative console

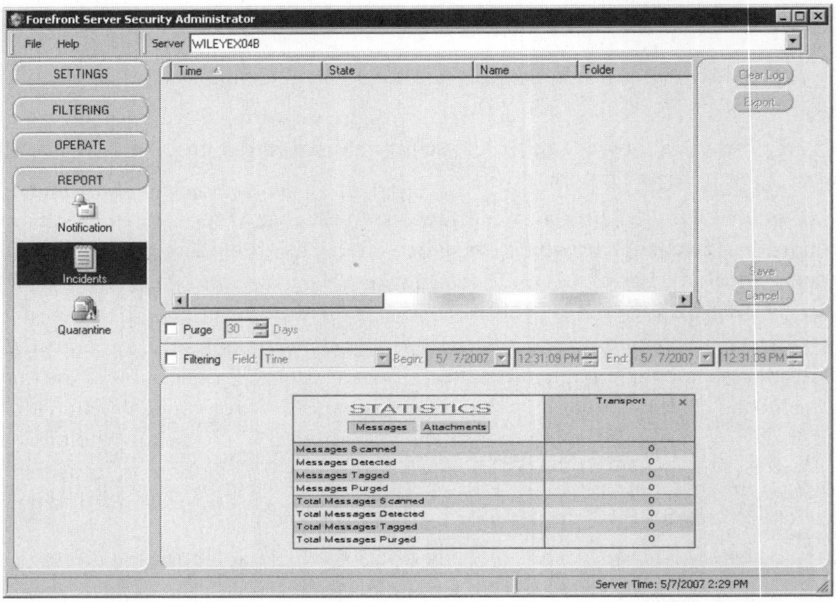

FIGURE 5.42 The Quarantine area of the administrative console

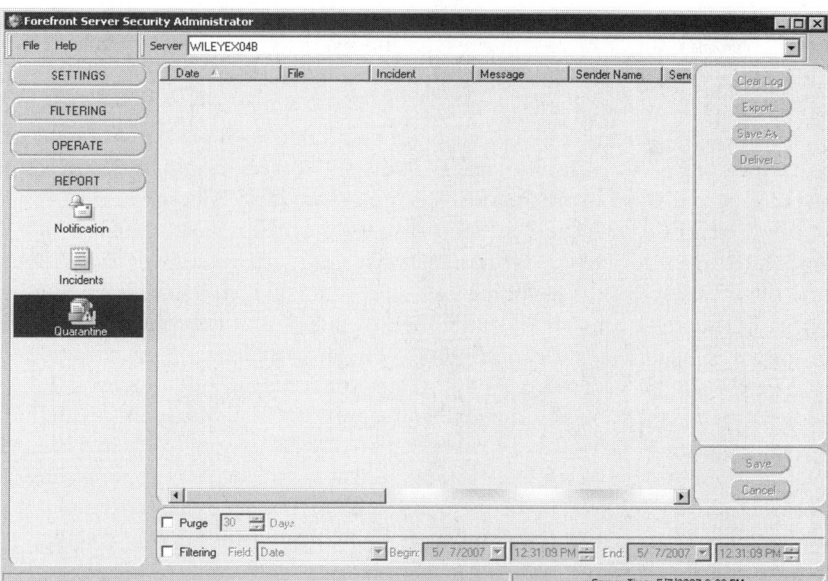

Real World Scenario

Using Exchange's Built-in Power

As you have seen throughout the course of this chapter, the Edge Transport server provides you with a powerful antispam solution right out of the box. How powerful and effective that solution is, however, will depend on how much time you spend assessing the available options and configuring them in a way that makes the most sense for your organization. If you take the time to evaluate and document your needs thoroughly and then take the time to plan your required configuration, you could get away without even needing to purchase or install an additional antispam product for your Exchange organization. Of particular note are the IP Block List and Attachment Filtering options. You can use these two areas to block the majority of all spam entering your organization. Whatever path you decide to choose when it comes to spam control, do your organization a favor and take your time. The spam problem will not be going away any time soon, but you can definitely make a difference to your users if you understand the powerful options Exchange Server 2007 gives you and configure them to their maximum potential.

Summary

In this chapter, you examined the role of the Edge Transport server in your Exchange organization. The Edge Transport server, a new dedicated Exchange Server 2007 role, is responsible for routing and scanning all inbound and outbound SMTP messages to and from your Exchange organization. Although they cannot be made highly available through network load balancing or Microsoft Clustering Services, multiple Edge Transport servers should be deployed for redundancy with the required DNS entries made in your external DNS zones.

When configured for EdgeSync, Edge Transport servers will obtain all connector information and domain information from Hub Transport servers. Additionally, a specialized ADAM installation on the Edge Transport server will be used to contain all recipient information for your Exchange organization in a protected format, thereby increasing the security of your internal network resources. When EdgeSync is configured, you don't need to perform the otherwise time-consuming edge cloning process to keep Edge Transport servers configured identically.

For additional security, you should install some antivirus and antispam product on your Edge Transport servers. Microsoft Forefront Security for Microsoft Exchange is a perfect fit and is fully supported by Microsoft, but you may find other third-party applications that meet your needs as well. You might not even end up using Edge Transport servers at all if your organization already has a functional virus and spam control solution in place today.

Exam Essentials

Know your antispam options. One of the best features of the Edge Transport server is the wealth and variety of antispam options it provides you. Be sure to thoroughly investigate each one and understand the pros and cons of using each. You'll want to be able to differentiate between the options as well when given an exam question asking which option would be best used to perform a specific task.

Understand EdgeSync. The EdgeSync process is a huge benefit to any messaging administrator. By taking the time to configure the Hub Transport servers with the desired settings and going through the EdgeSync process, you can greatly increase the performance and security of your Exchange organization. Be sure to understand the steps and reasons for each step involved in the EdgeSync process.

Learn the PowerShell commands. Take advantage of this information, and learn how to use the Exchange Management Shell to your advantage. As you've shown in this chapter, you must perform certain configuration options that you cannot do from the Exchange Management Console. You should expect to be tested on these items.

Review Questions

1. Which Forefront antivirus bias setting would you want to use if your requirement was to ensure that all messages routed through an Edge Transport server were scanned by the maximum number of scan engines?

   A. Absolute Performance

   B. Maximum Certainty

   C. Favor Performance

   D. Favor Certainty

   E. Maximum Performance

   F. Absolute Certainty

   G. Neutral

2. Of the antispam agents available on the Edge Transport server, which one must you configure and manage exclusively from the Exchange Management Shell?

   A. Content filtering

   B. Recipient filtering

   C. Sender reputation

   D. Attachment filtering

3. What software components must be installed on the Windows Server 2003 SP1 computer before the Edge Transport server role can be installed? (Choose all that apply.)

   A. PowerShell 1.0

   B. .NET Framework 2.0

   C. MMC 3.0

   D. ADAM with SP1

4. You have several Edge Transport servers for which you need to use edge cloning. Your Edge Transport servers are not configured to use EdgeSync. Which of the following commands would you need to use from the Exchange Management Shell to configure the answer file for the import process?

   A. `ImportEdgeConfig -CloneConfigData:"F:\CloneConfigData.xml" -IsImport $true -CloneConfigAnswer:"F:\CloneConfigAnswer.xml"`

   B. `ImportEdgeConfig -CloneConfigData:"F:\CloneConfigData.xml" -IsImport $false -CloneConfigAnswer:"F:\CloneConfigAnswer.xml"`

   C. `ExportEdgeConfig -CloneConfigData:"F:\CloneConfigData.xml"`

   D. `ExportEdgeConfig -CloneConfigData:"F:\CloneConfigData.xml" -IsImport $false -CloneConfigAnswer:"F:\CloneConfigAnswer.xml"`

5. Before installing Edge Transport servers in the DMZ and configuring EdgeSync on them, what ports should you ensure are open between the DMZ and the internal network? (Choose all that apply.)

   A. 50636

   B. 3389

   C. 25

   D. 50389

   E. 110

   F. 443

6. What PowerShell cmdlet will you need to use to create the EdgeSync subscription file?

   A. `New-EdgeSubscription`

   B. `Configure-EdgeSubscription`

   C. `Create-EdgeSubscription`

   D. `Enable-EdgeSubscription`

7. You are configuring a new Exchange Server 2007 organization for a small medical practice. Since many medical terms and drugs are common spam words, you've been asked to try to configure Exchange to pass messages containing some specific common spam words as nonspam items. What antispam agent can you configure on the Edge Transport server that could help you accomplish this request?

   A. Attachment filtering

   B. Content filtering

   C. Recipient filtering

   D. Sender filtering

   E. IP block list providers

   F. IP allow list providers

   G. IP block list

8. You are currently planning an upgrade from Exchange Server 2003 to Exchange Server 2007. You currently have four Mailbox servers and two front-end servers providing Outlook Web Access. All inbound mail from the Internet is routed directly to one of your Mailbox servers currently. What benefits could you realize by using Edge Transport servers in your Exchange Server 2007 upgrade plan? (Choose all that apply.)

   A. Fewer physical servers are required.

   B. Reduced load on the Mailbox servers.

   C. Reduced load on the front-end servers.

   D. No direct Internet connectivity to the Mailbox servers.

   E. No direct Internet connectivity to the front-end servers.

9. After the EdgeSync process has been completed and the ADAM instance on the Edge Transport server has completed replication, what types of items does the Edge Transport server now know about that it did not know beforehand? (Choose all that apply.)
   A. All configured internal accepted domains
   B. All configured remote domains
   C. All configured external domains
   D. All configured message classifications
   E. All configured send connectors
   F. All configured receive connectors
   G. All mailbox-enabled users in the domain

10. What must you do with the edge subscription file that was created on the Edge Transport server?
    A. Copy it to the `C:\Program Files\Microsoft\Exchange Server\Bin` directory on all Hub Transport servers.
    B. Copy it to any location on any Hub Transport server, and use the `Set-TransportConfig` cmdlet to complete the process.
    C. Copy it to the `C:\Program Files\Microsoft\Exchange Server\TransportRoles` directory on all Hub Transport servers.
    D. Copy it to any location on any Hub Transport server and New Edge Subscription Wizard.

11. Once EdgeSnyc has been completely configured, how often will configuration data be synchronized?
    A. Every 120 minutes
    B. Every 240 minutes
    C. Every 60 minutes
    D. Every 180 minutes

12. You have recently used a custom PowerShell script to create 2,500 new mailbox-enabled users for a special project your company is launching. You need these mailboxes to begin accepting SMTP messages from Internet hosts immediately. What should you do to make this happen?
    A. Use the `Start-EdgeSynchronization` cmdlet.
    B. Right-click a Hub Transport server in the Exchange Management Console, and select the Synchronize Now item from the context menu.
    C. Use the `Refresh-EdgeSynchronization` cmdlet.
    D. Select a Hub Transport server from the listing in the Exchange Management Console, and then click the Refresh link.

13. You were just assigned a new junior systems administrator today to help out by performing some lower-level tasks. You have asked him to add several new words to the content filtering antispam agent on your Edge Transport servers so that those words will not be considered in the SCL score. After some time, you start getting calls from several hundred upset users saying they are getting a large influx of spam messages. You check several of the reported messages, and none of them contains the words you asked the new administrator to add. What option in the content filtering agent did the new administrator most likely change to cause users to start getting spam when they previously were not?

    A. The list of custom words that are always allowed

    B. The list of custom words that are always blocked

    C. The list of recipients that will not have content filtered

    D. The actions to take at various SCL levels

14. You want to configure your Edge Transport servers to use Spamhaus as a resource when determining whether a message should be considered spam. What antispam agent do you need to configure to make this change effective?

    A. Attachment filtering

    B. Content filtering

    C. Recipient filtering

    D. Sender filtering

    E. IP block list providers

    F. IP allow list providers

    G. IP block list

15. You want to configure your Exchange organization with a listing of all valid Hub Transport servers before enabling EdgeSync. What cmdlet will you need to use to perform this configuration?

    A. `Configure-SenderIDServers`

    B. `Configure-EdgeSubscription`

    C. `Set-TransportConfig`

    D. `Set-SenderIDConfig`

16. Once you create the EdgySync subscription file on an Edge Transport server, within what time frame must you complete the process on a Hub Transport server?

    A. 24 hours

    B. 12 hours

    C. 6 hours

    D. 1 hour

17. You want to ensure that only those messages addressed to valid recipients currently working at your company are delivered to your Mailbox servers. What antispam agent should you configure to accomplish this?

    A. Attachment filtering
    B. Content filtering
    C. Recipient filtering
    D. Sender filtering
    E. IP block list providers
    F. IP allow list providers
    G. IP block list

18. Once EdgeSnyc has been completely configured, how often will recipient data be synchronized?

    A. Every 120 minutes
    B. Every 240 minutes
    C. Every 60 minutes
    D. Every 180 minutes

19. What network protocol does the ADAM instance on an Edge Transport server use to perform replication with Active Directory after the EdgeSync process has been completely configured?

    A. SMTP
    B. LDAP
    C. SNTP
    D. IMAP4
    E. RPC

20. You have several Edge Transport servers for which you need to use edge cloning. Your Edge Transport servers are not configured to use EdgeSync. When you configure the EdgeSnyc subscription file, what file format will it be in?

    A. `.hta`
    B. `.csv`
    C. `.txt`
    D. `.xml`
    E. `.bin`

Answers to Review Questions

1. B. Since the requirement is to ensure that all messages routed through an Edge Transport server are scanned by the maximum number of scan engines, you will need to configure the Maximum Certainty bias option. With this option configured, each item is scanned with all the selected scan items. This option provides the best protection but will result in the slowest performance.

2. D. No Exchange Management Console configuration is available for the attachment filtering agent. You will need to configure and manage this antispam agent exclusively from the Exchange Management Shell.

3. A, B, C, D. As with all the other Exchange Server 2007 roles, you must have the .NET Framework 2.0, PowerShell 1.0, and MMC 3.0 installed before you can install the Edge Transport server role. Additionally, you must also have ADAM with SP1 installed for Edge Transport servers. The Exchange setup routine will prompt you to install any missing components it detects before allowing you to install the Edge Transport server.

4. B. The `ImportEdgeConfig -CloneConfigData:"F:\CloneConfigData.xml" -IsImport $false -CloneConfigAnswer:"F:\CloneConfigAnswer.xml"` command would be the correct one to use to create the XML answer file. The `-CloneConfigAnswer` item specifies that an answer file is to be used/created, while the `-IsImport $false` item specifies that this action is not an actual import and is thus an answer file creation process.

5. A, B, C. You will need to ensure that ports 25 (SMTP), 3389 (RDP), and 50636 (S-LDAP) are open on the firewall between the DMZ and the internal network. Port 25 is required for SMTP traffic, port 3389 is required for Remote Desktop connections for remote management, and port 50636 is required for secure LDAP replication between Active Directory and the ADAM instance running on the Edge Transport server.

6. A. To create the edge subscription file, you will need to use the Exchange Management Shell cmdlet `New-EdgeSubscription`. If you wanted to save the file to the F drive, your entry might look like this: `New-EdgeSubscription -FileName "F:\EdgeSubscription.xml"`.

7. B. The Custom Words tab of the Content Filter allows you to enter a list words that will modify the default behavior of the content filter. In the top area of this tab, you can enter words that will never be blocked, such as those that might otherwise typically be blocked by the content filter. You can enter the requested spam-like words in this section and prevent the Edge Transport server's antispam agents from considering those words in the overall SCL rating of the message.

8. B, D. By using Edge Transport servers to route all inbound and outbound SMTP traffic, you can prevent direct connections to or from the Internet or to or from your Mailbox servers, which is always a better configuration. In addition, the Mailbox servers will be less utilized because of the elimination of the many spam and virus-laden messages before they actually enter your internal network and are processed by the Mailbox servers.

9. A, B, D, E, G. After EdgeSync is configured, the Edge Transport server contains the following information in its ADAM database:

   The following information is replicated to the ADAM database on the Edge Transport server once EdgeSync has been configured:

   - A listing of all internal accepted domains
   - A listing of all remote domains
   - Any configured message classifications
   - Information about internal send connectors that have been configured
   - A listing of all valid internal SMTP addresses for the domain, which includes mailbox-enabled users, mail users, mail contacts, mail-enabled groups, and mail-enabled public folders.
   - The list of safe and blocked sender lists that have been configured for each of these users

10. D. To complete the edge subscription process, you need to copy the edge subscription file created on the Edge Transport server to a Hub Transport server and use the New Edge Subscription Wizard. You can also use the `New-EdgeSubscription` cmdlet to complete the process.

11. C. Configuration data will be synchronized every 60 minutes (hourly) once EdgeSync has been completely configured.

12. A. You can use the `Start-EdgeSynchronization` cmdlet to force EdgeSync synchronization to happen outside its regular schedule.

13. D. In this scenario, the most obvious possible issue is that the actions to take at the configured SCL levels have been changed or that the SCL levels at which to take specific actions have been changed. In the case where all actions were unchecked on the Actions tab of the Content Filtering dialog box, even if a message scored a 9 on the SCL rating, it would still be allowed to pass. Also possible, but much less likely because of the logistics of manually entering that many email addresses, would be that the new administrator configured those recipients to never have their messages filtered.

14. E. You will need to configure the IP Block List Providers item to allow the Edge Transport server to use Spamhaus or any other IP block list service.

15. C. You will need to use the `Set-TransportConfig` cmdlet. If your Hub Transport servers had IP addresses of 192.168.0.150 and 192.168.0.151, then the command you'd enter would look like this: `Set-TransportConfig -InternalSMTPServers 192.168.0.150,192.168.0.151`. You need to perform this action from a Hub Transport server, not from an Edge Transport server. Once EdgeSync is enabled, most information related to routing messages will be overwritten on the Edge Transport server.

16. A. You need to complete the EdgeSync process within 1440 minutes (24 hours) of creating the EdgeSync subscription file on the Edge Transport server.

17. C. The Recipient Filtering antispam agent has an option named Block Messages Sent to Recipients Not Listed in the Global Address List that is not enabled by default. You should enable this option to reject all messages that are not addresses to valid recipients in your GAL.

18. B. Recipient data will be synchronized every 240 minutes (every four hours) once EdgeSync has been completely configured.

19. B. ADAM uses Lightweight Directory Access Protocol (LDAP) to communicate with Active Directory for replication. The LDAP session is SSL secured as it passes through the internal firewall for security.

20. D. The EdgeSync subscription file will be an `.xml` file that can be easily opened in Notepad for inspection. You must manually transfer the resulting XML file to a Hub Transport server to complete the EdgeSync configuration process.

Configuring and Managing Exchange Recipients

MICROSOFT EXAM OBJECTIVES COVERED IN THIS CHAPTER:

✓ **Configuring Recipients and Public Folders**

- Configure recipients.
- Configure mail-enabled groups.
- Configure resource mailboxes.
- Configure public folders.

Some of an administrator's most important tasks are creating and configuring Exchange *recipients*. A recipient is an object in Active Directory that references a resource that can receive a message. The resource might be a mailbox in a mailbox database, such as in the case of a user, or a public folder in the public folder database that is shared by many users. No matter where an actual resource exists, though, a recipient object is always created in Active Directory and configured within Exchange.

In this chapter, we will discuss the types of Exchange recipients, their creation, and their properties. Exchange has four basic types of recipients:

Users A *user* is an Active Directory object that typically represents a person who uses the network. Once Exchange is installed and updates the schema, each user in the Active Directory can be mailbox-enabled, mail-enabled, or neither. A *mailbox-enabled user* has an associated mailbox in a mailbox database on an Exchange server. Each user's *mailbox* is a private storage area that allows an individual user to send, receive, and store messages. A *mail-enabled user* is one who has an email address but does not have a mailbox on an Exchange server. These users send and receive email by using an external ISP.

Groups A *group* in Active Directory is like a container to which you can assign certain permissions and rights. You can then place users (and other groups) into that group, and they automatically inherit the group's permissions and rights. Exchange uses the concept of mail-enabled groups to form distribution groups. Messages sent to a group are redirected and sent to each member of the group. These groups allow users to send messages to multiple recipients without having to address each recipient individually.

Contacts A *contact* is a pointer object that refers to an email address for a non-Exchange recipient. Contacts are most often used for connecting your organization to foreign messaging systems such as the Internet. As an administrator, you would create contacts so that frequently used email addresses are available in the global address list (GAL) as real names. This makes it easier to send mail because users do not need to guess at cryptic email addresses.

Public folders A *public folder* is like a public mailbox. It is a container for information to be shared among a group of people. Public folders can contain email messages, forms, word-processing documents, spreadsheet files, and files of many other formats. Public folders can also be configured to send information to other recipients.

In short, an Exchange recipient is any object that has an email address, whether it's a mailbox user, a public folder, a distribution group, or a contact. In this chapter, we'll examine all of those items except for public folders, which we'll discuss in Chapter 8, "Configuring and

Managing Client Connectivity and Public Folders." The main subjects of this chapter are as follows:

- Configuring mailbox-enabled and mail-enabled user accounts
- Configuring mail-enabled groups
- Configuring mail contacts
- Configuring resource mailboxes

Configuring User Accounts and Mailboxes

User mailboxes are the most common type of Exchange recipient object that you'll be working with, so naturally it makes sense for our discussion of recipient management to begin there. As you no doubt know by now, there were some drastic changes made to the user account and mailbox creation, configuration, and management processes with the release of Exchange Server 2007. Previously (in Exchange Server 2003), you could create user accounts and mailbox-enable them all within the Active Directory Users and Computers console. Those days are no more, because many organizations asked for a wider separation of permissions between the administrators who take care of Active Directory and those who take care of Exchange. In many organizations, they are the same person or group of people, but in other organizations they are completely separate groups of administrative staff. The end result is that you now have a slightly disjointed user account and mailbox creation and management processes with Exchange Server 2007. In the following sections of the chapter, we will dive deep into user account creation and mailbox configuration.

Mailbox-Enabled vs. Mail-Enabled

Every user in an organization needs access to an Exchange-based mailbox in order to send and receive messages using the Exchange server. Two of the principal administrative tasks in Exchange are creating and managing these mailboxes. In Exchange Server 2007, a user with an associated mailbox is called a *mailbox-enabled user*. Mailbox-enabled users are able to send and receive messages, as well as to store messages on an Exchange server.

A mail-enabled user is simply a user who has an email address but not a mailbox on an Exchange server. This means the user can receive email through their custom address but cannot send mail using the Exchange system. You cannot mail-enable a user during account creation. The only way to create a mail-enabled user is first to create a new user that is not mailbox-enabled and then to enable mail for that user.

Managing User Accounts and Mailboxes

Before you can have an Exchange mailbox, you must have an Active Directory user account. The mailbox is really just an extension of the properties and attributes that the user account object has. That fact is not new, having been the case since the introduction of Exchange Server 2000, but the means by which you create and manage mailboxes is new in Exchange Server 2007. Although you can still create and manage user accounts from the Active Directory Users and Computers console, which you'll explore in a bit, you must now create and manage all messaging-related options and functionality from within the Exchange Management Console or Exchange Management Shell.

Creating Accounts and Mailboxes with the Exchange Management Console

In the Exchange Management Console, you will find mailboxes and their corresponding management options listed in the Microsoft Exchange ➢ Recipient Configuration ➢ Mailbox node, as shown in Figure 6.1.

The default view is to list all recipients within the organization, although your initial view may not display them all depending on how many mailboxes you've configured to be displayed. The default setting is 1,000 mailboxes and can be changed by clicking the Modify the Maximum Number of Recipients to Display link under the mailbox options in the Actions pane on the right of the Exchange Management Console.

FIGURE 6.1 Viewing Exchange mailboxes

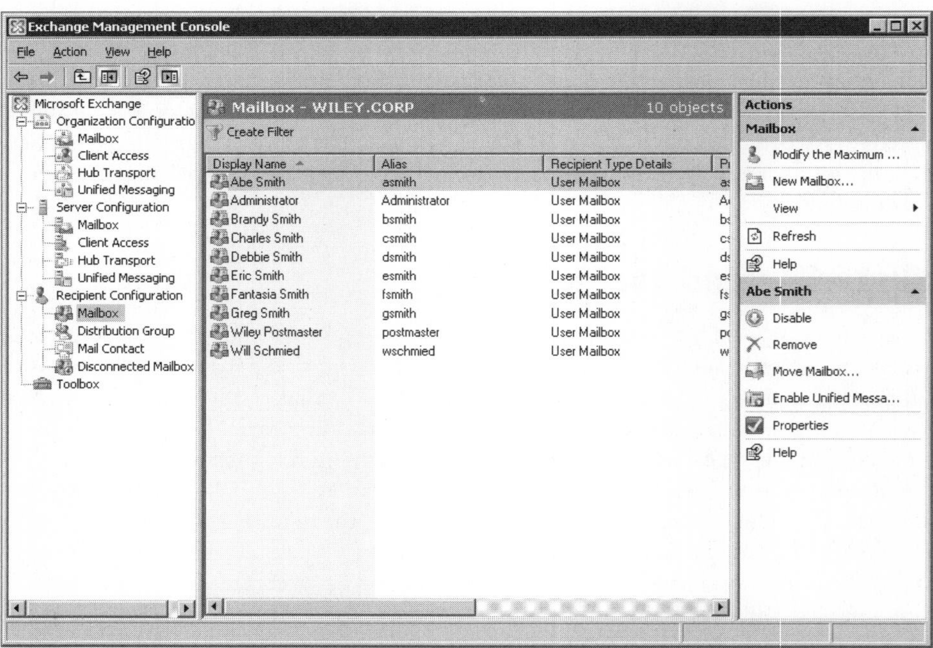

Other options you have in the Actions pane on the right of the Exchange Management Console include creating a new mailbox; if you've selected a mailbox, then you have the following additional options: Disable, Remove, Move Mailbox, Enable Unified Messaging, and Properties. We'll examine all these options in the following sections.

Exercise 6.1 outlines the steps for creating a new user account that will be mailbox-enabled.

EXERCISE 6.1

Creating a New Mailbox-Enabled User

1. Click Start ➢ Programs ➢ Microsoft Exchange Server 2007, and then select Exchange Management Console.
2. Expand the Microsoft Exchange root object, expand the Recipient Configuration folder, and then click the Mailbox node.
3. In the Actions pane on the right, click the New Mailbox link. The New Mailbox Wizard starts.

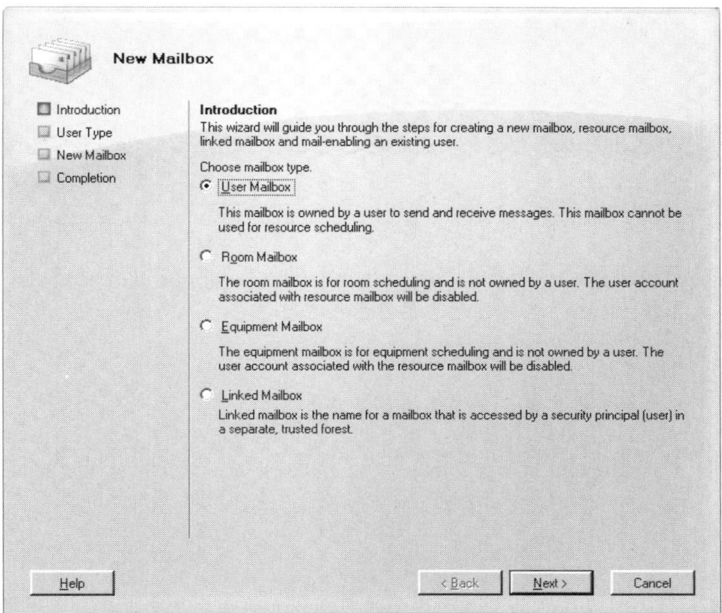

EXERCISE 6.1 *(continued)*

4. For the time being, you're going to be working only with user mailboxes, a mailbox that is assigned to an actual user. You'll examine resource mailboxes later in this chapter. Select the User Mailbox option, and click Next to continue to the User Type page shown here.

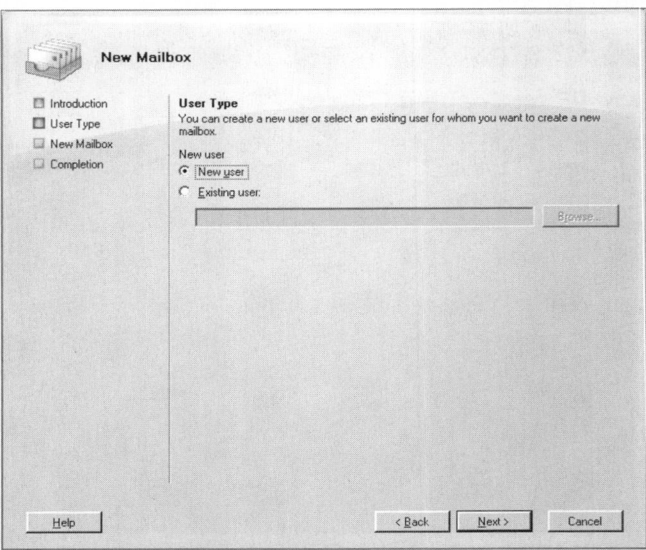

5. Since you want to create a new user account and mailbox-enable it in this exercise, select the New User option, and click Next. The User Information page appears, as shown here.

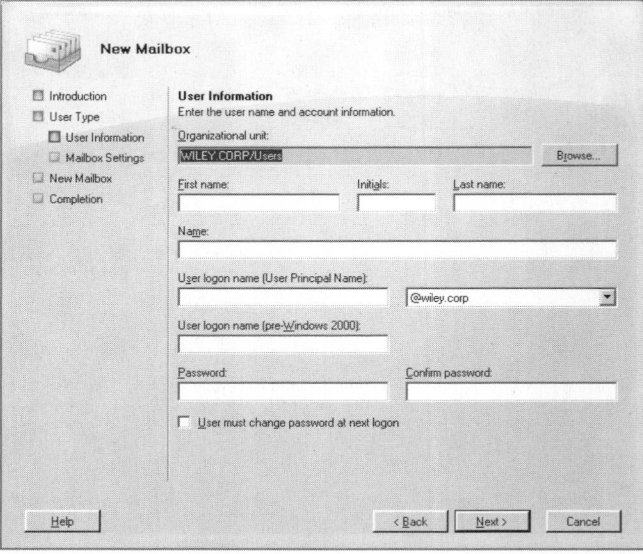

EXERCISE 6.1 *(continued)*

6. Enter all the required information: first name and last name, full (display) name, logon name, and password. If you do not want to create the user object in the default Users container of Active Directory, click the Browse button to open the Select Organizational Unit dialog box shown here.

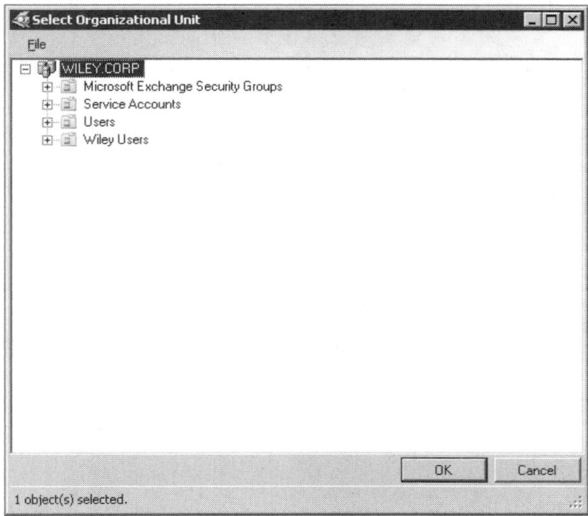

7. After you've correctly entered all the required information, click Next to continue to the Mailbox Settings page shown here.

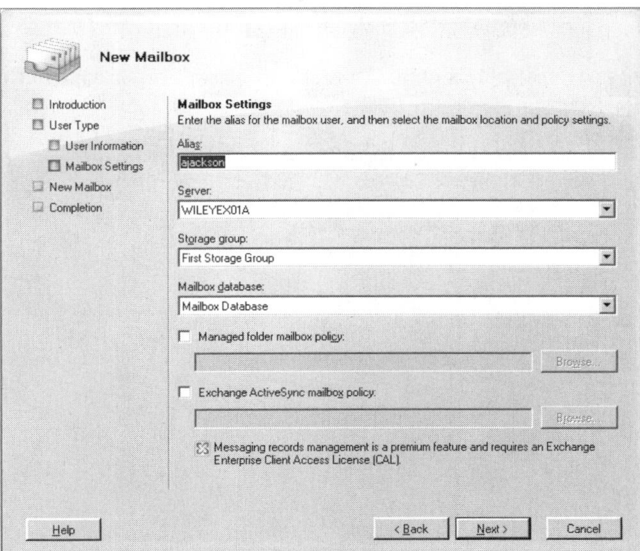

EXERCISE 6.1 *(continued)*

8. On the Mailbox Settings page, you will need to select the Mailbox server, storage group, and mailbox database in which the user's mailbox should be created. After making your selections, click Next to proceed to the New Mailbox page.
9. On the New Mailbox page, review all your configuration entries, and click New if you are satisfied. You can click Back to change any of the entries you made. When you click New, the Completion page appears.
10. As always, Exchange displays for you the PowerShell code it used to perform the user account and mailbox creation. Click Finish to close the wizard.

If you have user accounts that already exist in Active Directory but are not mailbox-enabled, you can perform the steps detailed in Exercise 6.2 to create a mailbox for those accounts.

EXERCISE 6.2

Mailbox-Enabling an Existing User

1. Click Start ➢ Programs ➢ Microsoft Exchange Server 2007, and then select Exchange Management Console.
2. Expand the Microsoft Exchange root object, expand the Recipient Configuration folder, and then click the Mailbox node.
3. In the Actions pane on the right, click the New Mailbox link. The New Mailbox Wizard starts.
4. Select the User Mailbox option, and click Next to continue to the User Type page.
5. On the User Type page, select Existing User, and then click the Browse button to open the Select User dialog box shown here.

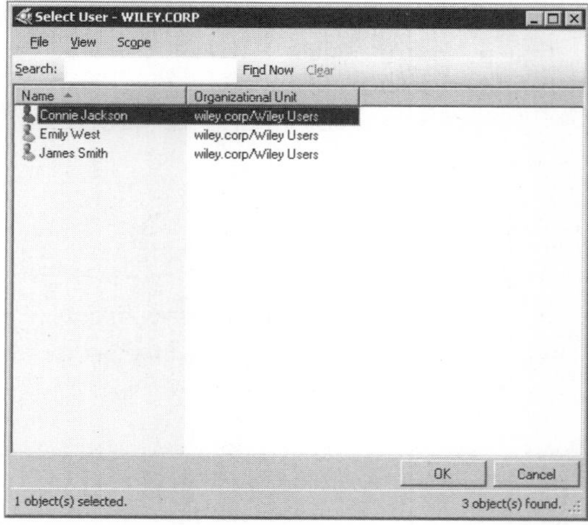

EXERCISE 6.2 *(continued)*

6. From the Select User dialog box, you will be able to select from a list of the user accounts in Active Directory that are not disabled and do not already have a mailbox assigned. Select a user account, and click OK to return to the User Type page. Click Next to go to the Mailbox Settings page.
7. On the Mailbox Settings page, you will need to select the Mailbox server, storage group, and mailbox database in which the user's mailbox should be created. After making your selections, click Next to proceed to the New Mailbox page.
8. On the New Mailbox page, review all your configuration entries, and click New if you are satisfied. You can click Back to change any of the entries you made. When you click New, the Completion page appears.
9. As always, Exchange displays for you the PowerShell code it used to perform the user account and mailbox creation. Click Finish to close the wizard.

Remember that disabled Active Directory user accounts will not be displayed when you try to mailbox-enable an existing user account and you've selected the User Mailbox option.

Creating Accounts and Mailboxes with the Exchange Management Shell

Of course, anything you can do within the Exchange Management Console, you can do in the Exchange Management Shell as well. Creating mailbox-enabled user accounts and mailbox-enabling existing users are no exceptions. To create a new Active Directory user account that is mailbox-enabled, you need to use the `new-Mailbox` cmdlet within the Exchange Management Shell; the code would look something like this:

```
New-Mailbox -Name 'Bradley Jackson' -Alias 'bjackson'
-OrganizationalUnit 'WILEY.CORP/Wiley Users'
-UserPrincipalName 'bjackson@WILEY.CORP'
-SamAccountName 'bjackson' -FirstName 'Bradley' -Initials '' -LastName 'Jackson'
-ResetPasswordOnNextLogon $false
-Database 'CN=Mailbox Database,CN=First Storage Group,CN=InformationStore,
CN=WILEYEX01A,CN=Servers,CN=Exchange Administrative Group (FYDIBOHF23SPDLT),
CN=Administrative Groups,CN=WILEY,CN=Microsoft Exchange,CN=Services,
CN=Configuration,DC=WILEY,DC=CORP'
```

Figure 6.2 displays the resulting output of this command.

FIGURE 6.2 Creating a new mailbox-enabled user account with the Exchange Management Shell

```
Machine: WILEYEX01A | Scope: WILEY.CORP
[PS] C:\>New-Mailbox -Name 'Bradley Jackson' -Alias 'bjackson' -OrganizationalUn
it 'WILEY.CORP/Wiley Users' -UserPrincipalName 'bjackson@WILEY.CORP' -SamAccount
Name 'bjackson' -FirstName 'Bradley' -Initials '' -LastName 'Jackson' -ResetPass
wordOnNextLogon $false -Database 'CN=Mailbox Database,CN=First Storage Group,CN=
InformationStore,CN=WILEYEX01A,CN=Servers,CN=Exchange Administrative Group (FYDI
BOHF23SPDLT),CN=Administrative Groups,CN=WILEY,CN=Microsoft Exchange,CN=Services
,CN=Configuration,DC=WILEY,DC=CORP'

cmdlet New-Mailbox at command pipeline position 1
Supply values for the following parameters:
Password: **********

Name                   Alias            ServerName        ProhibitSendQuo
                                                          ta
----                   -----            ----------        ---------------
Bradley Jackson        bjackson         wileyex01a        unlimited


[PS] C:\>_
```

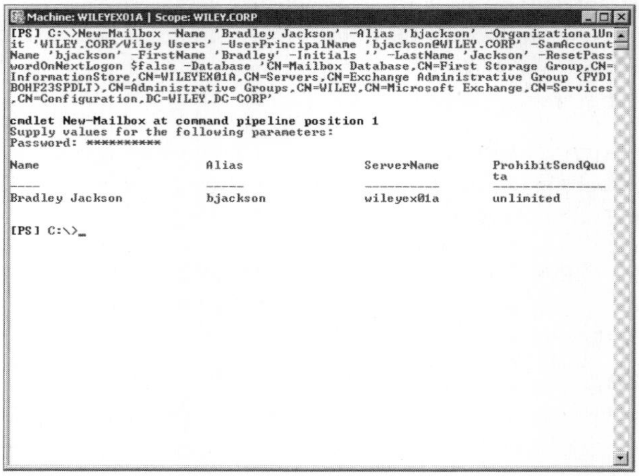

There is no way to create passwords for accounts created from the PowerShell as you could previously. In other words, you cannot directly provide the password using the `-Password` parameter. You have two options available to you in this scenario:

- Enter the password manually as shown in Figure 6.2 previously.
- Use a variable before entering the command(s) to create your mailbox-enabled user account(s), as illustrated in Figure 6.3. If you go this route, you could write a new PowerShell script that actually contains the line with the `$password` variable, thus prompting for the password to be used and containing another line that uses the `Import-CSV` cmdlet to import a list of entries such as the password that should be passed to the `new-Mailbox` cmdlet.

FIGURE 6.3 Using a password variable to create mailbox-enabled user accounts with the Exchange Management Shell

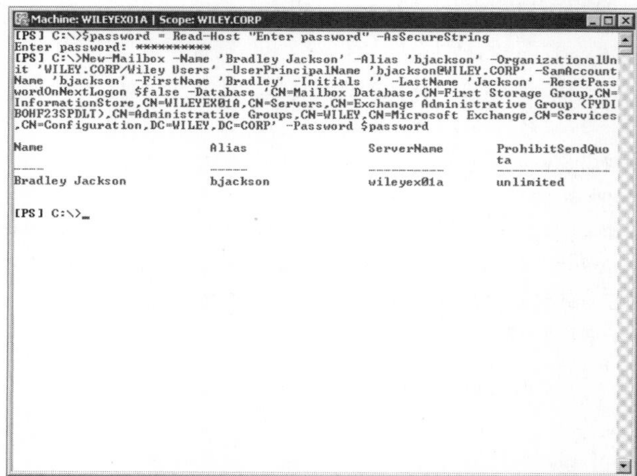

For an example of how to create mailbox-enabled user accounts in Exchange Server 2007 using a CSV import file, see "Managing mailboxes in Exchange Server 2007" located at `http://www.msexchange.org/tutorials/Managing-mailboxes-Exchange-Server-2007-Part1.html`. Be sure to also check out the TechNet reference for the `New-Mailbox` cmdlet, located at `http://technet.microsoft.com/en-us/library/aa997663.aspx`.

If you need to mailbox-enable only an existing Active Directory user account object, the code and process are much simpler because you don't need to worry about messing with passwords. You'll use the `Enable-Mailbox` cmdlet, and the code would look something like this:

```
Enable-Mailbox -Identity 'WILEY.CORP/Wiley Users/James Smith' -Alias 'jsmith'
-Database 'CN=Mailbox Database,CN=First Storage Group,CN=InformationStore,
CN=WILEYEX01A,CN=Servers,CN=Exchange Administrative Group (FYDIBOHF23SPDLT),
CN=Administrative Groups,CN=WILEY,CN=Microsoft Exchange,CN=Services,
CN=Configuration,DC=WILEY,DC=CORP'
```

Figure 6.4 displays the resulting output of this command.

FIGURE 6.4 Mailbox-enabling an existing user account with the Exchange Management Shell

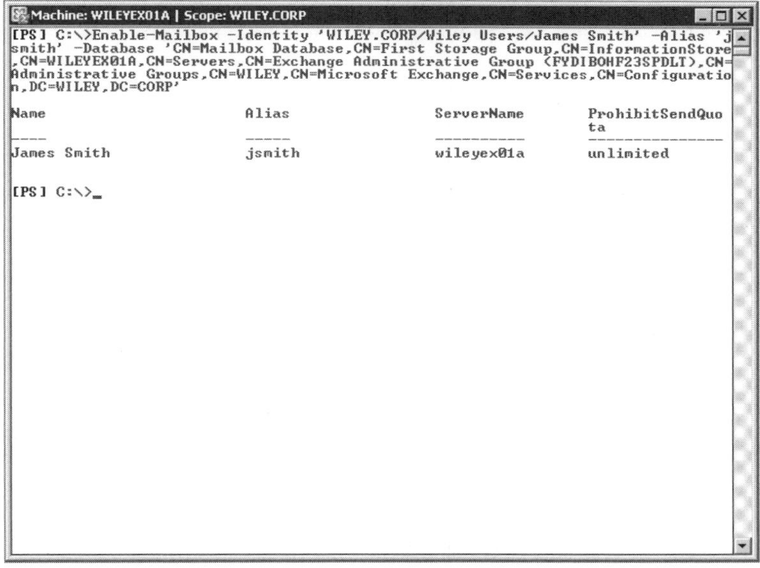

Creating Accounts with the Active Directory Users and Computers Console

Of course, you can still (and will) create and manage user accounts from the Active Directory Users and Computers console. That's the whole rationale behind moving the messaging-specific functions back into the Exchange management tools, where they previously were in Exchange Server 5.5 and older versions. In larger organizations, some administrators will manage only Active Directory, and other administrators will manage only Exchange. In that case, the first group would be responsible for creating user accounts per the organizational standards in place, and the second group would be responsible only for managing the messaging attributes of those user accounts. Or you might find it easier, if you manage both Active Directory and Exchange, to continue using whatever method you currently have in place for creating user accounts, such as using the `dsadd` command or VBScript, and then mailbox-enabling the accounts later using the PowerShell `Enable-Mailbox` cmdlet. You can call other commands from within a PowerShell script, and you could actually wrap the whole process into a single PowerShell script that uses some of the old and new methods available to you.

When you use the dsadd command, you can actually specify the initial password to be used by using the `-pwd` switch—something that makes scripting account creation a lot easier than what the Exchange Management Shell currently offers with the `new-Mailbox` cmdlet.

As an example of what a typical `dsadd` command might look like to create a new Active Directory user account, consider the following example, which not only creates the new user account object but also assigns group memberships, a logon script, and a home folder:

```
dsadd user "CN=Smith\, Albert,OU=Sales,OU=Departments,DC=mycompany,DC=local"
-samid "amsith" -pwd *asmith042* -mustchpwd yes -fn "Albert" -ln "Smith"
-display "Smith, Albert" -desc "Sales"
-memberof "CN=Sales Group,OU=User Groups,DC=mycompany,DC=local"
-hmdrv "H:" -loscr "script.bat" -hmdir "\\SERVER42\SALES$\AMSITH"
-empid "42042" -dept "Sales" -company "My Company"
```

However, if you want to create and configure a new user account using the Active Directory Users and Computers console, then Exercise 6.3 has the steps you'll need to follow.

EXERCISE 6.3

Creating a New User Account in Active Directory Users and Computers

1. Log in to a domain controller or a computer that has the Windows Server 2003 SP1 or SP2 Administrative Tools installed. You will need the correct version that corresponds to the service pack level of your domain controllers, which must be at least Windows Server 2003 SP1 to install Exchange Server 2007 in the domain.

EXERCISE 6.3 *(continued)*

2. Click Start ➢ Programs ➢ Control Panel ➢ Administrative Tools, and then select Active Directory Users and Computers. The Active Directory Users and Computers console opens.

3. Navigate to the organizational unit where you want the new user account to be created in, and then click the New User button at the top of the console, as shown here.

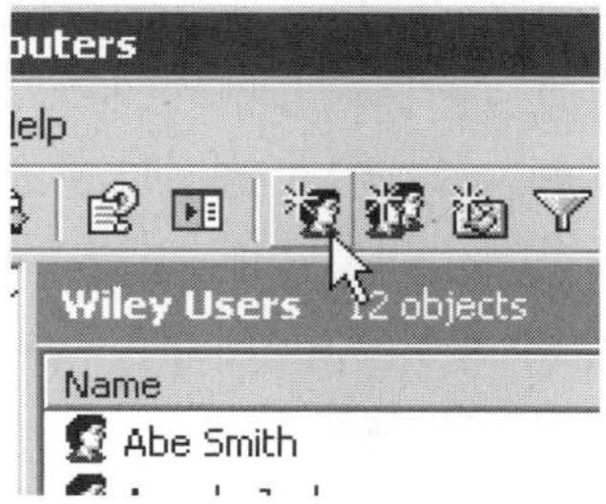

4. The New Object – User dialog box opens, as shown here.

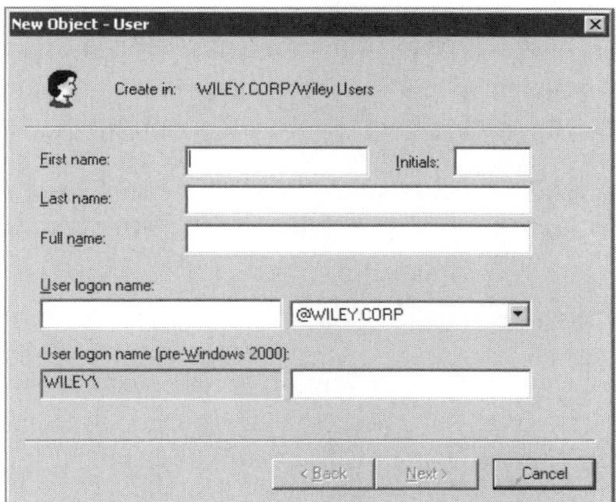

EXERCISE 6.3 *(continued)*

5. Enter all the required information: first name and last name, full (display) name, and logon name. Click Next to continue to the password page, as shown here.

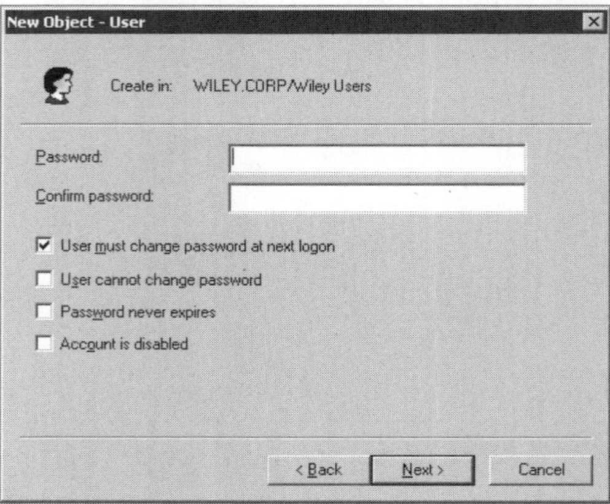

6. Enter the password for the user, and select any password-related options that are required. Click Next to summary page.

7. On the summary page, click Finish to create the user if all the details displayed are correct. If you need to make any changes, click the Back button.

Of course, after the user account has been created, you can then mailbox-enable it from either the Exchange Management Console or the Exchange Management Shell, as you learned earlier.

Modifying Mailbox-Enabled User Accounts

It only stands to reason that once you have mailbox-enabled users in your Exchange organization that you're eventually going to have to manage or modify their configurations. We'll discuss just that in the following sections.

Performing Basic Management from the Exchange Management Console

You do all mailbox management from the Exchange Management Console from the Microsoft Exchange ➢ Recipient Configuration ➢ Mailbox node, as shown previously in Figure 6.1. When a mailbox is selected in the middle of the console, you'll have mailbox-specific options that become available on the right side of the console, as shown in Figure 6.5. Of course, all these options are also available by right-clicking the mailbox of concern and selecting them from the context menu.

The Disable option is actually used to remove all messaging attributes from the user account object, not to disable the account itself. To disable the user account, and thus make it unable to be used for login, you'll need to visit the Active Directory Users and Computers console. If you click the Disable link in the Exchange Management Console, you'll be prompted to consider your action and whether you want to continue. You can accomplish the same effect using the `Disable-Mailbox` cmdlet.

FIGURE 6.5 Mailbox management options in the Exchange Management Console

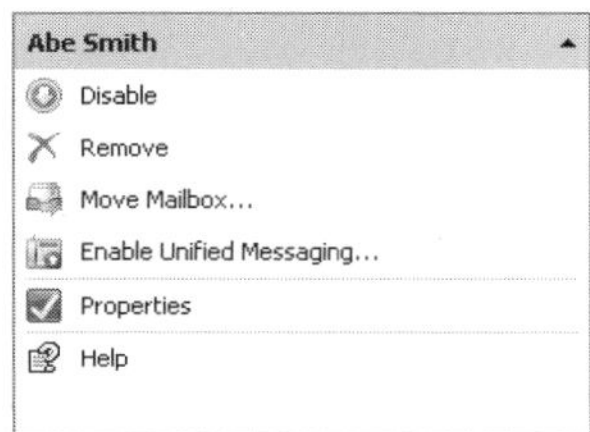

The Remove option actually causes the Active Directory user account object to be deleted from Active Directory along with the corresponding mailbox. If you click the Remove link in the Exchange Management Console, you'll be prompted to consider your action and whether you want to continue. You can accomplish the same effect using the `Remove-Mailbox` cmdlet.

The Move Mailbox option allows you to move the selected mailbox to a different mailbox database on the same server or a different server within the Exchange organization. We'll talk in depth about moving mailboxes in Chapter 9, "Managing and Maintaining the Exchange Organization." Since we don't discuss unified messaging in this book, we won't look at the Enable Unified Messaging option.

Managing Mailbox Properties

When you click the last item available for a mailbox, Properties, the mailbox's Properties dialog box opens to the General tab. We'll examine each tab, and the configurable items found on each, in the following sections.

General

The General tab of the mailbox's Properties dialog box, shown in Figure 6.6, contains all the basic identifying information about the mailbox, although you can change only the display name field at the top of the tab and the Alias field at the bottom of the tab. You can also opt to have the mailbox hidden from view in the GAL, a common configuration for certain types of resource mailboxes or when an employee has been terminated from the organization but the mailbox has not yet been deleted.

Other useful information you'll find on the General tab includes the following:

- The organizational unit in which the Active Directory user account is located
- Who the last user was to log in to the mailbox

FIGURE 6.6 The General tab of the mailbox's Properties dialog box

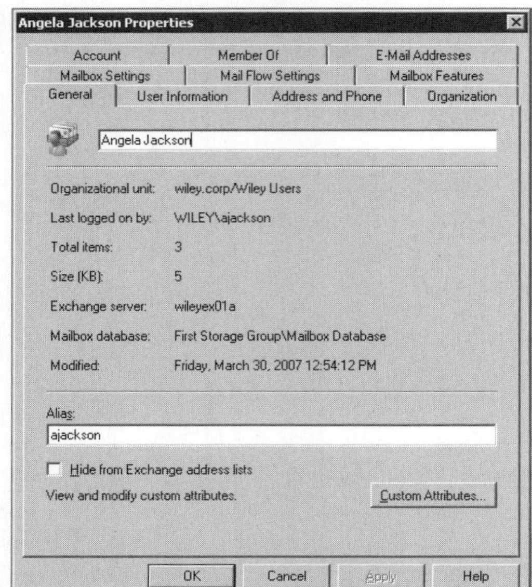

- How many items are contained within the mailbox and how large the entire mailbox is
- The Exchange Mailbox server, storage group, and database in which the mailbox is located
- The last time the mailbox properties were modified

By clicking the Custom Attributes button, the Custom Attributes dialog box will open. Custom attributes are beyond the scope of this exam and will not be discussed.

User Information

The User Information tab of the mailbox's Properties dialog box, shown in Figure 6.7, allows you to configure various basic information about the user who owns the mailbox. You can configure the following information on this tab:

- The user's first name, initials, and last name
- A name that is displayed within Active Directory (this setting does not impact the display name in the GAL)
- A simple display name for the GAL that contains only ASCII characters and no Unicode characters
- The user's web page
- Notes about the mailbox and user that are not displayed anywhere else

Address and Phone

The Address and Phone tab of the mailbox's Properties dialog box, shown in Figure 6.8, contains various information fields that you can configure with the user's address and contact phone numbers, such as an office home, home phone, and mobile phone.

FIGURE 6.7 The User Information tab of the mailbox's Properties dialog box

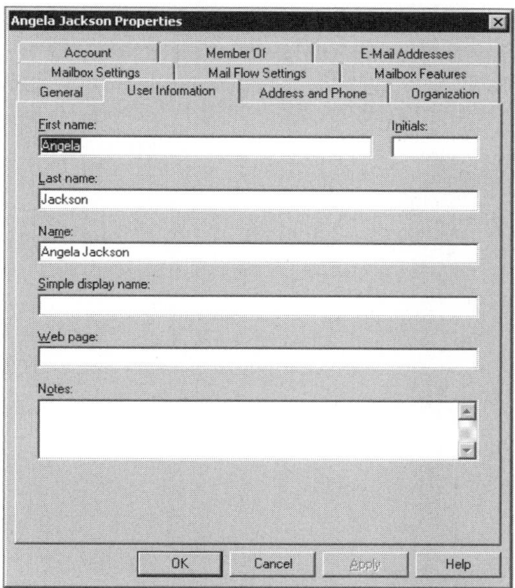

FIGURE 6.8 The Address and Phone tab of the mailbox's Properties dialog box

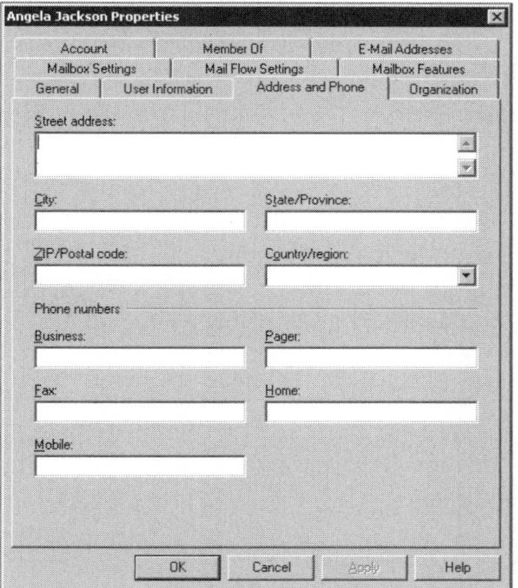

Organization

The Organization tab of the mailbox's Properties dialog box, shown in Figure 6.9, contains organizational information fields that you can configure about the user such as title, company, and manager. The Direct Reports field is not directly configurable but is populated using reverse links from those Active Directory user account objects that have the Manager field configured.

Mailbox Settings

The Mailbox Settings tab of the mailbox's Properties dialog box, shown in Figure 6.10, contains two items to configure: Messaging Records Management and Storage Quotas.

FIGURE 6.9 The Organization tab of the mailbox's Properties dialog box

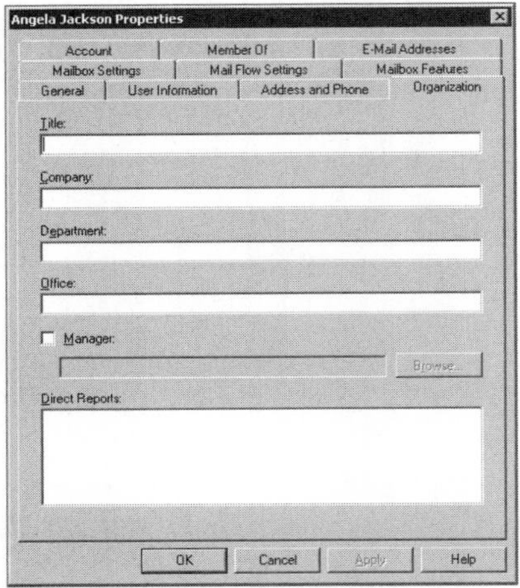

FIGURE 6.10 The Mailbox Settings tab of the mailbox's Properties dialog box

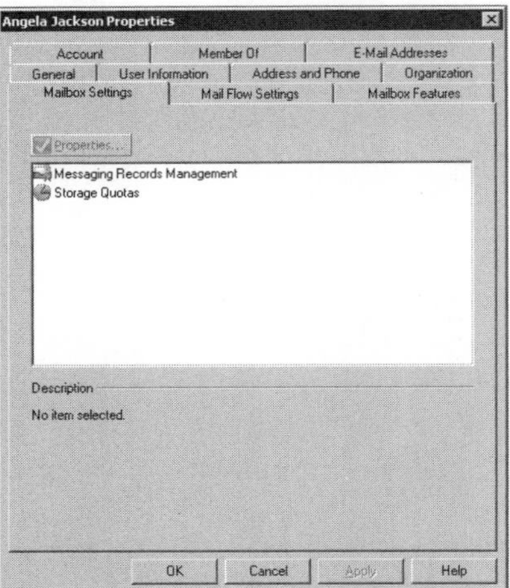

By selecting the Messaging Records Management option and clicking the Properties button, the Messaging Records Management dialog box opens, as shown in Figure 6.11. We will discuss these settings in Chapter 7, "Configuring Exchange Server Rules and Policies."

By selecting the Storage Quotas option and clicking the Properties button, the Storage Quotas dialog box opens, as shown in Figure 6.12. From here you can override the default storage quota limits put in place on the mailbox store that contains the user's mailbox. You might do this if a user is out of the office for an extended period of time and has no means to archive or delete messages. Alternatively, you might configure special storage quotas for certain users in your company, such as the chief information officer (CIO).

FIGURE 6.11 The Messaging Records Management dialog box

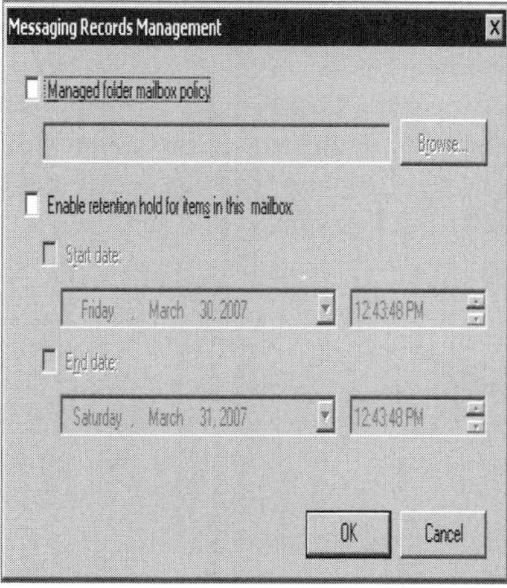

FIGURE 6.12 The Storage Quotas dialog box

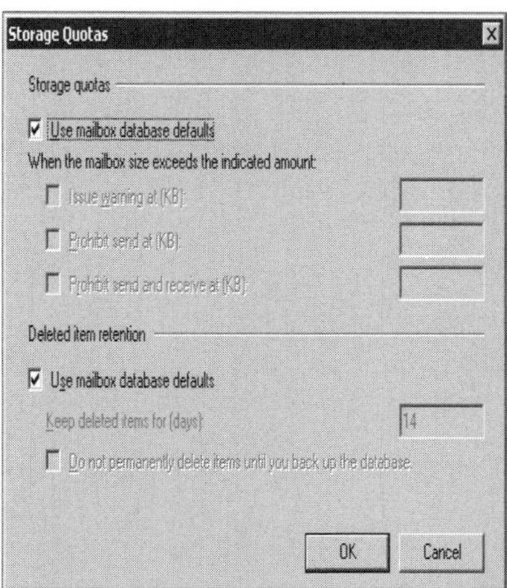

Mail Flow Settings

The Mail Flow Settings tab of the mailbox's Properties dialog box, shown in Figure 6.13, allows you to configure specific settings that determine how messages to or from this mailbox-enabled user are handled.

By selecting the Delivery Options option and clicking the Properties button, the Delivery Options dialog box opens, as shown in Figure 6.14. From here you can delegate the rights to Send on behalf of this user to other mailbox-enabled users in Active Directory. This is commonly done to let, for example, an administrative assistant send replies on behalf of the chief executive officer (CEO) of the company. Additionally, you can configure a forwarding location for the mailbox so that all messages received in the mailbox are delivered to another location, which can be another mailbox or a mail-enabled contact. You have the option of keeping a copy of the message in both mailboxes or just in the mailbox to which you are forwarding. Lastly, you have the option to limit how many recipients can be included in any message the user tries to send—this might be helpful if you have a user who keeps sending messages to large numbers of users, a la spam.

By selecting the Message Size Restrictions option and clicking the Properties button, the Message Size Restrictions dialog box opens, as shown in Figure 6.15. From here you can configure mailbox-specific send and receive size limits that are applied only to the mailbox and that override those applied at the organizational or SMTP connector level.

FIGURE 6.13 The Mail Flow Settings tab of the mailbox's Properties dialog box

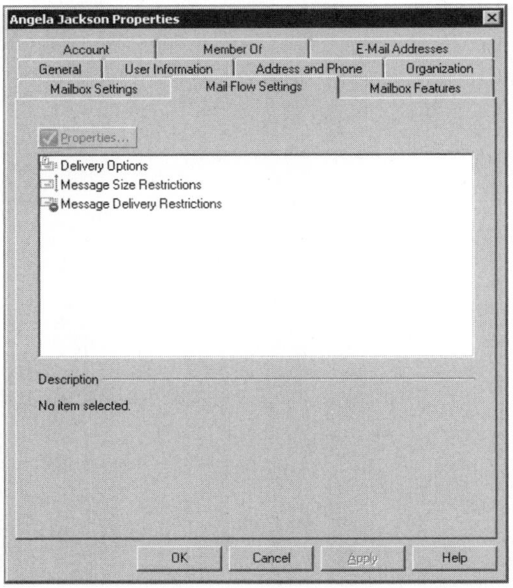

If you've tried to locate where you can configure organizational-level message size restrictions for your Exchange Server 2007 organization and have not found it, then you're not alone. There is no location within the Exchange Management Console where you can view and/or configure this information. The default values for send and receive size for messages are unlimited, meaning there is no limit in place. You can change this value using the `Set-TransportConfig` cmdlet on the Edge Transport and Hub Transport servers. For more information about how to configure organizational-level send and receive limits with the `Set-TransportConfig` cmdlet, see the following TechNet Web page: `http://technet.microsoft.com/en-us/library/bb124151.aspx`.

FIGURE 6.14 The Delivery Options dialog box

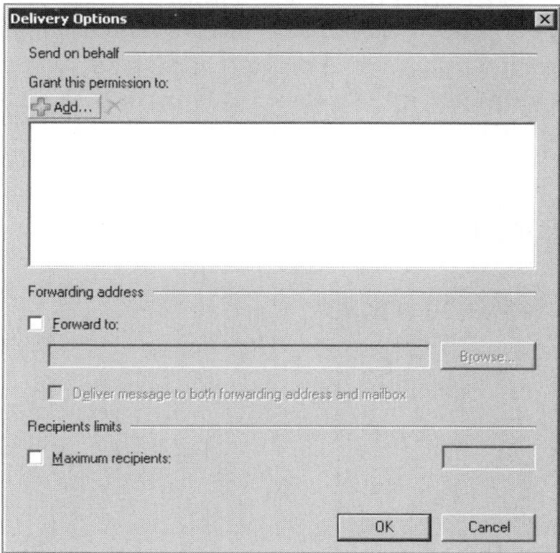

FIGURE 6.15 The Message Size Restrictions dialog box

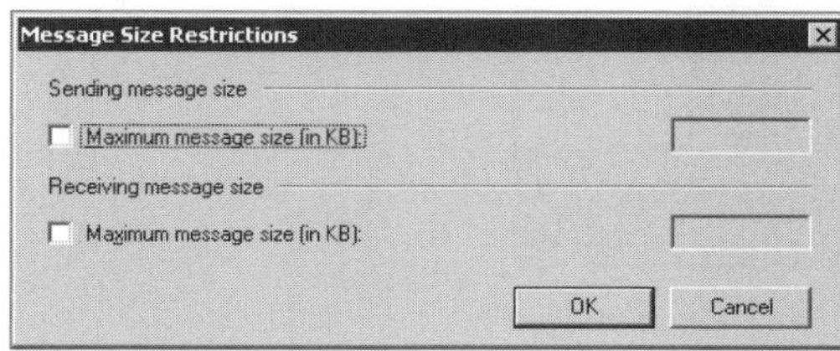

If you want to configure the limits on a specific SMTP connector, you'll need to use either the `Set-SendConnector` cmdlet to change the limit from its default value of 10MB or the `Set-ReceiveConnector` cmdlet to change the limit from its default value of 10MB. You can find out more information about using these cmdlets at `http://technet.microsoft.com/en-us/library/aa998294.aspx` and `http://technet.microsoft.com/en-us/library/bb125140.aspx`, respectively.

By selecting the Message Delivery Restrictions option and clicking the Properties button, the Message Delivery Restrictions dialog box opens, as shown in Figure 6.16. From here you can configure which senders are allowed and not allowed to send messages to this mailbox. By default, there are no restrictions configured on the Message Delivery Restrictions dialog box.

Mailbox Features

The Mailbox Features tab of the mailbox's Properties dialog box, shown in Figure 6.17, allows you to enable or disable specific Exchange features at the mailbox level. These options are similar to the Outlook Web Access segmentation options discussed earlier in Chapter 4, "Configuring Exchange Server Roles," except that they impact only the specific mailbox being configured. If an item has any other configurable properties available, the Properties button will become available when the item is selected.

FIGURE 6.16 The Message Delivery Restrictions dialog box

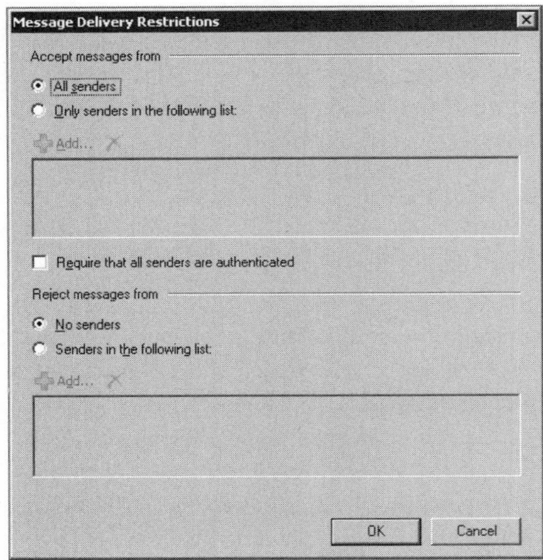

FIGURE 6.17 The Mailbox Features tab of the mailbox's Properties dialog box

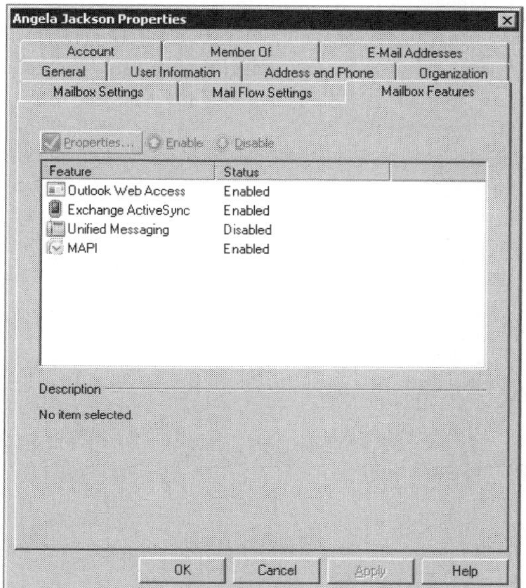

Account

The Account tab of the mailbox's Properties dialog box, shown in Figure 6.18, allows you to configure basic account information about the user. Items you can configure here include the User Principal Name logon name, the pre–Windows 2000 logon name, and whether the user must change their password at the next login attempt. Notice the lack of ability to actually reset a user's password—that's still definitely an action you'll be performing from the Active Directory Users and Computers console.

Member Of

The Member Of tab of the mailbox's Properties dialog box, shown in Figure 6.19, provides a read-only listing of all security and distribution groups of which the user is a member. Not listed on this tab is the built-in Domain Users group membership that all user accounts in the domain have by default. If you examined the user account from Active Directory Users and Computers, you'd see that group membership as well. To add a user to a distribution group, you'll need to work from the Distribution Group node of the Recipient Configuration node in the Exchange Management Console or use the Active Directory Users and Computers console. Security groups can be added only via the Active Directory Users and Computers console.

Of course, you can use various scripting techniques such as the `dsmod group` command, VBScript, or the `Add-DistributionGroupMember` cmdlet to add user accounts to groups.

FIGURE 6.18 The Account tab of the mailbox's Properties dialog box

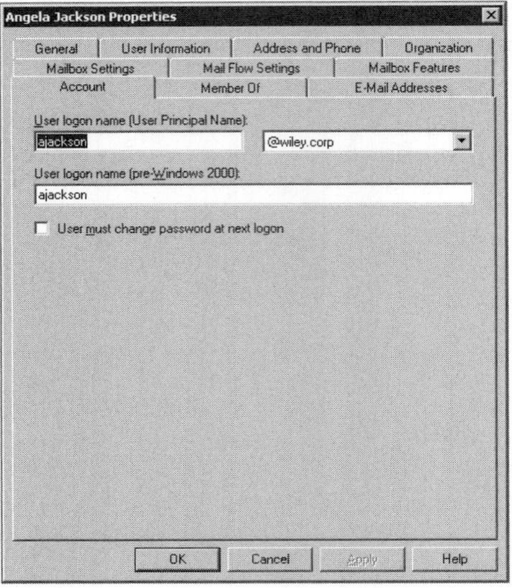

E-Mail Addresses

The E-Mail Addresses tab of the mailbox's Properties dialog box, shown in Figure 6.20, allows you to add, remove, and edit email addresses assigned to the mailbox. The only type of email address that Exchange Server 2007 supports by default is SMTP, but you can configure custom types, if needed in your organization, by clicking the down arrow next to the Add button.

FIGURE 6.19 The Member Of tab of the mailbox's Properties dialog box

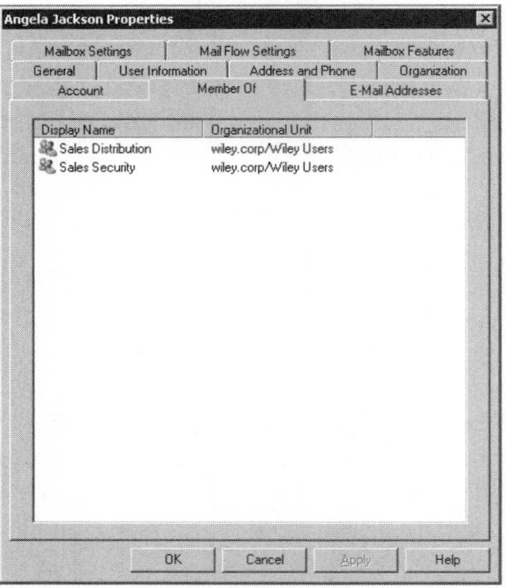

FIGURE 6.20 The E-Mail Addresses tab of the mailbox's Properties dialog box

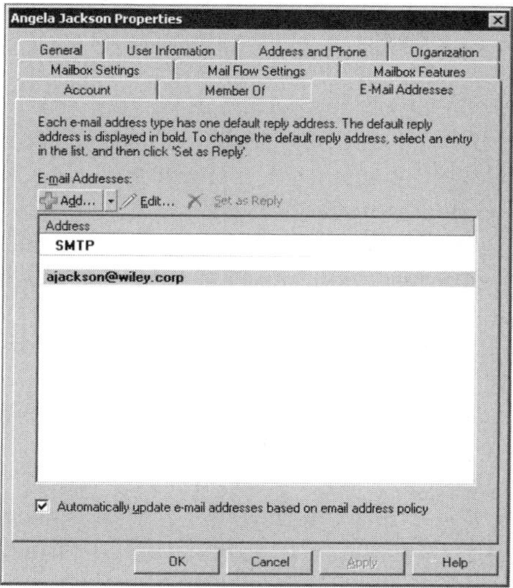

Working with Deleted Mailboxes

When you delete a user account that was mailbox-enabled or you disable a mailbox-enabled user account (which just removes the mailbox attributes from it), the mailboxes themselves are not actually deleted immediately by default. Deleted mailboxes are known as *disconnected* mailboxes until they are actually purged from the mailbox database. How a mailbox remains disconnected is determined by the settings configured on the Limits tab of the mailbox database's Properties dialog box, as shown in Figure 6.21. By default, the value is 30 days to retain deleted (disconnected) mailboxes.

FIGURE 6.21 The Limits tab of the mailbox database's Properties dialog box

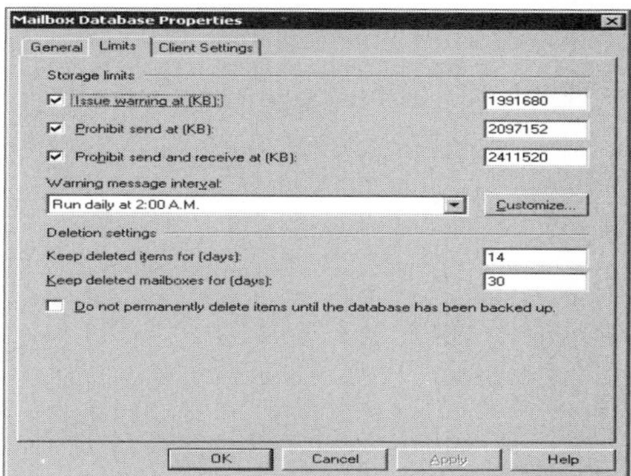

Refer to Chapter 4 if you want to review mailbox database configuration.

So then, where do these disconnected mailboxes go, and what can you do with them? The mailboxes are not visible under the Recipient Configuration ➤ Mailbox node of the Exchange Management Console, but they are visible in the Recipient Configuration ➤ Disconnected Mailbox of the Exchange Management Console, as shown in Figure 6.22.

If you want to permanently remove the mailbox, that is, to *purge* the mailbox in Exchange-speak, then you have two options: either wait for the retention period to pass, which is 30 days by default, or use the `Remove-Mailbox` cmdlet. This a two-step process, however, since you need some information about the disconnected mailbox that is not immediately available to you: the globally unique ID (GUID) of the mailbox. To get that information, you can use the `Get-MailboxStatistics` cmdlet to load a variable and then use the `Remove-Mailbox` cmdlet to purge the mailbox. Your code might look like the following:

```
$Temp = Get-MailboxStatistics | Where {$_.DisplayName -eq 'Connie Jackson'}
Remove-Mailbox -Database 'WILEYEX01A\First Storage Group\Mailbox Database'
-StoreMailboxIdentity $Temp.MailboxGuid
```

Figure 6.23 displays the resulting output of this command. Of course, once you purge a mailbox, the only way to recover it is to restore a backup of the mailbox database that was created before the mailbox was purged.

FIGURE 6.22 Viewing disconnected mailboxes

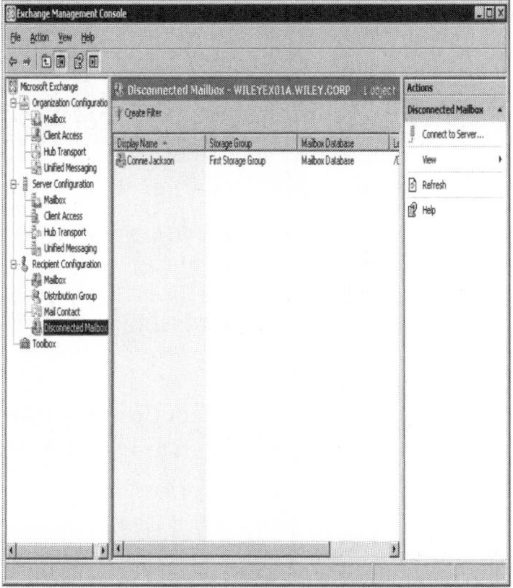

FIGURE 6.23 Permanently deleting a disconnected mailbox with the Exchange Management Shell

However, if you really did want to recover the mailbox, that is, to reconnect it to an existing Active Directory user account, you can easily do that from the Disconnected Mailbox node. Exercise 6.4 outlines the steps for reconnecting a disconnected mailbox.

You won't be able to perform the steps in Exercise 6.4 unless you have previously removed or disabled a mailbox, as discussed earlier in this chapter.

EXERCISE 6.4

Connecting a Disconnected Mailbox

1. Click Start ➢ Programs ➢ Microsoft Exchange Server 2007, and then select Exchange Management Console.
2. Expand the Microsoft Exchange root object, expand the Recipient Configuration folder, and then click the Disconnected Mailbox node.
3. Select the disconnected mailbox, and either right-click it and select Connect from the context menu or click the Connect link found in the Actions menu on the right. Either way, the Connect Mailbox Wizard starts.

EXERCISE 6.4 *(continued)*

4. On the User Type page, select the type of mailbox you are reconnecting. For this exercise, click User Mailbox. Click Next to continue to the Mailbox Settings page shown here.

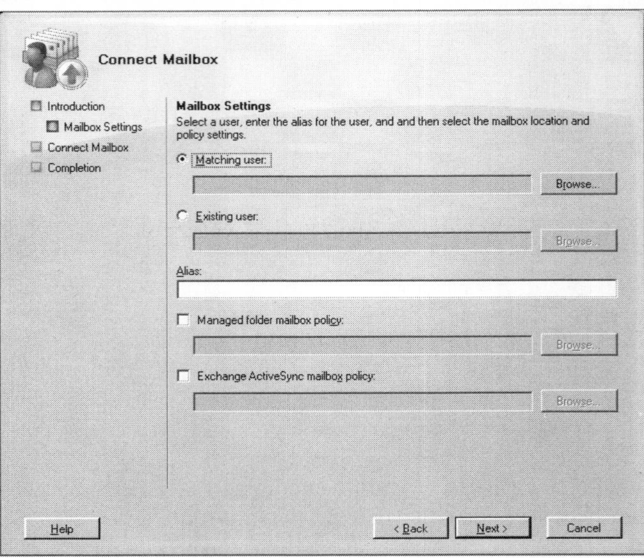

5. On the Mailbox Settings page, you will be able to select how to reconnect the mailbox. Use the Matching User option to allow you to browse to the user account that the mailbox originally belonged to, assuming that user account was not deleted. Use the Existing User option to allow you to browse to a list of all eligible Active Directory user accounts—those that are not currently mailbox-enabled. You'll also need to configure an alias for the mailbox and select any policies that may need to be applied to the mailbox. After entering your selections, click Next to continue to the Connect Mailbox page.

6. On the Connect Mailbox page, you'll have the chance to review the configuration. If everything is correct, click the Connect button. If you need to make changes, use the Back button.

7. As always, Exchange displays for you the PowerShell code it used to perform the user account and mailbox creation. Click Finish to close the wizard.

If you look at the PowerShell code that Exchange uses to perform the reconnection action, you'll see the GUID and how it would be difficult for you to remember it if you could find it in the first place. That code will look similar to the following:

```
Connect-Mailbox -Identity '39e169b0-5d41-4244-82e5-cb91152f505d'
-Database 'WILEYEX01A.WILEY.CORP\First Storage Group\Mailbox Database'
-User 'WILEY\bjackson' -Alias 'bjackson'
```

Managing Mail-Enabled User Accounts

As we discussed earlier, mail-enabled user accounts are those user accounts that have an email address configured but do not have a mailbox on an Exchange server. You might typically use a mail-enabled user account when you have a contractor coming into your organization for a period of time that needs an Active Directory account but wants to receive all messages using their normal email account.

Creating Mail Users with the Exchange Management Console

Exercise 6.5 outlines the steps for creating a new user account that will be mail-enabled.

EXERCISE 6.5

Creating a New Mail-Enabled User

1. Click Start ➢ Programs ➢ Microsoft Exchange Server 2007, and then select Exchange Management Console.
2. Expand the Microsoft Exchange root object, expand the Recipient Configuration folder, and then click the Mail Contact node.
3. In the Actions pane on the right, click the New Mail User link. The New Mail User Wizard starts.
4. Since you want to create a new user account and mail-enable it in this exercise, select the New User option, and click Next. The User Information page appears.
5. Enter all the required information: first name and last name, full (display) name, logon name, and password. If you do not want to create the user object in the default Users container of Active Directory, click the Browse button to open the Select Organizational Unit dialog box.
6. After you've correctly entered all the required information, click Next to continue to the Mail Settings page.
7. On the Mail Settings page, you will need to select the mail alias, which is provided by default for you, and then create an external email address to be assigned to the mail-enabled user. Click the Edit button to open the SMTP Address dialog box. Enter the correct external SMTP email address, and then click OK. Click Next to proceed to the summary page.
8. On the summary page, review all your configuration entries, and click New if you are satisfied. You can click Back to change any of the entries you made. When you click New, the Completion page appears.
9. As always, Exchange displays for you the PowerShell code it used to perform the user account and mailbox creation. Click Finish to close the wizard.

If you have user accounts that already exist in Active Directory but are not mailbox-enabled or mail-enabled, you can perform the steps detailed in Exercise 6.6 to mail-enable those accounts.

EXERCISE 6.6

Mail-Enabling an Existing User

1. Click Start ➢ Programs ➢ Microsoft Exchange Server 2007, and then select Exchange Management Console.
2. Expand the Microsoft Exchange root object, expand the Recipient Configuration folder, and then click the Mail Contact node.
3. In the Actions pane on the right, click the New Mail User link. The New Mail User Wizard starts.
4. Select the User Mailbox option, and click Next to continue to the User Type page.
5. On the User Type page, select Existing User, and then click the Browse button to open the Select User dialog box.
6. From the Select User dialog box, you will be able to select from a list of the user accounts in Active Directory that are not disabled and do not already have a mailbox assigned. Select a user account, and click OK to return to the User Type page. Click Next to Mail Settings page.
7. On the Mail Settings page, you will need to select the mail alias, which is provided by default for you, and then create an external email address to be assigned to the mail-enabled user. Click the Edit button to open the SMTP Address dialog box. Enter the correct external SMTP email address, and then click OK. Click Next to proceed to the summary page.
8. On the summary page, review all your configuration entries, and click New if you are satisfied. You can click Back to change any of the entries you made. When you click New, the Completion page appears.
9. As always, Exchange displays for you the PowerShell code it used to perform the user account and mailbox creation. Click Finish to close the wizard.

Creating Mail Users with the Exchange Management Shell

As you've seen countless times by now, anything you can do within the Exchange Management Console, you can do in the Exchange Management Shell as well. Creating mail-enabled user accounts and mail-enabling existing users are no exceptions. To create a new Active Directory user account that is mail-enabled, you need to use the `new-MailUser` cmdlet within the Exchange Management Shell. The code would look something like this:

```
New-MailUser -Name 'Alisha Smith' -Alias 'asmith1'
-OrganizationalUnit 'WILEY.CORP/Users' -UserPrincipalName 'asmith1@WILEY.CORP'
-SamAccountName 'amsith1' -FirstName ' Alisha' -Initials '' -LastName 'Smith'
-ResetPasswordOnNextLogon $false
-ExternalEmailAddress 'SMTP:alisha.smith@externalcompany.com'
```

Figure 6.24 displays the resulting output of this command.

FIGURE 6.24 Creating a new mail-enabled user account with the Exchange Management Shell

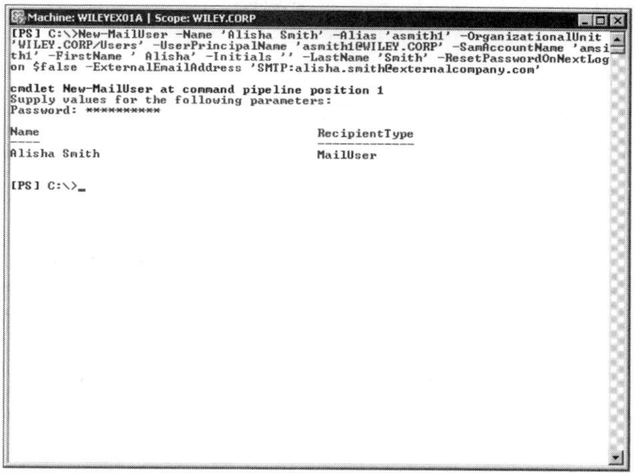

Of course, the same issue with passwords that you saw previously when creating mailbox-enabled user accounts from the PowerShell is still evident when creating mail-enabled user accounts.

If you need to mail-enable only an existing Active Directory user account object, the code and process is much simpler because you don't need to worry about messing with passwords. You'll use the `Enable-MailUser` cmdlet, and the code would look something like this:

```
Enable-MailUser -Identity 'WILEY.CORP/Wiley Users/Susan West' -Alias 'swest'
 -ExternalEmailAddress 'SMTP:susan.west@externalcompany.com'
```

Figure 6.25 displays the resulting output of this command.

FIGURE 6.25 Mail-enabling an existing user account with the Exchange Management Shell

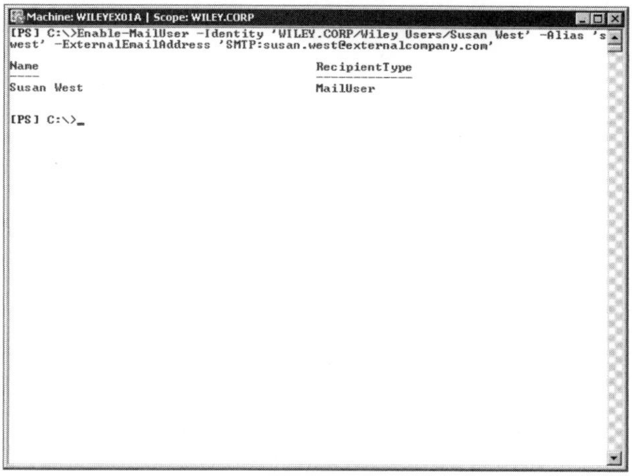

Managing Mail Users

If you have mail-enabled user accounts, or *mail users* as Exchange Server 2007 refers to them, then you're going to need to manage or change the configuration of some of them at some point in time. You'll examine the configuration options you have in the following sections.

Performing Basic Management from the Exchange Management Console

You do all mail user management from the Exchange Management Console from the Microsoft Exchange ➢ Recipient Configuration ➢ Mail Contact node, as shown in Figure 6.26. When a mail user is selected in the middle of the console, you'll have mailbox-specific options that become available on the right side of the console. Of course, all of these options are also available by right-clicking the mailbox of concern and selecting them from the context menu.

The Disable option is actually used to remove all messaging attributes from the user account object, not to disable the account itself. To disable the user account, and thus make it unable to be used for login, you'll need to visit the Active Directory Users and Computers console. If you click the Disable link in the Exchange Management Console, you'll be prompted to consider your action and whether you want to continue. You can accomplish the same effect using the `Disable-MailUser` cmdlet.

FIGURE 6.26 Mail user management options in the Exchange Management Console

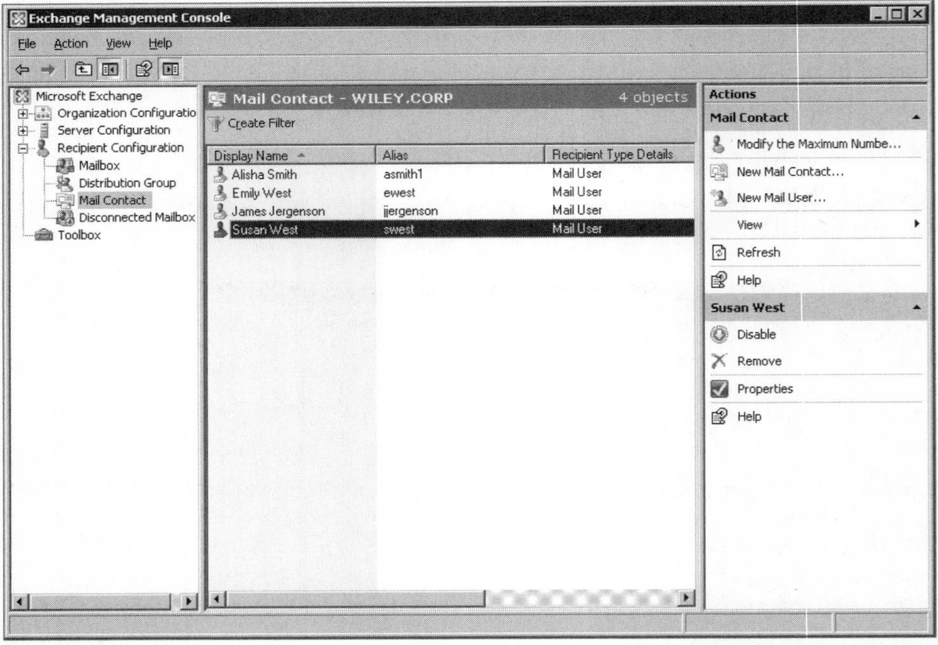

The Remove option actually causes the Active Directory user account object to be deleted from Active Directory along with the corresponding mailbox. You can accomplish the same using the `Remove-MailUser` cmdlet.

The Move Mailbox option allows you to move the selected mailbox to a different mailbox database on the same server or a different server within the Exchange organization. We'll talk in depth about moving mailboxes in Chapter 9. Since we don't discuss unified messaging in this book, we won't look at the Enable Unified Messaging option.

Managing Mail Users' Properties

When you click the last item available for a mail user, Properties, the mailbox Properties dialog box opens to the General tab, as shown in Figure 6.27. For the most part, these are the same tabs and options as shown previously when working with mailbox-enabled user accounts. To that end, we won't cover all the great items in detail here.

FIGURE 6.27 The General tab of the mail user's Properties dialog box

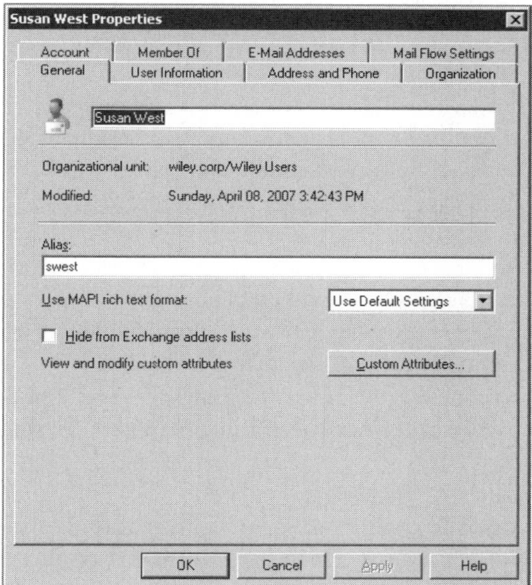

General

The General tab of the mailbox Properties dialog box contains all the basic identifying information about the mail user, although you can change only the display name field at the top of the tab and the Alias field at the bottom of the tab. You can also opt to have the mail user hidden from view in the GAL if desired.

Other useful information you'll find on the General tab includes the following:

- The organizational unit in which the Active Directory user account is located
- The last time the mail user properties were modified

By clicking the Custom Attributes button, the Custom Attributes dialog box will open. Custom attributes are beyond the scope of this exam and will not be discussed.

User Information

The User Information tab of the mailbox Properties dialog box allows you to configure various basic information about the user account. You can configure the following information on this tab:

- The user's first name, initials, and last name
- A simple display name for the GAL that contains only ASCII characters and no Unicode characters
- The user's web page
- Notes about the mailbox and user that are not displayed anywhere else

Address and Phone

The Address and Phone tab of the mailbox Properties dialog box contains various information fields that you can configure with the user's address and contact phone numbers, such as an office home, home phone, and mobile phone.

Organization

The Organization tab of the mailbox Properties dialog box contains organizational information fields that you can configure about the user such as title, company, and manager. The Direct Reports field is not directly configurable but is populated using reverse links from those Active Directory user account objects that have the Manager field configured.

Account

The Account tab of the mailbox Properties dialog box allows you to configure basic account information about the user. Items you can configure here include the user principal name logon name, the pre–Windows 2000 logon name, and whether the user must change their password at the next login attempt. Notice the lack of ability to actually reset a user's password—that's still definitely an action you'll be performing from the Active Directory Users and Computers console.

Member Of

The Member Of tab of the mailbox Properties dialog box provides a read-only listing of all security and distribution groups of which the user is a member. Not listed on this tab is the built-in Domain Users group membership that all user accounts in the domain have by default. If you examined the user account from Active Directory Users and Computers, you'd see that group membership as well. To add a user to a distribution group, you'll need to work from the Distribution Group node of the Recipient Configuration node in the Exchange Management Console or use the Active Directory Users and Computers console. Security groups can be added only via the Active Directory Users and Computers console.

E-Mail Addresses

The E-Mail Addresses tab of the mailbox Properties dialog box allows you to add, remove, and edit email addresses assigned to the mailbox. The only type of email address that Exchange Server 2007 supports by default is SMTP, but you can configure custom types, if needed in your organization, by clicking the down arrow next to the Add button.

Mail Flow Settings

The Mail Flow Settings tab of the mailbox Properties dialog box allows you to configure specific settings that determine how messages to or from this mailbox-enabled user are handled. By selecting the Message Size Restrictions option and clicking the Properties button, the Message Size Restrictions dialog box opens, allowing you to configure specific receive size limits that are applied only to this mail user and that override those applied at the organizational or SMTP connector level. By selecting the Message Delivery Restrictions option and clicking the Properties button, the Message Delivery Restrictions dialog box opens, allowing you to configure which senders are allowed and not allowed to send messages to this mail user. By default, there are no restrictions configured on the Message Delivery Restrictions tab.

Configuring Send As Permissions

Many times the user account that is tied to a mailbox may not be the only one that needs to be able to send messages as that account (user). Some common examples of this scenario are departmental mailboxes, project mailboxes, or customer comment and suggestion mailboxes. Additionally, you might opt to configure Send As permissions instead of using the Outlook delegation process to allow a delegate to send as someone else, perhaps their supervisor. In these cases, no matter who is actually managing the messages within the mailbox, any replies or new messages from that mailbox appear to be from that mailbox and not the actual user sending the message. This requires a change to the Send As permission on the user account associated with the mailbox of concern and must be performed from within the Active Directory Users and Computers console, as outlined in Exercise 6.7.

EXERCISE 6.7

Configuring Send As Permissions on a Mailbox

1. Log in to a domain controller or a computer that has the Windows Server 2003 SP1 or SP2 Administrative Tools installed.

2. Click Start ➢ Programs ➢ Control Panel ➢ Administrative Tools, and then select Active Directory Users and Computers. The Active Directory Users and Computers console opens.

3. On the View menu of the Active Directory Users and Computers console, select the Advanced Features option. This is needed to enable the display of the user account's Security tab in the Properties dialog box.

4. Navigate to the organizational unit where the mailbox-enabled user account for which you want to configure Send As permissions is. Once the account is located, right-click it, and select Properties to open the account's Properties dialog box.

EXERCISE 6.7 *(continued)*

5. Select the Security tab, as shown here.

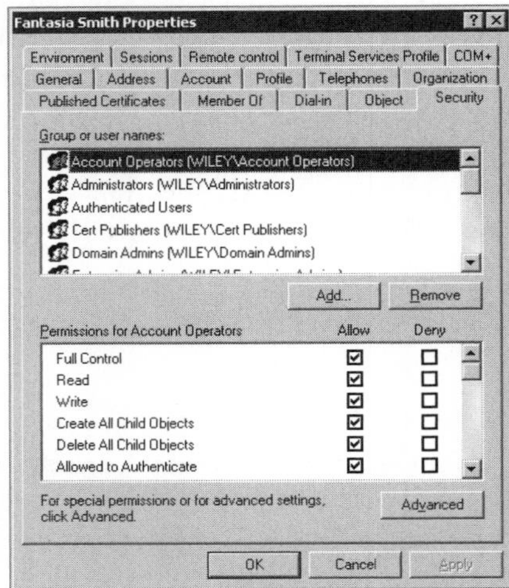

6. Click the Advanced button to open the Advanced Security Settings for *User* dialog box, shown here.

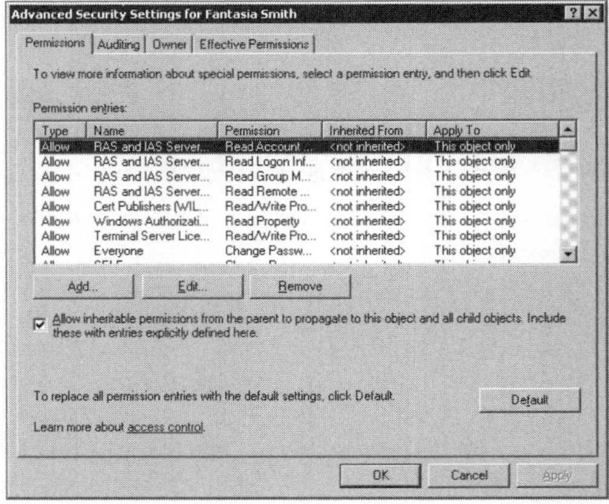

7. Click the Add button. Select the user account or security group from the Select User, Computer, or Group dialog box that you want to configure the Send As permissions for on the selected user account. Click Check Name to verify the correct spelling, and then click OK. The Permission Entry dialog box opens.

8. In the Permission Entry dialog box, select This Object Only from the Apply Onto drop-down list. Scroll down through the permissions list, and select the Allow check box for the Send As permission.

9. Click OK three times to accept all changes and close all open dialog boxes.

After configuring Send As permissions, it may take some time for them to become active because Active Directory replication must complete first. If you want to force the issue and make the changes effective immediately, you will need to stop and then restart the Microsoft Exchange Information Store service on the Mailbox server that houses the mailbox on which you configured Send As permissions. Note that this action will interrupt all access to all mailboxes and public folders on that Mailbox server temporarily—so you'll likely not want to do that during production hours.

Configuring Mail-Enabled Groups

In Windows Server 2003, a group is an Active Directory object that can hold users and other groups. In the case of security groups, permissions can be assigned to a group and are inherited by all the objects in that group. This makes the group a valuable Windows security construct. Exchange Server 2007 also uses the group for another purpose. A group can be made mail-enabled and then populated with other mail- or mailbox-enabled recipients to make a *distribution list*, a term you may be familiar with from earlier versions of Exchange Server. A group can contain users, contacts, public folders, and even other groups. When a message is sent to a mail-enabled group, the list of members is extracted, and the message is sent to each member of the list individually. Groups are visible in the GAL if they are configured properly to be mail-enabled.

Windows Server 2003 supports two distinct types of groups. A security group can be assigned permissions and rights and be mail-enabled. A distribution group can be mail-enabled only.

Understanding Group Types and Scopes

Before we can begin any discussion on creating and managing groups, a discussion on group types and group scopes is necessary. You will need to have a good understanding of how the two different group types and three different group scopes work before you can effectively use groups in your Exchange organization.

Group Types

As mentioned previously, there are two types of groups within Active Directory: security groups and distribution groups. The names of these groups are fairly descriptive in regard to their usage.

Security Groups

Security groups, as the name implies, are used primarily to configure and assign security settings for those user and group objects placed within the group. An administrator can configure the desired rights and permissions on the group, and these settings will then automatically be applied to all group members without needing to manually configure the settings on the individual objects. As you can see, this is a benefit both from an administrative point of view (less work to be done) and from an accuracy point of view (fewer chances of configuring individual object permissions incorrectly). Security groups can also be mail-enabled if desired, therefore allowing their mailbox-enabled and mail-enabled members to receive all messages that are sent to the security group.

Distribution Groups

Distribution groups, as their name implies, are used only for sending messages to a large number of objects without having to manually select each user, group, or contact. You can place all members of a specific department or geographical location into a distribution group and then send one message to the group that will be distributed to all members. Since distribution groups are not access control list (ACL)–enabled like security groups are, you cannot assign user rights or permissions to them.

You can change a distribution group into a security group at any time with no loss in functionality. However, changing a security group into a distribution group will result in the rights and permissions that have been configured on that group being lost. You will be warned of this when attempting to make the change.

Group Scopes

Within Active Directory, three different group scopes exist. The scope of the group determines who may be members of the group from an Active Directory standpoint. From an Exchange standpoint, the group scope determines who will be able to determine group membership when multiple domains exist within the organization.

Domain Local Groups

The membership of domain local groups is not published to the global catalog servers in the organization, thus preventing Exchange users from being able to determine the group membership of mail-enabled domain local groups outside the domain in which their user account is located. In most cases, if your organization consists of multiple domains, then you may opt to not use domain-local groups for Exchange distribution purposes. The membership of domain-local groups is dependent on the domain functional level of the domain but typically can include accounts from any domain in the forest.

Global Groups

The membership of global groups is also not published to the global catalog servers in the organization. In most cases, if your organization consists of multiple domains, then you may opt to not use global groups for Exchange distribution purposes. The membership of global groups is dependent on the domain functional level of the domain but typically can include only those accounts from the same domain in the forest in which the group was created.

Universal Groups

Only universal groups have their membership information published to the global catalog servers in the organization. This then allows Exchange users who are located in any domain in the forest to be able to determine the group membership of any group in the forest, regardless of the domain in which it has been created. The ability to create, and therefore use, universal groups is dependent on the domain functional level of the domain in that they can be created only when the domain functional level is at Windows 2000 native or Windows Server 2003. If your organization is capable of using universal groups, you'll want to consider their usage for Exchange distribution groups, especially when creating query-based distribution groups, as discussed later in this chapter. Universal groups can contain members from any domain in the forest.

There is a lot more to be said about group scopes, including how the domain functional level impacts your ability to work with the different scopes. You can find more information about group scopes by searching the Windows Server 2003 help files for *group scopes* or by visiting this website: `http://technet2.microsoft.com/windowsserver/en/library/79d93e46-ecab-4165-8001-7adc3c9f804e1033.mspx`.

Managing Mail-Enabled Groups

Once you have mailbox-enabled and mail-enabled users (and perhaps mail contacts, as you'll examine later in this chapter), you'll likely want to start using mail-enabled groups to make messaging really work in your organization. Commonly, every department in an organization has at least one distribution group created for it, such as the "Sales distribution group," which would contain all members of the sales department. Although you can still create and manage groups from the Active Directory Users and Computers console, which you'll explore now, you must now create and manage all messaging-related options and functionality from within the Exchange Management Console or Exchange Management Shell.

Creating Distribution Groups with the Exchange Management Console

In the Exchange Management Console, you will find distribution groups and their corresponding management options listed in the Microsoft Exchange ➢ Recipient Configuration ➢ Distribution Groups node, as shown in Figure 6.28.

FIGURE 6.28 Viewing Exchange distribution groups

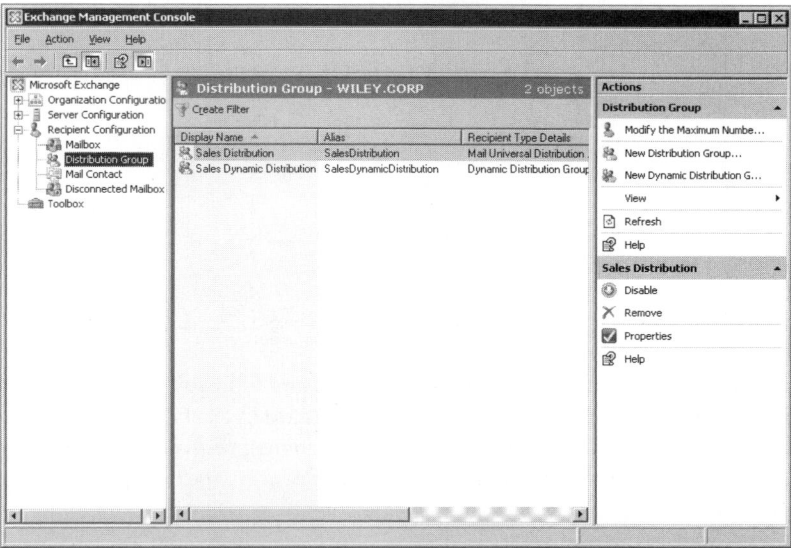

The default view is to list all distribution groups within the organization, although your initial view may not display them all depending on how many mailboxes you've configured to be displayed. The default setting is 1,000 mailboxes and can be changed by clicking the Modify the Maximum Number of Recipients to Display link under the mailbox options in the Actions pane on the right of the Exchange Management Console.

Other options you have in the Actions pane on the right of the Exchange Management Console include creating a new distribution group and creating a new dynamic distribution group; if you've selected a distribution, then you have the following additional options: Disable, Remove, and Properties. We'll examine all these options in the following sections.

Exercise 6.8 outlines the steps for creating a new distribution group.

EXERCISE 6.8

Creating a New Distribution Group

1. Click Start ➢ Programs ➢ Microsoft Exchange Server 2007, and then select Exchange Management Console.

2. Expand the Microsoft Exchange root object, expand the Recipient Configuration folder, and then click the Distribution Group node.

3. In the Actions pane on the right, click the New Distribution Group link. The New Distribution Group Wizard starts.

4. Select the New Group option, and click Next to continue to the Group Information page shown here.

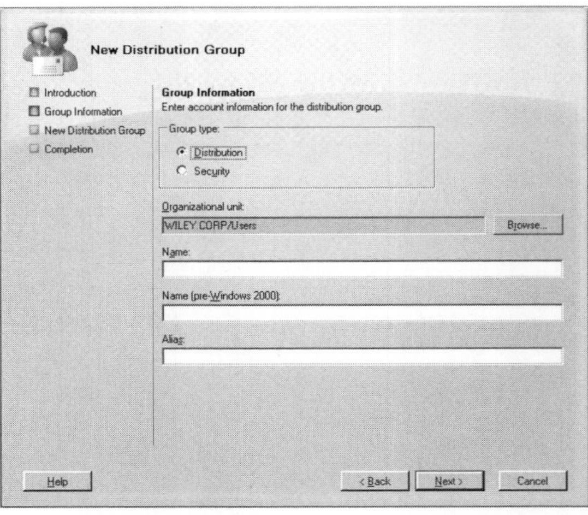

5. On the Group Information page, select Distribution, and then select the location within Active Directory where the new group should be created by clicking the Browse button. You'll also need to supply the group name from which the pre–Windows 2000 name and group alias will be automatically created, though you can change these values. Click Next to continue to the summary page.

EXERCISE 6.8 *(continued)*

6. On the summary page, review all your configuration entries, and click New to create the new distribution group. If you need to change any entries, you can click the Back button.
7. As always, Exchange displays for you the PowerShell code it used to perform the user account and mailbox creation. Click Finish to close the wizard.

If you have security groups that already exist in Active Directory but are not mail-enabled, you can perform the steps detailed in Exercise 6.9 to mail-enable those groups.

EXERCISE 6.9

Mail-Enabling an Existing Security Group

1. Click Start ➢ Programs ➢ Microsoft Exchange Server 2007, and then select Exchange Management Console.
2. Expand the Microsoft Exchange root object, expand the Recipient Configuration folder, and then click the Distribution Group node.
3. In the Actions pane on the right, click the New Distribution Group link. The New Distribution Group Wizard starts.
4. On the Introduction page, select Existing Groups, and then click the Browse button to open the Select Group dialog box shown here. Note that the security group will need to be universal in scope in order to be displayed.

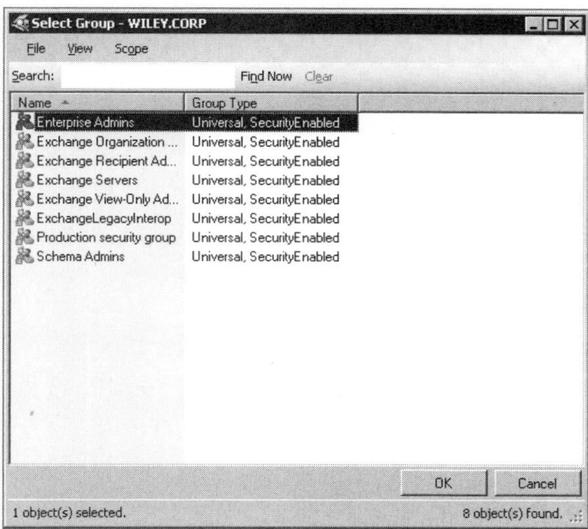

EXERCISE 6.9 *(continued)*

5. From the Select Group dialog box, you will be able to select from a list of the universal security groups in Active Directory that are not mail-enabled. Select a group, and click OK to return to the Introduction page. Click Next to Group Information page.
6. On the Group Information page, the only value you'll be able to change is the alias. Click Next to continue to the summary page.
7. On the summary page, review all your configuration entries, and click New if you are satisfied. You can click Back to change any of the entries you made. When you click New, the Completion page appears.
8. As always, Exchange displays for you the PowerShell code it used to perform the user account and mailbox creation. Click Finish to close the wizard.

Even though every step of this process in Exercise 6.9 discusses distribution groups, by completing the wizard you are only mail-enabling the security group (adding an email address to it). You are not changing the group type from security to distribution, which is something that you can do from the Active Directory Users and Computers console if desired later.

Of course, you can create a new security group using the process outlined previously in Exercise 6.8 if you want. You'll need to manage the group membership of security groups from the Active Directory Users and Computers console, though.

Creating Distribution Groups with the Exchange Management Shell

Creating distribution groups from the Exchange Management Shell is a fairly simple task that you may want to undertake if a large number of groups must be created. To create a distribution group, you need to use the `new-DistributionGroup` cmdlet within the Exchange Management Shell. The code would look something like this:

```
new-DistributionGroup -Name 'Sales distribution group' -Type 'Distribution'
-OrganizationalUnit 'WILEY.CORP/Wiley Users'
-SamAccountName 'Sales distribution group' -Alias 'Salesdistributiongroup'
```

Figure 6.29 shows the resulting output of this command.

If you need to mail-enable only an existing group object, you'll use the `Enable-DistributionGroup` cmdlet, and the code would look something like this:

```
Enable-DistributionGroup -Identity 'WILEY.CORP/Wiley Users/Sales security group'
-Alias 'Salessecuritygroup'
```

Figure 6.30 shows the resulting output of this command.

FIGURE 6.29 Creating a distribution group with the Exchange Management Shell

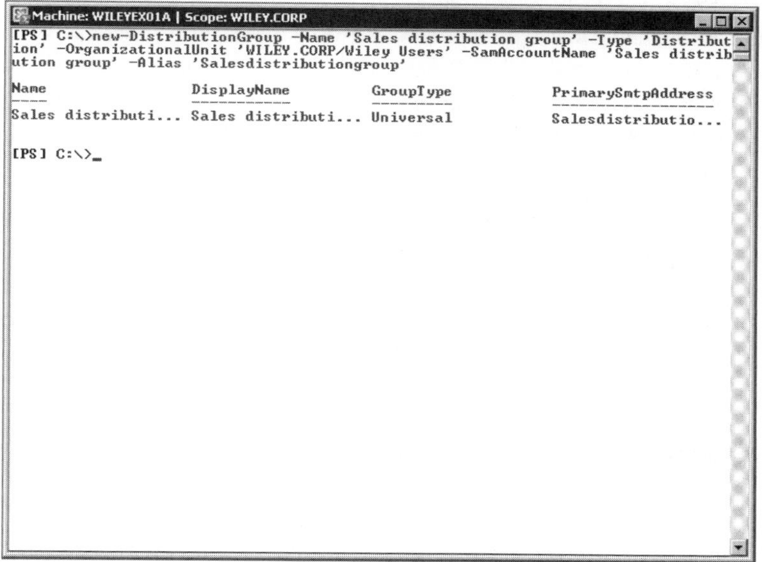

FIGURE 6.30 Mail-enabling an existing security group with the Exchange Management Shell

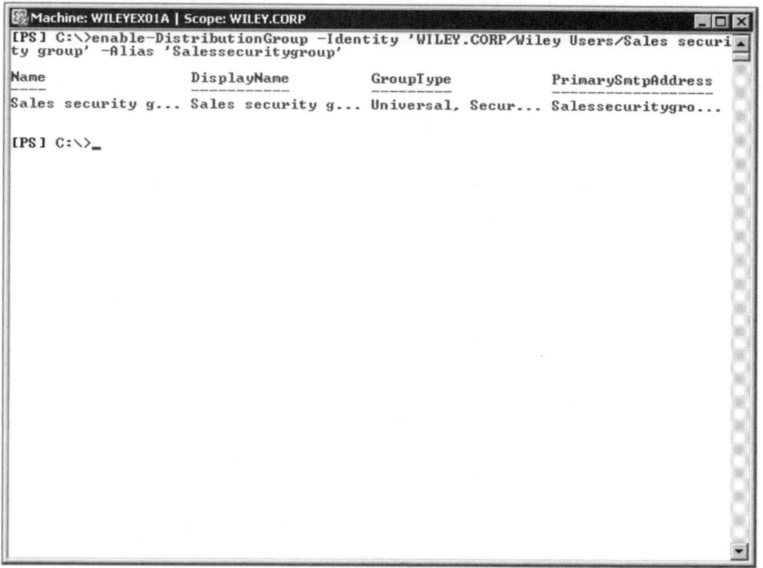

Creating Groups with the Active Directory Users and Computers Console

Of course, you can still (and will) create and manage groups from Active Directory Users and Computers. That's the whole rationale behind moving the messaging-specific functions back into the Exchange management tools, where they previously were in Exchange Server 5.5 and older versions. In larger organizations, some administrators will manage only Active Directory, and other administrators will manage only Exchange. In that case, the first group would be responsible for creating groups per the organizational standards in place, and the second group would be responsible only for managing the messaging attributes of those groups. Or you might find it easier, if you manage both Active Directory and Exchange, to continue whatever method you currently have in place for creating user accounts, such as using the `dsadd` command or VBScript, and then mail-enable the accounts later using the PowerShell `Enable-DistributionGroup` cmdlet.

Exercise 6.10 outlines the steps for creating a new group using Active Directory Users and Computers.

EXERCISE 6.10

Creating a New Group in Active Directory

1. Log in to a domain controller or a computer that has the Windows Server 2003 SP1 or SP2 Administrative Tools installed.

2. Click Start ➢ Programs ➢ Control Panel ➢ Administrative Tools, and then select Active Directory Users and Computers. The Active Directory Users and Computers console opens.

3. Navigate to the organizational unit in which you want the new group to be created, and then click the New Group button at the top of the console.

4. The New Object – Group dialog box opens, as shown here. In the Group Name field, type a name that represents the members of the group you are creating. Notice that Windows automatically fills in a group name that's compatible with pre–Windows 2000 versions.

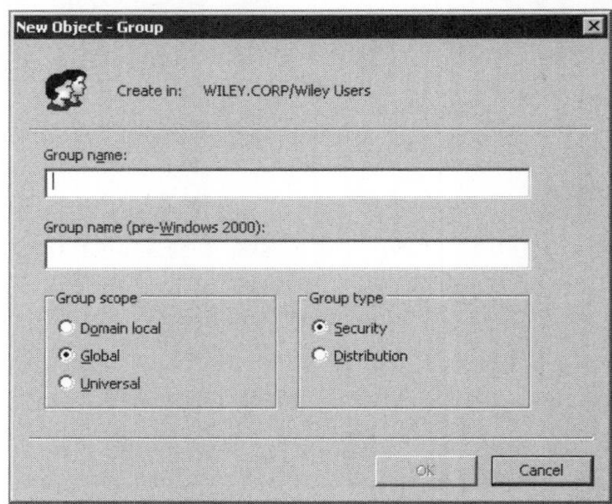

EXERCISE 6.10 *(continued)*

5. Next, you must choose a group scope. This determines at what level the group will be available in Active Directory—local, global, or universal. With Exchange Server 2007, it is usually best to make the group universal in scope so that it will be available throughout the organization. Otherwise, you may find that the group is limited by domain boundaries. Note that a domain must be running in the Windows 2000 native or Windows Server 2003 domain functional level to support universal groups.

6. Next, you must define a group type. This determines whether the group is for security or distribution purposes. A *security group* can be made mail-enabled and used for distribution purposes. Recall that security groups can also be assigned permissions and made part of ACLs for resources. A *distribution group* is used for email purposes only and cannot be used for security purposes. Security groups can be converted later into distribution groups, with a loss of all configured ACL entries. Likewise, distribution groups can be converted later into security groups if desired.

7. When you have entered all options, click OK to create the new group.

Even if you select distribution as the group type, no messaging configuration options are available in the group creation process. This is a direct result of the messaging attribute management being moved back to the Exchange Management Console in Exchange Server 2007.

Modifying Distribution Groups

It only stands to reason that once you have distribution groups in your Exchange organization, you're eventually going to have to manage or modify their configurations. We'll discuss just that now.

Performing Basic Management from the Exchange Management Console

You do all distribution group management from the Exchange Management Console from the Microsoft Exchange ➤ Recipient Configuration ➤ Distribution Group node, as shown previously in Figure 6.28. When a distribution group is selected in the middle of the console, you'll have specific options that become available on the right side of the console. Of course, all these options are also available by right-clicking the mailbox of concern and selecting them from the context menu.

The Disable option is actually used to remove all messaging attributes from the group object, not to disable the group itself since you can't disable a group in the same way that you would a user account. If you click the Disable link in the Exchange Management Console, you'll be prompted to consider your action and whether you want to continue. You can accomplish the same effect using the `Disable-DistributionGroup` cmdlet.

The Remove option actually causes the Active Directory group account object to be deleted from Active Directory along with the corresponding mail attributes. You can accomplish the same effect using the `Remove-DistributionGroup` cmdlet.

Managing Group Properties

When you click the last item available for a distribution, Properties, the distribution group's Properties dialog box opens to the General tab. We'll examine each tab, and the configurable items found on each, in the following sections.

General

The General tab of the distribution group's Properties dialog box, shown in Figure 6.31, contains some the basic identifying information about the distribution, although you can change only the display name field at the top of the tab and the Alias field at the bottom of the tab.

By clicking the Custom Attributes button, the Custom Attributes dialog box will open. Custom attributes are beyond the scope of this exam and will not be discussed.

FIGURE 6.31 The General tab of the distribution group's Properties dialog box

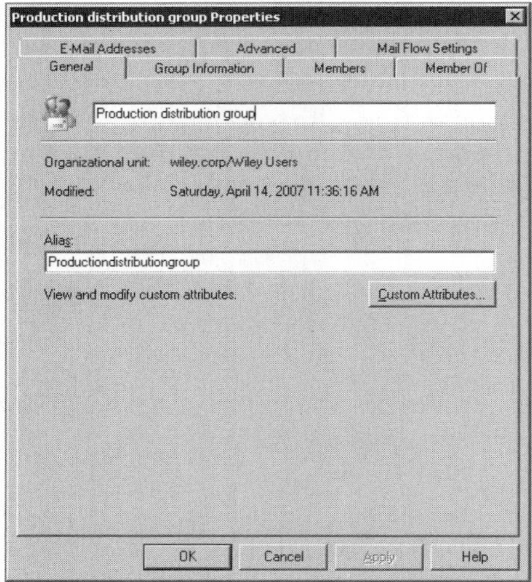

Group Information

The Group Information tab of the distribution group's Properties dialog box, shown in Figure 6.32, allows you to configure various basic information about the distribution group. You can configure the following information on this tab:

- The group name, which is limited to 64 characters
- The pre–Windows 2000 group name, which is limited to 20 characters and which cannot contain any of the following characters:

  ! # $ % ^ & - . _ { } | ~

- A user or security group who can manage the membership of this distribution group using Microsoft Outlook
- Notes about the distribution group that are not displayed anywhere else

Members

The Members tab of the distribution group's Properties dialog box, shown in Figure 6.33, is likely where you'll spend the majority of your group configuration time. You can add new members by using the Add button. You can remove existing members by using the delete (X) button.

FIGURE 6.32 The Group Information tab of the distribution group's Properties dialog box

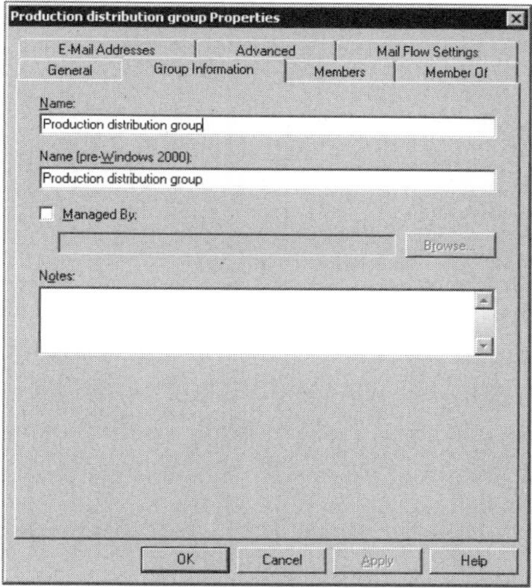

FIGURE 6.33 The Members tab of the distribution group's Properties dialog box

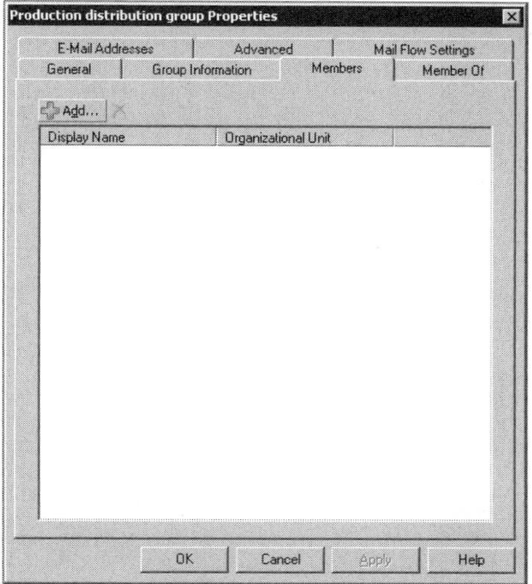

Member Of

The Member Of tab of the distribution group's Properties dialog box, shown in Figure 6.34, contains read-only information displaying a listing of any other groups of which this distribution group is a member. This information is automatically populated as you add this distribution to the Members tab of other distribution groups.

E-Mail Addresses

The E-Mail Addresses tab of the distribution group's Properties dialog box, shown in Figure 6.35, allows you to add, remove, and edit email addresses assigned to the distribution group. The only type of email address that Exchange Server 2007 supports by default is SMTP, but you can configure custom types, if needed in your organization, by clicking the down arrow next to the Add button. If multiple addresses exist, you can also configure one to be the default reply address using the Set as Reply button.

Advanced

The Advanced tab of the distribution group's Properties dialog box, shown in Figure 6.36, contains some useful configuration options that you'll likely find yourself using more than once for distribution groups.

Options that can be configured on this tab include the following:

- *Simple Display Name*: This contains only ASCII characters and no Unicode characters.
- *Expansion Server*: Whenever a message is sent to a group, the group must be expanded so that the message can be sent to each member of the group. A categorizer performs this expansion. The default choice is Any Server in the Organization. This choice means that the home server of the user sending the message always expands the group. You can also designate a specific server to handle the expansion of the group. The choice of a dedicated expansion server is a good one if you have a large group. In this case, expansion could consume a great amount of server resources, which can compromise performance for busy servers.

FIGURE 6.34 The Member Of tab of the distribution group's Properties dialog box

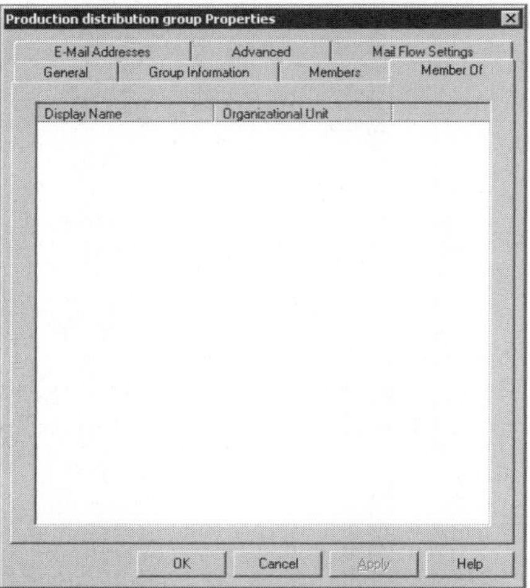

- *Hide Group from Exchange Address Lists*: If you enable this option, the group is not visible in the GAL.
- *Send Out-of-Office Messages to Originator*: Users of Outlook clients can configure rules that enable the clients to automatically reply to messages received while the users are away from their office. When this option is enabled, users who send messages to groups can receive those automatic out-of-office messages from members of the list. For particularly large groups, it's best not to allow out-of-office messages to be delivered because of the excess network traffic they generate.
- *Send Delivery Reports to Group Manager*: If you enable this option, notification is sent to the manager of the group whenever an error occurs during the delivery of a message to the group or to one of its members. Note that this option has no functionality if the group has not been assigned a manager.
- *Send Delivery Reports to Message Originator*: If you enable this option, error notifications are also sent to the user who sent a message to the group.
- *Do Not Send Delivery Reports*: If you enable this option, error notifications will not be sent.

FIGURE 6.35 The E-Mail Addresses tab of the distribution group's Properties dialog box

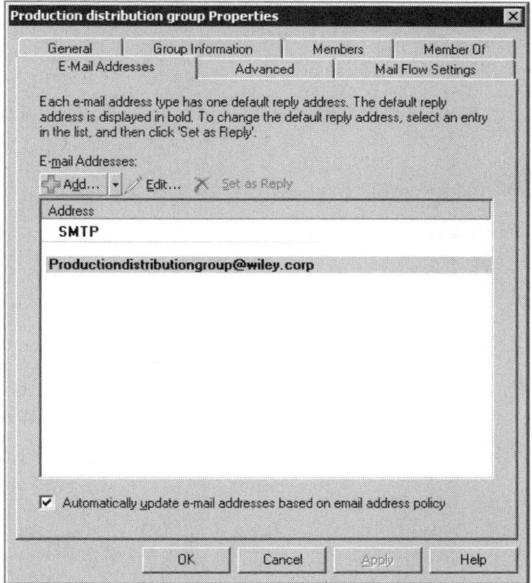

Mail Flow Settings

The Mail Flow Settings tab of the distribution group's Properties dialog box, shown in Figure 6.37, allows you to configure specific settings that determine how messages to this distribution group are handled.

FIGURE 6.36 The Advanced tab of the distribution group's Properties dialog box

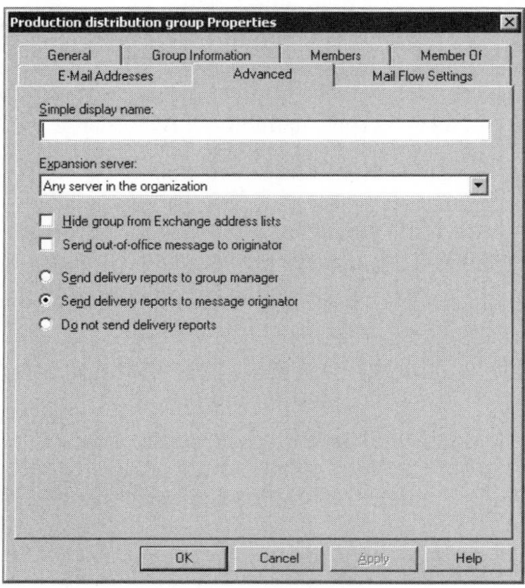

FIGURE 6.37 The Mail Flow Settings tab of the distribution group's Properties dialog box

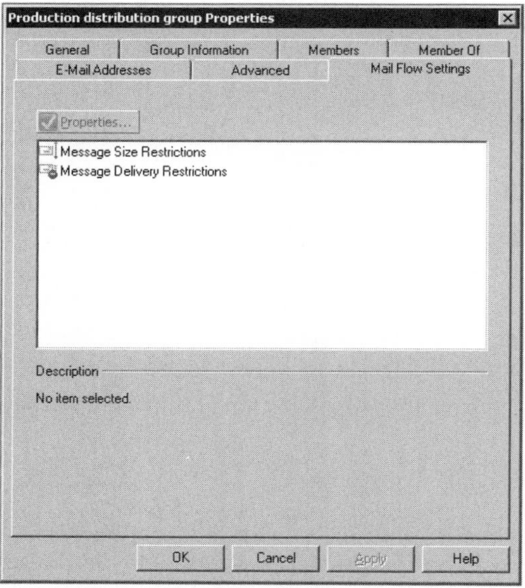

By selecting the Message Size Restrictions option and clicking the Properties button, the Message Size Restrictions dialog box opens. From here you can configure distribution group–specific receive size limits that are applied only to the distribution group and that override those applied at the organizational or SMTP connector level.

By selecting the Message Delivery Restrictions option and clicking the Properties button, the Message Delivery Restrictions dialog box opens. From here you can configure which senders are allowed and not allowed to send messages to this distribution group. By default, there are no restrictions configured on the Message Delivery Restrictions dialog box.

Managing Dynamic Distribution Groups

Dynamic distribution groups were first introduced in Exchange Server 2003 as query-based distribution groups. One of the biggest problems with using static distribution groups in the past was the amount of work and time that it took to maintain an accurate and up-to-date group membership. Dynamic distribution groups aim to correct that problem. As the name implies, a dynamic distribution group is a mail-enabled distribution group that has its membership defined by the results of an LDAP query that is made against the content of Active Directory.

The obvious advantage to using a dynamic distribution is that it provides a way to dynamically configure the membership of a group from all Exchange recipients based on a configured LDAP query. You can create a query, for example, that might limit the membership of a group to those users who are part of the accounting department of your organization. By that same logic, you could also create a dynamic distribution group that specifies membership should be limited to those users, contacts, and distribution groups that are located in a specific building or in a specific geographical area (such as a state or city) within your organization. By being able to quickly create, and change, the queries used to create these groups, you save time and energy over maintaining larger standard distribution groups. As well, dynamic distribution groups are much more accurate in their group membership because all the work is done by the results of the query you create.

As you might suspect by now, there is a trade-off to the power and flexibility that dynamic distribution groups provide. This trade-off comes in the form of increased loading on your global catalog servers. Each time an email is sent to a dynamic distribution group, the LDAP query you have configured must be run against the global catalog to determine the membership of the group.

Unlike query-based distributions in Exchange Server 2003, when you create a dynamic distribution group in Exchange Server 2007, you have a fairly small number of object attributes you can query on. These attributes are as follows:

- State or province (from the Address and Phone tab of the object's Properties dialog box)
- Department (from the Organization tab of the object's Properties dialog box)
- Company (from the Organization tab of the object's Properties dialog box)
- Custom attributes 1–15 (from the General tab of the object's Properties dialog box)

Creating Dynamic Distribution Groups with the Exchange Management Console

In the Exchange Management Console, you will find dynamic distribution groups and their corresponding management options listed in the Microsoft Exchange ➤ Recipient Configuration ➤ Distribution Groups node, as shown previously in Figure 6.28.

Exercise 6.11 outlines the steps for creating a new dynamic distribution group.

EXERCISE 6.11

Creating a New Distribution Group

1. Click Start ➤ Programs ➤ Microsoft Exchange Server 2007, and then select Exchange Management Console.
2. Expand the Microsoft Exchange root object, expand the Recipient Configuration folder, and then click the Distribution Group node.
3. In the Actions pane on the right, click the New Dynamic Distribution Group link. The New Dynamic Distribution Group Wizard starts.
4. Enter the name and alias for the new dynamic distribution group, and click Next to continue to the Filter Settings page shown here.

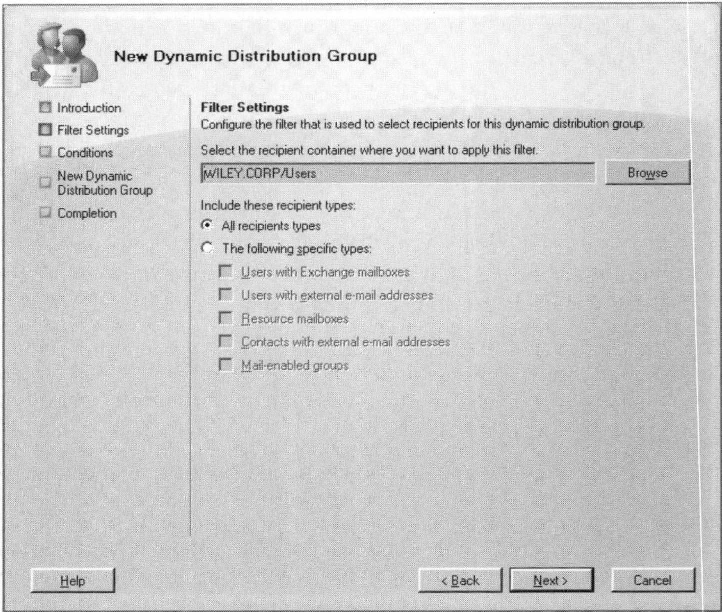

EXERCISE 6.11 *(continued)*

5. On the Filter Settings page, select the scope of the filter, such as particular organizational unit or an entire Active Directory domain. You can also select which specific types of recipients you want to include, such as just user mailboxes or just mail contacts. Typically, you'll use the default selection to include all recipients. Click Next to continue to the Conditions page shown here.

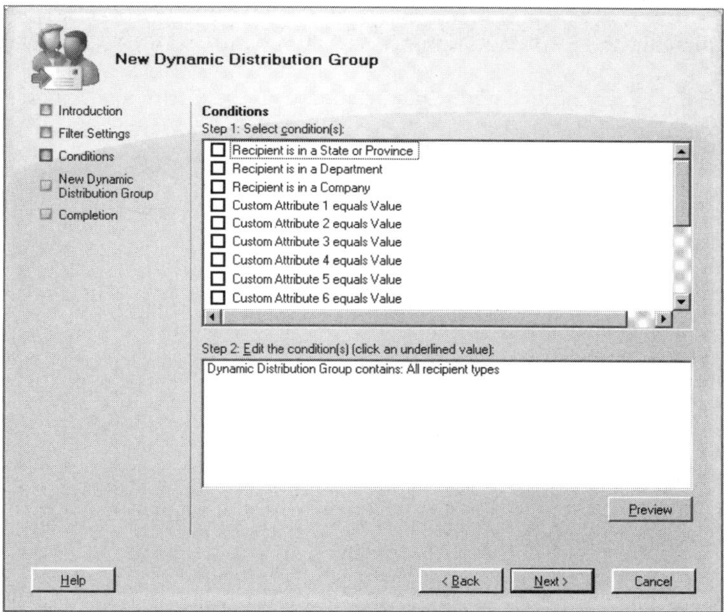

6. On the Conditions page, select the conditions you want to filter on in the Step 1 area, such as State. Once you've selected a condition, you need to enter a value for this condition in the Step 2 area of the page. Once you've configured your desired conditions, click Next to continue to the summary page.

7. On the summary page, review all your configuration entries, and click New to create the new dynamic distribution group. If you need to change any entries, you can click the Back button.

8. As always, Exchange displays for you the PowerShell code it used to perform the user account and mailbox creation. Click Finish to close the wizard.

Creating Dynamic Distribution Groups with the Exchange Management Shell

Creating dynamic distribution groups from the Exchange Management Shell is a fairly simple task, as you saw previously in Exercise 6.11. To create a new dynamic distribution group that uses the department condition you saw in Exercise 6.11, you need to use the `new-DynamicDistributionGroup` cmdlet within the Exchange Management Shell. The code would look something like this:

```
new-DynamicDistributionGroup -Name 'Sales dynamic distribution group'
-IncludedRecipients 'AllRecipients' -ConditionalDepartment 'Sales'
-OrganizationalUnit 'WILEY.CORP' -Alias 'Salesdynamicdistributiongroup'
-RecipientContainer 'WILEY.CORP/Wiley Users'
```

Figure 6.38 displays the resulting output of this command.

FIGURE 6.38 Creating a dynamic distribution with the Exchange Management Shell

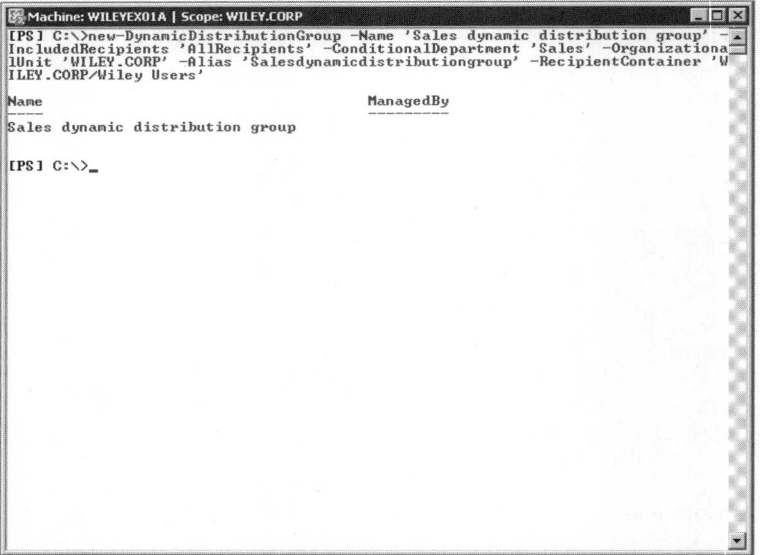

Modifying Dynamic Distribution Groups

It only stands to reason that once you have dynamic distribution groups in your Exchange organization that you're eventually going to have to manage or modify their configurations. We'll discuss just that now.

Performing Basic Management from the Exchange Management Console

You do all dynamic distribution group management from the Exchange Management Console from the Microsoft Exchange ➢ Recipient Configuration ➢ Distribution Group node, as shown previously in Figure 6.28. When a dynamic distribution group is selected in the middle of the console, you'll have specific options that become available on the right side of the console. Of course, all these options are also available by right-clicking the mailbox of concern and selecting them from the context menu.

Selecting the Remove option actually causes the Active Directory group object to be deleted from Active Directory along with the corresponding mail attributes. You can accomplish the same effect using the `Remove-DynamicDistributionGroup` cmdlet.

Managing Group Properties

When you click the only other item available for a distribution, Properties, the distribution group's Properties dialog box opens to the General tab. We'll examine the tabs specific to dynamic distribution groups, and the configurable items found on each, in the following sections.

Filter

The Filter tab of the dynamic distribution group's Properties dialog box, shown in Figure 6.39, allows you to change the scope of the filter that defines the dynamic distribution group.

FIGURE 6.39 The Filter tab of the dynamic distribution group's Properties dialog box

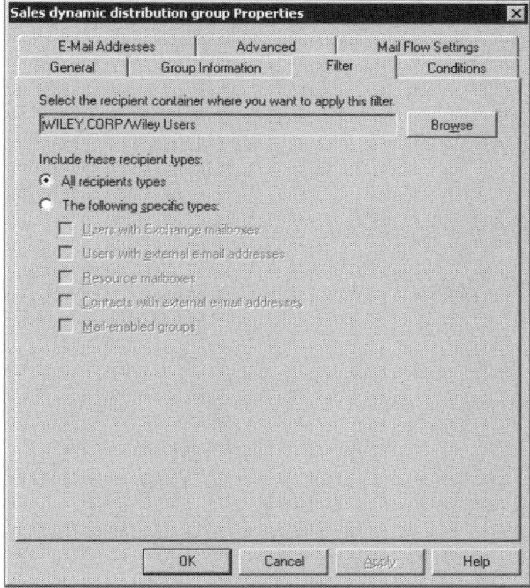

Conditions

The Conditions tab of the distribution group's Properties dialog box, shown in Figure 6.40, allows you to change the filter conditions that define the membership of the dynamic distribution group.

Once you've configured a filter scope and the conditions, you'll want to use the Preview button to open the Dynamic Distribution Group Preview dialog box, as shown in Figure 6.41. From here you'll be able to determine how effective your filter and conditions were at getting the recipients you wanted. It's at this time that the importance maintaining accurate information in Active Directory for all Exchange recipients starts to become very clear to most administrators.

FIGURE 6.40 The Conditions tab of the distribution group's Properties dialog box

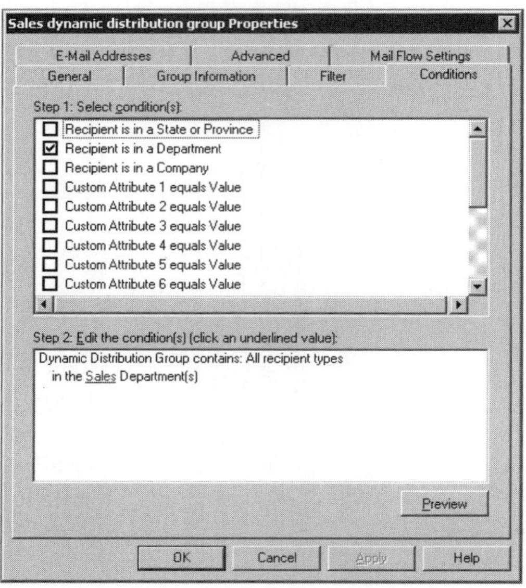

FIGURE 6.41 Previewing the membership of a dynamic distribution group

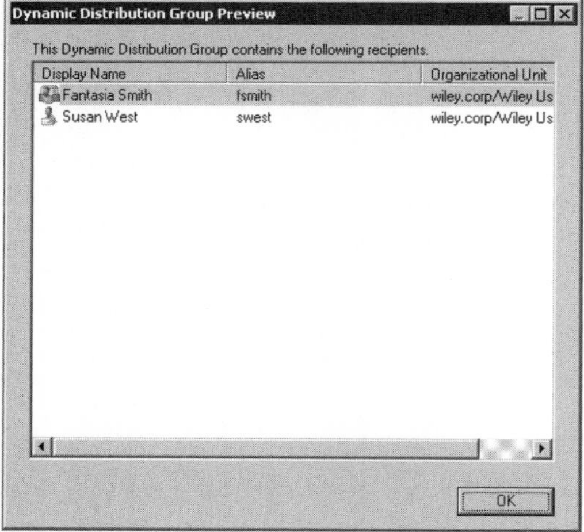

Configuring Mail Contacts

Mail-enabled contacts are commonly created to represent people outside your organization that users inside your organization commonly communicate with via email. Another common implementation of mail contacts is to provide a means to route messages to mobile phones and pagers from monitoring programs via the Exchange infrastructure. Although you can still create and manage contacts from the Active Directory Users and Computers console, which you'll explore next, you must now create and manage all messaging-related options and functionality from within the Exchange Management Console or Exchange Management Shell.

Creating Contacts with the Exchange Management Console

In the Exchange Management Console, you will find contacts and their corresponding management options listed in the Microsoft Exchange ➢ Recipient Configuration ➢ Mail Contact node, as shown in Figure 6.42.

The default view is to list all contacts within the organization, although your initial view may not display them all depending on how many mailboxes you've configured to be displayed. The default setting is 1,000 contacts and can be changed by clicking the Modify the Maximum Number of Recipients to Display link under the mailbox options in the Actions pane on the right of the Exchange Management Console.

Other options you have in the Actions pane on the right of the Exchange Management Console include creating a new mail contact and creating a new mail user (which we've already examined); if you've selected a contact, then you have the following additional options: Disable, Remove, and Properties. We'll examine all these options in the following sections.

FIGURE 6.42 Viewing Exchange contacts

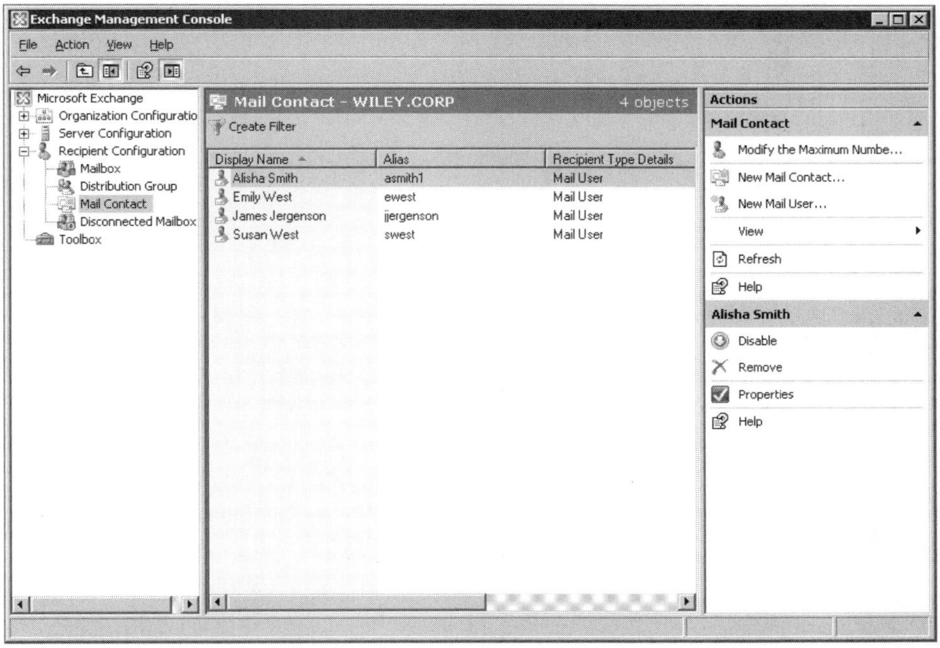

Exercise 6.12 outlines the steps for creating a mail contact.

EXERCISE 6.12

Creating a New Mail Contact

1. Click Start ➤ Programs ➤ Microsoft Exchange Server 2007, and then select Exchange Management Console.
2. Expand the Microsoft Exchange root object, expand the Recipient Configuration folder, and then click the Mail Contact node.
3. In the Actions pane on the right, click the New Mail Contact link. The New Mail Contact Wizard starts.
4. Since you want to create a mail contact in this exercise, select the New Contact option, and click Next. The Contact Information page appears, as shown here.

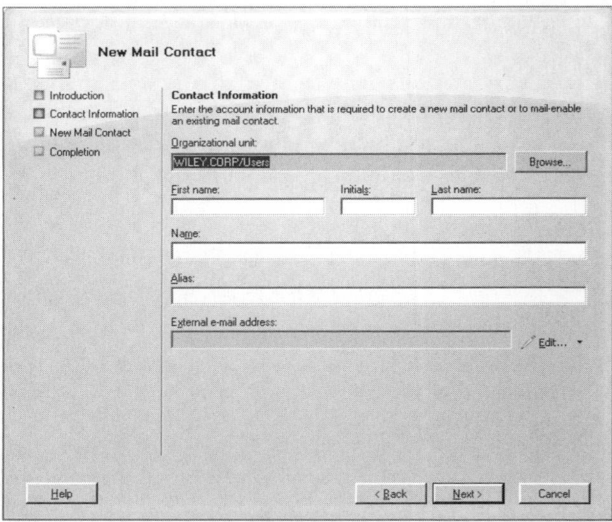

5. Enter all the required information: first name and last name, display name, alias, and external address. If you do not want to create the user object in the default Users container of Active Directory, click the Browse button to open the Select Organizational Unit dialog box. After you've correctly entered all the required information, click Next to continue to the summary page.
6. On the summary, review all your configuration entries, and click New if you are satisfied. You can click Back to change any of the entries you made. When you click New, the Completion page appears.
7. As always, Exchange displays for you the PowerShell code it used to perform the user account and mailbox creation. Click Finish to close the wizard.

If you have contact objects that already exist in Active Directory but are not mail-enabled, you can perform the steps detailed in Exercise 6.13 to mail-enable those contacts.

EXERCISE 6.13

Mail-Enabling an Existing Contact

1. Click Start ➢ Programs ➢ Microsoft Exchange Server 2007, and then select Exchange Management Console.
2. Expand the Microsoft Exchange root object, expand the Recipient Configuration folder, and then click the Mail Contact node.
3. In the Actions pane on the right, click the New Mail Contact link. The New Mail Contact Wizard starts.
4. Select the User Mailbox option, and click Next to continue to the User Type page.
5. On the Introduction page, select Existing Contact, and then click the Browse button to open the Select Contact dialog box.
6. From the Select Contact dialog box, you will be able to select from a list of the contact objects in Active Directory that are not currently mail-enabled. Select a contact, and click OK to return to the Introduction page. Click Next to go to Contact Information page.
7. On the Contact Information page, you will be able to change only the alias and configure an external address. After you've correctly entered all the required information, click Next to continue to the summary page.
8. On the summary, review all your configuration entries, and click New if you are satisfied. You can click Back to change any of the entries you made. When you click New, the Completion page appears.
9. As always, Exchange displays for you the PowerShell code it used to perform the user account and mailbox creation. Click Finish to close the wizard.

Creating Contacts with the Exchange Management Shell

To create a new mail contact using PowerShell, you need to use the `New-MailContact` cmdlet within the Exchange Management Shell. The code you would use would look something like this:

```
New-MailContact -ExternalEmailAddress 'SMTP:rickjones@bigcorp.net'
-Name 'Rick Jones' -Alias 'RickJones'
-OrganizationalUnit 'WILEY.CORP/Wiley Users'
-FirstName 'Rick' -Initials '' -LastName 'Jones'
```

If you need to mail-enable only an existing Active Directory contact object, you'll use the `Enable-MailContact` cmdlet, and the code would look something like this:

```
Enable-MailContact -Identity 'WILEY.CORP/Wiley Users/Andrea Jones'
-ExternalEmailAddress 'SMTP:andreajones@bigcorp.net' -Alias 'AndreaJones'
```

Creating Contacts with the Active Directory Users and Computers Console

Of course, you can still (and will) create and manage contacts from Active Directory Users and Computers. If you want to create and configure a new user account using the Active Directory Users and Computers console, then Exercise 6.14 has the steps you'll need to follow.

EXERCISE 6.14

Creating a New Contact in Active Directory Users and Computers

1. Log in to a domain controller or a computer that has the Windows Server 2003 SP1 or SP2 Administrative Tools installed.
2. Click Start ➢ Programs ➢ Control Panel ➢ Administrative Tools, and then select Active Directory Users and Computers. The Active Directory Users and Computers console opens.
3. Navigate to the organizational unit in which you want the new user account to be created. Right-click the desired organizational unit, and select New ➢ Contact from the context menu. The New Object – Contact dialog box opens, as shown here.

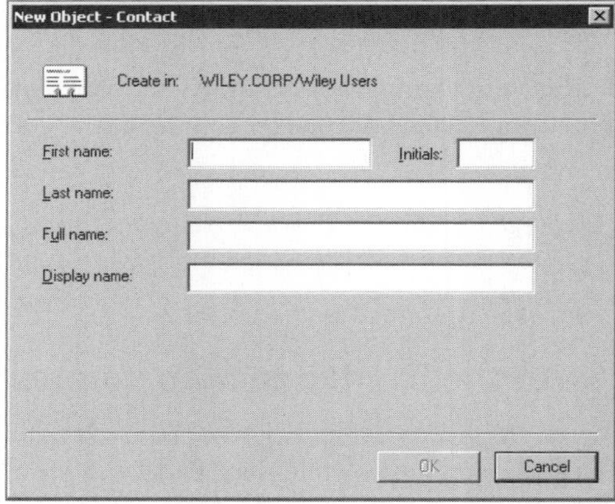

4. Enter all the required information: first name and last name, full name, and display name.
5. When you have entered all the information, click OK to create the new contact.

Of course, after the contact has been created, you can then mail-enable it from either the Exchange Management Console or the Exchange Management Shell, as you've learned previously.

Modifying Mail Contacts

It only stands to reason that once you have mailbox-enabled users in your Exchange organization that you're eventually going to have to manage or modify their configurations. We'll discuss just that now.

Performing Basic Management from the Exchange Management Console

You do all mail contact management from the Exchange Management Console from the Microsoft Exchange ➢ Recipient Configuration ➢ Mail Contact node, as shown previously in Figure 6.42. When a mailbox is selected in the middle of the console, you'll have mailbox-specific options that become available on the right side of the console. Of course, all of these options are also available by right-clicking the mailbox of concern and selecting them from the context menu.

The Disable option is actually used to remove all messaging attributes from the mail contact. If you click the Disable link in the Exchange Management Console, you'll be prompted to consider your action and whether you want to continue. You can accomplish the same effect using the `Disable-MailContact` cmdlet.

The Remove option actually causes the contact object to be deleted from Active Directory. You can accomplish the same effect using the `Remove-MailContact` cmdlet.

Managing Mailbox Properties

When you click the last item available for a mail contact, Properties, the mail contact's Properties dialog box opens to the General tab. We'll examine each tab, and the configurable items found on each, in the following sections.

General

The General tab of the mail contact's Properties dialog box, shown in Figure 6.43, contains all the information about the mail contact. You have the option to change the display name field at the top of the tab and the Alias field at the bottom of the tab. Additionally, you can also opt to have the mailbox hidden from view in the GAL, change the MAPI settings, or configure the custom attributes.

Contact Information

The Contact Information tab of the mail contact's Properties dialog box has the same basic configuration options as shown previously for mailbox users in Figure 6.7. You can configure the following information on this tab:

- The mail contact's first name, initials, and last name
- A name that is displayed within Active Directory (this setting does not impact the display name in the GAL)

- A simple display name for the GAL that contains only ASCII characters and no Unicode characters
- The user's web page
- Notes about the mailbox and user that are not displayed anywhere else

FIGURE 6.43 The General tab of the mail contact's Properties dialog box

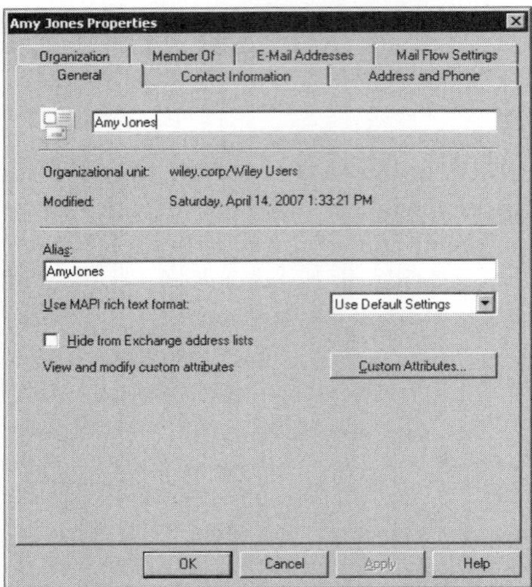

Address and Phone

The Address and Phone tab of the mail contact's Properties dialog box has the same basic configuration options as shown previously for mailbox users in Figure 6.8. From here, you can configure the user's address and contact phone numbers, such as an office home, home phone, and mobile phone.

Organization

The Organization tab of the mail contact's Properties dialog box has the same basic configuration options as shown previously for mailbox users in Figure 6.9. From here you can configure organizational information fields about the mail contact such as title, company, and manager. The Direct Reports field is not directly configurable but is populated using reverse links from those Active Directory user account objects that have the Manager field configured.

Member Of

The Member Of tab of the mail contact's Properties dialog box is a view-only listing of all groups that the mail contact is a member of, as shown previously for mailbox users in Figure 6.19.

E-Mail Addresses

The E-Mail Addresses tab of the mail contact's Properties dialog box, shown in Figure 6.44, allows you to add, remove, and edit internal and external email addresses assigned to the mail contact. The only type of email address that Exchange Server 2007 supports by default is SMTP, but you can configure custom types, if needed in your organization, by clicking the down arrow next to the Add button. Each mail contact must have at least one internal and one external email address associated with it to ensure proper mail flow.

FIGURE 6.44 The E-Mail Addresses tab of the mail contact's Properties dialog box

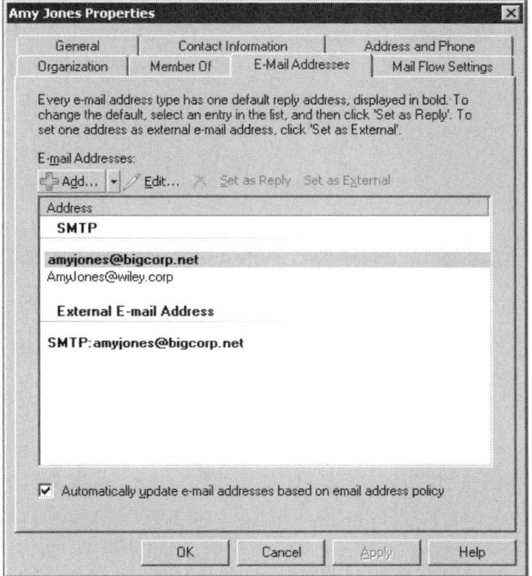

Mail Flow Settings

The Mail Flow Settings tab of the mail contact's Properties dialog box allows you to configure specific settings that determine how messages to this mail contact are handled, as shown previously for mailbox users in Figure 6.13.

By selecting the Message Size Restrictions option and clicking the Properties button, the Message Size Restrictions dialog box opens. From here you can configure specific receive size limits that are applied only to the mail contact and that override those applied at the organizational or SMTP connector level.

By selecting the Message Delivery Restrictions option and clicking the Properties button, the Message Delivery Restrictions dialog box opens. From here you can configure which senders are allowed and not allowed to send messages to this mail contact. By default, there are no restrictions configured on the Message Delivery Restrictions dialog box.

Configuring Resource Mailboxes

New in Exchange Server 2007 is the formal concept of a resource mailbox. Previously, many Active Directory and Exchange administrators had used resource mailboxes, but in all reality they're no different from any other mailbox-enabled user account. In Exchange Server 2007, they have been designated as their own type of recipient and are handled slightly differently than normal users who have mailbox-enabled user accounts are handled.

Creating Resource Mailboxes with the Exchange Management Console

In the Exchange Management Console, you will find mailboxes and their corresponding management options listed in the Microsoft Exchange ➢ Recipient Configuration ➢ Mailbox node, as shown previously in Figure 6.1. The basic management processes associated with resource mailboxes are the same as those for regular user mailboxes, so we'll examine only the differences in the remaining portion of this section.

Exercise 6.15 outlines the steps for creating a new user account that will be mailbox-enabled.

EXERCISE 6.15

Creating a New Resource Mailbox

1. Click Start ➢ Programs ➢ Microsoft Exchange Server 2007, and then select Exchange Management Console.
2. Expand the Microsoft Exchange root object, expand the Recipient Configuration folder, and then click the Mailbox node.
3. In the Actions pane on the right, click the New Resource Mailbox link. The New Mailbox Wizard starts.
4. For this exercise, select the Room Mailbox option, and click Next to continue to the User Type page.
5. Since you want to create a new user account and mailbox-enable it in this exercise, select the New User option, and click Next. The User Information page appears.
6. Enter all the required information: first name and last name, full (display) name, logon name, and password. If you do not want to create the user object in the default Users container of Active Directory, click the Browse button to open the Select Organizational Unit dialog box.
7. After you've correctly entered all the required information, click Next to continue to the Mailbox Settings page.
8. On the Mailbox Settings page, you will need to select the Mailbox server, storage group, and mailbox database in which the user's mailbox should be created. After making your selections, click Next to proceed to the New Mailbox page.
9. On the New Mailbox page, review all your configuration entries, and click New if you are satisfied. You can click Back to change any of the entries you made. When you click New, the Completion page appears.
10. As always, Exchange displays for you the PowerShell code it used to perform the user account and mailbox creation. Click Finish to close the wizard.

If you have disabled user accounts that already exist in Active Directory but are not mailbox-enabled, you can perform the steps detailed previously in Exercise 6.2 to create a mailbox for those accounts. You'll just need to select Room or Equipment for the mailbox type.

Remember that enabled Active Directory user accounts will not be displayed when you try to mailbox-enable an existing user account and you've selected the Room or Equipment option.

Creating Accounts and Mailboxes with the Exchange Management Shell

Creating resource mailboxes from the Exchange Management Shell is almost identical to the process you used previously to create mailbox-enabled users. You'll still need to use the `new-Mailbox` cmdlet within the Exchange Management Shell, but you'll need to configure an additional parameter: whether the mailbox is a room mailbox or an equipment mailbox. The code you would use would look something like this to create a room mailbox:

```
New-Mailbox -Name 'Conference Room 42A' -Alias 'cr42a'
-OrganizationalUnit 'WILEY.CORP/Users' -UserPrincipalName 'cr42a@WILEY.CORP'
-SamAccountName 'cr42a' -FirstName 'Conference Room 42A' -Initials ''
-LastName '' -Database 'CN=Mailbox Database,CN=First Storage Group,
CN=InformationStore,CN=WILEYEX01A,CN=Servers,
CN=Exchange Administrative Group (FYDIBOHF23SPDLT),CN=Administrative Groups,
CN=WILEY,CN=Microsoft Exchange,CN=Services,CN=Configuration,DC=WILEY,DC=CORP'
-Room
```

Figure 6.45 displays the resulting output of this command; notice that no password is required to be entered.

FIGURE 6.45 Creating a new resource mailbox with the Exchange Management Shell

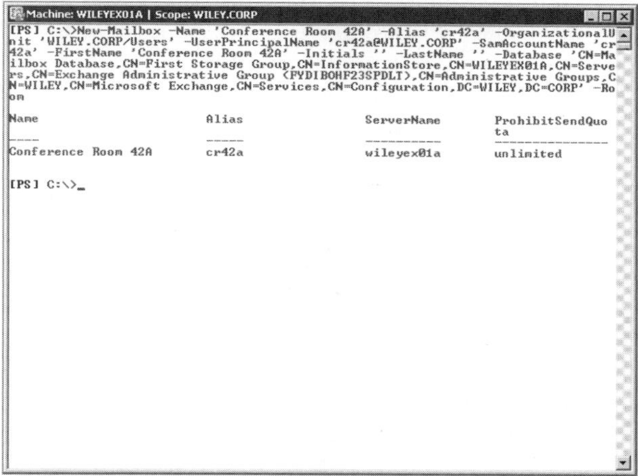

If you need to mailbox-enable only an existing disabled Active Directory user account object to be a resource mailbox, you'll use the `Enable-Mailbox` cmdlet, and the code would look something like this for an equipment mailbox:

```
Enable-Mailbox -Identity 'WILEY.CORP/Wiley Users/Projector 1'
-Alias 'projector1' -Database 'CN=Mailbox Database,CN=First Storage Group,
CN=InformationStore,CN=WILEYEX01A,CN=Servers,
CN=Exchange Administrative Group (FYDIBOHF23SPDLT),CN=Administrative Groups,
CN=WILEY,CN=Microsoft Exchange,CN=Services,CN=Configuration,DC=WILEY,DC=CORP'
-Equipment
```

Modifying Resource Mailboxes

If you have resource mailboxes in your Exchange organization, then you're going to need to manage or modify their configurations at some point in time. We'll discuss just that now.

Performing Basic Management from the Exchange Management Console

You do all mailbox management from the Exchange Management Console from the Microsoft Exchange ➢ Recipient Configuration ➢ Mailbox node, as shown previously in Figure 6.1. When a mailbox is selected in the middle of the console, you'll have mailbox-specific options that become available on the right side of the console. Of course, all these options are also available by right-clicking the mailbox of concern and selecting them from the context menu.

The Disable option removes all messaging attributes from the user account object; it doesn't disable the account itself. To disable the user account, and thus make it unable to be used for login, you'll need to visit the Active Directory Users and Computers console. If you click the Disable link in the Exchange Management Console, you'll be prompted to consider your action and whether you want to continue. You can accomplish the same effect using the `Disable-Mailbox` cmdlet.

The Remove option actually causes the Active Directory user account object to be deleted from Active Directory along with the corresponding mailbox. You can accomplish the same effect using the `Remove-Mailbox` cmdlet.

The Move Mailbox option allows you to move the selected mailbox to a different mailbox database on the same server or a different server within the Exchange organization. We'll talk in depth about moving mailboxes in Chapter 9. Since we don't discuss unified messaging in this book, we won't look at the Enable Unified Messaging option.

Managing Resource Mailbox Properties

When you click the last item available for a resource mailbox, Properties, the resource mailbox's Properties dialog box opens to the General tab. With the exception of a single new tab, the Resource Information tab, resource mailboxes have the same configuration properties available as any other mailbox-enabled account. To that end, we'll cover only the Resource Information tab here. If you need to review the other properties, refer to the "Modifying Mailbox-Enabled User Accounts" section earlier in this chapter.

Resource Information

The Resource Information tab of the mailbox's Properties dialog box, shown in Figure 6.46, contains configuration options that allow you to provide information to your users about the capabilities of the resource. The Resource Capacity field is used to specify how many people a room or resource can accommodate and accepts only numerical input ranging from 0 through 2,147,483,647.

FIGURE 6.46 The Resource Information tab of the mailbox's Properties dialog box

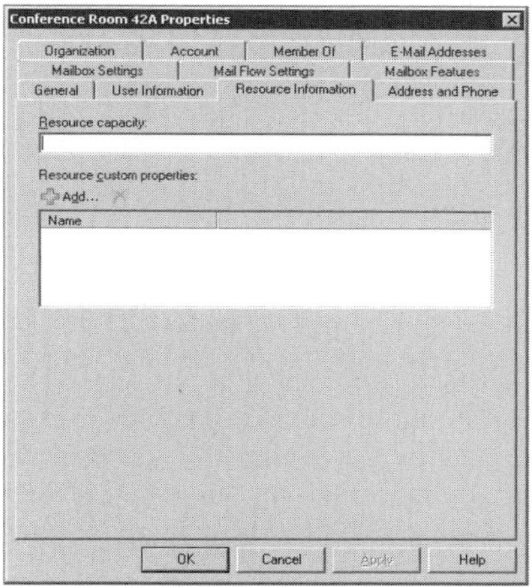

The Resource Custom Properties field allows you to select custom properties that have been defined in your Exchange organization and to indicate that this resource has those properties. Some examples might be selecting AV to indicate that the room has that capability or ConferenceCall to indicate the room has a conference call–quality phone. By default, there are no options configured to select from here, so you'll have to configure them yourself from the Exchange Management Shell by using the `Set-ResourceConfig` cmdlet. Unfortunately, if you simply use the cmdlet in its most basic format, you'll just end up setting the resource custom property to be the last entry you made. If you want to have multiple options available to select from, you'll have to get more creative, perhaps using code similar to that displayed here, which reads the current custom properties in, adds some custom properties in an array, and then writes the array out:

```
$ResourceConfiguration = Get-ResourceConfig
$ResourceConfiguration.ResourcePropertySchema.Add("Room/AV")
$ResourceConfiguration.ResourcePropertySchema.Add("Room/TV")
$ResourceConfiguration.ResourcePropertySchema.Add("Room/Whiteboard")
$ResourceConfiguration.ResourcePropertySchema.Add("Room/ConferenceCall")
$ResourceConfiguration.ResourcePropertySchema.Add("Equipment/Projector")
$ResourceConfiguration.ResourcePropertySchema.Add("Equipment/Computer")
Set-ResourceConfig -Instance $ResourceConfiguration
```

Once you create resource custom properties, you'll be able to select them by clicking the Add button to open the Select Resource Custom Property dialog box, as shown in Figure 6.47. Note that the custom properties will be shown only for the type of resource mailbox being configured, so you won't find the Projector option displayed when working with a conference room based on the PowerShell code used here. The configuration you end up with is limited only by your needs and imagination.

FIGURE 6.47 The Select Resource Custom Property dialog box

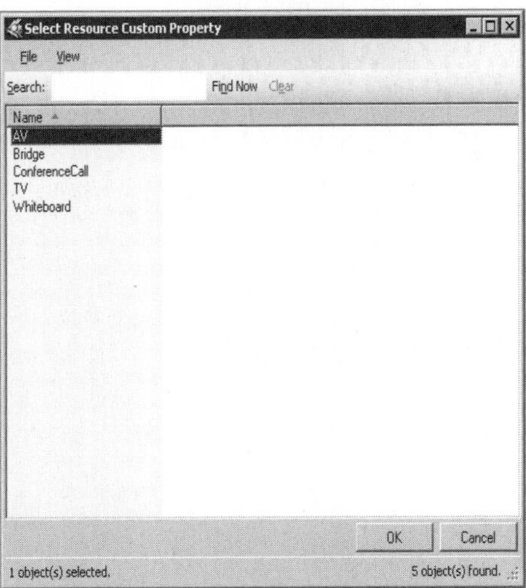

Once you've created and done basic configuration on your resource mailboxes, you should perform one additional step to enable their full functionality. To finish the configuration of the resource mailbox, you will need to log in to it via Outlook Web Access. Before you can do that, you'll need to change the password on the resource mailbox user account to one that meets your domain security policies and then enable it. You must perform these actions from the Active Directory Users and Computers console. Once you've done that, log in to the resource mailbox using Outlook Web Access, and click the Options button. In the Options area, select the Resource Settings option on the left side of the window to display the advanced resource options you need to configure for the resource mailbox. Figure 6.48 and Figure 6.49 display these options.

All of these settings are also available from the Exchange Management Shell by using the `Set-MailboxCalendarSettings` cmdlet, although using Outlook Web Access may prove to be an easier route if the number of resource mailboxes to be configured is low. If you've ever used the Exchange Server 2003 Auto Accept Agent, many of these configuration settings will be familiar to you. If you haven't, they will still be useful to use as you configure how resources should behave when users send meeting requests to them. At the bare minimum, you need to enable the Automatically Process Meeting Requests and Cancellations option, or else the resource won't be very useful to your users. After making any changes, be sure to click the Save button at the top of the screen. Also, be sure to disable the associated user account once again after you've made your changes.

FIGURE 6.48 Configuring resource mailbox properties via Outlook Web Access

Resource Scheduling Options

Automatically process meeting requests and cancellations
Disable Reminders
Maximum number of days: 180
Always decline if end date is beyond this limit
Limit meeting duration
Maximum allowed minutes: 1440
Allow scheduling only during working hours
Allow conflicts
Allow recurring meetings
Allow up to this number of individual conflicts: 0
Allow up to this percentage of individual conflicts: 0

Resource Scheduling Permissions

Specify users and groups which have permissions to schedule this resource by sending a meeting request
These users can schedule automatically if the resource is available:
Everyone
Select Users and Groups:
These users can submit a request for manual approval if the resource is available:
Everyone
Select Users and Groups:
These users can schedule automatically if the resource is available and submit a request for manual approval if the resource is unavailable:
Everyone
Select Users and Groups:
For requests requiring approval:
Always forward to delegates
Always tentatively accept these requests

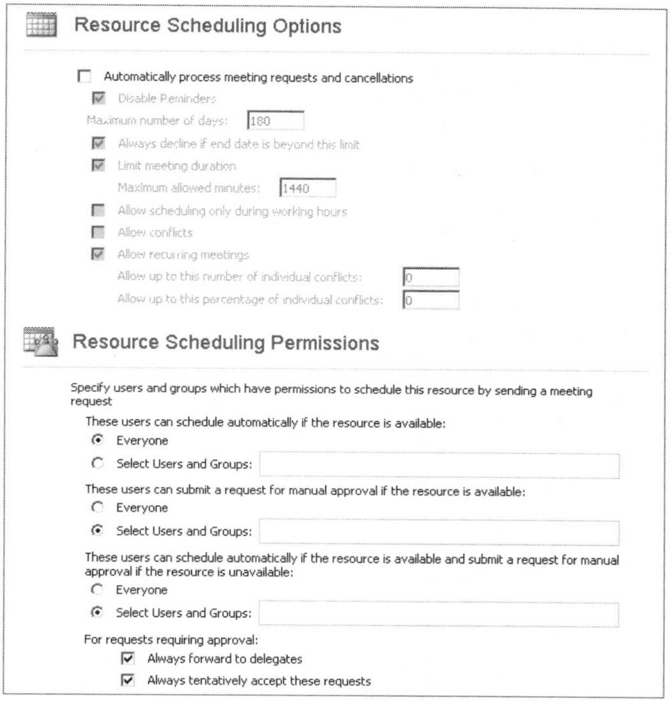

FIGURE 6.49 Configuring resource mailbox properties via Outlook Web Access

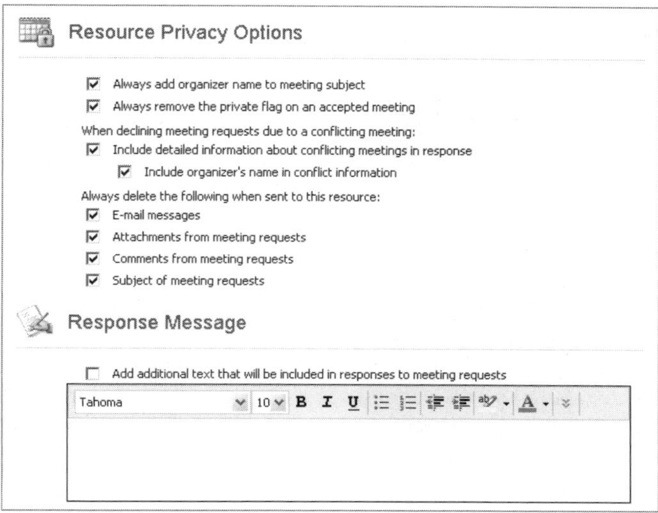

Real World Scenario

Using Resource Mailboxes

Although many administrators have been using the term *resource mailbox* for many years, why do you really need to go through the steps to create and configure one? In the past, before the Auto Accept Agent (or similar third-party methods), if you wanted to reserve a room or piece of equipment, you needed to manually make an entry on that item's calendar—assuming that it even had a mailbox.

By using resource mailboxes and taking the time to fully and properly configure them, you can empower users and resource managers to be able to use and manage these resources as they need. Do you need to book a conference room for a week that has AV and conference calling capabilities? It's no problem if the resource mailboxes that correspond to the conference rooms in your organization have been set up properly. Using resource mailboxes properly also ensures that there can be no conflicts for that resource—a conflicting meeting request that contains that resource will be denied by that resource mailbox. Since the scheduling information for a resource mailbox is available via Free/Busy, anyone trying to schedule a meeting or otherwise book any of these resources will be able to see when the desired resource is available before finalizing the meeting request, therefore ensuring that meetings won't have to be updated or rescheduled because the needed conference room or projector wasn't available at that time.

Take the time to properly implement and configure resource mailboxes for all your resources that can be reserved. When that's done, be sure to provide the user community with adequate instruction on how to leverage this functionality. When the dust settles, you'll have a happier, more productive user community, and your resource owners will be happy to be out of the business of scheduling resource usage.

Summary

Recipients are Active Directory objects that reference resources that can receive messages. The three main types of recipients discussed in this chapter are as follows:

- Users
- Groups
- Contacts

A user is an Active Directory object that usually represents a person with an Exchange mailbox. A mailbox-enabled user has an associated mailbox in a mailbox database on an Exchange server. Each user mailbox is a private storage area that allows an individual user to send, receive, and store messages. A mail-enabled user is one who has an email address and can receive, but not send, messages.

A group is a container into which you can place other recipients. Recipients in a group automatically inherit that group's permissions and rights. Exchange uses mail-enabled groups to form distribution lists. Messages sent to a group are redirected and sent to each member of the group. These groups allow users to send messages to multiple recipients without having to address each recipient individually.

Dynamic distribution groups allow Exchange administrators to create distribution groups that maintain their group membership dynamically. Once the LDAP query has successfully been created for the query-based distribution group, the applicable objects (those that meet the filter query criteria) will automatically be members of the query-based distribution group. Every time an email message is sent to a query-based distribution group, the LDAP query is performed to determine the current group membership to which the message should be expanded.

A contact is a pointer to an email address for a non-Exchange recipient. Contacts are most often used for connecting your organization to recipients who exist outside your Exchange organization. As an administrator, you would create contacts so that frequently used email addresses are available in the global address list as real names.

Exam Essentials

Understand group types and scopes. It is important that you understand fully the different group types and group scopes that can exist within Active Directory. As well, you should understand how the use of a particular group scope can impact your Exchange organization by limiting who can determine group membership.

Know the difference between mail-enabled and mailbox-enabled. Although the concepts are simple in nature, many people get confused when it comes to remembering the difference between a mailbox-enabled object and a mail-enabled object. Mailbox-enabled objects can send and received email messages using the Exchange organization and store their messages in an Exchange mailbox. Mail-enabled objects can send and receive email messages but do not have an associated Exchange mailbox. Some mail-enabled objects, such as contacts, send and receive email using an external ISP account. Other mail-enabled objects, such as distribution groups, use the Exchange organization to receive mail but have no mailbox themselves.

Get nit-picky with recipient management. Many tasks in Exchange Server 2007 require very specific knowledge or conditions to be in place before they can be performed. As an example, creating a resource mailbox requires that the associated user account be disabled. Be sure that you know and understand all the "little" nuances that go along with recipient management in Exchange Server 2007 before exam day.

Learn the PowerShell commands. Almost every configuration or management action you perform from the Exchange Management Console will present you with the PowerShell code that was used to perform the action. Take advantage of this information, and learn how to use the Exchange Management Shell to your advantage. Some of these commands are likely to make an appearance on your exam as well.

Know where to go for configuration and management tasks. Many times on the exam you are likely to be asked what configuration is needed to produce the required results. The Exchange Management Console has been completely redesigned to make it easier to navigate and get to tasks, but that doesn't mean it won't be difficult to remember later. Take the time as you review the material in this book to think about what types of configuration and management tasks you find yourself performing in each major node of the Exchange Management Console.

Review Questions

1. You need to create a new mailbox-enabled user account within your Exchange organization. What method would you need to use to perform this action with the fewest number of steps?

   A. Create the mailbox-enabled user account from the Active Directory Users and Computers console.

   B. Create the mailbox-enabled user account from the Exchange Management Shell using the `New-Mailbox` cmdlet.

   C. Create the mailbox-enabled user account from the Exchange Management Console.

   D. Create the mailbox-enabled user account from the command line using the `dsadd` command.

2. Your CIO has directed you to configure all user accounts belonging to management personnel in your organization to correctly show the employees they supervise. Every employee in your organization has an Active Directory account, but not all of them have mailboxes. How will you configure this information?

   A. Using the Exchange Management Console, select each manager's user account, and enter the list of employees who work for that manager in the Direct Reports field.

   B. Using the Exchange Management Console, select each employee's user account, and enter the user's manager in the Manager field.

   C. Using the Active Directory Users and Computers console, select each employee's user account, and enter the user's manager in the Manager field.

   D. Using the Active Directory Users and Computers console, select each manager's user account, and enter the list of employees who work for that manager in the Direct Reports field.

3. You are the Exchange administrator for your organization. During the summer months, your company hires several thousand temporary employees to help out as business increases. These temporary employees typically work for only two to four months and then are let go. Each employee has a mailbox-enabled user account. Your organization's default retention policy for deleted mailboxes is 90 days, but you don't want these mailboxes to be retained for this long. What is the best way to permanently delete these mailboxes that belonged to the temporary employees immediately?

   A. Change the deleted mailbox retention period to one day, and let the regular Exchange maintenance routines delete them.

   B. Select them and delete them from the Disconnected Mailboxes node of the Exchange Management Console.

   C. Use the `Remove-Mailbox` cmdlet from the Exchange Management Shell.

   D. Use the `dsrm user` command from a command prompt.

4. Your organization has several resource mailboxes that multiple users need to be able send messages from so that the messages appear to be coming from that mailbox. Where will you need to go to perform the required configuration to allow these users to send as the resource mailbox?

   A. The Exchange Management Shell

   B. The Exchange Management Console

   C. The Active Directory Users and Computers Console

   D. Any of these locations

5. You are in the process of creating several new mail contacts in your Exchange organization that will represent external vendors that users routinely communicate with. When speaking of mail contacts, which of the following statements is true?

   A. A mail contact must have at least one internal email address and has no other requirements.

   B. A mail contact must have at least one internal email address and at least one external email address.

   C. A mail contact must have at least one external email address and has no other requirements.

   D. None of these statements is true.

6. What cmdlet will you use in the Exchange Management Shell to create a new user account with a mailbox?

   A. `New-Mailbox`

   B. `Enable-MailUser`

   C. `Enable-Mailbox`

   D. `Connect-Mailbox`

   E. `New-MailUser`

7. What cmdlet will you use in the Exchange Management Shell to mailbox-enable an existing Active Directory user account?

   A. `New-MailUser`

   B. `Connect-Mailbox`

   C. `Enable-MailUser`

   D. `Enable-Mailbox`

   E. `New-Mailbox`

8. You have recently created several universal distribution groups from the Active Directory Users and Computers console. After several days, the groups still do not have email addresses associated with them and do not show up in the global address list. What should you do to correct this problem? (Choose two; each answer presents a complete solution.)

   A. Use the `New-DistributionGroup` cmdlet from the Exchange Management Shell.

   B. Use the Exchange Management Shell to start the New Distribution Group Wizard.

   C. Locate the distribution group in the Exchange Management Console, and mail-enable it.

   D. Use the `Enable-DistributionGroup` cmdlet from the Exchange Management Shell.

   E. Use the Exchange Management Console to start the New Distribution Group Wizard.

9. You are trying to create a new resource mailbox from the Exchange Management Shell by using the `New-Mailbox` cmdlet. When you create the resource mailbox, you are asked to supply a password. Later when you go to configure the calendar options for the resource mailbox in Outlook Web Access, those options are not available. What is the most likely problem?

   A. You must use the `New-ResourceMailbox` cmdlet to create resource mailboxes, not the `New-Mailbox` cmdlet.

   B. You cannot perform the initial creation of a resource mailbox from the Exchange Management Shell; you will need to use the Exchange Management Console.

   C. You did not specify that the mailbox was to be a resource mailbox by using the `-Resource` switch with the `New-Mailbox` cmdlet.

   D. You did not specify that the mailbox was to be a resource mailbox by using the `-Room` or `-Equipment` switch with the `New-Mailbox` cmdlet.

10. You are planning to create several dynamic distribution groups for use in your organization. What filter conditions are available to you by default and do not require any custom PowerShell code? (Choose all that apply.)

    A. Mailbox server

    B. Department

    C. Description

    D. Manager

    E. State or province

    F. Company

    G. Last name

    H. Mailbox database

11. You need to disable the user account of a salesperson who has left your organization. The salesperson had a mailbox on one of your Exchange Mailbox servers. You do not want to make any changes to the mailbox at this time. What method could you use to disable the user account?

    A. Use the `Disable-Mailbox` cmdlet from the Exchange Management Shell.

    B. Use the Disable link for the mailbox in the Exchange Management Console.

    C. Use the `Disable-MailUser` cmdlet from the Exchange Management Shell.

    D. Use the Active Directory Users and Computers console to disable the user account.

12. Your organization recently extended the contracts for three on-site contractors for an additional year. In the past, these contractors had mailboxes on one of your Exchange Mailbox servers. Going forward, the contractors will need only an Active Directory user account and will not need to have a mailbox. What should you do to remove the mailbox only, leaving the user account functional?

    A. Use the `Remove-Mailbox` cmdlet from the Exchange Management Shell.

    B. Use the `Disable-Mailbox` cmdlet from the Exchange Management Shell.

    C. Use the `Remove-MailUser` cmdlet from the Exchange Management Shell.

    D. Use the `Disable-MailUser` cmdlet from the Exchange Management Shell.

13. Which of the following types of objects can a distribution group contain? (Choose all that apply.)
    A. User
    B. Group
    C. Contact
    D. Public folder

14. Which of the following statements is true regarding security and distribution groups?
    A. Only a security group can be mail-enabled.
    B. Only a distribution group can be mail-enabled.
    C. Both types of groups can be mail-enabled.
    D. Neither type of group can be mail-enabled.

15. You are the Exchange administrator for your organization. During the summer months, your company hires several thousand temporary employees to help out as business increases. These temporary employees typically work for only two to four months and then are let go. Each of these employees needs to be able to receive company-wide email announcements that are sent on a fairly routine basis. These employees do not have any access to the network. What should you do to ensure that the temporary employees receive the required email messages? (Choose two; each answer is part of the overall solution.)
    A. Create a mail-enabled user account for each one of them, and enter their external email address. Configure the user account to be a member of the temporary employees department.
    B. Create a distribution group, and add each of the temporary employees to it.
    C. Create a mail-enabled contact for each of them. Configure the contact to be a member of the temporary employees department.
    D. Create a dynamic distribution group with a filter that adds each of the temporary employees to it by department.

16. Your company has hired an outside marketing agency to create marketing materials. Many of your employees often need to email messages to people in this marketing agency. Since both the marketing agency and your network have Internet access, Internet email seems the best method. However, you want to set it up so that the people in the marketing agency appear in the Exchange global address list. What type of recipient object would you configure to achieve this?
    A. Mailbox
    B. Mail-enabled user
    C. Contact
    D. A mailbox with a foreign owner

17. You are the Exchange administrator for your organization. During the winter months, your company hires several hundred new employees to help out as business increases. A network administrator from the Active Directory group creates the user accounts for each new employee and configures them with all organizational information. A network administrator from the Exchange group then creates mailboxes for all the user accounts. You need to ensure that all new employees always receive email messages that are sent to their departments. What type of group should you create?

    A. You should create a distribution group for each department. You should then place the members of the department in their respective distribution groups.

    B. You should create a security group for each department. You should then place the members of the departments in their respective distribution groups.

    C. You should create a dynamic security group for each department that filters group membership based on the Exchange object's Department attribute value.

    D. You should create a dynamic distribution group for each department that filters group membership based on the Exchange object's Department attribute value.

18. You've just completed creating more than 200 resource mailboxes that represent various conference rooms and other equipment items your organization has that can be reserved. You've instructed the users in your organization to book these resources by including them as resources on all meeting requests. Users complain to you that when they book resources, they never get any notification of whether the booking was accepted and that sometimes when they go to use the resource they booked someone else is already using it and stating that they also booked that resource for that period of time. What is the most likely cause for this problem?

    A. The user accounts associated with the resource mailboxes are not disabled.

    B. You did not perform any advanced configuration on the resource mailboxes using the `Set-MailboxCalendarSettings` cmdlet.

    C. You did not hide the mailboxes from the global address list.

    D. The Mailbox server that contains the resource mailboxes is not operating properly.

19. You have become aware that a few of your users have signed up for a daily newsletter published by a user in another department of your company that often includes large file attachments. You would like to prevent all messages from this newsletter from reaching these users. What is the best way to do this?

    A. Configure delivery restrictions for the users that allow all messages except those from the newsletter's email address.

    B. Configure delivery restrictions for the users that allow only messages from within the Exchange system and from select originators outside the system.

    C. Configure a size limit on messages that can be sent to these users.

    D. Configure a storage limit on these users' mailboxes.

20. A user named Aaron leaves your company. Management would like a user named Bobbi to assume Aaron's responsibilities. What could you do so that Bobbi can receive Aaron's email messages? Select the best answer.

A. Make Bobbi's mailbox an alternate recipient for Aaron's mailbox.

B. Disable Aaron's user account, and give Bobbi profile permission to access Aaron's mailbox.

C. Delete Aaron's mailbox, and forward all undeliverable messages to Bobbi.

D. Create a rule in Aaron's mailbox so that all of Aaron's mail is forwarded to Bobbi.

Answers to Review Questions

1. B. By using the `New-Mailbox` cmdlet, you can create the new user account and mailbox-enable it all at once. No other method presented affords you that ability.

2. C. Since some employees do not have Exchange mailboxes, you will need to use the Active Directory Users and Computers console to allow you to configure all of them. The actual configuration change that must be done is to enter the manager's name into the Manager field on the Organization tab of each user's account.

3. C. Although it is no small task when dealing with a number of disconnected mailboxes, the best way to delete them immediately is to use the `Remove-Mailbox` cmdlet. You cannot delete them using any other method except through the regular Exchange maintenance routines that depend on the deleted mailbox retention period. Changing the retention period to allow you to quickly delete the mailboxes belonging to the temporary employees will also likely cause you to delete other disconnected mailboxes you did not intend on deleting.

4. C. You will need to go to the Active Directory Users and Computers console to configure Send As permissions on the resource mailbox user accounts. You will configure the permissions from the Security tab.

5. B. For email messages to be properly routed to a mail contact, the contact must have at least one internal email address and at least one external email address. You will configure the external email address manually when you create the mail contact, and Exchange will stamp the internal email address on the mail contact for you automatically after that.

6. A. You can use the `New-Mailbox` cmdlet to create and mailbox-enable a user account in one step.

7. D. You can use the `Enable-Mailbox` cmdlet to mailbox-enable an existing user account.

8. D, E. You can either use the `Enable-DistributionGroup` cmdlet from the Exchange Management Shell or use the Exchange Management Console to start the New Distribution Group Wizard. Either method will configure the messaging-related properties on the distribution group and resolve the issue you're experiencing.

9. D. In this scenario, given that you were prompted for a password and the resource calendar options do not show up in Outlook Web Access, the most likely problem is that you did not specify that the mailbox was to be a resource mailbox by using the `-Room` or `-Equipment` switch with the `New-Mailbox` cmdlet.

10. B, E, F. By default, you have the following filter conditions to select from when creating a new dynamic distribution group from either the Exchange Management Console or the Exchange Management Shell:

    - State or province
    - Department
    - Company
    - Custom attributes 1–15

    If you need to create and sort of conditions, you'll need to perform the configuration from the Exchange Management Shell using the parameter `-RecipientFilter` in the `New-DynamicDistributionGroup` or the `Set-DynamicDistributionGroup` cmdlet.

11. D. The only option listed that actually disables the user account and does not change any mail-related settings is to disable the user account from the Active Directory User and Computers console.

12. B. You should use the `Disable-Mailbox` cmdlet from the Exchange Management Shell. Using the `Remove-Mailbox` cmdlet from the Exchange Management Shell will actually cause the user account to be deleted as well.

13. A, B, C, D. A distribution group can contain any other type of recipient object, including other distribution groups.

14. C. Any type of group can be mail-enabled.

15. C, D. You should create a mail-enabled contact object for each of the temporary employees and configure the Department attribute to be Temporary Employees. You should then create a dynamic distribution group that uses a filter query based on the value of the Department attribute.

16. C. A contact is a pointer object that holds the address of a non-Exchange mail recipient. Contacts are made visible in the global address list and, therefore, permit Exchange clients to send messages to non-Exchange mail users.

17. D. The best solution to this situation is to create a dynamic distribution group that uses an LDAP filter query based on the value of the Department attribute to determine group membership. In this way, a group configured with a filter for all Exchange objects that belong to the marketing department will dynamically place all these objects in the group. In the same way, another group configured with a filter for all Exchange objects that belong to the maintenance department would dynamically place these objects in the group. There is no such thing as a dynamic security group.

18. B. By default, a newly created resource mailbox will not automatically accept and schedule meeting requests that it receives. You will need to configure this behavior by using the `Set-MailboxCalendarSettings` cmdlet or by logging into the resource mailbox using Outlook Web Access.

19. A. The default delivery restrictions are to accept messages from everyone and reject messages from nobody. You can enter specific originators from whom you want to block messages for individual users. You could configure a size limit on inbound messages to these users, but this would likely still allow some messages from the newsletter to be delivered.

20. A. Making Bobbi's mailbox an alternate recipient ensures that both mailboxes receive a copy of all messages sent to Aaron's mailbox. Creating a rule in Aaron's mailbox that forwards mail to Bobbi would also work but would require more configuration on your part.

Chapter 7

Configuring Exchange Server Rules and Policies

MICROSOFT EXAM OBJECTIVES COVERED IN THIS CHAPTER:

✓ **Configuring the Exchange Infrastructure**

- Configure transport rules and message compliance.
- Configure policies.

Thanks to government regulations, companies such as Enron, and an overabundance of lawyers, we find ourselves in a world with a great many rules and compliance requirements. Exchange Server 2007 comes stocked with a plethora of improvements and added features to help you thrive in this regulated world. The main focus of the Exchange Server 2007 compliance features set is regulatory compliance, applied in business sectors such as publicly traded companies, financial services companies, and medical companies. The compliance feature set also focuses on protecting private information and providing solutions that ensure that corporate governance principles are being maintained.

The feature set is basically "compliance in transport." A design change in Exchange Server 2007 now forces every message in an Exchange organization to travel through a Hub Transport server. Even messages sent between mailboxes in the same database and on the same Mailbox server have to travel through a Hub Transport server. This was a deliberate design change in Exchange Server 2007 that allows "stuff" to be done to every message in an Exchange organization. The "stuff" that can be done to messages is what enables you to be compliant and regulated in Exchange bliss.

The main subjects of this chapter are as follows:

- Messaging records management
- Server-based rules
- Message classifications
- Server based policies
- Transport Rules

Configuring Message Compliance and Record Management

Corporate compliance requirements are becoming increasingly important across business sectors and geographies. In the United States, the market focus has primarily been on regulatory compliance for publicly traded companies and companies operating in regulated sectors, such as health care and financial services. In addition to compliance requirements, additional attention is being focused on protecting private information and in providing solutions that ensure corporate governance principles are being maintained.

Most compliance-based market attention is focused on the requirements to comply with regulations such as the Health Insurance Portability and Accountability Act (HIPAA), Sarbanes-Oxley (SOX) Act, the EU Data Protection Act, and California SB 1386. However, the broader demand is driven by the need to maintain controlled access and show both information and process integrity for electronic communications. This section will cover the basic compliance feature concepts and how to configure the compliance features offered by Exchange Server 2007.

Message compliance in Exchange Server 2007 is facilitated by messaging records management (MRM). MRM is an Exchange feature set that controls the contents of custom and default managed folders. Managed folders are folders that appear in users' mailboxes and are controlled by the administrator. You can create custom *managed folders* or work with the default folders. Folder contents are controlled by the *managed content settings* that control the life span of a message by moving, deleting, and archiving/journaling messages when you say so. Groups of managed folders can be conveniently assigned to users' mailboxes by means of *managed folder mailbox policies*. All the settings and tasks are then applied to the folders when you want them to be applied by the *managed folder assistant*.

Exchange MRM depends on users to classify their own messages. One of the keys to successful MRM deployment is coupling the right folder structure with effective retention limits so users can correctly designate messages that need to be retained. The other key is effective training and simplification of the categorization process so that users will not have issues determining how to classify a message.

When it comes to planning and deploying MRM, you should consider these key planning points:

- For MRM and messaging policies to be truly effective, you need to prohibit personal folders (`.pst`) on your network. You cannot control the messages in a personal folder. Because you cannot control them, they present a bit of a hole in any effort to comply with a compliance requirement or in any effort to control messages.
- Apply content settings and policies to default folders. This provides retention actions for message types stored in the default set of user folders. Everyone has these folders, and this is where you can make the most automated impact on messages. If you don't want to automatically delete items from the default folders, you should at least consider creating a Review And Then Delete folder into which Inbox mail is moved after a given period of time.
- Create any custom managed folders that you might need in order to comply with any corporate governing body's compliance requirements. With custom folders created, you should create content settings and apply them to the default and custom folders to ensure that needed items will be properly retained while still maintaining good storage management practices.
- Consider creating a custom self-service web page that uses Exchange web services to allow users to subscribe to their own managed custom folders. Eventually there will probably be prepackaged web pages for this, but for now, this will mean some custom development work.
- With all these settings and mail manipulations in place, how will you know whether they are working? To be best informed, you should develop a tracking plan that monitors how messages are being retained, moved, and dealt with.

Real World Scenario

Rules and MRM Used for International Biotech's Compliance

We consult on occasion for a large, international biotech company that works in the medical field and on classified projects. This leads to some complex message retention needs. For example, one agency wants all messages to be secure, another agency wants everything to be retained for seven years if it has to do with a project, and another organization requires that certain messages are limited in where they can be sent. This is just a small example of the requirements this company faces. Prior to deploying Exchange Server 2007, this company used a number of third-party tools and manual employee systems to attempt to comply.

This company was excited to have Exchange Server 2007 and Outlook 2007 because it allowed the company's employees to classify messages based on project and compliance needs. And that was all the user had to do. Once the messages were classified, MRM moved the messages where they needed to be to have the right content setting applied and then to be retained in the proper manner. Transport rules help the company limit where messages go and safeguard against sending certain messages where they are not supposed to go. Transport rules also allow the company to automatically classify some of the messages in case a user misses something.

MRM, message classification, and transport rules allow this company to free up resources from the compliance effort so they can focus on efforts that have a more positive effect on the company's bottom line.

Configuring Managed Folders

The Exchange Server 2007 managed folders feature enables you to create message retention folders that better organize and manage email messages. Managed email folders are automatically created in target users' mailboxes. An automated process scans the Inbox and these folders in order to retain, expire, or journal messages based on managed content settings. Once you've created the managed folders, users choose in which retention folder a given item should be placed. This is why it is important to preplan the folder names and structure of your managed folders.

Two types of managed folders are available in Exchange Server 2007:

- *Managed custom folders*: Custom managed folders are folders you create and push to users' mailboxes. Managed custom folders are controlled by the administrator and cannot be renamed, moved, or deleted by the user. Managed custom folders should be given names that reflect their intended purpose—remember that users will decide what goes in these folders. Think like a user, and make the names as short and descriptive as possible.
- *Managed default folders*: Managed default folders are the folders that Exchange creates by default and include folders such as the Sent Items, Deleted Items, and Inbox folders. The administrator and the users can't create new, or rename, default managed folders.

Before covering how to create custom managed folders, we should note that custom folders are not required; they are optional. Although you cannot change the name of the default folders, you can replace them with custom managed folders. The custom folder replacement will just have the same name. For example, you could apply a content setting of Delete After 30 Days to the Inbox of your store checkers and then create another custom Inbox called Year Inbox. The Year Inbox folder would be created as a type that corresponds to the folder you want to replace; for this example, that would be type Inbox, and it could be given to users based on a managed mailbox policy. The policy would determine which Inbox folder the users would see, the 30-day one or Year Inbox. The Year Inbox folder would replace the default Inbox folder but would still be named Inbox to the users. In this example, users would always see the standard default folder name Inbox in their mailboxes, regardless of whether the mailbox policy specified the 30-day Inbox or Year Inbox folder. In addition, you can specify only one Inbox; you cannot have two instances of any default folders in a user's mailbox.

To create a managed folder, perform the steps outlined in Exercise 7.1 and Exercise 7.2.

EXERCISE 7.1

Creating a Managed Folder Using the Exchange Management Console

1. Open the Exchange Management Console, and click the Mailbox node in the Organization Configuration section. In the Actions pane to the right, select New Managed Custom Folder or New Managed Default Folder. This will launch in the wizard to create a new managed folder.

2. On the first page of the New Managed Folder Wizard, fill out the Name field, and then select the default folder type of the folder you plan on replacing with the new managed folder. For some of the folder types, you will be able to add a message that will be displayed in Outlook or OWA. Once you've filled out this page, click New, and you will create the managed folder.

3. On the first page of the New Managed Custom Folder Wizard, fill in the name and the Outlook display name, set a storage limit if you need one, and then add the Outlook or OWA message if needed. Once you've filled out this page, click New, and you will create the new custom managed folder.

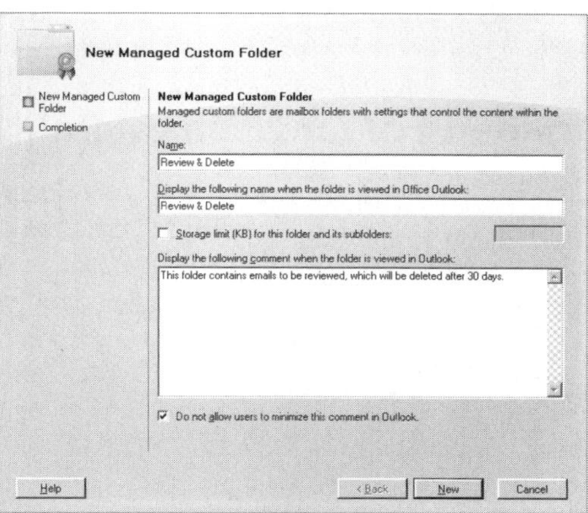

EXERCISE 7.2

Creating a Managed Folder Using the Exchange Management Shell

1. Open the Exchange Management Shell, and run one of the following commands (make sure to change the parameters enclosed in brackets):

```
New-ManagedFolder -Name<Folder_Name> -FolderName <Folder_Name_Visable_To_User>

New-ManagedFolder -Name<Folder_Name> -DefaultFolderType <Default_Folder_Type>
```

Configuring Managed Content Settings

The Exchange Server 2007 MRM message content settings allow you to control the life span of messages. You can control a message's life span in two ways:

- By controlling how long a message is retained in a folder before it is moved or deleted.
- By controlling the journaling or archival of a message to an archival location. Message content settings can be applied to both default and user-created custom managed folders.

Each managed folder should have a managed content setting applied to it that defines what should be done with the messages in the folder. Managed content settings can apply to all items in a folder or to specific message types (message types examples are voicemail messages, email messages, and task items). The managed content settings for a folder specify three retention settings:

- The period of time a message should be retained in the folder.
- When the retention period starts. Does it start once a message is placed in *x* folder, when the message is created, or after the message has been in a folder for *x* days?
- What action should be taken at the end of the retention period? Should the message be deleted or moved or placed somewhere else, possibly in an archival system?

As an example, you could create a managed content setting that moves all messages in everyone's Sent Items folder to a custom managed folder called Review & Delete. You could then specify that everything in the Review & Delete folder be deleted after 30 days. To create a new managed content setting, follow the steps outlined in Exercise 7.3 and Exercise 7.4.

Configuring Managed Folder Mailbox Policies

You can use managed folder mailbox policies to create a group of folders that you can then apply to single or groups of users. Say you have salespeople that all need the same folders: the folders 100 Days to Delete, Keep Forever, and Keep for X Years. If you created a policy that had each folder in it, you could simply apply that policy to the sales group, and then they would all have the folders. Otherwise, you have to add each folder one at a time for every sales user. In this section, first we will cover how to create a managed folder mailbox policy, and then we will cover how to apply the policy to a user. To create and apply a managed folder mailbox policy, follow the steps outlined in Exercise 7.5, Exercise 7.6, Exercise 7.7, and Exercise 7.8.

EXERCISE 7.3

Creating a Managed Content Setting Using the Exchange Management Console

1. Open the Exchange Management Console, and click the Mailbox node in the Organization Configuration section. Select the Default or Custom Managed Folder tab, and then select the folder to which you want to apply the setting. In the Actions pane to the right, select New Managed Content Setting. This will launch the New Content Setting Wizard.

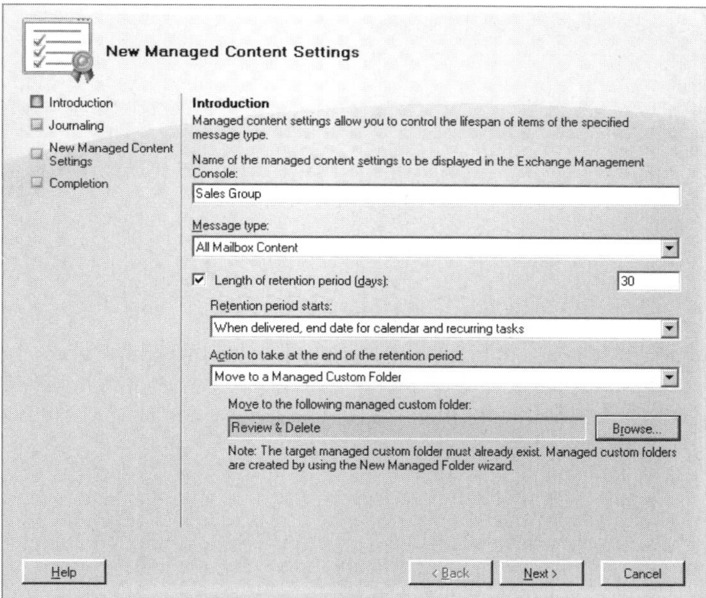

2. On the first page of the New Managed Content Settings Wizard, enter the name of the content setting, select the type of messages you want to change in the folder, and then configure the retention periods and actions. Click Next.

3. On the second page of the wizard, you can configure journaling by selecting a message format for a journaling mailbox. Click Next.

4. On the summary page, verify that all the settings are correct, and then click New to create the custom content setting.

EXERCISE 7.4

Creating a Managed Content Setting Using the Exchange Management Shell

1. Open the Exchange Management Shell, and run one of the following commands (make sure to change the parameters enclosed in brackets):

```
New-ManagedContentSettings -FolderName <Folder_To_Apply_Setting_TO>

-MessageClass <Item_Type> -Name <Setting_Name> -RetentionEnabled $true

-RetentionAction <Action> -AgeLimitForRetention
  <Age_Of_Item_Before_Action_Is_Taken>
```

EXERCISE 7.5

Creating a Managed Folder Mailbox Policy Using the Exchange Management Shell

1. Open the Exchange Management Console, and click the Mailbox node in the Organization Configuration section. In the Actions pane to the right, select New Managed Folder Mailbox Policy. This will launch the New Managed Folder Mailbox Policy Wizard.

2. On the first page of the New Managed Folder Mailbox Policy Wizard, enter the name for the policy, click the Add button, and add the folders you want in the policy. Once everything is filled out, click the New button to create the managed folder mailbox policy.

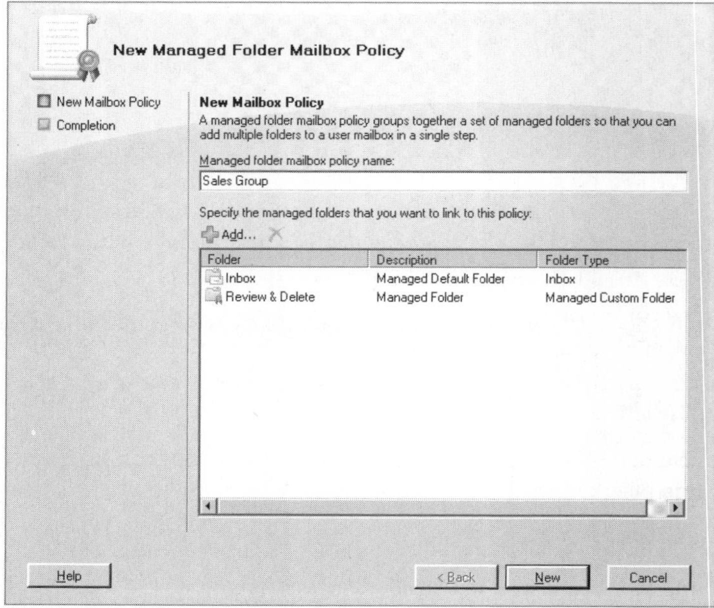

EXERCISE 7.6

Creating a Managed Folder Mailbox Policy Using the Exchange Management Shell

1. Open the Exchange Management Shell, and run one of the following commands (make sure to change the parameters enclosed in brackets):

```
New-ManagedFolderMailboxPolicy -Name <Policy_Name>

-ManagedFolderLinks <Folder_Names>
```

EXERCISE 7.7

Applying a Managed Folder Mailbox Policy Using the Exchange Management Console

1. Open the Exchange Management Console, and click the Recipients node in the Recipients Configuration section. In the Actions pane, right-click a user, and select Properties. Select the Mailbox Settings tab.

2. On the Mailbox Settings tab, select Managed Records Management, and then fill in the Managed Folder Mailbox Policy box.

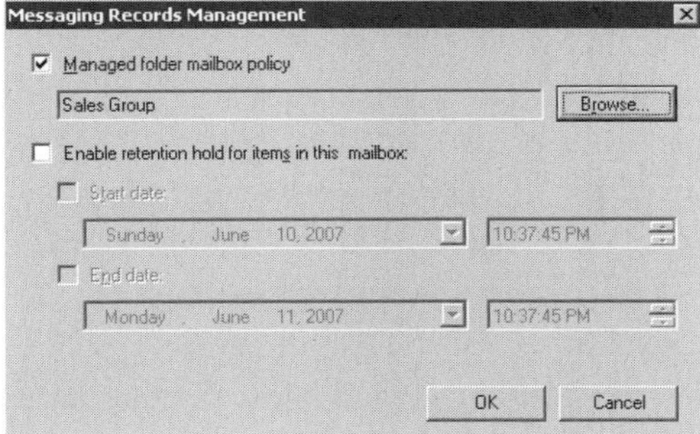

EXERCISE 7.8

Applying a Managed Folder Mailbox Policy Using Exchange Management Shell

1. Open the Exchange Management Shell, and run one of the following commands (make sure to change the parameters enclosed in brackets):

```
Set-Mailbox -Identity <Mailbox_Name>

-ManagedFolderMailboxPolicy <Managed_folder_Mailbox_Policy_Name>
```

Configuring the Managed Folder Assistant

The managed folder assistant is the Exchange Server 2007 function that creates managed folders in mailboxes and then applies managed content settings. When the managed folder assistant is run, it will process every mailbox on the server. The assistant can be scheduled to run with a start time and an end time; if it does not complete processing all of the mailboxes on a server in the allotted time, the next time it starts, it will continue where it left off. Keep in mind that the assistant is not scheduled by default; you must manually enable it, or the managed content settings won't ever be applied.

Be aware that the managed folder assistant is a resource-intensive process. The process has to read the date on every object in a mailbox, calculate how that date relates to the managed content settings, and then act on the actions in the settings. The managed folder assistant should be run only when the server can tolerate the extra load. It doesn't have to run every night; you should run the assistant just enough to satisfy your compliance obligations. To schedule the managed folder assistant, perform the steps outlined in Exercise 7.9 and Exercise 7.10.

EXERCISE 7.9

Scheduling the Managed Folder Assistant Using the Exchange Management Console

1. Open the Exchange Management Console, and click the Mailbox node in the Server Configuration section. Right-click a server that you want to schedule the assistant to run on, and select Properties. Select the Managed Records Management tab.

2. On the Messaging Records Management tab, click the Customize button, and schedule when you want to run the assistant.

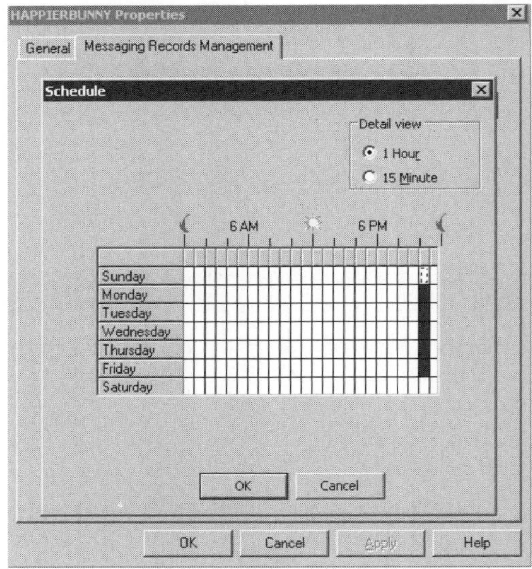

EXERCISE 7.10

Scheduling the Managed Folder Assistant Using the Exchange Management Shell

1. Open the Exchange Management Shell, and run one of the following commands (make sure to change the parameters enclosed in brackets):

```
Set-MailboxServer -Identity <Mailbox__Server_Name>
-ManagedFolderAssistantSchedule <Day_StartTime_Day_StopTime>
```

Configuring Rights Management Service (RMS) Exchange Agents

Information rights management (IRM) is a useful collateral technology that can be used to protect email messages and documents against improper disclosure. IRM embeds usage information in the document so that access restrictions, expiration information, and policy controls travel with the document. Microsoft's implementation of IRM is based on the Windows Rights Management Server, plus on the client-side support built into Office 2003, Office 2007, and SharePoint Server 2007. IRM is particularly useful for protecting sensitive content from being improperly forwarded or copied; it also allows for documents and messages that expire past a specified date.

In Exchange Server 2007, you no longer need to configure Exchange Server to support Windows Rights Management Server.

Configuring Message Classifications

The Exchange Server 2007 message classification feature allows administrators to create classifications for users to apply to messages. This allows users to classify messages according to their content or intended purpose. When a user applies a classification in Outlook 2007 or OWA 2007, metadata is added to the message. The added metadata gives directions to the recipients and/or to the transport server to help them make decisions about what to do with the messages.

When the recipient opens the message in Outlook or OWA, the classification metadata is used to retrieve and then display a classification message to the recipient. This classification message helps the recipient determine how to treat the message. One of the default classifications is Company Confidential. The Company Confidential classification has a classification message that says, "This message contains sensitive information, the distribution of which should be limited." This message should help the user to not send this message to competitors or people who should not see it. The following is an example of what a client would see when viewing a classified message.

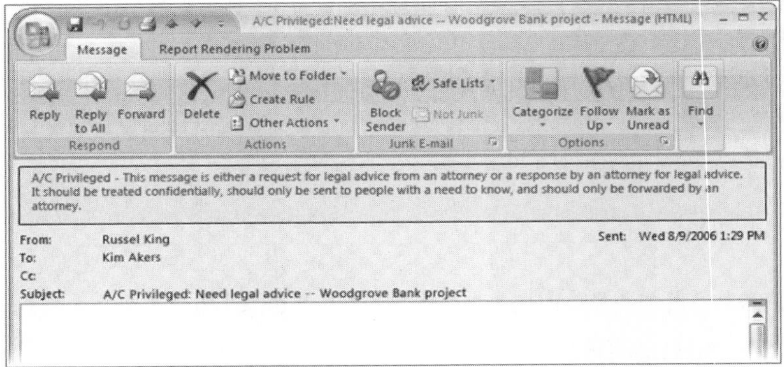

Message classifications can also be applied or acted upon by server-based transport rules. As an example, you could have a rule that removed attachments from messages that were deemed inappropriate. After the rule removed the attachment, it could apply another rule that would then tell the user what happened to the message attachment. You could also have a rule that looked for messages with a Company Confidential classification on them, kept those messages from leaving the company, and then forwarded the message to a compliance officer. The compliance officer could then deal with the employee as needed.

Exchange Server 2007 ships with a default set of five classifications, as outlined in Table 7.1.

TABLE 7.1 Exchange Server 2007 Default Classifications

Default Classification	Default Classification Message
A/C Privileged	This message contains legally sensitive information that is privileged between an attorney and a client.
Attachment Removed	This message had one or more attachments that were removed for security purposes.
Company Confidential	This message contains sensitive information, the distribution of which should be limited.
Company Internal	This message contains information that should not be forwarded or disseminated outside the company.
Partner Mail	This message contains content from or to business partners.

You can modify classifications and the classification messages based on your company needs, and you can create new classifications using the Exchange Management Shell command `New-MessageClassification`. Here is an example of an Exchange management shell command that can be used to create a new message classification:

```
New-MessageClassification -Name "Glue" -DisplayName "You are glue"
-SenderDescription "This message should be considered glued in to
 recipients inbox only the systems admin can remove, move, or forward
this message from the inbox" -RecipientDescription "this message is
glued to your inbox, you cannot move if from your inbox by way of
deletion, or forwarding, or moving. This message is here until the
System admin decides to remove it."
```

You can assign precedence to classifications to help determine in which order classifications should be applied in the event that a message has more than one classification. You must add classifications manually as an XML file on the client's computer before Outlook 2007 will present them to the user. You can do this by editing the file or by using Active Directory Group Policy. But before Outlook can see this XML file, you need to add a registry key to the computer to turn on this functionality and tell Outlook where the file is. But wait, there's more—the registry key is in the `HKEY_Current_User` hive, so this has to be added for each user on a given computer. The registry keys are as follows:

```
[HKEY_CURRENT_USER\Software\Microsoft\Office\12.0\Common\Policy]
"AdminClassificationPath"="c:\Exchange\Classifications.xml"
"EnableClassifications"=dword:00000001
"TrustClassifications"=dword:00000001
```

Once the registry key is in place, the user's Outlook needs to be restarted in order to read the XML file. The XML file is generated manually with an Exchange Management Shell script. The script is in the scripts folder where Exchange is installed on your server. From the folder that has the script, run the following command to create the XML file:

```
./Export-OutlookClassification.ps1 > c:\exports\Classifications.xml
```

Now that you have the XML file, `Classifications.xml`, you need to copy it to the folder specified in the `AdminClassificationPath` registry key. If you make any changes to any classifications in the future, you will need to do this process all over again. We hope this is made simpler in the SP1 or SP2 version of Exchange Server 2007.

One last bit about classifications: Exchange Server 2007 is a localized server product; almost everything in Exchange can be localized, including the message classification messages. You do this by using the `-Locale` switch when you create a new classification with the `New-MessageClassification` Exchange Management Shell command.

Configuring Transport Rules

Transport rules are just like Outlook rules, but they are applied to messages during transport by the Hub and Edge Transport server roles, and they are under complete control of the administrator. There was a design change in Exchange Server 2007 with the addition of the Edge Transport role that allowed for the birth of server rules. Every message in an Exchange organization must travel through a Hub Transport server. It does not matter even if you are bored and sending messages to yourself. Those messages still need to leave the Mailbox server and travel through the Hub Transport server where they are then sent right back to the same Mailbox server. Every message is touched by a Hub Transport server, which puts the Hub Transport server in a position to consistently do "stuff" to messages.

There is one uniform rule applied throughout the organization that every Hub Transport server has to work with. There is no way to keep one Hub Transport server from processing rules while letting all the other servers process them. Transport rules are stored in the Configuration container of Active Directory, which is replicated to all of the global catalog servers in a forest.

The Exchange teams says rules are a tool for compliance, and as administrators, we see rules as a great tool for not only having compliance control over messages but also for having some control over users. The following is a list of some actions you can use rules to accomplish:

- You can create ethical walls to limit the interaction of certain groups of users.
- You can filter personal information (SSNs, account numbers, and so on) in emails from being sent.
- You can set up message classifications that can be acted upon by transport rules.
- You can add items to messages using transport rules such as legal disclaimers, notes, or subjects.
- You can forward, copy, and blind copy messages to additional recipients.
- You can create mail flow rules for enforcing encryption and routing policies.
- You can perform message hygiene functions on an Edge Transport server.

You can do a lot more with rules; they are a flexible tool for controlling email. The Exchange Management Console rule GUI is similar to the interface used in Outlook. If you don't like the idea of working with rules in the GUI, you can also write rules in the Exchange Management Shell.

Each transport rule contains three components:

- *Conditions* specify which email message attributes, headers, recipients, senders, or other parts of the message are used in identifying which messages a rule should take action on. If no condition is applied to a transport rule, the transport rule applies the configured action unless the message matches a configured exception.
- *Exceptions* specify messages that should be exempt from a transport rule, even if the message matches a transport rule condition. Exceptions are optional.

- *Actions* specify what should happen to email messages that match all the conditions and none of the exceptions that are present on a transport rule. Actions modify some aspect of the message or the message's delivery. Every transport rule must have at least one action configured. Actions include the ability to modify the message header or body, add or remove recipients, apply classifications, add disclaimers, bounce the message with an NDR, or silently drop the message.

You can specify conditions and exceptions using a large number of criteria that allow the rule to match messages according to specific AD objects (such as sender or addressee), patterns of text (either literal or using regular expressions), or other conditions.

Edge Transport rules are basically the same as Hub Transport rules except that they use a different set of actions and conditions and they are not replicated to any other Edge Transport server.

Before configuring transport rules, you should consider these few design and planning tips:

- Every Hub Transport server will have to evaluate every rule on every message that passes through it. Rules are cached in RAM. Large numbers of rules will therefore require large allocations of RAM on the Hub Transport servers.
- The official limit to rules is 1,000 per forest. Note that this rule was based on limited performance testing and is more a recommendation than a set-in-stone limit. You should monitor server performance and message transport times to determine the magic number of rules for your Hub Transport servers.
- If you are going to use regular expressions in rules, be very careful; it's easy to make a mistake that causes unexpected or unwanted behavior. Also, note that using regular expressions can add to the processing requirements of a rule.
- When a rule is created, it might not show up on all the other Hub Transport servers instantly because of AD replication timing.
- If you configure a transport rule to use a distribution group, you must specify a universal security group. This is required because transport rules are forest-wide, so you need to use a group that is also forest-wide.

To create a new Hub Transport rule, follow the steps outlined in Exercise 7.11 and Exercise 7.12.

EXERCISE 7.11

Creating a New Transport Rule Using the Exchange Management Console

1. Open the Exchange Management Console, and click the Hub Transport node in the Organization Configuration section. Select the Transport Rules tab.

EXERCISE 7.11 *(continued)*

2. In the Actions pane to the right, click New Transport Rule, and the New Transport Rule Wizard will guide you through creating a rule.

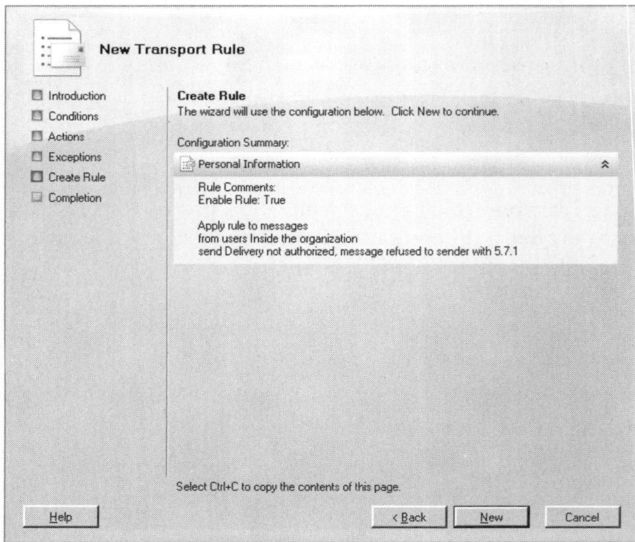

3. At the end of the wizard, you have the option of enabling the rule. A rule will not do anything until it is enabled, so if you did not enable the rule at the end of the wizard, you can do it later by right-clicking the rule and selecting Enable Rule.

EXERCISE 7.12

Creating a New Transport Rule Using the Exchange Management Shell

1. Open the Exchange Management Shell, and run the following commands (make sure to change the parameters enclosed in brackets):

```
New-TransportRule -Name <Rule_Name> -Condition <Conditions>

-Exception <Exceptions> -Action <Actions>
```

Configuring Email Address–Generation Policies

Email address policies assign email addresses to users. One major change in Exchange Server 2007 vs. Exchange 2000 and Exchange 2003 is that the Recipient Update Service (RUS) no longer exists. For anyone who worked with previous 2000/2003 versions, this is something

Real World Scenario

Kevin Miller Shares His Real-Life Rule Story:

"I host Exchange at home for my family and a number of friends. With about 30 people on the server, I configured a server using stretched LCR between my house and my parents' house. The stretch is done using an iSCSI mounted disk. My wife has full enterprise administrator permissions to the home network, and she knows how to use them. As part of writing this chapter, I started a war with her to see how well we could harass each other with message rules.

"The first rule I created incorrectly for our game was simple. It prepended the words *[Love me]* to the subject field of every message I sent her. It was cute, and we both got a laugh out of it—until later in the day when I could not send her messages anymore. The messages were all being NDRed, saying the Subject field was too long. After looking more closely at the message, I saw that my rule was doing what I had told it to do, not what I had hoped it would do. I needed to add an exception to the rule telling it to not add the text if it was already there.

"My wife created the second rule that went wrong. She was trying to make me feel the burden of some of the spam that she was getting because I had turned off IMF for some testing. So, she set up a rule to send all the messages sent to her with an SCL of 5 or less to my email box instead of hers. This in itself would not have been that bad, but previously she had created a rule that sent her a copy of all the messages that were sent to my Inbox. This created a loop and pretty much crashed our server."

We share these stories to demonstrate the power of transport rules and encourage you to plan for all your rules and how they will work. Rules will do what you tell them to do regardless of how harmful that might be to you. With every rule you create, spend some time to figure out how it might go wrong and what exceptions you might need.

you will want to get up and clap about; for the rest of you, know that this is a good thing. The RUS was a phantom Exchange service that applied address policies and seemed to work whenever it wanted to work. The RUS had to touch a user's mailbox before the user could get email. With the RUS, you could create a new mailbox and wait hours before the RUS would stamp the mailbox and the user could receive email.

In Exchange Server 2007, the process that creates a mailbox applies the email address policy to the mailbox as one of the last steps of the mailbox creation process. When you make a change to the policy, you can tell it to run immediately or have it run at some other time. You can also update the email address with the `Update-EmailAdressPolicy` command. To create a new email address policy, follow the steps outlined in Exercise 7.13 and Exercise 7.14.

EXERCISE 7.13

Creating a New Email Address Policy Using the Exchange Management Console

1. Open the Exchange Management Console, and click the Hub Transport node in the Organization Configuration section. Select the E-mail Address Policy tab.

2. In the Actions pane to the right, click New E-mail Address Policy, and the New Email Address Policy Wizard will guide you through creating a policy.

3. On the first page of the New E-Mail Address Policy Wizard, choose the name of the policy and the recipient types that will be affected by the policy, such as Exchange Mailboxes, Resource Mailboxes, External Accounts, and more. Once you fill out this page, click Next.

4. On the second page, select the conditions that must be met by the objects that the policy will apply to. You can apply policies based on State, Company, Department, and Custom Attributes 1–15. Clicking the Preview button will display of list of objects that will be affected by the conditions. Click Next when you are satisfied with the conditions.

5. On the third page, enter the email address that will be applied to the objects that meet the conditions set on the last page. Click the Add button to add addresses. Select how the email address will be formatted. When all the desired email addresses are entered, click Next.

6. On the next page, you are presented with the option of applying the policy immediately or scheduling it to be applied later. Once you have configured when the policy will be applied, click New, and the policy will be created.

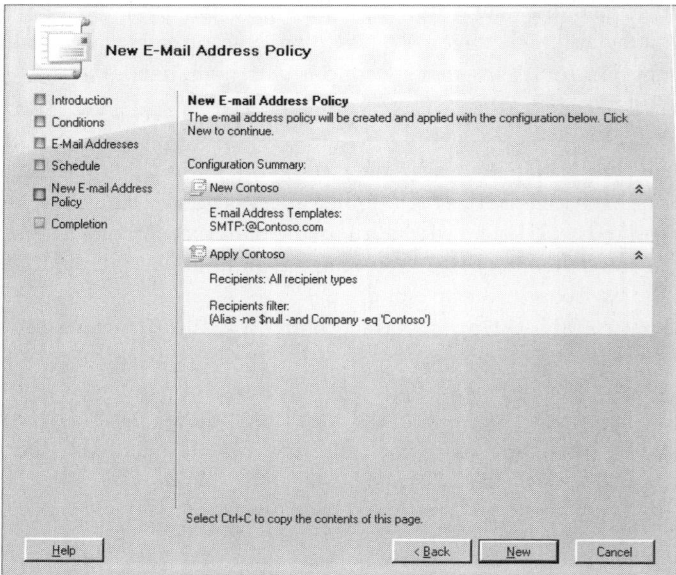

EXERCISE 7.14

Creating a New Email Address Policy Using the Exchange Management Shell

1. Open the Exchange Management Shell, and run one of the following commands (make sure to change the parameters enclosed in brackets):

```
New-EmailAddressPolicy -Name <Policy_Name> -IncludedRecipients

<Who_To_Apply_Policy_To> -EnabledPrimarySMTPAddressTemplate

<Email_Address_To_Apply>
```

Configuring Address Lists

An *address list* is a collection of recipient and other AD objects such as groups, contacts, users, and rooms. You can use address lists to organize recipients and resources, making it easier for users to find the recipients and resources they want. Address lists are updated dynamically based on LDAP queries. This is beneficial because objects don't have to be manually added to the lists when they are created in your organizations. One of the more popular default address lists for an organization is the global address list (GAL). The GAL should contain all the objects in your organization that are Exchange-enabled and not set to be hidden from address lists. There are a number of other default address lists, but none has its own acronym like the GAL. These lists are for the most part self-explanatory:

- *The All Contacts list*: All the Exchange-enabled nonhidden contacts in the Exchange organization
- *The All Groups list*: All the Exchange-enabled nonhidden groups in the Exchange organization
- *The All Rooms list*: All the Exchange-enabled nonhidden rooms in the Exchange organization
- *The All Users list*: All the Exchange-enabled nonhidden users in the Exchange organization
- *The Public Folders list*: All the Exchange-enabled nonhidden contacts in the Exchange organization
- *The default global address list*: All the Exchange-enabled objects in the Exchange organization

Address lists are stored on the server and accessed from the server. Disconnected users (home users, dial-up users, or mobile users) do not generally have access to the server to perform lookups in the GAL. To facilitate this, Exchange allows you to create an Offline Address Book (OAB). You can load the OAB onto the Outlook client and use it as a local query source for address book lookups.

Outlook cached mode uses the OAB by default to cut down on network requests over the wire. This has both advantages and disadvantages. The OAB is generally generated once a night (customizable), so users who are using the OAB will see address list changes only once a day after they have downloaded the new version, which could possibly lead to a negative consequence, such as users not seeing any changes made to the address lists until they download a new OAB copy. The OAB is a positive thing because of the amount of saved server load in the form of LDAP queries made against Exchange and global catalog servers by using the local address lists instead.

To create a new address list, follow the steps in Exercise 7.15 and Exercise 7.16.

EXERCISE 7.15

Creating a New Address List Using the Exchange Management Console

1. Open the Exchange Management Console, and click the Mailbox node in the Organization Configuration section. Select the Address Lists tab.

2. In the Actions pane to the right, click New Address List, and the New Address List Wizard will guide you in creating an address list.

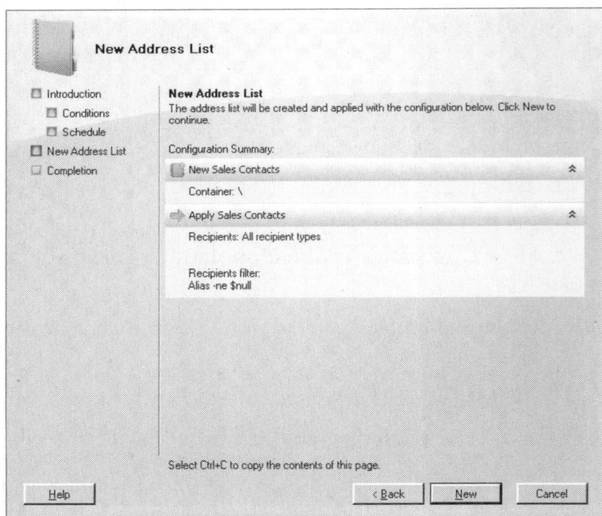

EXERCISE 7.16

Creating a New Address List Using the Exchange Management Shell

1. Open the Exchange Management Shell, and run one of the following commands (make sure to change the parameters enclosed in brackets):

```
New-AddressList -Name <Address_List_Name>

<Query> -Container <Where_To_Place_The_Address_List>  -ConditionalCustomAttribute1
```

Configuring Mobile Device Policies

Exchange ActiveSync mailbox policies let you apply a number of settings to a user's or group of users' mobile devices. The settings are there to allow you to have some control over the phones that attach to your organization and how secure they are.

Table 7.2 lists all the available ActiveSync settings.

TABLE 7.2 ActiveSync Settings

Setting	Description
Allow Nonprovisionable Devices	This allows older Windows mobile devices that do not support ActiveSync push.
Allow Simple Password	This enables or disables the ability to use passwords based on simple patterns, such as sequential numbers like 5678 (numbers in order) or 0852 (patterns on the phone).
Alphanumeric Password Required	This requires that a password be more complex and contain at least one non-numerical character.
Attachments Enabled	If enabled, this setting allows attachments to be downloaded to the mobile device. If your phones are on pay-for-bit data plans, this might be good to disable to help reduce bandwidth costs on the phones
Device Encryption Enabled	If this setting is enabled, it forces the device to use encryption when communicating with the Exchange servers
Password Enabled	If this setting is enabled, it forces the device to have a password.
Password Expiration	This setting sets the length of time after which a device password will expire and then must be changed.

TABLE 7.2 ActiveSync Settings *(continued)*

Setting	Description
Password History	This sets how many passwords are saved in order to limit the user from reusing a previous password.
Policy Refresh Interval	This setting defines how frequently the device will connect to the Exchange server and update mobile device policy information.
Maximum Attachment Size	This setting specifies the maximum size of attachments that will be automatically downloaded to the device.
Maximum Failed Password Attempts	This setting specifies how many times an incorrect password can be entered before a device wipe is performed.
Maximum Inactivity Time Lock	This setting specifies the length of time a device can go without user input before the device will be locked and require a password to unlock it.
Minimum Password Length	This setting specifies the minimum length that a password must be.
Password Recovery	This enables the device password to be recovered from the server.
UNC File Access	This setting, if enabled, allows the device to access files stored on Universal Naming Convention (UNC) shares on the company network.
WSS File Access	This setting, if enabled, allows the device access to files stored on Microsoft Windows SharePoint Services sites on the company network.

To create an ActiveSync mailbox policy, follow the steps outlined in Exercise 7.17 and Exercise 7.18.

EXERCISE 7.17

Creating an ActiveSync Mailbox Policy Using the Exchange Management Console

1. Open the Exchange Management Console, and click the Client Access node in the Organization Configuration section. Select the Exchange ActiveSync Mailbox Policy tab.
2. In the Actions pane to the right, click New Exchange ActiveSync Mailbox Policy, and the New ActiveSync Policy Wizard will guide you through creating a policy.

EXERCISE 7.17 *(continued)*

3. On the first page of the New ActiveSync Policy Wizard, set the name of the policy, and then set all the settings listed in Table 7.2. Once all settings have been configured, click New to create the policy.

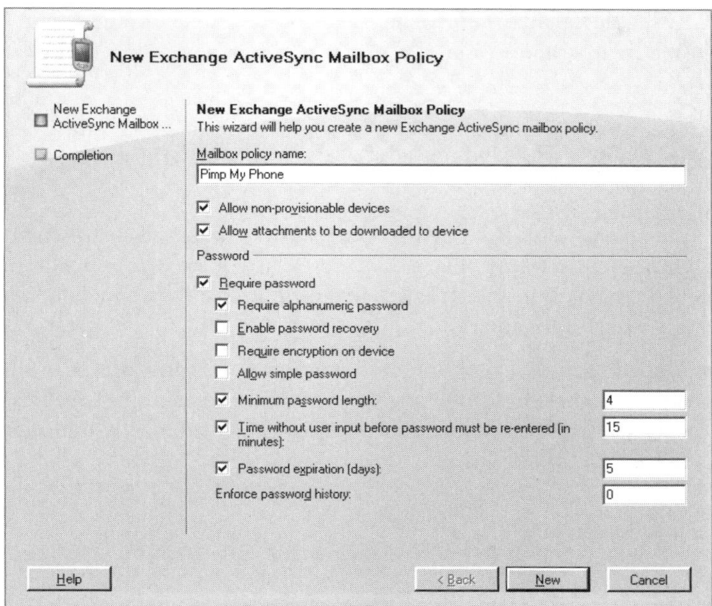

EXERCISE 7.18

Creating an ActiveSync Mailbox Policy Using the Exchange Management Shell

1. Open the Exchange Management Shell, and run one of the following commands (make sure to change the parameters enclosed in brackets):

```
New-ActiveSyncMaiboxPolicy -Name <Policy_Name>

-DevicePasswordEnabled:$false

-AlphanumericDevicePasswordRequired:$false
```

Summary

We covered a decent amount of ground in this chapter, focusing on the basic configuration and management of MRM, rules, and server policies. Every organization that deploys Exchange Server 2007 will have Hub Transport, CAS, and Mailbox servers. This chapter also covered some of the tools available to you to control messages as they travel through an organization and while they are stored in an organization.

Exam Essentials

Understand all of the parts of MRM. MRM consists of default and custom managed folders, content settings, and managed folder policies. All these components are important tools for managing the life span of a message in an Exchange organization. Understand what all of these components are and how they fit together.

Know the parts of a rule action, exception, and condition. Transport rules have three different configurable parts: the condition triggers the rule, the exception specifies what part of the condition to exclude, and the action says what to do with the email message if it fits the condition and is not excluded from the rule.

Review Questions

1. How do you rename the Inbox folder and apply a different retention policy to it?

   A. You have to reformat the server because you can select the folder names only when you install Exchange.

   B. You create a new managed folder, specify Inbox as the folder, then apply your settings to it as desired.

   C. You can change the settings on the Inbox folder, but you cannot rename it.

   D. None of the above.

2. When should the MRM mailbox assistant be run?

   A. It should be run after you have deleted or moved a number of mailboxes as part of a mailbox cleanup operation.

   B. It should be run every Monday morning when you have the biggest load on the Mailbox server, because MRM functions better where there is extra server load.

   C. It is automatically run when it needs to be run; you shouldn't have to worry about when it runs.

   D. You should run it when the server has the least load because it is a resource-intensive operation.

3. What is a managed folder mailbox policy used for?

   A. It allows you to apply a grouping of folders to users all at once instead of one at a time.

   B. It allows you to group folders and then apply a single mailbox content setting to them. This eliminates having to create the same set of content settings over and over again.

   C. Mailbox policies apply settings to new folders as they are created to make sure the new folders all have uniform settings.

   D. It allows you to create a group of default settings that are applied to all newly created custom managed folders.

4. Your server has issues with the network time servers due to an error at the Navy time sources, and it somehow jumps forward a few hours during the time that the managed folder assistant is running. This time shift causes the server to stop the assistant before it has a chance to complete. What will happen the next time the managed folder assistant runs?

   A. The assistant will not start, and an error with event ID 1299 will be entered in the Application log stating that the assistant failed to start because of a failure.

   B. The assistant will start up right where it left off.

   C. The assistant will start back from the beginning because things might have changed since last time.

   D. The assistant will simply restart after it failed.

5. If an enabled transport rule has no condition, what will it do when it runs?
   A. Currently a message that has no condition will cause the transport service to stop responding; this is a known issue and will be fixed in Exchange Server 2007 SP1.
   B. The rule will do nothing at all.
   C. The rule will act on every message.
   D. An event log entry with event ID 1966 will be entered in the event log stating the rule has no condition and that it has been disabled.
6. Email address policies are applied by what?
   A. The RUS
   B. The address policy service
   C. The `Update-EmailAddress` command
   D. None of the above
7. GAL stands for what?
   A. Global address locator
   B. Group attribute locale
   C. Group address book
   D. Global address list
8. What is the recommended limit to the number of rules in an organization?
   A. 1,000 per server
   B. 10,000 per AD domain
   C. 500 per Exchange organization
   D. 1,000 users per AD forest
9. You have two groups of users to which you want to apply different Inbox content settings. One group wants items in their Inbox to be maintained for only 30 days, and the other group wants to maintain their email for 392 days. How would you do this?
   A. Create a separate managed content setting for each group of people, and apply them to the managed mailbox policy for each group.
   B. Create a new default managed folder, and apply the content settings to each default folder as needed.
   C. Create new custom managed folders, replace the Inbox folders with the custom folders, and then apply the content settings to each custom folder as needed.
   D. None of the above.

10. When you delete a custom managed folder in the Exchange management console, what happens to the folders in the user's mailbox?

    A. The folders are deleted along with all the messages in them.

    B. Nothing happens to the folder.

    C. When you delete a custom managed folder, you are prompted to enter an expiration date for the folder.

    D. When you delete a custom managed folder, you have the option to pick what happens.

11. Managed content settings can do all of the following except which action?

    A. Delete mail items.

    B. Move mail items.

    C. Mark mail items as read.

    D. Send mail items to a journaling location.

12. The Maximum Inactivity Time Lock setting performs what action when applied on an Exchange server policy?

    A. Allows you to monitor and then disable mailboxes that are not accessed by anyone for a given amount of time

    B. Logs users out of OWA if there has been no activity for a given amount of time

    C. Locks a mobile device if it has no activity for a given amount of time

    D. Disconnects an SMTP session if there has been no activity for a given amount of time

13. What's an OAB good for?

    A. The Object Attribute Block list stores all of the junk email blocked addresses and domains that are configured on every Outlook client in an Exchange organization. The list is used on the Edge Transport server to block spam messages.

    B. The Offline Address Book is used as a local copy of the Exchange address lists by Outlook clients to cut down on network requests to Exchange and global catalog servers.

    C. The Offline Address Book gives offline users access to email address and company contact information stored in their online contacts folder.

    D. None of the above.

14. Which of the following is not an available method to classify a message?

    A. The user can use the Exchange Management Shell command `Classify-Message`.

    B. The user can manually classify a message via OWA 2007.

    C. The user can manually classify a message using Outlook 2007 properly configured.

    D. Administrators can classify messages using server transport rules.

15. Yesterday you created a new rule on your Hub Transport server located in Hawaii, and the rule does not seem to be working on your Hub Transport server in Cape Town. You know that your connections are all good and that mail is being routed between the two locations. You can log in to both servers from your location. What could be keeping your Cape Town server from running the rule that you made on the Hawaii server?

    A. The RUS.

    B. The HubSync service might not be running on both servers. Without this service, rules do not replicate.

    C. You should check AD replication to be sure that the GC that Cape Town is talking to has replicated from the server that Hawaii is connected to.

    D. None of the above.

16. You've created a transport rule that adds the text *[CONFIDENTIAL]* to the subject line of every message sent between the R&D department and the marketing department. About a week goes by, and you start to get complaints that users in both departments are not able to send messages to each other. What is most likely the cause of messages not being sent?

    A. A routing error must be taking place on the transport server.

    B. The subject line has exceeded the maximum allowed size.

    C. The antispam agents on the Edge Transport server must be blocking the messages.

    D. There is not enough information given in the question to answer this question.

17. Your boss comes into your office and says, "I want you to delete all messages in everyone's Sent Items folder older than 43 days." He then leaves your office. What MRM feature would you use to make this happen?

    A. Custom managed folders

    B. Custom mailbox policy

    C. Managed content setting

    D. Both A and C

18. Your boss comes back into your office, and he is excited after you completed your last task so quickly. He now says, "I don't want anyone but my assistant and my daughter to be able to send email to me. I want all the rest of the emails to me to be sent to my assistant instead." How would you do this?

    A. Use mailbox security settings.

    B. Assign your boss a secret email address, and give it only to his assistant and his daughter.

    C. Use a Hub Transport server transport rule or two.

    D. You apologize to your boss and say you cannot do that.

19. To create a new custom managed folder using the Exchange Management Shell, which command would you use?

    A. `Create-NewCustomManagedFolder`

    B. `New-CustomManagedFolder`

    C. `New-ManagedFolder -Type Custom`

    D. None of the above

20. Your manager is concerned about the impact a stolen mobile device might have on company information. If a phone is stolen, he wants to make sure that the thief can't access any information on it. What ActiveSync setting could you set to make your manager more comfortable?

    A. You could set the Device Encryption Enabled setting to Enabled, which would make the data on the mobile device secure.

    B. You could set the maximum failed password attempts to three, which would erase all the information on the device if the incorrect password was typed more than three times.

    C. You could set the Password Inactivity setting to three days, which would make the phone reformat itself if it has not correctly logged into Exchange in more than 72 hours.

    D. None of the above.

Answers to Review Questions

1. D. You cannot rename the default folders, but you can replace them with custom managed folders.

2. D. You should run the MRM mailbox assistant when there is the least load on the server because it is a resource-intensive operation. It is best to run it during nonpeak business hours.

3. A. Managed folder mailbox policies make it simpler to push folders to users' mailboxes.

4. B. The assistant will restart where it left off.

5. C. Setting a condition is optional. Without a condition, a rule will act on every message unless the exception expects the message.

6. D. The correct Exchange Management Shell command to apply an email address policy is the `update-emailaddresspolicy` command.

7. D. The correct answer is the global address list, which is the address that lists all the nonhidden Exchange-enabled objects in the organization.

8. D. The correct answer is 1,000 rules per forest. Rules are forest-wide applied to each and every Hub Transport server in the forest. This is a recommended limit, and you should base your limit on this and the performance testing of your Hub Transport servers.

9. B. The correct answer is to replace the Inbox of each group with a new default managed folder that has the content settings needed.

10. B. When the custom folder is deleted, the folders in the user's Inbox will stay there until you manually delete them.

11. C. Managed content settings cannot mark items as read. Content settings can be used to move, delete, and journal messages.

12. C. The Maximum Inactivity Time Lock setting is an ActiveSync policy and allows you to force mobile devices to become locked after a given amount of time with no activity and require a password before they can be used again.

13. B. The Offline Address Books contain offline copies of address lists that can be used by Outlook. OABs are customizable on the server and can contain whatever address lists they need to contain. The OAB allows offline clients access to the address lists, and they allow online clients to access the address lists locally, cutting down on network traffic.

14. A. There is no PowerShell command to classify a message.

15. C. Hub Transport servers store their rules in the AD configuration container and are replicated to Exchange servers based on AD site replication.

16. B. The rule you created is missing an exception that tells it to not add the text to the subject line if the text is already there. This has caused the subject lines to become larger than Exchange will allow you to send.

17. C. Managed content settings allow you to perform actions on messages in folders based on criteria such as the age of a message.

18. C. You could configure a Hub Transport rule to redirect all of your boss's email to his assistant. To allow email from his daughter and his assistant to reach him, you could place an exception on the rule so that the rule runs when his daughter or his assistant is listed on the From line.

19. D. The correct Exchange Management Shell command to create a new managed custom folder is `New-ManagedFolder`

20. B. Setting the maximum failed password attempts is the best way to secure the data on a mobile device because it deletes all the information on the device if the password is not typed correctly. You should also set the Maximum Inactivity Time Lock setting so that the phone will lock itself if it is inactive.

Configuring and Managing Client Connectivity and Public Folders

MICROSOFT EXAM OBJECTIVES COVERED IN THIS CHAPTER:

✓ **Configuring the Exchange Infrastructure**

- Configure public folders.
- Configure client connectivity.

✓ **Monitoring and Reporting**

- Monitor client connectivity.

Although the main subject areas of this chapter might not seem like a logical fit, they really are in more than one way. For starters, both public folder and client connectivity configuration and management are something that is more often than not done once and forgotten. This is for good reason—they usually just work after that point. Another tie that binds these otherwise different subject areas together is that most Exchange administrators don't enjoy working with them, and furthermore, most Exchange administrators don't maintain a high proficiency level with these subjects. We'll try to bring the topics together in this chapter, presenting the information you'll need on exam day and also some useful reference material for use later as you administer Exchange Server 2007. The main subjects of this chapter are as follows:

- Managing public folders
- Configuring client connectivity services
- Configuring mobile devices

Managing Public Folders

For many companies, public folders are a major part of their Exchange Server deployments. Public folders are a powerful way to share knowledge and data throughout your organization, and they've been a staple of Exchange Server. They are a great way to share content and information with many users, and since they can be mail-enabled, they can also be an easy way for third-party application developers to hook into Exchange. Just use the MAPI libraries to connect to Exchange as a user with permissions to the specified public folder, and you have the ability to send and receive messages—and share them with multiple users—without doing a lot of coding.

At the same time, public folder management has been a weakness in previous versions of Exchange Server:

- There is a distinct lack of freely available command-line tools for managing public folders and public folder stores. Some tools were available from PSS, but they weren't advertised and weren't generally supported for versions of Exchange past 5.5.
- The public folder support in the legacy Exchange System Manager lacked effective bulk operation support; you could not, for example, easily add a new public folder store to the replica list of a given folder and its subfolders without visiting each folder in turn or without overwriting the replica lists of the subfolders with copies of the initial folder's list.
- There was no easy way to export or import properties, permissions, or other settings from one public folder or server to another.

- The public folder replica and replication information displayed by the legacy System Manager were often incomplete, misleading, or just plain wrong.
- The installable file system (IFS, or M drive) introduced by Exchange 2000 allowed administrators to access Exchange store objects as if the store were a file system. Unfortunately, this allowed them to use inappropriate tools to make their management tasks "easier" and introduced a whole new category of problems that could break public folders.

Unfortunately, Microsoft's announcement that it was deemphasizing support for public folders in Exchange 2007 has caused a lot of worry and confusion. When you combine this with the lack of any GUI public folder management tools in the initial release of Exchange 2007, a lot of people have concluded that you just can't do public folders anymore. If you have a large public folder deployment in your organization, this is obviously an area of concern for you. Be assured that public folders are alive and well, and in some ways they're even better in Exchange 2007 than they ever have been. The new EMS cmdlets for handling public folders are definitely worth the price of admission, and even the lack of built-in GUI functions is offset by the wonderful tool known as PFDAVAdmin.

Creating the Public Folder Database

If you did not select to install public folders on your Exchange Server 2007 Mailbox server during the initial installation, you can return later and create a public folder database. We'll examine that process briefly here because it is similar to the mailbox database creation process covered in detail in Chapter 4, "Configuring Exchange Server Roles."

If you start with only Outlook 2007 clients, you don't have a requirement to have public folders in your Exchange organization. However, if you later add other clients such as Outlook 2003 to your organization, you will need to create a public folder database and public folder tree to house the Offline Address Book (OAB) and free/busy information. You might also just want to have public folders for other uses too. If you're adding public folders for older clients, such as Outlook 2003, you'll need to restart the Microsoft Exchange Information Store service on the Mailbox server with the public folder database installed before these older clients will be able to see and connect to the public folder tree just created.

To create the storage group that will house your new public folder database, simply perform the steps outlined in Exercise 4.1 in Chapter 4. To create the new public folder database, perform the steps outlined in Exercise 8.1.

If you install Exchange Server 2007 Mailbox servers into an existing Exchange Server 2003 organization, a public folder database will be created automatically on the Mailbox server in a separate storage group. This ensures backward compatibility and cannot be changed or prevented.

EXERCISE 8.1

Creating a New Public Folder Database

1. Click Start ➤ Programs ➤ Microsoft Exchange Server 2007, and then select Exchange Management Console.
2. Expand the Microsoft Exchange root object, expand the Server Configuration folder, and then click the server containing the storage group in which you want to create a new database.
3. Right-click the storage group object in which you want to create the database, and select the New Public Folder Database option from the context menu. This opens the New Public Folder Database Wizard. Alternatively, you can click the New Public Folder Database link under the storage group options in the Actions pane on the right of the Exchange Management Console.
4. Type a name for the new public folder database, and select the database file path by clicking the Browse button. Remember, the database should be on a different physical volume than its storage group's transaction logs if possible. To ensure the database is available for immediate use, leave the Mount This Database option checked. Click New to complete the database creation process.
5. As usual, Exchange displays a summary page showing the success or failure of the actions you instructed it to perform. Notice this time, however, two actions are performed: creating the database and mounting the database.
6. Click Finish to close the wizard.

Exploring the Public Folder Management Options

When Microsoft announced it was "deemphasizing" support for public folders in Exchange Server 2007, a lot of Exchange administrators immediately got worried. What was the future of public folders? Would Exchange Server 2007 continue to support them? If not, what would the migration path look like?

Happily, Microsoft has clarified its position on public folder support. Public folders are still fully supported in Exchange Server 2007 (and will be through 2016), although they may not be included in future releases of Exchange Server. However, Exchange Server 2007 is the first version to provide support for Microsoft Windows SharePoint Services integration as an alternative method of seamlessly sharing data within your organization and making it available to Outlook 2007 and Outlook Web Access (OWA) users.

In the meantime, you can go forward with your Exchange 2007 migration secure in the knowledge that you will be able to continue using your public folder infrastructure. You can continue to use the Exchange 2003 System Manager console to create, manage, and delete public folders, or you can use the functionality built into Exchange 2007.

Understanding Native Exchange 2007 Support

Although the Exchange Management Console (EMC) offers minimal support for public folders, Exchange 2007 provides the bulk of its built-in support via Exchange Management Shell (EMS) cmdlets. Don't worry; they're not difficult to use, even if you're not a script or command-line guru.

Before we show you how to use the new public folder cmdlets, though, we'll cover exactly what you can do in the EMC. Be warned that it isn't much: you can create and delete public folder stores on your Mailbox servers and manage the basic properties of these stores. You can't view the public folder hierarchy, add or delete public folders, set folder properties, manage access permissions, or view and manage replication. To do all those tasks, you'll need some other tool such as Outlook to manage individual folders or EMS to deal with public folders from the server.

If you're missing the GUI and feeling left high and dry, ponder the plight of POP3 or IMAP4 GUI management. Exchange 2007 includes no GUI interface for managing those protocols, and EMS is the only way to go. At least with public folders, if you don't feel up to tackling EMS, you can always use the Exchange 2003 System Manager console.

Using the Exchange Management Shell

The Exchange Management Shell, as you've seen many times up to this point, is built on the Windows PowerShell technology. Because it's a specialized application of PowerShell, it uses the same format as standard PowerShell cmdlets. That format is as follows:

```
verb-noun
```

By combining the noun and verb in the name of the cmdlet, each cmdlet describes both the type of operation it performs as well as the object it manipulates. Verbs produce a standard behavior regardless of the object to which they're applied. For example, the `Get` verb will always provide a read-only list of the object's properties, while the `Set` verb will always allow you to modify those properties—even when those properties vary from object to object.

In some of the following examples, you'll see lines terminated by a backtick (`) character. PowerShell uses this character for line termination; it tells the shell that the logical line of input will be continued on the next physical line. This allows you to break up long lines for display and still ensure that they work correctly when you enter them. As a result, the same verbs and nouns tend to be used over and over again; this helps you learn your way around more quickly. Many of the properties are common across multiple objects, so you'll quickly get used to how to use them. The help page for each cmdlet lists all parameters that can be used with that cmdlet.

Performing General Public Folder Tasks

These cmdlets apply to the entire public folder hierarchy at once and provide broad control of your public folder infrastructure:

- `Get-PublicFolderStatistics`: This cmdlet provides a detailed set of statistics about the public folder hierarchy on a given server, such as `Get-PublicFolderStatistics -Server "WILEXEX01A"`.
- `Resume-PublicFolderReplication`: This cmdlet reenables all public folder content replication when it has been suspended.
- `Suspend-PublicFolderReplication`: This cmdlet suspends all public folder content replication.
- `Update-PublicFolderHierarchy`: This cmdlet starts the content synchronization process for the public folder hierarchy on the specified server, such as `Update-PublicFolderHierarchy -Server "WILEXEX01A"`.

Manipulating Individual Public Folders

These cmdlets are designed to work with a specific public folder:

- `Get-PublicFolder`: This cmdlet retrieves the properties for the specified public folder. If you don't name a public folder by specifying a value for the `-Identity` property, it will default to the root public folder. If you need to see system folders, you'll need to set the `-Identity` property to a value beginning with the string `\NON IPM SUBTREE`.
    - `Get-PublicFolder-Identity "\Jobs\Posted" -Server "WILEXEX01A"`
    - `Get-PublicFolder-Recurse`
    - `Get-PublicFolder -Identity \NON IPM SUBTREE -Recurse`

By default, the `Get-PublicFolder` cmdlet returns the values for only a single folder. The `-Recurse` switch changes the behavior to report on all subfolders as well.

- `New-PublicFolder`: This cmdlet creates a new public folder. The `-Path` property is required and provides the name and location of the new public folder, such as `New-PublicFolder -Identity "\Jobs\New" -Server "WILEXEX01A"`.
- `Remove-PublicFolder`: This cmdlet deletes a public folder. The `-Path` property is required and provides the name and location of the public folder to be deleted, such as `Remove-PublicFolder -Identity "\Jobs\Old" -Server "WILEXEX01A"`.

By default, the `Remove-PublicFolder` cmdlet removes only the named public folder. The `-Recurse` switch will delete all subfolders as well, which is handy for removing an entire group of folders at once.

- `Set-PublicFolder`: This cmdlet allows you to set most of the properties for the named public folder, such as limits, replicas, replication schedules, and more, such as `Set-PublicFolder -Identity "\Jobs\Posted" -Server "WILEXEX01A"`.

You cannot use the `Set-PublicFolder` cmdlet to mail-enable a public folder or to change its mail-related attributes. See the next section, "Manipulating Public Folder Mail Attributes," for the cmdlets to use for these tasks.

- `Update-PublicFolder`: This cmdlet starts the content synchronization process for the named public folder. The `-Identity` property is required, such as `Update-PublicFolder -Identity "\Jobs\Posted"`.

Manipulating Public Folder Mail Attributes

These cmdlets are designed to work with a specific public folder and modify the attributes it receives when it is mail-enabled:

- `Disable-MailPublicFolder`: This cmdlet takes an existing mail-enabled public folder and renders it mail-disabled, such as `Disable-MailPublicFolder -Identity "\Jobs\New"`.
- `Enable-MailPublicFolder`: This cmdlet takes an existing public folder and renders it mail-enabled. The optional `-HiddenFromAddressListsEnabled` switch allows you to hide the folder from your address lists, such as `Enable-MailPublicFolder-Identity "\Jobs\New" -HiddenFromAddressListsEnabled $true -Server "WILEXEX01A"`.

You set the mail-related attributes separately using the `Set-MailPublicFolder` cmdlet.

- `Get-MailPublicFolder`: This cmdlet retrieves the mail-related properties for the specified public folder. If you don't name a public folder by specifying a value for the `-Identity` property, it will default to the root public folder, such as `Get-MailPublicFolder -Identity "\Jobs\Old" -Server "WILEXEX01A"`.

You set the mail-related attributes separately.

- `Set-MailPublicFolder`: This cmdlet allows you to set the mail-related properties for the named public folder, such as alias, email addresses, send and receive sizes, permitted and prohibited senders, such as `Set-PublicFolder-Identity"\Jobs\Posted" -Server "WILEXEX01A" -AliasPostedJobs -PrimarySmtpAddress "postedjobs\commatcontoso.com"`.

Once you have set the mail-related attributes for a public folder, you must still mail-enable it using the `Enable-MailPublicFolder` cmdlet.

Managing Public Folder Databases

These cmdlets allow you to manage the public folder databases:

- `Get-PublicFolderDatabase`: This cmdlet provides the functionality used by the Exchange Management Console and allows you to view the properties of existing public folder databases, such as `Get-PublicFolderDatabase -Server "WILEXEX01A"`.

The `-Identity`, `-Server`, and `-StorageGroup` parameters are not compatible with each other. Use only one of the three to narrow down your selection.

- `New-PublicFolderDatabase`: This cmdlet allows you to create a new public folder database.

You can see the `New-PublicFolderDatabase` cmdlet in action by using the Exchange Management Shell to create a new database; it will show you the exact syntax it used with the cmdlet, as shown previously in the chapter.

- `Remove-PublicFolderDatabase`: This cmdlet deletes an existing public folder database from the active configuration of the server, such as `Remove-PublicFolderDatabase -Identity "Public Folder Database"`.

The corresponding EDB file is not deleted by the `Remove-PublicFolderDatabase` cmdlet; you have to manually remove it from the hard drive.

- `Set-PublicFolderDatabase`: This cmdlet provides the underlying functionality used by the Exchange Management Console to update the properties of existing public folder databases, such as `Set-PublicFolderDatabase -Identity "PublicFolderDatabase" -Name "New and Improved PF Database"`.

Managing Public Folder Permissions

These cmdlets allow you to modify and monitor the permissions on your public folders. Administrative and client permissions are handled through two separate sets of nouns. The Exchange 2007 documentation contains the list of specific permissions that you can apply.

- `Add-PublicFolderAdministrativePermission`: This cmdlet lets you add an administrative permission entry to a given public folder, such as

`Add-PublicFolderAdministrativePermission-User 'Jim' -Identity "\Jobs\Posted" -AccessRights "ViewInformationStore, AdministerInformationStore".`

You can specify a single access right or list multiple rights at once using the syntax shown in the example for the `Add-PublicFolderAdministrativePermission` cmdlet.

- `Add-PublicFolderClientPermission`: This cmdlet lets you add a client permission entry to a given public folder, such as `Add-PublicFolderClientPermission -User "Greg.Smith" -Identity "Jobs\Posted" -AccessRights "CreateItems".`
- `Get-PublicFolderAdministrativePermission`: This cmdlet lets you view the administrative permission entries on a given public folder, such as `Get-PublicFolderAdministrativePermission -Identity "\Jobs\Posted".`
- `Get-PublicFolderClientPermission`: This cmdlet lets you view the client permission entries on a given public folder, such as `Get-PublicFolderClientPermission -Identity "\Jobs\Posted".`
- `Remove-PublicFolderAdministrativePermission`: This cmdlet lets you remove an administrative permission entry from a given public folder, such as `Remove-PublicFolderAdministrativePermission-User "Fran.Jones" -Identity "\Jobs\Posted" -AccessRights "ViewInformationStore".`
- `Remove-PublicFolderClientPermission`: This cmdlet lets you remove a client permission entry from a given public folder, such as `Remove-PublicFolderClientPermission -User "Nathan.Smith" -Identity"\Jobs\Posted" -AccessRights "CreateItems".`

Using Additional Scripts for Complicated Tasks

Although the cmdlets described in the preceding sections are certainly great for single-folder operations, performing common operations on entire groups of folders starts getting sticky. Since most of us aren't scripting gurus, Exchange 2007 provides some example Exchange Management Shell scripts that allow you to perform more complicated server and management tasks that affect groups of folders:

- `AddReplicaToPFRecursive.ps1` adds the specified server to the replica list for a given public folder and all folders underneath it.
- `AddUsersToPFRecursive.ps1` allows you to grant user permissions to a folder and all folders beneath it.
- `MoveAllReplicas.ps1` finds and replaces a server in the replica list of all public folders, including system folders.
- `RemoveReplicaFromPFRecursive.ps1` removes the specified server from the replica list for a given public folder and all folders underneath it.

- `ReplaceReplicaOnPFRecursive.ps1` finds and replaces a server in the replica list of a given public folder as well as all subfolders.
- `ReplaceUserPermissionOnPFRecursive.ps1` finds and replaces one user in the permissions on a given public folder and all its subfolders with a second user; the original user permissions are not retained.
- `ReplaceUserWithUserOnPFRecursive.ps1` copies one user's access permissions on a given public folder and all its subfolders to a second user while retaining permissions for the first user; it's confusingly named.
- `RemoveReplicaFromPFRecursive.ps1` removes the given user's access permissions from the given public folder and all its subfolders.

You can find these scripts in the Scripts subfolder of the Exchange 2007 installation folder. Note that with the default Windows PowerShell configuration, you just can't click these scripts and run them; you must invoke them from within the Exchange Management Shell, usually by navigating to the folder and calling them explicitly.

Using Outlook

Exchange public folders can also be created by mailbox-enabled users in their email clients. We'll show you how to create a public folder using the Outlook client.

Open Outlook, and make sure the folder list is displayed. Next, double-click Public Folders in the folder list, or click the plus icon just in front of Public Folders. Notice that the plus sign becomes a minus sign when a folder is expanded to show the folders within it.

You've now expanded the top-level folder for public folders, which contains two subfolders: Favorites and All Public Folders. Expand the All Public Folders folder, and you'll see that it has at least one subfolder: Internet Newsgroups. If your organization uses public folders, you probably have at least one other subfolder here as well.

If your Exchange organization has a large number of public folders, you can drag the ones you use often to your Favorites subfolder. This makes them easier to find. Folders in the Favorites folder are also the only ones that are available when you work offline without a connection to your Exchange server.

To create new public folders in the folder All Public Folders, follow the steps in Exercise 8.2.

EXERCISE 8.2

Creating New Public Folders with Outlook

1. Open the Outlook client.

EXERCISE 8.2 *(continued)*

2. Right-click the All Public Folders item, and then select New Folder from the context menu. The Create New Folder dialog opens, as shown here.

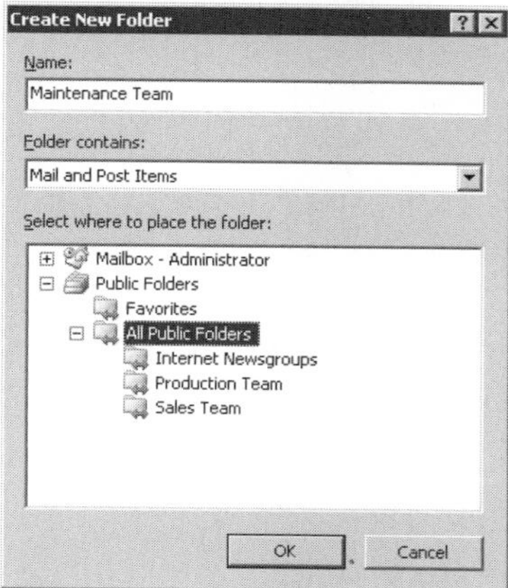

3. Enter a name for the folder; we've given ours the somewhat unimaginative name Maintenance Team.

4. When you're done creating your folder, click OK.

Note that the folder we just created here holds email and posted items, which is the default selection. Email items are messages. Posted items contain a subject and text. You can post an item in a folder designed to hold posts without dealing with messaging attributes such as to whom the item is sent. To post an item, click the down arrow near the New icon on the main Outlook window, and select Post in This Folder from the drop-down menu. If you wanted to create a public folder to house calendar items or contact items, you'd need to select the correct type of public folder contents from the Folder Contains drop-down list shown in Exercise 8.2.

If you're told you don't have sufficient permissions to create the folder, you need to assign those permissions using one of the other Exchange public folder management tools. If you have Exchange administrative permissions, you can make this change yourself.

The new public folder now shows up under the All Public Folders hierarchy. If you can't see the full name of your new folder, make the Folder List pane a little wider. Now right-click your new folder, and select the Properties option from the context menu. This opens the folder's Properties dialog box, shown in Figure 8.1.

FIGURE 8.1 Public folder properties

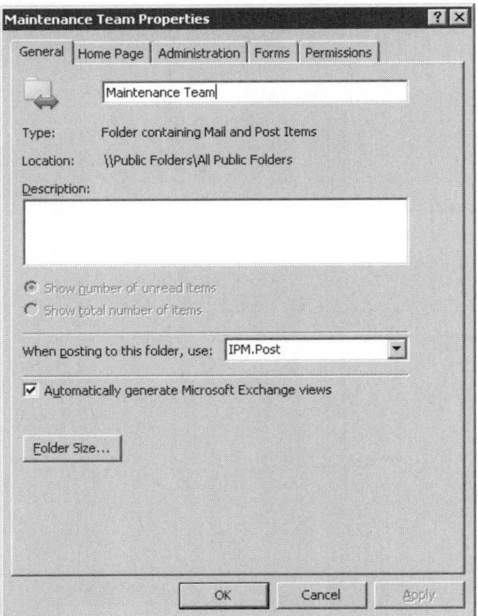

We're not going to spend a lot of time with this dialog box. Among other things, mailbox owners use the public folder's Properties dialog box to do the following:

- Add a description for other mailbox owners who access the folder.
- Make the folder available on the Internet.
- Set up a default view of the folder, including grouping by such things as the subject or sender.
- Set up some administrative rules on folder characteristics, access, and such.
- Set permissions for using the folder.

Go ahead and look around in the public folder's Properties dialog box. When you're done, click Cancel, unless you've made some changes you want to keep. If you have, then click OK to save your changes.

You create and manage private folders in mailboxes in the same way you create and manage public folders in the Public Folders hierarchy. 'Nuff said.

Using the Exchange Server 2003 System Manager

In Exchange 5.5, you could create public folders using only an email client. You couldn't create one in the Administrator program. Exchange 2003 lets you create public folders in Exchange System Manager as an Exchange administrator.

Launch the Exchange System Manager, expand the Administrative Groups node, expand the desired administrative group, and expand the Folders node. Right-click the Public Folders container, and select New ➤ Public Folder from the context menu to open the new public folder's Properties dialog box.

Let's take a look at the key tabs in this dialog box.

General

You use the General tab of the public folder's Properties dialog box, as shown in Figure 8.2, to name your folder and enter a description. The Path field shows where the folder is located in the Public Folder hierarchy after it has been created. If Maintain Per-User Read and Unread Information for This Folder is selected, each user will see items in the folder they have read in nonbold text. If this option is not selected, all items will show in bold text for all users whether or not they have been read.

FIGURE 8.2 The General tab of the public folder's Properties dialog box

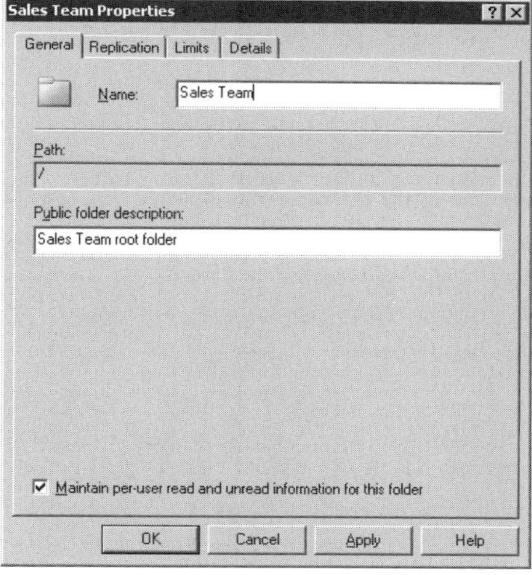

Replication

The Replication tab of the public folder's Properties dialog box, as shown in Figure 8.3, is an important property page because it is used to manage the replication of folders between this server and other Exchange servers. Replication enables you to put copies of the same folder on multiple Exchange servers. It is useful either for local load balancing or for limiting wide area network traffic and improving performance by placing copies of folders in routing groups at geographically distant sites.

FIGURE 8.3 The Replication tab of the public folder's Properties dialog box

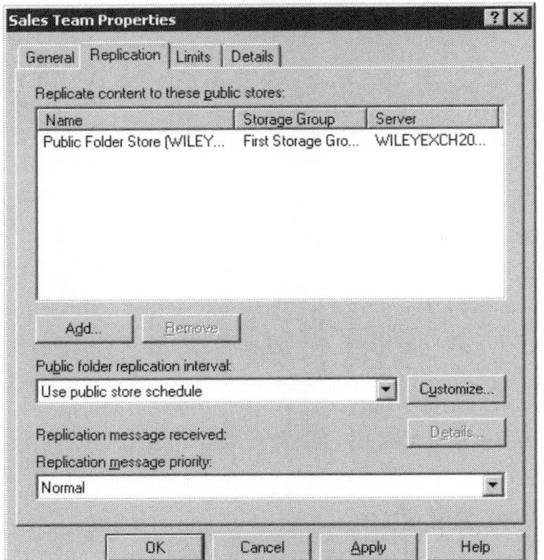

Limits

You've already seen the Limits tab, as shown in Figure 8.4. Let's look at each of the three types of limits on this page:

- *Storage Limits*: As with mailboxes, you can set thresholds at which warnings are sent and specify that posting to the folder is prohibited. You can also set a maximum posted-item size. If you want, you can choose to use the default storage limits settings for the public folder store where the folder resides.
- *Deletion Setting*: As with mailboxes, you can set the maximum number of days that a deleted item will be kept for recovery before being totally deleted. If you deselect the Use Public Store Defaults check box, you can enter a number of days that deleted items should be retained. If you don't want items retained at all, set the number of days to 0.
- *Age Limits*: This is the number of days that an item in the folder lives before being deleted. This is a handy tool for controlling storage usage.

When you're finished creating your public folder, click OK, and admire your handiwork in the Public Folders container. You should create folders in the Folders\Public Folders container, not in the public folder store. The public folder store holds created folders. You create new public folders in the Folders\Public Folders container. This seems simple, but if we had a dollar for every time we wrongly went to the public folder store to create a new public folder, well, we'd at least be on the beach in Hawaii right now.

FIGURE 8.4 The Limits tab of the public folder's Properties dialog box

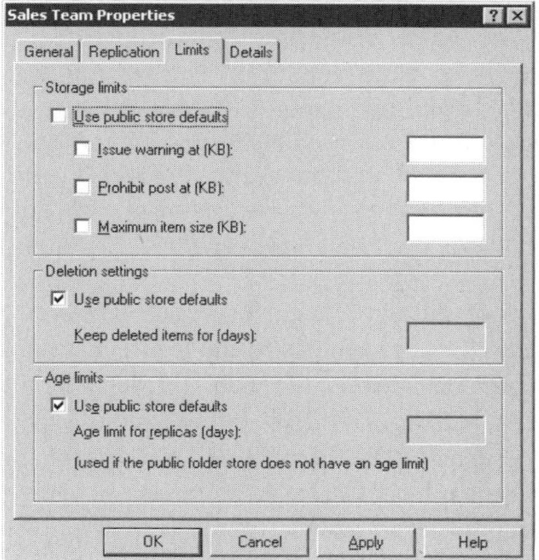

In some earlier versions of Exchange, the Windows group Everyone had rights by default to create folders in the Public Folders container. This right extends to both top-level folders (folders within and, thus, just below the Public Folders container) and subfolders within top-level folders. If you want to alter this right, right-click the Public Folders container, and select Properties. Use the Security tab in the public folder's Properties dialog box to add or remove users and groups or their rights in the Public Folders container. Even if you don't want to change the default, we strongly recommend you take a look at the Security tab. Many of the permissions on it are specific to public folders and are therefore quite different from the permissions for other types of Exchange recipients.

Using the Public Folder DAV Administration Tool

It is really unfortunate that the initial release of Exchange 2007 provides no GUI for public folder management. Although the Exchange Management Shell cmdlets are functional, it can take some time to master using them; in the meantime, you still have public folders to administer.

PFDAVAdmin requires the .NET Framework version 1.1 to be installed, which means you must maintain multiple versions of the .NET Framework on your management servers and workstations.

Happily, Microsoft has an outstanding freely available GUI tool, the Public Folder DAV Administrator (PFDAVAdmin), that it makes available. PFDAVAdmin is a .NET application that uses WebDAV instead of MAPI to access the public folder store.

You might now be wondering whether using PFDAVAdmin is a good idea, given its reliance on WebDAV. In Exchange 2007 support for the WebDAV protocol is "deemphasized," meaning that Microsoft doesn't promise it will be around for the next major version of Exchange. But it's still here in Exchange 2007—and it allows you to use this wonderful management tool.

PFDAVAdmin is a wonderfully flexible tool. At first glance, it seems to give you the ability to manage public folder permissions using a GUI that is close to the legacy Exchange System Manager. In addition to querying and setting permissions, you can add, replace, and remove individual access control entries (ACEs) across a set of folders without having to wholesale replace the access control lists (ACLs) in question. PFDAVAdmin will also notify you when an ACL is damaged or in noncanonical order (meaning that the ACEs aren't properly ordered) and allow you to fix them on more than one folder at once.

Administrators who used the installable file system (IFS)—otherwise known as the M drive—in Exchange 2000 Server and Exchange Server 2003 upgrades would often use the Windows Explorer permission tool to modify permissions on public folders. Unfortunately, this usually causes ACEs to get written in the wrong order, causing all sorts of subtle problems. PFDAVAdmin is the easy way to fix them, if you've got to deal with them and you don't have to wait until you have Exchange 2007 in your organization to do it! Luckily, Exchange 2007 makes the IFS go away, so once you fix the problems, they're not likely to return.

You can also use PFDAVAdmin to do the following:

- Perform bulk operations on folder properties. In addition, you can do bulk search and removal operations of per-item permissions.
- Apply changes to your list of replicas to a folder and all subfolders without overwriting each folder's replica list (that is, add or remove specific server entries without making each folder's replica list an exact copy of your starting point).
- Export folder permissions on folders, public folder stores, and mailbox stores.
- Export and import public folder replica lists.

Microsoft makes PFDAVAdmin freely available through the Microsoft Exchange tools download website. You can find the download link by searching for "PFDAVAdmin" at the following location: `www.microsoft.com/downloads/`.

Using Other Public Folder Tools

Exchange administrators have used a couple of other tools throughout the years. Although these tools work with legacy Exchange servers, many of them are not certified for use with Exchange 2003 (let alone Exchange 2007). However, you can still use them as long as you have legacy Exchange public folder servers in your organization. We'll mention two in particular:

- The PFAdmin tool (`PFAdmin.exe`) is a command-line tool for common administrative tasks. With it you can manage ACLs, manage replicas, and rehome folders. If you happen to have some old product CDs, you can find a copy of this tool on the BackOffice Resource Kit (BORK) 4.5 CD.
- The PFInfo tool (`PFInfo.exe`) is a GUI tool that provides reporting on a server's folder replicas and associated permissions. You can even use the output of this tool as input to PFAdmin, allowing you to provide a level of consistency across multiple servers.

Although you might be tempted to use PFAdmin and PFInfo in your Exchange 2007 organization (especially if you're already using them), we recommend you finally retire these tools before retiring your legacy Exchange public folder servers. The most compelling reason to use these tools with legacy Exchange servers was to provide the missing command-line and scripting capability for public folder management, and now that Exchange 2007 includes the EMS, you should really put the effort into mastering the public folder cmdlets it provides.

You might find one additional legacy tool of value. The Public Folder Migration Tool (`PFMigrate.wsf`) is a Visual Basic script that was introduced in the Exchange Server 2003 Deployment Tools (ExDeploy). This script was designed for one purpose: to provide a simple interface for performing bulk public folder replica transfers from Exchange Server 5.5 servers to Exchange Server 2003 servers. However, because it can handle cross-administrative group replica transfers, PFMigrate can move replicas to Exchange 2007 servers. The script is downloadable from the Microsoft website as part of the latest versions of the Exchange Server 2003 ExDeploy tools.

Working with the Public Folder Hierarchy

You can create public folders in any available public folder store on any Exchange Mailbox server. By default, public folder stores are not created on Exchange 2007 Mailbox servers unless you specify that the server will be used with clients running Outlook 2003 and earlier. When you create a new public folder store on an Exchange 2007 Mailbox server, you can create a new storage group for it or place it in a storage group that already has one or more mailbox stores in it.

A public folder hierarchy, or public folder tree, is a list of public folders and their subfolders that are stored in the default public folder stores on the Exchange servers in an Exchange organization. The hierarchy also includes the name of the server on which a copy of each folder resides. Because the hierarchy exists in Active Directory as a separate object, it does not contain any of the actual items in your various public folders. There is one organization-wide public folder hierarchy object, although in previous versions of Exchange, you could create additional public folder trees that were not visible through the Public Folder object in Outlook but could be accessed through other methods, such as NNTP.

You cannot create nonvisible public folder trees using the management tools in Exchange Server 2007; you will need to continue using the Exchange Server 2003 System Manager if you want to create these objects.

Replicating Public Folders

In an environment with a single Exchange server, the hierarchy exists and is stored on the Exchange server. In an environment with multiple public folder stores, each Exchange server that has a public folder store has a copy of the public folder hierarchy. Exchange servers work together to ensure that each Exchange server in an administrative group has an up-to-date copy of the public folder hierarchy. This process, called *public folder hierarchy replication*, is automatic. In Exchange 2000 Server and Exchange Server 2003, there were certain limitations with this process when replication crossed administrative and routing group boundaries. Once you've fully migrated to Exchange Server 2007, these limitations will be a thing of the past; all Exchange Server 2007 servers are in a single separate administrative group that has been created for backward compatibility with Exchange 2000 Server and Exchange Server 2003 servers in the organization.

The Exchange Server 2003 System Manager uses the public folder hierarchy to appropriately display public folder objects in various containers and to retrieve information about public folders, whether that information is stored in the hierarchy or on the server where the public folder physically resides. Email clients such as Outlook and OWA use the hierarchy to list public folders available on all servers in the organization and to access items in a specific folder. Security limits associated with a given public folder, of course, limit the actual access granted to administrators and users.

The public folder hierarchy also includes what are called *system folders*, such as the Schedule + Free Busy folder. We'll talk about it and the other system folders later in this chapter.

How public folders are accessed depends on the client version. By default, Outlook 2007 and Outlook Web Access clients use the new Exchange Server 2007 web services to determine the location of a public folder. Previous versions of Outlook will first look for a public folder on the user's public folder store, which might or might not be the same Exchange server where the user's mailbox is located. The default public folder store is configured on the General tab of the mailbox store's Properties dialog box, as shown in Figure 8.5.

If a specific public folder doesn't exist in the default public folder store, the client is directed to a server where the public folder resides. As you can imagine, when many public folders are accessed over a lower-bandwidth network, server and network loads can get pretty heavy as users access public folders on one or a limited number of Exchange servers. If you need to, you can replicate folders on one Exchange server to other Exchange servers.

FIGURE 8.5 The default public folder store property of a mailbox database in Exchange Server 2007

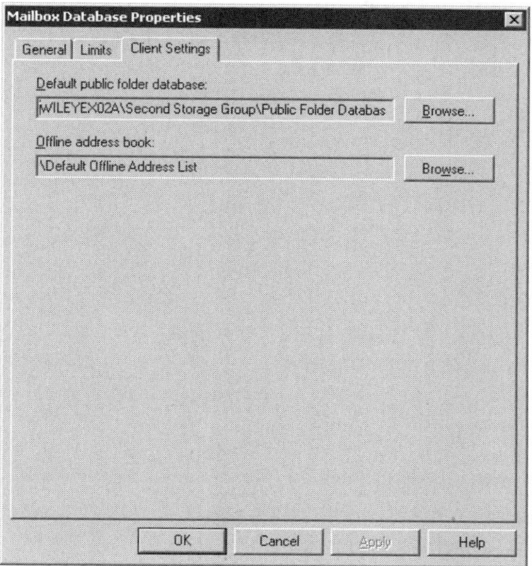

Why would you want to replicate public folders? Well, we can think of four reasons:

- When you need to balance public folder access loads on your Exchange servers. Having all your users connect to a single server for all their public folder access can quickly result in an overwhelmed server if you have a large number of users or if you have heavy public folder usage.
- When you have an Exchange server or group of Exchange servers separated from other servers in your organization by low-bandwidth links. In that case, you may be better off having limited replication traffic over your links and allowing users to connect to local replicas, keeping their traffic on the LAN.
- When IMAP4 clients see folders only on the Exchange server to which they connect, including public folders. If you want an IMAP4 client to be able to see a specific public folder, you must create a replica of that folder on the IMAP4 user's Mailbox server.
- When public folder replication is essential when you're planning to remove an Exchange server from your organization (like all those Exchange 2003 servers you're migrating away from). If the server you're removing hosts the only replica for a set of public folders and you don't want to lose those folders, you must replicate them to another Exchange server in your organization.

Now that we've whetted your appetite regarding public folder replication, we'll tackle the subject in further detail in the next section.

Managing Public Folders

All of what we said about public folders in single administrative group environments in an earlier section of this chapter ("Replicating Public Folders") applies to public folders in multiadministrative group environments. Again, remember that with Exchange Server 2007 you may have multiple administrative groups while you're in the process of upgrading your organization from an earlier version of Exchange, but you will end up with a single administrative group when you've finally switched completely to Exchange Server 2007. Until that day, though, you'll need to use the Exchange 2003 Exchange System Manager to fully manage some of the complications listed in this section.

Public folder management gets to be more complex as additional administrative groups are created and connected by routing groups. Two issues come immediately to mind.

First, an Exchange organization's one and only MAPI-based default public folder tree can remain in the administrative group where it was originally created or can be moved to another administrative group. In either case, when the default public folder tree has been moved to a new administrative group, control of its management can be delegated to a specially constituted Windows 2003 group.

Do not delete the administrative group where the Exchange public folder hierarchy is found. Public folders *will* stop working.

Second, as Exchange organizations grow in size and complexity, nothing becomes more important on the public folders side than the location of public folders and replicas of public folders. You can significantly reduce network traffic and decrease folder access times by replicating heavily accessed public folders to Exchange servers in different routing groups with relatively low-bandwidth links to the Exchange servers where the public folders currently reside.

Let's take a closer look at public folder tree management and public folder replication.

Accessing Public Folders Using the Exchange 2003 System Manager

You can still create and manage public folders using the Exchange Server 2003 System Manager; many administrators will be more comfortable with this option than with using the Exchange Management Shell, at least at first. For the most part, public folder management is straightforward in multiserver Exchange Server environments.

Look at Figure 8.6 and Figure 8.7, which show the public folders on the two servers WILEYEXCH2003A and WILEYEX02A, an Exchange Server 2003 server and an Exchange Server 2007 server, respectively.

First, notice that WILEYEXCH2003A has many public folders that don't exist on WILEYEX02A. This should demonstrate that by default the Public Folders container on each Exchange server contains only those folders that have replicas located in that store.

FIGURE 8.6 Public folders on WILEYEXCH2003A

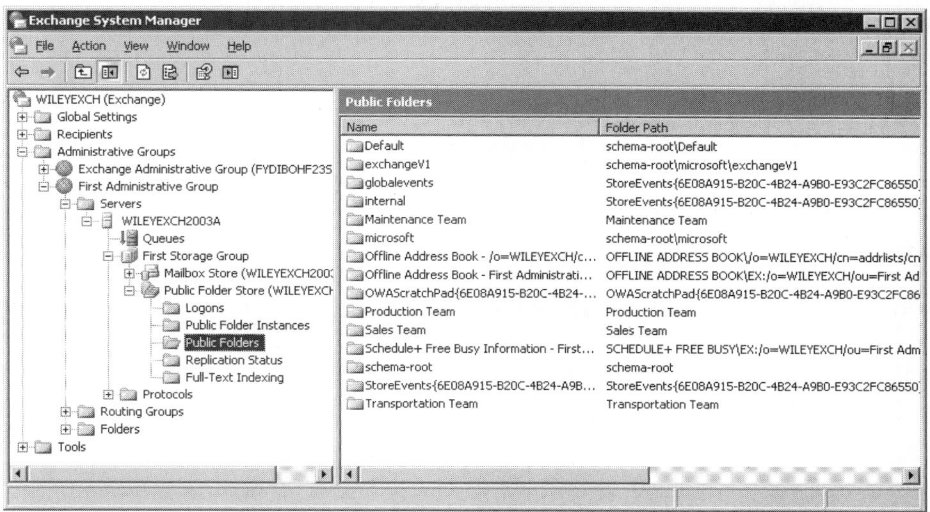

FIGURE 8.7 Public folders on WILEYEX02A

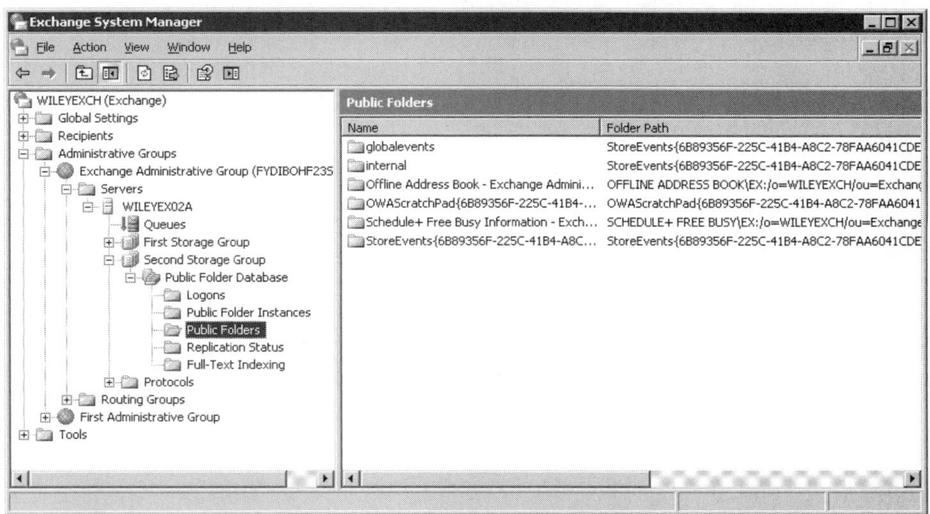

Performing Public Folder Replication

Technically, all copies of a public folder, including the one on the Exchange server where the folder was originally created, are called *replicas*. There's good reason for this. After a folder has been replicated, users will place items into it via the replica on their own default public folders server or on the nearest server as calculated using connector costs. So, no replica of the folder can be considered a master copy. The replicas of a folder update each other on a regular basis, reinforcing the idea that there is no master copy.

You can set up replication of a public folder on either the server that will provide the folder or the server that will hold the new replica of the public folder. To replicate a folder, follow the steps outlined in Exercise 8.3.

EXERCISE 8.3

Creating Public Folder Replicas

1. On a computer with the Exchange Server 2003 System Manager installed, click Start ➢ Programs ➢ Microsoft Exchange ➢ System Manager.
2. Expand the Administrative Groups node, and locate the Exchange Server 2003 Administrative Group that has the default public folder tree in it, as shown here.

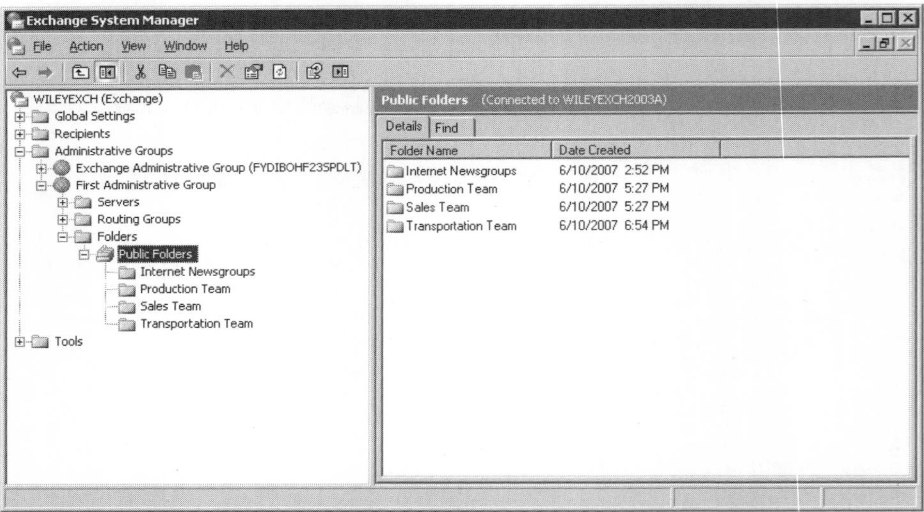

3. Right-click the folder to be replicated, and select Properties from the context menu. This opens the Properties dialog box for the public folder.

EXERCISE 8.3 *(continued)*

4. Switch to the Replication tab, as shown here.

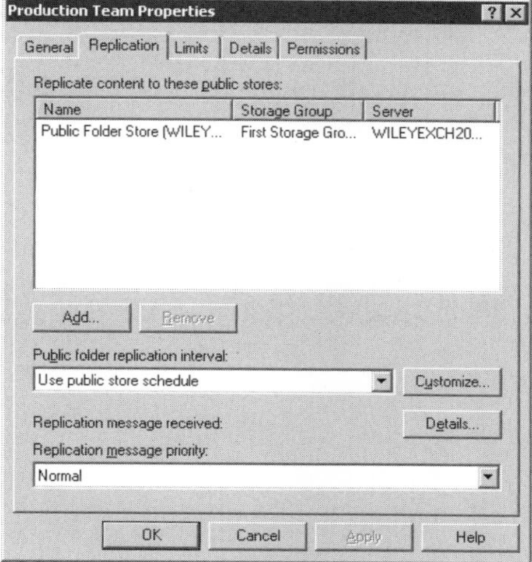

5. To add a replica of the public folder to another public folder database, in this case to replicate it from WILEYEXCH2003A (in our Exchange 2003 administrative group) to WILEYEX02A (in the Exchange 2007 administrative group), click the Add button to open the Select a Public Store dialog box, as shown here.

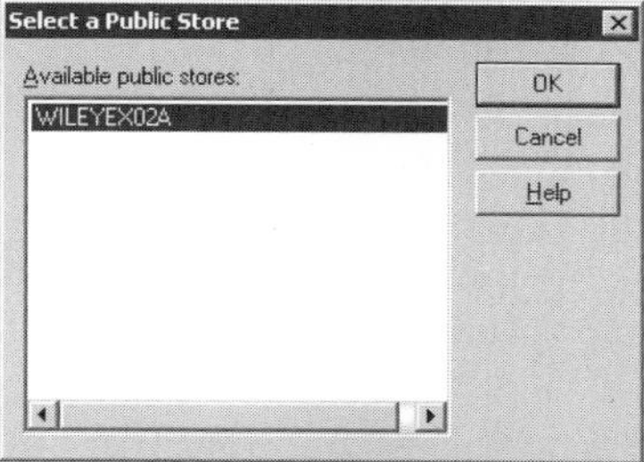

6. Select the server to add the replica to, and click OK.

7. Click OK to close the public folder's Properties dialog box.

Some of the other properties dealing with public folder replication you can configure include the schedule to replicate and the replication priority, as shown in Figure 8.8. The public folder replication interval is based on a schedule you can set. Depending on the importance of the contents of the folder and the available network bandwidth, you can accept the default

Always Run, select other options from the drop-down list, or create your own custom schedule for replication of this folder. You can give replication messages for a folder higher or lower transmission priority. Options include Not Urgent, Normal, and Urgent. Select Normal or Urgent for folders with contents of some importance to your organization; select Not Urgent for messages of lesser importance.

FIGURE 8.8 The Replication tab of the public folder's Properties dialog box

Verifying Public Folder Replication

To verify replication is working properly, you have several methods available to you. Going back to the Replication tab of the public folder's Properties dialog box, referring to Figure 8.8, you can click the Details button to open the Replication Status dialog box, as shown in Figure 8.9.

FIGURE 8.9 The Replication Status dialog box

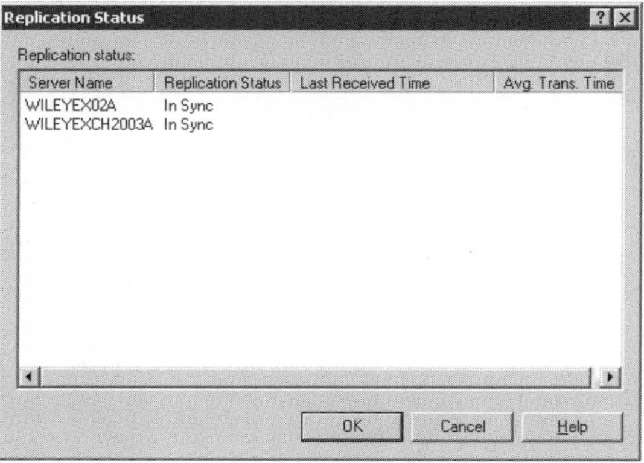

You can verify the existence of a replica on the Exchange Server 2007 Mailbox server by using the `Get-PublicFolderStatistics` cmdlet. Alternatively, you can just use the Exchange Server 2003 System Manager to examine the Public Folders node of the public folder database. The replicated public folder will show up for viewing as well.

That's really all there is to public folder replication. Monitoring replication is a matter of attending to the replication status of your replicas and, of course, ensuring that the connectors between your routing groups are up and running.

The legacy Exchange systems use a special type of public folder to hold information used by Exchange servers and their clients. However, these system folders are normally invisible to the Exchange Server 2003 System Manager. To see the system folders, right-click Public Folders in the Folders container, and select View System Folders. Some of these folders must be replicated to assure smooth functioning of your Exchange system. One of these is the Schedule + Free Busy folder, which holds calendar information for every mailbox in the administrative group. If this folder isn't available to other Mailbox servers, users will not be able to schedule meetings while looking at the free/busy times for people they want to invite. This folder's absence can also cause some Outlook clients to issue regular and very annoying warnings about not being able to find free/ busy information. Ensure that at the least the free/busy folder is visible across administrative groups, and if that's going to be a problem, consider replicating it. Do remember, though, that Exchange Server 2007 no longer requires system public folders to handle free/busy information for users on Exchange Server 2007 Mailbox servers when dealing with newer clients (Outlook 2007 and newer). Be careful about most of the other system folders. Unless you know what you're doing, let the system replicate them.

Sometimes replication doesn't seem to be happening, even though the Exchange System Manager says all is well. You can push replication along in two ways. First, make sure there is at least one item in the public folder you're replicating. Second, in the Folders\Public Folders subcontainer, right-click the folder you're interested in, and select All Tasks ➢ Send Contents. Use the Send Contents dialog box that pops up to select the server or servers you want to synchronize and the number of days into the past that you want to resend the contents.

Setting Public Folders Options

Although a good deal of public folder management has to do with replication and limits, there is more to public folder life. Let's take a look at some of the public folder configuration options available to you. You can use the Exchange Management Shell cmdlets to set these options, but we'll continue to show examples using the Exchange 2003 System Manager.

The tabs you'll see when you go to manage the properties of a public folder will depend on whether it has been mail-enabled. The General, Replication, Limits, Details, and Permissions tabs are available for all public folders, regardless of whether they've been mail-enabled. The

Exchange General, E-mail Addresses, Exchange Advanced, and Member Of tabs exist only for mail-enabled public folders. We'll cover only a few key tabs here; the rest are either secondary in nature or fairly self-explanatory.

GENERAL

The only option on this page that wasn't on the General tab of the public folder's Properties dialog box that you used to create the folder is the Address List Name field, as shown in Figure 8.10. As it is, the Address List Name field will be available only if the public folder has been mail-enabled.

FIGURE 8.10 The General tab of the public folder's Properties dialog box

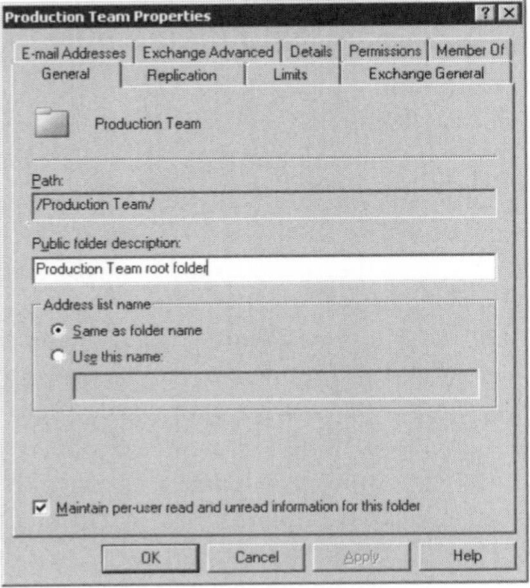

The Address List Name field allows you to have Exchange display a different name for the folder in Exchange's address lists than the name you gave the folder when you created it.

EXCHANGE GENERAL

The Exchange General tab, shown in Figure 8.11, is very much like the Exchange General tab for a mailbox. It has buttons for opening property pages for delivery restrictions (size of incoming and outgoing messages and from where messages will be received) and delivery options (delegate send-on-behalf-of permissions and set a forwarding address). These pages look and behave just like the same pages for a mailbox.

EXCHANGE ADVANCED

The Exchange Advanced tab, shown in Figure 8.12, is similar to the same tab for a mailbox. You can use it to set a simple display name and to unhide and hide a public folder from Exchange address lists. By default, a new public folder is hidden from address lists. You must deselect Hide from Exchange Address Lists to expose it to the address lists. The Exchange Advanced tab contains a Custom Attributes button. Click it to enter custom information for this recipient.

FIGURE 8.11 The Exchange General tab of the public folder's Properties dialog box

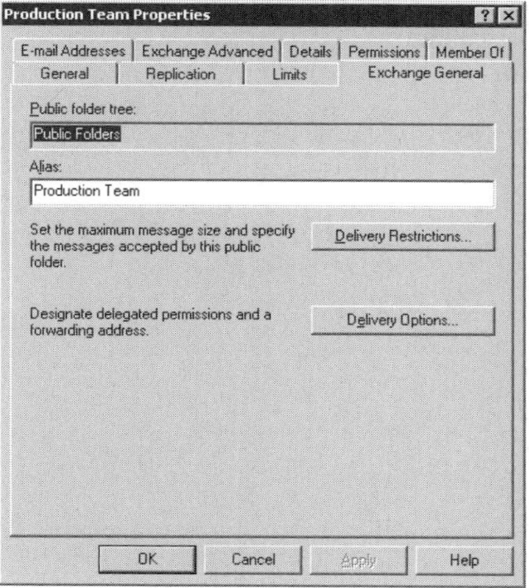

FIGURE 8.12 The Exchange Advanced tab of the public folder's Properties dialog box

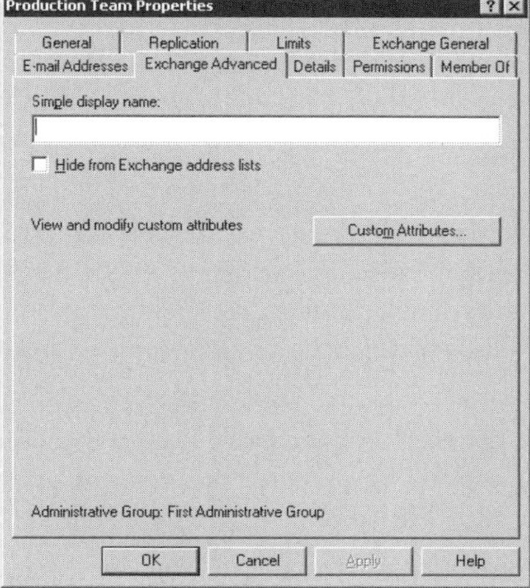

PERMISSIONS

The Permissions tab, shown in Figure 8.13, includes a range of security options. These options cover client permissions, directory rights, and administrative rights. We'll cover each of these here.

FIGURE 8.13 The Permissions tab of the public folder's Properties dialog box

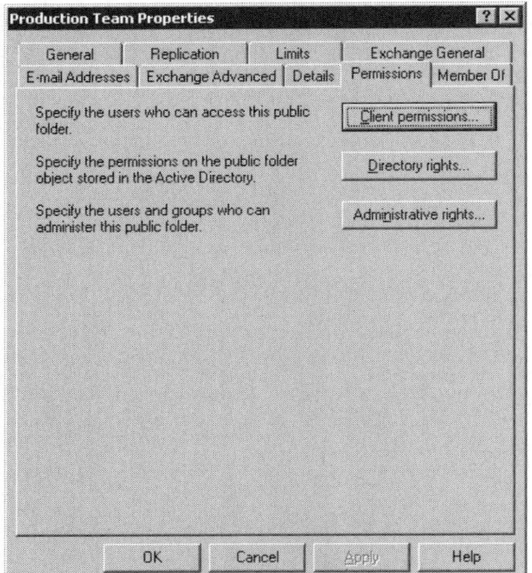

Client Permissions When you click the Client Permissions button, you open a separate Client Permissions dialog box where you assign specific folder access rights to Exchange users and distribution groups, who can then work with a public folder using their Outlook clients. For emphasis, we'll restate what we just said in a somewhat different form: you grant public folder access permissions to Exchange recipients, not to Windows 2003 users and groups. Once access to a public folder is granted, Exchange recipients access the folder in their Outlook clients while connected to their mailboxes.

To see this in action, click Add in the Client Permissions dialog box to start adding a new user or group that will have access to this public folder. This action opens a dialog box that looks very much like the Outlook Address Book that you use to select recipients to send a message to, not the dialog box that you use to select Windows 2003 users and groups. Click Cancel to exit the Add Users dialog box.

If you created the public folder in Exchange System Manager while logged in as the domain administrator, then the administrator is given the role of Owner. The owner of a public folder has complete control over the folder.

If a user has the correct permissions on a public folder, that user can change access permissions on the folder for other users. You can modify permissions on a public folder in two places. You can modify them from within the Outlook client using the Permissions tab for a public folder, and you can modify them using the Client Permissions dialog box that is available in Exchange System Manager.

Which of these you use depends on your security rights. If you are an Exchange user with no extraordinary permissions who is an owner of a public folder, you manage permissions for the folder in Outlook using the Permissions tab for a public folder. If you're an Exchange administrative user, you can change permissions on any public folder using the Client Permissions dialog box.

A group named Default includes all Exchange recipients not separately added to the Name list. When the folder is created, this group is automatically given the default role of Author. Note that Authors don't own the folder and can't create subfolders. Also note that Authors can edit and delete only their own folder items.

Microsoft has come up with several interesting roles— including Owner, Publishing Editor, Editor, Publishing Author, Author, Nonediting Author, Reviewer, Contributor, and Custom— each with a different combination of client permissions. Table 8.1 describes these permissions, descending from the permission with the most capabilities to the permission with the fewest capabilities. The word *items*, as used in this table, refers to the contents of the public folder, such as email messages, forms, documents, and other files. Table 8.2 lists the predefined groupings of permissions according to role.

TABLE 8.1 Public Folder Permissions

Permission	Description
Create Items	Can create new items in a folder.
Read Items	Can open and view items in a folder.
Create Subfolders	Can create subfolders within a folder.
Folder Owner	Can change permissions in a folder and perform administrative tasks, such as adding rules and installing forms on a folder.
Folder Contact	Receives email notifications relating to a folder. Notifications include replication conflicts, folder design conflicts, and storage limit notifications.
Folder Visible	Determines whether the folder is visible to the user in the public folder hierarchy.
Edit Items	Can edit (modify) items in a folder.
Delete Items	Can delete items in a folder.

TABLE 8.2 Predefined Roles and Their Permissions

Role	Create Items	Read Items	Create Subfolders	Folder Owner	Folder Contact	Folder Visible	Edit Items	Delete Items
Owner	Yes	Yes	Yes	Yes	Yes	Yes	All	All
Publishing Editor	Yes	All	Yes	No	No	Yes	All	All
Editor	Yes	All	No	No	No	Yes	All	All
Publishing Author	Yes	Yes	Yes	No	No	Yes	Own	Own
Author	Yes	Yes	No	No	No	Yes	Own	Own
Nonediting Author	Yes	Yes	No	No	No	Yes	None	None
Contributor	Yes	No	No	No	No	Yes	None	None
Reviewer	No	Yes	No	No	No	Yes	None	None
None	No	No	No	No	No	Yes	None	None

Custom roles consisting of any combination of individual permissions may also be assigned.

When a public folder is created, the following three users are included on the permissions list by default:

The user who created the public folder This user is automatically assigned the Owner role.

A special user named Default This user represents all users who have access to the public folder store but aren't explicitly listed in the permissions list. In top-level folders, the Default user is automatically granted the Author role (this can be modified). Below the top-level folders, the Default user automatically inherits the permissions it has at its parent folder.

A special user named Anonymous The Anonymous user represents all users logged on with Anonymous access. For example, an Exchange server could contain public folders holding promotional information for public viewing. People without user accounts could use a web browser or newsreader program and the Anonymous account to access the Exchange server and read the promotional information. Any permissions assigned to the Anonymous account are applied to these users.

Exchange administrators can always designate themselves as the owners of public folders. This is especially important if the recipient who is the owner of a public folder (or all Active Directory accounts that are on the permissions list of that recipient) is deleted.

Directory Rights Users and groups with appropriate permissions at the directory rights level can change the properties of a public folder object in Active Directory. The Directory Rights tab that pops up when you click the Directory Rights button is the same as the Security tab for other Exchange recipients. That's why public folders don't have a Security tab.

Administrative Rights Administrative rights are permissions to manage a public folder using Exchange System Manager. Click the Administrative Rights button to open the Administrative Rights tab. Administrative permissions include rights to modify the public folder access control list and the public folder administrative access control list. These rights include permission to use the Directory Rights tab and the Administrative Rights tab, the very tab we're talking about right now. Permissions also include the right to set the deleted-item retention time and space quotas for the public folder. You had the option of exercising both of these rights on the Limits tab when you created your public folder earlier in this chapter.

We'll conclude this section by pointing out that administrative rights are granted to Windows 2003 users and security groups, not to Exchange recipients and distribution groups as in versions of Exchange prior to Exchange Server 2000.

Configuring Client Connectivity

As has been said about numerous things over time, build it, and they will come. This is of course true about your Exchange organization when referring to clients wanting to access the data contained within. If your only worry was supporting Outlook MAPI clients and Outlook Web Access HTTP clients, then you'd really have nothing to worry about. In real life, that's almost certainly not going to be the case. You're likely to have IMAP4 or even POP3 clients in your organization, especially if you support Apple computers on your network. As well, you could certainly expect to see Windows Mobile devices start to make an appearance on your network as the push to make as much data accessible all the time continues. Even if you don't end up supporting other client protocols, you'll still have a need to learn about the new features of Autodiscover and the Availability service, so don't skim the following sections too quickly!

Using Autodiscover

Exchange 2007 introduces a new feature called Autodiscover that Outlook 2007 and newer clients can use. Autodiscover is a web service that resides on the Exchange 2007 Client Access server role. The popular notion of Autodiscover is that it helps Outlook 2007 automatically locate an Exchange 2007 server, and that is correct. However, Autodiscover actually helps Outlook locate a number of different types of Exchange resources, including the following:

- User's home Mailbox server
- Outlook Anywhere URL
- URL (internal or external) for the Offline Address Book
- URL (internal or external) for unified messaging
- URL (internal or external) for the Availability service

When a user launches Outlook 2007 for the first time, they are prompted for some basic information (email address or domain/username and password). Outlook 2007 contacts the Autodiscover web service and looks up information such as the home Mailbox server, display name, and URLs for Outlook features such as free/busy information, and the Offline Address Book. If this information is changed, then the Outlook client gets updated information (including the home Mailbox server name) from the Autodiscover service.

When the user specifies their email address, they should use their default SMTP address. Autodiscover may not work for additional SMTP addresses.

Internal vs. External Autodiscover

Outlook 2007 uses two approaches to locate an Autodiscover site and determine the necessary information. It uses the first approach when the Windows computer is a member of the Active Directory forest in which the Exchange server exists. Figure 8.14 shows the process that Outlook uses to locate resources. In this example, the computer on which Outlook 2007 is installed is a member of the Active Directory forest. This is considered the service process for internal clients.

In step 1 in Figure 8.14, Outlook is launched for the first time, and there is no Outlook profile for the user account. Outlook contacts Active Directory to find a service connection point (SCP). A *service connection point* is an Active Directory object that can be used to publish and locate network services. The SCP object will provide Outlook with the fully qualified domain names of Client Access servers; Outlook contacts a Client Access server in its local Active Directory site.

FIGURE 8.14 The Autodiscover process when a client is in the same Active Directory forest

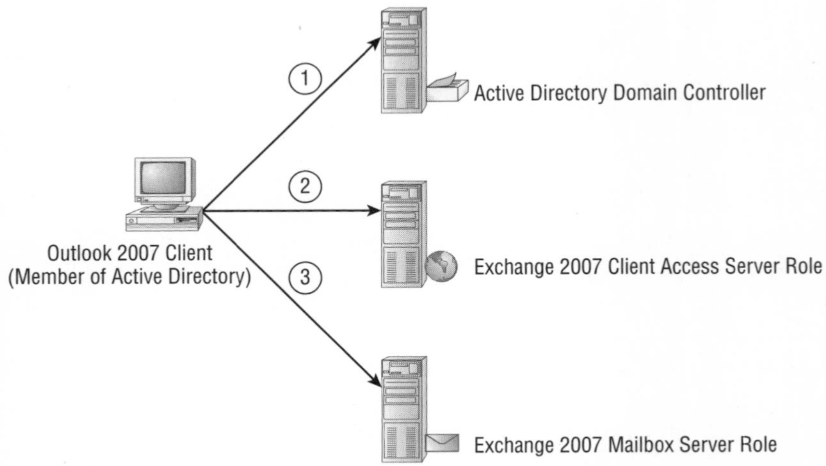

In step 2, the Outlook 2007 client queries the Client Access server to retrieve the user's home server. The username and domain name are used to locate the user's home Mailbox server. Outlook also retrieves information about the location of the Availability service and the distribution points for the OAB. From this information, the Outlook profile is created.

In step 3, Outlook connects to the user's home Exchange server.

If the desktop client is not a member of the Active Directory or is outside the corporate network and cannot contact a domain controller, then Outlook 2007 uses a different approach. This is the Autodiscover service process for external access. In this approach, DNS is used to locate the Autodiscover service. Figure 8.15 shows an example of how the Autodiscover service is located for an external client. In this example, the user must provide their email address since it cannot be provided for them using their Active Directory user account.

In step 1, Outlook tries to contact an Active Directory domain controller (if the client is a member of the Active Directory). If Active Directory cannot be located or the computer is not a member of the Active Directory, the user is presented with the Add New E-mail Account dialog box, as shown in Figure 8.16. In this dialog box, the user must enter their primary STMP address, their name, and their account password. The email address is important because the STMP domain name is used in step 2.

FIGURE 8.15 The Autodiscover process when a client is not in the same Active Directory forest

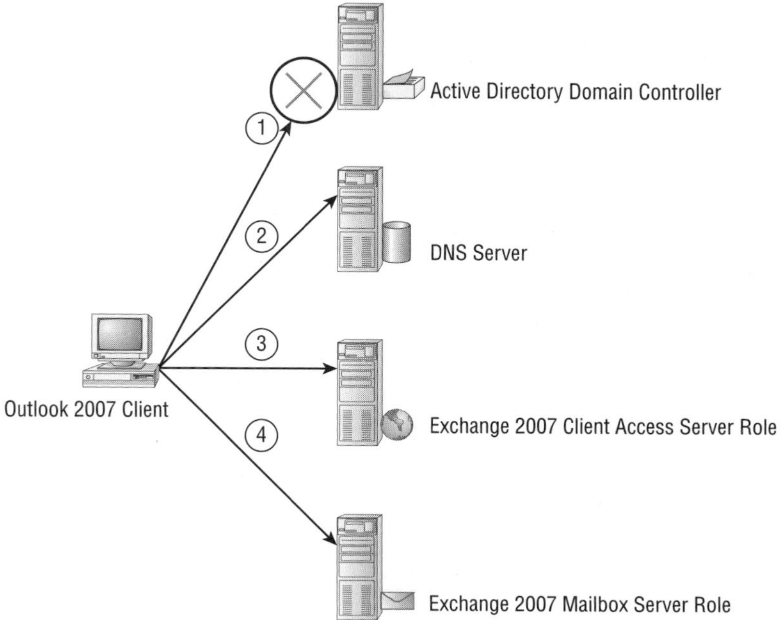

FIGURE 8.16 Providing account information manually to Outlook

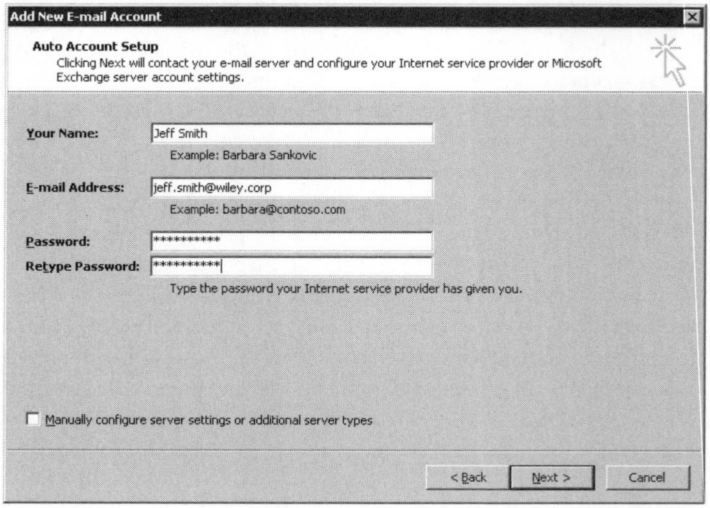

In step 2, the Outlook 2007 client performs a DNS query and uses the SMTP domain name. In our example, the domain name is wiley.corp. Outlook will use the following URLs to try to connect in order to locate the Autodiscover server:

```
https://wiley.corp/autodiscover/autodiscover.xml
https://autodiscover.wiley.corp/autodiscover/autodiscover.xml
```

These URLs will need to be resolvable in DNS and accessible from outside your network for external clients. If you will use the DNS approach for "external" clients on your inside network, you will want to make sure that one of these two URLs is resolvable using your internal DNS.

The Client Access server that hosts the Autodiscover URL will then return the Outlook Anywhere information necessary to configure Outlook 2007 as well as external URL locations for the Availability service and the Offline Address Book distribution point.

Configuring Autodiscover

When an Exchange 2007 Client Access server is installed, an SCP record is created in Active Directory for it. This includes the internal Outlook Anywhere settings, the internal URL for the OAB, and the internal URL for Exchange web services. However, depending on your environment, you may need to configure additional settings, if, for example, you needed to enable Outlook Anywhere (formerly RPC over HTTP) or define external URLs for other web services.

Configuring Autodiscover Virtual Directories

An Autodiscover virtual directory is automatically created on each Exchange 2007 Client Access server. The only way to configure this is through the Exchange Management Shell. The `Get-AutoDiscoverVirtualDirectory` cmdlet will let you view the Autodiscover virtual directories.

Configuring Outlook Anywhere and Autodiscover

By default, Outlook Anywhere is not enabled on the Client Access servers. To enable Outlook Anywhere, locate each Client Access server in the Server Configuration work center in the Exchange Management Console, and select the Enable Outlook Anywhere task in the Actions pane. This launches a wizard that prompts you for the external hostname and the type of authentication and gives you the option to use SSL offloading, as shown in Figure 8.17.

FIGURE 8.17 Enabling Outlook Anywhere

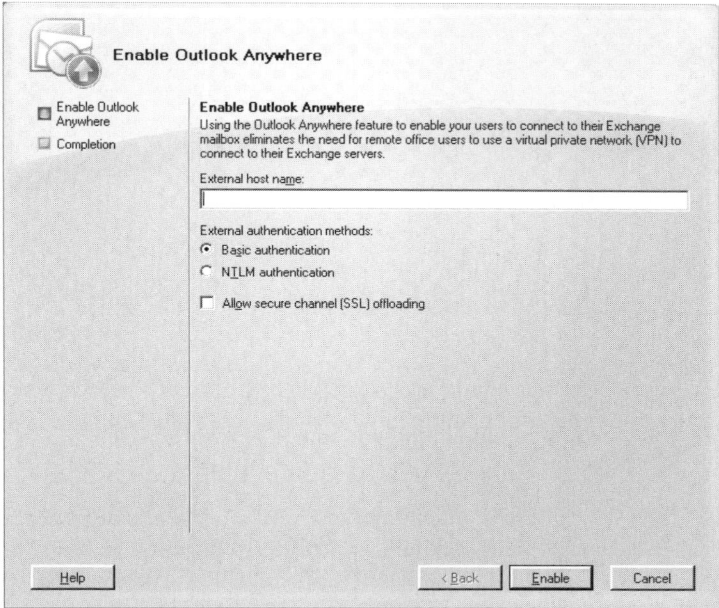

If you are using network load balancing, the external hostname will be the fully qualified domain name that the clients will use externally. When you have completed the information required by the wizard, you can click the Enable Outlook Anywhere button.

Optionally, you could enable Outlook Anywhere using the `Enable-OutlookAnywhere` cmdlet. Here is an example:

```
Enable-OutlookAnywhere -Server "WILEYEX02A"
-ExternalHostname "outlook.wiley.com"
-ExternalAuthenticationMethod "Basic" -SSLOffloading $false
```

Once Outlook Anywhere is enabled, you can select the properties of the Client Access server and view the Outlook Anywhere properties of that particular Client Access server. Figure 8.18 shows an example.

FIGURE 8.18 Configuring the external hostname for Outlook Anywhere

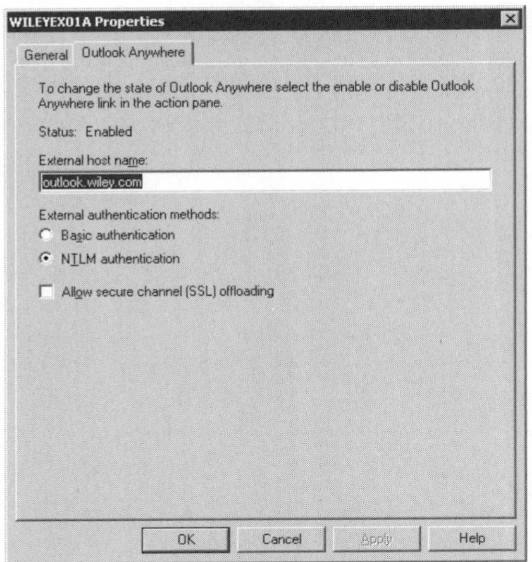

Refer to Chapter 4 for some additional discussion on Outlook Anywhere.

You can retrieve the same information (and more) using the `Get-OutlookAnywhere` cmdlet. When configuring the external hostname for Outlook Anywhere, remember that this is the URL that will be referred to external Outlook 2007 clients when Autodiscover is used.

Configuring Offline Address Books and Autodiscover

The Offline Address Book distribution points by default contain only the internal URL used to locate them. You can set these using the graphical user interface by selecting the properties of the Offline Address Book virtual directory in the Exchange Management Console. Figure 8.19 shows the URLs tab of the OAB (Default Web Site) virtual directory's Properties dialog box for a Client Access server.

You can also set this parameter using the cmdlet `Set-OABVirtualDirectory`. Here is an example:

```
Set-OABVirtualDirectory "WILEYEX02A\OAB (Default Web Site)"
-ExternalURL https://outlook.wiley.com/OAB -RequireSSL:$True
```

You can view the configuration of the Offline Address Book virtual directory using the `Get-OABVirtualDirectory` cmdlet.

FIGURE 8.19 Setting the external URL for Offline Address Book distribution

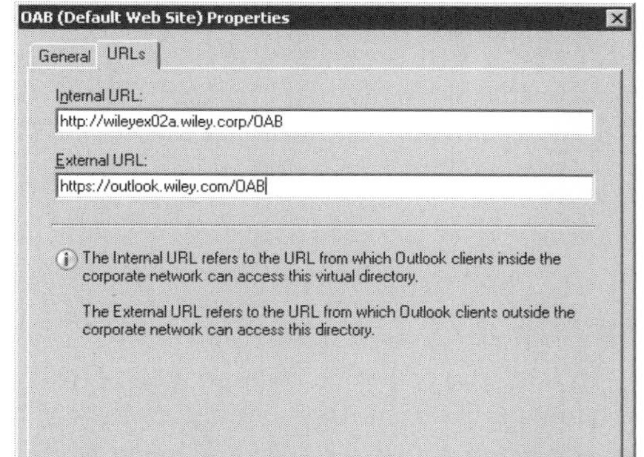

Configuring Web Services and Autodiscover

If remote or external clients will need access to custom web services, you should configure the external URL for web services. You can do this only via the Exchange Management Shell. The following cmdlet is an example for setting the external URL for a Client Access server:

```
Set-WebServicesVirtualDirectory "WILEYEX02A\EWS (Default web site)"
-ExternalUrl "https://ooutlook.wiley.com/EWS/Exchange.asmx"
-BasicAuthentication:$True
```

To check the configuration of the Web Services virtual directory, you can use the `Get-WebServicesVirtualDirectory` cmdlet.

Configuring Autodiscover and Secure Sockets Layer

If you have tried to deploy both internal and external URLs already, then you are already wondering how Secure Sockets Layer is supposed to work if the FQDN of the internal location is different from the external FQDN. After all, if certificates are requested, you usually provide only one name in the certificate-signing request. There is a workaround, however, that allows you to have more than one DNS domain name for a Client Access server. To do this, you have to use the `New-ExchangeCertificate` cmdlet. The command line is fairly involved; here is an example:

```
New-ExchangeCertificate -generaterequest
-subjectname "dc=com,dc=wiley,o=Wiley Publishing, cn=outlook.wiley.com"
-domainname WILEYEX02A, WILEYEX02A.wiley.corp,outlook.wiley.com,
autodiscover.wiley.com -path c:\certrequest-WILEYEX02A.txt
```

This cmdlet creates a certificate request with multiple hostnames. In this case, the hostnames include outlook.wiley.com, autodiscover.wiley.com, WILEYEX02A, and WILEYEX02A.wiley.corp.

You can take the contents of this file and get a certificate signed and issued by a trusted certificate authority, or you could sign it yourself using Windows Certificate Server. The result will be a file that is returned to you from the certification authority (in this case, certnew.cer). Here is an example of using the `Import-ExchangeCertificate` cmdlet to import the signed certificate into the certificate store:

```
Import-ExchangeCertificate -path c:\certnew.cer -friendlyname "WILEYEX02A Cert"
```

If you are used to creating certificate requests using the Internet Information Services Manager console, then there is a new step you may not be familiar with. The `Import-ExchangeCertificate` cmdlet imports the certificate into the computer's personal certificate store, but it does not assign it to the default website. You will need to perform the steps in Exercise 8.4 to associate the certificate with the default website.

EXERCISE 8.4

Installing an SSL Certificate

1. Click Start ➢ Programs ➢ Administrative Tools ➢ Internet Information Services (IIS) Manager.
2. Open the Web Sites container, right-click Default Web Site, and select Properties.
3. Select the Directory Security tab.
4. Click the Server Certificate button, and then click Next.
5. Select the Assign an Existing Certificate radio button, and click Next.
6. In the Select a Certificate list, select the certificate you have just imported using the `Import-ExchangeCertificate` cmdlet. When you have selected the certificate, click Next.
7. Confirm that port 443 is the SSL port, which is usually the case. Click Next.
8. On the Certificate Summary page, you can see some of the details of the certificate. When you are ready, click Next, and then click Finish.

Congratulations! The certificate is now installed and associated with the default website. On the Directory Security tab, you can click the View Certificate button to see more details about the certificate.

Supporting POP3 and IMAP4 Clients

POP3 and IMAP4 are probably the most basic email protocols in use. With SMTP, they are the most straightforward of the email delivery mechanisms, and virtually every email server available supports them. However, they do have their drawbacks, particularly when used with Exchange.

For example, if you collect your email with POP3 from your Exchange mailbox, all email in the mailbox will be marked as read whether or not the message has actually been read on the client.

The other major issue with POP3 is that it is designed to remove the email from the server and store it locally. It is easy to make an error in configuration and remove all the email from the server. Although there are options to leave email on the server, it's easy to overlook them.

Things are a little better with IMAP4 because the email is actually stored on the server. However, you still are limited on the functionality from Exchange compared to the full Outlook client or Outlook Web Access.

As such, POP3/IMAP4 access should be the last access protocol of choice, and where possible you should not be supporting it. However, in some environments such as academic environments, POP3 and IMAP4 clients are popular and must still be supported.

POP3 and IMAP4 are disabled by default in Exchange 2007, and there is no GUI configuration available through the Exchange Management Console. You must configure the protocols using the Exchange Management Shell.

You can configure SMTP for use by POP3/IMAP4 clients using the Management Console. However, you may want to look at deploying TLS/SMTP because the standard port 25 is often blocked for accessing remote SMTP servers from home user–type connections, meaning the POP3/IMAP4 clients will be unable to send email through your server.

Either way, because of the nature of the protocols, keeping a copy of the messages for compliance reasons is almost impossible. The user could send the message through another SMTP server, so there will be no trace of the message on your server.

If you need to track email messages for compliance reasons, you should look at using a MAPI connection such as Outlook Web Access or Outlook Anywhere.

Configuring Exchange to Support POP3 and IMAP4 Clients

Configuring Exchange Server 2007 to support POP3 or IMAP4 clients requires a couple of steps. These include enabling the services and configuring the Client Access servers to support these protocols.

Enabling the Services

Before clients can connect to the POP3 or IMAP4 services, the services must be enabled and started because they are set to start manually. You can enable POP3 and IMAP4 in two ways. As with Exchange 2003, you can change the service in the Services console, shown in Figure 8.20, from Disabled to Automatic and then start the service.

You can also enable the services through the Exchange Management Shell. To enable POP3, use the following command:

```
Set-Service msExchangePOP3 -startuptype automatic
```

Once it's enabled, you need to start the service by using the following command:

```
Start-Service -service msExchangePOP3
```

For IMAP4, the procedure is almost identical:

```
Set-Service msExchangeIMAP4 -startuptype automatic
```

FIGURE 8.20 Configuring POP3 and IMAP4 services

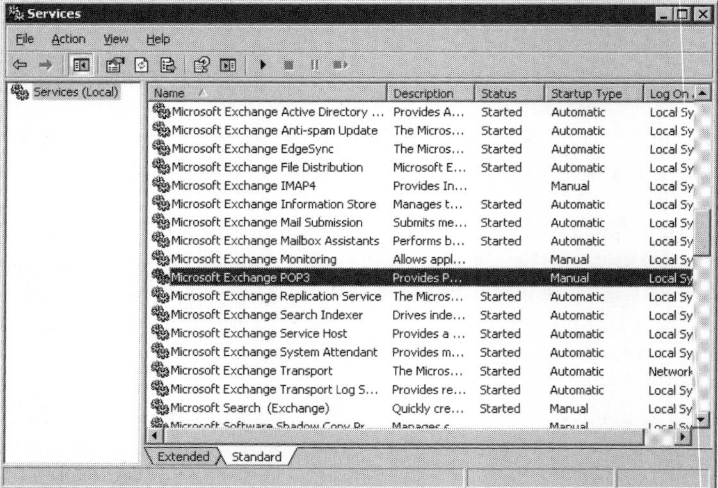

To start the service, use the following command:

```
Start-Service msExchangeIMAP4
```

Configuring POP3 and IMAP4: Server

Once you have enabled the services, you can configure them. You must do this through the Exchange Management Shell. The default settings may be suitable for you. You can check the current settings using the following commands:

- POP3: `Get-PopSettings`
- IMAP4: `Get-ImapSettings`

The only additional configuration you may want to cover is enabling TLS/SSL support, which we won't be discussing here.

You can find more information about securing POP3 and IMAP4 at the following TechNet location: `http://technet.microsoft.com/en-us/library/bb430779.aspx`.

Configuring POP3 and IMAP4: Mailboxes

By default, all user accounts are enabled for POP3 and IMAP4 access. Therefore, you may want to review the accounts and disable that functionality for those users who will not be accessing Exchange using POP3 or IMAP4. You do this using the `Set-CASMailbox` command.

For example, to disable POP3 for a user robert.jones@wiley.com, use the following command:

```
Set-CASMailbox -identity robert.jones@wiley.com -POPEnabled:$false
```

You can view the status of the mailboxes simply by entering the command `Get-CASMailbox`, which will display all mailboxes in the Exchange organization and whether they are enabled.

Configuring a Receive Connector for Use with POP3 and IMAP4

POP3/IMAP4 clients need to have an SMTP connector through which to send their outbound email. For Exchange 2007, that means a receive connector must be configured to accept their messages and allow them to be relayed through the server to the clients.

There should already be a connector configured that is suitable for use, which is called Client *servername*. You can see this using the Exchange Management Console or using the Management Shell command `Get-ReceiveConnector`.

This default connector should require little configuration. Note that this connector is configured to use port 587, which is the TLS port. It uses the certificate that is installed on the Exchange server during installation. If you intend to have clients relay email through the server on this port, then you need to either import the certificate to their machine so that it is trusted or replace the certificate with one from a trusted CA.

If you want to use the standard TCP port 25 to relay email, you need to review the configuration of the server connector. In all cases, basic authentication needs to be enabled on the connector because it is the only type of authentication that SMTP clients support. You can also use basic authentication requiring TLS.

Configuring a POP3 or IMAP4 Client

You will no doubt be familiar with the configuration of POP3/IMAP4 clients and SMTP. For Exchange, it is almost the same as any Internet email account you may have configured. For the server address of the POP3, IMAP4, and SMTP servers, you should use a hostname.

Although you can use an IP address, if you ever need to change the IP address of the server, it is far easier to change a single DNS entry than to try to get many users to update their email client configurations.

What you use for your hostnames is up to you—as long as they resolve correctly on the Internet. You may already have a hostname setup that points to your Exchange server used for MX records. If so, you could use the same hostname in the account settings. Alternatively, if you think you might change the configuration in the future so that the servers are different, you may want to use pop3.domain.com, imap4.domain.com, and smtp.domain.com, with them all pointing at the same IP address. If you need to change them later, simply adjust the DNS records.

If you are using TLS/SSL for account access, ensure that you change the port setting in the email client to use the alternative port. This is often found in the advanced settings.

Finally, you need to enter credentials. For Exchange, these credentials need to be in a specific format:

- For POP3 and IMAP4 access, it is in the format of *`domain\username\alias`*.
- For SMTP access, it is in the format of *`domain\username`*.
- In both cases, you can also use the UPN, *`username@domain.local`*.

The choice of authentication format is up to you and what you think will be easiest to support. We suggest deciding on one format and then sticking to it so it is easier to write documentation and help guides while maintaining some consistency.

Configuring Windows Mobile Devices and ActiveSync

Currently two ActiveSync applications are available from Microsoft. First, the traditional ActiveSync is an application that is installed on the desktop machine and allows synchronization through Outlook. Second, with Exchange 2003, Microsoft introduced Exchange ActiveSync (EAS), which allows synchronization directly to the Exchange server over a network or Internet connection. This was initially on-demand sync, but Exchange 2003 Service Pack 2 enabled the "push mail" feature using HTTP or HTTPS. Push email enables email to be synchronized with the device as new messages arrive; when a message arrives in the user's Inbox, the Exchange server notifies connected mobile devices that a new message must be synchronized to the device.

Exchange 2007 takes EAS and has further enhanced it; however, to take full advantage of the new features in EAS, you need to be using Windows Mobile 6.0.

Exchange ActiveSync was available with Windows Mobile 2003 but really became popular only with Windows Mobile 5. To use the push technology, you need to have a device with the Messaging and Security Feature Pack (MSFP) installed. This is not available as a separate download but will be part of a software update from the handset supplier.

You must obtain Microsoft Messaging and Security Feature Pack updates for mobile devices or Windows Mobile 6 updates from the device vendor or the cell phone provider, not Microsoft.

If you have purchased a device since approximately June 2006, it almost certainly will come with a version of Windows Mobile 5.0 with MSFP. Many devices that run Windows Mobile 5 can be upgraded to the MSFP version.

How Can You Tell Whether Your Device Has the MSFP?

You can identify whether your handset has the MSFP update in two ways. In both cases you need to look at the version information. You can find this by selecting Settings ➢ System in the About applet.

You need to look at the version information. You will see a string that is something like OS 5.1.195 (Build 14847.2.0.0), as shown in Figure 8.21. With some handsets, the build number says Messaging and Security Feature Pack. If that is the case, you know for sure. If yours does not, then you need to look at the build number. The key element is the last three digits. To have the MSFP installed, it needs to be 2.0.0 or higher. Build 2.0.0 was the first build to have the MSFP update.

We wrote this chapter using Windows Mobile 5.0 and are presuming you are using a Windows Mobile–based device with at least that version of the software. You can find instructions for the older versions of Windows Mobile on Microsoft's website at `www.microsoft.com`.

Configuring Exchange to Support ActiveSync

Exchange ActiveSync should be enabled by default from the standard installation of the Client Access server role. You can confirm whether this is the case by checking for the presence of a number of elements in Internet Information Services (IIS) Manager. In the IIS Manager under Default Web Site, as shown in Figure 8.22, check to see whether the virtual directory Microsoft-Server-ActiveSync exists.

FIGURE 8.21 Viewing the Windows Mobile version information

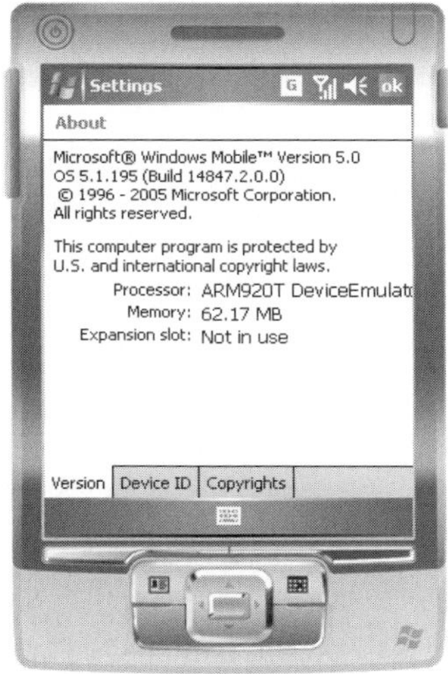

FIGURE 8.22 Viewing the Exchange virtual directories and application pools

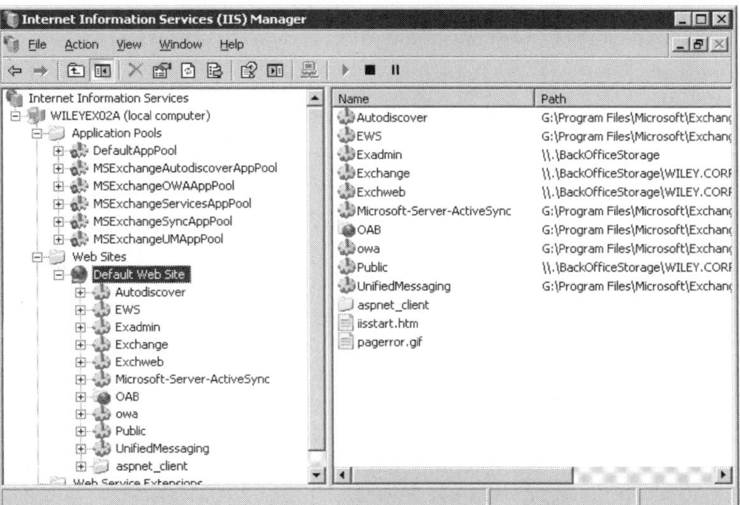

As an administrator, you will want to test Windows Mobile for yourself; however, getting hold of a device with the relevant software may be difficult. Microsoft has released an emulator for Windows Mobile, which was originally designed for developer use but is now available as a stand-alone product. You can install this on your workstation and connect to the Exchange server over your network. At the time of this writing, you can download the emulator from the Microsoft downloads site by searching for "Standalone Device Emulator 1.0 with Windows Mobile OS Images" at `www.microsoft.com/downloads/`.

You can also check the Exchange-related application pools by right-clicking an application pool, such as the `MSExchangeSyncAppPool` application pool. If Start is available, then EAS is not running. Choose Start to enable the application pool.

You can do additional configuration of ActiveSync through the Exchange Management Console. Under Server Configuration, choose the Exchange ActiveSync tab. Right-click the virtual directory listed, and choose Properties. You'll see three tabs. The first tab, General, allows you to set the internal and external URL for ActiveSync. The second tab, Authentication, allows you to control authentication, including whether to use client certificates. The third tab allows you to control remote file server access. This is identical in operation to remote file server access through Outlook Web Access but is not available with the current versions of Windows Mobile.

For Exchange Management Shell configuration, you use two cmdlets:

- The cmdlet `New-ActiveSyncVirtualDirectory` will allow you to create a new virtual directory for another website on the same server.
- The cmdlet `Set-ActiveSyncVirtualDirectory` allows you to change settings for the ActiveSync virtual directory. This includes settings not available to you through the Exchange Management Console. This command will enable basic authentication on a server named WILEYEX02A:

```
Set-ActiveSyncVirtualDirectory
-Identity "EXCHANGE01\microsoft-server-activesync"
-BasicAuthEnabled:$true
```

Defining an ActiveSync Policy

An ActiveSync policy allows you to define certain settings for the devices. With Exchange 2003, the policy applied to all devices, or there were exceptions for certain users. The level of control was very low. You can now have different settings for different users, allowing you more control over the devices—possibly depending on each user's job function.

ActiveSync policies are Exchange organization-wide, so you set them in the Organization Configuration ➤ Client Access node of the Exchange System Manager, as shown in Figure 8.23.

The policy is divided into two main areas: access and password.

The General tab of the ActiveSync policy's Properties dialog box, as shown in Figure 8.24, is for access-related settings. You can define whether attachments are downloaded to the device, configure access to Universal Naming Convention (UNC) and Windows SharePoint Services (WSS) servers, and choose whether nonprovisionable devices can be configured.

FIGURE 8.23 Viewing ActiveSync policies

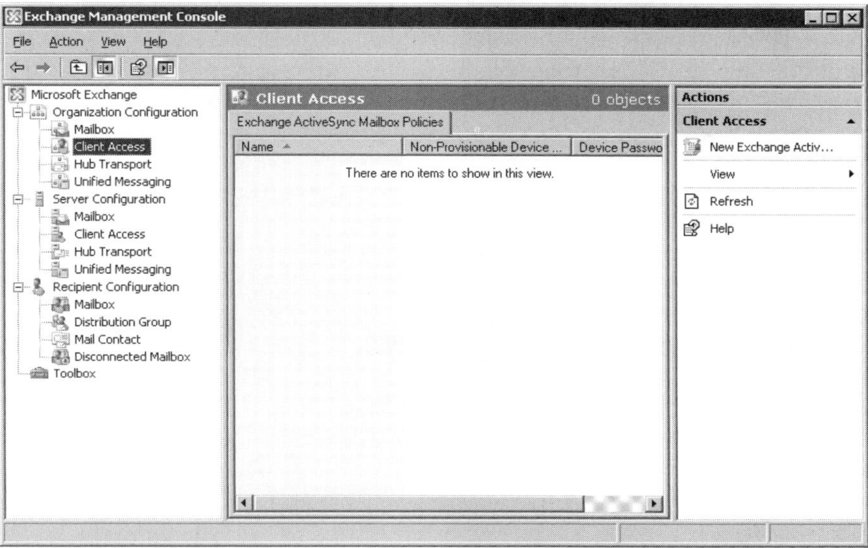

FIGURE 8.24 The General tab of the ActiveSync policy's Properties dialog box

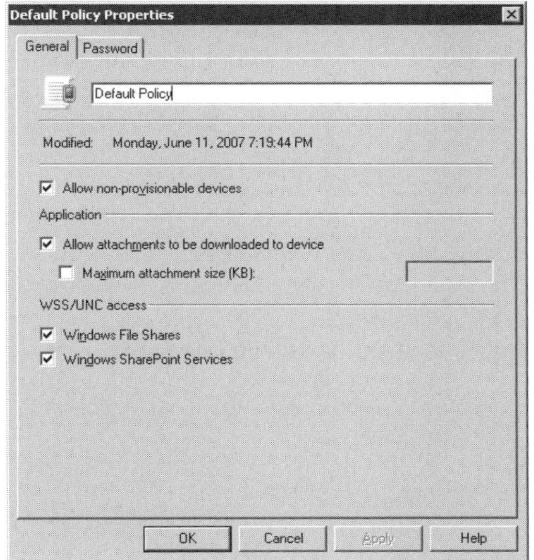

Nonprovisionable devices are devices that do not support the Autodiscover service. Most sites will need to enable nonprovisionable devices, at least initially until their devices or all users are using a version of Windows Mobile that supports provisioning via Autodiscover.

The Password tab of the ActiveSync policy Properties dialog box, as shown in Figure 8.25, is for the password policy. The settings on this tab are fairly self-explanatory. If you want to take advantage of the remote wipe features, you need to require a password. If you do not, when you attempt to wipe the device, the user will be asked to allow enforcement of a password policy. By saying no, they can maintain access to the device. Allow Simple Password is a policy that allows the user to set a password such as 1234. If you have policies regarding passwords, you may not want to enable that option.

FIGURE 8.25 The Password tab of the ActiveSync policy's Properties dialog box

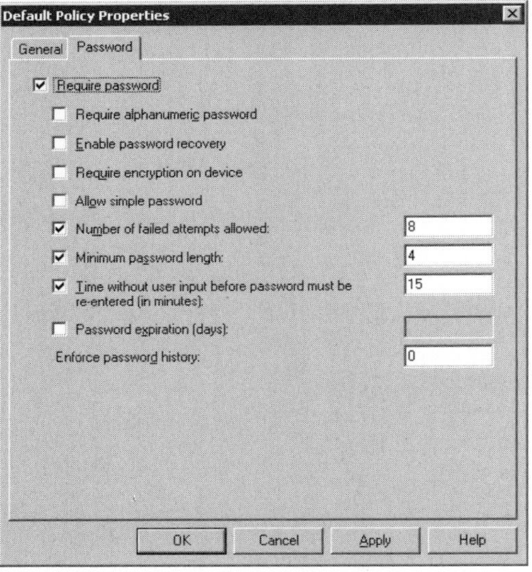

You can have more than one ActiveSync policy; to create another one, select New ActiveSync Policy from the Actions pane in the Exchange Management Console, or run the cmdlet `New-ActiveSyncPolicy` with the required parameters.

This command will create a new policy called Sales, with Device Password enabled:

```
New-ActiveSyncMailboxPolicy -Name:"Sales" -DevicePasswordEnabled:$true
```

You can assign a policy to each user as required. To set a policy to a user through the Exchange Management Console, follow the steps in Exercise 8.5.

EXERCISE 8.5

Assigning an ActiveSync Policy to a User

1. Click Start ➢ Programs ➢ Microsoft Exchange Server 2007, and then select Exchange Management Console.
2. Expand the Microsoft Exchange root object, expand the Recipient Configuration folder, and then click the Mailbox node.
3. In the Actions pane on the right, click the Properties link to open the mailbox user's Properties dialog box.
4. Click the Mailbox Features tab, as shown here.

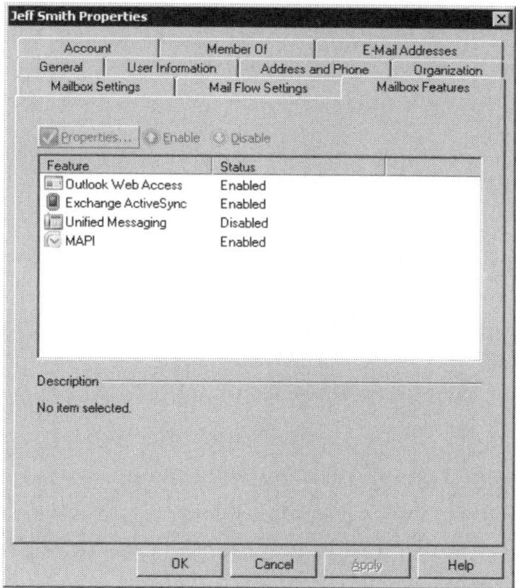

5. Click the Exchange ActiveSync item, and then click the Properties button. The Exchange ActiveSync Properties dialog box opens, as shown here.

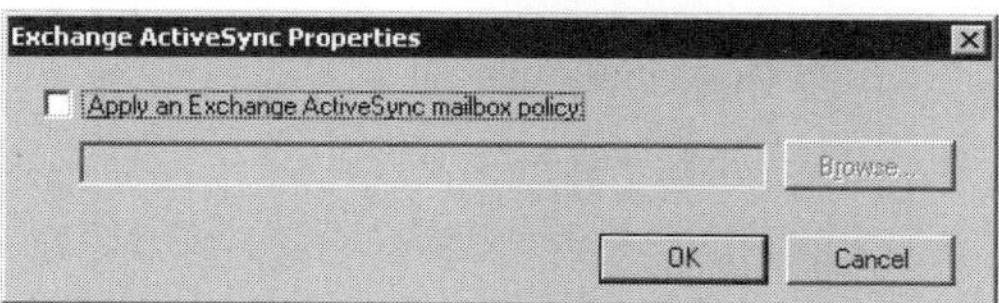

6. Click the Apply an Exchange ActiveSync Policy option, and then click Browse to locate a policy to apply.
7. Click OK to close the Exchange ActiveSync Properties dialog box.
8. Click OK to close the mailbox user Properties dialog box.

If you want to set multiple users at the same time, you need to use the Exchange Management Shell. To set the policy through the Exchange Management Shell, use the `Set-CASMailbox` command. For example, to set the policy Sales on user rick.jones, run the following:

```
Set-CASMailbox Rick.Jones -ActiveSyncMailboxPolicy
(Get-ActiveSyncMailboxPolicy "Sales").Identity
```

If you want to set a policy to all users, which may be a good way to start off, you have to use a combination of commands. This command will set the policy Default Policy on all users:

```
Get-Mailbox | Set-CASMailbox -ActiveSyncMailboxPolicy
(Get-ActiveSyncMailboxPolicy "Default Policy").Identity
```

Configuring a Windows Mobile Device

This section guides you through configuring a Windows Mobile device. These instructions and screen shots were created using the Windows Mobile 5.0 emulator, which is running build 2.0.0.

Therefore, you may find that a few screens look slightly different from what is shown here. The entries are identical, so it should be easy enough to adapt to the later versions of Windows Mobile that are released after this book is published.

To configure your device to sync with Exchange, follow the steps outlined in Exercise 8.6.

EXERCISE 8.6

Configuring ActiveSync on a Mobile Device

1. Select ActiveSync from Programs. If this is the first time you have configured ActiveSync, you should simply select the text Set Up Your Device to Sync with It, as shown here. If you already have ActiveSync configured to synchronize with a desktop, then you can change the settings from the menu or use ActiveSync on the desktop to configure synchronization with a server.

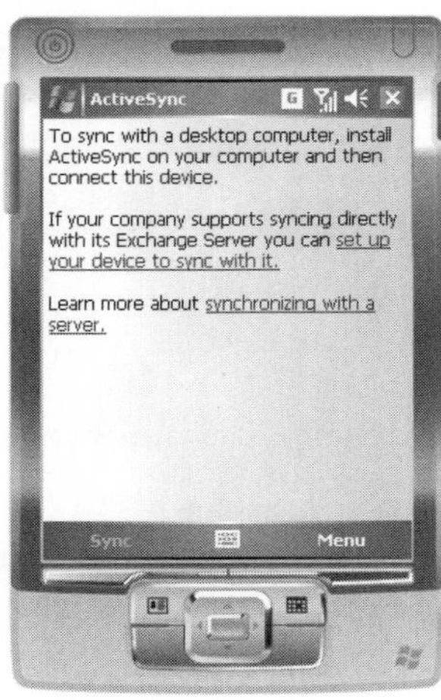

EXERCISE 8.6 *(continued)*

2. You will be asked for the server address, as shown here. This needs to be the external name of the Exchange server—for example, mail.domain.com. If you are going to use SSL, then the name needs to match what is on the certificate. The certificate also needs to be trusted by the device (either because you are using a commercial certificate that has a root certificate in the device or because you have imported the root or client certificate into the device in advance).

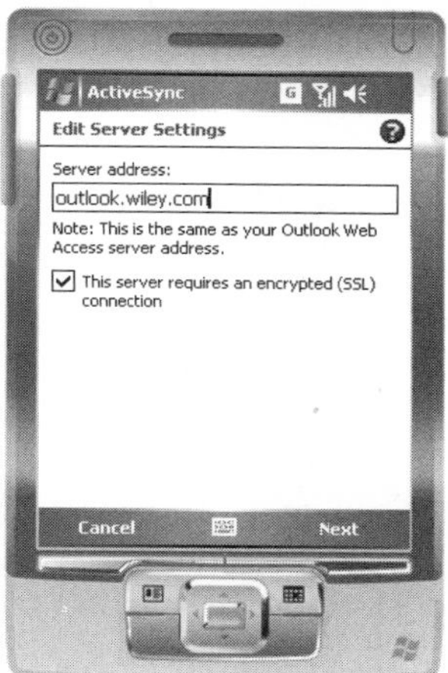

3. Enter the username, password, and domain for the account that is being used, as shown here. If you want to sync automatically, you will need to save the password.

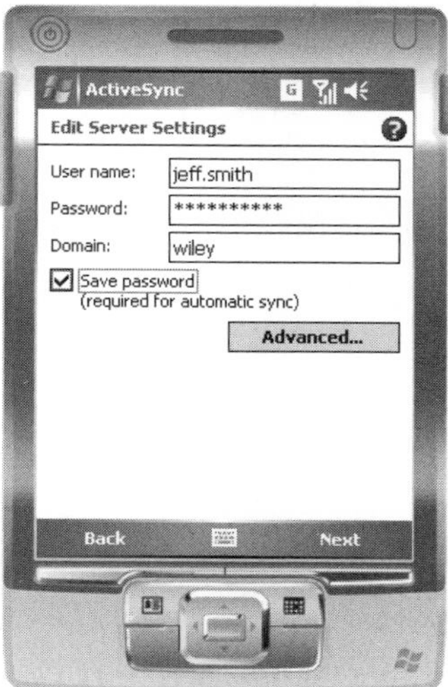

EXERCISE 8.6 ***(continued)***

4. Whether you want to set the advanced settings, as shown here, is up to you. Advanced settings deal with item conflict (the default is Replace the Item on My Device) and event logging (the default is None).

5. On the last screen, shown here, you can set what is synchronized over the server connection. Most users will be configuring all four options (Inbox, Calendar, Contacts, and Tasks). You cannot sync the Notes folder over the air, so if you are using the Notes feature in Outlook, you will need to continue to use the desktop ActiveSync as well.

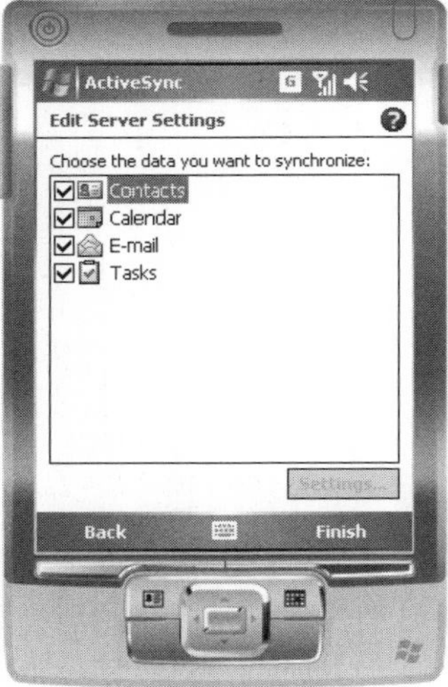

EXERCISE 8.6 *(continued)*

6. You can adjust how much is synchronized for some of the types, such as Calendar and E-mail. Select the type, and then select Settings to adjust. Calendar allows you to change how much of your calendar is synchronized. E-mail, shown here, allows you to change how much old email is synchronized and whether attachments come across.

7. After you select Finish, the device will attempt to sync for the first time, as shown here. If there is a lot of email to come across, then you should have the device connected to the network via USB ActiveSync for that first sync.

Exchange ActiveSync will sync over a wireless network connection. However, the push technology for email does not operate over wireless. That requires a mobile phone connection. Furthermore, if you have ActiveSync set to push, you will need to initiate a manual sync to sync over the wireless network.

Managing a Windows Mobile Device

At some point, one of your users will lose their device, or you will need to wipe it. The management of Windows Mobile devices is now built in to Exchange. You can manage the devices in three ways.

First, the end user can manage it through Outlook Web Access. The administrator can turn off this option if they want. However, if you have lots of remote users, you may want to enable this feature so the users can wipe the devices as soon as they realize they have lost it. Mobile device management is within the options of OWA, as shown in Figure 8.26, once the user has logged in.

Refer to Chapter 4 for more information about configuring the options that users will see in OWA.

FIGURE 8.26 Managing a mobile device via OWA

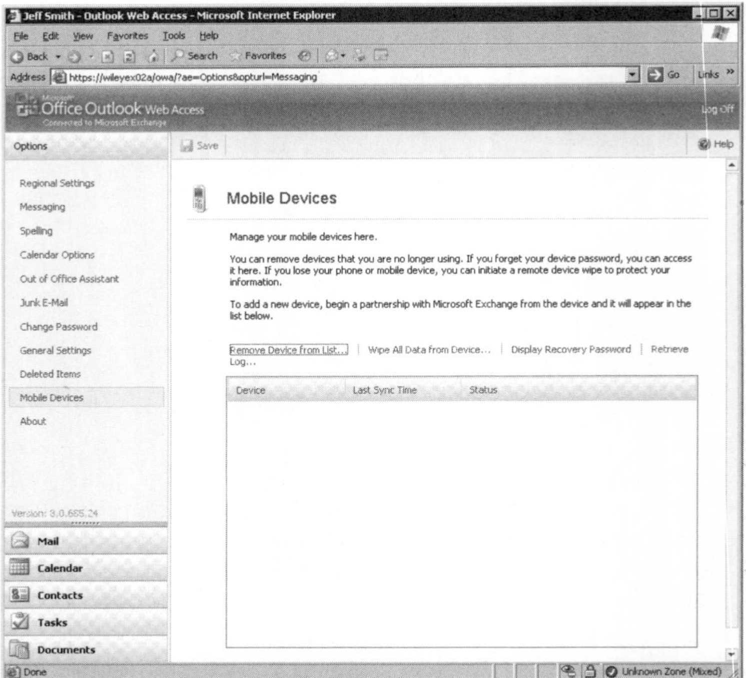

Second, you can manage the device through the Exchange Management Console. You can manage the device by right-clicking the user in the Recipients Configuration ➢ Mailbox node center and choosing Manage Mobile Device; this runs the Manage Mobile Device Wizard.

The Manage Mobile Device task option appears only if there is a mobile device associated with a mailbox.

On the bottom of the Manage Mobile Device Wizard page, click Perform a Remote Wipe to Clear Mobile Device Data, and then click the Clear button. You can return to this page to confirm that the wipe has taken place.

Finally, you can manage the device through the Exchange Management Shell. A series of commands will allow you to wipe the device. To wipe the device through the Exchange Management Shell, you need to perform the steps outlined in Exercise 8.7.

EXERCISE 8.7

Wiping a Mobile Device

1. Get the identity of the device. To get the identity of the device that is used by user Jeff.Smith, run the following command:

```
Get-ActiveSyncDeviceStatistics-Mailbox Jeff.Smith

| FL Identity
```

2. After you have the device ID, you can send the wipe command. To wipe a device with the ID of WM Jeff.Smith11, use this command:

```
Clear-ActiveSyncDevice -Identity WM Jeff.Smith11
```

3. To confirm that the wipe was successful, use the following command:

```
Get-ActiveSyncDeviceStatistics -Mailbox Jeff.Smith
```

Real World Scenario

Should You Keep an Exchange Server 2003 Server?

If your organization has a large number of public folders or has public folder content that is not readily supported by Microsoft Office SharePoint Share (MOSS), then the question of whether to keep one or more public folder servers running Exchange Server 2003 is a valid one. Given the current (before Exchange Server 2007 SP1) state of management of public folders in Exchange Server 2007, it's a much easier task to just keep public folders on Exchange Server 2003 servers.

Even though you can create replica sets of public folders on Exchange Server 2007 Mailbox servers, you still have little to no real management capability available. Thus, you might very well wind up back at the question of whether you should keep one or more Exchange Server 2003 servers to host your public folders—for the time being at least. Although the preferred choice is to move the public folder content into MOSS, that's not always going to be possible within your organization for many reasons, political and content issues being among the primary detractors of moving into MOSS.

Of course, keeping Exchange Server 2003 servers in the Exchange organization is no simple task either, especially if you consider that users may (and likely will) be prompted twice for their credentials as they move from one version of Exchange to another while accessing content. An alternative to that problem might be to host replicas of all your public folders on an Exchange Server 2007 Mailbox server but perform all configuration and management of those public folders from a replica set on an Exchange Server 2003 server and let replication do the rest.

Whatever choice you make, make it after you've considered the pros and cons of the situation—there is really no easy or simple choice at this point in time. Let's hope the release of SP1 for Exchange Server 2007 will make things significantly easier for public folder management.

Summary

If you're new to Exchange 2007 or don't have a lot of investment in public folders in your current Exchange organization, then you probably haven't been too worried about the rumors of the demise of public folders in Exchange 2007. These rumors are fortunately not true; public folders are still supported in Exchange, even if the out-of-the box management options aren't all that we could want.

By concentrating its effort on providing solid support for public folder management in the Exchange Management Shell, Microsoft has finally provided the missing command-line management interface that can simplify dealing with one-off public folder management tasks. These cmdlets also make it easy to do large-scale scripted and bulk management operations.

The lack of a native GUI is offset by Microsoft's continued development and support of the PFDAVAdmin tool, which provides a familiar interface for those who are used to the legacy Exchange System Manager. However, it also gives you a lot more power, providing sophisticated bulk operations and import/export capabilities that make managing large public folder deployments smoother. While you still have legacy servers in your organization, you can continue using the legacy System Manager to manage your public folder replicas.

Outlook 2007 is a pretty user-friendly electronic-messaging client with lots of bells and whistles, such as task and calendaring capabilities and contacts. When Exchange Server 2007 is installed properly on a server, a user can easily install Outlook on a workstation and begin using it without having to respond to a single installation query. The Exchange service Autodiscover should reduce the support burden for Outlook 2007 users by reducing the number of calls to the help desk and the confusion surrounding getting an initial Outlook profile configured when they first start using a new desktop computer.

Access to email away from the desktop is now important to most users. Exchange 2007 provides more options than ever before for that access. Users now have full access to their email wherever and whenever they need it, and the security of the network is maintained. Windows Mobile and ActiveSync users can be provided with access to their mailboxes from their mobile devices. They can synchronize their mailboxes from anywhere they can get cell phone or Wi-Fi signals.

Finally, although in some organizations POP3 and IMAP4 clients have been replaced completely by web browser–based clients or Outlook, many organizations still use POP3 and IMAP4. Exchange continues to support these clients.

Exam Essentials

Know the different types of public folder permissions. Public folders, like most other objects in Active Directory, can be configured with permissions to determine access to the public folder itself. Public folders have three different sets of permissions that can be configured on them: client permissions, directory rights, and administrative rights. Permissions are configured from the Permissions tab of the public folder's Properties dialog box. Client permissions determine which users are allowed to perform specific tasks in the public folder, such as posting new items and creating new child folders. Directory rights are used to configure the NTFS permissions that determine who can perform modifications on the public folder object that is stored in Active Directory. Administrative rights allow you to assign NTFS permissions to users and groups that determine who is actually allowed to perform administrative tasks on the public folder.

Get nit-picky. Many tasks in Exchange Server 2007 require specific knowledge or conditions to be in place before they can be performed. As an example, creating a resource mailbox requires that the associated user account be disabled. Be sure that you know and understand all the "little" nuances that go along with recipient management in Exchange Server 2007 before exam day.

Learn the PowerShell commands. Almost every configuration or management action you perform from the Exchange Management Console will present you with the PowerShell code that was used to perform the action. Take advantage of this information, and learn how to use the Exchange Management Shell to your advantage. Some of these commands are likely to make an appearance on your exam as well.

Know where to go. Many times on the exam you will likely to be asked what configuration is needed to produce the required results. The Exchange Management Console has been completely redesigned to make it easier to navigate and get to tasks, but that doesn't mean it won't be difficult to remember later. Take the time as you review the material in this book to think about what types of configuration and management tasks you find yourself performing in each major node of the Exchange Management Console.

Review Questions

1. A user named Perry is the owner of a public folder named Research. Perry leaves your company, and another administrator deletes Perry's user account. What would you as an administrator have to do to modify the permissions on the Research folder?

   A. Create a new account with the same user information as the deleted account.

   B. Restore a backup tape of the server that was created before Perry was deleted.

   C. Designate your account as the owner of the Research folder.

   D. Create a new public folder, and move the contents of the Research folder to it.

2. Which cmdlet can you use to get a complete listing of all public folders on a Mailbox server?

   A. `Get-PublicFolderStatistics`

   B. `Get-PublicFolder`

   C. `Get-PublicFolderStatus`

   D. `Get-PublicFolderListing`

3. What two actions must be completed before an IMAP4 client can connect to an Exchange Client Access server?

   A. The service must be set to automatic start.

   B. The service must be set to manual start.

   C. The service must be installed.

   D. The service must be started.

4. What would be the proper command to issue to mail-enable the Activities public folder and have it be hidden from the global address list?

   A. `Enable-MailPublicFolder-Identity "\Activities" -HiddenFromAddressLists: $false`

   B. `Enable-MailPublicFolder-Identity "\Activities" -ShownInAddressLists: $true`

   C. `Enable-MailPublicFolder-Identity "\Activities" -HiddenFromAddressLists: $true`

   D. `Enable-MailPublicFolder-Identity "\Activities" -HiddenFromAddressListsEnabled`

5. What Exchange feature provides the connectivity with Windows Mobile devices?

   A. ActiveSync

   B. ExchangeSync

   C. ExchangeMobile

   D. ActiveExchange

6. Which of the following predefined public folder roles enable a user to delete items other than the items they created? (Choose all that apply.)
   A. Owner
   B. Reviewer
   C. Editor
   D. Publishing Author

7. Which cmdlet will you need to use to configure most of the properties of a public folder?
   A. `Put-PublicFolder`
   B. `Update-PublicFolder`
   C. `Configure-PublicFolder`
   D. `Set-PublicFolder`

8. Which two client protocols can the Client Access server support that is not enabled by default?
   A. POP3
   B. SNMP
   C. NNTP
   D. IMAP4
   E. RPC

9. To enable POP3 access for the user Robert Jones, which of the following commands must you issue?
   A. `Set-CASMailbox -identity robert.jones@wiley.com -POPEnabled:$false`
   B. `Set-Mailbox -identity robert.jones@wiley.com -POPEnabled:$true`
   C. `Set-CASMailbox -identity robert.jones@wiley.com -POPEnabled:$true`
   D. `Set-Mailbox -identity robert.jones@wiley.com -POPDisabled:$false`

10. From which of the following tools can you configure replicas for public folders?
    A. Exchange Management Console
    B. Active Directory Users and Computers
    C. Exchange System Manager
    D. PFDavAdmin

11. What kind of permissions must you configure to give Exchange recipients the ability to manage and create content within public folders?
    A. Directory rights
    B. Recipient rights
    C. Administrative rights
    D. Client rights

12. Which cmdlet will you need to use to add client permissions to a public folder?
   A. `Add-PublicFolderClientPermission`
   B. `Put-PublicFolderClientPermission`
   C. `Configure-PublicFolderClientPermission`
   D. `Set-PublicFolderClientPermission`

13. Which three users are included by default on the permissions list of a new public folder?
   A. The user who created the folder
   B. The local Administrator account
   C. A special user account named Default
   D. A special user account named Anonymous
   E. The Exchange Administrator account

14. Which of the following tasks can the PFDavAdmin tool be used for? (Choose all that apply.)
   A. Export and import public folder replica lists.
   B. Export folder permissions on folders, public folder stores, and mailbox stores.
   C. Perform bulk operations on folder properties. In addition, you can do bulk search and removal operations of per-item permissions.
   D. Apply changes to your list of replicas to a folder and all subfolders without overwriting each folder's replica list.

15. Your organization has a public folder named Safety Issues that employees use to post notices about safety hazards that have been located within your buildings and warehouses. You want all employees in the company to be able to post new items into this folder and read any existing items but perform no other actions. What role do you need to configure for the Default user on this public folder?
   A. Contributor
   B. Author
   C. Nonediting Author
   D. Editor

16. To set the "Default Policy" ActiveSync policy for all recipients, which of the following commands would you need to use?
   A. Use this:
   ```
   Get-Mailbox | Put-CASMailbox -ActiveSyncMailboxPolicy
   (Get-ActiveSyncMailboxPolicy "Default Policy").Identity
   ```
   B. Use this:
   ```
   Get-Mailbox | Set-CASMailbox -ActiveSyncMailboxPolicy
   (Get-ActiveSyncMailboxPolicy "Default Policy").Identity
   ```

C. Use this:

```
Get-Mailbox | Set-ActiveSyncMailboxPolicy
(Get-ActiveSyncMailboxPolicy "Default Policy").Identity
```

D. Use this:

```
Get-Mailbox | Set-Mailbox -ActiveSyncMailboxPolicy
(Get-ActiveSyncMailboxPolicy "Default Policy").Identity
```

17. Where in System Manager would you go to find out the current replication state of public folders on a server?

A. The property pages for that server

B. The property pages for the public folder

C. The property pages for the public folder store

D. The Replication Status subcontainer of the public folder store

E. The Public Folders subcontainer of the public folder store

18. You recently created a public folder that employees of your company can use to post personal announcements, such as marriages and births. You have now become aware that a number of people are also posting large attachments to messages in the form of photos or other documents. This is causing the public folder to swell considerably in size. People enjoy the Announcements folder, and you want to keep it available. However, you want to keep users from posting large messages or attachments. What is your best option?

A. Set a limit on the size of messages that each user may send by using the property pages for that user.

B. Set a limit on the size of messages that can be posted in the public folder by using the folder's property pages.

C. Set a limit on the maximum size that a public folder can reach before new posts are prohibited, and then manually delete large posts.

D. Set a limit on the maximum size that a public folder can reach before new posts are prohibited, and then create a script that deletes large posts automatically.

19. Which of the following things does Autodiscover help to configure? (Choose all that apply.)

A. The internal URL for the Availability service

B. The external URL for the Offline Address Book (OAB)

C. A user's home Mailbox server

D. The Outlook Anywhere URL

20. The age limit on your public folders is set to 14 days. The deleted-item retention time is set to 7 days. A user deletes an item 12 days after it was created. That same user then recovers the deleted item 7 days later. How long will it be until the item expires?

A. The item will expire immediately.

B. 2 days.

C. 5 days.

D. 14 days.

Answers to Review Questions

1. C. An administrator has the permission to change the owner of a folder. Once the administrator takes ownership of the folder, they can then perform administrative tasks, such as adding rules and installing forms.

2. A. You will use the `Get-PublicFolderStatistics` cmdlet to get a listing of all public folders on a server.

3. A, D. You need to configure the IMAP4 server for automatic start so it will start every time the Client Access server is rebooted. After that, you need to manually start the IMAP4 service for the first time before clients will be able to connect to the Client Access server via IMAP4.

4. D. To mail-enable the Activities public folder and cause it to be hidden from the global address list, you would use the `Enable-MailPublicFolder-Identity "\Activities" -HiddenFromAddressListsEnabled` command.

5. A. ActiveSync is the piece of Exchange Server 2007 that communicates with Windows Mobile devices.

6. A, C. Only the Owner, Editor, and Publishing Editor of a public folder can delete items other than their own. The Publishing Author, Author, and Nonediting Author can delete their own items only. All other roles cannot delete any items.

7. D. The `Set-PublicFolder` cmdlet allows you to set most of the properties for the named public folder, such as limits, replicas, replication schedules, and more, such as `Set-PublicFolder -Identity "\Jobs\Posted" -Server "WILEXEX01A"`.

8. A, D. POP3 and IMAP4 are disabled by default in Exchange 2007, and no GUI configuration is available through the Exchange Management Console. You must configure the protocols using the Exchange Management Shell.

9. C. You will need to issue the following command to enable POP3 access for the user: `Set-CASMailbox -identity robert.jones@wiley.com -POPEnabled:$true`.

10. C. Of the available tools, only the Exchange System Manager provides a means to configure public folder replication options.

11. D. Client permissions assign access rights to Exchange users and distribution groups, who can then work with a public folder using their Outlook clients.

12. A. To configure client permissions on a public folder, you will need to use the `Add-PublicFolderClientPermission` cmdlet.

13. A, C, D. When a public folder is created, the user who created the folder is given the role of folder owner. The Default user represents all users who have access to the public folder store and aren't explicitly listed in the permissions list. The Anonymous user represents all users logged on with anonymous access.

14. A, B, C, D. You can use the PFDAVAdmin tool to do the following:

    - Perform bulk operations on folder properties. In addition, you can do bulk search and removal operations of per-item permissions.
    - Apply changes to your list of replicas to a folder and all subfolders without overwriting each folder's replica list (that is, add or remove specific server entries without making each folder's replica list an exact copy of your starting point).
    - Export folder permissions on folders, public folder stores, and mailbox stores.
    - Export and import public folder replica lists.

15. C. The Nonediting Author role will allow users to read existing items in the public folder and create new items but will not allow them any other permissions on the public folder

16. B. To apply the "Default Policy" ActiveSync policy to all recipients in your organization, you would need to use the following command:

    ```
    Get-Mailbox | Set-CASMailbox -ActiveSyncMailboxPolicy

    (Get-ActiveSyncMailboxPolicy "Default Policy").Identity
    ```

17. D. The Replication Status subcontainer lists all folders and the number of servers that contain a replica of each folder. It also lists the current replication state and the time of the last replication.

18. B. The Limits tab for a public folder contains several settings that govern public folder limits. One setting allows you to specify the maximum size of messages that can be posted to the public folder. This is the best way to ensure that large posts are not made. Setting a limit on the size of the messages that users can send would also restrict the sending of regular email messages. Deleting posts, whether done manually or automatically, might be considered intrusive and arbitrary by users.

19. A, B, C, D. Autodiscover actually helps Outlook locate a number of different types of Exchange resources, including these:

    - User's home Mailbox server
    - Outlook Anywhere URL
    - URL (internal or external) for the Offline Address Book
    - URL (internal or external) for unified messaging
    - URL (internal or external) for the Availability service

20. D. Since the item was recovered after the original expiration date, a new expiration date is set equal to the original expiration period. If the item had been recovered before the original expiration date, it would have then expired on the original expiration date.

Managing and Maintaining the Exchange Organization

MICROSOFT EXAM OBJECTIVES COVERED IN THIS CHAPTER:

✓ **Configuring Recipients and Public Folders**

- Move mailboxes.
- Implement bulk management of mail-enabled objects.

✓ **Monitoring and Reporting**

- Monitor mail queues.
- Perform message tracking.

As the size and complexity of your Exchange organization grows, you'll likely find yourself facing new challenges, both for normal and abnormal operations. In this chapter, we'll examine some of the tools and processes you will most likely encounter while managing the Exchange organization. The main subjects of this chapter are as follows:

- Managing message queues
- Using message tracking
- Moving mailboxes
- Performing scheduled and impromptu bulk management of recipients

Managing Mail Queues and Message Tracking

Eventually it will happen—message flow in your Exchange organization will stop working correctly. Maybe it will be because a particular mailbox database is dismounted or otherwise not available, or maybe it will be because there is a problem with the addressing of external recipients or domains. Regardless of how you get to that point, examining the Exchange message queues will be your first stop in troubleshooting the problem. In the following sections of the chapter, we'll examine the queues found on an Exchange Server 2007 Hub Transport server and show how you can interact with them. We'll also spend some time examining how to configure and use the message tracking functionality of Exchange Server 2007.

Introducing the Exchange Queues

A *queue* is a temporary staging location for those messages in transit that are between processing steps. There are multiple queues found on each Hub Transport server, and each one represents a set of messages to be processed in a specific way. Queues can be managed from both the Exchange Management Console and the Exchange Management Shell, as you'd expect. The queues are Extensible Storage Engine (ESE) databases, the same as the mailbox and public folder databases within Exchange Server 2007, thus allowing Exchange Server to interact with them at a very low level.

There are also queues on the Edge Transport servers for messages that are coming inbound from the Internet or going outbound to the Internet. For all intents, the management of the queues on the Edge Transport server is the same as for the Hub Transport server. We'll be working with Hub Transport servers only for this chapter.

On the Hub Transport server, you can find the following types of queues:

- *Submission queue*: This is a persistent (always present) queue that is used by the categorizer to group all messages that have just been submitted for transport. The categorizer is an Exchange component that processes these messages and determines what to do and where they need to be routed, such as expanding the membership of a distribution group for messages queued on the Hub Transport server. Once the categorizer has determined the required information it needs about the message, including recipients, it can then apply any transport policies and route the message properly.
- *Mailbox delivery queue*: This queue holds the messages that are being attempted for delivery to a Mailbox server. Multiple mailbox sever queues can exist on a Hub Transport server; however, they will exist only for Mailbox servers located in the same Active Directory site as the Hub Transport server. The next hop for messages located in a mailbox delivery queue is to the Mailbox server to which they are destined.
- *Remote delivery queue*: This queue holds messages that are being routed to remote SMTP destinations, such as servers that are located outside the Active Directory site containing the Hub Transport server. Remote delivery queues are dynamically created and removed as needed depending on the messages that are in routing on that server. The next hop for messages located in a remote delivery queue is a remote Active Directory site or SMTP domain or smart host.
- *Poison message queue*: This queue holds messages that have been determined to be potentially harmful to the Exchange organization after a server failure has occurred, such as messages that contain errors that are potentially fatal to the Exchange organization. When no messages meeting this condition are found, this queue does not exist on the Hub Transport server, although the queue is in a ready state should it be needed. Messages placed into the poison message queue are not attempted for delivery, and their status is set to suspended, allowing the messages to be examined and deleted or released by the administrator after further review. The next hop for messages located in the poison message queue that have been released is the submission queue.
- *Unreachable queue*: This queue holds messages that cannot be routed to their destinations for any reason, such as changes in the routing path that block message transport.

Managing Exchange Queues and Queued Items

You have many options available to you as to how to manage the queues as a whole or how to manage individual messages in the queues. Which action you take will depend largely on the scenario you are facing and, to a smaller degree, which queue you are working with. In the following sections, we'll examine queue and queued item management in depth.

You can access the Queue Viewer from the Exchange Management Console by navigating to the Tools section, as shown in Figure 9.1. Once you've located the Queue Viewer tool, simply double-click it to open the Queue Viewer, as shown in Figure 9.2.

FIGURE 9.1 Locating the Queue Viewer in the Exchange Management Console

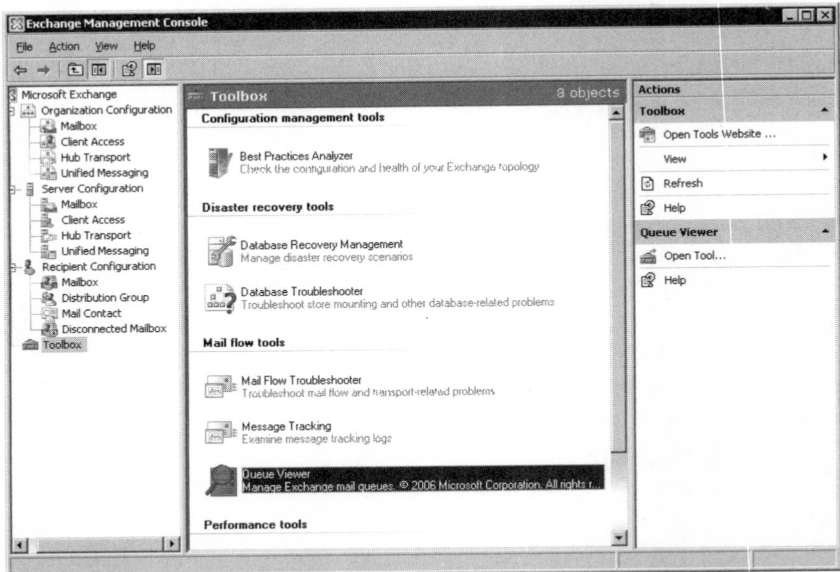

FIGURE 9.2 Examining the Queue Viewer window

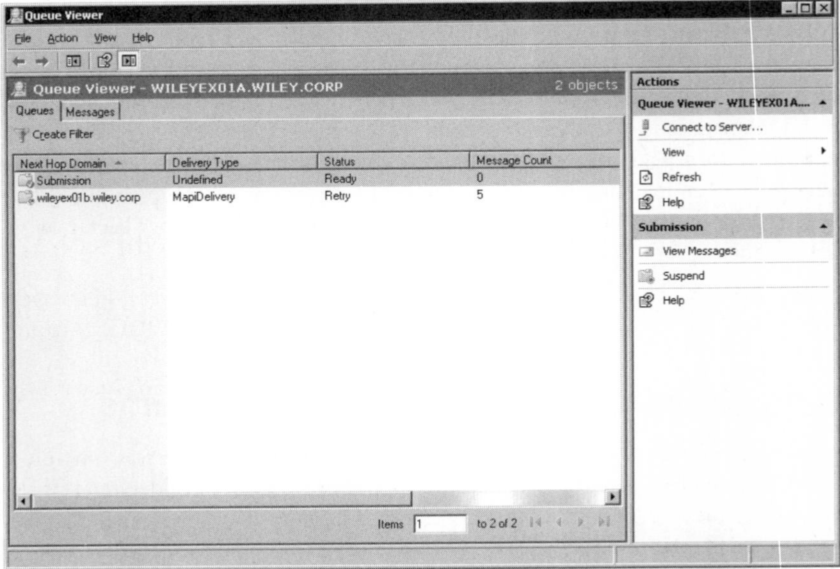

By default, the Queue Viewer opens to a display the queues on that Hub Transport server, but you can change this view by clicking the Connect to Server link in the Actions pane on the right side of the Queue Viewer window.

Managing Queues

Once in the Queue Viewer, you can quickly determine the status of each queue that exists on that Hub Transport server. The main display of the Queue Viewer provides a wealth of information about the status of each queue on the server, which will be important knowledge in your monitoring and troubleshooting efforts. The following data fields are available in the Queue Viewer for each queue present:

- *Next Hop Domain*: Provides information about the destination of messages in the selected delivery queue. Possible values here include the following:
  - An Active Directory site name
  - The fully qualified domain name (FQDN) of an Exchange Mailbox server
  - A connector name
  - A routing group name
  - A remote SMTP domain name
  - An Exchange server name
- *Delivery Type*: Provides information about the next hop destination. Possible values here include the following:
  - *MapiDelivery*: Messages are queued for delivery to recipients with mailboxes in the local Active Directory site.
  - *DNSConnectorDelivery*: Messages are queued for delivery to an external recipient via an SMTP connector configured to use DNS for message routing.
  - *NonSmtpGatewayDelivery*. Messages are queued for delivery to an external recipient using a non-SMTP connector.
  - *SmartHostConnectorDelivery*: Messages are queued for delivery to an external recipient via an SMTP connector configured to use a smart host for message routing.
  - *SmtpRelayWithinAdSitetoEdge*: Messages are queued for delivery to an external recipient using an SMTP connector on an Edge Transport server that has an EdgeSync subscription to Active Directory.
  - *SmtpRelayWithinAdSite*: Messages are queued for delivery to another Hub Transport server in the same Active Directory site.
  - *SmtpRelaytoRemoteAdSite*: Messages are queued for delivery to another Exchange server in a remote Active Directory site.
  - *SmtpRelaytoTiRg*: Messages are queued for delivery to an Exchange Server 2003 routing group.
  - *Undefined*: Messages are located in the submission queue, and the next hop has not yet been determined.
  - *Unreachable*: Messages are located in the unreachable queue, where a route to the recipient could not be determined.

- *Status*: Provides the current status of the queue. Possible values here include Active, Suspended, Ready, and Retry.
- *Message Count*: Provides the number of message items currently in the queue.
- *Next Retry Time*: Provides the date and time of the next connection attempt for a queue in a Retry status.
- *Last Error*: Provides the last recorded error for the queue.
- *Last Retry Time*: Provides the date and time of the last connection attempt for a queue in a Retry status.

To drill down into a specific queue and see the messages contained within, you can double-click it, or you can click once to select it and then click the View Messages link in the Actions pane on the right side of the window. Either way, a new tab opens for the selected queue and displays information about the items contained within that queue, as shown for the mailbox delivery queue for server wileyex01b.wiley.corp in Figure 9.3.

We'll discuss message-level management tasks in the next section of this chapter, so for now let's backtrack to the Queue Viewer's main window, shown previously in Figure 9.2. By selecting a specific queue of interest, a number of queue management tasks become available in the Actions pane on the right side of the Queue Viewer, as shown in Figure 9.4.

FIGURE 9.3 Examining messages in a specific queue

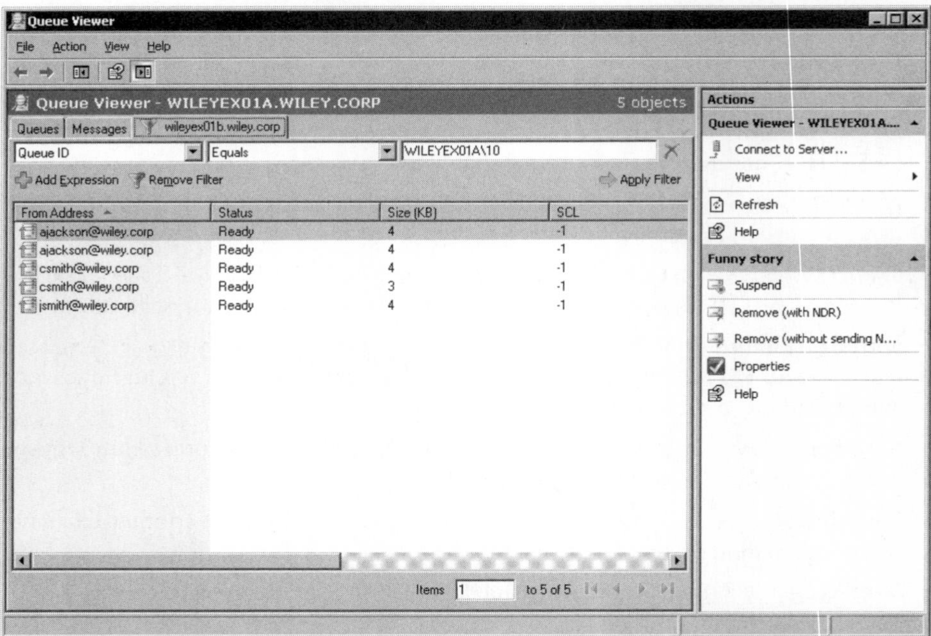

FIGURE 9.4 Exploring the message queue tasks

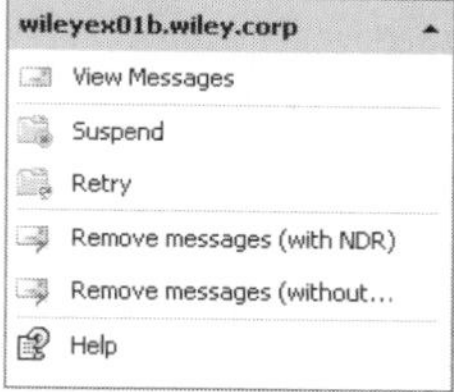

These tasks are as follows:

- *View Messages*: Clicking this link will open the selected queue in another tab, shown previously in Figure 9.3.
- *Suspend*: Clicking this link will temporarily prevent any messages in the selected queue from being delivered. New messages can enter the queue, but no messages can leave the queue while in a suspended state.
- *Resume*: Clicking this link enables messages in the selected suspended queue to be delivered and routed as required.
- *Retry*: Clicking this link will cause messages in a queue with a retry status to have delivery attempted before the next regularly scheduled retry event. If delivery is successful, the messages will be routed. If delivery is not successful, the retry timer will be reset for the next retry time.
- *Remove Messages (with NDR)*: Clicking this link will cause all messages in the selected queue to be deleted and sends a nondelivery report (NDR) for each message. NDR messages are not sent for NDR messages that are in the queue at the time of deletion.
- *Remove Messages (Without Sending NDR)*: Clicking this link causes all messages in the selected queue to be deleted silently, without sending an NDR.

Of course, you can perform all these tasks from the Exchange Management Shell as well.

To get a detailed listing of all queues on the local server, you will use the `Get-Queue | format-list` cmdlet, which produces output like that shown in Figure 9.5.

You can accomplish the remaining tasks using the following PowerShell cmdlets:

- To suspend a queue, use the `Suspend-Queue` cmdlet:
  - To suspend a queue with a next hop domain of wiley.com that is in a retry status, you would use the following cmdlet: `Suspend-Queue -Filter {NextHopDomain -eq "wiley.com" -and Status -eq "retry"}`.
  - To suspend all queues on the server wileyex01a.wiley.corp that have more than 2000 messages in them, you would use the following cmdlet: `Suspend-Queue -Server wileyex01a.wiley.corp -Filter {MessageCount -gt 2000}`.
- To resume a suspected queue, use the `Resume-Queue` cmdlet:
  - To resume a suspended queue on the server wileyex01a.wiley.corp that contains messages destined for the wrox.com domain, you would use the following cmdlet: `Resume-Queue -Server wileyex01a.wiley.corp -Filter {NextHopDomain -eq "wrox.com"}`.

- To retry a queue, use the `Retry-Queue` cmdlet:
  - To force a retry attempt on a queue that contains messages destined for the wrox.com domain, you would use the following cmdlet: `Retry-Queue -Filter {NextHopDomain -eq "wrox.com" -and Status -eq "retry"}`.
- To remove messages from a queue, with or without sending an NDR, use the `Remove-Message` cmdlet. The value of the `withNDR` parameter determines whether an NDR is sent and can be either $true or $false:
  - To remove messages from a queue on the server wileyex01a that contains messages destined for the wileyex01b.wiley.corp Mailbox server, use the following cmdlet: `Remove-Message -Filter {Queue -eq "wileyex01a\wileyex01b.wiley.corp"} -withNDR $false`.

FIGURE 9.5 Viewing message queues from the Exchange Management Shell

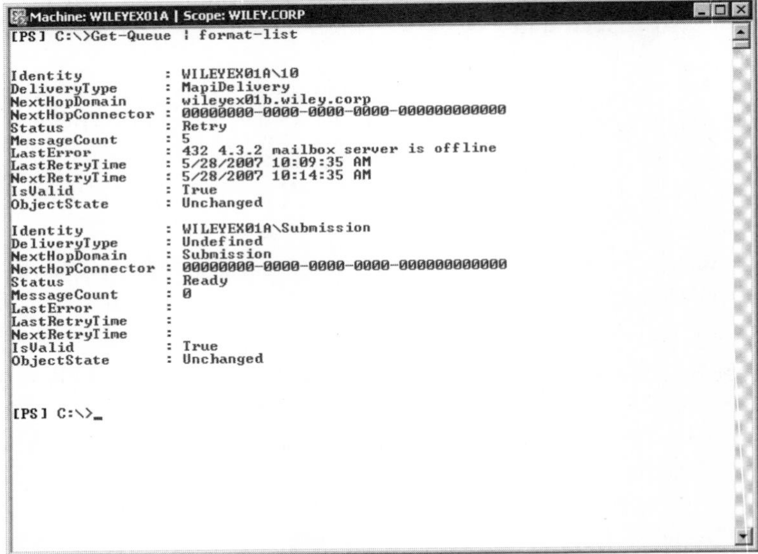

Managing Queued Messages

Of course, you may need or want to manage only specific messages in a selected queue and not the entire queue itself. Once you select the tab belonging to specific queue of concern in the Queue Viewer, you'll have a listing of messages that are currently in the queue, as shown previously in Figure 9.3. Each queue in the Queue Viewer has the following data fields available:

- *Date Received*: This is the date and time the message was received on the server.
- *Expiration Time*: This is the data and time the message will be deleted from the queue if it is not delivered first.

- *From Address*. This is the SMTP address of the sender of the message.
- *Internet Message ID*: The message GUID and SMTP address of the sending server are combined to make a unique ID that you can find in the message header.
- *Last Error*: This is the value of the last error that was recorded for the message.
- *Message Source Name*: This is the value of the component that submitted the message to the queue.
- *Queue ID*: This is the identity of the queue where the message is located.
- *SCL*: This is the value between 0 and 9 that specifies how likely the message is spam.
- *Size (KB)*: This is the size of the message in kilobytes (KB).
- *Source IP*: This is the IP address of the originating server that submitted the message.
- *Status*: This is the current status of the message. Possible values here include the following:
  - *Active*: The message is currently being delivered to its destination or being processed by the categorizer.
  - *Suspended*: The message is currently suspended.
  - *PendingRemove*: The message was selected for deletion but was already in a delivery status. If the message delivery attempt fails, the message will be deleted.
  - *PendingSuspend*: The message was selected for suspension of delivery but was already in a delivery status. If the message delivery attempt fails, the message will be suspended.
  - *Ready*: The message is waiting to be processed.
  - *Retry*: The message was not successfully delivered on the last attempt and is awaiting the next queue retry.
- *Subject*: This is the subject value of the message.

When a message (or group of messages) is selected, management tasks become available in the Actions pane on the right side of the Queue Viewer, as shown in Figure 9.6.

FIGURE 9.6 Queued message tasks

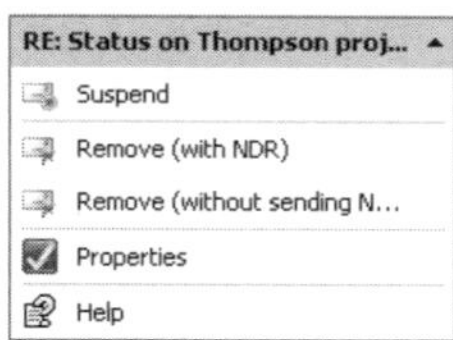

These tasks are as follows:

- *Suspend*: Clicking this link temporarily prevents the selected message(s) from being delivered out of the queue.
- *Resume*: Clicking this link enables the delivery of the selected suspended messages.
- *Remove (with NDR)*: Clicking this link causes all selected messages to be deleted and sends an NDR for each message.

- *Remove (Without Sending NDR)*: Clicking this link causes all selected messages to be deleted silently, without sending an NDR.
- *Properties*: Clicking this link opens a new dialog box, shown in Figure 9.7, which displays header and recipient information for the selected message. This can be useful when trying to determine to whom the message is addressed.

FIGURE 9.7 Viewing queued message properties

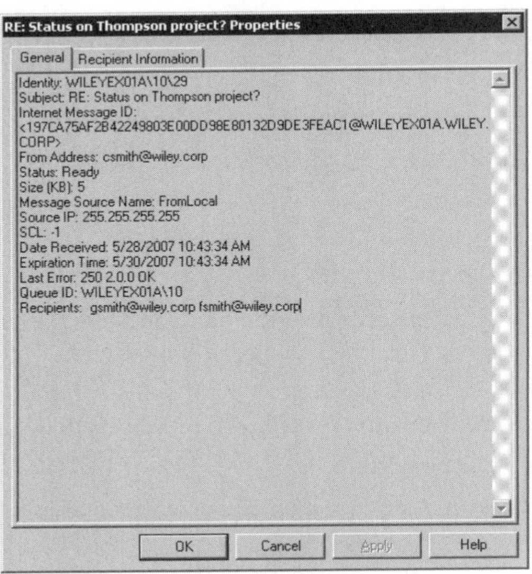

As you'd expect, you can perform all these tasks from the Exchange Management Shell as well:

- To suspend a message, use the `Suspend-Message` cmdlet:
  - To suspend all messages in all queues that are from the SMTP sender loanstoday@moremoney.biz, use the following cmdlet: `Suspend-Message -filter {FromAddress -eq "loanstoday@moremoney.biz"}`.
- To resume suspended messages, use the `Resume-Message` cmdlet:
  - To resume all messages in all queues that are from the SMTP sender ceo@wiley.corp, use the following cmdlet: `Resume-Message -filter {FromAddress -eq "ceo@wiley.corp"}`.
- To remove messages, with or without sending an NDR, use the `Remove-Message` cmdlet:
  - To remove all messages with the subject of "Get Bigger Faster!" from all queues, use the following cmdlet: `Remove-Message -filter {Subject -eq "Get Bigger Faster!"} -WithNDR $false`.
- To view the properties of one or more messages, use the `Get-Message` cmdlet:
  - To view the properties of all messages in all queues that were sent from the wiley.corp SMTP domain, use the following cmdlet to produce the results shown in Figure 9.8: `Get-Message -Filter {FromAddress -like "*@wiley.corp"} | format-list`.

- To view the properties of a specific message in any queue that has a subject of "RE: Lunch with vendor?" use the following cmdlet: `Get-Message -Filter {Subject -eq "RE: Lunch with vendor?"} | format-list`.

FIGURE 9.8 Viewing queued message properties in the Exchange Management Shell

```
Machine: WILEYEX01A | Scope: WILEY.CORP
[PS] C:\>Get-Message -Filter {FromAddress -like "*@wiley.corp"} | format-list

Identity           : WILEYEX01A\10\28
Subject            : RE: Lunch with vendor?
InternetMessageId  : <197CA75AF2B422498O3E00DD98E80132D9DE3FEAC0@WILEYEX01A.WILE
                     Y.CORP>
FromAddress        : csmith@wiley.corp
Status             : Ready
Size               : 5197B
MessageSourceName  : FromLocal
SourceIP           : 255.255.255.255
SCL                : -1
DateReceived       : 5/28/2007 10:43:30 AM
ExpirationTime     : 5/30/2007 10:43:30 AM
LastError          : 250 2.0.0 OK
RetryCount         : 0
Queue              : WILEYEX01A\10
Recipients         :
IsValid            : True
ObjectState        : Unchanged

Identity           : WILEYEX01A\10\29
Subject            : RE: Status on Thompson project?
InternetMessageId  : <197CA75AF2B422498O3E00DD98E80132D9DE3FEAC1@WILEYEX01A.WILE
                     Y.CORP>
FromAddress        : csmith@wiley.corp
Status             : Ready
Size               : 5735B
MessageSourceName  : FromLocal
SourceIP           : 255.255.255.255
SCL                : -1
DateReceived       : 5/28/2007 10:43:34 AM
ExpirationTime     : 5/30/2007 10:43:34 AM
LastError          : 250 2.0.0 OK
RetryCount         : 0
Queue              : WILEYEX01A\10
Recipients         :
IsValid            : True
ObjectState        : Unchanged
```

You can also export a suspended message from a queue using the Exchange Management Shell, a task you cannot perform from the Exchange Management Console. By using the `Export-Message` cmdlet, you can save a copy of a queued message to an EML file that can be examined in its entirety or passed along to a user to be opened in Outlook. To export a specific message in any queue that has a message identity of WILEYEX01A\10\28, use the following cmdlet: `Export-Message -Identity WILEYEX01A\10\28 -Path "c:\mymessage.eml"`.

You can determine the message identity of a specific message by using the output of the `Get-Message | format-list` cmdlet.

Configuring Queue Properties

You can configure only two properties within the Exchange Management Console that control the behavior of the Queue Viewer. You can access these items once the Queue Viewer is open by selecting Tools ➢ Options. The Queue Viewer Options dialog box opens, as shown in Figure 9.9. You can change the refresh interval and the number of messages that are displayed per page from here.

You can find the actual queue database files (in a default installation) in the location shown in Figure 9.10.

FIGURE 9.9 Setting Queue Viewer options

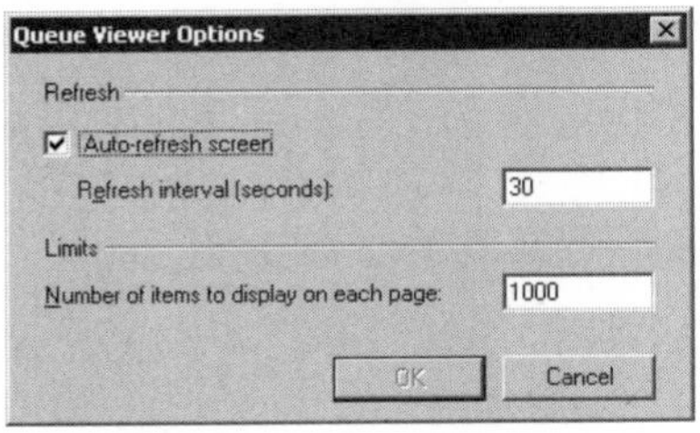

Queue Viewer Options
Refresh
Auto-refresh screen
Refresh interval (seconds): 30
Limits
Number of items to display on each page: 1000
OK Cancel

FIGURE 9.10 Viewing the queue database files

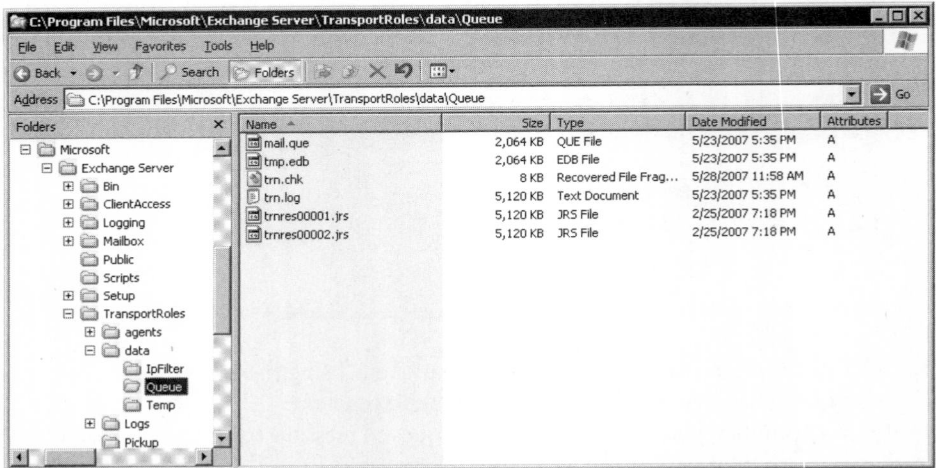

The files that make up the queue database are similar to those that make up mailbox and public folder databases; they include the following:

- `Mail.que`: The actual queue database file.
- `Tmp.edb`: A temporary database file used to verify the queue database schema during service start-up on the Exchange server.
- `Trn.log`: The active transaction log file.
- `Trntmp.log`: An empty transaction log file that has been provisioned to be the next `Trn.log` file.
- `Trn`*nnn*`.log`: An old transaction log file that has reached its maximum capacity.
- `Trn.chk`: The checkpoint file that keeps track of all transaction log entries that have already been committed to the queue database file.
- `Trnres00001.jrs` and `Trnres00002.jrs`: Reserve transaction logs that act as placeholders to ensure adequate space exists to shut down the queue database cleanly should the drive containing it run out of free space.

The behavior of the queue database cannot be configured by either the Exchange Management Shell or the Exchange Management Console but instead is configured via an XML file named `EdgeTransport.exe.config` that is located in `C:\Program Files\Microsoft\Exchange Server\Bin` by default. Figure 9.11 displays some of the contents of this XML file.

FIGURE 9.11 Viewing the queue database configuration file

```
EdgeTransport.exe.config - Notepad
File  Edit  Format  View  Help
<configuration>
  <runtime>
    <gcServer enabled="true" />
  </runtime>
  <appSettings>
    <add key="AgentLogEnabled" value="true" />
    <add key="ResolverRetryInterval" value="30" />
    <add key="DeliverMoveMailboxRetryInterval" value="30" />
    <add key="ResolverLogLevel" value="Disabled" />
    <add key="ExpansionSizeLimit" value="1000" />
    <add key="MaxIdleTimeBeforeResubmit" value="12:00:00" />
    <add key="MailboxDeliveryQueueRetryInterval" value="00:05:00" />
    <add key="QueueGlitchRetryInterval" value="00:01:00" />
    <add key="QueueGlitchRetryCount" value="4" />
    <add key="PFReplicaAgeThresholdHours" value="48" />
    <add key="DeferredReloadTimeoutSeconds" value="5" />
    <add key="MaxDeferredNotifications" value="20" />
    <add key="MaxQueueViewerQueryResultCount" value="250000" />
    <add key="RoutingConfigReloadInterval" value="12:00:00" />
    <add key="DumpsterAllMail" value="false" />
    <add key="DumpsterAllowDuplicateDelivery" value="false" />
    <add key="DatabaseCheckPointDepthMax" value="20971520" />
    <add key="DatabaseMaxCacheSize" value="134217728" />
    <add key="DatabaseCacheFlushStart" value="3" />
    <add key="DatabaseCacheFlushStop" value="5" />
    <add key="QueueDatabaseBatchSize" value="40" />
    <add key="QueueDatabaseBatchTimeout" value="100" />
    <add key="QueueDatabaseMaxConnections" value="4" />
    <add key="QueueDatabaseLoggingFileSize" value="5242880" />
    <add key="QueueDatabaseLoggingBufferSize" value="524288" />
    <add key="QueueDatabaseMaxBackgroundCleanupTasks" value="32" />
    <add key="QueueDatabaseOnlineDefragEnabled" value="true" />
    <add key="QueueDatabaseOnlineDefragSchedule" value="1:00:00" />
    <add key="QueueDatabaseOnlineDefragTimeToRun" value="3:00:00" />
    <add key="QueueDatabasePath" value = "C:\Program Files\Microsoft\Ex
    <add key="QueueDatabaseLoggingPath" value = "C:\Program Files\Micro
    <add key="IPFilterDatabasePath" value = "C:\Program Files\Microsoft\
    <add key="IPFilterDatabaseLoggingPath" value = "C:\Program Files\Mi
```

Editing the `EdgeTransport.exe.config` file is certainly only for the most advanced Exchange administrators. If you choose to edit this file, take care to check the correct syntax and spelling of your changes. You can get more information about the available parameters and options by visiting the following TechNet article: `http://technet.microsoft.com/en-us/library/aa996006.aspx`. As well, after you make any changes to the `EdgeTransport.exe.config` file, you'll need to restart the Microsoft Exchange Transport service to make the changes live on the server.

Common changes that you might make to the `EdgeTransport.exe.config` file would be to change the retry, resubmit, and expiration intervals of messages. The following TechNet article provides guidance on these tasks: `http://technet.microsoft.com/en-us/library/aa998043.aspx`.

Another common change you might want to make is to move the queue database to a different location. You should reference the following TechNet article for more information about that task: `http://technet.microsoft.com/en-us/library/bb125177.aspx`.

Managing Message Tracking

The message tracking tool has been a staple for Exchange administrators for some time, and its usefulness is not likely to change anytime soon. To access the message tracking interface, simply go back to the Toolbox shown previously in Figure 9.1, and double-click the Message Tracking item. The first time you run the message tracking tool, you'll be prompted to check for updates. Once you've done this and you are in the tool itself, you'll have an interface to work with like that shown in Figure 9.12. Note how the actual `Get-MessageTrackingLog` cmdlet that will be used to perform the tracking action is already displayed and changes as you select parameters. PowerShell is everywhere in Exchange Server 2007!

FIGURE 9.12 Viewing the message tracking interface

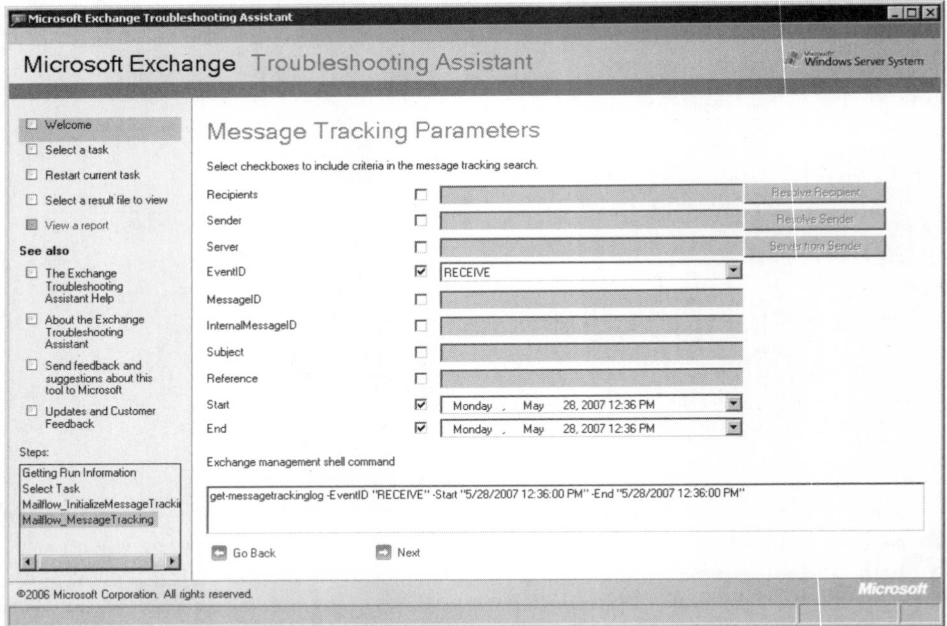

Performing Message Tracking

The actual process to use message tracking hasn't really changed much from Exchange Server 2003, so administrators with experience using it there should be able to jump right into it in Exchange Server 2007. Even if you haven't had a lot of experience with tracking messages, the interface is fairly straightforward to put parameters into, so you can get right to work.

As an example, if you wanted to check the delivery status of all messages sent from Angela Jackson (ajackson@wiley.corp) to Will Schmied (wschmied@wiley.corp) during the time frame of 1:30 p.m. on May 21, 2007, to 1:30 p.m. on May 28, 2007, you might configure the message tracking parameters like those shown in Figure 9.13.

The resulting output is a bit difficult to work with at first, but eventually you will get used to the more detailed and less user-friendly display that Exchange Server 2007 provides, as shown in Figure 9.14.

The corresponding cmdlet to execute this search is `Get-MessageTrackingLog -Recipients:wschmied@wiley.corp -Sender "ajackson@wiley.corp" -EventID "DELIVERY" -Start "5/21/2007 1:30:00 PM" -End "5/28/2007 1:30:00 PM" | format-list`, which produces the result shown in Figure 9.15.

FIGURE 9.13 Configuring message tracking parameters

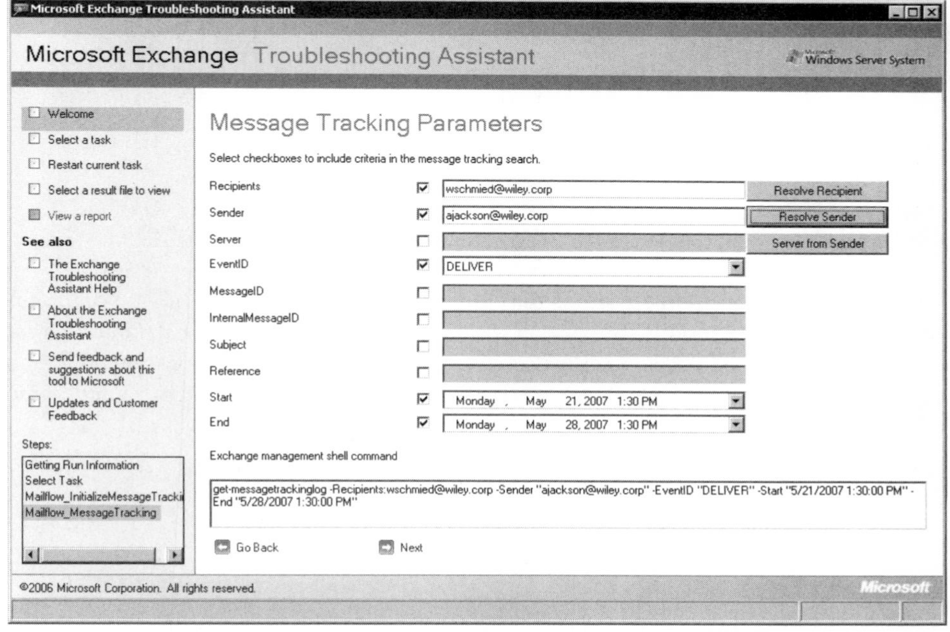

FIGURE 9.14 Viewing message tracking output

Message Tracking Results

Selected row will populate parameters for next message tracking search.

	Timestamp	EventId	Source	SourceConte	MessageId	MessageSubj	Sender	Recipients	InternalMe
▶	2007/05/28	DELIVER	STOREDRIV		<197CA75AF	RE: Inventory	ajackson@wil	fsmith@wiley.	30
	2007/05/28 1	DELIVER	STOREDRIV		<197CA75AF	RE: Funny st	ajackson@wil	fsmith@wiley.	31
	2007/05/28 1	DELIVER	STOREDRIV		<197CA75AF	Please updat	ajackson@wil	wschmied@w	32

FIGURE 9.15 Viewing message tracking output from the Exchange Management Shell

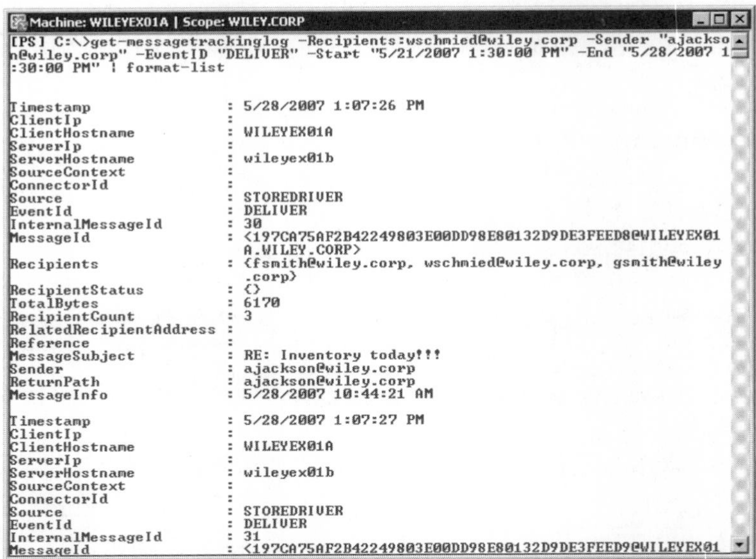

The EventID field is searchable and is oftentimes the piece of information you're looking for when it comes to determining the final status of a specific message. Was the message that Jim claimed to never have received really delivered? You can answer that question, and many others, through message tracking. The EventID field has the following values, each of which will tell you the exact status of that particular line in the tracking logs:

- *BADMAIL*: The message could not be delivered or returned to sender.
- *DELIVER*: The message was delivered to the recipient's mailbox.
- *DEFER*: The delivery of the message was delayed.
- *DSN*: A delivery status notification was generated for the message.
- *EXPAND*: The membership of a distribution was expanded to determine the final recipients of the message.
- *FAIL*: Delivery of the message has failed permanently.
- *POISONMESSAGE*: The message was put into or removed from the poison message queue.
- *RECEIVE*: The message was received and committed to the database.
- *REDIRECT*: The message was redirected to another recipient.
- *RESOLVE*: The message's recipient was resolved to a different email address.
- *SEND*: The message was sent using SMTP to a different server.
- *SUBMIT*: The message was submitted to the Hub Transport server from a Mailbox server or Edge Transport server.
- *TRANSFER*: The recipients of the message were moved to a forked message because of recipient limits or conversion of the message content.

Note that the DELIVER status in the EventID field is your confirmation that a message was actually delivered to a recipient's mailbox—no matter what they try to tell you!

Configuring Message Tracking

The actual message tracking logs are located (in a default installation) at the following location, as shown in Figure 9.16: `C:\Program Files\Microsoft\Exchange Server\TransportRoles\Logs\MessageTracking`.

The logs are formatted as comma-separated-value (CSV) files, so you can open them in any text editor, as shown in Figure 9.17, or even in Microsoft Excel for advanced sorting and grouping if you want, although you'll most commonly access the logs using the message tracking interface.

FIGURE 9.16 Locating the message tracking logs

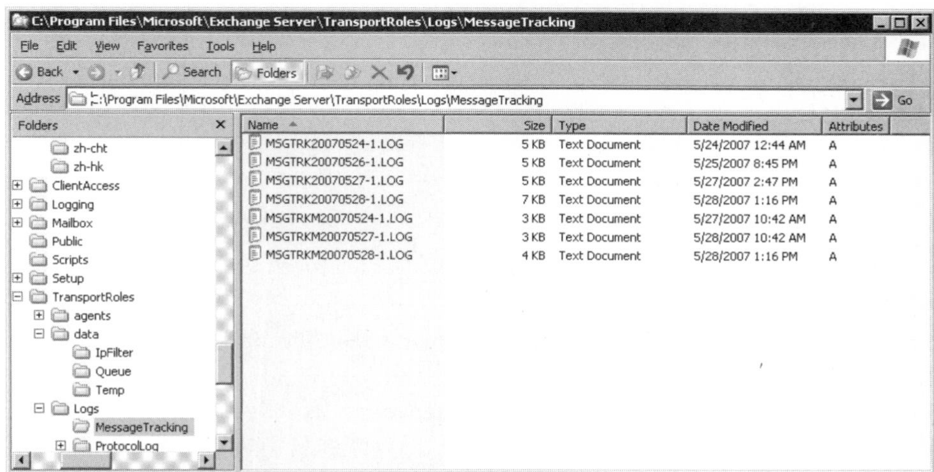

FIGURE 9.17 Examining a message tracking log

MSGTRKM20070528-1.LOG - Notepad

File Edit Format View Help

```
#Software: Microsoft Exchange Server
#Version: 8.0.0.0
#Log-type: Message Tracking Log
#Date: 2007-05-28T15:42:02.127Z
#Fields: date-time,client-ip,client-hostname,server-ip,server-hostname,so
2007-05-28T15:42:02.127Z,192.168.0.151,WILEYEX01A,,WILEYEX01A,"MDB:353c60
2007-05-28T15:42:09.158Z,192.168.0.151,WILEYEX01A,,WILEYEX01A,"MDB:353c60
2007-05-28T15:43:30.392Z,192.168.0.151,WILEYEX01A,,WILEYEX01A,"MDB:353c60
2007-05-28T15:43:34.345Z,192.168.0.151,WILEYEX01A,,WILEYEX01A,"MDB:353c60
2007-05-28T15:44:25.361Z,192.168.0.151,WILEYEX01A,,WILEYEX01A,"MDB:353c60
2007-05-28T15:44:30.361Z,192.168.0.151,WILEYEX01A,,WILEYEX01A,"MDB:353c60
2007-05-28T18:16:33.861Z,192.168.0.151,WILEYEX01A,,WILEYEX01A,"MDB:353c60
```

You may want to perform a few configuration actions for tracking logs that we'll discuss here:

- Disabling or enabling message tracking on a server
- Changing the location of the tracking logs
- Changing the maximum size of the each tracking log
- Changing the maximum size of the tracking log directory
- Changing the maximum age for tracking logs
- Disabling or enabling message subject tracking in message tracking logs

Disabling or Enabling Message Tracking on a Server

By default, message tracking is enabled on all Edge Transport, Hub Transport, and Mailbox servers. You can disable (or enable) message tracking by using the following commands for Edge Transport and Hub Transport servers:

- To disable message tracking, use `Set-TransportServer` *`servername`* `-MessageTrackingLogEnabled:$false`.
- To enable message tracking, use `Set-TransportServer` *`servername`* `-MessageTrackingLogEnabled:$true`.

You can disable (or enable) message tracking by using the following commands for Mailbox servers:

- To disable message tracking, use `Set-MailboxServer` *`servername`* `-MessageTrackingLogEnabled:$false`.
- To enable message tracking, use `Set-MailboxServer` *`servername`* `-MessageTrackingLogEnabled:$true`.

Changing the Tracking Log Location

To change the location of the tracking logs from their default location, you can use the following commands:

- `For hub transport or Edge Transport servers, use Set-TransportServer` *`servername`* `-MessageTrackingLogPath "T:\Message Tracking".`
- For Mailbox servers, use `Set-MailboxServer` *`servername`* `-MessageTrackingLogPath "T:\Message Tracking"`.

Changing the Tracking Log Maximum Size

To change the maximum size of each individual tracking log, you can use the following commands:

- For Hub Transport or Edge Transport servers, use `Set-TransportServer` *`servername`* `-MessageTrackingLogMaxFileSize 15MB.`
- For Mailbox servers, use `Set-MailboxServer` *`servername`* `-MessageTrackingLogMaxFileSize 15MB.`

By default, each message tracking log created has a maximum size of 10MB. You can use values in bytes (B), kilobytes (KB), megabytes (MB), gigabytes (GB), or terabytes (TB) when configuring the maximum size of each message tracking log.

Changing the Tracking Log Directory Maximum Size

To change the maximum size of the folder containing the message tracking logs, you can use the following commands:

- For Hub Transport or Edge Transport servers, use `Set-TransportServer` *`servername`* `-MessageTrackingLogMaxDirectorySize 5GB`.
- For Mailbox servers, use `Set-TransportServer` *`servername`* `-MessageTrackingLogMaxDirectorySize 5GB`.

Changing the Tracking Log Maximum Age

To change the message tracking log age, you can use the following commands:

- For Hub Transport or Edge Transport servers, use `Set-TransportServer` *`servername`* `-MessageTrackingLogMaxAge 45.00:00:00`.
- For Mailbox servers, use `Set-MailboxServer` *`servername`* `-MessageTrackingLogMaxAge 45.00:00:00`.

The value entered has a format of dd.hh:mm:ss, where d = days, h = hours, m = minutes, and s = seconds. If the value is set 00:00:00, Exchange will not automatically prune tracking logs because of age.

Disabling or Enabling Message Subject Logging

By default, message subject logging is enabled, but you can disable or enable it if you want. You can disable (or enable) subject logging by using the following commands for Edge Transport and Hub Transport servers:

- To disable subject logging, use `Set-TransportServer` *`servername`* `-MessageTrackingLogSubjectLoggingEnabled $false`.
- To enable message tracking, use `Set-TransportServer` *`servername`* `-MessageTrackingLogSubjectLoggingEnabled $true`.

You can disable (or enable) message tracking by using the following commands for Mailbox servers:

- To disable message tracking, use `Set-MailboxServer` *`servername`* `-MessageTrackingLogSubjectLoggingEnabled $false`.
- To enable message tracking, use `Set-MailboxServer` *`servername`* `-MessageTrackingLogSubjectLoggingEnabled $true`.

Moving Mailboxes

Most Exchange administrators have their own pattern or method for placing mailboxes on Exchange servers. Some place them on a specific Mailbox server or in specific mailbox databases by department or geographical location. Other administrators randomly assign mailboxes to Mailbox servers and mailbox databases. Whatever method you use, at some time you're going to need to move one or more mailboxes for some reason.

Using the Exchange Management Console

The most common, and familiar, method of moving mailboxes is to move them as needed using the GUI, in this case the Exchange Management Console. To move a mailbox from the Exchange Management Console, perform the steps outlined in Exercise 9.1.

EXERCISE 9.1

Moving a Mailbox with the Exchange Management Console

1. Click Start ➢ Programs ➢ Microsoft Exchange Server 2007, and then select Exchange Management Console.
2. Expand the Microsoft Exchange root object, expand the Recipient Configuration folder, and then click the Mailboxes node.
3. Select the mailbox to be moved in the center area of the window.
4. In the Actions pane on the right, click the Move Mailbox link. The Move Mailbox Wizard opens, as shown here.

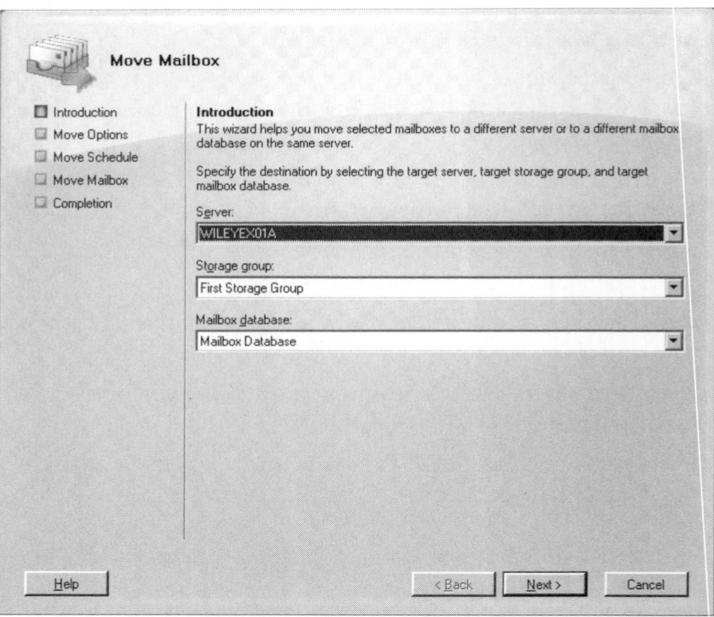

EXERCISE 9.1 *(continued)*

5. From the available options, select the destination Mailbox server, storage group, and mailbox database. After making your selections, click Next to continue to the Move Options page, as shown here.

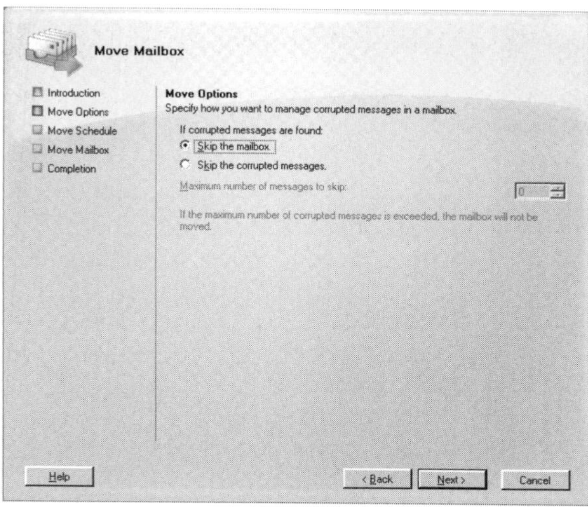

6. On the Move Options page, you'll be able to determine what to do if errors are encountered during the mailbox move process. Usually you'll want to leave the default selection of Skip the Mailbox selected, allowing you to return to the mailbox for a closer examination later if errors are encountered. After making your selection, click Next to continue to the Move Schedule page, as shown here.

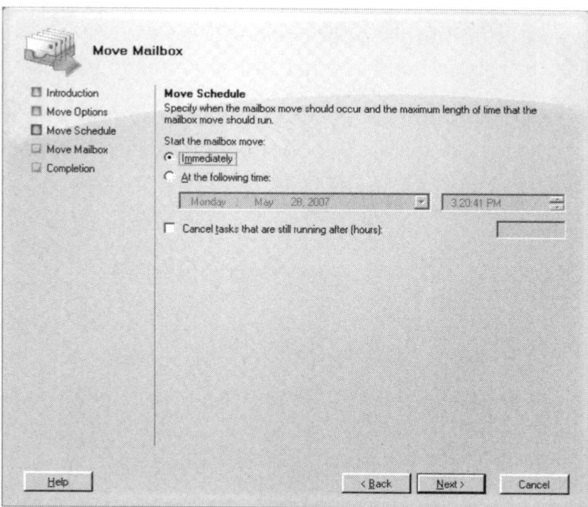

EXERCISE 9.1 *(continued)*

7. On the Move Schedule page, you will be able to start the move process immediately or schedule it for another time such as off-usage hours when the user will likely not be using their mailbox. Selecting to move the mailbox at a later time is also commonly used when large groups of mailboxes are being moved. After making your selection, click Next to continue to the Move Mailbox page, as shown here.

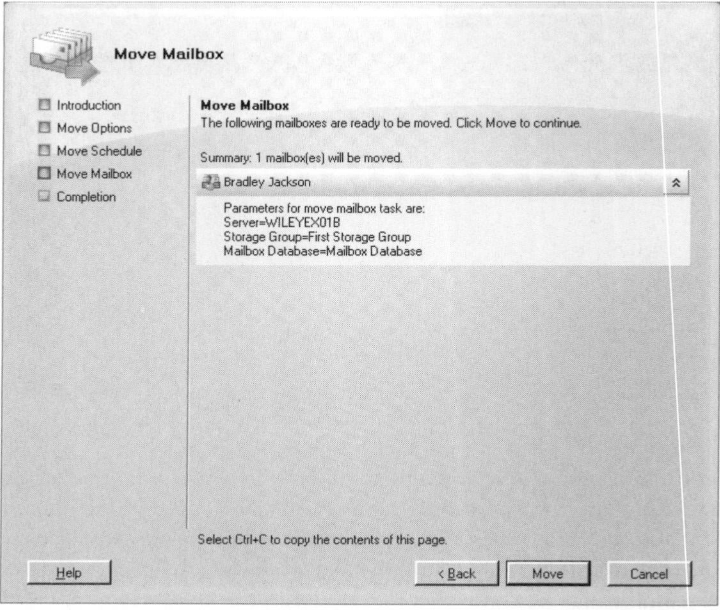

8. The Move Mailbox page summarizes your choices. Click Move to start or schedule the move process. Click Back if you need to make any changes to your selections.

9. If the move was set to occur immediately, you will be presented with the Completion page within a few minutes. Otherwise, the Completion page will appear after the scheduled move event. Click Finish to close the Move Mailbox Wizard.

Using the Exchange Management Shell

Of course, you can also perform the mailbox move process from the Exchange Management Shell, but the ease or difficulty of doing so depends on the number of mailboxes to be moved. If you are moving only a single mailbox, the process is simple and uses the `Move-Mailbox` cmdlet with no piped input, such as the following command to move the mailbox for James Smith (jsmith) to the default mailbox database on the server named wileyex01a:

```
Move-Mailbox jsmith
-TargetDatabase "WILEYEX01A\First Storage Group\Mailbox Database"
```

Figure 9.18 illustrates the output you'll see from this process.

FIGURE 9.18 Moving a mailbox from the Exchange Command Shell

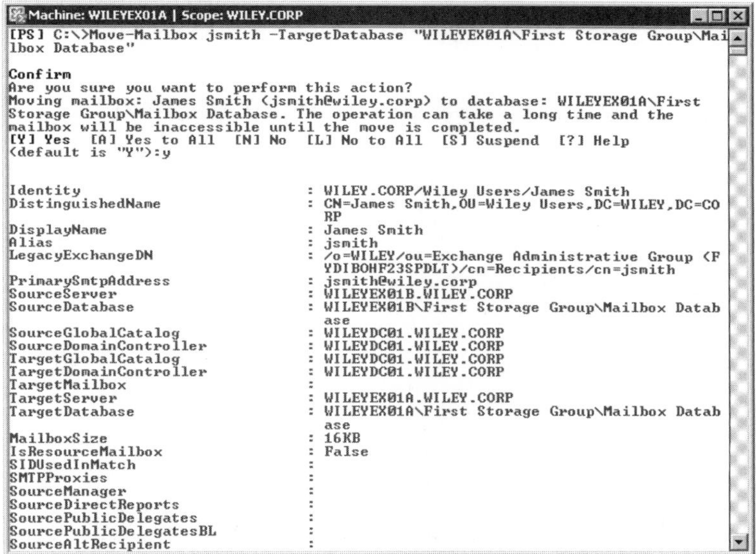

As you can see, all you needed to know was some identifying information about the mailbox to be moved, such as the alias, the user principal name or email address, and the destination location into which the mailbox should be moved. For the destination, you will need to specify at least the storage group name and the mailbox database name for same-server moves. If the move spans different servers, you'll need to provide the destination server name as well, as shown in the example.

This discussion of moving mailboxes from the Exchange Management Shell assumes the move is taking place within the same forest. For more advanced mailbox move operations, see the TechNet article at `http://technet.microsoft.com/en-us/library/bb124797.aspx`.

If you want to move multiple mailboxes from the Exchange Management Shell, you have a few different options available to you depending on what you want to accomplish. If, for example, you wanted to move all the mailboxes for users with a last name of Jackson from one mailbox database to another, you could use a command similar to the following:

```
Get-Mailbox -Filter {alias -like "*jackson"} | Move-Mailbox
-TargetDatabase "WILEYEX01A\First Storage Group\Mailbox Database"
```

Figure 9.19 shows the output of this command. Notice how you were able to specify the mailboxes to be moved by using the `Get-Mailbox` cmdlet with a filter set on the alias. Once the list of mailboxes to moved was available, the output was then piped to the `Move-Mailbox` cmdlet as input for the identity of the mailboxes to be moved.

FIGURE 9.19 Moving two mailboxes from the Exchange Command Shell

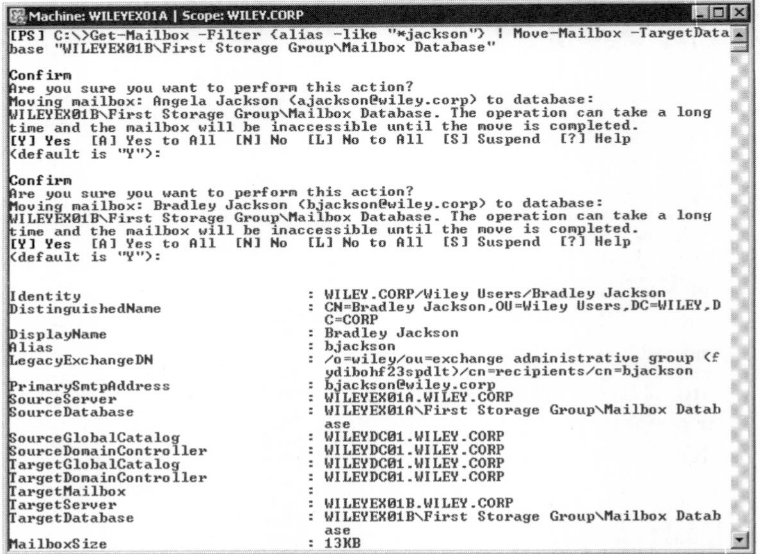

You might want to specify some options when using the `Move-Mailbox` cmdlet:

- The `-BadItemLimit` option specifies how many failed items are allowed before the mailbox will be skipped for moving. An example of this is as follows: `Move-Mailbox jsmith -TargetDatabase "WILEYEX01A\First Storage Group\Mailbox Database" -BadItemLimit 10`.
- `If the mailbox being` moved is larger than allowed in the destination mailbox database, the move will fail unless you use the `-MailboxSizeLimitOptions PreserveSource` option. This will allow the move to succeed and configure the mailbox to have the same size limit as originally configured in the source mailbox database.
- For some unknown reason, the `Move-Mailbox` cmdlet does not delete the source mailbox after the move has been completed. To enable this function, you must use the `-SourceMailboxCleanupOptions DeleteSourceMailbox` option as part of the

Move-Mailbox cmdlet. You should always use this option to ensure that the mailbox database stays as small as it can.

- To keep the recipient policies on the mailbox that existed in the source mailbox database, you'll need to use the -IgnorePolicyMatch $true option as part of the Move-Mailbox cmdlet.

Performing Bulk Management

If there is anything that can make an administrator's life easier, it's accomplishing multiple tasks with a single action. When we use the phrase *bulk management*, that's what we're talking about: executing a single action that performs that action against multiple objects. One of the design priorities in Exchange Server 2007 was to emphasize the ability to make changes in bulk, thereby saving time and increasing efficiency and accuracy. In the following sections, we'll cover some (but likely not all) of the bulk management tasks that you can perform in Exchange Server 2007.

Moving Mailboxes

Moving mailboxes can be a complicated and time-consuming process. But if done in bulk, it can be much easier and more efficient than if done interactively as we previously examined. Consider the following examples from the Microsoft Exchange team blog for mailbox move scenarios:

- If you wanted to place all of the mailboxes for users that were in the Finance department into their own mailbox database (and storage group), you could use the following bulk management command: Get-User | Where { $_.Department -ilike "Finance" } | Move-Mailbox -TargetDatabase "WILEYEX02C\Finance Storage Group\Finance Mailbox Database".
- If you wanted to move all the mailboxes for users that were located in the Finance OU into their own mailbox database (and storage group), you could use the following bulk management command: Get-User | Where { $_.OU -ilike "*Finance" } | Move-Mailbox -TargetDatabase "WILEYEX02C\Finance Storage Group\Finance Mailbox Database".
- If you had multiple companies represented within your Exchange organization, say subsidiaries or divisions and you wanted to move all the mailboxes for the Small Corp company to their own Mailbox server, you could use the following bulk management command: Get-User | Where { $_.Company -ilike "Small Corp" } | Move-Mailbox -TargetDatabase "WILEYEX07A\Small Corp Storage Group\Mailbox Database".
- If you wanted to reorganize the server and mailbox database location of your users' mailboxes by their office location, you could use the following bulk management command to move all users in the Memphis office: Get-User | Where { $_.City -ilike "Memphis" } | Move-Mailbox -TargetDatabase " "WILEYEX09B\Memphis Storage Group\Mailbox Database".

- You can perform the same geographical filtering by using the ZIP (postal) code or state/province information as well by using the `Where { $_.PostalCode -Eq "38105" } or Where { $_.StateOrProvince -ilike "TN" }` filter.

You can, and definitely should, spend time on the Microsoft Exchange team blog, called "You Had Me At EHLO!" You can find it at `http://msexchangeteam.com`. The previous examples were modified from those originally published at `http://msexchangeteam.com/archive/2006/10/27/429522.aspx`.

Of course, the possibilities here are limited only by the attributes of the user object in Active Directory and your willingness to experiment.

You can, of course, schedule a large number of mailboxes to be moved using the Move Mailbox Wizard you examined earlier in this chapter. This may be an attractive solution if you know which mailboxes you're interested in moving but don't want to create the required PowerShell cmdlets to perform the work.

Creating Mailboxes

In Chapter 6, "Configuring and Managing Exchange Recipients," you examined the mailbox-enabled user creation process. At that time, we noted that creating multiple users in bulk was a problematic process in Exchange Server 2007, something that was not necessarily the case in Exchange Server 2003. You can get around this problem in two ways: create the mailbox-enabled users in a two-step process (simpler overall but more work) or create the mailbox-enabled users in a one-step process (more complicated overall but less work). We'll examine both options here, and you can decide which one you want to use in your environment.

Using the Two-Step Process

In Exchange Server 2003, recipients were mailbox-enabled after they were created, and the user account creation process was completely independent of the mailbox-enablement process. Many companies created customized in-house procedures to provision new user accounts and mailbox-enable them. One of the more unique we've seen is an Excel spreadsheet that uses variable substitutions from several sheets to create the `dsadd user` command that is ultimately used to create and configure the user account with the exception of Exchange and Terminal Services items. This isn't such a bad way to create and configure user accounts because it is easy and provides guaranteed repeatability as long as the underlying information in the spreadsheet is kept up-to-date, such as department to group memberships, department to home folder locations, department to OU relationships, and so on.

An example of the resulting `dsadd user` command that you might get from this process is presented here for review:

```
dsadd user "CN=Smith\, Albert,OU=Sales,OU=Departments,DC=mycompany,DC=local"
-samid "amsith" -pwd *asmith042* -mustchpwd yes -fn "Albert" -ln "Smith"
```

```
-display "Smith, Albert" -desc "Sales"
-memberof "CN=Sales Group,OU=User Groups,DC=mycompany,DC=local" -hmdrv "H:"
-loscr "script.bat" -hmdir "\\SERVER42\SALES$\AMSITH" -empid "42042"
-dept "Sales" -company "My Company"
```

So, if the spreadsheet (in this example) were created properly and the empty rows were prepopulated with the formulas to create the required `dsadd user` command, then all you'd need to do would be to enter the uniquely identifying information about the user, such as the first and last name, department, and initial password. In the case of this specific Excel spreadsheet, the password was also automatically created based on the first and last names of the user and a random string of characters. The command could then be copied and pasted into a command interpreter window, and the account would be created almost without effort (well, beyond the extensive effort that went into creating and configuring the spreadsheet initially).

That's the first step of the two-step process: creating the user account. It doesn't really matter how you created the user account in bulk, as long as you had it created.

The second step of the two-step process is to mailbox-enable the newly created user accounts using the `Enable-Mailbox` cmdlet:

```
Enable-Mailbox -Identity 'WILEY.CORP/Wiley Users/James Smith' -Alias 'jsmith'
-Database 'CN=Mailbox Database,CN=First Storage Group,CN=InformationStore,
CN=WILEYEX01A,CN=Servers,CN=Exchange Administrative Group (FYDIBOHF23SPDLT),
CN=Administrative Groups,CN=WILEY,CN=Microsoft Exchange,CN=Services,
CN=Configuration,DC=WILEY,DC=CORP'
```

Of course, you'll need to know the full LDAP path to the mailbox database you want to create the mailbox in, but you can script this using variable substitution to create multiple mailboxes as part of the overall user creation process.

The primary advantage of the two-step method is that you can assign a unique password to each mailbox-enabled user account being created. Additionally, you can assign the user and mailbox provisioning processes to different administrators for separating administrative responsibilities. A significant downside to the two-step method is the overall complexity and length of time required to create and implement the solution.

Using the One-Step Process

If you want to speed things up for account and mailbox provisioning or you just want to use native Exchange Server 2007 methods, you can use the one-step process to create and mailbox-enable the accounts in one action.

The TechNet article at `http://technet.microsoft.com/en-us/library/bb310752.aspx` explains in detail how to create mailbox-enabled accounts in some detail, but we'll examine the process here using a modified version of the commands presented there.

To create accounts in bulk using a PowerShell cmdlet, you'll need to first create and save a CSV text file containing the values to be read in to create the user accounts. An example of what this file might look (containing just a name and a username) is presented here for analysis:

```
Name,UserName
Greg Jones,gjones
```

```
Amy Mathis,amathis
Geoff Anderson,ganderson
Matthew Perkins,mperkins
Patrick Malone,pmalone
```

When this CSV file is read in using the `Import-CSV` cmdlet and piped into the `New-Mailbox` cmdlet using the `ForEach-Object` cmdlet, such as the following command, the new mailbox-enabled user accounts will be provisioned in one fell swoop:

```
Import-CSV "C:\NewUsers.csv" | ForEach-Object
-Begin {$Temp = ConvertTo-SecureString "pass@word1" -asPlainText -force}
-Process
{New-Mailbox -Name $_.Name -UserPrincipalName "$($_.UserName)@wiley.corp"
-OrganizationalUnit "wiley.corp/Wiley Users"
-Database "wileyex01a\Second Storage Group\Second Mailbox Database"
-Password $Temp -ResetPasswordOnNextLogon $true}
```

Figure 9.20 shows the resulting output.

FIGURE 9.20 Creating user accounts and mailboxes in bulk using the Exchange Command Shell

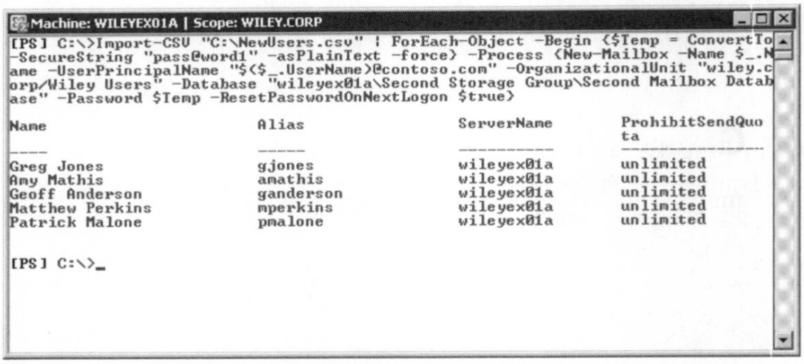

```
Machine: WILEYEX01A | Scope: WILEY.CORP
[PS] C:\>Import-CSV "C:\NewUsers.csv" | ForEach-Object -Begin {$Temp = ConvertTo
-SecureString "pass@word1" -asPlainText -force} -Process {New-Mailbox -Name $_.N
ame -UserPrincipalName "$($_.UserName)@contoso.com" -OrganizationalUnit "wiley.c
orp/Wiley Users" -Database "wileyex01a\Second Storage Group\Second Mailbox Datab
ase" -Password $Temp -ResetPasswordOnNextLogon $true}

Name                    Alias           ServerName      ProhibitSendQuo
                                                        ta
----                    -----           ----------      ---------------
Greg Jones              gjones          wileyex01a      unlimited
Amy Mathis              amathis         wileyex01a      unlimited
Geoff Anderson          ganderson       wileyex01a      unlimited
Matthew Perkins         mperkins        wileyex01a      unlimited
Patrick Malone          pmalone         wileyex01a      unlimited

[PS] C:\>_
```

The one-step method has a few variations, such as supplying the password for the new accounts ahead of time using the `$Password = Read-Host -AsSecureString` command within the Exchange Management Shell before performing the CSV file read. You would then use a slightly modified bit of code, as shown here:

```
Import-CSV "C:\NewUsers.csv" | ForEach-Object
{New-Mailbox -Name $_.Name -UserPrincipalName
   "$($_.UserName)@wiley.corp.com"
-OrganizationalUnit "wiley.corp/Wiley Users"
-Database "wileyex01a\Second Storage
   Group\Second Mailbox Database"
-Password $Password -ResetPasswordOnNextLogon $true}
```

Figure 9.21 shows the resulting output.

The primary advantage to using the one-step process to provision new user accounts and mailboxes is the simplicity of executing the command. Of course, that simplicity does come at the cost of every user account having the same password—unless you come up with a way to handle that via a randomly generated password, which is certainly possible. The possibilities are limited only by your imagination when it comes to using PowerShell to manage Exchange Server 2007.

FIGURE 9.21 Using an alternative method for creating user accounts and mailboxes in bulk using the Exchange Command Shell

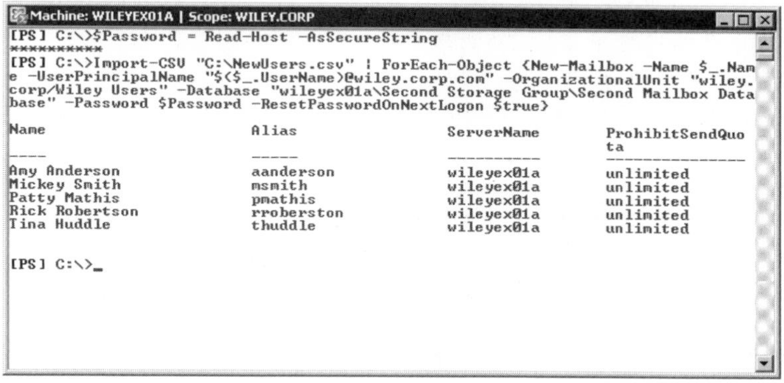

```
Machine: WILEYEX01A | Scope: WILEY.CORP
[PS] C:\>$Password = Read-Host -AsSecureString
**********
[PS] C:\>Import-CSV "C:\NewUsers.csv" | ForEach-Object {New-Mailbox -Name $_.Nam
e -UserPrincipalName "$($_.UserName)@wiley.corp.com" -OrganizationalUnit "wiley.
corp/Wiley Users" -Database "wileyex01a\Second Storage Group\Second Mailbox Data
base" -Password $Password -ResetPasswordOnNextLogon $true}

Name                    Alias              ServerName       ProhibitSendQuo
                                                            ta
----                    -----              ----------       ---------------
Amy Anderson            aanderson          wileyex01a       unlimited
Mickey Smith            msmith             wileyex01a       unlimited
Patty Mathis            pmathis            wileyex01a       unlimited
Rick Robertson          rroberston         wileyex01a       unlimited
Tina Huddle             thuddle            wileyex01a       unlimited

[PS] C:\>_
```

Populating Groups

One of the most common tasks Exchange administrators often find themselves performing is the maintenance of distribution group memberships. Of course, using query-based distribution groups can sometimes alleviate or eliminate this problem, but they're not always the solution. Sometimes you may need to know with absolute certainty who is in a group, something you can guarantee and keep static by using traditional distribution groups. Of course, if you're looking to quickly populate a security group, you cannot use an LDAP query like you can with the dynamic distribution groups, so PowerShell can help there as well.

Suppose you want to populate a distribution group with all mailbox-enabled users who have various management-level titles or are members of the board department. That would be a fairly difficult combination to enact with a dynamic distribution group, but you can easily populate a distribution group by using a command such as the following:

```
Get-User -Filter {((Title -like '*Manager*') -or (Title -like '*Director*')
-or (Title -like '*Board Member*') -or (Department -eq 'Board'))
-and (RecipientTypeDetails -eq 'UserMailbox')}
| ForEach-Object -Process {Add-DistributionGroupMember -Identity
"Management Team" -Member $_.Name}
```

Viewing Mailbox Sizes

One of the most annoying things you'll quickly notice about Exchange Server 2007 is that you cannot easily view the sizes of your users' mailboxes. This used to be a common task in Exchange Server 2003 using the Exchange System Manager—but now the information is unavailable for viewing.

To get the information you need, you'll need to first determine what you want. It sounds simple, but it really makes a difference when you start to construct your PowerShell commands for viewing mailbox information. If all you want is a basic report that includes the size, last login information, and status of the mailbox (less than or greater than the quotas that have been set), then the following code from the Exchange Server 2007 wiki will probably do the trick for you:

```
Get-Mailbox | Get-MailboxStatistics
| Select-Object DisplayName,TotalItemSize,StorageLimitStatus,LastLogonTime
```

Figure 9.22 displays the resulting output.

FIGURE 9.22 Viewing mailbox size and login information

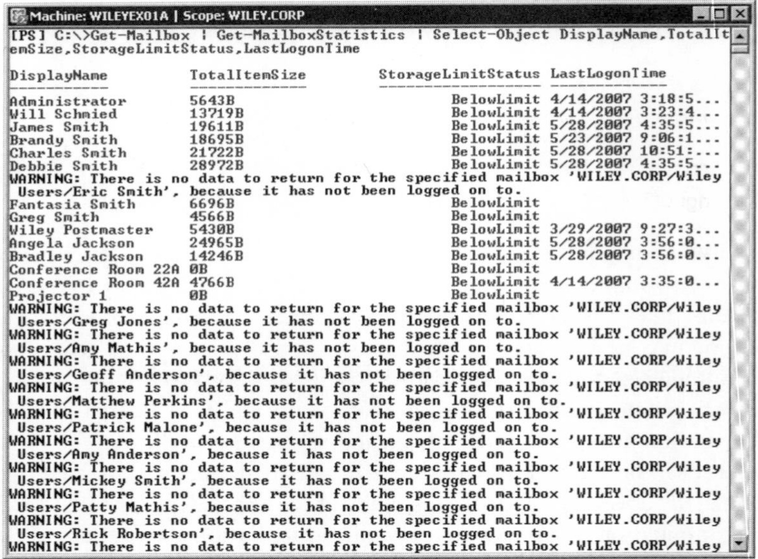

You can visit the Exchange Server 2007 wiki at www.exchangeninjas.com.

You could even pipe the output to a CSV file using the `Export-CSV` cmdlet, producing the code shown here:

```
Get-Mailbox | Get-MailboxStatistics
| Select-Object DisplayName,TotalItemSize,StorageLimitStatus,LastLogonTime
| Export-CSV C:\MailboxStats.csv
```

Figure 9.23 shows what the resulting CSV file will look like.

FIGURE 9.23 Examining exported mailbox size information

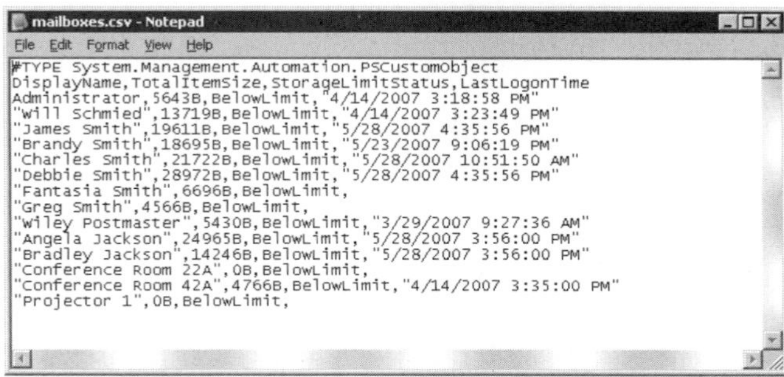

mailboxes.csv - Notepad

File Edit Format View Help

```
#TYPE System.Management.Automation.PSCustomObject
DisplayName,TotalItemSize,StorageLimitStatus,LastLogonTime
Administrator,5643B,BelowLimit,"4/14/2007 3:18:58 PM"
"Will Schmied",13719B,BelowLimit,"4/14/2007 3:23:49 PM"
"James Smith",19611B,BelowLimit,"5/28/2007 4:35:56 PM"
"Brandy Smith",18695B,BelowLimit,"5/23/2007 9:06:19 PM"
"Charles Smith",21722B,BelowLimit,"5/28/2007 10:51:50 AM"
"Debbie Smith",28972B,BelowLimit,"5/28/2007 4:35:56 PM"
"Fantasia Smith",6696B,BelowLimit,
"Greg Smith",4566B,BelowLimit,
"Wiley Postmaster",5430B,BelowLimit,"3/29/2007 9:27:36 AM"
"Angela Jackson",24965B,BelowLimit,"5/28/2007 3:56:00 PM"
"Bradley Jackson",14246B,BelowLimit,"5/28/2007 3:56:00 PM"
"Conference Room 22A",0B,BelowLimit,
"Conference Room 42A",4766B,BelowLimit,"4/14/2007 3:35:00 PM"
"Projector 1",0B,BelowLimit,
```

If you want to display the quota information for each mailbox, you will need to use a slightly different command, such as the one shown here:

```
Get-Mailbox | Format-Table
 Name,IssueWarningQuota,ProhibitSendQuota,ProhibitSendReceiveQuota
```

Figure 9.24 shows the resulting output.

FIGURE 9.24 Examining mailbox quota information

Machine: WILEYEX01A | Scope: WILEY.CORP

```
[PS] C:\>Get-Mailbox | Format-Table Name,IssueWarningQuota,ProhibitSendQuota,Pro
hibitSendReceiveQuota

Name                IssueWarningQuota   ProhibitSendQuota   ProhibitSendReceive
                                                            Quota
----                -----------------   -----------------   -------------------
Administrator       unlimited           unlimited           unlimited
Will Schmied        unlimited           unlimited           unlimited
James Smith         unlimited           unlimited           unlimited
Brandy Smith        unlimited           unlimited           unlimited
Charles Smith       unlimited           unlimited           unlimited
Debbie Smith        unlimited           unlimited           unlimited
Eric Smith          unlimited           unlimited           unlimited
Fantasia Smith      unlimited           unlimited           unlimited
Greg Smith          unlimited           unlimited           unlimited
Wiley Postmaster    unlimited           unlimited           unlimited
Angela L. Jackson   unlimited           unlimited           unlimited
Bradley Jackson     unlimited           unlimited           unlimited
Conference Room 22A unlimited           unlimited           unlimited
Conference Room 42A unlimited           unlimited           unlimited
Projector 1         unlimited           unlimited           unlimited
Greg Jones          unlimited           unlimited           unlimited
Amy Mathis          unlimited           unlimited           unlimited
Geoff Anderson      unlimited           unlimited           unlimited
Matthew Perkins     unlimited           unlimited           unlimited
Patrick Malone      unlimited           unlimited           unlimited
Amy Anderson        unlimited           unlimited           unlimited
Mickey Smith        unlimited           unlimited           unlimited
Patty Mathis        unlimited           unlimited           unlimited
Rick Robertson      unlimited           unlimited           unlimited
Tina Huddle         unlimited           unlimited           unlimited


[PS] C:\>_
```

Real World Scenario

Planning Ahead to Save Time (and Prevent Problems) Later

Although you've looked at several methods to move mailboxes one at a time or in large groups in this chapter, sometimes you're better off not having to move mailboxes. Or perhaps a better way to phrase that would be, you're better off not moving mailboxes if you can plan ahead of time to place the mailboxes where you want them.

Although the move process is almost always painless and error-free, there are always exceptions to that rule. In fact, more often than not, it is during a mailbox move that you'll find out there is corruption in a mailbox—not exactly the news you were hoping for during what was supposed to be a stress-free move process. Of course, you can configure a specific number of corrupted items to be skipped and still allow the mailbox to be moved, but you're still going to have to deal with an unhappy user and possibly a restore evolution. That is not to say you should never move mailboxes for fear of corrupt items, but it's something to consider. Other issues that can arise from mailbox moves include large amounts of disk space usage because of transaction log growth, interruption to user access during the move process, and the time and effort involved to process the moves on your part—just to name a few.

Before you start to think you should never move a mailbox, that's not the point we're trying to get across here. We just want to point out some of the downsides to mailbox moves, especially when you're moving large quantities of mailboxes. There are certainly many good reasons to move mailboxes, such as server decommission, migration to a newer version of Exchange, or mailbox distribution across multiple servers. However, you can prevent that last reason from occurring for the most part by just taking the time (ahead of time) to properly plan and size your servers. Do you really want to put 4,000 recipients on a single server, or would you rather create several Mailbox servers (or better yet, several Mailbox server clusters) and then distribute the mailboxes evenly across them?

Although a mailbox move, more often than not, is really just a mailbox move, you should always strive to do it right the first time if at all possible. You'll thank yourself later when your Mailbox servers run smoothly.

Summary

Although you'll be performing many administrative tasks as an Exchange administrator, some are more common than others. Some of the most common tasks you'll need to understand and be able to perform well include the following:

- Moving mailboxes
- Tracking messages through the Exchange organization
- Managing and configuring message queues

These three tasks were the main focus of this chapter, although we did take a brief amount of time to examine some of the many, many possibilities for bulk management of Exchange Server 2007. The few items we examined in no way represent all the possibilities, and the list of tasks that can be carried in such a fashion will no doubt continue to grow as more administrators find creative ways to make repetitive tasks faster and more efficient.

Exam Essentials

Know your queues. You should have a good understanding of the purpose and function of each of the queues you're likely to encounter on your Exchange servers. Each one has a different purpose and will provide you with a wealth of information in your troubleshooting and routine monitoring tasks.

Practice message tracking. Although the message tracking interface in Exchange Server 2007 is not as user-friendly or usable to some administrators, it's still a powerful tool and one you need to understand how to configure, use, and interpret. Message tracking is oftentimes overlooked or undervalued, but the first time you need to absolutely determine what happened to a message, you'll find out how useful and important message tracking can be. Take some time to learn how to use it, and you'll be rewarded many times over.

Get nit-picky. Many tasks in Exchange Server 2007 require very specific knowledge or conditions to be in place before they can be performed. As an example, creating a resource mailbox requires that the associated user account be disabled. Be sure you know and understand all the "little" nuances that go along with recipient management in Exchange Server 2007 before exam day.

Learn the PowerShell commands. Almost every configuration or management action you perform from the Exchange Management Console will present you with the PowerShell code that was used to perform the action. Take advantage of this information, and learn how to use the Exchange Management Shell to your advantage. Some of these commands are likely to make an appearance on the exam as well.

Know where to go. Many times on the exam you are likely to be asked what configuration is needed to produce the required results. The Exchange Management Console has been completely redesigned to make it easier to navigate and get to tasks, but that doesn't mean it won't be difficult to remember later. Take the time as you review the material in this book to think about what types of configuration and management tasks you find yourself performing in each major node of the Exchange Management Console.

Review Questions

1. Which of the following queue types would be used for messages being routed to a different Active Directory site than the one the Hub Transport server is in that contains the queue?
   - A. Mailbox delivery queue
   - B. Remote delivery queue
   - C. Submission queue
   - D. Unreachable queue
   - E. Remote site queue
   - F. Poison message queue

2. A queue that contains messages that are destined for delivery to an external recipient using an SMTP connector configured to use a smart host for routing will have what delivery type associated with it?
   - A. MapiDelivery
   - B. DNSConnectorDelivery
   - C. NonSMTPGatewayDelivery
   - D. SmartHostConnectorDelivery
   - E. SMTPSmartHostDelivery

3. What action could you take on a queue on one of your Hub Transport servers if you did not want any of the messages in the queue to be attempted for delivery but you did not want them to be deleted either?
   - A. Resume.
   - B. Suspend.
   - C. Retry.
   - D. View messages.
   - E. Remove messages (with NDR).

4. You recently found out that your company has been swamped with spam that somehow made it through your spam filters. All the spam is promoting a new herbal enhancement product, and you've identified the most common subject headers of the messages. To stop the delivery of the messages, you've suspended all your mail queues, which is also causing legitimate messages to be held for delivery. If you wanted to remove all the suspect messages from the queues so you could allow delivery of the remaining messages, what cmdlet could you use?
   - A. `Remove-Message -filter {Subject -eq "`*`subject`*`"} -WithNDR $false`
   - B. `Purge-Message -filter {Subject -eq "`*`subject`*`"} -WithNDR $false`
   - C. `Delete-Message -filter {Subject -eq "`*`subject`*`"} -WithNDR $false`
   - D. `Drop-Message -filter {Subject -eq "`*`subject`*`"} -WithNDR $false`

5. To track messages from the Exchange Management Shell, what cmdlet must you use?
   A. `View-MessageTrackingLog`
   B. `Track-Message`
   C. `Get-MessageTracking`
   D. `Get-MessageTrackingLog`

6. If you wanted to remove all the messages from a specific queue and not send an NDR to any of the senders, what cmdlet would you need to use?
   A. `Remove-Queue -Filter {Queue -eq "`*`server\queue`*`"} -noNDR $true`
   B. `Remove-Message -Filter {Queue -eq "`*`server\queue`*`"} -withNDR $false`
   C. `Delete-Message -Filter {Queue -eq "`*`server\queue`*`"} -withNDR $false`
   D. `Empty-Queue -Filter {Queue -eq "`*`server\queue`*`"} -noNDR`

7. What EventID in the message tracking log indicates that a message was committed to the database on the destination Mailbox server?
   A. Deliver
   B. Receive
   C. Committed
   D. Written

8. You're looking at the queues on one of your Hub Transport servers and need to find the one corresponding to a particular Mailbox server. The Mailbox server and Hub Transport server are located in the same Active Directory site. What pieces of information in the main window of the Queue Viewer can help you determine which queue is the correct one? (Choose all that apply.)
   A. The Next Hop Domain value should indicate the fully qualified domain name of the Mailbox server.
   B. The Next Hop Domain value should indicate the Active Directory site name.
   C. The Delivery Type should indicate DNSConnectorDelivery.
   D. The Status should indicate Suspended.
   E. The Delivery Type should indicate MapiDelivery.
   F. The Message Count should indicate no messages are in the queue.

9. By default, what size will each message tracking log be limited to in Exchange Server 2007?
   A. 5MB
   B. 1MB
   C. 10MB
   D. 20MB

10. If you wanted to move a group of mailboxes based on the department configured for the user account, what two cmdlets would you need to use? (Choose two correct answers.)

A. `Get-Mailbox`

B. `Select-Mailbox`

C. `Move-Mailbox`

D. `Find-Mailbox`

E. `Get-User`

11. To delete a mailbox from the source mailbox database after it has been moved from the Exchange Management Shell, what option must you specify with the `Move-Mailbox` cmdlet?

A. `-DeleteSourceMailbox $true`

B. `-SourceMailboxCleanupOptions DeleteSourceMailbox`

C. `-SourceMailboxCleanupOptions DeleteSourceMailbox $true`

D. `-SourceMailboxCleanupOptions $true`

12. If you wanted to create new mailbox-enabled users in bulk, what two Exchange Management Shell cmdlets would you need to use? (Choose two correct answers.)

A. `Import-CSV`

B. `New-Mailbox`

C. `New-User`

D. `Read-CSV`

E. `Make-Mailbox`

F. `Get-CSV`

13. To view the sizes of all mailboxes in your Exchange organization, what three Exchange Management Shell cmdlets must you use? (Choose three correct answers.)

A. `Show-Information`

B. `Get-MailboxStatistics`

C. `Get-MailboxInformation`

D. `Get-Mailbox`

E. `Show-MailboxStatistics`

F. `Select-Object`

G. `List-Mailbox`

14. What EventID in the message tracking log indicates that a message was originally sent to an SMTP address that belongs to a distribution group?

A. Explode

B. Receive

C. Committed

D. Expand

15. From which of the following locations can you perform mailbox moves for mailboxes located on an Exchange Server 2007 Mailbox server? (Choose all that apply.)
    A. The Exchange Management Shell
    B. The Active Directory Users and Computers console
    C. The Exchange System Manager
    D. The Exchange Management Console
    E. The command interpreter

16. When looking at the status of a queue for messages being delivered to a Mailbox server, which one of the following status messages would not be seen?
    A. Retry
    B. Resumed
    C. Suspended
    D. Ready
    E. Active

17. What EventID in the message tracking log indicates that a message was placed in the recipient's mailbox on the database on the destination Mailbox server?
    A. Deliver
    B. Receive
    C. Committed
    D. Written

18. A queue that contains messages that are destined for delivery to a different Hub Transport server in the same Active Directory site will have what delivery type associated with it?
    A. MapiDelivery
    B. SmtpRelayWithinAdSite
    C. SmtpRelaytoRemoteAdSite
    D. SmtpRelaytoHubTransport
    E. SmtpRelaytoTiRg

19. What cmdlet would you need to use to prevent all messages in a selected queue from being attempted for delivery?
    A. `Resume-Queue`
    B. `Freeze-Queue`
    C. `Hold-Queue`
    D. `Suspend-Queue`
    E. `Stop-Queue`

20. If messages are placed into a specific queue, they are not attempted for delivery. These messages are available for administrative review and can be released manually by an administrator. Which of the listed queues is this?

A. Mailbox delivery queue

B. Remote delivery queue

C. Submission queue

D. Unreachable queue

E. Suspect queue

F. Poison message queue

Answers to Review Questions

1. B. The remote delivery queue holds messages that are being routed to remote SMTP destinations, such as servers that are located outside the Active Directory site containing the Hub Transport server. Remote delivery queues are dynamically created and removed as needed depending on the messages that are in routing on that server. The next hop for messages located in a remote delivery queue is a remote Active Directory site or SMTP domain or smart host.

2. D. A delivery type of SmartHostConnectorDelivery will be indicated for queues containing messages for delivery to an external recipient using an SMTP connector configured to use a smart host for message routing. If the SMTP connector were configured to use DNS MX records instead, the delivery type would indicate DNSConnectorDelivery

3. B. If you were to suspend the queue, this would temporarily prevent any messages in the queue from being delivered. New messages can enter the queue, but no messages can leave the queue while in a suspended state.

4. A. To remove all messages with a specific subject line from all queues, you would use the `Remove-Message -filter {Subject -eq "subject"} -WithNDR $false` cmdlet.

5. D. You need to use the `Get-MessageTrackingLog` cmdlet to track messages from the Exchange Management Shell. An example of how the cmdlet would be used is as follows: `Get-MessageTrackingLog -Recipients:wschmied@wiley.corp -Sender "ajackson@wiley.corp" -EventID "DELIVERY" -Start "5/21/2007 1:30:00 PM" -End "5/28/2007 1:30:00 PM" | format-list`.

6. B. To remove all the messages from a specific queue and not send NDRs to the senders, you would need to use the `Remove-Message` cmdlet as follows: `Remove-Message -Filter {Queue -eq "server\queue"} -withNDR $false`.

7. B. The Receive status in the message tracking log indicates the message was received and committed to the database.

8. A, E. Since this is delivery from a Hub Transport server to a Mailbox server in the same Active Directory domain, you can look for two key pieces of information about the queues to determine which one is for delivery to that Mailbox server. The Next Hop Domain value should indicate the fully qualified domain name of the Mailbox server, and the Delivery Type value should indicate MapiDelivery.

9. C. The default size of the message tracking logs in Exchange Server 2007 is 10MB. You can change that value by using the `Set-TransportServer servername -MessageTrackingLogMaxFileSize size cmdlet`.

10. C, E. To selectively move a group of mailboxes based on the department information found on the user's account, you need to use the `Get-User` and `Move-Mailbox` cmdlets. For example, if you wanted to place all the mailboxes for users in the Finance department into their own mailbox database (and storage group), you could use the following bulk management command: `Get-User | Where { $_.Department -ilike "Finance" } | Move-Mailbox -TargetDatabase "WILEYEX02C\Finance Storage Group\Finance Mailbox Database"`.

11. B. You would need to use the `-SourceMailboxCleanupOptions DeleteSourceMailbox` option as part of the `Move-Mailbox` cmdlet.

12. A, B. To create mailbox-enabled users in bulk, you would need to have the configuration for each mailbox in a CSV file. Then you would use the `Import-CSV` cmdlet to pipe input into the `New-Mailbox` cmdlet for processing.

13. B, D, F. To get the size information on each mailbox in your Exchange organization, you need to use the `Get-Mailbox` cmdlet to pipe input to the `Get-MailboxStatistics` cmdlet. The output of the `Get-Mailbox` cmdlet should then be piped to the `Select-Object` cmdlet to display the specific information you're interested in, such as `TotalSize, DisplayName,` or `LastLogonTime`.

14. D. The EventID of Expand indicates the membership of a distribution was expanded to determine the final recipients of the message.

15. A, D. In Exchange Server 2007, you can move mailboxes by using the Move Mailbox Wizard in the Exchange Management Console or by using the `Move-Mailbox` cmdlet from the Exchange Management Shell.

16. B. The status of a queue can be only one of the following four values: Active, Suspended, Ready, Retry.

17. A. The Delivery status in the message tracking log indicates the message was delivered to the recipient's mailbox.

18. B. A queue that contains messages that are being routed to a different Hub Transport server in the same Active Directory site will have a delivery type of SmtpRelayWithinAdSite. If the queue contained messages for delivery to a Hub Transport server in a different Active Directory site, it would have a delivery type of SmtpRelaytoRemoteAdSite. The delivery type of SmtpRelaytoTiRg is used when the queue contains messages queued for delivery to an Exchange Server 2003 routing group.

19. D. You would need to use the `Suspend-Queue` cmdlet. As an example, to suspend a queue with a next hop domain of wiley.com that is in a retry status, you would use the following cmdlet: `Suspend-Queue -Filter {NextHopDomain -eq "wiley.com" -and Status -eq "retry"}`.

20. F. The poison message queue holds messages that have been determined to be potentially harmful to the Exchange organization after a server failure has occurred, such as messages that contain errors that are potentially fatal to the Exchange organization. When no messages meeting this condition are found, this queue does not exist on the Hub Transport server, although the queue is in a ready state should it be needed. Messages placed into the poison message queue are not attempted for delivery, and their status is set to suspended, allowing the messages to be examined and deleted or released by the administrator after further review. The next hop for messages located in the poison message queue that have been released is the submission queue.

Creating, Managing Highly Available Exchange Server Solutions

MICROSOFT EXAM OBJECTIVES COVERED IN THIS CHAPTER:

✓ **Installing and Configuring Microsoft Exchange Servers**

- Install Exchange.

✓ **Configuring Disaster Recovery**

- Configure high availability.

High availability (HA) is discussed often, but few administrators understand what it really means. Administrators have been conditioned by article after article to think high availability means the same thing as clustering. In fact, many administrators think high availability is a code word for clustering technologies. High availability is much more than what most administrators think it is. Although Microsoft server clustering and network load balancing are highly available platforms for applications, they do not provide high availability by themselves. Every administrator should understand that clustering is only a piece of high availability.

High availability requires the implementation of strong management processes, proper testing procedures, and well-planned implementation processes. An organization cannot achieve high availability just by implementing clustering technologies. The most important requirement in achieving high availability is implementing a high-availability philosophy or spirit within the organization where administrators stop, think, evaluate, collaborate, and then decide what to do in the event of a major failure or when changing the configuration of an application or server. Proper change control, for example, is part of that spirit.

Many organizations go through a process called *risk management* or *risk identification* where they list everything that could possibly go wrong or that would cause Exchange Server 2007 services to not be available. For example, an organization may list disk failure as a possible risk and then take steps to mitigate that risk by using redundant array of inexpensive disks (RAID) controllers and configuring all disks in fault-tolerant arrays. Another example would be where an organization lists main board failure as a risk and then decides to implement a server clustering solution to mitigate that risk.

In a nutshell, *high availability* is the combination of well-defined, planned, tested, and implemented processes, software, and fault-tolerant hardware focused on supplying and maintaining application availability.

As a high-level example, consider messaging in an organization. A poor implementation of Exchange is usually slapped together by purchasing a server that the administrator thinks is about the right size and installing Exchange Server 2007 on it. Messaging clients are installed on network-connected desktops, and profiles are created. The Exchange server might even be successfully configured to connect to the Internet. It is possible to install an Exchange messaging environment over a short business week and even overnight in some cases. It is easy to do it fast and get it done, but lots of important details are missed.

By contrast, in a high-availability environment, the deployment of messaging is well designed. Administrators research organizational messaging requirements. Users are brought into discussions with administrators and managers. Messaging is considered a possible solution to many company ills. Research may go on for an extended period while consultants are brought in to help build a design and review the design of others. Vendors are brought in to discuss how their products (antivirus and content management solutions, for example) will keep the messaging environment available and not waste messaging resources processing spam and spreading viruses. Potential third-party software is tested and approved after a large investment of administrator and end user time. Hardware is sized and evaluated based on performance requirements and expected loads. Hardware is also sized and tested for disaster recovery and to meet service-level agreements for both performance and time to recovery in the event of a disaster. Hardware selected will often contain fault-tolerant components such as redundant memory, drives, network connects, cooling fans, power supplies, and so on. A high-availability environment will incorporate lots of design, planning, and testing. A high-availability environment will often, but not always, include additional features such as server clustering, which decreases downtime by allowing for rolling upgrades and allowing for a preplanned response to failures. A top-notch high-availability messaging environment will also consider the messaging client software and its potential configurations that lead to increased availability for users. For example, Outlook 2003 offers a cache mode configuration that allows users to create new messages, respond to existing mail in their Inboxes, and manage their calendars (amongst many other tasks) without having to maintain a constant connection to the Exchange server. Cache mode allows users to continue working even though the Exchange server might be down for a short time, and it also allows for the more efficient use of bandwidth.

All critical business systems have to be analyzed to understand the cost incurred when they are unavailable. If there is a significant cost, then the organization should take steps to minimize downtime. Taking this view to the extreme, the goal is really to provide *continuous availability (CA)* of applications and resources for the organization. Doesn't everyone want email to always be available for processing messaging traffic and helping the people in the organization collaborate? Of course, that is what we want. We want applications and their entire environment to continue running forever. We strive for continuous availability, and we settle for high availability.

Obviously, continuous availability just isn't possible over extremely long periods of time. Hardware will always fail; it is just a matter of when. Software becomes obsolete over time, too. You should understand that high availability includes not just the hardware and software solution but also the backup/restore solution and failover processing. Most high-availability experts will also add that a true high-availability environment includes a well-documented development, test, and production migration process for any changes made in production environments. All and all, there is much to achieving high availability, but you can achieve high levels of application availability through well-designed, planned, tested, and implemented processes, software, and hardware.

Another example is if you use *network load balancing (NLB)* to provide application availability to your users. In Exchange Server 2007, you can use NLB for the Edge Transport server role and for the Client Access server role. NLB helps keep the applications available to your users. The same can be said for server clustering; however, you need to take into account the nonavailability during the actual failover of your application in the event of hardware or software failures. Sometimes, failover is a matter of seconds; in other cases, it can be several minutes. In all cases, a clustering solution will significantly drive down nonavailability and increase the uptime of your application as run on your servers. Many experts state that for any application or system to be highly available, the parts need to be designed around availability, and the individual parts need to be tested before being put into production. As an example, if you are using third-party products with your Exchange environment that have not been properly tested, you may find that they are a weak link that results in the loss of availability. Implementing a cluster will not necessarily result in high availability if there are problems with the software, as was discussed previously.

High availability is so much more than just slapping a couple of servers together in a cluster. Please keep in mind all the details behind a top-notch high-availability environment.

Exchange Server 2007 includes many new features that enhance availability. *Local continuous replication (LCR)*, *cluster continuous replication (CCR)*, and *single copy cluster (SCC)* are three features that increase the reliability and thus the availability of Exchange Server 2007 services.

This chapter covers an extremely large amount of material. Microsoft Windows server clustering and NLB require complete books to cover them properly. In this chapter, you'll learn what high availability really is, some of the basics of configuring NLB, and some of the basics of configuring server clustering. The main subjects of this chapter are as follows:

- Local continuous replication
- Cluster continuous replication
- Single copy cluster

Installing Server Clustering

The topic of server clustering will be a significant portion of this chapter because a basic understanding of server clustering for Windows Server 2003 is vital. Without a properly built and configured server cluster, it is not possible to properly install Exchange Server 2007 in the cluster and have it be reliable. Installing server clustering requires several steps:

1. Installing and configuring the hardware, which includes installing and configuring the server nodes, configuring the network, setting up the disk structure, and making sure all the firmware is up-to-date.
2. Installing and configuring the operating system. This step includes some basics of server hardening (which won't be covered in detail here because this is best covered in a Windows Server 2003 book) and includes some other steps to prepare for clustering.
3. Configuring the *cluster service*. This step is where you find out whether your hardware and operating system will work for you. Once this step is complete, you will have a cluster, but nothing running on it.
4. Installing and configuring applications. This step will be covered in detail later in the chapter.

Installing and Configuring Cluster Hardware

To build a Microsoft Windows *server cluster*, you must first provide all the hardware components. This is not a simple task in Windows Server 2003 since the *hardware compatibility list* that administrators know so well is not really used to identify supported hardware. In fact, the support model actually requires a much more stringent hardware requirement. The Windows Server Catalog (`www.windowsservercatalog.com`) lists entire cluster solutions. Approved cluster solutions include hardware that has been tested as a complete solution along with the operating system. To receive full support for Windows Server 2003 clusters, you must purchase a complete solution from the list; this includes the following:

- The operating system, which will be either Windows Server 2003 Enterprise, Windows Server 2003 Enterprise R2, Windows Server 2003 Datacenter, or Windows Server 2003 Datacenter R2
- The server nodes, which will include the brand, model number, and CPU configuration
- The *host bus adapter (HBA)* brand and model number for each server
- The fiber switch or hub
- The storage, which is usually the most expensive part of server clustering

Some server clusters do not require storage, so it is much cheaper and easier to purchase the hardware in those cases since the HBA, switch (or hub), and storage device will not be required. This will be important to note later when we cover CCR.

Hooking Up the Hardware

The hardware has been purchased and now is ready to be hooked up. This is not a difficult step. You must build each server node, install the network cards, install the HBAs, and put the servers into the server rack. The following tips will be useful in this process:

Network Each node of the cluster is connected to two different networks for clustering purposes. Each node is connected to the public network, which is where clients can connect to the cluster nodes and attach to applications and services running on the cluster as if the virtual servers were normal servers. The second network is the private network, also referred to as the *heartbeat network*. This network connects all nodes of the cluster so they can keep track of the availability of the nodes in the cluster. It is through this heartbeat network that a passive server node can detect whether the active server node has failed and then take action to start the virtual servers on it. It is possible that other networks also are used for such things as dedicated backups, but they are not used for cluster purposes.

Many organizations use network adapter teaming software to improve network adapter reliability. If teaming software is used on the public network adapters, it should be configured for fault-tolerant mode only and should never be configured for load balancing. Network teaming software is not supported on the heartbeat network.

Disk Disk hardware is usually the largest investment when it comes to clustering. Although you can use SCSI devices, we do not recommend SCSI because *iSCSI* and fiber are much better choices and are capable of providing more flexibility in the disks that they can provide to the nodes. Future versions of clustering will not support directly attached and shared parallel SCSI devices. Only iSCSI and fiber connections, along with serially attached SCSI devices, will be supported in the future. *Multipathing* configurations are an area of dispute when discussing disk environments. Many organizations will install two fiber adapters to connect to the SAN device in their networks. While multipathing can increase performance, it adds another layer of complexity to the environment that may not be worth it. Keep in mind that each of the clustered disks should be a *logical unit number (LUN)* on a *storage area network (SAN)*. If you are carving them up yourself, we highly recommend using RAID-1 sets for the transaction logs, Simple Mail Transfer Protocol (SMTP) queues, and RAID-5 for the mailbox stores. Do not create physical disk resources that are partitions on the same physical drives.

When it comes to disk sizing, we highly recommend reading Nicole Allen's blog entry at `http://blogs.technet.com/exchange/archive/2004/10/11/240868.aspx`. She does a fantastic job of explaining how to size disks for Exchange. You can also see similar information on storage optimization at `www.microsoft.com/technet/prodtechnol/exchange/2003/library/optimizestorage.mspx`.

One of the disks provided by the storage environment is the *quorum* disk. This disk is required for most server clustering environments. The quorum and disks for the database and transaction logs are needed for Exchange Server 2007 for SCC configurations.

Redundant and fault-tolerant hardware components Another hardware concern is that you should use redundant and fault-tolerant hardware components when possible. For example, all nodes should be connected to an uninterruptible power supply and should have redundant power supplies, redundant fans, and internal RAID drives for the operating system.

"Two of three" rule Once the nodes and the external SCSI device are running and clustering is not configured, it is a good idea to limit situations where the two nodes both attempt to access the external storage. To do this, you should implement the "two of three" rule. This rule means that only two of the three devices (node1, node2, and external storage) should be powered up and running at the same time. After the cluster service is installed, then all three can run at once without any issues.

Installing and Configuring the Operating System

Windows Server 2003 Enterprise Edition will be the main operating system most people use when implementing clustering. Although clustering can be configured using the Datacenter Edition of Windows, it is extremely rare. Windows Server 2003 is also available in an x64 edition, and the R2 version will be released shortly. Clustering is installed on all these operating systems when installed on new hardware out of the box. Clustering, although it is installed, is not configured.

You should have a complete infrastructure already installed and in place before installing cluster nodes and then clustering. Cluster nodes should be treated as highly valued systems and should not have unnecessary extra software installed on them. The high-availability philosophy dictates a "keep it simple" principle.

When it comes to clustering, people are usually interested in achieving high availability. To achieve high availability, you need to follow best practices and not shortcut anything because that would reduce the uptime of the environment in most cases. High availability is a philosophy, and if you are embracing it for an application, the cost of a separate domain controller should not dissuade the organization from achieving its goals. Domain controllers are highly available in that with multiple domain controllers you will have a writable copy of Active Directory (AD) as long as one is up and available.

This chapter will not cover the basics of server hardening because that is best covered in a book about Windows Server 2003. The basics of server hardening do apply, though, for cluster nodes. As with all servers, patches, service packs, firmware updates, driver updates, antivirus updates, and other tools must be properly tested before putting them into a production cluster environment. A failure because of lack of testing can result in significant downtime, which defeats the whole goal of clustering.

TCP/IP Configuration for the Public Network

At a minimum, as part of properly configuring the hardware, a cluster must have a public network that is accessible by clients. All networks used in clustering should be forced to a setting, such as 100MB Full Duplex, and not allowed to be set to automatically sense the speed. The following are other concerns:

IP address IP addresses for cluster nodes should always be statically mapped. Although Microsoft does not support DHCP-provided addresses for the nodes or for any cluster resources, Microsoft does support permanent DHCP leases and static IP addresses. There is some risk involved in depending on DHCP, so subscribing to the high-availability philosophy, you should look for ways to remove or mitigate the risk. It is a best practice to use static IP addresses only.

Subnet mask The subnet mask will, of course, be dependent on the public network segment used for the public network adapter. Note that all public network adapters must be on the same network segment.

Default gateway The public network interface should be configured with a default gateway; otherwise, it will be able to communicate only with computers in the same network segment.

DNS The public network interface should be configured with a primary and a secondary DNS server to provide proper host name resolution.

WINS The public network interface should be configured with a primary and a secondary WINS server to provide proper NetBIOS name resolution.

It is important to note that the Cluster Administrator MMC uses NetBIOS naming to make connections, so WINS can be very valuable. Also, even though the tool requires WINS, it is possible to connect to an individual node of a cluster using the remote desktop protocol and manage the Cluster Administrator on a node of the cluster, so WINS is not necessarily required. In fact, cluster security best practices call for removing NetBIOS dependencies for all nodes of the cluster.

Basically, yes, NetBIOS is needed for the Cluster Administrator tool to be used for remote management, but it is not supposed to be used for security reasons. Since we are talking about an Exchange Server 2007 cluster that might be using email clients that require NetBIOS, then we will want to implement WINS.

Network priority It is important that the network binding order be set correctly for clustering so it does not have a negative impact on performance. To set the network priority, open the Network Connections applet in Control Panel, and select the Advanced menu item. On the Adapters and Bindings tab, make sure the public network is listed first, with the private network after it, as shown in Figure 10.1.

FIGURE 10.1 Network priority configuration

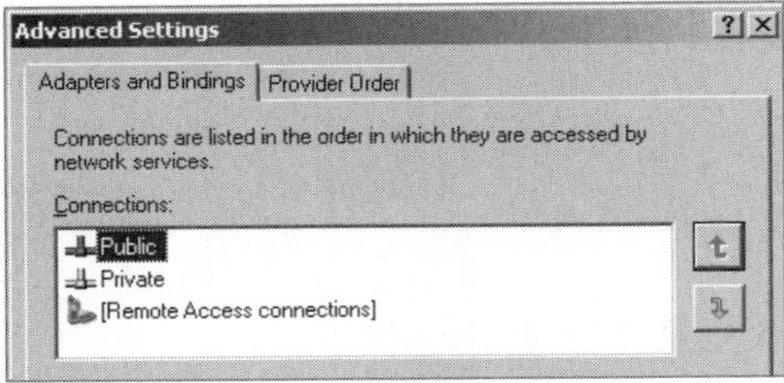

TCP/IP Configuration for the Private Network

At a minimum, as part of properly configuring the hardware, a cluster must have a private network that handles the heartbeat traffic between the nodes. As mentioned previously, all networks used in clustering should be forced to a setting, such as 100MB Full Duplex, and not be set to automatically sense the speed. Here are some additional tips:

IP address IP addresses should always be statically mapped. DHCP is not an option since the private network will contain the network adapters for cluster nodes for private communication only. The network segment used should be nonroutable and should not exist anywhere else in the organization.

The recommended ranges, per RFC 1918, include the following:

- From 10.0.0.0 to 10.255.255.255 (10/8)
- From 172.16.0.0 to 172.31.255.255 (172.16/12)
- From 192.168.0.0 to 192.168.255.255 (192.168/16)

Subnet mask The subnet mask will, of course, depend on the private network segment used for the private network adapter.

Default gateway The private network interface should not be configured. Heartbeat traffic has no need to exist anywhere but in the private network.

DNS DNS information is not needed for the private network. However, it is important to go to the DNS tab in the TCP/IP properties. On the DNS tab, make sure the Register This Connection's Address in DNS check box is not selected.

WINS The private network interface does not require any name resolution at all, so there is no need for WINS entries. However, it is important that the Disable NetBIOS Over TCP/IP radio button is selected on the WINS tab in the TCP/IP properties.

Services To keep the private network as clean as possible, the Client for Microsoft Networks and the File and Printer Sharing for Microsoft Networks options should be removed from the connection properties.

Service Account for Server Cluster

The cluster service account must be a domain account so that each of the nodes of the cluster can use the account to start the cluster service once clustering is configured. The wizard used to configure clustering will ask for the account information during the configuration of clustering.

The cluster service account must have the following permissions associated with it:

- The account must include these permissions for all nodes of the cluster:
  - Log on as a service
  - Act as part of the operating system
  - Adjust memory quotas for a process
  - Backup files and directories
  - Restore files and directories
  - Increase scheduling priorities
- The account should be limited for security so it can log onto the nodes only and not onto any other computers.
- The password should be a complex password, and it should not be set to expire. As with any service account, it is also a good idea to configure it so that its password cannot be changed, although this won't prevent an administrator from changing the password if need be.
- The account must be a local administrator on each of the nodes of the cluster.

- The account must be a member of the domain (Windows NT 4.0, Windows 2000 AD, or Windows 2003 AD), but it does not need to be a domain administrator.
- The account must have the proper permissions for installing the application.

Cluster Disk Configuration

Using the two of three rule discussed earlier, keep the cluster disks unavailable until the operating systems are installed on all cluster nodes, and then all nodes should be turned off once they are fully installed and all hardening processes have been run. Once it is time to configure clustering, then configure the disks so they are available to each and every node. Turn on one node, and make sure the node can see the disks in disk manager. Do not format the disks at this time. After the first node is verified, perform the same test on the second node. Again, do not partition or format the disks at this time.

Once all nodes have been tested to make sure they can see the disks properly, use the first node of the cluster and partition and format the disks. Leave the disks as basic disks, and do not change them to dynamic disks. If they are converted to dynamic disks, they will not be usable for clustering.

Configuring the Cluster Service

Unlike previous versions of Windows, the server cluster service is installed by default. Nothing needs to be done to install it. All that is required is that the cluster is configured using the tools available. Exercise 10.1 shows how to install and configure a cluster service.

EXERCISE 10.1

Installing and Configuring the Cluster Service

1. Click Start ➢ Administrative Tools ➢ Cluster Administrator to start the Cluster Administrator MMC. Once the Cluster Administrator is open, it will automatically provide a drop-down box and request what action you want to take. In this case, select Create a New Cluster, and then click OK, as shown here. This step will start the New Server Cluster Wizard.

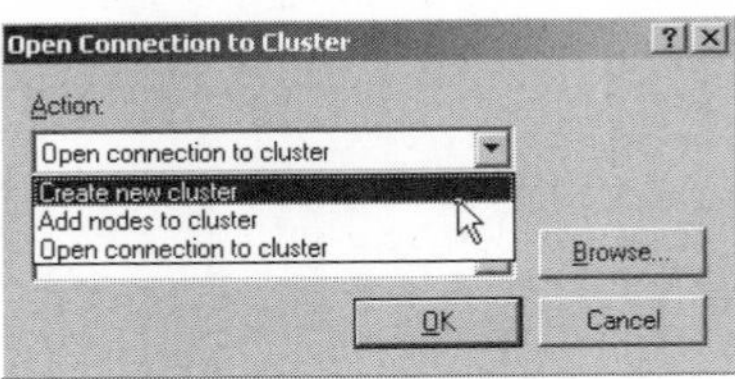

EXERCISE 10.1 *(continued)*

2. In the New Server Cluster Wizard, you are presented with several options. The first option is to enter the cluster name and domain for the cluster, as shown here.

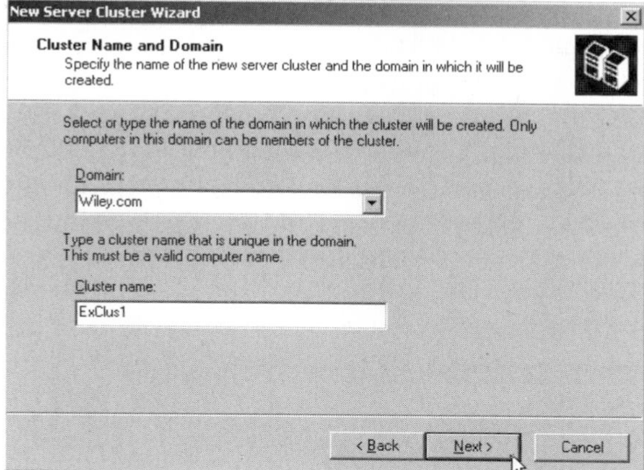

3. The Domain entry is the easy part. All that needs to be entered here is the domain name of the Active Directory domain (or NT 4.0 domain name) where the nodes and the server cluster will live. The cluster name is a bit tougher. This name is really used only to address the entire cluster using the Cluster Administrator (for connecting to the cluster, for example) or when using the `cluster.exe` command-line utility to create, configure, and maintain a server cluster. After you enter the name information, click Next.

4. The next step in the wizard is to collect the computer name of the first computer to be added to the cluster. You can manually enter the name, or you can use the Browse button to browse for the node name. Of course, using the Browse button requires using NetBIOS naming, so if you have locked down your nodes so they can't use NetBIOS, it will be best if you just manually enter the name. You can click the Advanced button to select whether you want to perform a typical (full) configuration of the cluster, which is the default option. If you select Typical, then the wizard will try to configure the cluster completely without any interference or prompts for information. The other option is the Advanced (minimum) configuration, which will enable you to manually enter the location of all storage to be managed by the server, including the quorum. Once the first computer name (or node name) is entered, click Next. At this point, the wizard will analyze the node and its hardware configuration, and it will then do the following:

   - Check for existing cluster.
   - Establish node connection(s).
   - Check node feasibility.

EXERCISE 10.1 *(continued)*

- Find common resources on nodes.
- Check cluster feasibility.

5. After the tasks are complete, you will get a green bar if everything passes feasibility testing. You may see some caution signs. You should always check the caution signs to make sure it is nothing that will cause the installation to fail, as shown here. In this case, there is a caution sign for the Finding Common Resources on Nodes item. Expanding the caution sign will show, in this case, that the wizard has found a suitable quorum device but it does not meet size requirements for best practices. This warning is a common one. Microsoft best practices say that the quorum must be at least 500 megabytes (MB) and formatted using NTFS. If you actually select 500MB when creating the logical unit number, it will be slightly less than 500MB after it is formatted.

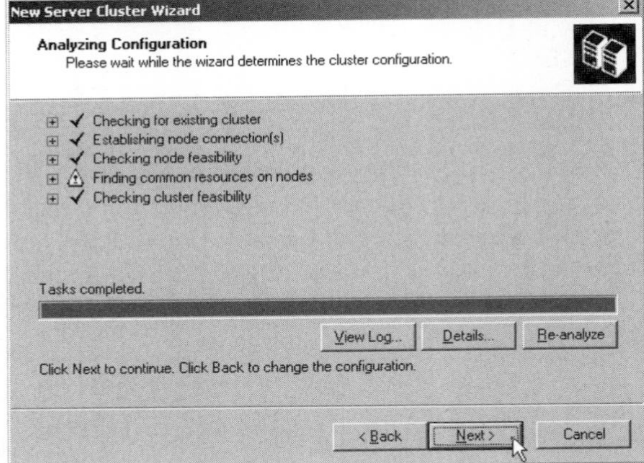

6. Click Next to enter the IP address of the cluster. This IP address will correspond to the cluster name provided earlier, and the cluster name will resolve to this IP address in DNS if it is entered dynamically or manually. Enter the IP address, and click Next.

7. Enter the Cluster Service Account information on the next page of the New Server Cluster Wizard. This account, as discussed earlier, must be a domain account and must be a local administrator account on each node of the cluster. Enter the account name, password, and domain name, and then click Next.

EXERCISE 10.1 *(continued)*

8. You should read the information on the Proposed Cluster Configuration page, as shown here, and verify that all the information you entered is entered without mistakes and verify that the proper drives have been identified as managed drives (drives that will be managed by the cluster service and shared between the nodes for clustered applications) and the quorum. In this case, you can see that Q was selected to be the quorum and that the S, T, and W drives were identified as shared drives that will be managed by the cluster service. Click Next.

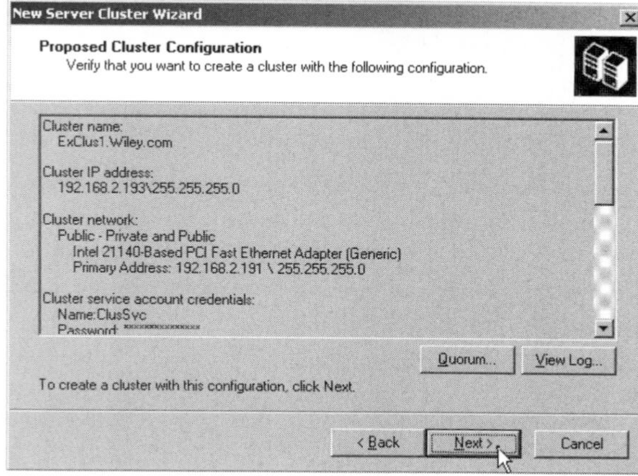

9. If the cluster configuration found extra physical disks, each one of the extra disks will be put into a new cluster group. You can easily move the disks later, and you can delete the cluster groups to clean up the interface.

10. Finally, the New Server Cluster Wizard will run a verification process, and then you can click Finish after it is completed.

11. At this point, the cluster is built, but it is only a single-node cluster. Opening the Cluster Administrator MMC will show the completed cluster configuration, as shown here.

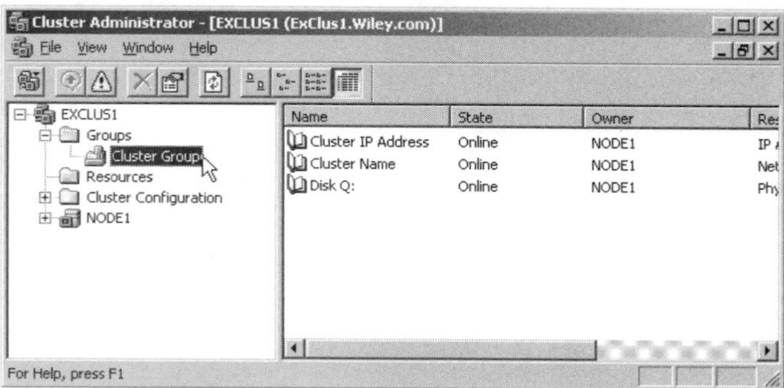

EXERCISE 10.1 *(continued)*

12. To add another node, open the Cluster Administrator, and right-click the cluster name. Select New ➢ Node, as shown here, and then use the Add Node Wizard to join another node to the cluster.

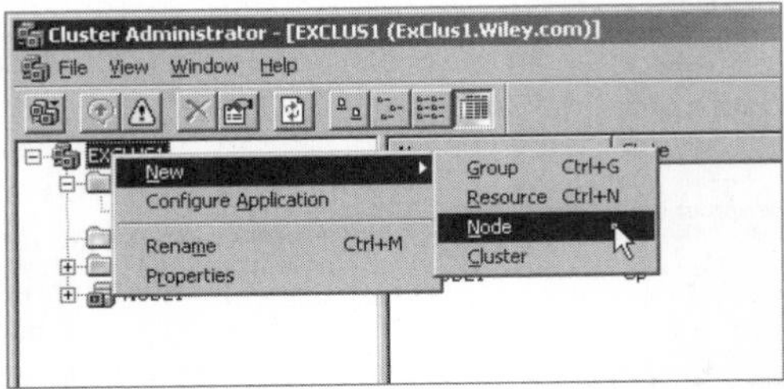

13. After entering the new node name, or multiple node names if it is a large cluster, click Next to run through the Analyzing Configuration tool. The tool will check the cluster to make sure everything is visible and able to connect. Once the green bar appears again, click Next, and enter the cluster service account information again. Click Next a few more times, and then click Finish. The cluster is completed, as shown here.

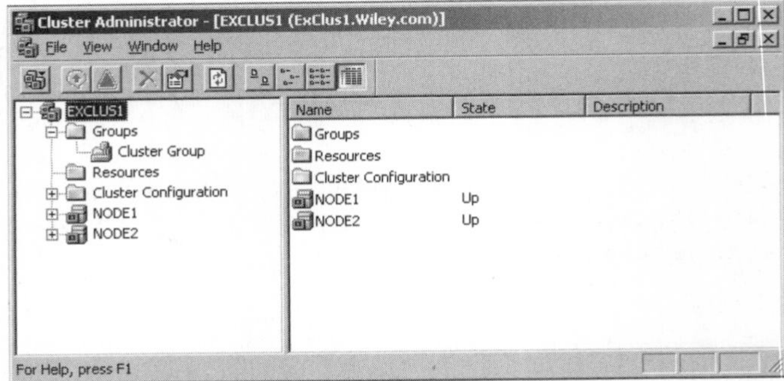

At this point, the cluster is built and fully configured. You can test it to make sure the cluster service properly fails over the default cluster group. Once the cluster has been fully tested and documented, then you can install applications such as Exchange Server 2007.

Installing and Configuring Network Load Balancing

Many organizations have applications that are critical to daily operations such as databases, messaging systems, and file/print services. There are some places where technologies such as NLB are more appropriate than using server clustering to achieve high availability for those applications.

Internet server programs supporting mission-critical applications and services must run 24 hours a day, 7 days a week. In addition, network applications and servers need the ability to scale performance to handle large volumes of client requests without creating unwanted delays. Network load balanced clusters enable you to manage a group of independent servers as a single system for higher availability, easier manageability, and greater scalability.

NLB is a fully distributed, software-based solution and does not require any specialized hardware or network components. At this time, there are not even any additional licensing costs associated with using NLB. All members of the Windows Server 2003 family have NLB built into their operating systems at no additional cost. NLB doesn't require a centralized device because all hosts receive inbound packets, and redundancy is provided according to the number of hosts within the cluster.

Exchange Server 2007 is somewhat limited in its use of NLB. The Edge Transport server role and the Client Access server role can both use NLB and are fully supported for NLB. However, since the Client Access server role is usually combined with other roles, there is seldom a need for it in production messaging environments. The Edge Transport server role is a good example of where we would use NLB in Exchange Server 2007 because no other roles can be hosted on an Edge Transport server and because of its need for high availability for handling large amounts of inbound and outbound traffic.

A typical NLB cluster looks much like the one shown in Figure 10.2. Two or more nodes are connected to the perimeter network with a separate connection for server management. The management network is used to patch or perform other maintenance on the NLB nodes.

FIGURE 10.2 NLB architecture

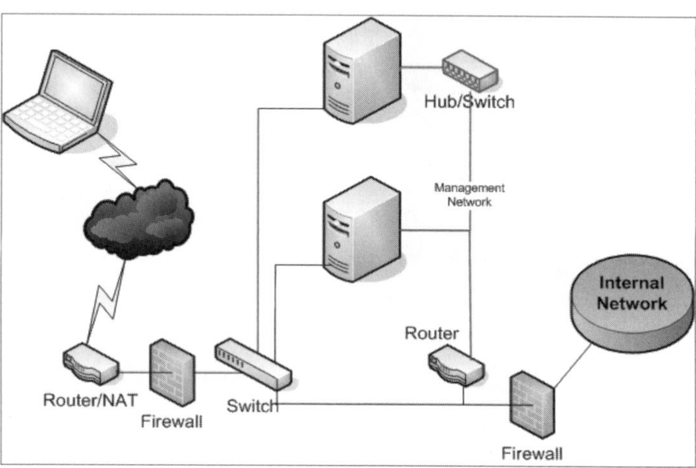

In NLB, the network adapters that are configured to be part of the NLB cluster all share the same IP address as well as the same MAC address. It just isn't possible to use the NLB network interface and predictably attach to a specific node to perform maintenance.

What makes NLB clustering work is the NLB driver. NLB is configured on all the NLB cluster nodes so it is identical with the exception of the priority number, which runs from 1 to 32 (thus, there is a limit of 32 nodes per NLB cluster). With the NLB driver enabled and configured alike on all the nodes, the nodes go through a process called *convergence* where they all agree on an algorithm that divides up the network traffic. At that point, clients, as shown in Figure 10.3, connect to the NLB cluster, and because of issues with the nodes having the same IP address and same MAC address, the switch floods all of its ports, and each node then receives the same packets. The NLB driver, which sits right before the TCP/IP stack, then decides whether it should process the packet or drop it based upon the algorithm. The filtering process for NLB is very efficient in the way it handles packets in comparison to a centralized device that has to process them and then retransmit them. Because of the way the NLB driver works, NLB provides higher bandwidth on similar network configurations that use a centralized device.

If the NLB driver decides it is supposed to process the packet and the packet meets the port rules for the NLB cluster, then it passes the packet to the TCP/IP layer and through the rest of the network model.

The biggest problem with NLB, though, is that it is not capable of looking into the individual nodes and testing to see whether an application or service is running properly. If an application or service (such as the World Wide Web Service) fails, NLB will continue to include the node in the NLB cluster, and some connections will fail.

FIGURE 10.3 Network load balancing behavior

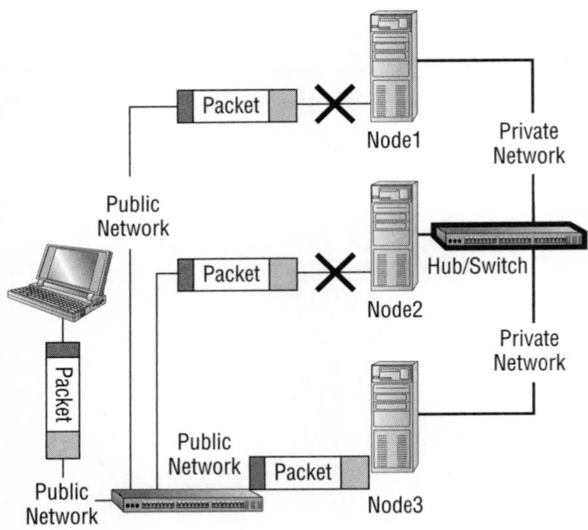

Installing and Configuring the Network Load Balancing Driver

Since the driver is installed on all Windows Server 2003 family members, it just needs to be enabled. In Control Panel, open Network Connections, and select the properties of the network card that will be part of the NLB cluster.

Enabling NLB requires selecting the check box shown in Figure 10.4.

FIGURE 10.4 Enabling NLB behavior

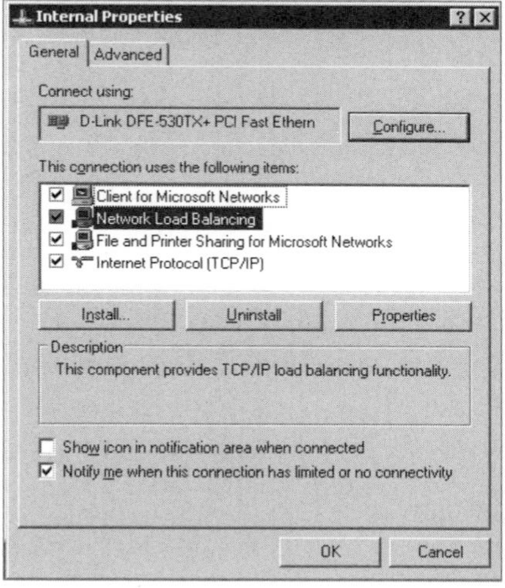

Now, there are a few more steps to perform. At this point, highlight Network Load Balancing, as shown in Figure 10.4, and then click the Properties button. It is here that NLB is configured. You'll see three tabs: Cluster Parameters, Host Parameters, and Port Rules.

Cluster Parameters

On this tab, you need to enter several pieces of information, and they all need to be alike for every node in the NLB cluster. The IP address is the address of the entire NLB cluster. This is the shared IP address that will be configured for each node. This IP address will need a DNS record created that matches the Full Internet Name field, as shown in Figure 10.5.

The full Internet name could be something as simple as smtp.wiley.com (if your company domain name is Wiley). After creating the DNS name, a MX record could also be created for the DNS name so email could be sent to this address once it is fully configured. Obviously, this is how an Edge Transport server is deployed and used with NLB.

The Unicast and Multicast radio buttons are key when it comes to network behavior and the use of IP addresses and MAC addresses.

FIGURE 10.5 Cluster Parameters tab

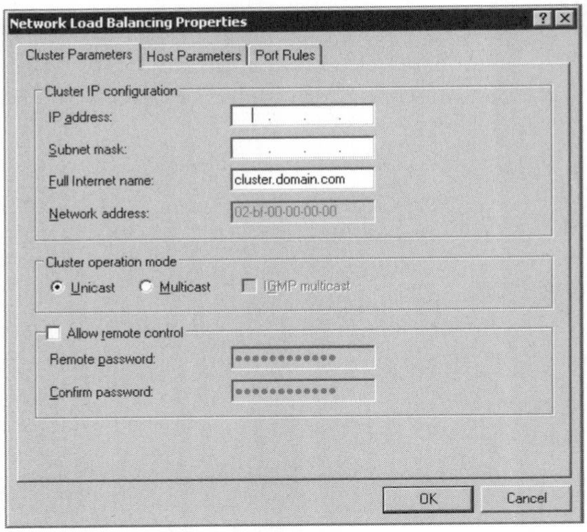

Unicast

When you enable unicast support, the unicast mode changes the cluster adapter's MAC address to the cluster MAC address that is shown on the tab. It can be hard to read because it is grayed out. This cluster address is the same MAC address that is used on all cluster hosts. When this change is made, clients can no longer address the cluster adapters by their original MAC addresses.

Multicast

When you enable multicast support, NLB adds a multicast MAC access to the cluster adapters on all the cluster hosts. At the same time, the cluster adapters retain their original MAC addresses. You cannot change the MAC addresses on some network adapters; check the hardware specifications for your network adapter.

Internet Group Management Protocol

Internet Group Management Protocol (IGMP) establishes host membership to a multicast group. If routers or switches support RFC 1112, it is possible to configure NLB to use IGMP and prevent port flooding.

Almost all packets are sent as unicasts or broadcasts. Unicasts have a single-destination IP address pointing to a single recipient. Broadcasts are destined for all hosts on a subnet.

Multicast packets also must fit the model for either unicast or broadcast. The big difference between multicast packets and unicast (or broadcast) packets is that the destination IP address includes a group of hosts rather than a single host or a network segment. When the application sends multicast traffic, you need to check the destination IP address—the only way to distinguish that traffic—that identifies the specific multicast group for which the datagram was meant.

A multicast-aware router or switch, when using IGMP, will track which ports are members of the multicast group. So, a properly configured (and aware) environment can use IGMP and not experience port flooding.

The problem with NLB is that it does not use multicast IP ranges (Class D addresses, from 224 to 239), so many devices refuse to treat it like a standard multicast. So, using IGMP in those cases will not work and will not prevent switch flooding.

HOST COMMUNICATION

For unicast, there is no host-to-host communication within the NLB cluster.

For multicast, host-to-host communication is possible.

MAC ADDRESSES

When configuring NLB, part of the process includes adding or replacing MAC addresses on a network adapter in each NLB host.

- Unicast changes the network adapter's MAC to the NLB cluster MAC, and it is shared by all nodes in the NLB cluster.
- Multicast adds another MAC to its existing MAC so it has two MACs on the network adapter.

You can easily see the MAC being used by NLB by pinging the NLB IP address and then running `arp -a` to display the MACs associated with IP addresses that have recently been resolved.

For example, you might see 02-bf-c0-a8-1e-fa. This breaks down as follows:

- The first number is the type: 01 = IGMP, 02 = Unicast, 03 = Multicast.
- The second number (bf) is unknown in origin.
- The next four numbers are the IP address in hexadecimal: c0 = 192, a8 = 168, 1e = 30, fa = 250, which comes to 192.168.30.250.

In this case, if the cluster IP address was configured to be 192.168.30.250, then the MAC address for the cluster would be 02-bf-c0-a8-1e-fa. Of course, this is assuming that unicast was selected.

Host Parameters

Entering the information for the host parameters is pretty simple. This is the IP address configuration information for the NLB cluster node that is being configured. The hardest part of entering this information is remembering to do an IPConfig command, write down the results, and then enter them. The next hardest part is to enter the priority number so it is unique for each host that will be part of the NLB cluster. You can also, as shown in Figure 10.6, set the default state. Almost all the time, it will be set to Started because you want to join the NLB cluster.

Port Rules

NLB uses port rules to differentiate between the types of traffic that are to be load balanced and those traffic types that can be ignored. NLB configures all ports for load balancing by default, but you can modify the configuration of the NLB driver that determines which incoming traffic is load balanced on a per-port basis by creating port rules for each group of ports or individual ports. These rules set load balancing for clients requesting a port covered by the port range parameter. How an application is load balanced is determined by the port rules, which are created on each host. Figure 10.7 shows the default configuration.

FIGURE 10.6 Host Parameters tab

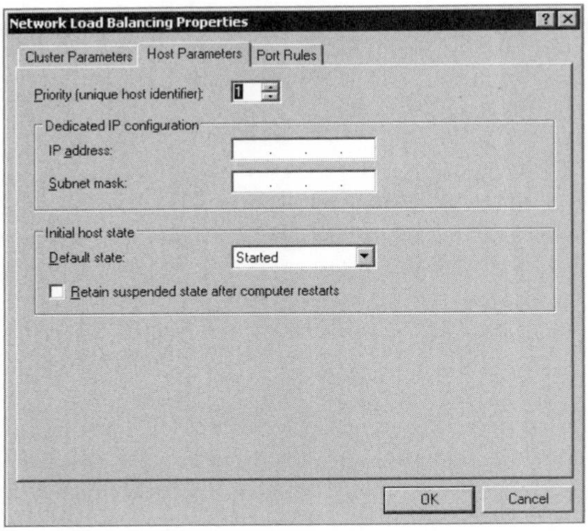

FIGURE 10.7 Port Rules tab

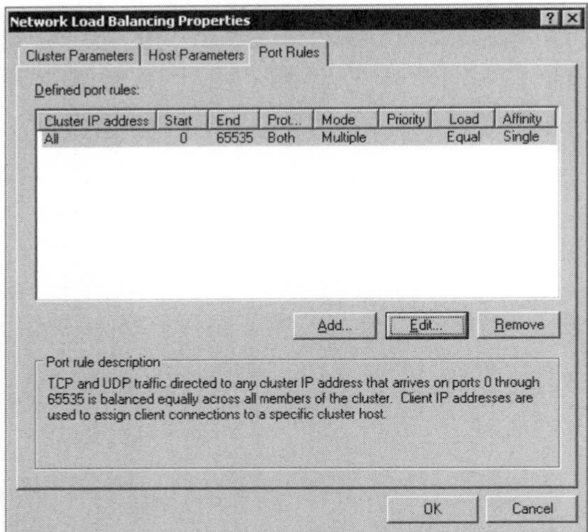

In the case of an Edge Transport server, for example, port 25 would be configured for inbound SMTP traffic. Other ports might be needed depending on the applications that are run on the NLB cluster.

You can apply port rules to a specific IP address (if the NLB cluster supports multiple IP addresses), and you can configure them to either accept a port or disable a port or port range. You can also use port rules based on TCP or UDP, as shown in Figure 10.8.

FIGURE 10.8 Adding or editing port rules

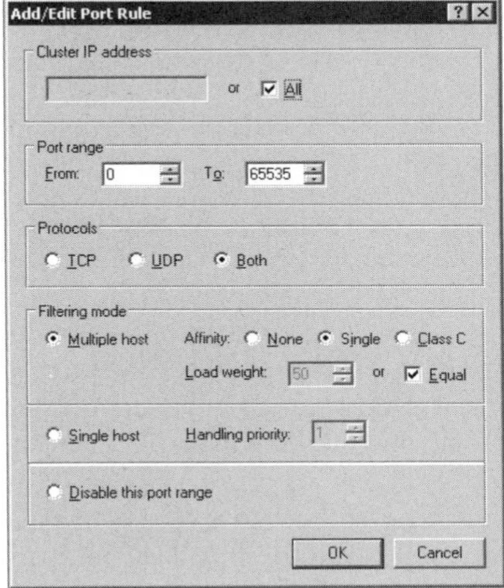

You can add port rules or update parameters by taking each host out of the cluster in turn, updating its parameters, and then returning it to the cluster. Remember, the host joining the cluster handles no traffic until convergence is complete. If a rule is added, it does not take effect until all hosts have been updated and have rejoined the cluster.

NLB preserves session state through client affinity settings for each port rule. These settings direct all TCP connections from a given client address or class of client addresses to the same cluster host. Unless the client changes its IP address or the NLB cluster node fails, the client will continue to use the same server. Directing the connections to the same cluster host allows the server applications in the designated host memory to correctly maintain the session state.

Affinity is important for web applications using session state to provide "stickiness" for client connections, and it is vital for SSL connectivity.

Affinity can be set to None, Single, or Class C. When set to None, affinity is not kept, and clients may visit multiple servers instead of being tied to a single server. In single affinity, the affinity is based on the single IP address of the client. The clients of the NLB cluster will continue to go to the same node so long as their IP addresses don't change or there is a failure of a node or a new node is added to the cluster that would require a reconvergence and a selection of a new algorithm for distribution. When set to Class C, affinity sends all clients from the same Class C address to a single node. This rule is often used because of the large number of proxy servers around the Internet. If Single is selected, then a proxy server would appear as a single IP, and one NLB cluster node might get hammered because there are many hundreds of clients behind the proxy server while other servers are lightly used.

Network Load Balancing Host TCP/IP Properties

Once you have made all the changes for the NLB configuration and clicked the OK button, a message will appear stating that you must add the NLB cluster IP address to the TCP/IP configuration for the host. Click the Advanced button from the TCP/IP properties, and manually enter the IP address for the NLB cluster in the IP Settings tab.

Network Concerns/Switch Flooding

In many networks where collapsed backbone switching technology is used, large port counts are available. Typically in these environments individual computers are allocated a single switch port to provide maximum possible bandwidth to the computer.

If NLB cluster hosts are directly connected to a switching hub or combined switch/router to receive client requests, the switch is unable to properly map the MAC address to a single port so it is forced to flood all ports to find the right port (which includes all ports that are connected to NLB cluster hosts) and will continue to do that until it is able to find one port where the MAC address exists (which it can't).

After a switch has identified which port a particular host (recognized by its MAC address) is connected to, it will no longer duplicate inbound traffic to all the ports. The NLB service prevents a switch from identifying the host's port by masking the source MAC address by using a different MAC address in reply. Masking the source MAC address results in the switch continuing to send inbound data to all the ports, which is called *switch flooding*. If the switch has ports associated with computers other than cluster hosts, these ports will also have the inbound traffic reflected on them, consuming bandwidth on ports where the traffic will be discarded.

Switch flooding can be limited by the following:

- Using a hub between all NLB cluster hosts
- Setting up a VLAN and putting all NLB cluster hosts in the VLAN
- Using port mirroring

When using a hub, if a hub is placed between the switch and the NLB ports and all NLB connections are hooked up to the hub, then the switch will see that the MAC address belongs to a single port on the switch and will send all NLB traffic to the hub. This creates a couple of problems, though:

- A hub typically cannot be managed or monitored, thus failures will be harder to proactively detect and react to.
- Hubs all run at half duplex, and there can and will be collisions.

When using a VLAN, if all the ports are combined into a VLAN, then port flooding will not impact any ports other than those that participate in the NLB cluster. The issues here are as follows:

- Now you have a new network segment and need routes to it.
- Another administrator might screw up the VLAN when working on other parts of the switch configuration.

Port mirroring is a rather new technology available in limited switch and router models. Basically, a network administrator can configure the switch so any traffic that comes in for one port is mirrored on other ports. This will eliminate flooding problems, too. The problems with this configuration are as follows:

- Limited support. Less than a handful of ports can be mirrored per switch fabric.
- Administrators have limited knowledge of the technology.

Using DNS Round-Robin

In DNS round-robin, there are multiple entries for the same name. For example, DNS would have a host record entry for Server1 with an IP address of 192.168.2.50, and there would be a second server providing the same services that would have a host record entry in DNS for Server1 with an IP address of 192.168.2.51.

Users of Server1 would be alternated between the two IP addresses and thus load balanced between the two addresses. If the two Server1s were overloaded, another server could be installed, and DNS could be configured with another Server1 host record with an IP or 192.168.2.52. What happens is that the first client receives the first address, the second client receives the second address, the third client receives the third address, the fourth client receives the first address, and they continue to loop. Using DNS round-robin, it is possible to spread the load among multiple servers.

The problem with round-robin DNS is that it is completely unable to handle a down server. In the event one of the servers fails, its address will continue to be given to clients, and a portion of the clients will basically be pointed to an invalid address so a portion of the clients will fail to connect.

Configuring Local Continuous Replication

LCR is not really a high availability solution. LCR does, however, provide mitigation against several possible failures. LCR provides mitigation against database disk failure and database corruption.

LCR uses a process called *log shipping* to send logs of completed transactions from the disk where the production storage group exists to another disk that holds a copy. The copy is updated by replaying the logs to maintain an exact copy of the production storage group and to keep it updated, as in Figure 10.9.

FIGURE 10.9 LCR overview

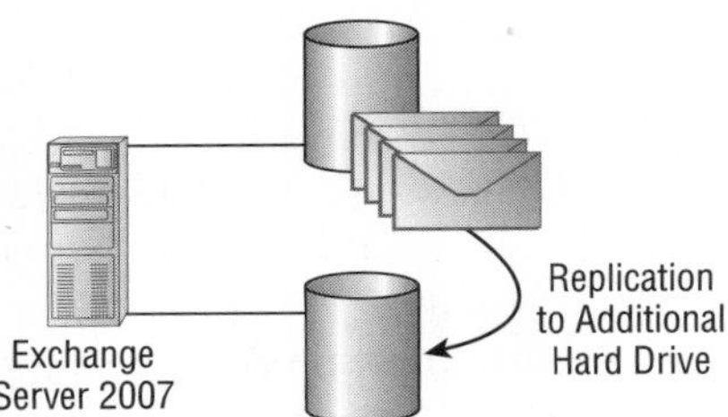

In the event of a disk failure or problems with database corruption, you can use LCR to significantly reduce the time it would take to restore the storage group from tape and return the Exchange Server 2007 server to production. In an LCR environment, you can use a manual process to remove the broken disk or corrupted storage group and replace the failed disk or storage group with the copy.

LCR improves availability and reduces total cost of ownership by doing the following:

- It reduces the time it takes to recover from a failed disk or corrupted database.
- It reduces the number of backups that must be taken of the storage group, although it is probably a good idea to continue with daily backups.
- It improves performance during the backup process by using the copy for the backup instead of the production so the production storage group is not impacted by the backup process.

You can stream backups using the production database only. You can create VSS backups using either the production database or the copy databases. Backups done using the copy database will truncate only the log files that have been written into the copy database. Transactions not committed to the database will be left in their existing transaction logs.

Overall, LCR is an excellent feature for organizations requiring quick recovery of disk and database failures. However, because moving to the copy from production requires downtime, the organization must be able to handle the outage time. LCR is an inexpensive solution, in most cases, and is highly recommended when not using a server clustering solution because of the following:

- Recovery to the copy storage group is a fairly quick process.
- Although there is an increase in I/O requirement, it is minimal.
- It is possible to run backups against the copy and not impact the production storage group at all during the backup process.
- Users requiring the additional protection can be grouped in the same storage group.
- Administration is available via the Exchange Management Console or the Exchange Management Shell.

Preparing for Local Continuous Replication

Preparing for LCR requires building the proper storage group and database structure. To detect disk or database failure, a monitoring solution should be in place so the failure can be identified quickly and the downtime is reduced. Microsoft Operations Manager (MOM), NetIQ, Tivoli, OpenView, and other monitoring and management tools can provide monitoring services. Proper disk, memory, and CPU should be provided to meet the performance service-level agreements for Exchange services.

Microsoft recommends disk structures that are capable of handling the additional input/output for LCR. Since LCR generates more I/O through the copy of the log information and the writing of the log information on the target, keeping the databases a reasonable size is important. Also, since the copy is often used to capture backups, the disks used for the copy should be similar to the disks used for the production storage group. Any supported type of storage can be used with LCR, including direct-attached storage, serially attached SCSI, and iSCSI. You can also use volume mount points instead of using drive letters. Using mount points may be a better solution for LCR because you can then just take the disk used for the copy and mount it to the same point as the production storage group after it is removed.

Disk recommendations and restrictions exist for LCR and include the following:

- Each storage group can contain only one database. This is a limitation for CCR as well as SCC. However, it is not really a big limitation since you can have up to 50 storage groups under Exchange Server 2007.
- If you have more than one public folder database in the Exchange organization, you will not be able to use LCR because if you have two or more public folder databases, then the public folders use public folder replication. Replication is always occurring even if they are not configured to replicate.
- Use RAID-0 or create your disk partitions so they are spread over multiple disks. This will increase performance for I/O, which is always something you should consider with Exchange Server 2007. It is also considered a best practice to separate the log files from the database by putting them on separate physical disks. Microsoft recommends you partition your disks and your data to improve performance and fault tolerance. To make troubleshooting easier, you should spread out your data so it is located on separate disks as follows:
    - The operating system files should be on RAID-1.
    - The Exchange binaries should be on either RAID-5 or RAID-1.
    - The database files for the production storage group should be on their own set of disks.
    - The transaction logs for the production storage group should be on another set of disks.
    - The database files for the copy should be on another set of disks.
    - The transaction logs for the copy should also be on another set of disks.
- Size the copy disks so they are approximately the same size as the production storage group disks. Both the production disks and the copy disks should be sized to allow for defragmentation and to allow for growth of the databases. Microsoft recommends a maximum database size of 100 gigabytes (GB) for servers running LCR. For other mailbox servers not running LCR, Microsoft recommends a maximum of 200GB for the database.

Memory requirements for Exchange Server 2007 and LCR will need to be increased to handle the additional processing of LCR since both the production storage group and the copy are on the same server. To make sure there is enough RAM to provide for the increased requirements, Microsoft recommends an additional 1GB of RAM for servers running LCR.

CPU requirements for Exchange Server 2007 and LCR will also need to be increased to handle the additional processing of LCR. Microsoft recommends increasing CPU by 20 percent over similar systems with similar loads that are not using LCR.

Enabling Local Continuous Replication

There are two main scenarios you could have when implementing LCR:

- Existing storage group
- New storage group

In each scenario, the account used must have the appropriate Exchange Server 2007 permissions, and the account must be an Exchange Server administrator as well as a local administrator for the Exchange server that will be enabled for LCR.

Existing Storage Group

You can configure LCR for an existing storage group using the Exchange Management Console or the Exchange Management Shell (PowerShell). In Exercise 10.2, you'll configure an existing Exchange Server 2007 server with an existing storage group to start using LCR and generate the copy in the location entered using the Exchange Management Console.

EXERCISE 10.2

Using the Exchange Management Console to Configure LCR for an Existing Storage Group

1. Start the Exchange Management Console.
2. Expand Microsoft Exchange ➤ Server Configuration, and select Mailbox.
3. Select the Mailbox server containing the target storage group for LCR.
4. Right-click the target storage group, and select Enable Local Continuous Replication to start the Enable Storage Group Local Continuous Replication Wizard.
5. Click Next on the Introduction page.
6. On the Set Paths page, set the locations for the LCR log files and LCR system files by clicking Browse. Click Next.
7. On the database page, use Browse to set the path for the LCR database file. Click Next.
8. Verify the information on the Configuration Summary on the Enable page. Click Enable.
9. Click Finish to close the wizard upon completion.

In Exercise 10.3, you'll configure an existing Exchange Server 2007 server with an existing storage group to start using LCR and generate the copy in the location entered by using the Exchange Management Shell.

EXERCISE 10.3

Using the Exchange Management Shell (PowerShell) to Configure LCR for an Existing Storage Group

1. Configure the database copy: Enable-DatabaseCopy - Identity <Server>\<StorageGroup>\<Database> -CopyEDBFilePath:<FullPathWithDatabaseFileNameAndExtension>.
2. Configure the storage group copy: Enable-StorageGroupCopy -Identify <Server>\<StorageGroup> -CopyLogFolderPath:<FullPath -CopySystemFolderPath:<FullPath>.

New Storage Group

You can configure LCR for a new storage group using either the Exchange Management Console or the Exchange Management Shell (PowerShell). In Exercise 10.4, you'll configure an existing Exchange Server 2007 server to create a new storage group, to configure it for LCR, and to generate the copy in the location entered by using the Exchange Management Console.

EXERCISE 10.4

Using the Exchange Management Console to Create a Storage Group and Enable It for LCR

1. Open the Exchange Management Console.
2. Expand Microsoft Exchange ➤ Server Configuration, and select Mailbox.
3. Right-click the target server for the new storage group, and select New Storage Group to start the New Storage Group Wizard.
4. On the New Storage Group page, enter the name for the new storage group in the Storage Group Name box.
5. Select the location for the log files and system files using the Browse buttons.
6. Select the Enable Local Continuous Replication for This Storage Group check box.
7. Set the locations for the copy of the log files and system files using the Browse buttons, and click New.
8. Click Finish to close the wizard.

In Exercise 10.5, you'll configure an existing Exchange Server 2007 server to create a new storage group, to configure it for LCR, and to generate the copy in the location entered by using the Exchange Management Shell.

EXERCISE 10.5

Using the Exchange Management Shell (PowerShell) to Create aStorage Group and Enable It for LCR

1. Run the following command: `New-StorageGroup -server <Server> -name <StorageGroupName> -HasLocalCopy:$true - CopyLogFolderPath <PathforLCRLogFiles> -CopySystemFolderPath <PathforLCRSystemFiles>`.

Disabling Local Continuous Replication

Sometimes it is necessary to disable replication. In some cases, it is necessary for maintenance purposes. In other cases, it is necessary to disable LCR so that the production database can be replaced with the copy. To disable LCR, the account used must have the appropriate Exchange Server 2007 permissions. The account must be an Exchange Server administrator and must be a local administrator for the Exchange server that is currently enabled for LCR.

After disabling LCR, you have to manually delete the files in the copy storage group and all the databases, as shown in Exercise 10.6.

EXERCISE 10.6

Using the Exchange Management Console to Disable LCR

1. Open the Exchange Management Console.
2. Expand Microsoft Exchange ➤ Server Configuration, and select Mailbox.
3. Select the Mailbox server that contains the production storage group you want to disable for LCR.
4. Right-click the target storage group, and then click Disable Local Continuous Replication.
5. Click Yes to confirm.
6. Click OK to acknowledge the Microsoft Exchange warning.
7. Manually delete the LCR storage group and database files.

You can also use the Exchange Management Shell (PowerShell) to disable LCR on an Exchange Server 2007 server, as shown in Exercise 10.7. In many cases, using the Exchange Management Shell is preferred once administrators become familiar with it.

EXERCISE 10.7

Using the Exchange Management Shell to Disable LCR

1. Run the following command: `Disable-StorageGroupCopy -Identity <StorageGroup>`.
2. Manually delete the LCR storage group and database files.

Seeding a Local Continuous Replication Copy

Seeding is the process of creating a blank database for the copy or making a copy of the production database and then initiating the copy process to update the seeded database with the live production database. When configuring LCR initially, seeding is not needed. However, seeding is required in the following situations:

- When Exchange Server 2007 has discovered corrupted log files that cannot be replayed into the database copy
- When running an offline defragmentation of the production database
- When page scrubbing a database on the production database occurs and you want to push the changes to the copy

The time needed to seed the copy depends on the size of the production database, the available bandwidth, and the overall load on the server. You can seed the copy using any of these methods:

- Use `Run Update-StorageGroupCopy` to make a copy backup of the storage group. After the copy process is done, it can be moved to the LCR database folder.
- Using `Running Enable-StorageGroupCopy` on the server will seed the copy database by default. You can use the `-SeedingPostponed` option to stop the automatic seeding. The `Enable-StorageGroupCopy` command includes the steps of the `Update-StorageGroupCopy` command. When the `Enable-StorageGroupCopy` cmdlet is run on a Mailbox server, it seeds the database by default, unless the `-SeedingPostponed` option is used.
- The copy database can also be manually copied from the production database by taking the database offline or stopping all Exchange services. Of course, by using this process, the Exchange server will not be able to process messages until the production database is brought back online.

In Exercise 10.8, you'll use the Exchange Management Shell to suspend the copy process, clean up files in the copy location, seed the copy location, and then restart the replication process.

EXERCISE 10.8

Seeding the LCR Database Using the Exchange Management Shell

1. Open the Exchange Management Shell.
2. Run `Suspend-StorageGroupCopy -Identity:<Server>\<StorageGroupName> -SuspendComment:"Seeding"` to suspend replication.

EXERCISE 10.8 *(continued)*

3. Delete all the database and log files as well as all the checkpoint files from the LCR location. Delete all `*.log`, `*.jrs`, and `*.chk` files, as well as the `.edb` file, from the LCR folder.
4. Run `Update-StorageGroupCopy -Identity:<Server>\<StorageGroupName>` to seed the LCR location. This command will automatically restart replication. Use the `-ManualResume` parameter to stop the copy from starting automatically.
5. If the replication was not resumed automatically, run `Resume-StorageGroupCopy -Identity:<Server>\<StorageGroupName>`.
6. After the `Update-StorageGroupCopy` command is complete and the storage group copy is resumed, verify that replication is working correctly by using the `Get-StorageGroupCopyStatus` cmdlet.

In Exercise 10.9, you'll use the Exchange Management Console to dismount the copy database, suspend replication, delete the copy information, copy the production database to the copy location, and resume replication.

EXERCISE 10.9

Seeding the LCR Database Using the Exchange Management Console

1. Open the Exchange Management Console.
2. Expand Microsoft Exchange ➢ Server Configuration, and select Mailbox.
3. Select the server containing the LCR copy, right-click the storage group containing the LCR copy, and select Dismount Database.
4. Suspend the replication process by right-clicking the storage group containing the LCR copy, selecting Suspend Local Continuous Replication, and then selecting Yes to confirm.
5. Remove the database files, log files, and checkpoint files from the copy, and delete the `*.log`, `*.jrs`, and `*.chk` files, as well as the `.edb` file, from the LCR database folder.
6. After dismounting the database and deleting the files in the LCR database folder, copy the database file from the production storage group to the copy location.
7. Once the copy process is complete, right-click the database, and select Mount Database.
8. Right-click the copy database and select Resume Local Continuous Replication.

Once the previous exercise is complete, the replication process should start up. Log shipping and replay will start automatically.

Testing the Health of the Local Continuous Copy Process

A standard practice for general maintenance should be to test the health of the LCR process. After all, if it isn't keeping up and is taking too long to catch up during peak hours, then it becomes less useful or even useless. In Exercise 10.10, you'll test the health of LCR.

EXERCISE 10.10

Testing Health of LCR Using Exchange Management Console

1. Open the Exchange Management Console.
2. Expand Microsoft Exchange ➢ Server Configuration, and select Mailbox.
3. Select the Mailbox server containing that copy.
4. Right-click the storage group, and select Properties.
5. Click the Local Continuous Replication tab to view the status of LCR.

Getting the same information using the Exchange Management Shell is pretty simple. From the shell, enter the command `Get-StorageGroupCopyStatus -Identity <Server>\<StorageGroup>`, and then view the resulting information.

They key information for the copy status includes the following:

- Summary status
- Copy queue length
- Replay queue length

It is important to capture this information on a regular basis. Administrators can use this information to establish baselines for times of the day, for weeks, and for months. With solid baseline information, administrators can easily tell whether processes are possibly problematic and need additional attention.

Switching to the Copy Database

The whole point of implementing LCR is to mitigate against the failure of the production database or the corruption of the database. Once failure of the database has been identified through monitoring or through user reports, it is up to administrators to run a manual process to switch the Exchange server to the copy database and make it the production database.

With quick notification and rapid response, it is possible to recover using the copy database in ten minutes or less.

You can make this change in many ways, as is true for most processes. In this case, there are Exchange Management Shell commands that Microsoft supports but does not necessarily recommend. For example, the `Restore-StorageGroupCopy` command includes a `ReplaceLocations` parameter. Instead of using this process and changing the location that Exchange uses for the database, Microsoft recommends that the database be changed to the old location by resetting the letter of the drive so that it equals the old production drive letter.

Exercise 10.11 covers the steps required to switch to the copy database and make it the production database.

EXERCISE 10.11

Recovering from Corrupt Database to the Copy

1. Identify the source of the corruption if possible. Some simple things to check include making sure the log and database drives are online. If the log drive is not available at the time of failure, it is possible that data might be lost. If the log files are still available, and they should be if they were properly deployed on a separate disk from the actual database, then there should be no loss of data.
2. Dismount the corrupt production database in the production storage group using the `Dismount-Database` cmdlet in the Exchange Management Shell or using the Dismount option from the context menu for the database in the Exchange Management Console.
3. Use the Exchange Management Shell to activate the copy. An Exchange administrator can run the `Restore-StorageGroupCopy -Identity:<Server>\<StorageGroupName>` cmdlet. This command will disable LCR for the production storage group.
4. Use the disk management tool or other tools to change the drive letter and possibly the folder structure so that the copy database is in the same logical location as the previous production database.
5. Once everything is properly placed, mount the copy database, and it will now become the production database.

The steps to recover from a failed production disk or corrupt database take only a few minutes to run. Since there is no need to copy data, the process is not constrained by the size of the database.

Configuring Single Copy Cluster

A *single copy cluster* is just like the cluster technology used for Exchange Server 2003 server clustering with a few minor exceptions. One big exception is that with Exchange Server 2007 it is possible to have an extremely large number of databases. Exchange Server 2007 allows for 50 storage groups of up to 5 stores per storage group. However, for SCC, storage groups are limited to a single store per storage group, but that still allows for up to 50 separate databases. That is a significant amount of data storage available.

In Exchange Server 2003, it was possible to use server clustering for everything except for the front-end role, which used NLB to provide scalability and high availability. In Exchange Server

2007, there are now five roles: Mailbox Server, Client Access, Hub Transport, Unified Messaging, and Edge Transport. The only role that can be used for server clustering in Exchange Server 2007 is the Mailbox role. To install the clustered mailbox environment, you need to have both a Hub Transport role and a Client Access server role in the same site. Exchange now requires more hardware for large environments that want to take advantage of high availability.

The basic architecture of an SCC looks like Figure 10.10. In a typical SCC there are two nodes, but there can be as many as eight nodes. In between each node is a private network that handles the heartbeat traffic and a public network used by clients to access the nodes and the virtual server(s) running in the cluster. In the case of Figure 10.10, there is only one virtual server. Client machines connect to the cluster using the virtual server's name and IP address.

FIGURE 10.10 SCC overview

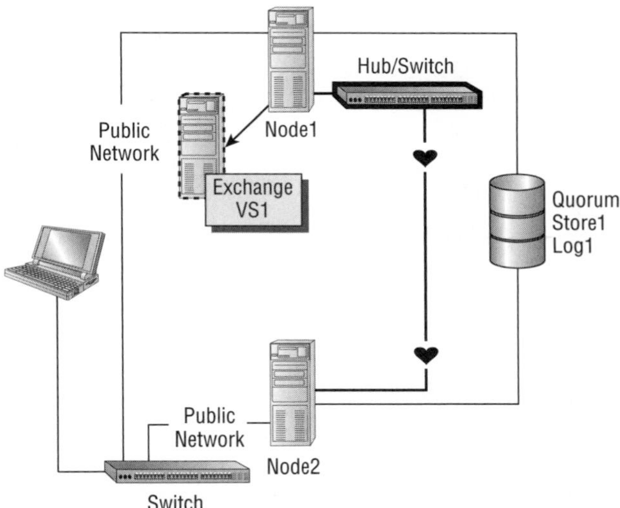

One of the big differences between server clustering in Exchange Server 2003 and Exchange Server 2007 is that Exchange Server 2007 no longer supports active/active clustering where there are two virtual servers with one running on each node. In Exchange Server 2007 there must be a passive node whether it is a two-node cluster or whether it is an eight-node cluster.

Meeting Basic Requirements for Single Copy Cluster

The following are the basic requirements for SCC.

Domain

You can install SCC only in a domain that supports Exchange Server 2007. All nodes of SCC must belong to the same Active Directory domain. SCC nodes cannot be members of a workgroup or belong to different domains. Exchange Server 2007 is not supported if the nodes for SCC are domain controllers. The nodes must be member servers.

Compatibility

Although you can install Exchange Server 2007 in an Exchange Server 2003 environment, the cluster cannot contain both versions of Exchange, and it cannot contain Exchange 2000. It must solely be Exchange Server 2007. Also, an Exchange Server 2007 cluster cannot contain any version of Microsoft SQL Server.

Exchange Server 2007 requires 64-bit hardware and 64-bit operating system versions. Exchange Server 2003 and Exchange 2000 both use 32-bit hardware and operating systems. It is not possible to mix 32-bit hardware and 64-bit hardware in a cluster.

Software

The SCC cluster must be installed on a 64-bit version of Windows Server 2003 Enterprise or Windows Server 2003 Enterprise R2. The operating system files need to be installed in the same locations. The boot and system files need to be in the same locations on all nodes. The Exchange binaries must be installed on the same locations on all nodes.

Network and Disk

We covered the network requirements and disk requirements for server clustering earlier in this chapter. You must follow the basic requirements for server clustering.

Installing SCC

You can install SCC the command line or the graphical interface. We'll show both here.

In Exercise 10.12, you'll install SCC on an existing Windows Server 2003 server cluster.

EXERCISE 10.12

Installing SCC on Active Node and on Passive Node Computers Using the Exchange Management Shell

1. Log onto the first node of the cluster.

2. Open a command prompt, navigate to the source code for Exchange Server 2007, and run `setup /r:mailbox` to make sure the Active Directory schema is updated and all the proper Exchange server files for the mailbox role are copied onto the first node.

3. At the command prompt, change to the location of the bin folder on the first node's hard drive. By default, the location will be `<systemdrive>:\Program files\Microsoft\Exchange Server\bin`. From this location, run the following (all on one line):

```
Setup /newcms /CMSname:<NameofClusteredMailboxServer>

/CMSIPAddress:<ClusteredMailboxServerIPAddress>

/CMSSharedStorage /CMSDataPath:<PathToSharedStorageForDatabase>
```

EXERCISE 10.12 *(continued)*

4. In Cluster Administrator, create the proper physical disks inside the new SCC group or move them from another location if they were previously created.

5. Log onto the second node of the cluster.

6. Open a command prompt, navigate to the source code for Exchange Server 2007, and run `setup /r:mailbox` to make sure the Active Directory schema is updated and all the proper Exchange server files for the mailbox role are copied onto the second node. If there are multiple nodes, perform the same step on each.

If Exchange Server 2007 needs to be installed in another location on each node, make sure to specify the location. To change the location, run `setup /r:mailbox /targetdir:<filepath>`, and make sure the same file path is used on all nodes.

In Exercise 10.13, you'll install SCC using the `setup` command and using the graphical setup interface. The process is a little more complex; however, it is important to go through the process to see the individual steps taken when using the GUI.

EXERCISE 10.13

Installing SCC on Active Node and on Passive Node Computers Using the Exchange Management Console

1. Connect to the installation media, and run setup from a command line to start the Exchange install on the active node of the cluster. During the Exchange setup wizard, click Next on the Introduction page, click Next to accept the license agreement, click Next on the Error Reporting page, select the Custom Exchange Server Installation option, and click Next, as shown here.

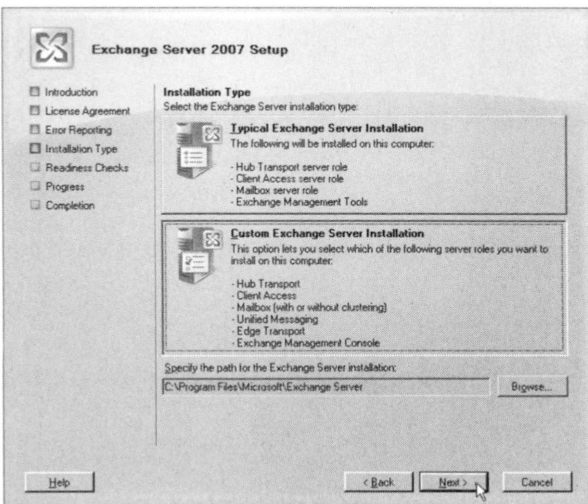

EXERCISE 10.13 *(continued)*

2. On the Server Role Selection page, select Active Clustered Mailbox Role, select the file installation path, and click Next. The file installation path needs to point to the drive letter of one of the shared disks in the cluster that already exists or that will be created later.
3. Select the Single Copy Cluster option on the Cluster Setting Selection page, and enter the following information for the virtual server for the SCC installation:
   - Clustered mailbox server name
   - IP address
   - Shared storage location for the database files
4. On the Client Settings page, click Yes or No depending on whether your organization will have Outlook 2003 or Entourage clients. Click Next to start the checks and the installation.
5. Click Install once all the checks are completed on the Readiness Checks page, as shown here.

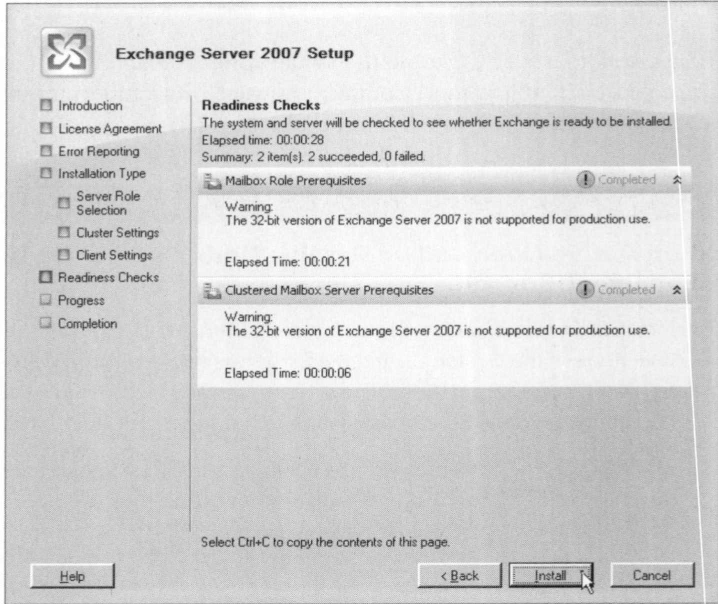

6. The Progress page will show the steps being performed, and once they are completed, click Finish.
7. The next step will be to click Step 5: Get Critical Updates for Microsoft Exchange, which must be run to download any updates. Once all updates are completed, click Close to complete the installation.

EXERCISE 10.13 *(continued)*

8. Create the physical disk resources for the new Exchange cluster group, or move the disks from another location in the Cluster Administrator MMC. Make sure the Affect the Group check box is cleared while setting up the disk resources.

9. Install the passive node using steps 1–7, but in step 2, select the Passive Clustered Mailbox Role during installation, as shown here.

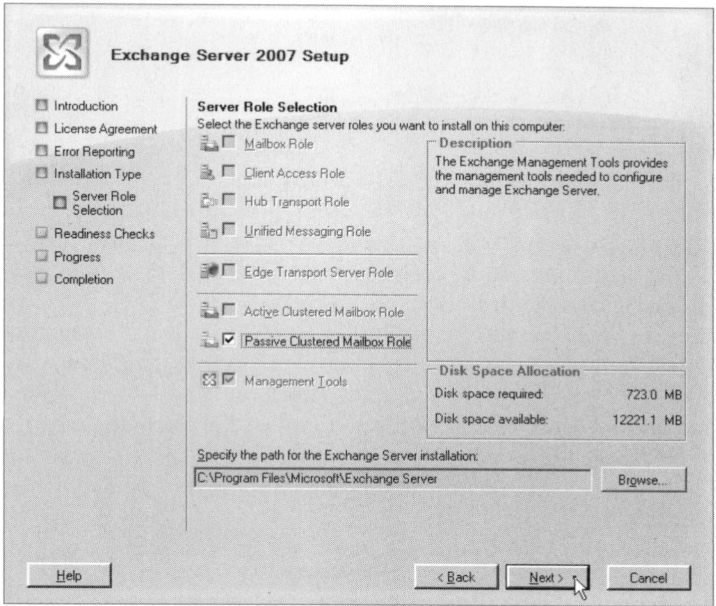

It is important that the information in step 3 be correct. It is easy to mistakenly give the information for the default cluster group that was created when the cluster was built. This is not correct. This information must be unique because it will be used for the new virtual server that will be created for the SCC installation.

Installing the passive node will follow the same steps as the active node. Once it is complete, the end result will be two nodes in an SCC. You can see the results of the work in the Cluster Administrator MMC, as shown in Figure 10.11.

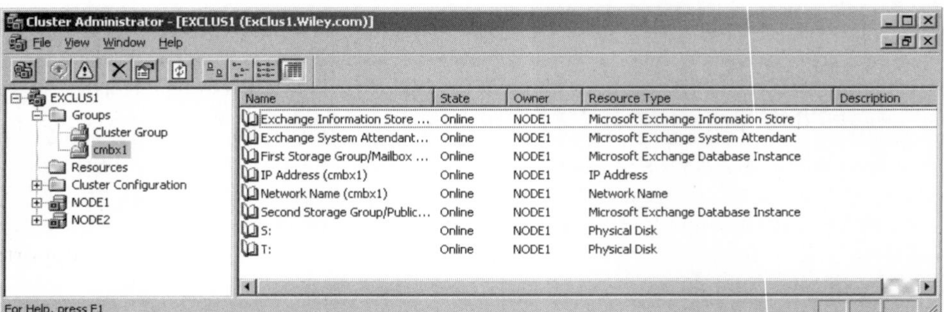

FIGURE 10.11 Cluster Administrator MMC

The SCC can manage many more users than an Exchange Server 2003 cluster of similar node size. Of course, capacity depends upon the user types, how much data they require, how often they send and receive mail, and the equipment. With increased scalability from increased RAM utilization that leads to increased caching, it is not unusual to see more than 5,000 mailbox users on a single SCC implementation.

After installation, use the Exchange Server 2007 command shell, and use the following command to move the mailbox role from the active node to the passive node: `Move-Clustered MailboxServer`.

It is possible to use the Cluster Administrator console to perform the move, or *handoff* as it is called for Exchange Server 2007; however, the Cluster Administrator console is not Exchange 2007 aware. As a best practice, you should always move the mailbox role in as SCC using the command shell.

Configuring Cluster Continuous Replication

Many organizations in the past tended to shy away from server clustering for a few reasons. A single point of failure concern around the SAN environment and the disks provided by the SAN, which include the quorum and the cluster disks used for database and transaction log storage, is one major concern. Another major concern is related to geographically dispersed clustering, also called *geoclustering*.

CCR is capable of providing high availability in a single data center or in two datacenters by using geographically dispersed clustering. In either case, CCR provides a solution with the following attributes:

- Has no single point of failure. With majority node set quorum and the replication capability provided in Exchange Server 2007, the cluster has no single point of failure.
- Has no special hardware requirements for a complete solution like in the Windows Server Catalog. Each node should be similar in capability and must have the same general disk

structures, but there is no requirement to use the clustering solutions or geographically dispersed clustering solutions from the Windows Server Catalog. Each piece of hardware should still be purchased from the hardware compatibility list, though.

- Has no special disk infrastructure requirements such as a SAN or multiple SANs with replication capabilities. The biggest change is that with log shipping capabilities CCR does not require a SAN to provide shared disks and doesn't need multiple SANs for a geocluster.
- Can be used to reduce backup times, the load on production during backup times, and the recovery time to return to full production. The copy location, the passive node, can be used to perform backups. This takes the load off of the production environment and increases the performance of backups. Volume shadow copy (VSS) backups are supported for the passive node, but streaming backups will not work.

Many organizations that depend on email want the capability of having clusters that span distance locations so in the event of the loss of a datacenter, it is still possible for email users to access their email and continue doing business. To make a geocluster work, both sites must have purchased an approved solution from the Windows Server Catalog, and those solutions are extremely expensive because they involve multiple SANs and software to manage the SANs for replication and for locking.

Figure 10.12 best illustrates the challenges. In this figure, there are two sites with one node for the cluster in each site. Geoclustering has a few issues that make the implementation a challenge:

- The quorum disks must remain replicated over the sites.
- The quorum disks must maintain locks so that only the active node is able to access its quorum disks.
- The data disks must remain replicated over the sites.
- The data disks must maintain locks so that only the active node is able to access its data disks.
- The network latency must be less than 500 milliseconds round-trip.
- The public network for all nodes must be in the same network segment, and doing this over remote locations requires using *virtual local area networks (VLANs)*.
- The private network for all nodes must be in the same network segment, and doing this over remote locations requires using VLANs.

Configuring Majority Node Set

Microsoft implemented *majority node set (MNS)* quorums to address the first two issues. Instead of selecting a shared physical disk to host the quorum, it is possible to select the MNS option to create a server cluster. From the perspective of Windows, MNS looks just like a single quorum disk, but the quorum data is actually stored on multiple disks across the cluster. MNS is designed and built so it ensures that the cluster data stored remains consistent across the different disks. Since MNS can use locally attached disks, nodes do not require expensive shared disks to maintain clustering information in the quorum. Locally attached disks can be internal to the node or external and directly attached. There is no requirement for a SAN fabric or arbitrated loop.

FIGURE 10.12 Geographically dispersed cluster

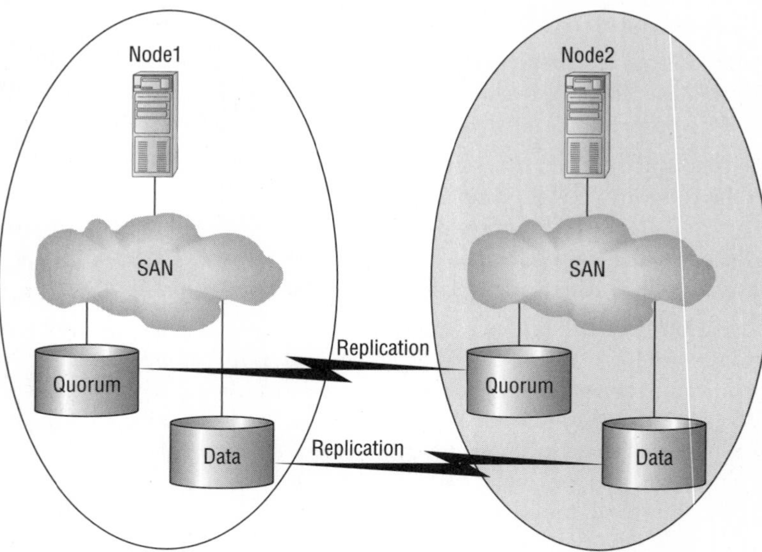

MNS has several limitations, including the following:

- Covers only quorum. One of the biggest concerns with MNS is that although it provides a nice geographically dispersed method to handle the quorum, it doesn't provide anything for data that would normally be shared by nodes.
- Requires a minimum of three nodes or two nodes and a *file share witness (FSW).*
- *Uses file sharing technology, which in turn uses server messenger blocks.*

The limitations of MNS are minor compared to the new capabilities it brings to clustering and Exchange Server 2007 CCR in particular.

Building a cluster using MNS is similar to building a standard cluster with a shared disk quorum. To properly install CCR, the cluster must first be configured using an MNS quorum. After the cluster is established using the first node, the second node must be installed, and then the cluster will be ready to install CCR for Exchange Server 2007.

Exercise 10.14 shows how to install a two-node MNS cluster.

EXERCISE 10.14

Installing a Two-Node MNS Cluster

1. Open the Cluster Administrator MMC, and then click File ➢ New ➢ Cluster. Click Next to start the New Cluster Wizard.
2. Enter the domain name and the cluster name. Click Next.

EXERCISE 10.14 *(continued)*

3. Enter the name of the first node, or use the Browse button to select the name. Click Next.
4. The Analyzing Configuration step will take place. Since there are no shared disks, there will be a couple of warnings stating that a suitable quorum device could not be found and that a local quorum will be created.
5. Enter the IP address, and click Next.
6. Enter the cluster service account information, and click Next.
7. On the Proposed Cluster Configuration page, click the Quorum button, select Majority Node Set from the drop-down box, and click OK. Click Next.
8. Once the tasks are completed on the Creating the Cluster page, click Next.
9. Click Finish on the last page of the wizard to complete the installation of the cluster with the first node.
10. In the Cluster Administrator, expand the group, and then select the default cluster group to show the resources.
11. Right-click Cluster Group, and select New ➤ Node to open the Add Nodes Wizard. Click Next.
12. Enter the name of the second node in the Select Computers page, click Add to select the node, and then click Next.
13. Once the Analyzing Configuration process completes, click Next.
14. Enter the password for the Cluster Service account, and click Next.
15. Click Next on the Proposed Cluster Configuration page.
16. Click Next once the Adding Nodes to the Cluster process is complete.
17. Click Finish to close the Add Nodes Wizard and complete the process.

Once the MNS cluster is built and configured, then it is possible to install CCR with Exchange Server 2007. However, at this point, if there is a node failure, MNS will not be able to provide for Majority, so the cluster service will fail. After all, one out of two is not greater than 50 percent. This is where the FSW comes in.

File Share Witness

To allow for the failure of a node in a MNS quorum, there must be enough surviving nodes to constitute more than one half of the number of original nodes. In a two-node MNS implementation, there is no room for failure. In the past, another node had to be installed to provide at least three production nodes. However, since the MNS quorum really is nothing more than a file share, somebody had the bright idea to actually use a file share to provide the third piece of the MNS so that there could be a failure of one of the three and the cluster would still continue running.

The file share witness, as defined in KB 921181, requires a hotfix to be installed on both cluster nodes if running Service Pack 1. The hotfix is included in Service Pack 2. Microsoft recommends using a Hub Transport server for the FSW, but any number of servers will work just fine as long as they are running the server service. Microsoft also recommends that the FSW be in a different site than either of the two CCR nodes if implementing geoclustering.

Exercise 10.15 shows how to implement FSW.

EXERCISE 10.15

Implementing File Share Witness

1. Download and install the hotfix from the link in MS KB 921181 and run it on both nodes if running Service Pack 1; skip this step if running Service Pack 2. Once it is completed, restart the node.

2. Create a share on the server to be used for the FSW. The share should be named something along the lines of FSW-CCRClusterName. The share should be configured for Everyone with Full Control.

3. From one of the nodes, it does not matter which one is used, run `Cluster.exe res "Majority Node Set" /priv MNSFileShare=\\FSWServerName\FSW-CCRClusterName`, and press Enter. The resource name for the MNS might be different. Refer to the Cluster Administrator MMC to see what the resource is named.

Introducing CCR

In a basic CCR implementation, two nodes are used along with a file share witness. With two nodes and the file share witness, then you can use MNS to provide a redundant quorum for the cluster. One of the drawbacks of MNS is that it does not address the data requirements for a cluster. Using CCR, which has its own replication capability for Exchange mailbox data, removes any issues of clustering with MNS. In a CCR implementation, such as the one shown in Figure 10.13, there is no requirement for a SAN environment to provide shared disk access. In CCR, the active node uses its own local disks to provide Exchange mailbox services, and it uses replication in the form of log shipping to send updated transactions from the active server to the passive server. The passive server then receives the logs and replays them into its database. The process is pretty much like LCR, but now the copy is being sent to another server in a cluster.

The replication process is asynchronous. This means it is possible that the failure of the production environment could result in loss of messages. This potential for lost messages led to another technology to overcome any lost message. The transport dumpster is a feature of the Hub Transport service.

FIGURE 10.13 CCR

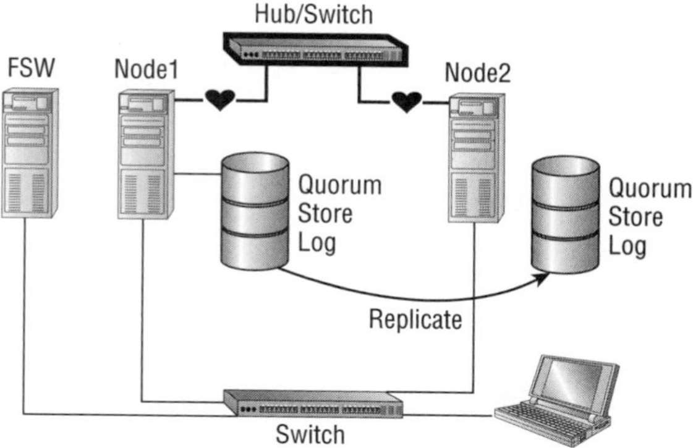

Transport Dumpster

Since all messages must be handled by the Hub Transport role so that messages can be scanned properly to meet corporate hygiene requirements and so that all transport rules are applied evenly throughout the Exchange organization, this seems like a logical place to do some message caching. The transport dumpster is a required component for CCR implementations. The queue size in the Hub Transport role is controlled by time/space limitations that the Exchange administrator can set. When a failover is experienced in CCR, the surviving clustered mailbox server automatically requests every Hub Transport server in the Active Directory site to resubmit mail from the transport dumpster cache/queue. As the messages are received by the mailbox server, the information store deletes any duplicates and redelivers only the mail that was lost.

The transport dumpster is used only for CCR implementations. It is not used in LCR or in SCC because neither of these implementations use asynchronous replication. CCR is the only technology that is susceptible to lost messages without the transport dumpster functionality. The transport dumpster is configured to be used automatically in CCR implementations, and its default settings are a `MaxDumpsterSizePerStorageGroup` setting of 18MB and a `MaxDumpsterTime` setting of seven days. These settings are usually sufficient for the vast majority of organizations, but you can modify them.

Microsoft recommends that you set the default size limit to 1.5 times the maximum message size. For example, if your organization sets a limit on message size at 5MB, then you should set the transport dumpster to a maximum of 7.5MB. Exercise 10.16 shows how to identify the current settings.

EXERCISE 10.16

Identifying Current Transport Dumpster Settings

1. Open the Exchange Management Shell.
2. Run `Get-Transportconfig`.

Exercise 10.17 shows how to set the transport dumpster configuration using the Exchange Management Shell.

EXERCISE 10.17

Setting Transport Dumpster Settings

1. Open the Exchange Management Shell.
2. Run `Set-transportconfig -MaxDumpsterSizePerStorageGroup <size> -MaxDumpsterTime <time>`.

The size should be listed as number of megabytes, as in 20MB. The duration should be listed as days.hours:minutes:seconds, with days being a two-digit number, such as 07.00:00:00.

Other Issues and Limitations of CCR

CCR is a new technology; however, it has been well tested, and several issues were discovered during the testing and development periods. It is important to note that there are several limitations when deploying CCR:

- Just like in LCR, there can be only a single database in each storage group so that there is a direct mapping from the database to the transaction logs for the database. However, since Exchange Server 2007 is now capable of handling 50 storage groups, the limitations are not drastic.
- There are several limitations of public folders in a CCR implementation because of conflicts between CCR replication and standard public folder replication:
  - If there is only one mailbox server (the CCR cluster), then it can host a public folder store because public folder replication is disabled.
  - If there are multiple mailbox servers and only one hosts a public folder store (the CCR cluster), then it can host it because public folder replication is disabled.
  - If there are multiple mailbox servers and there are multiple public folder stores, then no public folders can be hosted on the CCR cluster.
- Mailbox server names are limited to 15 characters or less to provide down-level support for email clients.
- CCR cannot be hosted in the same cluster as Exchange Server 2003, Exchange 2000, or any version of SQL Server.
- CCR nodes are not supported on nodes that are also domain controllers or global catalog servers.
- The same version of Exchange Server 2007 must be installed on all nodes, and all nodes must use the same drives and paths for the Exchange binary files, the databases, and the transaction logs.

- The performance of the network will be important when configuring the disk structures. Microsoft recommends using Gigabit Ethernet for connections between nodes. However, this is not always possible, especially when configuring CCR for geoclustering. The network speed is extremely important if there is a failure of the production server such that its drive must be replaced. In this case, the new production server must reseed the new passive server. The faster the network, the faster the reseeding process.

Installing CCR Cluster

Now that the biggest steps have been completed, installing the cluster service using MNS and configuring the FSW, it is time to actually create the CCR cluster.

Exercise 10.18 will walk through the steps to configure the CCR cluster.

EXERCISE 10.18

Installing a CCR Cluster

1. Install the preliminary components: .NET Framework 2.0 or higher, Microsoft Management Console (MMC) 3.0, and Microsoft Windows PowerShell.

2. Connect to the installation media, and run `setup` from a command line to start the Exchange install on the active node of the cluster. During the Exchange setup wizard, click Next on the Introduction page, click Next to accept the License Agreement, click Next on the Error Reporting page, select the Custom Exchange Server Installation option, and then click Next, as shown here.

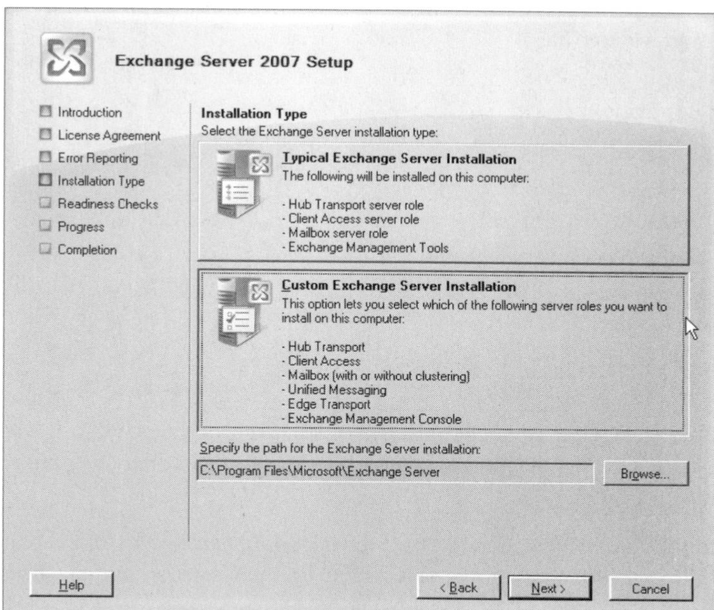

EXERCISE 10.18 *(continued)*

3. On the Server Role Selection page, select Active Clustered Mailbox Role, select the file installation path, and click Next. The file installation path needs to point to the drive letter and path for where the Exchange binaries will be installed.

4. On the Cluster Settings page, select the Continuous Copy Replication option, and enter the following information for the virtual server for the CCR installation:

   - Clustered mailbox server name
   - IP address
   - Storage location for the database files, which will be a local hard drive

5. On the Client Settings page, click Yes or No depending on whether the organization will have Outlook 2003 or Entourage clients. Click Next to start the checks and the installation.

6. Click Install once all the checks are completed on the Readiness Checks page, as shown here.

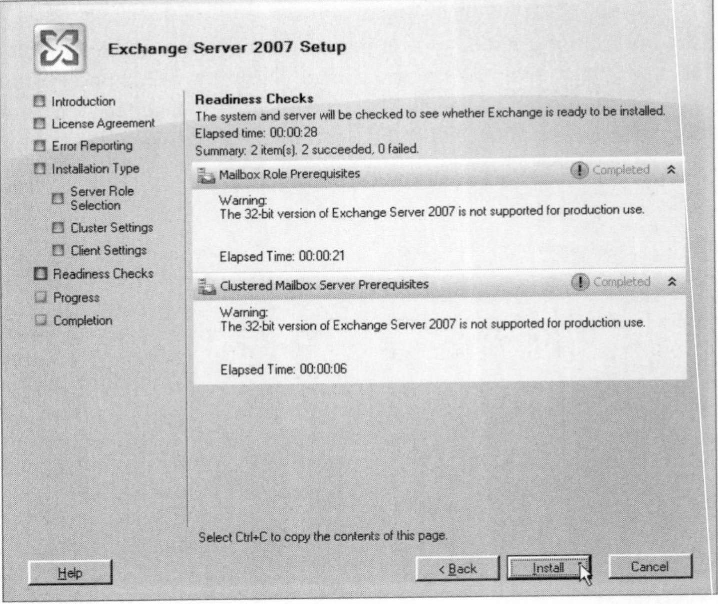

7. The Progress page will show the steps being performed, and once they are completed, click Finish.

8. The next step will be to click Step 5: Get Critical Updates for Microsoft Exchange, which must be run to download any updates. Once all updates are completed, click Close to complete the installation.

EXERCISE 10.18 *(continued)*

9. Install the passive node using steps 1–7, but in step 2, select the Passive Clustered Mailbox Role during installation, as shown here.

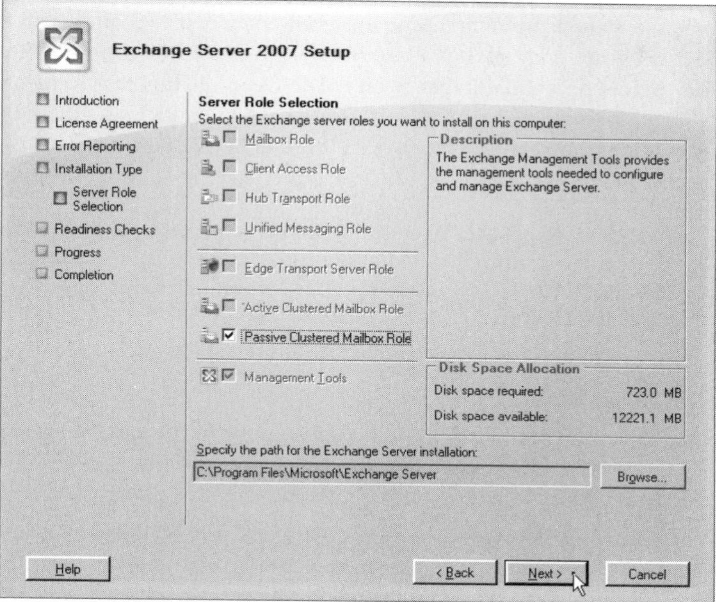

Exchange Server 2007 does not support placing the databases or the transaction logs at the root of a drive. A directory must be created to hold these files.

Dealing with CCR Outages

There are basically two types of outages regarding CCR, and the behaviors are a bit different for each type of outage. The two main types of outages are scheduled and unscheduled.

Scheduled Outage

The architecture of CCR allows for extended scheduled outages of a specific node without an extended outage of the clustered mailbox server. Because one node can be offline, the other node is capable of providing mailbox services while the offline node is repaired or undergoes ordinary maintenance. Scheduled outages make sure that all log data on the active node is successfully copied to the passive node before the active node is allowed to take itself offline. Scheduled outages should never result in the loss of data even though the replication is asynchronous.

In a two-node CCR solution, only one node can be taken offline at a time. A second node being taken offline or failing will cause the mailbox services provided by the cluster to stop, and clients will no longer be able to access their email. With the redundancy built into MNS with the file share witness, either the file share witness or the passive node can be taken offline for maintenance, updates, and repairs without the entire cluster failing. Of the two nodes and the file share witness, only one can be down at a time for maintenance. If two of the three are brought down, then the entire cluster will fail. It is a best practice to check moving the clustered mailbox to the passive node before doing maintenance on the active node. It is easy to identify the active node using the Cluster Administrator MMC. It is also easy to check using the Exchange Management Shell by running the `Get-ClusteredMailboxServerStatus` cmdlet.

The standard process of shutting down a Windows server node in a CCR cluster does not automatically handle moving the clustered mailbox from an active CCR mailbox node to the passive node. It is important to manually move the clustered mailbox before shutting down the active server node.

Setting *AutoDatabaseMountDial*

Microsoft has implemented controls to handle the behavior in the case of an active mailbox server failing. CCR has an attribute that can be used to control unscheduled failures. The attribute, `AutoDatabaseMountDial`, has three possible values:

- *Lossless*: When set to Lossless, the passive node waits for the failed node to come back online before its databases are mounted. In this mode, it is vital that there is no loss of messages. For the process to succeed, the failed node must come back online with all logs available. When the unscheduled outage occurs, the passive node becomes the active node, and the Information Store is brought online using standard clustering technologies. The new active node then checks to see whether all the databases can be mounted without any lost data. If it is possible to mount the databases without any lost data, then the information store will mount the databases and make sure the clustered mailbox is available to clients. If the databases cannot be mounted without lost data, then the active node of the CCR cluster will look to the other node and try to copy logs from it to bring itself fully up-to-date. If the failed server comes back online with all its logs available, then this process will eventually update the active node. If the failed node comes back online and its logs are not available, then the database will not mount. In this environment, it is possible for the Exchange administrator to manually mount the databases.
- *Good Availability*: When set to Good Availability, the cluster provides fully automatic recovery if replication is working properly and the logs are replicating as fast as they are being created.
- *Best Availability*: Best Availability is the default setting. It allows automatic recovery even if replication has some latency. In this case, in a failure, the new active node might be slightly behind the state of the old active node after the failover and some loss experienced.

The `Move-ClusteredMailboxServer` cmdlet checks and verifies the health of the passive node to make sure it has a good copy of the database and it is relatively current. If, for some reason, the passive node is missing a significant amount of data, the time for the move is increased to allow the rest of the replication that is out of sync to catch up.

Scheduled moves are sometimes used to force the update of the passive copy and to move to the passive copy to perform maintenance on a corrupted database.

The `Move-ClusteredMailboxServer` cmdlet prompts the Exchange administrator for information regarding the move. This information is then copied to the event logs. The cmdlet requires the Exchange administrator to specify the server node for the new location. This step is used to prevent the clustered mailbox from being moved when it is already running in the correct location.

Do not use `cluster.exe` or the Cluster Administrator MMC to move Exchange Server 2007 clustered mailboxes. These tools can cause serious problems with replication.

Restoring Replication Activity After a Scheduled Outage

Once the scheduled outage is complete, moving the clustered mailbox to its original location is often part of the testing of the changes made. After making all the changes and performing the scheduled maintenance, the node should be restarted. There are two scenarios:

- *Successful outage*: The Scheduled outage was completely successful, no problems were found during the move of the clustered mailboxes, and the database came online and mounted without any problems. In this situation, both nodes had consistent storage groups and databases. Once the outage is complete, and the old passive node has become active, then it will begin replicating to the old active node, which is now passive. Once replication is caught up, then the clustered mailbox can be moved to its original location, and maintenance can be performed on the other node if necessary.
- *Partially successful outage*: In this case, the scheduled outage was not completely successful. It is possible that there was database corruption prior to the outage. The outage could not verify that all logs on the source were made available to the target before mounting the database. CCR can automatically recover from some inconsistencies. Replication will start and process any available logs. If replication cannot recover automatically, the copy is marked as broken and creates an event in the event log identifying the issue. If the database can be used, then reseeding might be required.

Unscheduled Outage

Unscheduled outages happen because of failures of the dependent services or the resources. CCR minimizes failures based on items that are not likely to be real issues that would normally have caused a failover in Exchange Server 2003 server clustering. CCR focuses its automatic recovery on situations where there is a high degree of confidence that the clustered mailbox would experience improved performance and reliability. In an unscheduled outage, the clustered mailbox is moved to the passive node, and the database is mounted. After mounting, the clustered mailbox becomes the active databases, and all updates and new information are processed. The formerly active node becomes the passive node, and all updates are sent to the new passive node and read into its database.

Since CCR uses asynchronous replication, unscheduled outages result in some data loss. The lost data will include, at a minimum, the active logs being written to by the active server. To address this lost information, CCR controls the failover behavior and provides the ability to recapture the transactions that would be most likely lost. The process evaluates whether database on the passive node will be mounted and used. The options include the following:

- *Lossless*: When set to Lossless, the passive node waits for the failed node to come back online before its databases are mounted. In this mode, it is vital that there is no loss of messages. For the process to succeed, the failed node must come back online with all logs available. When the unscheduled outage occurs, the passive node becomes the active node, and the Information Store is brought online using standard clustering technologies. The new active node then checks to see whether all the databases can be mounted without any lost data. If it is possible to mount the databases without any lost data, then the information store will mount the databases and make sure the clustered mailbox is available to clients. If the databases cannot be mounted without lost data, then the active node of the CCR cluster will look to the other node and try to copy logs from it to bring itself fully up-to-date. If the failed server comes back online with all of its logs available, then this process will eventually update the active node. If the failed node comes back online and its logs are not available, then the database will not mount. In this environment, it is possible for the Exchange administrator to manually mount the databases.
- *Good Availability*: When set to Good Availability, the cluster provides fully automatic recovery if replication is working properly and the logs are replicating as fast as they are being created.
- *Best Availability*: Best Availability is the default setting. It allows automatic recovery even if replication has some latency. In this case, in a failure, the new active node might be slightly behind the state of the old active node after the failover and some loss experienced.

The default configuration is Good Availability. When set to Good Availability, the node will mount all databases that are synchronized. In most cases, Good Availability will bring a database online if, during the time it took to generate a new log, the last generated log was replicated. This means Good Availability will mount the database if changes are being applied as fast as they are being generated on the production server before the failure. Best Availability allows for more variation in the inconsistency between the two copies. Lossless guarantees the copy is not brought online unless it can be confirmed that there will be no data loss. If Lossless is used, automatic recovery will occur only when the original server is operational again and all log data is available and not corrupted.

The Lossless setting can result in long outages. In some cases, it does not make sense to use Lossless because the downtime will cause major impacts on organizational production. After all, why would an organization use high-availability platforms but still allow for long outages?

As in the scheduled outage, if the databases are not automatically mounted in a failover, an Exchange administrator can still manually mount the databases. The administrator must check the state of the copy and then issue two commands.

Summary

Exchange Server 2007 has taken some great strides toward filling in some of the holes that previous versions of Exchange did not address for high availability. In particular, several different levels of high availability are provided for in Exchange Server 2007, including local continuous replication to cluster continuous replication.

Local continuous replication provides the protection from database corruption that administrators have been looking for since the release of Exchange. Previous high-availability solutions did not address the concern of administrators when it came to database corruption. Now, it is fairly inexpensive to protect an organization against database corruption or against a complete drive failure of the messaging database.

Single copy clustering is a fine solution and meets most organizations' needs of high availability. However, like the legacy server cluster solution for Exchange Server 2003, this solution also has problems related to the corruption of the database and the clustered disk architecture providing single points of failure for the solution. SCC provides for clusters from two to eight nodes with up to seven virtual servers hosting clustered mailboxes.

Cluster continuous replication clustering is a definite step in the right direction. With CCR, there are no longer single points of failure around the disk architecture like those found in a typical server clustering configuration. Combining the file share witness with the capabilities of the transport dumpster, CCR is a fairly inexpensive and extremely trustworthy solution.

Exchange Server 2007 has definitely taken some large steps forward in helping to keep messaging up and running so it is available for users around the clock.

Exam Essentials

Understand the differences between LCR, SCC, and CCR. While all these are considered high-availability components when talking about Exchange Server 2007, each one fits a particular need.

Know how to implement LCR, SCC, and CCR. Knowing how to install these components is only part of the process. It is also important to understand how to recover from a failure in each situation. You should also understand how server clustering works in general with Windows Server 2003 Enterprise Edition. There are many changes to clustering in Windows Server 2008, but it has not yet been released.

Know which roles can be used in LCR, SCC, and CCR. It is important to understand how the different roles are supported or not supported when it comes to high availability.

Review Questions

1. You are planning to upgrade your current Exchange Server 2003 organization to Exchange Server 2007. Your company uses public folders extensively and is not ready to move them into Microsoft Office SharePoint Server (MOSS) just yet. What are your options regarding creating a CCR cluster of mailbox servers in Exchange Server 2007? (Choose all that apply; each answer presents a complete solution.)

   A. Create one or more Exchange Server 2007 mailbox servers that house public folders only, without any mailbox databases. Create a CCR cluster with additional Exchange Server 2007 mailbox servers that have only mailbox databases.

   B. Leave the public folders on Exchange Server 2003 servers. Create a CCR cluster with additional Exchange Server 2007 mailbox servers that have only mailbox databases.

   C. Move all public folders to an Exchange Server 2007 mailbox server, configuring no replicas for the public folders. Create a CCR cluster that includes this server.

   D. Move all public folders to an Exchange Server 2007 mailbox server, configuring multiple replicas for the public folders. Create a CCR cluster with additional Exchange Server 2007 mailbox servers that have only mailbox databases.

2. You moved your file server from its switch to another switch that also hosts network load balanced web servers. Users report that the file server is extremely slow. What should you do?

   A. Move the file server to another switch.

   B. Add another NIC to the file server, and implement network teaming.

   C. Create a special VLAN for all file server clients.

   D. Defragment the hard drives on the file server.

3. Your company has had problems with Exchange databases becoming corrupted. In each case, the lost data has caused management to become very upset. What technology should you implement to mitigate against corruption of mailbox data?

   A. Single copy clustering

   B. Local continuous replication

   C. Network load balancing

   D. RAID-5 drives for databases

4. Your company has two identical servers. You have installed Windows Server 2003 Enterprise Edition on the first one and installed Exchange Server 2007 on it as well. You install Windows Server 2003 Enterprise on the second server, but you are unable to configure single copy clustering. What should you do?

   A. Select the Custom installation method on the second node, select the Passive Cluster Mailbox Role, select Single Copy Cluster, and run the installation to completion.

   B. Rerun the Exchange install on top of the existing server, select the role for Active Cluster Mailbox, install the second node, select the Passive Cluster Mailbox Role, then select Single Copy Cluster, and run the installation to completion.

   C. Uninstall all roles other than the mailbox role on the first computer, then rerun the installation, select the role for Active Cluster Mailbox, then install the second node, select the Passive Cluster Mailbox Role, select Single Copy Cluster, and run the installation to completion.

   D. Reformat and rebuild the first server so that it has just the operating system on it, configure clustering, and then install Exchange Server 2007 using SCC.

5. You need to provide high availability for an Edge Server. What technology should you use?

   A. Network load balancing

   B. Local continuous replication

   C. DNS round-robin

   D. Single copy clustering

6. You intend to configure two server nodes into a single copy cluster for Exchange Server 2007. Which of the following are required? (Choose all that apply.)

   A. A minimum of two network adapters

   B. A minimum of two identical nodes

   C. Windows Server 2003 Enterprise for both nodes

   D. Shared disk architecture such as a storage area network

7. You are configuring the network for a two-node continuous copy replication cluster. You configure the public network for Node1 with 192.168.2.20/24, and you configure the public network for Node2 with 192.168.3.35/24 in a remote site. You configure the private network for Node1 with 10.10.10.1/24 and the private network for Node2 with 10.10.10.2/24. When you try to create the cluster, you are unable to make it work. What should you do to make it work properly? (Choose all that apply.)

   A. Put the two public adapters in the same network segment.

   B. Configure the public network with a VLAN.

   C. Configure the private network with a VLAN.

   D. Implement a shared disk quorum using the letter Q.

8. You need to patch the current single copy cluster that you have running. What should you do?

   A. Apply the patch to the active node, and restart the active node. Then apply the patch to the other node, and restart it.

   B. Apply the patch to both nodes, and restart them at the same time.

   C. Apply the patch to both nodes, and restart them by restarting the active node first and waiting for it to fully restart before restarting the other node.

   D. Patch the passive node, use the PowerShell command to move the clustered mailbox, then patch the other node, and use the PowerShell command to move the clustered mailbox to its original location.

9. You need to move the clustered mailbox from Node1 to Node2 for maintenance. What should you do?

   A. Use the Cluster Administrator MMC, right-click the clustered mailbox cluster group, and select Move.

   B. Use the Cluster Administrator MMC, right-click the clustered mailbox cluster group, and select Take Offline.

   C. Use PowerShell, and run `Move-Clustered MailboxServer`.

   D. Use `cluster.exe`, and run `Cluster Group <groupname> /Move`.

10. You are designing a two-node single copy cluster for Exchange Server 2007. How many IP addresses do you need for the public network?

    A. 2

    B. 3

    C. 4

    D. 5

11. You are configuring a Windows Server 2003 cluster for Exchange Server 2007 CCR. You must create a service account for the cluster service. Which of the following should you do? (Choose all that apply.)

    A. Create a standard domain user account.

    B. Make the account a local administrator on all cluster nodes.

    C. Configure the account so it can log onto the cluster nodes only.

    D. Let the cluster installation set the rest of the rights during configuration.

12. You have configured your cluster, but you find that there is not enough bandwidth between the cluster nodes and the storage area network. What should you do? (Choose all that apply.)

    A. Add another HBA to each server node, and use multipathing software.

    B. Add another network adapter to each server node, and implement load balanced network adapter teaming.

    C. Add another HBA to the SAN device itself, and configure multipathing.

    D. Implement RAID-1+0 instead of RAID-5 for databases.

13. What are the different control levels that can be implemented in Exchange Server 2007 for CCR to manage potential data loss during a failover?

    A. Lossless

    B. Good Availability

    C. Best Availability

    D. Fast Failover

14. Under which situations can you install public folders on a clustered mailbox?

    - If there is only one mailbox server (the CCR cluster), then it can host a public folder store because public folder replication is disabled.
    - If there are multiple mailbox servers and only one hosts a public folder store (the CCR cluster), then it can host it because public folder replication is disabled.
    - If there are multiple mailbox servers and multiple public folder stores, then no public folders can be hosted on the CCR cluster.

    A. If there is only one mailbox server (the CCR cluster)

    B. If there are multiple mailbox servers and only one hosts a public folder store (the CCR cluster)

    C. If there are multiple mailbox servers and there are multiple public folder stores

    D. If there is one mailbox servers other than the CCR cluster

15. Which of the following properties can be configured with a public store system policy? (Choose all that apply.)

    A. The public folder tree associated with the store

    B. Support for S/MIME signatures

    C. The database associated with a store

    D. Storage limits

    E. Replication intervals

16. The file share witness hotfix needs to be run where? (Choose all that apply.)

    A. Active node of the cluster

    B. Passive node of the cluster

    C. On the server to host the file share witness

    D. On the domain controller

17. You have just run the command in PowerShell to view the status of LCR. Which of the following are available to view? (Choose all that apply.)

    A. Data copied in last hour

    B. Summary status

    C. Copy queue length

    D. Replay queue length

18. You have implemented network load balancing for your Edge Transport servers in the perimeter network. You need to limit the port flooding so it does not impact other servers. What should you do?

    A. Configure a VLAN on a switch, and put all the NLB cluster nodes in that VLAN only.

    B. Set up a hub and connect all NLB cluster nodes to the hub, and then connect the hub to the switch environment.

    C. Implement port mirroring on the switch device.

    D. Manually change the MAC addresses on the NLB cluster nodes.

19. What address range is usually used for multicasting?

    A. Class A, from 1 to 126

    B. Class B, from 128 to 191

    C. Class C, from 192 to 223

    D. Class D, from 224 to 239

20. What is the best practice configuration for network load balancing?

    A. One network adapter and multicast

    B. Two network adapters and multicast

    C. One network adapter and unicast

    D. Two network adapters and unicast

Answers to Review Questions

1. A, B, C. There are several limitations related to public folders in a CCR implementation because of conflicts between CCR replication and standard public folder replication, including the following:
   - If there is only one mailbox server (the CCR cluster), then it can host a public folder store because public folder replication is disabled.
   - If there are multiple mailbox servers and only one hosts a public folder store (the CCR cluster), then it can host it because public folder replication is disabled.
   - If there are multiple mailbox servers and multiple public folder stores, then no public folders can be hosted on the CCR cluster.
2. A. NLB clusters cause port flooding that can cause other devices on the same switch as NLB nodes to degrade in performance as they try to process all the packets sent to them.
3. B. Local continuous replication (LCR) copies the database to another physical disk using log shipping. Since it is not using block-level replication, the corruption itself should never be copied to the LCR location.
4. D. You cannot install an application in a cluster until clustering has been installed first.
5. A. Network load balancing or DNS round-robin will work for Edge Transport. However, DNS round-robin does not provide high availability.
6. A, B, C, D. All of the options are required for a single copy cluster.
7. A, B, C. A requirement for all Windows Server 2003 clusters is that all public network connections be in the same network segment, and the only way to get that to work is to use VLANs. The same is true of the private network.
8. D. It is always a best practice to patch the passive node first; that way, if for some reason the clustered mailbox does not start up properly on the patched node, it can be restarted in its original location until troubleshooting reveals the problem.
9. C. When permissions are not specifically configured for a user or group on an object, they will be inherited from the parent object.
10. C. You need a minimum of four IP addresses for the public network. You need one for each server node for a total of two. You also need one for the cluster itself, and then you need one more during the setup of Exchange Server 2007 for clustering. That's a total of four.
11. A, B, C, D. All the options are considered to be best practices for configuring the cluster service account.
12. A, C. The only way to increase bandwidth to the disk structure is to add more paths and configure multipathing.
13. A, B, C. Lossless, Good Availability, and Best Availability are the three levels for controlling potential data loss during a failover of a CCR cluster.

14. A, B, C. The clustered mailbox can host a public folder only in situations where public folder replication is not run.

15. B, D, E. The General, Database, Replication, Limits, and Full-Text Indexing pages of a public store are available for configuration, but not all the properties on those pages are available. You cannot configure a public folder tree or the database associated with a store because these are parameters that apply only to a specific store and cannot be applied to multiple stores using a policy.

16. A, B. The hotfix is run on all nodes of the cluster, but it is not run on the server hosting the file share witness.

17. B, C, D. `Get-StorageGroupCopyStatus` retrieves the summary status, copy queue length, and replay queue length.

18. A, B, C. Manually changing the MAC address would actually break NLB. It also is not an option through the GUI; you would have to do it through the `netsh` command.

19. D. Usually, multicasting is done using the address ranges found in Class D.

20. D. The best practice for NLB is to use two NICs, one for the NLB network and the other for a management network, and to configure the NLB network for unicast.

Disaster Recovery Operations for Exchange Server

MICROSOFT EXAM OBJECTIVES COVERED IN THIS CHAPTER:

✓ **Configuring Disaster Recovery**

- Recover server roles.
- Recover messaging data.
- Configure backups.

Now that your Exchange Server 2007 organization has been properly installed and configured, you need to create your disaster recovery plans. For many organizations, messaging services are business-critical. The loss of such a business-critical application could result in the loss of productivity and earnings. Even the smallest part of your Exchange organization not being available could significantly impact your company.

A proper basic disaster recovery plan should cover how to back up your data, your servers, and your configuration, as well as how to restore these items. Once that foundation is in place, you should then plan what to do in the event you lose your data center, lose a building, lose the power, or (as in the case of Hurricane Katrina in New Orleans, Louisiana, in 2005) all of your offices end up underwater. This planning should be well documented and practiced so that in the event of a disaster you will be able to make the best decisions in a limited time frame.

In this chapter, we will examine the Windows Server 2003 backup application Backup. The main subjects of this chapter are as follows:

- Understanding what disaster recovery is, how it applies to Exchange Server 2007, and how Exchange Server 2007 fits into an overall company disaster plan
- Configuring backups, including how to create, modify, perform, and monitor backup jobs
- Recovering messaging data, including how to recover messages and mailboxes, reconnect mailboxes, recover mailbox and messaging queue Extensible Storage Engine (ESE) databases, and repair a damaged database
- Backing up and recovering different server roles, including how to recover a Client Access server (CAS), a Hub Transport server, an Edge Transport server, and a Mailbox server

What Is Disaster Recovery?

Disaster recovery means different things to different people, and it is applied differently at different companies, depending on experience and company requirements. For the purpose of the Exchange Server 2007 server certification exams, *disaster recovery* means having enough data in a recoverable format to recover from the loss of any Exchange server data or Exchange server. This can be limited to the loss of a single email message or can encompass the loss of an entire data center. To properly create a disaster recovery plan, you need to consider any possible disaster situation and plan for and protect against that situation.

You need to keep backups for a number of reasons such as data loss, hardware failure, site loss, and compliance. Data seems to have a way of becoming corrupted, lost, or needed after it has been deleted. Although you may never experience one of these situations, it is best to be prepared for them just in case. You do not want to find yourself creating a resume-generating event (RGE) when the owner of the company loses all their email and asks for it back and you have no way of getting back what was lost.

Depending on the government that you live under and the field you work in, you might be required to keep a copy or copies of every bit of data pertaining to certain regulations for a number of years such as the Health Insurance Portability and Accountability Act (HIPAA), the Sarbanes-Oxley Act, the EU Data Protection Act, and California SB 1386. When considering a disaster recovery plan, you should determine all the regulator and compliance requirements that might affect your plan. For more information about how Exchange Server 2007 can help with compliance, see Chapter 7.

To properly plan for a disaster in Exchange Server 2007, you need to consider the following:

- You need to understand what kind of disasters you might be recovering from, including the loss of a single mail item, a mailbox, a server, a data center, or your only office location.
- You need to understand how Exchange relies on Active Directory and whether there is a plan in place to protect Active Directory.
- You need to understand how Exchange relies on Active Directory's directory service for both server configuration and for user setting and configuration data.
- You need to know how to establish a service-level agreement (SLA). If you are offering no more than five hours of downtime a year, you will plan differently than you would if you were offering guaranteed uptime during business hours.
- You need to understand the ESE database technology that Exchange uses to store data. The ESES database is a transactional-based database that writes data to a to log file before the data is commits to the database.
- You need to know what backup technology is available to your organization and how your choices will affect your backup implementations. Different companies have different budgets, requirements, and needs for backup, which will affect what you use to back up your system.
- You need to understand the backup technologies in Exchange and how they can solve some of your backup needs.

Overall, you need to have backups of your Exchange server's configuration and your Exchange databases. You then need to have a plan to rebuild your servers and recover your Exchange databases. This chapter will teach you how to use Exchange Server 2007, Windows NT backup, and the Exchange Management Shell to back up everything you need; it will also teach you how to restore those backups.

Avoiding Disasters and Reacting to Them

The best way of dealing with something that you fear, or that might be uncomfortable, is to be prepared enough with the right knowledge and tools that you can completely avoid the fear and deal with it. Fear tends to vanish with knowledge. This chapter will empower you to understand the tools and features available in Exchange Server 2007 to deal with disasters. Exchange Server 2007 offers a number of technologies that help you avoid data obstacles or be able to quickly and easily overcome them.

Avoiding Data Loss

The first step to avoiding data loss is to design your Exchange hardware and I/O disk systems to be as redundant as possible. You have many different choices and methods for accomplishing a good redundancy plan. We have assessed a number of them in the past and have found that no one method is better than the next when implemented and maintained properly. The best method is always the method that you have the expertise and knowledge to support the best. The following are some recommendations for designing highly redundant hardware solutions:

- Purchase the best hardware your budget will allow. This includes hardware with more than one processor, separate memory buses, dual network connections, hardware that has the ability to autocorrect or to run even with hardware errors, and any other redundancy you can afford.
- Consider the support agreement that comes with the hardware. Find out how soon parts can be shipped or whether parts can be stored on-site to fix the problem. Find out within how many hours (4, 8, 24, 38, 72, or more) a support call issue will be fixed after an issue is reported.
- Know how quickly the hardware can be replaced. With blade server technology and servers booting and running entirely from a SAN, you could install your Exchange server on blade hardware and have a hot-swappable spare blade available, which in the event of a hardware failure automatically replaces the entire server minus the disk subsystem.
- Make sure your operating system is always on a mirrored RAID-1 drive set to protect against the loss of a hard drive.
- Make sure your database and transaction logs are on a redundant disk solution. This might be a RAID solution where the loss of a disk does not mean the loss of all your data. It could also mean that your data is stored on a SAN or NAS solution where the entire disk subsystem replicates to another site. However you design it, there should always be redundancy in your Exchange Server 2007 disk subsystem.
- Keep in mind that the best hardware in the world can still fail. Constantly monitor your hardware for any signs of failure. You should react quickly to any sign that there might be a failure on the horizon.

Exchange Server 2007 has a number of new and improved availability technologies that can help you almost completely avoid the need to recover your data in the event of a hardware failure or data loss situation. Local continuous replication (LCR) and cluster continuous replication (CCR) allow you to have a near-real-time replica of your Exchange database on separate hardware.

LCR creates a copy of your Exchange database on a locally attached volume. This volume can be a direct-attached hard drive internal to the hardware, a mounted SAN or network attached storage volume, or a mounted iSCSI volume on separate hardware. The downside of LCR is that the data replica is only a replica. To do something with the replica, you need a running server. In the event of server or hardware failure, you might be looking at rebuilding your server before you can mount the LCR replica.

CCR creates a replica of the Exchange database on separate disks, and those disks are attached to a backup Exchange Server 2007 server that waits for your main server to fail so it can take over. With proper support and understanding, this can lead to a server solution that results in very little downtime, even if you lose an entire Exchange site.

For more information about LCR and CCR, see Chapter 10, "Creating and Managing Highly Available Exchange Server Solutions."

Reacting to Disasters

How you react to a disaster greatly affects the amount of downtime and loss of productivity your organization could experience. One of the best things you can do to react the most efficiently is to know and practice your disaster recovery procedure. Exchange Server 2007 offers a number of new and improved tools to help you react to a disaster quickly and efficiently. Some of these are as follows:

- *Dial-tone recovery*: If you compare email to a phone system, then the dial tone of the phone system is the ability to send and receive email. You can quickly mitigate the loss of an Exchange database by mounting an empty database that will facilitate the ability of users to send and receive email. With Outlook running in cached mode, users will have a local copy of their email that they can work with and the ability to send and receive email while you work to recover and/or restore the Exchange database.
- *Database portability*: Databases can be moved to, or mounted on, any Exchange Server 2007 server in an organization. If one Mailbox server fails but you still have access to your Exchange databases, you could quickly mount the databases on a new server and run the `Move-Mailbox -ConfigurationOnly` Exchange Management Shell command to point your users to the new location.
- *Deleted items retention*: When a user deletes an item, it appears deleted to the user. However, a copy of the deleted item is kept in the mailbox database for a specified period of time, which allows the item to be quickly and easily recovered if it was deleted unintentionally.
- *Deleted mailbox retention*: When a mailbox is deleted, it appears deleted to the user. However, a copy of the mailbox is kept in the mailbox database for a specified period of time, which allows the mailbox to be recovered if it was deleted unintentionally.
- *Setup.com /M:RecoverServer*: Almost all the configuration information for your Exchange Server 2007 servers is stored in Active Directory. In the event of a server loss, you can quickly reinstall Exchange on a server with the same settings by running `Setup.com /M:RecoverServer` and applying all the configuration information stored in Active Directory to the new server.

`Setup.com /M:RecoverServer` will not work on an Edge Transport server because the Edge Transport server is not attached to Active Directory. It also will not recover any of the modifications made to IIS on a Client Access server. In addition, any local configuration settings applied to any server role in areas such as the registry or XML configuration files will not be recovered.

- *Database technology*: The Exchange database is designed to alert you to problems and recover from failure. For example, before a disk fails, you will receive -1081 errors that indicate possible errors in the disk subsystem. After a database has failed, you can use Exchange-provided tools, such as the Disaster Recovery Analyzer, ISInteg, and ESEUtil, that can repair most errors in the database. If you need to recover from a point-in-time backup, you can apply all the transaction logs since that backup and recover almost to the point of failure.
- *Outsourced dial tone*: A number of companies offer outsourced dial-tone functionality. In the event that your server or site goes down, this company will take over sending and receiving email for you and offer a web interface to interact with your email. Once the failure is over and your site or server is restored, the company will then send you all the email that it dealt with for you while you were down. We know of a number of companies that existed this way for more than a year after Hurricane Katrina in 2005.

Understanding these tools and knowing which one is best for any given situation will allow you to react quickly, correctly, and efficiently in the event that a disaster does happen. That being said, sometimes you might not have enough experience to properly judge what to do. To assist, numerous consulting companies specialize in dealing with disasters. We mention this only to give you all the tools you need to best deal with a disaster.

Real World Scenario

Be Prepared

Kevin Miller tells his disaster recovery story:

"Many years ago, when I worked for a large northwest real-estate company, I was once in a disaster situation that called for a dial-tone recovery. My Exchange databases (200GB worth of mail data) failed, and it was going to take me a significant amount of time to recover them (because of the cheap, slow tape backups that I was not allowed to replace at the time). So, I quickly created empty Exchange databases (dial-tone databases) that allowed my users to send and receive email and continue working. In this situation, that was about the only thing I did right.

"After creating the dial-tone databases, I built a new Exchange server in my restore domain and recovered all the databases. At this time, I should have swapped the recovered databases with the dial-tone databases and then merged the data from the dial-tone databases into the recovered databases. It was late (hour 20 of the day), I had not practiced enough, I had no written recovery procedure, and I was not altogether thinking straight. I used Exmerge to merge all the data from the recovered databases to disk and then copied that data to the production Exchange server. Once the data was copied to the production server, I used Exmerge to merge all the recovered data into the dial-tone databases on the running server. This took another 40 hours to complete because (I thought) we had a large amount of data to move.

"In hindsight (actually, on the drive home after working a 60-hour day recovering email and making all the users happy), I realized another error. During the disaster, I had moved my restore lab from the server room into the IT conference room and hooked it all up in a rush. I used a small eight-port hub to hook up everything that I needed to have in there, and it turned out that the eight-port hub was running at 10MB per second, which is why it took so long to transfer all the data.

"I share this story to illustrate how important it is to have a written recovery plan that is tested and practiced. You should not repeat my mistake of reacting without being prepared. My restore should have taken only five hours; instead, it took me nearly 60 hours to complete. Be prepared, know what your options are, and practice them as often as you can. How you react in a disaster can greatly affect the outcome of the disaster."

Configuring Backups

By far the most important information to back up is your Exchange database. Your Exchange database holds all the email, calendaring, contact, and task data associated with the users' mailboxes stored in that database. Without this mailbox data, all you really have are some routing and data access tools. The importance of the database makes it the focus of most disaster recovery plans for the backup and recovery of the Exchange mailbox database.

Exchange Server 2007 offers two different backup technologies to back up your Exchange database:

- *Legacy streaming backups*: A legacy streaming backup backs up the Exchange database while the database is mounted and in use by making a copy of the EDB file. A streaming backup reads every page of the Exchange database and checks the database for consistency in the process. Streaming backups are being deemphasized in Exchange going forward because they take so long to stream the database to a backup. They are considered a legacy technology with a mature feature set. Very little development time is being invested in this type of backup. Legacy streaming backups are the only supported Exchange-aware backup type offered by Windows Server Backup.

- *Volume Shadow Copy Service (VSS)*: VSS was introduced in Exchange 2003, and a great deal of development time and improvements have been implemented with Exchange Server 2007. The VSS backup engine pauses all write operations to the Exchange database and log files, prepares the backup for the snapshot, and then takes a snapshot of the database. It takes only a few seconds to take a snapshot, and then the database resumes normal operations. Windows Server Backup does not support Exchange-aware VSS backups. Because of this lack of support, Windows Server VSS backups are not the recommended method to back up Exchange Server 2007. Third-party Exchange-aware VSS backups are the recommended method. See the Exchange Server team blog article at `http://msexchangeteam.com/archive/2004/06/25/166104.aspx`.

In addition to choosing a backup technology and software product, you need to consider a number of variables when designing your backup process. A proper backup plan needs to back up all needed information and data without having much noticeable impact on your users. Those backups then need to be used to return your systems to full working order when they are needed or to get data that is not available online. When creating your backup plan, keep in mind the following:

- Consider the duration of time that your backups will take to complete and the time allocated to restore those backups. You should have an established expectation with your company of how long a database can be down—20 minutes, 2 hours, 2 days, or something else. Once you know that, you should then determine how much data you could restore in that given time. That size should be your maximum database size.
- Consider the required resources needed to complete a backup and what you will need to complete with those resources. Exchange runs an online maintenance process by default at night, which checks the database for errors and defragments. You should be aware of when this process runs and how it might compete with your backups, if they happen to run at the same time, because this can overburden a server. A backup can be a very CPU- and I/O-intensive operation, so it is not recommended that you run it during times of user load on the server. Watch the system CPU, I/O load, and network bandwidth to determine the best window of time to perform your Exchange backups.
- Define recovery point objectives. Recovery point objectives should cover the expected and minimum data losses that your company can tolerate, including how much data you must recover and how much you are expected to recover. If the loss of more than one day's worth of data is not acceptable, you will need a different backup scheme than if the loss of no more than one hour of data is acceptable.
- Consider the backup hardware you have and how it helps you support the recovery requirements. Older, slower tape technology might limit what you can offer in the form of recovery point objectives. Newer disk or optical-based backup technology might allow faster and more regular backup and restore operations. LCR might be able to allow for faster recovery times by offering a near-real-time replica of your database.
- Consider the backup applications you are using. Different software can support different backup types and media, which might allow for faster or more efficient backups and restores.

- You should have a copy of your data off-site in some format; you need to determine what business requirements mandate that you need this and do your best to satisfy those needs. In addition to business requirements, you need to determine whether any government or regulatory bodies might have influence over your company that require a specific data retention policy. With this information in mind, you then need to create a media rotation policy. A typical media rotation schedule will be based on tape devices and will require a number of tapes. Table 11.1 shows an example of a tape rotation schedule for a company that takes a log file backup every day of the week and then a full backup every week, month, and year. The full backups are rotated as needed. This is only an example; the needs of your organization might be very different from this, so please do not take this example as the only way to do it.

TABLE 11.1 Tape Rotation Schedule

Tape Name	Tape Usage
Weekly Even	This tape is used every day except Friday of an even week to back up the log files.
Weekly Odd	This tape is used every day except Friday of an odd week to back up the log files.
Friday 1–5	These tapes are Friday full backup tapes numbered 1–5 to cover every week of a month.
Monthly 1–12	These tapes are monthly month-end tapes numbered 1–12, so you will have one for each month of the year.
Yearly 1–7	These tapes are yearly year-end tapes numbered 1–7, so you will have one for each month of the year.

After considering the previous points, you then need to determine the best backup type to use to back up your Exchange databases. Each backup type has inherent advantages and disadvantages that you should consider. Exchange Server 2007 supports four backup types that have different backup and recovery times, require different amounts of backup space, and allow you to customize your backups to better fit your needs:

- *Full backup*: A full backup is a complete backup that captures all the data in a given database. This includes the EDB file and all necessary log files. Log files older than the checkpoint at the time of the backup are deleted after the backup completes. Perform a full backup on a daily basis to ensure that log files do not build up and consume all the space in the log file drive. The full backup is the simplest backup to work with because it requires only a single backup set for both backup and restore. It takes the longest to complete because it captures all the data.

The Windows Server Backup application terms this *normal* backup.

- *Copy backup*: A copy backup is the same as a full backup except that log files are not deleted at the completion of the backup. You can perform a copy backup to capture a specific point in time. Copy backups should be used before performing maintenance on the database.
- *Incremental backup*: An incremental backup is a change-only backup that archives the transaction log files only since the last full or incremental backup. Log files older than the checkpoint are deleted after the backup is complete. You cannot perform an incremental backup when circular logging is enabled because circular logging limits and reuses log files. An incremental backup can be used to support a short data loss window by allowing you to perform backups, on an hourly or shorter basis, that do not take very long to complete or have major user impact. The downside is that you need to have the last full backup and all the incremental backups since that full backup to fully restore the database.
- *Differential backup*: A differential backup is a change-only backup that archives only the transaction log files since the last full or incremental backup. The difference between an incremental and a differential backup is that the differential does not delete the log files after it completes a backup. Incremental and differential backups are the smallest backup files and take the shortest time to complete.

You now know what technologies are available for backup, what types of backups are available, the performance impacts, and your backup and restore needs. Now that you know this, you can map out your backup and recovery plan and then move on to configuring your backup jobs.

Your backups should ideally be run in a given window of time at night when your servers have the fewest users connected. You should capture all your Exchange databases and any server data you might need to restore your servers.

For a majority of small- to mid-sized organizations, using streaming full backups on a nightly basis is the ideal solution. Decent backup hardware should be able to stream close to .5GB to 2GB of data in a minute. With that speed, you should be able to support backing up or restoring up to 120GB to 480GB of data in a four-hour period.

Mid- to large-sized organizations might want to consider VSS snapshot backups because they support a backup and restore window measured in minutes instead of hours. That reduced amount of time comes with a much larger price tag, however, and an added layer of complexity. The need and resulting cost of the VSS third-party software, adequate hardware storage, and more experienced employees is why we suggest that this is geared more toward larger organizations. Snapshot backup sizes are limited only by Exchange database limitations and what your backup hardware and software can support. Even with snapshot backups, you might still need to take full backups or to back up the snapshots to keep backups at an off-site location.

Creating, Modifying, and Performing Backup Jobs

At the core of any Exchange backup plan is backing up the mailbox database. You can rebuild any server role if it comes down to it, but you cannot rebuild your mailbox data; if you lose your mailbox data, no one is going to be happy with you.

Windows Server's Backup utility is the only Microsoft-included method of Exchange backup. Right out of the box Exchange can be backed up only via Windows Server Backup using the legacy streaming backup method. With the addition of third-party backup software, however, you can use the Windows built-in VSS engine and perform the more time-efficient VSS snapshot backup.

Microsoft generally does not provide exam questions that reference third-party software; therefore, for this exam, backup questions that relate to an application will be based on Windows Server Backup. All the backup technologies and types discussed here are Microsoft supported, so you should expect to see questions about VSS and legacy streaming backups.

To use Windows Server Backup to back up an Exchange server, you need to install the Exchange Management Console on the server on which you are going to run backups. Installing the Exchange Management Console installs the Windows Server Backup APIs, which allow Windows Server to back up an Exchange database.

Exercise 11.1 outlines the basic steps to create, modify, and schedule a backup job using Windows Server Backup.

EXERCISE 11.1

Backing Up the Exchange Server Mailbox Database with Windows Server Backup

1. Open Windows Server Backup in the Advanced mode. (The Wizard mode does not allow you to select an Exchange database.)

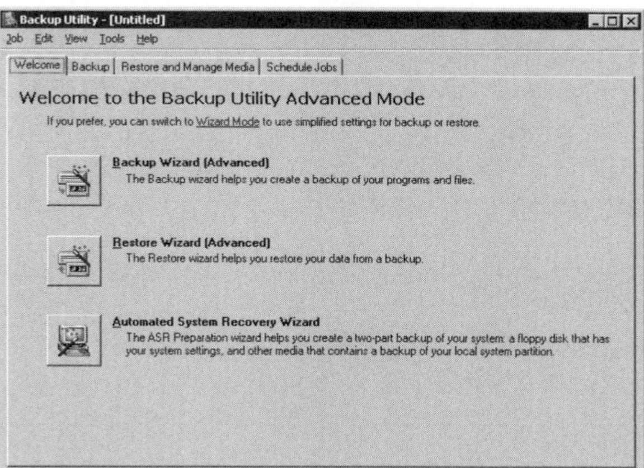

EXERCISE 11.1 *(continued)*

2. Select the Backup tab, expand Microsoft Exchange Server, and then expand the Exchange database you want to back up. Select an entire storage group, or expand the storage group and select a database in the storage group.

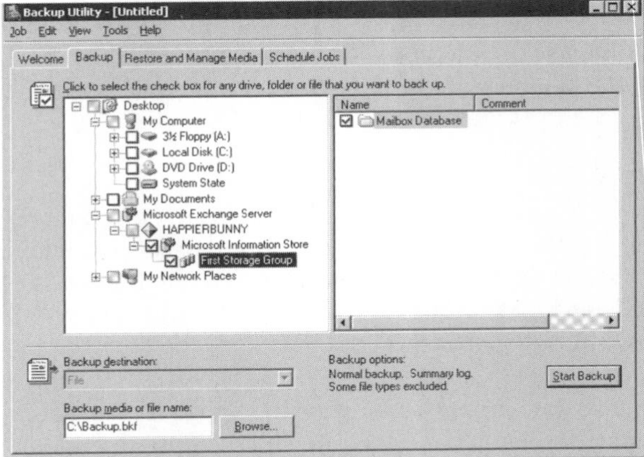

3. Once you have selected what you want to back up, choose the type of media and then the media designation to which you are going to back up the data. In the Backup Destination drop-down box, choose the media type to which you want to back up. Your options are generally Tape or Disk. In the Backup Media or File Name box, select the tape to which you want to back up or the file to which you want to back up.

4. After you have selected what to back up and where to back it up, you can save the job and schedule or launch it later. Alternatively, you can click Start Backup to start the backup job, or you can schedule it right now.

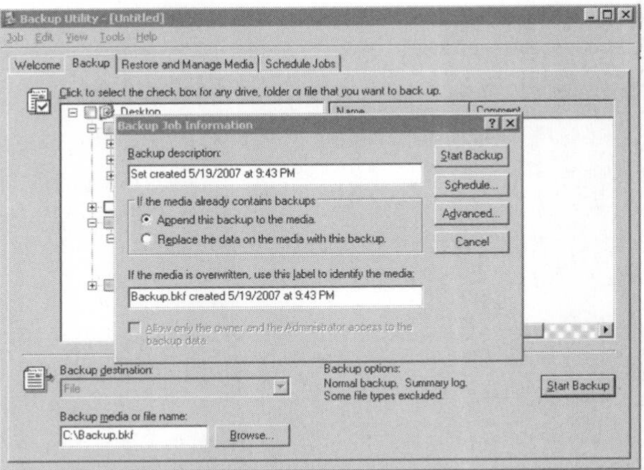

Monitoring and Validating Backup Jobs

You should never consider a backup a backup unless you have tested it and verified that there is restorable data in the backup. It might not be the best use of your time to restore every backup, but you should try to take the time to restore a backup at least once every few months. In the meantime, you can perform a number of tasks to feel more confident that your backups are running properly.

The Windows Server Backup utility writes backup confirmations and errors to a backup log file and to the Windows server event log. You should check both the backup log file and the server event logs on a daily basis. Almost every backup application should have some sort of logging, so regardless of whether you are using Windows Server Backup or a third-party application, you should still expect to see a backup log file in addition to the event log entries. When monitoring and validating your backup job, you should look for the following:

1. First you should make sure there are no errors in the log. Errors indicate, well, that there was an error in the backup process. They should also give you enough information to begin to determine what went wrong.
2. Next, make sure the backup that completed was the backup you had configured to run. If you back up the wrong data, it is as useless as though you had not run a backup at all.
3. Verify that the size of the backup is close to the size of the data you are backing up.

The Exchange backup engine writes a number of events to the Application event log. These indicate when a backup started, when it completed, the log files that successfully purged, the backup type used, and more. Look for events from source ESE and ESE backup. You need to research ESE and ESE backup errors or warning events to determine whether a problem has occurred. If a problem has occurred, then you need to fix that problem.

Real World Scenario

Test Your Backups

Kevin Miller shares his story:

"Long ago in the land of 5-inch floppies, I worked with a school district that would back up all its student records to two 5-inch floppy disks. The district had a disaster recovery plan. It made a full backup every night, and the person in charge of the backups would take a copy home with them at night and rotate the copy that was at home into the backup schedule. They had three sets of backups that rotated in the rotation.

"At first the records all fit on one 1.2MB 5-inch floppy, but after time that was not enough, and the backup started to need more disks. The person in charge of the backup would read the screen that said, "Please remove the disk and insert another disk." They would remove it and insert another disk. The disk was then formatted, and the data for disk 2 was writing on disk 2. All was well, and the employee now had a backup that spanned two disks.

"Then one day one of the hard disk drives in the server died, and we needed to recover from backup. The backups had never been tested until then. When we went to restore the backups, we had three sets of the two disks in the backup. Of the three sets, none had more than one disk that was good. The formatting and writing to the disk over the course of a year wore out most of the disks. The backups were all useless; there was nothing there to restore.

"We had to send the disk away to a data recovery company that read the disks in a clean room with special tools and returned the data to us on a good hard drive. This took three days and cost about $3,000 to recover the data. I share this story to illustrate how important it is to monitor that your backups are complete and validate that the backups actually contain valid restorable data. Had we ever tested a restore, we would have realized the disks were bad and replaced them with working disks, and we could have avoided this costly lesson."

Repairing a Damaged Exchange Database

Repairing an Exchange database is often a complex, frustrating, and time-consuming process. The Exchange database repair process begins by determining what the error is in the database. You can usually find a somewhat descriptive error message in the Application event log, which will populate when you try to mount the database. Armed with the error message, you can then follow one of two paths. You can search the Internet and find more information about the event ID and the HEX error in the event description, or you can contact someone who is experienced in disaster recovery. At the time of this writing, a call to Microsoft Customer Support Services (CSS) costs $245. This is a very small price to pay to have Microsoft walk you through the database repair process.

After determining which path to take, whether contacting Microsoft or going it alone, your next step is to run the actual file repair process. After the database has been repaired, you then get to see whether your dice roll paid off by attempting to mount the database. At this point, you are confronted with two possible outcomes: you are elated and excited as the database mounts, and you get to play superhero and save the day, or you are presented with another error in the Application event log, and you get to start the repair process all over again. Knowing what to run, when to run it, and how long it will take to run is the key to having a successful database repair.

Database repair might sound simple when we break it down as "find, research, and fix the problem and then mount the database," but in reality, it is not simple at all. It is almost always better to recover a failed database from backup than it is to repair a database. When you recover from a backup, you get a known good database at the end of the recovery process. When you repair a database, you are gambling that you will have anything usable at the end of the process. Most times, you have a usable database, but sometimes you do not. Even when you do end up with a usable database after a repair, you run the risk of missing data.

Understanding the Exchange Database Structure

The Exchange Database is referred to as the ESE database, which in turn was referred to, prior to 2007, as the Joint Engine Technology (JET) database. The ESE database stores all the user data and almost all the configuration data that Exchange Server 2007 uses. There are databases on the Edge Transport server, the Hub Transport server, and the Mailbox server.

The JET database at one time was a single B-tree database product inside Microsoft. It then diverged into a number of different databases as different product groups wanted to use the JET database. These product groups had different needs and requirements and wanted to do different things with the JET code. The birth and division of the JET database into what we use now were once called JET Blue and JET Red. Simplistically put, Blue was for Exchange, and Red was for Microsoft Access. When Active Directory came about, the Windows Server Active Directory team borrowed some resources from the Exchange team who had already implemented an x.400 directory structure in Exchange. Windows NT Server had already used the JET database for a number of features such as DHCP and WINS, and the Exchange team was very comfortable with the JET database, so it was decided that JET would be the database for Active Directory.

Figure 11.1 illustrates the files that make up the Exchange database.

FIGURE 11.1 The Exchange database

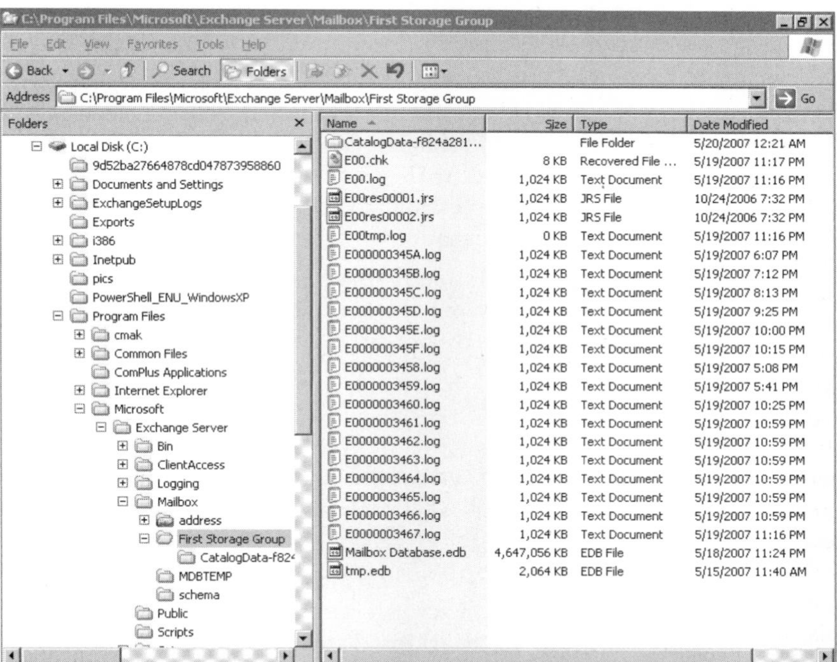

The ESE Exchange databases on the Edge Transport, Hub Transport, and Mailbox servers consist of the same database with a few minor configuration differences. Regardless of the server roles, databases consist of a number of files. The main files are as follows:

- *The EDB file (.edb)*: The `.edb` file is *the* file where all the data is stored. It has a size limit of 16TB based on the ESE database design, but the actual database size limit that you enforce should be much smaller. This allows time for backups and restores to complete without disrupting business and within time limits specified in your SLAs.
- *The temporary database (Tmp.edb)*: The temporary database is used to process transactions as they are being committed to the `.edb` database file.
- *The checkpoint file (EOO.chk)*: The `E00.chk` file maintains the checkpoint for the storage group. This checkpoint file keeps track of the last-committed transaction log file. If you are ever forced to perform a recovery, this file contains the point at which the replaying of transaction logs must start. The `00` after the `E` is the designation for the storage group.
- *Transaction log files (.log files)*: All changes made to the Exchange database are first committed to memory and then to transaction log files. Once the server has time, the log files are applied to the `.edb` file. The total number of transaction log files created depends on the transaction load on the server. There are three types of transaction logs:
  - *Working log file (E00.log)*: This is the current transaction log being written for the storage group. Once the log file reaches 1MB in size, it is renamed and a new `E00.log` file is created. The 00 after the E is the designation for the storage group.
  - *Transaction Log (E007FFFFFFF.log)*: This is the main transaction logs. They are numbered sequentially starting with E0000000001. Transaction log files are created and named based on an *E* followed with a two character sequence followed by a hexadecimal number from 1 to 0x7FFFFFFF, allowing for a total of 2,147,483,647 log files in the log stream. Transaction files are 1MB in size with Exchange Server 2007 to better support log shipping technology in LCR and CCR. (Previous versions had 5MB log files.) The `00` after the `E` is the designation for the storage group.
  - *Reserved log files (E00res00001.jrs and E00res00002.jrs)*: These are the reserved log files. In the event that the disk runs out of space, then the last transactions are written to these log files while the database dismounts. The `00` after the `E` is the designation for the storage group.

Using the Recovery Tools

Exchange Server 2007 includes two main command-line tools and two GUI wrappers for those tools to repair and work with your Exchange databases. The two tools, ESEUtil and ISIntag, are the main tools for working with the Exchange database.

ESEUtil The Exchange Server Database Utility (`ESEUtil.exe`) is a command-line tool that you can use to repair, view, and modify an Exchange database at the page level. ESEUtil is located in the Bin directory under your Exchange installation. In the past, ESEUtil could be used to work only with mailbox and public folder databases. To perform most of the operations that ESEUtil performs, ESEUtil will create a new temporary database and write all the fixed information to that new database. It is recommended that you have 1.2 times as much free space as there is data in your Exchange database before performing ESEUtil operations. You can determine the size of your database by looking for event IDs 1221 and 1224 in your event log and subtracting the whitespace reported from the total file size. For example, if your database is 45GB and the 1221 event for the database says that you have 12GB of whitespace in the database, then your database is 33GB, and you should ensure you have approximately 40GB of free space to perform ESEUtil operations on the Exchange database.

You can load ESEUtil with a number of switches; you can see them by running `eseutil /?` from a command prompt. The following is a brief explanation of the switches:

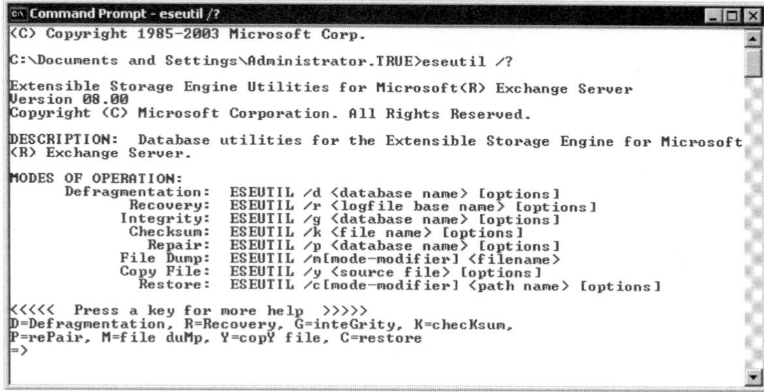

- `/D Defragmentation`: Defragments the database offline. This mode reduces the size on the disk of the `.edb` file by discarding the whitespace in the database and then rebuilding the indexes. It is not recommended that you run defragmentation as a regular maintenance operation. An online defrag is run every night, and the only difference between the online and offline defrag is that the offline defrag recovers whitespace. To recover whitespace in a database, it is better to create a new database and then move users to it.
- `/R Repair`: Repairs a corrupt offline database by discarding any pages that cannot be fixed. In repair mode, the ESEUtil tool fixes individual tables but does not maintain the relationships between tables. Use the ISInteg tool to check and fix links between tables in the repaired database.
- `/R Recovery`: Replays transaction log files to restore a database to internal consistency.
- `/G Integrity`: Verifies the page-level and ESE-level logical integrity of the database. Does not verify the integrity at the application level. You can verify application-level logical integrity with the ISInteg tool.

- `/M File Dump`: Displays headers of database files, transaction log files, and checkpoint files. Also displays database page header information, and database space allocation and metadata.
- `/K Checksum`: Verifies checksums on all pages in the database, log files, and checkpoint files.
- `/C Restore`: Allows you to run hard recovery on a database restored from a streaming backup. It also allows you to view some of the `Restore.env` file.
- `/Y Copy File`: Copies large files much faster than the normal Windows copy routine. It copies larger blocks at a time to accomplish the greater speed. You can use this switch to copy more than just Exchange files.

ISInteg The Information Store Integrity Checker (`ISInteg.exe`) finds and eliminates errors from the Exchange database at the application level. The ISInteg tool works at the logical schema level, and it can recover data that ESEUtil cannot. This is because data that is valid for the ESEUtil tool at the physical schema level can be invalid at the logical schema level. ISInteg is most often used after running the ESEUtil repair operation. The ISInteg tool repairs information, relationships, and index tables between pages in the database at the application level.

```
Command Prompt

C:\Documents and Settings\Administrator.TRUE>isinteg.exe /?
Microsoft Exchange Information Store Integrity Checker v08.00.0685.005
Copyright (c) 1986-2000 Microsoft Corp.    All rights reserved.
Usage:
 isinteg -s ServerName [-fix] [-verbose] [-l logfilename] -test testname[[, test
name]...]
    -s                ServerName
    -fix              check and fix (default - check only)
    -verbose          report verbosely
    -l filename       log file name (default - .\isinteg.pri/pub)
    -t refdblocation (default - the location of the store)
    -test testname,...
       folder message aclitem mailbox(pri only) delfld acllist
       rcvfld(pri only) timedev rowcounts attach morefld ooflist(pri only)
       global searchq dlvrto replstate(pub only)
       peruser artidx(pub only) search newsfeed(pub only) dumpsterprops
       Ref count tests: msgref msgsoftref attachref acllistref aclitemref
       newsfeedref(pub only) fldrcv(pri only) fldsub dumpsterref
       Groups tests: allfoldertests allacltests
 isinteg -dump [-l logfilename] (verbose dump of store data)
```

The two GUI wrappers—Exchange Database Recovery Management and Exchange Database Troubleshooting Assistant—are tools in their own rights. They are based on the Exchange Best Practice Analyzer (ExBPA) engine, which has grown into the Exchange Analyzer family of tools. that trouble shoot mail flow, performance, databases, and more. The two database tools in the toolbox analyze the current state of the server by reading event log files, database headers, user-added information, and log files. Once a problem has been identified, the tools react to the problem based on best practices established by Microsoft CSS, the Exchange team, and the Exchange communities. On occasion, the tools do not have the prescriptive advice or steps to repair your Exchange database, in which case you are again presented with the option of calling Microsoft CSS or working on the problem yourself.

You can download the GUI tools with the ExTRA tool, or you can find them in the Exchange Management Console in the Toolbox section, as shown here.

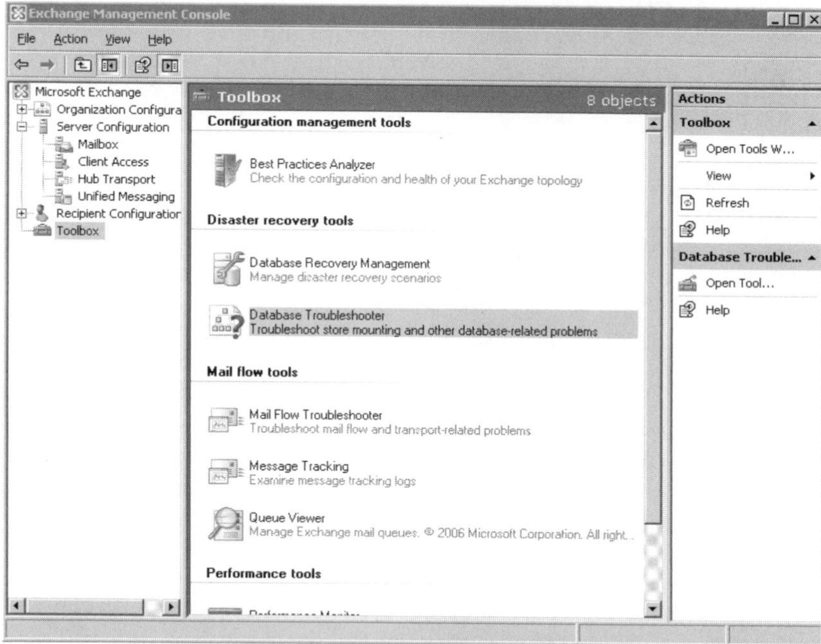

Features are always being added based on CSS-reported issues; this helps relieve call volume by automating the most common or simplest restore or repair situations. You should download the latest version of the tools before starting any restore or repair operation. Here's what the two tools do at the time of this writing:

- *Exchange Database Recovery Management*: This tool assists working with recovery storage groups and restoring databases. It can also perform a dial-tone database swap and merge for you, creating a dial-tone database, recovering a database to a recovery storage group (RSG), swapping the two, and finally merging the dial-tone database information into the recovered database.
- *Exchange Database Troubleshooting Assistant*: This tool is the tool you would use to help repair a damaged Exchange database. The troubleshooter can analyze the event logs for you and help determine what the error is. It can read the database and checkpoint files to determine the current state of the database and how best to deal with the database and transaction log files.

With the introduction of the Exchange Database Troubleshooting Assistant and the large amount of possible issues that might cause you to need to repair a database, it is not really possible to cover everything about the tool in this chapter of the book. Armed with the Exchange Database Troubleshooting Assistant, Internet searching skills, and the understanding of the ESE database laid out in this section, you should be able to repair most database problems you may encounter.

Recovering Messaging Data

The simplest way to recover deleted messaging data is with Exchange Server 2007's message retention and mailbox retention features. These features basically provide a server dumpster that holds every deleted message and mailbox for a given period of time. At the end of that period, this dumpster will be emptied—but not until an Exchange-aware backup has completed. You can turn off this feature by checking Do Not Permanently Delete Items Until This Database Has Been Backed Up, but that is not recommended. By default message data retention is configured to 14 and 30 days, with a minimum of 0 days (highly not recommended) and a maximum of 24,855 (69 years, not really recommended either).

Message and mailbox retention settings can be configured on per-database basis, as well as a per-user basis, which is useful if, for example, your board of directors has different retention requirements than your sales force. Per-user mailbox retention settings will always override per-database settings, which makes it simple to mix and match settings to better service your end users. If a message or mailbox is deleted and it is no longer in the retention dumpster, then the recovery process becomes much more involved. Figure 11.2 shows the dialog box where you can set the mailbox and item retention settings.

Recovering messages or mailboxes that are no longer in the retention dumpster involves first restoring the database to an RSG or a test server. Once you have done that, you can export the message or mailbox to PST, or in the case of mounting to an RSG, you can attach the mailbox to a user account. Although performing this process may provide you with needed practice performing restore operations, it can be time-consuming and just plain annoying.

FIGURE 11.2 Dialog box to set mailbox and item retention settings

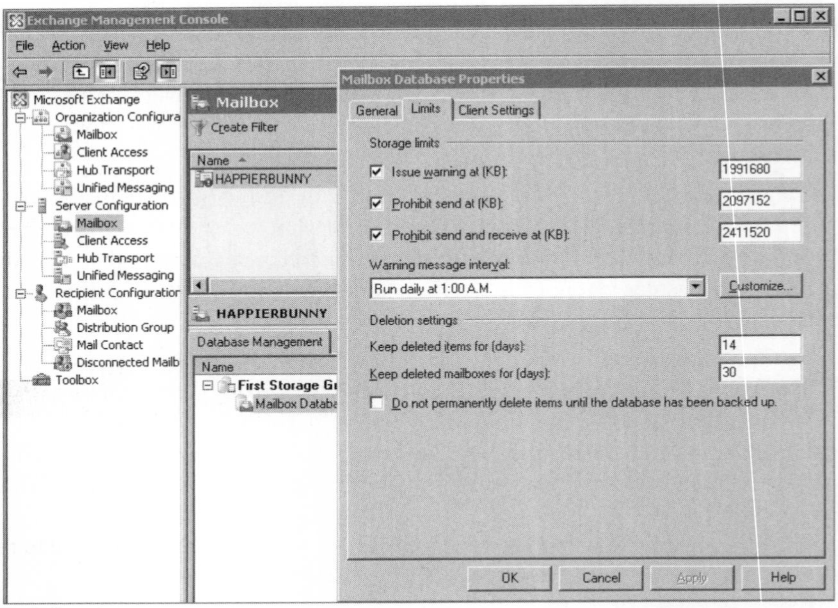

Recovering Messages with Deleted Items Retention

To a user, an email message appears to be gone once it's deleted and emptied from the Deleted Items folder. Similarly, when a user deletes an item while holding down the Shift key, the item instantly appears to be gone from the folder from which it was deleted. Although both actions will place the message in the server retention dumpster, a Shift+Delete will bypass the Deleted Items folder.

By default, Outlook enables deleted item recovery from the Deleted Items folder only. If you press Shift+Delete on a message from your Inbox, the message does not go to the Deleted Items folder; instead, it is deleted from the folder it was in when it was deleted. You can use the DumpsterAlwaysOn registry value on the client computer to enable recovery of items that have been deleted using Shift+Delete in a folder other than the Deleted Items folder. The instructions in Microsoft Knowledge Base article 246153 at `http://support.microsoft.com/kb/246153` cover this procedure. In Outlook Web Access (OWA), deleted items recovery is available only in the Deleted items folder.

Exercise 11.2 and Exercise 11.3 illustrate how to recover deleted items from the OWA and Outlook clients

EXERCISE 11.2

Recovering Deleted Items in Outlook Web Access

1. In Outlook Web Access (Premium Edition), click the Options button next to your mailbox name in the top-right corner of the screen.
2. Select Deleted Items in the options pane to the left.
3. You are now presented with a list of deleted items. Select the items you want to recover, and click Recover to Deleted Items folder.

Deleted item recovery in OWA is available only in the Premium Edition.

EXERCISE 11.3

Recovering Deleted Items in Outlook

1. In Outlook, select Tools ➢ Recover Deleted Items.
2. You are now presented with a list of deleted items. Select the items you want to recover, and click the Recover Selected Items button.

Recovering Deleted Mailboxes with Deleted Mailbox Retention

Exchange Server 2007's deleted mailbox retention feature, in our opinion, is to most importantly safeguard against company management, human resources, or the legal department deciding that a mailbox that was requested to be deleted previously should not have been deleted. Although deleted message retention is useful to protect against accidental end user message deletions, it is unlikely that an Exchange admin would accidentally delete a whole mailbox.

Deleted mailbox retention will hold a mailbox until the mailbox deletion period for that mailbox database says that the mailbox can be deleted and a full Exchange-aware backup has completed, if the Do Not Permanently Delete Items Until This Database Has Been Backed Up setting is set. If this is not quick enough to remove a deleted mailbox, you can purge the mailbox from the database. This will immediately delete the mailbox from retention.

Exercise 11.4 and Exercise 11.5 illustrate how to recover a deleted mailbox using the Exchange Management Console and the Exchange Management Shell.

EXERCISE 11.4

Recovering a Deleted Mailbox Using the Exchange Management Console

1. In the Exchange Management Console tree, expand Recipient Configuration, and then click Disconnected Mailboxes.

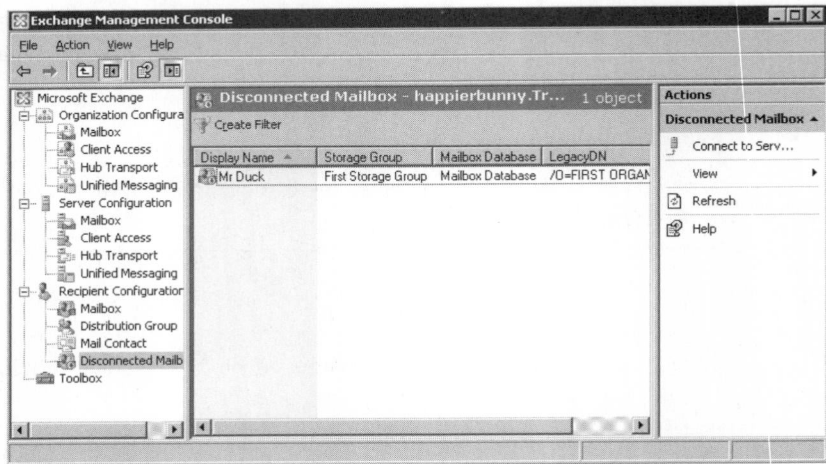

2. In the Actions pane, you will now see all the disconnected mailboxes on the current selected server.

EXERCISE 11.4 *(continued)*

3. Select the mailbox you want to recover, and then in the Actions pane, click Connect Mailbox to start the Connect Mailbox Wizard.

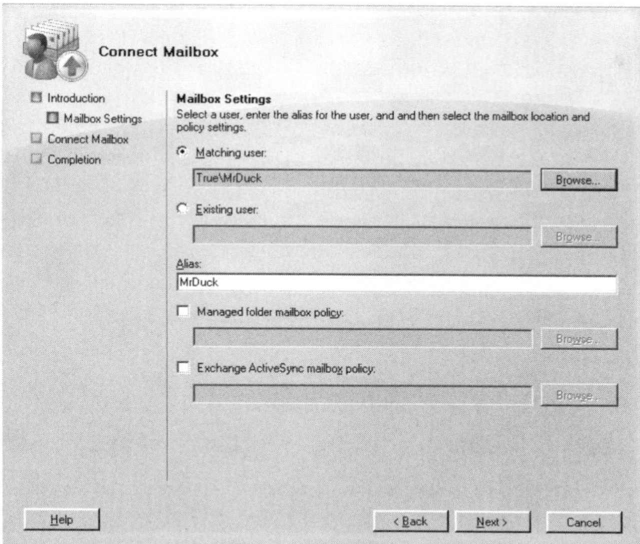

4. Follow the instructions to reconnect the disconnected mailbox in the Connect Mailbox Wizard to reconnect the deleted mailbox.

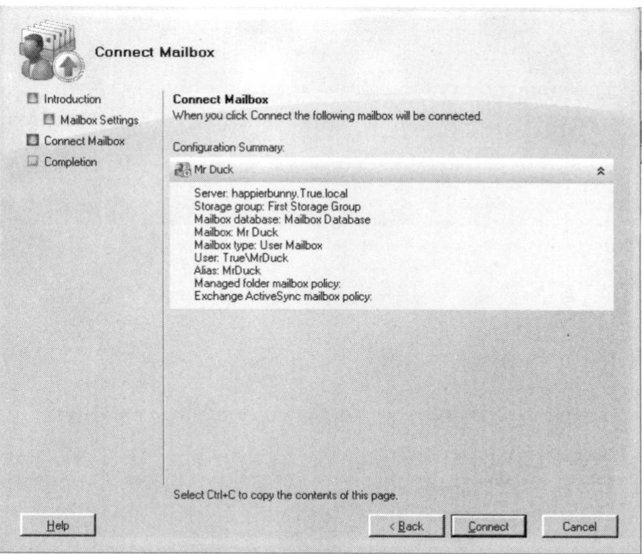

EXERCISE 11.5

Recovering a Deleted Mailbox Using the Exchange Management Shell

1. To find all the disconnected mailboxes on a given server, you need to run the `Get-MailboxStatistics` command piped to a SQL `where` statement that searches for mailboxes that have `DisconnectDate` not set to null. To do this, run the following Exchange Management Shell command:

```
Get-MailboxStatistics -Server <server> | where { $_.DisconnectDate -ne $null } |

select DisplayName,DisconnectDate
```

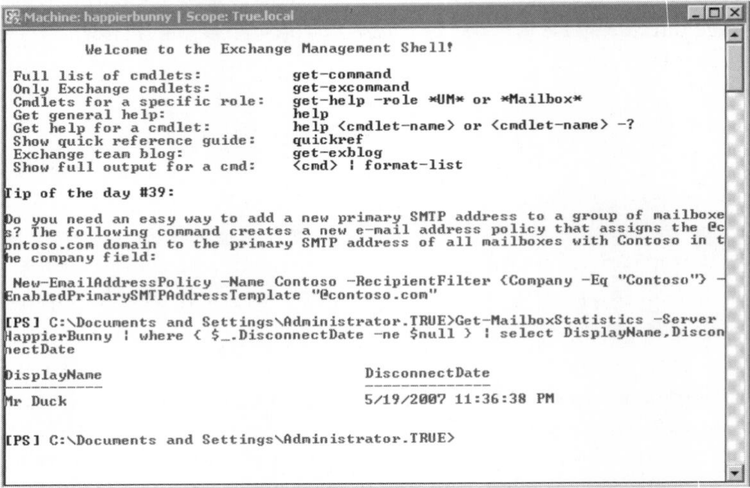

2. To reconnect a disconnected mailbox where the user object is still in Active Directory directory service, run the following Exchange Management Shell command:

```
Connect-Mailbox -Database <Mailbox_Database > -Identity <Deleted_Mailbox>
```

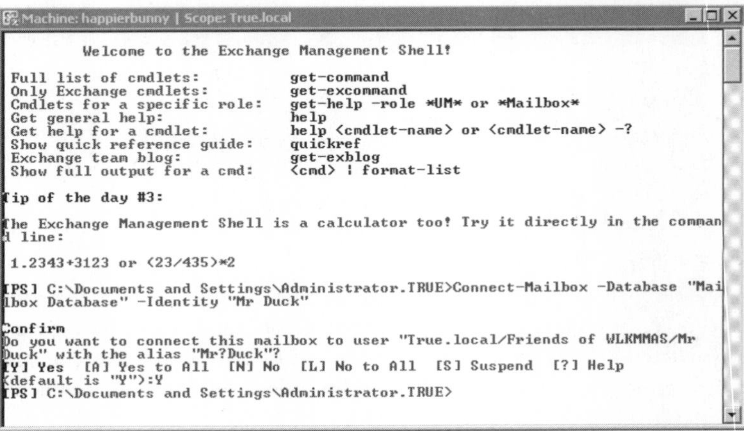

Recovering Mailbox Databases

Recovering an Exchange Server 2007 mailbox database is a somewhat simple process; it is by no means as complicated as attempting to repair an Exchange database. Before you start to restore a database, it helps to understand why you are restoring the database. Different restoration needs will require a different restoration process and will be approached differently. Reasons that might motivate you to restore an Exchange database from backup including the following:

- A hardware or site failure to the point that your Exchange server needs to be rebuilt. Once the server is rebuilt, mailbox databases are restored to the server so that it can serve data to users and receive email.
- A minor system failure, including power, hard disk, software, or hardware that caused the Exchange database to be corrupted. It is usually simpler in this case to restore from backup and replay the log files into the restored database than it is to attempt to repair the database.
- Something was deleted from the mailbox database that was deleted past the point of time where it might be in the retention dumpsters.

Once you've determined the motivation for the backup, then you can determine the best approach to restoring the data. You will approach recovering a single mailbox or mail item differently than you would approach restoring 10 mail servers in a data center that was down for a number of days because of some failure. The following are some situations and some different approaches you might take:

- Manager Les comes to you and says, "KrisJ left the company two months ago, and she just called and asked whether we could send her a copy of her contacts. We agreed to do that." In this case, you would need to find a backup taken before KrisJ left the company, restore it to an RSG, and then place her contacts in a mailbox. Once the contacts were in the mailbox, you could open that mailbox in Outlook and extract the contacts to a PST file. In the future (Exchange Server 2007 Service Pack 1), you should be able to extract her contacts to a PST file via an Exchange Management Shell command.
- Your Exchange databases are stored on the SAN, and some drives in your array have crashed. This caused you to lose one of the five databases on your Exchange server. In this situation, the first thing you should do is create a dial-tone database so users can continue to send and receive email. Once that is in place, you should then recover the database from the most recent backup. That backup might be in the form of a full backup or in the form of a full backup plus a number of incremental backups. Either way you should next restore the database to an RSG. After the restored database is mounted to the RSG and brought up to the most consistent state possible, by playing any recovered log files into the database, you can use the Database Recovery Management tool in the Toolbox section of the Exchange Management Console to swap the dial-tone and restored databases and then merge the two databases.
- Your servers were in a building that was hit by a hurricane, and all the server hardware was destroyed. Your mail is subsequently being temporarily dealt with by a third-party dial-tone provider. To reestablish your company's Exchange environment, your first steps would be to rebuild the site and then to replace the hardware. With replaced hardware,

you would then restore all the destroyed Exchange server's data. Backups were probably stored off-site. The off-site backups of the Exchange databases you would then restore to the production locations on the replaced servers. Users can then be told to start accessing email on the servers again. Finally, contact the third-party dial-tone provider to have it push all the data it has collected to your email server. Different providers will have different methods for doing this.

- An Exchange server in your organization has failed. In this situation, you should create dial-tone databases on another Exchange server and then use the `Move-Mailbox -ConfigurationOnly` command to redirect all your users to the new database. This allows users to send and receive email and continue working. Ever the optimist, you determine that the failed server was not really needed and that this is a good chance to consolidate. You then restore the backups to an RSG on the new server. After the restored database is mounted to the RSG and brought up to the most consistent state possible, by playing any recovered log files into the database, you can use the Database Recovery Management tool in the Toolbox section of the Exchange Management Console to swap the dial-tone and restored databases and then merge the two databases.

In these examples, you need to approach each situation a little bit differently. Although the approaches might have been slightly different, a few key concept and technologies stand out. Understanding these concepts will allow you to create better disaster recovery plans and to deal skillfully with situations as you are confronted with them. The key concepts and technologies that will help you the most with an Exchange database restore revolve around having as little noticeable impact on a user as possible. The goal is to quickly create a manual level of functionality to the user in order to give you the time to properly deal with the overall situation. The technologies and concepts that make this possible are as follows:

- *Recovery storage group*: The RSG is a special storage group on an Exchange server that allows you to mount a database that is not connected to any user accounts or that might have come from another Exchange server in the same organization. Once a database is mounted in an RSG, mailboxes can be linked to users and moved to a production database or extracted and merged into an existing user's mailbox.

You cannot restore an Exchange database from a different Exchange organization or a different version of Exchange to an RSG. You can mount Exchange Server 2007 databases from the same Exchange Server 2007 organization only to an RSG.

- *Dial tone*: The goal in any disaster situation is to recover as much functionality as possible as quickly as possible. The dial tone allows you to quickly recover from the loss of an Exchange database by mounting an empty database that will allow users to send and receive email.
- *The Move-Mailbox –ConfigurationOnly command*: If you don't have room on the server or the server is missing, you can create a dial-tone database on an alternative server and then point users to that alternate server with the `Move-Mailbox -ConfigurationOnly` command. In the past, this was a complicated process using ADSIEdit to resolve. In Exchange Server 2007, it is much simpler.

- *Third-party dial tone*: Some companies might not have the resources and might choose to outsource their dial-tone solution in the event of a disaster. A number of companies can help with this. A third-party dial-tone provider will receive all your email in event that your servers are no longer available. It will also offer methods to access that email as well as to send new emails. Once your servers are restored, the dial-tone provider will have a method to push all the email to your servers.

The basics of a mailbox recovery are to restore mail service using dial tone as quickly as possible, to recover as much previously stored mail data as possible, and finally to make that data available to your users. Before you can start your recovery, you should have the following in place:

- You need a server in place with enough disk space to hold the restored database and all the log files that might need to be restored.
- If the database that failed is still accessible, you should make a copy of it and the transaction log files associated with it, just in case they are needed later to recover. The log files—more than the database—might be needed to bring a restored database up-to-date.
- You need to locate the most recent backup that is relevant to the situation. Recovery last year or last month will most likely require a different backup.

Now let's look at one of the situations shown earlier where you lose a single database on a server; here we'll walk you through the steps to restore it. In Exercise 11.6, you will see how to recover an Exchange database.

EXERCISE 11.6

Recovering an Exchange Database

1. The first thing to do is to mount an empty database in place of the failed database as a dial-tone database. To do this, you must move the old database to a new location. So, to mount an empty database in the Exchange Management Console, in the navigation pane expand Server Configuration, and then select Mailbox in the Results pane. Select the server and then the mailbox database that failed. In the Actions pane, select Mount Database. You will be warned that you are creating an empty database, which is OK because you know what you are doing and you indeed want to do that.

2. With a dial-tone database mounted, your users will not be able to send and receive email. They might complain that they cannot see their old email. Before you can start the backup recovery, you need to create the recovery storage group. You can create an RSG either by using the Exchange Management Shell or by using the Database Recovery Management tool in the Toolbox section of the Exchange Management Console. To recover a mailbox database using the Exchange Management Shell, use the following steps:

   a. To create an RSG via the Exchange Management Shell, you need to first create a new recovery storage group by running the following commands:

```
New-StorageGroup -Name <RSG_Name> -Server <Server_Name> -LogFilePath <Log_
File_Path>

-SystemFolderPath <Storage_Group_Path>
```

EXERCISE 11.6 *(continued)*

b. You need to create a database in the storage group that you just created to recover the database to. This database should be named the same as the database you are restoring. Do this by running the following command:

```
New-MailboxDatabase -MailboxDatabaseToRecover
```

c. Once the database is created, you need to allow the database to be recovered to:

```
Set-MailboxDatabse <RSG_Name\Recovery_Database_Name> -AllowFileRestore
```

d. Next, restore your database using Windows Server Backup.

e. Once the database has been restored, you need to mount it using the following Exchange Management Shell command:

```
Mount-Database <RSG_Name\Recovery_Database_Name>
```

3. To recover a mailbox database using the Database Recovery Management tool, open the Database Recovery Management tool, and follow the wizard's steps. The tool is constantly being updated, so it's useful to document it step by step here because the steps might have changed by the time you read this book.

Backing Up and Recovering Different Server Roles

Disaster recovery planning has become more complicated and involved in Exchange Server 2007 with the introduction of different server roles. It is no longer just about backing up your Exchange database and being able to restore it and its mailboxes. You must now deal with a variety of other concerns:

- The Client Access server IIS Metabase is no longer synced with Active Directory, so you have to back up the IIS Metabase along with the system state on a Client Access server.
- Edge Transport server configuration is not stored in Active Directory but can be backed up into XML files with included PowerShell scripts.
- Transport queue databases are not stored in `.eml` files anymore but are now stored in an ESE database.
- The unified messaging custom audio files do not even have to be stored on an Exchange server. They just have to be accessible to the Unified Messaging server via a UNC path.
- Local configuration information on each server role is stored in the registry and in local files.

Backing Up and Recovering a Client Access Server

The Client Access server can be really simple or a mess to back up and restore. It depends on how much customization you have applied to your Client Access server. You can apply a number of different modifications to a Client Access server. You don't need to apply these, but if you do, you will then need to back them up or keep a log of the changes you made. Otherwise, it will be difficult to apply these changes after you have rebuilt your Client Access server.

If your Client Access server was not modified, then you can find everything you would need to recover your Client Access server stored in Active Directory. If this is the case, then your restore procedure is first to build a new server with the same name as the previous server and then to run `Setup /M:RecoverServer`. All of your settings will be applied to the server, and everything will be just as it was before the server had issues and needed to be recovered.

If there are modifications applied to your Client Access server, you should be aware of what they are and what kind of backup will be required for each modification. Some of the modifications on the Client Access server that will need to be backed up are as follows:

- *IIS settings*: The IIS Metabase stores configuration data for all the websites and web services on the Client Access server. Changes made to the IIS Metabase are not synchronized with Active Directory; they are stored locally only on the CAS sever where the changes were made. To back up the IIS Metabase, you should perform a system state backup of the Exchange server.
- *web.config*: The `web.config` file holds settings for the websites and web services on the Client Access server. If these are modified, you need to document the modifications so they can be reapplied to a server, or you should back them up with a file-level backup application.
- *Web pages*: For any web pages (for example, ASP or HTML files) that were modified, you need to document the modifications so they can be reapplied to a server, or you should back them up with a file-level backup application.

Installing an Exchange service pack or rollup hotfix might change the web pages, requiring that you reapply your web page modifications. If you have modified web pages, you should apply them to a test machine before applying them in production to see what is modified and how it affects any customizations you might have made.

- *POP3 and IMAP4 settings*: You can modify POP3 and IMAP4 configurations by modifying settings in XML files. If modified, then you need to document these XML file modifications so they can be reapplied to a server, or you should back them up with a file-level backup application.
- *Windows registry settings*: You can set some custom registry settings on a Client Access server. You need to document these settings so they can be reapplied to a server, or you should back them up with a system state backup.

If your Client Access server has been modified, you can recover it as shown earlier by running `Setup /M:RecoverServer`. Once you've done that, you will need to reapply all the modifications. How you reapply those will depend on how you backed up the modifications.

Included in the Exchange Server 2007 online help and in the application help files is an example script that you can use to easily back up a Client Access server, as well as all CAS custom modifications. The script functions much like the edge server export and import scripts. It does not make sense to include the Client Access server script here, because, with the release of Service Pack 1, the backup methods of a Client Access server will change. The help file will have the most up-to-date example of the script because the Exchange Server 2007 help files are updated on a regular basis. You should look at the example script to help plan your Client Access server disaster recovery.

Backing Up and Recovering a Hub Transport server

The Hub Transport server in our opinion has the best-designed disaster recovery solution. You can thank the Hub Transport server team for that. Almost everything in the Hub Transport server is stored in Active Directory. As long as your Active Directory is present and backed up, then your Hub Transport server is backed up. To restore your Hub Transport server, all you have to do is build a new server with the same name and then run `Setup /M:RecoverServer`. Once you've done that, your Hub Transport server is set up and ready to go again.

When we said almost everything on a Hub Transport server is stored in Active Directory, we meant almost everything. A few things are not captured and restored in a recovery scenario, but for the most part, those are not key to a Hub Transport server functioning. Those few things that you would miss and how they might impact are as follows:

- *The message queue database*: Data in the message queue database is transient information that exists in the database only while a message is in transport on that server or while messages are in a retry queue. A salvaged queue database can be mounted on any Hub Transport server in the organization, or messages can be extracted from the database via the Exchange Management Shell by using the command `Export-Message`. Keep in mind that the data you might recover could be minimal. You can find the message queue database in the `\Exchange server\TransportRoles\data\Queue` folder.
- *Windows registry settings*: You could set custom registry settings on a Hub Transport server. You need to document these settings so they can be reapplied to a server, or you can back them up so they can be reapplied.
- *The message tracking logs*: Each Hub Transport server has message tracking logs that hold a record of all the actions taken for every message that the server touched. The message tracking logs can be useful for performing diagnostic and forensic operations in an Exchange organization. If this data is valuable, then you should back it up on a regular basis with a file-level backup utility. You can find the message tracking logs in the `\Exchange Server\TransportRoles\Logs` folder.

Backing Up and Recovering an Edge Transport server

Unlike all the other Exchange Server 2007 server roles, the Edge Transport server role does not store configuration data in Active Directory. The Edge Transport server role uses Active Directory Application Mode (ADAM) to store configuration data. The ADAM database is a static copy of Active Directory and is never replicated to any other server. This means you cannot recover an Edge Transport server with the `Setup /M:RecoverServer` command. This also means that if you have more than one Edge Transport server, you must back up the configuration data for each server.

The Edge Transport team, being a brilliant team, decided that this was not a good story. *Story* is a common Microsoft buzzword used throughout the company. If someone asked you what the edge disaster recovery story was for a feature, they would be asking about the disaster recovery highlights, features, possible issues, design, and background. Someone might say that the Edge Transport server has a good disaster recovery story, which would mean the Edge Transport server role does not have many disaster recovery issues and addresses disaster recovery very well. This has been your Microspeak lesson of the day.

To recover the Edge Transport server, the Edge Transport team wrote and included, with Exchange Server 2007, two Exchange Management Shell scripts that back up and restore all of your Edge Transport server configuration data using XML files. You can back up and restore the Edge Transport server configuration by using the following scripts in the Exchange Management Shell:

- `ExportEdgeConfig.ps1`: This script exports all configuration data from an Edge Transport server and stores that data in an XML file.
- `ImportEdgeConfig.ps1`: This script imports all configuration data stored in the XML file that is created by the `ExportEdgeConfig.ps1` script and applies those settings to a new Edge Transport server.

The default location of the folder where you can find these scripts is `C:\Program Files\Microsoft\Exchange Server\Scripts`. The scripts capture almost all the configuration information stored on an Edge Transport server and write that information to an XML file. Once you have created this XML file, move the file off the server, and place it somewhere where it is backed up. What good is a backup of a server if you store it on the same server that crashes?

An added benefit of the XML file backup process for Edge Transport servers is a process that Microsoft calls the *cloned configuration process*. It allows you to configure one Edge Transport server and then clone its configuration to as many other Edge Transport servers as you need.

When your Edge Transport server configuration data is exported using the `ExportEdgeConfig.ps1` command, the Transport Configuration object is not extracted or written to the XML file. The Transport Configuration object has settings that apply to how an Edge Transport server deals with some transport issues server-wide. If you have not changed any of these settings, you do not need to back them up, because they are set to default values when you restore the XML file using the `ImportEdgeConfig.ps1` command. To back up and restore these settings, you use the `Get-TransportConfig` and the `Set-TransportConfig` Exchange Management Shell commands, please refer to the link in the following paragraph.

For more detailed information about what is captured and not captured by the ExportEdgeConfig.ps1 script, see the topic "Using Cloned Configuration Tasks for Edge Transport Server Disaster Recovery" at http://technet.microsoft.com/en-us/library/bb125150.aspx.

To capture the configuration of an Edge Transport server, run the ExportEdgeConfig.ps1 script. Running this script extracts the Edge Transport server configuration and places it in an XML file that can be backed up for later use. To reapply the XML backup to a newly installed Edge Transport server with the same server name, run the ImportEdgeConfig.ps1 script. Running this script will apply all the settings in the XML to your Edge Transport server. After the settings have been applied, you need to initiate EdgeSync to populate the ADAM database. Your Edge Transport server should now be restored and ready to go. Exercise 11.7 covers these steps in more details. Exercise 11.7 and Exercise 11.8 are a basic outline of the steps that you would take to back up and then restore an Edge Transport server.

EXERCISE 11.7

Backing Up an Edge Transport server

1. On the Edge Transport server that you want to back up, run the following Exchange Management Shell command:

```
./ExportEdgeConfig -cloneConfigData:"<Path_and_FileName_Of_XML_File>"
```

2. Place the XML file on a secure server in a location that is backed up.

EXERCISE 11.8

Restoring an Edge Transport server

1. Install a fresh install of Exchange Server 2007 Edge Transport server, giving the server the same name as the server you are replacing.
2. Place the XML backup file on the Edge Transport server that you want to restore.
3. On the Edge Transport server you want to restore, run the following Exchange Management Shell command:

```
./importedgeconfig.ps1 -cloneConfigData "C:\CloneConfigData.xml" -isImport
$true
```

4. Once your server has been configured with the restored settings, you need to repopulate the ADAM database by running the EdgeSync process to import all the user objects from Active Directory.

Backing Up and Recovering a Mailbox Server

Mailbox server recovery is a two-part process. Part one is recovering the server back to a usable state. Part two is recovering the mailbox database. We covered how to recover the mailbox database in a previous section of this chapter.

Almost all configuration data for the Mailbox server is stored in Active Directory. As long as your Active Directory is present and backed up, then your Mailbox server configuration is backed up. To restore your Mailbox server, all you have to do is build a new server with the same name and then run `Setup /M:RecoverServer`. Once that is done, your Mailbox server is set up and ready to go again—configuration-wise, that is. You will still need to recover or restore your mailbox or public folder databases to your server.

Summary

Disaster recovery for Exchange Server 2007 is an involved and complex concept that involves numerous levels of protection and different methods for recovery and restoration. With new server roles in Exchange Server 2007, disaster recovery has become more complex than in previous versions. Each server role requires different considerations to properly protect it in the event of a disaster.

The best way to deal with a disaster is to prevent it before it happens, with redundant reliable hardware, diligent monitoring, excellent planning, and knowledge. If a disaster cannot be prevented and you must cope with one, the best way to deal with it is to have well-documented and practiced procedures in place. Even with the best prevention and the best-laid plans, you still need to have good, verified backups.

Exam Essentials

Know your roles. Each server role stores valuable data differently, including the IIS Metabase and web pages for the Client Access server roles, the queue database on the edge and Hub Transport servers, everything in an XML file on the Edge Transport server, and the Exchange databases on the Mailbox server.

Know how to use Windows Server Backup. Windows Server Backup can back up and restore your Exchange server's databases, files, and system state. You need to know how Exchange Server backs up and from where it can backup, and then you need to know how to restore items and where it can restore items. You should be aware of all the options available to you for backups, including streaming, VSS, full, incremental, and differential.

Understand Exchange's disaster recovery features. Know what the new and updated disaster recovery features are, including dial-tone recovery, database portability, the recovery storage group, the disaster recovery analyzer wizards, deleted items retention, deleted mailbox retention, `Setup /M:RecoverServer`, the Edge Transport server scripts, LCR, and CCR.

Plan for and verify everything. You should never consider a backup to be an actual backup unless it is restorable. You need to test your backups to prove that they are usable backups. You should test your backups and use that as an opportunity to test and refine your disaster recovery plans.

Review Questions

1. A database on your Exchange Server 2007 Mailbox server becomes dismounted. The error in the Application log reports that your database was taken offline because it ran out of disk space. Searching for items to delete, you find a folder with thousands of 1MB files with names like `E0000FA344.log`. How can you delete these files?

   A. That's simple, because they are just logs of things that have been done to the Exchange database and can all be deleted.

   B. The files are all locked and in use by the Information Store service. You need to stop that service before you can delete the files.

   C. You should run an Exchange-aware backup. That backup will deal with the log files for you.

   D. Both B and C are correct.

2. You should always use an Exchange-aware backup solution to back up your Exchange databases. With Windows Server Backup, what are the available backup methods for Exchange Server 2007?

   A. Volume Shadow Copy Service (VSS) backups.

   B. The Streaming Backup API.

   C. Full and incremental, but not differential backups.

   D. All the above methods are supported Exchange-aware backup solutions.

3. For Exchange Server 2007 storage groups and databases to show up in Windows Server Backup, what application needs to be installed?

   A. You need to install the Exchange Server 2007 backup drivers by running `ExBackup.exe` found on the Exchange Server 2007 installation DVD.

   B. You need to install Exchange backup support for Windows Server by opening Control Panel, selecting Add or Remove Programs, selecting Add/Remove Windows Components, and then adding Exchange Backup Support for Windows Server Backup.

   C. You have to install the Exchange Management Console API by running Exchange Server 2007 setup and selecting only the Management Console.

   D. You have to install the Exchange Server 2007 Mailbox server role on the backup server to allow the Windows Server Backup to back up an Exchange database.

4. If your Mailbox server is configured with 3 storage groups and 18 mailbox databases, how many sets of transaction log files would your server have?

   A. 3

   B. 15

   C. 54

   D. 18

5. You come to work and find that one of your Mailbox servers has crashed. After further inspection, you determine that nothing is recoverable from the Mailbox server. To provide dial tone to the users whose mailboxes were on the failed server, you've decided to create new dial-tone databases on an existing Mailbox server in your Exchange organization. To do this, what Exchange Management Shell command would you run?

   A. `Move-Mailbox -<Mailbox_Name> -DialToneMove -MailboxDatabase <Destination_database>`

   B. `Get-MailboxStatistics -Database <Missing_Database_Name> | Move-Mailbox -ConfigurationOnly -TargetDatabase <New_Database_Name>`

   C. `Move-Mailbox -Database <Missing_Database_Name> -TargetDatabase <New_Database_Name>`

   D. `Move-Mailbox -ConfigurationOnly -Database <Missing_Database_Name> -TargetDatabase <New_Database_Name>`

6. While deleting inappropriate emails and spam messages from his Inbox, your CEO accidently deleted a message from his wife telling him where he is meeting her tonight for their anniversary dinner. He was holding down the Shift key while he deleted his messages. Your CEO is already in trouble and cannot let his wife know that he forgot again where they are meeting. Thankfully, you have configured deleted item retention for 60 days, so you instruct your CEO to select Tools ➢ Recover Deleted Items in Outlook 2003. He says he cannot find his message in there. What is wrong?

   A. Your CEO is using the wrong version of Outlook. Exchange Server 2007 supports deleted item recovery only from Outlook 2007. You should tell your CEO to use OWA to recover his message.

   B. The local deleted items cache on your CEO's computer is out-of-date and needs to be refreshed. You should instruct your CEO to reboot his computer and try again.

   C. If the message is not there, then it is gone and cannot be recovered. You should ask your CEO to call his wife and ask what was in the email.

   D. You need to add the `DumpsterAlwaysOn` registry key to your CEO's computer and then restart Outlook. Then his deleted item will be accessible.

7. While playing basketball in the server room, one of your interns unplugged your Exchange server rack. After restoring power, one of your Exchange databases did not mount, and the error leads you to believe that your database has become corrupted. Your backups all seem to be bad for this database. To repair the database, which would be the best tool to use?

   A. `ESEUtil /D`

   B. `ISInteg -patch`

   C. Exchange Database Troubleshooter

   D. Both A and B

8. Where does the Edge Transport server store configuration information that should be backed up?

   A. The ADAM database on the Edge Transport server.

   B. XML files on the Edge Transport server.

   C. The Windows Server registry.

   D. All the above places hold configuration information that should be backed up on an Edge Transport server.

9. Once you've restored all your Edge Transport server configuration information, what else needs to be reestablished on an Edge Transport server?
   - **A.** You need to reconfigure your SMTP connectors to receive email from the Internet.
   - **B.** You need to run EdgeSync to repopulate the ADAM database.
   - **C.** You need to reinitialize the hub and Edge Transport server transport connectors so that your Edge Transport server can send messages to your Hub Transport servers.
   - **D.** You need to manually rebuild your Edge Transport server's real-time IP block list cache.

10. Your Internet connection is down because of a rogue backhoe digging up the Internet cable to the building. With some time to kill, you take your Hub Transport server to the local tanning salon so it can get a good base tan for summer. While at the tanning salon, your Hub Transport server experiences a freak tanning oil accident that totally destroys the mirrored OS drive set. Since you had a downed Internet connection, your Hub Transport server had considerable email in the outbound message queue waiting to be sent. Once your Internet connection is back up, what could you do to send these messages?
    - **A.** The only way to send the messages on the Hub Transport server is to rebuild the Hub Transport server by creating a new server OS with the same name and then installing Exchange by running `Setup /M:RecoverServer`.
    - **B.** Even though the messages were stored on a different drive set, which survived the tanning oil accident, they cannot be sent again. The messages are stored in an encrypted format that is linked to the SID of the server.
    - **C.** The Hub Transport server's queue database is server agnostic. All you have to do is mount the database on another Hub Transport server, and that Hub Transport server will process the messages.
    - **D.** None of the above answers are correct.

11. Which of the following is not true for a recovery storage group?
    - **A.** Users can access all their email once a database is mounted in the recovery storage group.
    - **B.** You can mount a database created on any Exchange Server 2007 server in an organization.
    - **C.** You cannot manage a recovery storage group from inside the Exchange Management Shell.
    - **D.** You can have only one recovery storage group on a server at a time.

12. To restore an Edge Transport server, you could do any of the following except what?
    - **A.** Copy your backup XML files, and run the `ImportConfig.ps1` script.
    - **B.** Create a server with the same server name, and set up Exchange by running `Setup /M:RecoverServer`.
    - **C.** Keep a detailed log of all the modifications made to your server. Rebuild the server, and then apply all the modifications in the log to the server.
    - **D.** All the above are valid Edge Transport server restore scenarios.

13. You are pulling an overnighter cleaning up all the wiring in your server room, and your can of soda that was on top of one of your Exchange servers spilled all over the floor. You slipped on the soda and pulled all the drives out your Mailbox server's mailbox disk array. After looking at the drives, you realize that you have no idea in what order they need to be put back into the disk array. Your Mailbox server locks up because it cannot attach to any of the databases. You are now missing 300GB of mailbox data. Which of the following technologies would help you quickly recovery from this situation?

A. CCR

B. Windows Server Backup

C. ESEUtil

D. Exchange Database Troubleshooter

14. The last Exchange 2003 Mailbox server in your Exchange Server 2007 organization is missing from the server room. You suspect foul play, because someone on the server team had motive. The executive management team does not really care. All the executives care about is retrieving their mailboxes that were on the missing Exchange 2003 server. Which of the following approaches would be a viable solution to recover their mailboxes?

A. Restore the databases to an Exchange Server 2007 storage group, and merge them with the executive team's.

B. Build a server with the same name, reinstall Exchange Server 2007 with `Setup /M:RecoverServer`, and then restore the databases to that server.

C. Build an Exchange 2003 server with the same name, and then restore the database to that server.

D. Create new databases on one of your Exchange Server 2007 servers with the same name as the missing databases, mark those databases so that they can be overwritten, and then restore the databases to that server.

15. On a Client Access server, which of the following items should be backed up but don't have to be backed up to restore a Client Access server?

A. The message tacking logs

B. The transport queue database

C. The SMTP tracking logs

D. None of the above

16. The police called saying that they have recovered your missing Exchange server. When you get it back, you determine that your server does not work anymore, but you can read data from the hard disks. You want to see what has been done to your databases. Which of the following would you run to read the database header information on your databases?

A. `ESEUtil /M`

B. `ISINteg -header`

C. `Get-MailboxDatabase -name <Databae_Name> -DatabaseHeader`

D. Both A and C

17. ESE is short for what?

    A. Exchange Storage Engine

    B. Enterprise Storage Extension

    C. Extreme Storage Engineers

    D. Extensible Storage Engine

18. You have heavily modified IIS on your Client Access server. You know that CAS does not store everything in Active Directory. Which of the following places might the Client Access server use to store your modifications?

    A. The IIS XML configuration files

    B. The IIS Metabase

    C. The ADAM database

    D. The Client Access server mailbox on the Mailbox server

19. `Setup /M:RecoverServer` is a great tool to rebuild your Exchange servers. Which of the following statements is not true about this tool?

    A. `Setup /M:RecoverServer` extracts server configuration information from the Configuration node of Active Directory and applies it to your Exchange servers.

    B. For `Setup /M:RecoverServer` to recover a server, you need to build the server with the same server name as the server you are recovering.

    C. To run `Setup /M:RecoverServer`, you need to have the Exchange Server 2007 server installation files.

    D. `Setup /M:RecoverServer` can rebuild the following server roles: CAS, Edge Transport, and Mailbox. It cannot be used to recover a Hub Transport server.

20. You work for an email sales–based company. Missing any email is a horrible problem for your company, so you've been asked to support a backup solution where no more than five minutes of email data can be lost in the worst-case scenario. Which of the following backup methods would be the best fit to support this?

    A. Volume shadow copy backups every five minutes taken with Windows Server Backup

    B. Local continuous replication

    C. Streaming full backups every five minutes taken with Windows Server Backup

    D. Copy backups taken every five minutes with Windows Server Backup

Answers to Review Questions

1. C. You should never delete the transaction log files unless you've been directed to do so by CSS, or you fully understand what the ramifications are. The best way to delete the log files is to run an Exchange-aware backup utility that will fully commit all the files to the database and then delete them.

2. B. The Windows Server Backup application supports both VSS and streaming backups; however, it does not support VSS as an Exchange-aware backup method. The only Exchange-aware backup solution supported by Windows Server Backup is the Exchange steaming backup method.

3. C. Installing the Exchange Management Console is all you need to do to be able to see your Exchange storage groups and Exchange databases in Windows Server Backup.

4. A. Transaction log sets are associated with storage groups. If your server has three storage groups, then it would have three sets of transaction logs.

5. D. The correct command is `Move-Mailbox -ConfigurationOnly`. You can use the `Get-MailboxStatistics` command to list all the mailboxes in a database and then send those mailbox names to the `Move-Mailbox` command by using the following command: `Get-MailboxStatistics -Database <Missing_Database_Name> | Move-Mailbox -ConfigurationOnly -TargetDatabase <New_Database_Name>`.

6. D. By default, deleted items are recoverable only from the Deleted Items folder. By holding down Shift while deleting his message, your CEO deleted his messages without first placing them in the Deleted Items folder. To see deleted items in folders, other than the Deleted Items folder, you need to set the `DumpsterAlwaysOn` registry key on the client computer.

7. C. The Exchange Database Troubleshooter would be the best tool to use when confronted with a corrupted Exchange database. The troubleshooter will evaluate the problem and then choose the best course of action to fix the database.

8. D. The Edge Transport server configuration information is stored in ADAM, in XML files, and in the registry. If you are going to properly back up an Edge Transport server, you should capture the data in all these locations.

9. B. After a failed Edge Transport server has been reconfigured, you need to run EdgeSync to populate the ADAM database with all the attributes that are needed from Active Directory.

10. C. Exchange Server 2007 Hub Transport servers store messages in an ESE database. That database can be mounted on any Hub Transport server in your Exchange organization. To recover the messages, all you would need to do is copy the queue database to another Hub Transport server and then mount that queue database.

11. A. Users cannot access any data in a recovery storage group. To access data in a recovery storage group, you need to merge that data into another user's mailbox or move the mailbox from the recovery storage group and place it in a live database attached to a user account.

12. B. `Setup /M:RecoverServer` extracts setup information from Active Directory and applies it to the server on which you are running it. The Edge Transport server does not store any configuration information in Active Directory.

13. A. CCR is the correct answer. Had your Mailbox server been configured in CCR cluster, your server would fail over to the other node in the cluster. That other node would be attached to the disk array with a replica of your Exchange database.

14. C. Currently you have to restore the databases to an Exchange 2003 server because you cannot mount an Exchange 2003 database in an Exchange Server 2007 recovery or normal storage group.

15. D. All the above listed items are items you should back up on a Hub Transport server but not on a Client Access server.

16. A. `ESEUtil /M` would, when run with the right information, be able to display the database header for you.

17. D. ESE is short for Extensible Storage Engine.

18. B. IIS stores its configuration information in the IIS Metabase. This database is not replicated and should be backed up if settings are changed that might need to be restored in the event of a server failure.

19. D. `Setup /M:RecoverServer` cannot be run on an Edge Transport server. It can be run on a Hub Transport server.

20. B. LCR would give you the most up-to-date backup of your Exchange databases.

Chapter 12

Monitoring and Reporting on the Exchange Server Infrastructure

MICROSOFT EXAM OBJECTIVES COVERED IN THIS CHAPTER:

✓ **Monitoring and Reporting**

- Monitor system performance.
- Create server reports.
- Create usage reports.

The one task you'll most likely do more than anything other than recipient management, once your Exchange Server 2007 organization is installed and running, is monitoring. You'll want to monitor your Exchange servers to keep track of healthy or unhealthy trends. In addition, management will likely want monitoring done to produce data for reports on the status of the Exchange infrastructure because of its high visibility in most organizations. Whatever your circumstances are, you'll need to have some monitoring and reporting skills in your toolset. The main subjects of this chapter are as follows:

- Monitoring the system performance of the Exchange organization and its servers
- Creating reports about Exchange servers, performance, databases, and queues
- Creating reports about Exchange recipients

Monitoring System Performance

The most common monitoring that Exchange administrators perform is typically performance monitoring. With that in mind, you should know that performance monitoring includes both hardware (servers) and software (operating system and Exchange itself) and is no longer limited to just using the Windows Performance console. Exchange Server 2007 builds in the tools available in Windows Server 2003 and brings several of its own to the table. We'll examine common monitoring tasks and tools in the following sections of the chapter.

Monitoring Server Services

At the heart of Exchange are several key services that run on the Exchange servers and provide the functionality of Exchange. Although we examined these services in Chapter 3, "Installing Exchange Server 2007," Table 12.1 reviews them.

TABLE 12.1 Exchange Server 2007 Services

Service	Server Role Where Found
Microsoft Exchange Active Directory Topology	Mailbox, Client Access, Hub Transport, Unified Messaging
Microsoft Exchange ADAM	Edge Transport

TABLE 12.1 Exchange Server 2007 Services *(continued)*

Service	Server Role Where Found
Microsoft Exchange Credential Service	Edge Transport
Microsoft Exchange EdgeSync	Hub Transport
Microsoft Exchange File Distribution Service	Client Access, Unified Messaging
Microsoft Exchange Anti-spam Update	Hub Transport, Hub Transport
Microsoft Exchange IMAP4	Client Access
Microsoft Exchange Information Store	Mailbox
Microsoft Exchange Mail Submission Service	Mailbox
Microsoft Exchange Mailbox Assistants	Mailbox
Microsoft Exchange Monitoring	Mailbox, Client Access, Hub Transport, Unified Messaging, Edge Transport
Microsoft Exchange POP3	Client Access
Microsoft Exchange Replication Service	Mailbox
Microsoft Exchange Search Indexer	Mailbox
Microsoft Exchange Service Host	Mailbox, Client Access
Microsoft Exchange Speech Engine	Unified Messaging
Microsoft Exchange System Attendant	Mailbox
Microsoft Exchange Transport	Hub Transport, Edge Transport
Microsoft Exchange Transport Log Search	Mailbox, Hub Transport, Edge Transport
Microsoft Exchange Unified Messaging	Unified Messaging
Microsoft Search (Exchange Server)	Mailbox

More often than not, you'll know fairly quickly when a key Exchange service fails, but in some cases a service might fail and you'll never know it without either having some sort of automated health-monitoring application in place (such as Microsoft Operations Manager 2005) or manually checking the health of your server services. Since Microsoft Operations Manager 2005 is outside of the scope of this exam, we'll focus instead here on some methods you can, and should, use to monitor the Exchange services on your Exchange servers.

Using Services Console

If you have only a few Exchange servers or you just like to look at things manually, than a visit to the Services console can give you some quick insight into the status of the services on that server. You can find the Services console in the Administrative Tools folder or as a node within the Computer Management console. Use the location that makes the most sense for you. Figure 12.1 shows the Services node of the Computer Management console; you can see that the Exchange services on the server are up and running as expected.

FIGURE 12.1 Viewing the Exchange services in the Services node of the Computer Management console

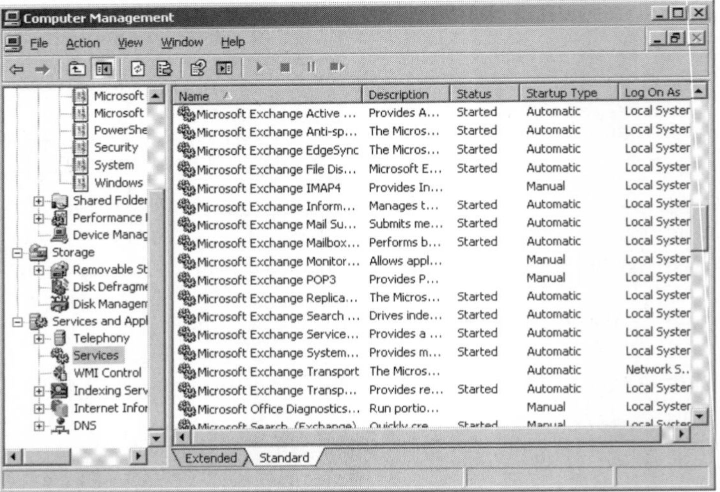

You can quickly open the Computer Management console by right-clicking the My Computer icon on the Desktop and selecting Manage from the context menu.

Using Event Viewer

Should you find a service that is not running, you will most often want to do two things: find out why it stopped and restart it. You can restart the service from the Services console shown in Figure 12.1, but if you want to get more information about what's going on with the service, then you will need to visit the Event Viewer, shown in Figure 12.2, which is also conveniently located in the Computer Management console and available as a stand-alone viewer in the Administrative Tools folder.

FIGURE 12.2 Exploring the Event Viewer node of the Computer Management console

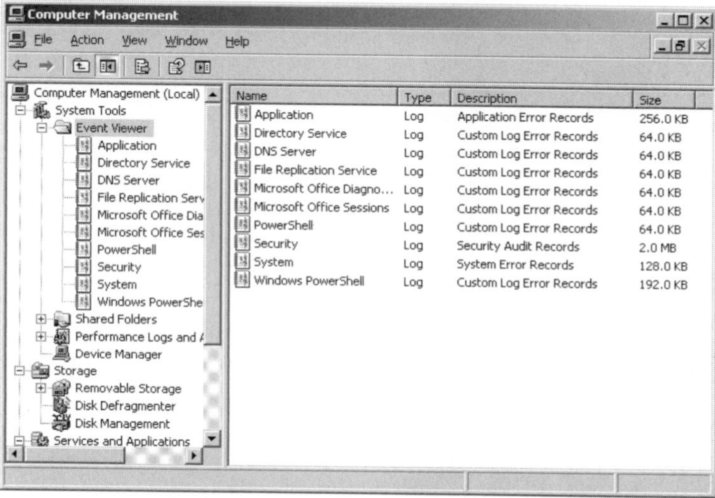

Typically, you'll find the most useful information about service status changes in the System log. The Application log will also often yield useful information. Figure 12.3 illustrates a sample event log entry you might find in the System log for a service that has stopped. By going forward and backward in the Event Viewer logs from a specific time of interest, you can find out what happened before and after an event you're interested in, such as the failure of a critical Exchange service.

FIGURE 12.3 Viewing an event log entry

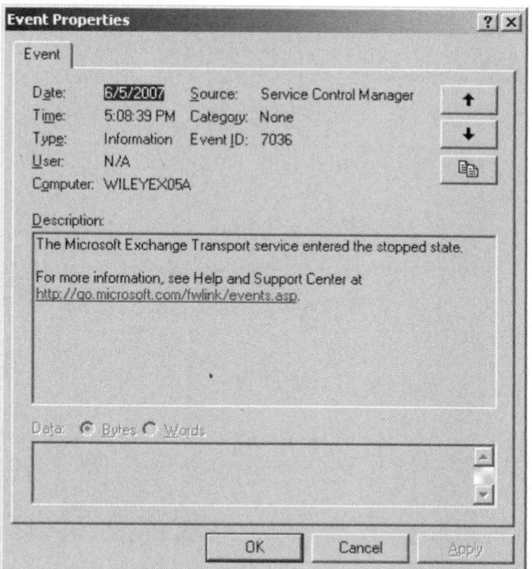

Using PowerShell

As with most other aspects of Exchange Server 2007 management, you can quickly and easily get service status information from the Exchange Management Shell using one or two PowerShell cmdlets. By just using the `Get-Service` cmdlet, you can view the status of all services installed on the server, including their status, short name, and display name. Figure 12.4 shows some sample output.

If you just want to view the Exchange-specific services, you can use the `Get-Service *Exchange*` cmdlet to return just a list of those services whose short names include the string *Exchange* in them, as shown in Figure 12.5.

FIGURE 12.4 Viewing services from the Exchange Management Shell

```
Machine: wileyex05a | Scope: wiley.corp
[PS] C:\>Get-Service

Status   Name               DisplayName
------   ----               -----------
Running  AeLookupSvc        Application Experience Lookup Service
Stopped  Alerter            Alerter
Stopped  ALG                Application Layer Gateway Service
Stopped  AppMgmt            Application Management
Stopped  aspnet_state       ASP.NET State Service
Stopped  AudioSrv           Windows Audio
Stopped  BITS               Background Intelligent Transfer Ser...
Running  Browser            Computer Browser
Stopped  CiSvc              Indexing Service
Stopped  ClipSrv            ClipBook
Stopped  clr_optimizatio... .NET Runtime Optimization Service v...
Stopped  COMSysApp          COM+ System Application
Running  CryptSvc           Cryptographic Services
Running  DcomLaunch         DCOM Server Process Launcher
Running  Dfs                Distributed File System
Running  Dhcp               DHCP Client
Stopped  dmadmin            Logical Disk Manager Administrative...
Running  dmserver           Logical Disk Manager
Running  DNS                DNS Server
Running  Dnscache           DNS Client
Running  ERSvc              Error Reporting Service
```

FIGURE 12.5 Viewing only Exchange services from the Exchange Management Shell

```
Machine: wileyex05a | Scope: wiley.corp
[PS] C:\>Get-Service *Exchange*

Status   Name               DisplayName
------   ----               -----------
Running  MSExchangeADTop... Microsoft Exchange Active Directory...
Running  MSExchangeAntis... Microsoft Exchange Anti-spam Update
Running  MSExchangeEdgeSync Microsoft Exchange EdgeSync
Running  MSExchangeFDS      Microsoft Exchange File Distribution
Stopped  MSExchangeImap4    Microsoft Exchange IMAP4
Running  MSExchangeIS       Microsoft Exchange Information Store
Running  MSExchangeMailb... Microsoft Exchange Mailbox Assistants
Running  MSExchangeMailS... Microsoft Exchange Mail Submission
Stopped  MSExchangeMonit... Microsoft Exchange Monitoring
Stopped  MSExchangePop3     Microsoft Exchange POP3
Running  MSExchangeRepl     Microsoft Exchange Replication Service
Running  MSExchangeSA       Microsoft Exchange System Attendant
Running  MSExchangeSearch   Microsoft Exchange Search Indexer
Running  MSExchangeServi... Microsoft Exchange Service Host
Stopped  MSExchangeTrans... Microsoft Exchange Transport
Running  MSExchangeTrans... Microsoft Exchange Transport Log Se...
Running  msftesql-Exchange  Microsoft Search (Exchange)

[PS] C:\>_
```

To further narrow down the status, because it is normal for some Exchange services to be in a stopped state, you can use the following cmdlets to return a listing of those Exchange-related services that are or are not currently running:

- To get a list of running Exchange services, use `Get-Service *Exchange* | Where-Object {$_.status -eq "Running"}`.
- To get a list of stopped Exchange services, use `Get-Service *Exchange* | Where-Object {$_.status -eq "Stopped"}`.

By using these filtered cmdlets, you might notice that the Microsoft Exchange Transport service wasn't running on the service, as shown in Figure 12.5 also. You could go a step further and use the `Start-Service MSExchangeTransport` cmdlet to start the stopped service and resume mail flow on your Hub Transport server.

Monitoring Performance

Although the Performance console has always been available to you in Windows Server 2003, Exchange Server 2007 gives you a customized Performance console called the Exchange Server Performance Monitor that you can access from the Toolbox node of the Exchange Management Console, as shown in Figure 12.6.

FIGURE 12.6 Using the performance and troubleshooting tools in the Toolbox node

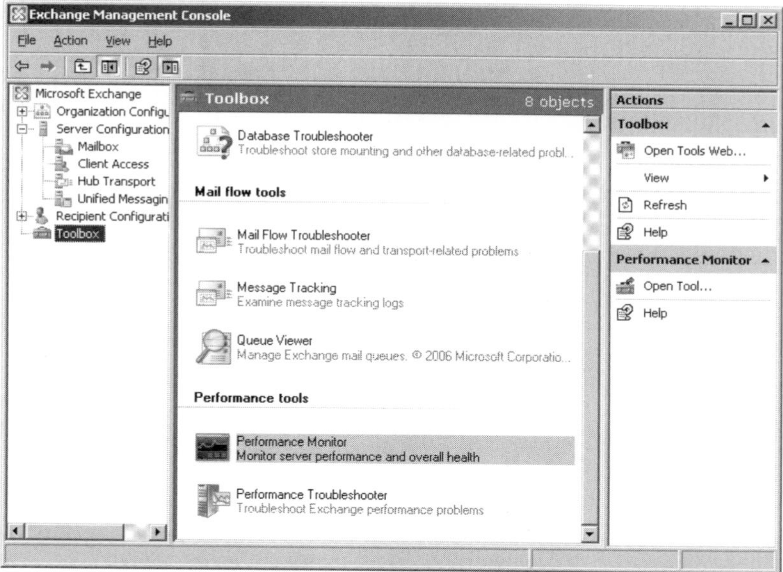

Double-clicking the Performance Monitor item opens the Exchange Server Performance Monitor, as shown in Figure 12.7. Several key Exchange performance counters are already loaded for you in the console, making it ready to use immediately.

FIGURE 12.7 Using the Exchange Server Performance Monitor

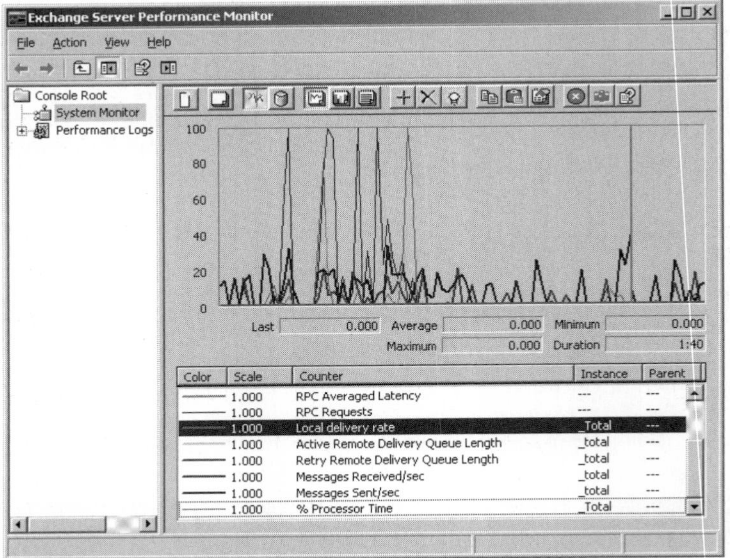

The counters listed in Table 12.2 are prepopulated in the Exchange Server Performance Monitor.

TABLE 12.2 Exchange Server Performance Monitor Counters

Counter	Description
LogicalDisk – Avg. Disk sec/Read	This counter displays the average time, in seconds, of a data read action from the disk. Typically, the average value of this counter should be less than 10 milliseconds. The maximum value of this counter should never exceed 50 milliseconds.
LogicalDisk – Avg. Disk sec/Write	This counter displays the average time, in seconds, of a data write action to the disk. Typically, the average value of this counter should be less than 10 milliseconds. The maximum value of this counter should never exceed 50 milliseconds.
Memory – Pages/sec	This counter displays the rate at which pages are read from or written to disk to resolve hard page faults. The value of this counter should never be more than 1,000.

TABLE 12.2 Exchange Server Performance Monitor Counters *(continued)*

Counter	Description
MSExchange Store Interface – RPC Latency average (msec)	This counter displays the average latency of RPC requests in milliseconds.
MSExchange Store Interface – RPC Requests outstanding	This counter displays the current number of RPC requests that are outstanding (not serviced) on the server.
MSExchangeIS – RPC Requests	This counter displays the current number of client requests that are being processed by the Information Store on the Exchange server.
MSExchangeIS – RPC Averaged Latency	This counter displays the latency, in milliseconds, of the last 1,024 RPC packets on the server.
MSExchangeIS Mailbox – Local delivery rate	This counter displays the rate at which messages are being delivered locally.
MSExchangeTransport Queues – Active Remote Delivery Queue Length	This counter displays the number of active items in the remove delivery queues on the server.
MSExchangeTransport Queues – Retry Remote Delivery Queue Length	This counter displays the number of items in a retry status on the remote delivery queues on the server.
MSExchangeTransport SmtpRecieve – Messages Received/sec	This counter displays the number of messages that are being received by the SMTP server each second.
MSExchangeTransport SmtpSend – Messages Sent/sec	This counter displays the number of messages that are being sent by the SMTP send connectors each second.
Processor – % Processor Time	This counter displays the percentage of time the processor(s) in the server spend executing threads that are not in an idle state.

To get a historical insight into server performance, you should monitor these counters for comparison monthly at the same time on the same day of the week for a two-hour (or more) period of time.

Using the Exchange Performance Troubleshooter

Should the time come when you start to get that dreaded complaint from your users—"the Exchange server is running so slowly today"—you'll be well equipped to deal with the issue by using the Performance Troubleshooter found in the Toolbox node of the Exchange Management Console. The Performance Troubleshooter is focused on only one thing: RPC-related issues within the Exchange organization. To perform a troubleshooting scan, follow the steps outlined in Exercise 12.1.

EXERCISE 12.1

Using the Exchange Performance Troubleshooter

1. Click Start ➢ Programs ➢ Microsoft Exchange Server 2007, and then select Exchange Management Console.
2. Expand the Microsoft Exchange root object, and click the Toolbox node.
3. Scroll down to the bottom of the list, and double-click Performance Troubleshooter. The Exchange Performance Troubleshooter opens, as shown here.

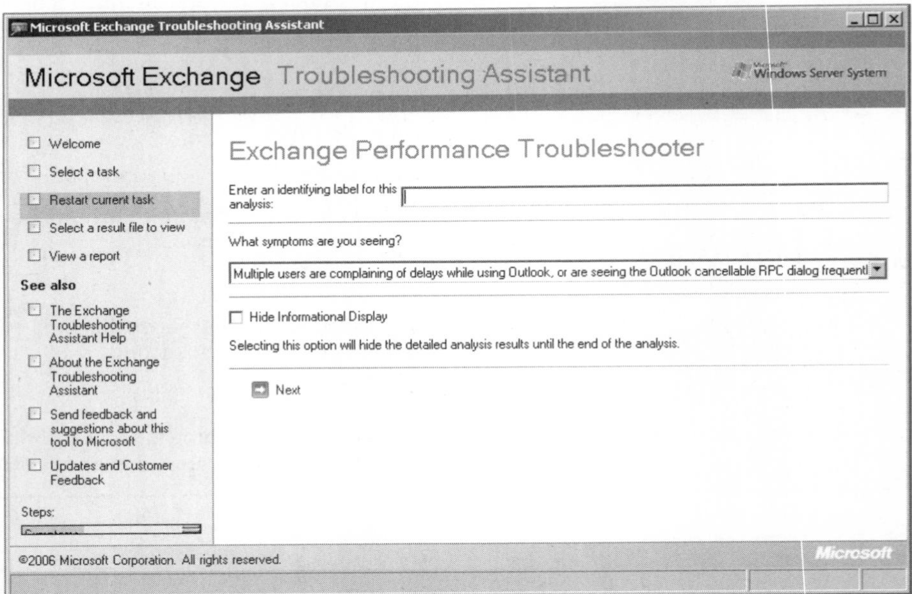

EXERCISE 12.1 *(continued)*

4. For easier identification later, enter some sort of descriptive name. From the symptoms drop-down list, select the symptom that most closely matches the problem you're having. For this exercise, select the default option of Multiple Users Are Complaining of Delays While Using Outlook, or Are Seeing the Outlook Cancellable RPC Dialog Frequently. Click the Next link to continue to the page shown here.

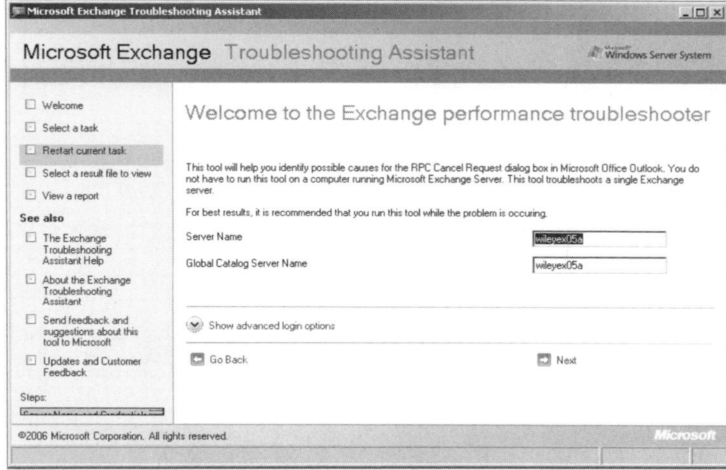

5. On this page, enter the name of the Exchange server you want to troubleshoot and the name of a global catalog server. After entering the server names, click the Next link.

6. The Performance Troubleshooter will perform some connectivity tests and then return a results page, as shown here.

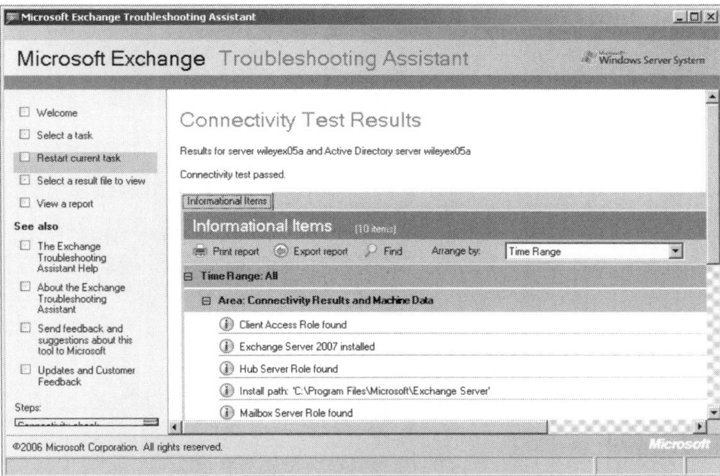

EXERCISE 12.1 *(continued)*

7. After reviewing the information presented, click the Next link at the bottom of the page to continue to the Configure Data Collection page, shown here.

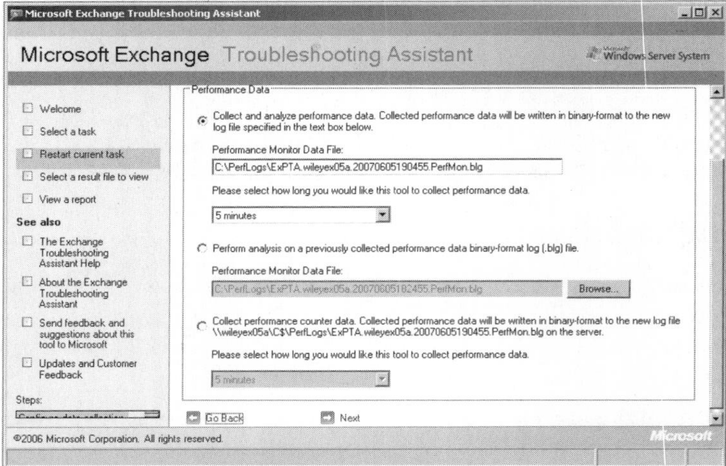

8. In most cases, you will want to collect and analyze performance data, which is the default selection. For this exercise, you'll do just that. Leave the default selection enabled, and click the Next link at the bottom of the page.

9. The Performance Troubleshooter will perform some additional counter and data path verification before starting the performance data collection process. After some time, the results page will appear, as shown here.

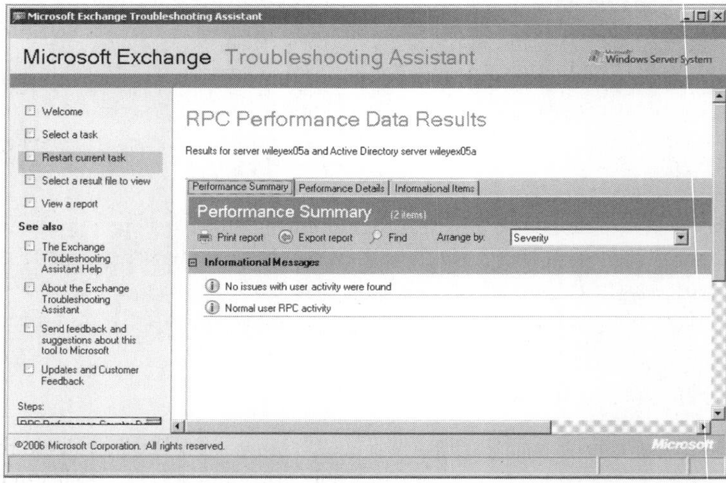

EXERCISE 12.1 *(continued)*

10. On the Performance Summary tab, you will be able to quickly determine whether any performance issues were found on the Exchange server. On the Performance Details tab, you can view more detailed information about each of the counter objects that were monitored. The Informational Items tab provides additional amplifying information to view.

11. When you're done viewing the report, you can either print it or export it to HTML or CSV. Be aware that these actions print or export only the currently viewed tab, so you'll need to print or export three times to save all the available information.

Monitoring Hardware

Hardware monitoring of your Exchange servers is every bit as important as monitoring services and performance. As it stands, though, it's not something that is included in Exchange Server 2007. Each major hardware vendor has an enterprise-quality monitoring and management application available for its hardware:

- Dell offers Dell OpenManage; see `www.dell.com/content/topics/global.aspx/sitelets/solutions/management/openmanage?`.
- HP offers HP Systems Insight Manager (SIM); see `http://h18013.www1.hp.com/products/servers/management/hpsim/index.html`.
- IBM offers IBM Director; see `www-03.ibm.com/systems/management/director/index.html`.

Several third-party platform-independent monitoring applications are available that use imported Simple Network Management Protocol (SNMP) management information books (MIBs). As well, you can often import a vendor's hardware-specific MIBs into another vendor's monitoring application. Whichever hardware platform you have your Exchange Server 2007 infrastructure on, you should seriously consider acquiring, installing, and configuring the corresponding management application.

Creating Server and Usage Reports

For any system, you'll at some time be asked to provide a report on the operational status of that system. The same is true for Exchange Server 2007, especially considering how critical and highly visible it is within most organizations. In the following sections, we'll cover some of the common types of server and usage reports you might be asked to prepare.

Creating Health Reports

Creating a server health report in Exchange Server 2007 is an easy task thanks to the Exchange Best Practices Analyzer (ExBPA), now a built-in tool. You can find the ExBPA in the Toolbox node of the Exchange Management Console, as shown previously in Figure 12.6. To create a health report using the ExBPA, follow the steps outlined in Exercise 12.2.

EXERCISE 12.2

Creating a Health Report

1. Click Start ➢ Programs ➢ Microsoft Exchange Server 2007, and then select Exchange Management Console.
2. Expand the Microsoft Exchange root object, and click the Toolbox node.
3. At the top of the list, double-click the Best Practices Analyzer item. The Exchange Best Practices Analyzer opens, as shown here.

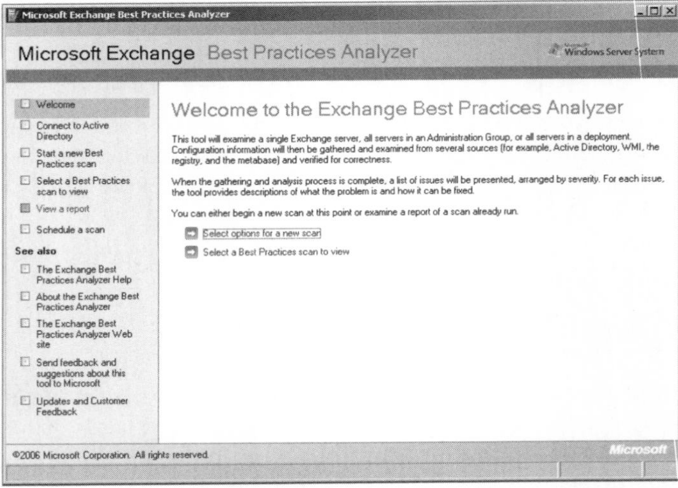

4. To get started, click the Select Options for a New Scan link. The Connect to Active Directory page opens, as shown here.

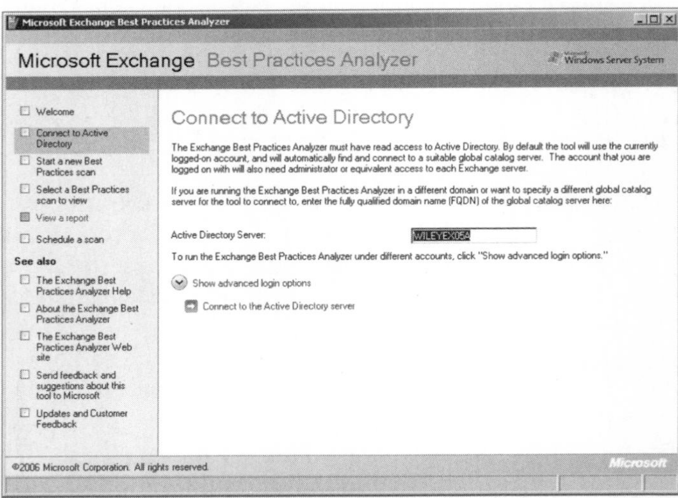

EXERCISE 12.2 *(continued)*

5. Enter the name of a global catalog server that the ExBPA should connect to, and then click the Connect to the Active Directory Server link. After a brief connectivity check, the Start a New Best Practices Scan page will appear, as shown here.

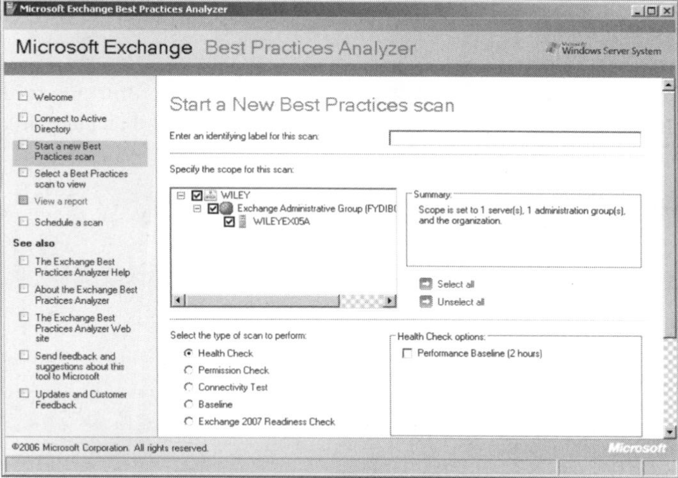

6. On the Start a New Best Practices Scan page, select the Health Check option, and select one or more Exchange servers on which to perform the health check. To make it easier to locate this ExBPA report later, you can give it a friendly label. After entering all selections, click the Start Scanning link at the bottom of the page.

7. A health check takes about two minutes per server to complete. After the check has completed, you will be presented with the option to view the report. Click the View a Report of This Best Practices Scan link to open the report, as shown here.

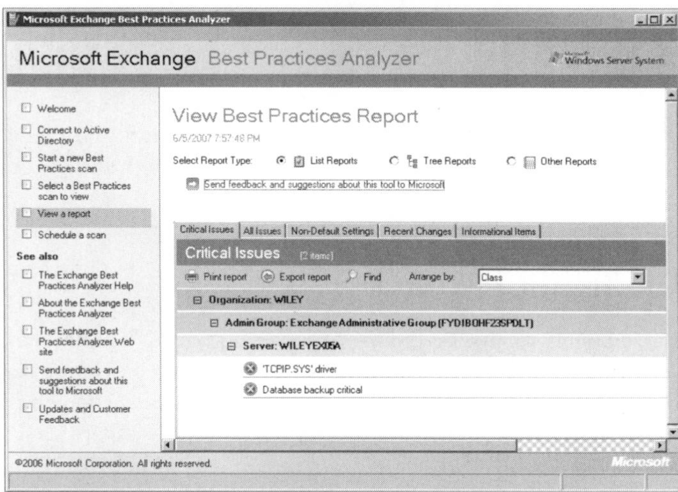

EXERCISE 12.2 *(continued)*

8. The first tab you'll see is the Critical Issues tab, and that's where you'll want to start focusing your efforts, if anything is listed there.

9. You can also print or export the ExBPA report to HTML, CSV, or XML. Exporting to HTML or CSV will export only the currently selected tab; exporting to XML will result in the entire scan report being exported.

10. Alternatively, you will have the ability to revisit scans later by returning to the Welcome page of the ExBPA and clicking the Select a Best Practices Scan to View link. A listing of all past scans will be made available, as shown here.

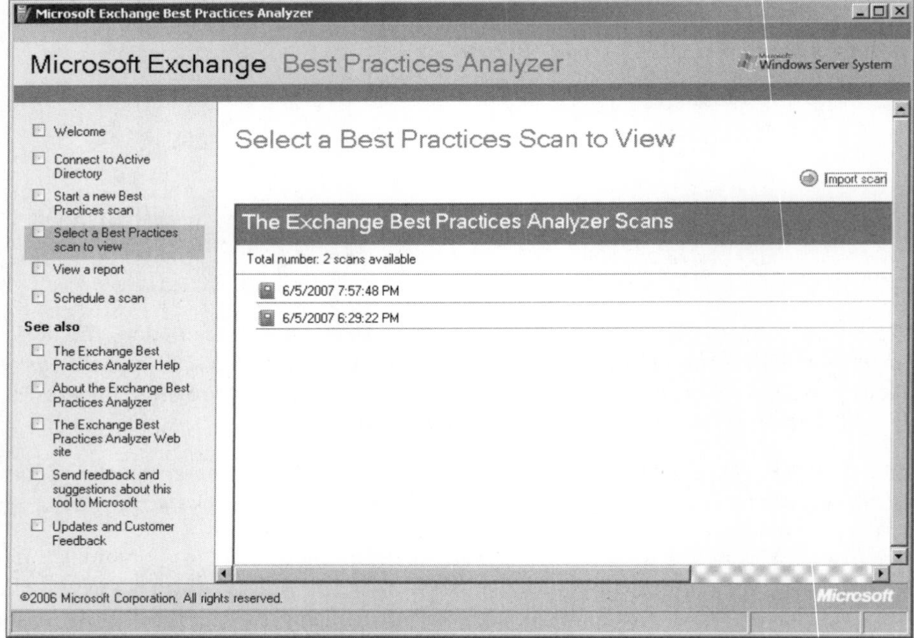

11. To view a previous scan report, click it to expand a list of options. You can view a report from the scan, export the scan as an XML file, delete the scan, or label it to make it easily identifiable.

Creating Availability Reports

To get true, usable availability reports on Exchange Server 2007, you'll need to use another application such as Microsoft Operations Manager (MOM) 2005 with the Exchange Server 2007 Management Pack (MP). MOM includes many reports on the Exchange environment. Table 12.3 lists the available reports in MOM 2005 with the Exchange Server 2007 MP.

TABLE 12.3 Microsoft Operations Manager Reports for Exchange Server 2007

Service Availability	Metrics	Antispam
Service Availability Summary	Client Performance	Attached File Filter
Mailbox Service Availability	Mailbox Count	Connection Filter
Mailflow Local Service Availability	RPC and Database Performance	Recipient Filter
Mailflow Remote Service Availability	Unified Messaging Call Summary	Sender ID
Outlook Web Access External Service Availability	Unified Messaging Message Summary	Sender Filter
Outlook Web Access Internal Service Availability		Content Filter
ActiveSync Internal Availability		Protocol Analysis
Unified Messaging Local Voice Service Availability		
Unified Messaging Local Fax Service Availability		
Unified Messaging Remote Voice Service Availability		

Working with MOM is beyond the scope of the 70-236 exam, but if your organization has more than a two or three Exchange servers, you should definitely take the time to explore how MOM could help you monitor Exchange, Active Directory, and many other key Microsoft products and services.

You can get more information about MOM at `http://www.microsoft.com/mom/default.mspx`. You can get more information about implementing MOM for Exchange Server 2007 monitoring at `http://technet.microsoft.com/en-us/library/bb201735.aspx`.

Creating Database and Message Queue Reports

You can create quick, useful reports on the status of all Exchange databases and queues on a server by using the Exchange Management Shell. To create a report showing all the information about all mailbox databases on a server, use the `Get-MailboxDatabase | Export-CSV` *`c:\mailboxdb.csv`* cmdlet, of course specifying your own location and name for the output file. Figure 12.8 shows an example of this report. Table 12.4 lists the report fields available.

TABLE 12.4 Mailbox database report fields

JournalRecipient	ExchangeLegacyDN	IssueWarningQuota
MailboxRetention	HasLocalCopy	EventHistoryRetentionPeriod
OfflineAddressBook	DeletedItemRetention	Name
OriginalDatabase	LastFullBackup	MinAdminVersion
PublicFolderDatabase	LastIncrementalBackup	AdminDisplayName
ProhibitSendReceiveQuota	MaintenanceSchedule	ExchangeVersion
Recovery	MountAtStartup	DistinguishedName
ProhibitSendQuota	Mounted	Identity
IndexEnabled	Organization	Guid
AdministrativeGroup	QuotaNotificationSchedule	ObjectCategory
AllowFileRestore	RetainDeletedItemsUntilBackup	ObjectClass
BackupInProgress	Server	WhenChanged
CopyEdbFilePath	ServerName	WhenCreated
DatabaseCreated	StorageGroup	OriginatingServer
Description	StorageGroupName	IsValid
EdbFilePath		

More than likely, however, that much information is going to be more than you really need to create the report you want. To create a report that contains just the specific fields of data you're interested in, you can use a cmdlet similar to the following: `Get-MailboxDatabase | Select-Object Name,Server,StorageGroup,Mounted,*Quota* | Export-CSV` *`c:\mailboxdb.csv`*.

The output from that more structured cmdlet would be much less and would be easier to work with. You can use any of the available fields listed for the `Select-Object` cmdlet.

FIGURE 12.8 Viewing a mailbox database report for a server

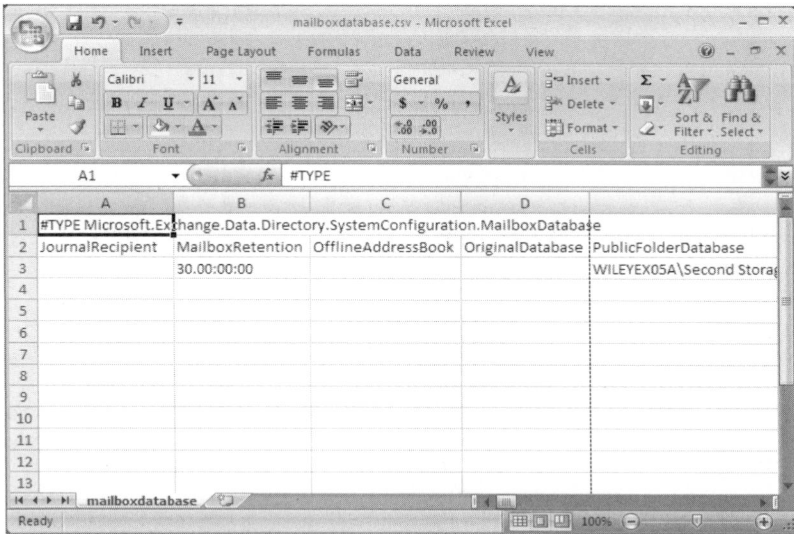

To create a report showing all the public folder databases on a server, you can use the `Get-PublicFolderDatabase | Export-CSV` *`c:\publicfolderdb.csv`* cmdlet, specifying your own location and name for the output file. Table 12.5 lists the report fields available.

TABLE 12.5 Public Folder database report fields

Alias	Description	StorageGroupName
FirstInstance	EdbFilePath	IssueWarningQuota
MaxItemSize	ExchangeLegacyDN	EventHistoryRetentionPeriod
ItemRetentionPeriod	HasLocalCopy	Name
ReplicationPeriod	DeletedItemRetention	MinAdminVersion
ProhibitPostQuota	LastFullBackup	AdminDisplayName
PublicFolderHierarchy	LastIncrementalBackup	ExchangeVersion
ReplicationMessageSize	MaintenanceSchedule	DistinguishedName
ReplicationSchedule	MountAtStartup	Identity

TABLE 12.5 Public Folder database report fields *(continued)*

UseCustomReferralServerList	Mounted	Guid
PublicFolderReferral ServerList	Organization	ObjectCategory
AdministrativeGroup	QuotaNotificationSchedule	ObjectClass
AllowFileRestore	RetainDeletedItemsUntil-Backup	WhenChanged
BackupInProgress	Server	WhenCreated
CopyEdbFilePath	ServerName	OriginatingServer
DatabaseCreated	StorageGroup	IsValid

To create a report detailing the current status of all the queues on the server, you can use the `Get-Queue | Export-CSV` *`c:\queues.csv cmdlet`*. Table 12.6 lists the report fields available.

TABLE 12.6 Server queue report fields

Identity	Status	NextRetryTime
DeliveryType	MessageCount	IsValid
NextHopDomain	LastError	ObjectState
NextHopConnector	LastRetryTime	

Creating Mailbox and User Usage Reports

Of the usage reports, most of them will involve users and/or mailboxes. You'll want to know how many mailboxes are located in a certain database, storage group, or server. You'll want to know who is using the most space in the mailbox database so that you gently remind your users how much they're exceeding their default quotas. This type of information will also be helpful when it comes to planning for server migrations or decommissioning.

The general cmdlet you can use to get information about mailboxes is the `Get-Mailbox` cmdlet. When run from the Exchange Management Console just like that, the cmdlet will return a small subset of data fields from what's really available to you. Figure 12.9 illustrates the feedback you'll get when using the `Get-Mailbox` cmdlet with no modification.

FIGURE 12.9 Viewing the output of the Get-Mailbox cmdlet

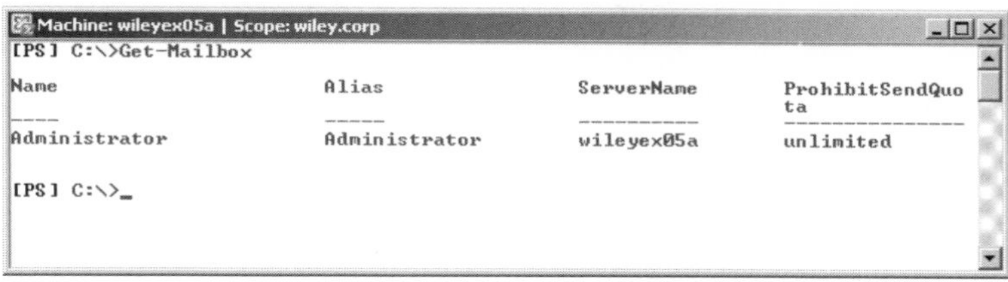

If you use the `Get-Mailbox | Export-CSV` *`c:\mailboxes.csv`* cmdlets, you'll get a CSV file that looks vaguely similar to that shown earlier in Figure 12.8 in that there will likely be more information than you need or want. Again, by using the `Select-Object` cmdlet to filter the information that is exported to the CSV file, you can get a much more usable report. Table 12.7 lists the report fields available.

TABLE 12.7 Server queue report fields

Database	SCLRejectEnabled	CustomAttribute7
DeletedItemFlags	SCLQuarantineThreshold	CustomAttribute8
UseDatabaseRetentionDefaults	SCLQuarantineEnabled	CustomAttribute9
RetainDeletedItemsUntil-Backup	SCLJunkThreshold	DisplayName
DeliverToMailboxAndForward	SCLJunkEnabled	EmailAddresses
RetentionHoldEnabled	AntispamBypassEnabled	GrantSendOnBehalfTo
EndDateForRetentionHold	ServerLegacyDN	HiddenFromAddressLists Enabled
StartDateForRetentionHold	ServerName	LegacyExchangeDN
ManagedFolderMailboxPolicy	UseDatabaseQuotaDefaults	MaxSendSize
ExchangeGuid	IssueWarningQuota	MaxReceiveSize
ExchangeSecurityDescriptor	RulesQuota	PoliciesIncluded
ExchangeUserAccountControl	Office	PoliciesExcluded

TABLE 12.7 Server queue report fields *(continued)*

ExternalOofOptions	UserPrincipalName	EmailAddressPolicyEnabled
ForwardingAddress	UMEnabled	PrimarySmtpAddress
RetainDeletedItemsFor	MaxSafeSenders	RecipientType
IsMailboxEnabled	MaxBlockedSenders	RecipientTypeDetail
Languages	Extensions	RejectMessagesFrom
OfflineAddressBook	AcceptMessagesOnlyFrom	RejectMessagesFromDL-Members
ProhibitSendQuota	AcceptMessagesOnlyFrom-DLMembers	RequireSenderAuthentication-Enabled
ProhibitSendReceiveQuota	AddressListMembership	SimpleDisplayName
ProtocolSettings	Alias	UMDtmfMap
RecipientLimits	OrganizationalUnit	WindowsEmailAddress
UserAccountControl	CustomAttribute1	IsValid
IsResource	CustomAttribute10	OriginatingServer
IsLinked	CustomAttribute11	ExchangeVersion
IsShared	CustomAttribute12	Name
LinkedMasterAccount	CustomAttribute13	DistinguishedName
ResourceCapacity	CustomAttribute14	Identity
ResourceCustom	CustomAttribute15	Guid
ResourceType	CustomAttribute2	ObjectCategory
SamAccountName	CustomAttribute3	ObjectClass
SCLDeleteThreshold	CustomAttribute4	WhenChanged
SCLDeleteEnabled	CustomAttribute5	WhenCreated
SCLRejectThreshold	CustomAttribute6	

A useful report on mailboxes might use the following cmdlet: `Get-Mailbox | Select-Object Name,SamAccountName,*Quota*,Database | Export-CSV` *`c:\mailboxes.csv`*. Of course, even this report will not tell you how big the mailboxes are. For that information, you'll have to expand your cmdlet even more, such as this one:

```
Get-Mailbox | Get-MailboxStatistics | Select-Object
DisplayName,TotalItemSize,ItemCount,StorageLimitStatus
| Export-CSV c:\mailboxes.csv
```

Real World Scenario

MOM Could Be Your Best Friend

Although Exchange Server 2007 offers a good number of monitoring and reporting tools and capabilities, it doesn't really offer enough tools or offer high enough quality tools and capabilities for the needs of most larger organizations. In addition, most organizations want automated monitoring and altering when things are not quite right with their Exchange servers because of the critical nature that Exchange has in most organizations. To meet these requirements, you should consider implementing MOM.

It's not just an Exchange-only benefit because MOM can monitor and report on almost any Microsoft product. The list of products that MOM has management packs for includes the following: Exchange, SQL Server, Windows, network load balancing, Active Directory, HP storage arrays, Windows Software Update Services (WSUS), SharePoint Services, Forefront for Exchange, File Replication Service (FRS), and many others.

MOM is not necessarily inexpensive, and it is not extremely quick and easy to implement—but if you spend the time and effort to do it right and customize it to your organization's needs, MOM will pay off with big dividends over time. So if you're looking for more monitoring or more reporting, get to know MOM to see what MOM can do for you.

Table 12.8 lists the report fields available when you use the `Get-MailboxStatistics` `cmdlet`.

TABLE 12.8 Mailbox statistics report fields

AssociatedItemCount	LastLogonTime	Database
DeletedItemCount	LegacyDN	ServerName
DisconnectDate	MailboxGuid	StorageGroupName
DisplayName	ObjectClass	DatabaseName

TABLE 12.8 Mailbox statistics report fields *(continued)*

ItemCount	StorageLimitStatus	Identity
LastLoggedOnUserAccount	TotalDeletedItemSize	IsValid
LastLogoffTime	TotalItemSize	OriginatingServer

Summary

In this chapter, we briefly covered some of the more common monitoring and reporting functionality that Exchange Server 2007 offers you. As is often said in management circles, you can't manage what you can't measure. That axiom holds true for every aspect of systems administration—if you don't know what's going on with your servers or applications, you can't effectively manage them or troubleshoot them.

Exam Essentials

Practice performance monitoring. Using the performance counters effectively is not something you can just start doing on your first try. To really get effective results out of your performance monitoring, you need to do it often, and you need to take the time to really understand what each counter is telling you. We covered some of the more specific counters relevant to Exchange Server 2007, but dozens of other counters are important to the Windows Server 2003 operating system as well. After all, if your server is not performing well, it stands to reason that Exchange won't be performing well. Take some time to learn which counters are pertinent to your organization, and make it a point to take performance measurements on a schedule to accurately get an indication of how your servers are performing.

Learn the PowerShell commands. Almost every configuration or management action you perform from the Exchange Management Console will present you with the PowerShell code that was used to perform the action. Take advantage of this information, and learn how to use the Exchange Management Shell to your advantage. Some of these commands are likely to make an appearance on the exam.

Know where to go. Many times on the exam you will likely be asked what configuration is needed to produce the required results. The Exchange Management Console has been completely redesigned to make it easier to navigate and get to tasks, but that doesn't mean it won't be difficult to remember later. Take the time as you review the material in this book to think about what types of configuration and management tasks you find yourself performing in each major node of the Exchange Management Console.

Review Questions

1. What performance counter would you most likely want to monitor to determine whether your Exchange Mailbox server has a problem with excessive paging?

   A. Processor – % Processor Time

   B. LogicalDisk – Avg. Disk sec/Write

   C. Memory – Pages/sec

   D. LogicalDisk – Avg. Disk sec/Read

2. What PowerShell cmdlet should you use to determine the status of services on a server?

   A. `Show-Service`

   B. `Get-Service`

   C. `List-Service`

   D. `Display-Service`

3. Which of the following PowerShell cmdlets will you need to use to create a CSV report that contains information about mailboxes, including the number of items and size of each mailbox? (Choose all correct answers.)

   A. `Get-Mailbox`

   B. `Get-MailboxStatistics`

   C. `Select-Object`

   D. `Export-CSV`

4. Which of the following tools in the Toolbox node of the Exchange Management Console would you use to create a health report on your Exchange Server 2007 servers?

   A. Performance Monitor

   B. Performance Troubleshooter

   C. Best Practices Analyzer

   D. Database Troubleshooter

5. To export the results of an ExBPA scan to a single file containing all the results, which file format must you use?

   A. CSV

   B. XML

   C. HTTP

   D. PDF

6. Which of the following would be the best choice for monitoring the status of hardware components in your Exchange servers?
   - A. Microsoft Operations Manager (MOM)
   - B. An application from the hardware vendor
   - C. Exchange Server Performance Monitor
   - D. A custom PowerShell script that creates CSV reports
7. Which logs in the Event Viewer will typically contain useful information for troubleshooting Exchange service issues? (Choose two.)
   - A. Application
   - B. PowerShell
   - C. Security
   - D. System
   - E. Windows PowerShell
8. Which of the following tools in the Toolbox node of the Exchange Management Console would you use to determine whether there are RPC problems on your Exchange Server 2007 servers?
   - A. Performance Monitor
   - B. Performance Troubleshooter
   - C. Best Practices Analyzer
   - D. Database Troubleshooter
9. Given that most of the installed Exchange services on an Exchange Mailbox server should normally be running, you want to quickly determine using the PowerShell which Exchange services are not running. Which of the following cmdlets would you need to use to perform this task?
   - A. `List-Service *Exchange* | Where-Status {-eq "Stopped"}`
   - B. `Get-Service *Exchange* | Where-Status {-eq "Stopped"}`
   - C. `List-Service *Exchange* | Where-Object {$_.status -eq "Stopped"}`
   - D. `Get-Service *Exchange* | Where-Object {$_.status -eq "Stopped"}`
10. When performing performance monitoring of your Exchange Mailbox server using the Exchange Server Performance Monitor, you see a lot of fluctuation in the values of the LogicalDisk – Avg. Disk sec/Write counter. What is the desired value that this counter should typically be less than?
   - A. 10 milliseconds
   - B. 20 milliseconds
   - C. 50 milliseconds
   - D. 75 milliseconds

Answers to Review Questions

1. C. The Memory – Pages/sec counter displays the rate at which pages are read from or written to disk to resolve hard page faults. The value of this counter should never be more than 1,000.

2. B. By using the `Get-Service` cmdlet with no modification, you can view the status of all services installed on the server, including each one's status, short name, and display name.

3. A, B, C, D. You'll actually need to use all four cmdlets to create the required report. For example, if you created the report and listed the name, item count, mailbox size, and over/under quota status, your cmdlet might look like this:

   ```
   Get-Mailbox | Get-MailboxStatistics | Select-Object
   DisplayName,TotalItemSize,ItemCount,
   StorageLimitStatus | Export-CSV c:\mailboxes.csv
   ```

4. C. You can quickly and easily create a server health report using the Exchange Best Practices Analyzer (ExBPA), which is located in the Toolbox node of the Exchange Management Console.

5. B. Only the XML export format will result in the entire ExBPA scan report being saved in a single file. Unfortunately, XML does not lend itself well to printing, so if your intent is to save and then print later, you'll want to save each tab of the report using the HTML format. The XML format is intended for exporting the report from one location and later importing it into another location for viewing and action.

6. B. Hardware monitoring of your Exchange servers is every bit as important as monitoring services and performance. As it stands, though, it's not something that is included within Exchange Server 2007. Each major hardware vendor has an enterprise-quality monitoring and management application available for its hardware. It's usually best to use the corresponding monitoring application from the vendor that supplied the hardware on which your Exchange servers are running.

7. A, D. Typically, you'll find the most useful information about service status changes in the System log. The Application log will also often yield useful information.

8. B. The Performance Troubleshooter is focused on only one thing: RPC-related issues within the Exchange organization.

9. D. By using the `Get-Service *Exchange* | Where-Object {$_.status -eq "Stopped"}`cmdlet, you can quickly get a listing of all the Exchange-related services that are not currently running. From this list, you can determine which ones should and should not be in a stopped state.

10. A. The LogicalDisk – Avg. Disk sec/Write counter displays the average time, in seconds, of a data write action to the disk. Typically, the average value of this counter should be less than 10 milliseconds. The maximum value of this counter should never exceed 50 milliseconds.

Glossary

A

accepted domain An email domain for which your Exchange servers accept inbound mail.

access control entries (ACEs) Entries on an access control list (ACL) that define a user's permission for an object.

access control list (ACL) A list of users and groups allowed to access a resource and the particular permissions each user has been granted or denied.

Active Directory Stores information about objects in a Windows Server 2003 network and makes this information easy for administrators and users to find and use.

address space The set of remote addresses that can be reached through a particular connector. Each connector must have at least one entry in its address space.

administrative group Used to define administrative boundaries within an Exchange 2000/2003 environment.

administrative rights NTFS permissions that determine what administrative tasks a user or group is permitted to perform on a public folder.

age limit A property that specifies the length of time a unit of data may remain in its container (for example, a public folder).

alias An alternative name for an object. In Exchange, an alias is usually generated for a user based on the user's name.

All Public Folders The name for the default public folder tree in an Exchange organization. This tree is accessible by all clients that can access public folders.

anonymous access Accessing a server by logging in using a Windows account set up for general access.

anonymous authentication See *anonymous access*.

application programming interface (API) A collection of programming classes and interfaces that provide services used by a program. Other programs can use a program's API to request services or communicate with that program.

architecture The description of the components of a product or system, what they are, what they do, and how they relate to each other.

archive A location and collection of data (messages) that needs to be preserved for a given time. An archive is generally not online and immediately accessible, but it is searchable and accessible if needed.

attribute A characteristic of an object. For example, attributes of a mailbox-enabled user include display name and storage limits. The terms *attribute* and *property* are synonymous.

auditing Windows Server 2003 can be configured to monitor and record certain events. This can help diagnose security events. The audit information is written to the Windows Security event log.

authentication A process whereby the credentials of an object, such as a user, must be validated before the object is allowed to access or use another object, such as a server or a protocol. For instance, the Microsoft Exchange Server POP3 protocol can be configured to allow access only to POP3 clients that use the Integrated Windows authentication method.

B

backfill The process used in public folder replication to fill in messaging data that is missing from a replica.

backup Typically a hard drive or backup tape that stores copies of files.

Bad Mail folder The folder in which SMTP stores undeliverable messages that cannot be returned to the sender.

Basic (clear-text) authentication Requires the user to submit a valid Windows username and password. The username and password are sent across the network as unencrypted clear text.

Basic over Secure Sockets Layer (SSL) authentication Extends the Basic (clear-text) authentication method by allowing an SSL server to encrypt the username and password before they are sent across the network.

C

cache mode A feature in Outlook 2003 and Outlook 2007 that allows clients to work disconnected from the Exchange server. Outlook will periodically reconnect to the Exchange server and synchronize any changes to the user's mailbox.

categorizer A component of the Exchange Server 2007 routing engine used to resolve the sender and recipient for a message, expanding any distribution groups as needed. In previous versions of Exchange Server, this task was performed by the MTA.

centralized model An administrative model in which one administrator or group of administrators maintains complete control over an entire Exchange organization.

certificate Allows verification of the claim that a given public key actually belongs to a given individual. This helps prevent someone from using a phony key to impersonate someone else. A certificate is similar to a token.

certificate authority (CA) The central authority that distributes, publishes, and validates security keys. The Windows Server 2003 Certificates Services component performs this role. See also *public key* and *private key*.

certificate revocation list (CRL) A list containing all certificates in an organization that have been revoked.

certificate store A database created during the installation of a certificate authority (CA) that is a repository of certificates issued by the CA.

certificate template Stored in Active Directory; defines the attributes for certificates.

certificate trust list (CTL) Holds the set of root CAs whose certificates can be trusted. You can designate CTLs for groups, users, or an entire domain.

challenge/response A general term for a class of security mechanisms, including Microsoft authentication methods, that use Windows Server 2003 network security and an encrypted password.

change number One of the constructs used to keep track of public folder replication throughout an organization and to determine whether a public folder is synchronized. The change number consists of a globally unique identifier for the Information Store and a change counter that is specific to the server on which a public folder resides.

checkpoint file The file (`EDB.CHK`) that contains the point in a transaction log that is the boundary between data that has been committed and data that has not yet been committed to an Exchange database.

child domain Any domain configured underneath another domain in a domain tree.

circular logging The process of writing new information in transaction log files over information that has already been committed. Instead of repeatedly creating new transaction logs, the Exchange database engine "circles back" and reuses log files that have been fully committed to the database. Circular logging keeps down the number of transaction logs on the disk. These logs cannot be used to re-create a database because the logs do not have a complete set of data. The logs contain only the most recent data not yet committed to a database. Circular logging is disabled by default.

client access license (CAL) Gives a user the legal right to access an Exchange server. Any client software that has the ability to be a client to Microsoft Exchange Server is legally required to have a CAL purchased for it.

client access server Non-MAPI clients, such as POP3, IMAP4, mobile, and web-based clients, must connect to the Mailbox servers via a Client Access server. In this way, the Client Access server is most like the front-end servers utilized in previous versions of Exchange Server. All requests from these non-MAPI clients are received by the Client Access server and then forwarded to the applicable Mailbox server for action.

cluster A group of servers (also called *nodes*) that function together as a single unit.

cluster continuous replication (CCR) This is a new cluster implementation that removes the requirement for a shared disk implementation such as a SAN. This configuration uses a majority node set quorum and log shipping to keep the data synced between the active and passive nodes.

cluster resource A service or property, such as a storage device, an IP address, or the Exchange System Attendant service, that is defined, monitored, and managed by the cluster service.

cluster service The software service used to manage all the cluster activity. The cluster service controls access to resources by the individual nodes of the cluster.

clustering A Windows service that enables multiple physical servers to be logically grouped for reasons of high availability.

committed When a transaction is transferred from a transaction log to an Exchange database, it has been committed.

compliance For the purpose of Exchange, compliance is the act of complying with government, agency, or corporate policies that dictate how communications and information should be handled.

Computer Management snap-in An administrative tool holding a variety of utilities, including Event Viewer and disk management tools.

contact A recipient object that represents a foreign message recipient. Contacts appear in the global address list (GAL) and allow Exchange clients to address messages to foreign mail users. Also referred to as a *mail contact*.

container object An object in the Exchange or Active Directory hierarchy that contains and groups other objects. For example, the organization object in System Manager is a container object that contains all other objects in the organization.

contiguous namespace When multiple entities share a common namespace. For example, Windows Server 2003 domain trees share a contiguous namespace; domain forests do not.

continuous availability (CA) The unattainable desire to never have applications unavailable.

convergence The process during which the active nodes in a cluster calculate a new, stable state among themselves after the failure of one or more cluster nodes.

copy backup During a copy backup, all selected files are backed up, regardless of how their archive bit is set. After the backup, the archive bit is not changed in any file.

D

daily backup During this backup, all files that changed on the day of the backup are backed up, and the archive bit is not changed in any file.

Data Encryption Standard (DES) A secret-key encryption method that uses a 56-bit key.

database There are two types of databases in Exchange Server 2007: public databases that hold public folders meant to be accessed by groups of users and mailbox databases that hold user mailboxes.

DAVEx An IIS component that passes client requests between W3svc and the Information Store.

DCDiag A command-line utility that can be used to analyze the state of all domain controllers in a forest and report problems that were found.

decentralized model Typically used to define administrative boundaries along real geographical or departmental boundaries. Each location would have its own administrators and its own administrative group.

decryption Translating encrypted data back to plain text.

dedicated public folder server An Exchange server whose primary purpose is to hold public folder databases and from which the mailbox databases have been removed.

deleted-item retention time The period that items in a public or private database deleted by users are actually retained on the Exchange server.

demilitarized zone (DMZ) See *perimeter network*.

dial-tone recovery A basic recovery that provides the ability to send and receive email but does not provide any historical email data. A dial-tone recover is used as a go-between to provide basic services and allow users to continue to work while a database restore takes place.

differential backup A method in which all files that have been changed since the last full backup are backed up. See also *incremental backup*.

digital signature A process of digitally signing data using public and private keys so that the recipient of the data can verify the authenticity of both the sender and the data.

directory A hierarchy that stores information about objects in a system. A directory service (DS) manages the directory and makes it available to users on the network.

directory replication Transferring directory information from one server to another. In Active Directory, directory information is replicated between domain controllers. In previous versions of Exchange, directory information is replicated between Exchange servers.

directory rights Used to configure the NTFS permissions that determine who can perform modifications on the public folder object that is stored in Active Directory.

disaster recovery Having enough data in a recoverable format to recover from the loss of any Exchange Server data or Exchange Server. This can be limited to the loss of a single email message or can encompass the loss of an entire data center.

Disaster Recovery mode A mode in which you can run Exchange Server 2007 setup that lets you recover an Exchange installation after a failure.

discovery The actions that are taken when a group or select messages or records are requested to comply with a given policy or form of governance.

discretionary access control list (DACL) A list of access control entries (ACEs) that give users and groups specific permissions on an object.

dismounting The process of taking a public or mailbox database offline.

distribution group An Active Directory group formed so that a single email message can be sent to the group and then sent automatically to all members of the group. Unlike security groups, distribution groups don't provide any security function.

DMZ See perimeter network.

DNS See *Domain Name Service (DNS)*.

domain A group of computers and other resources that are part of a Windows Server 2003 network and share a common directory database.

domain controller A computer running Windows Server 2003 that validates user network access and manages Active Directory.

domain forest A group of one or more domain trees that do not necessarily form a contiguous namespace but may share a common schema and global catalog.

Domain Name Service (DNS) The primary provider of name resolution within an organization.

domain tree A hierarchical arrangement of one or more Windows Active Directory domains that share a common namespace.

dynamic distribution group An email-enabled distribution group whose group membership is determined by the results of an LDAP query created when the group is configured.

E

Edge Transport server Designed to be deployed in the DMZ of your network, the Edge Transport server is used to provide a secure SMTP gateway for all messages entering or leaving your Exchange organization. As such, the Edge Transport server is responsible for antivirus and antispam controls, as well as protecting the recipient data held within Active Directory.

EHLO The ESMTP command used by one host to initiate communications with another host.

email Electronic messages sent between users of different computers.

encryption The process of scrambling data to make it unreadable. The intended recipient will decrypt the data into plain text in order to read it.

enterprise CA Acts as a certificate authority for an enterprise and requires access to the Active Directory. See also *certificate authority (CA)*.

Enterprise Edition The premier version of Exchange Server 2007 with support for up to 50 storage groups and 50 databases.

ethical walls A rule or system that prevents communication between specific groups in organization.

event log A set of three logs (Application, Security, and System) maintained by Windows Server. The operating system and many applications, such as Exchange Server 2007, write software events to the event log.

Exchange Management Console A snap-in for the Microsoft Management Console used to manage an Exchange Server 2007 organization.

expanding a distribution group The process of determining the individual addresses contained within a distribution group. This process is performed by the home server of the user sending the message to the group unless an expansion server is specified for the group.

extended permissions Permissions added to the standard Windows Server 2003 permissions when Exchange Server 2007 is installed.

Extensible Storage Engine (ESE) The database engine used by Exchange Server 2007.

F

failback The process of cluster resources moving back to their preferred node after the preferred node has resumed active membership in the cluster.

failover The process of moving resources off a cluster node that has failed to another cluster node. If any of the cluster resources on an active node become unresponsive or unavailable for a period time exceeding the configured threshold, failover will occur.

file share witness (FSW) KB 921181 describes this new feature. The FSW is nothing more than a file share on another computer that is not part of the cluster but can be used to allow for a failure and allow the cluster to still maintain a majority for MNS. The new file share witness feature allows for the creation of another quorum resource that will work with MNS quorum resources to provide more redundancy of the quorum. This new change allows the use of two nodes for the cluster, and a third server of some kind someplace on the network to provide another quorum resource to work with MNS. The file share witness is perfect for those clusters that have no need for shared storage for their data, or it can be provided via other methods. Now, you can have two nodes and still have a majority available in the case of a single node failure.

firewall A set of mechanisms that separate and protect your internal network from unauthorized external users and networks. Firewalls can restrict inbound and outbound traffic, as well as analyze all traffic between your network and the outside.

folder-based application An application built within a public folder by customizing properties of the folder, such as permissions, views, rules, and the folder forms library to store and present data to users.

foreign system A non-Exchange messaging system.

forest root domain The first domain installed in a domain forest and the basis for the naming of all domains in the forest.

forms registry Stores the Outlook Web Access (OWA) forms rendered by Internet Information Services (IIS) and passed to the client.

free/busy Terminology used in the Microsoft Schedule+ application to denote an unscheduled period of time (free) or a scheduled period of time (busy).

full-text indexing A feature that can be enabled for a database in which every word in the database (including those in attachments) is indexed for much faster search results.

fully qualified domain name (FQDN) The full DNS path of an Internet host. An example is `sales.dept4.widget.com`.

function call An instruction in a program that calls (invokes) a function. For example, MAPIReadMail is a MAPI function call.

G

GAL See *global address list (GAL)*.

general-purpose trees Public folder trees added to an Exchange organization beyond the default public folder tree. General-purpose trees are not accessible by MAPI clients such as Microsoft Outlook.

global address list (GAL) A database of all the recipients in an Exchange organization, such as mailboxes, distribution lists, custom recipients, and public folders.

global catalog Used to hold information about all objects in a forest. The global catalog enables users and applications to find objects in an Active Directory domain tree if the user or application knows one or more attributes of the target object.

group A collection of users and other groups that may be assigned permissions or made part of an email distribution list.

groupware Any application that allows groups of people to store and share information.

H

heartbeat A special communication among members of a cluster that keeps all members aware of one another's existence (and thus their operational states).

HELO The SMTP command used by one host to initiate communications with another host.

high availability (HA) The combination of well-defined, planned, tested, and implemented processes, software, and fault-tolerant hardware focused on supplying and maintaining application availability.

hierarchy Any structure or organization that uses class, grade, or rank to arrange objects.

host bus adapter (HBA) This adapter connects the server node to the storage area network using fiber or, potentially, an iSCSI SAN.

HTML See *HyperText Markup Language (HTML)*.

HTTP See *HyperText Transfer Protocol (HTTP)*.

HTTP Digest authentication An Internet standard that allows the authentication of clients to occur using a series of challenges and responses over HTTP.

Hub Transport server Routes messages for delivery within the Exchange organization. By moving message routing to another server (other than the Mailbox server), many new and needed features and functions become available. As an example, while messages are being routed through the Hub Transport server, they can have transport rules and filtering policies applied to them that determine where they'll wind up, such as being delivered to a compliance mailbox in addition to the recipient's mailbox, or what they'll look like, such as stamping a disclaimer on every outbound message.

HyperText Markup Language (HTML) The script language used to create content for the World Wide Web (WWW). HTML can create hyperlinks between objects on the Web.

HyperText Transfer Protocol (HTTP) The Internet protocol used to transfer information on the World Wide Web (WWW).

I

IIS metabase The database of configuration information maintained by Internet Information Services.

Inbox The storage folder that receives new incoming messages.

Inbox repair tool A utility (`Scanpst.exe`) used to repair corrupt personal folder (`.pst`) files.

incremental backup Method in which all files that have changed since the last normal or incremental backup are backed up. The archive bit is cleared after an incremental backup is performed.

Information Store See *Store.exe*.

infrastructure master An operations master role server that is responsible for updating references from objects in its domain to objects in other domains.

inheritance The process through which permissions are passed down from a parent container to objects inside that container (child objects).

installer package (MSI file) One of the files generated by Windows Installer; used to control configuration information during installation. The installer package contains a database that describes the configuration information. See also *installer transform (MST file)*.

installer transform (MST file) One of the files generated by Windows Installer; used to control configuration information during installation. The transform file contains modifications that are to be made as Windows Installer installs Outlook. See also *installer package (MSI file)*.

Integrated Windows authentication Requires the user to provide a valid Windows username and password. However, the user's credentials are never sent across the network. At the Windows 2000 native domain functional level or the Windows Server 2003 domain functional level, this method uses Kerberos v5.

Internet Information Services (IIS) A built-in component of Windows Server 2003 that allows access to resources on the server through various Internet protocols, such as POP3, IMAP4, and HTTP.

Internet Message Access Protocol version 4 (IMAP4) An Internet retrieval protocol that enables clients to access and manipulate messages in their mailbox on a remote server. IMAP4 provides additional functions over POP3, such as access to subfolders (not merely the Inbox folder) and selective downloading of messages.

ipconfig A command-line utility that can be used to display and modify TCP/IP information about all installed network adapters. Common uses include flushing the local DNS resolver cache and releasing and renewing DHCP leases.

K

Kerberos version 5 (v5) The primary form of user authentication used by Windows Server 2003.

key A randomly generated number used to implement advanced security, such as encryption or digital signatures. See also *key pair*, *public key*, and *private key*.

key pair A key that is divided into two mathematically related halves. One half (the public key) is made public; the other half (the private key) is known by only one user.

L

leaf object An object in a Microsoft Management Console window that does not contain any other objects.

Lightweight Directory Access Protocol (LDAP) An Internet protocol used for client access to an X.500-based directory, such as Active Directory.

local continuous replication (LCR) This is a single-server environment where the production storage group is copied to another physical disk on the same server using log shipping.

local procedure call (LPC) When a program issues an instruction that is executed on the same computer as the program executing the instruction. See also *remote procedure call (RPC)*.

lockbox The process of using a secret key to encrypt a message and its attachments and then using a public key pair to encrypt and decrypt the secret key.

log file replay A process in which Exchange examines the transaction log files for a storage group to identify transactions that have been logged and that have not been incorporated into a database. This process, also known as *playing back log files*, brings the databases up-to-date with the available transaction log files.

logical unit number (LUN) The logical unit number is the disk structure as defined on the SAN or NAS device used to provide disk resources to a cluster. For example, on the SAN, there may be 10 physical disks combined in a RAID format. These disks are then exposed from the SAN to the computer as one unit. The Windows computer then sees one large physical disk connected to it. See, now you are really confused.

M

Mail and Directory Management (MADMAN) MIB A specialized version of the base management information base that was created for monitoring messaging systems. See also *management information base (MIB)*.

mail exchanger (MX) record A record in a DNS database that indicates the SMTP mail host for an organization.

mailbox The generic term referring to a container that holds messages, such as incoming and outgoing messages.

mailbox database A database on an Exchange server that holds mailboxes. See also *database*.

mailbox server The primary function of the Mailbox server role is to provide users with mailboxes that can be accessed directly from the Outlook client. The Mailbox server also contains the databases that hold public folders if you are still using them in your organization, so, as a point of comparison, the Mailbox server is most like the back-end server from previous versions of Exchange.

mailbox-enabled user A user who has been assigned an Exchange Server mailbox.

mail-enabled user A user who has been given an email address but no mailbox.

majority node set cluster In Windows Server 2003 Enterprise Edition, Microsoft presented another option to the shared disk environment for the quorum. Instead of selecting a shared physical disk to host the quorum, it is possible to select the majority node set (MNS) option to create a server cluster. From the perspective of Windows, MNS looks just like a single quorum disk, but the quorum data is actually stored on multiple disks across the cluster. MNS is designed and built so it ensures that the cluster data stored is kept consistent across the different disks on different computers.

management information base (MIB) A set of configurable objects defined for management by SNMP.

MAPI See *Messaging Application Programming Interface (MAPI)*.

MAPI client A messaging client that uses the Messaging Application Programming Interface (MAPI) to connect to a messaging server. See also *Messaging Application Programming Interface (MAPI).*

MAPI subsystem The second layer of the MAPI architecture; this component is shared by all applications that require its services and is therefore considered a *subsystem* of the operating system.

message state information Information that identifies the state of a message in a public folder. Message state information consists of a change number, a time stamp, and a predecessor change list.

Messaging Application Programming Interface (MAPI) An object-oriented programming interface for messaging services, developed by Microsoft.

Microsoft Clustering Service (MSCS) A Windows service that provides for highly available server solutions through a process known as *failover*. An MSCS cluster consists of two more nodes (members) that are configured such that upon the failure of one node, any of the remaining cluster nodes can transfer the failed node's resources to itself, thus keeping the resources available for client access.

Microsoft Management Console (MMC) A framework application in which snap-ins are loaded to provide the management of various network resources. System Manager is an example of a snap-in.

Microsoft Office Outlook 2007 The premier client application for use with Exchange Server 2007.

Microsoft Search Service The service that performs full-text indexing of mailbox and public databases.

migration Moving resources, such as mailboxes, messages, and so on, from one messaging system to another.

mounting The process of bringing a mailbox or public database online. See also *dismounting*.

multimaster replication model A model in which every replica of a public folder is considered a master copy.

multipathing Multipathing is commonly used in Fiber SAN designs. Nodes will have two HBAs (remember, high availability requires redundancy) that are then joined using software. Some common products that you may have heard of include PowerPath (EMC) and SecurePath (HP). The two HBAs can be bound together and load balanced to improve throughput from 2GB to 4GB for a particular node. It is also fairly common, though, that the fiber array will also use two HBAs bound together to provide 4GB of throughput, which is then shared among all the servers that attach to the array for storage; 4GB may not be enough. In some cases, organizations will invest and provide four fiber connections from the SAN to the fabric, thus providing 8GB of throughput.

Multipurpose Internet Mail Extensions (MIME) An Internet protocol that enables the encoding of binary content within mail messages. For example, MIME could be used to encode a graphics file or word processing document as an attachment to a text-based mail message. The recipient of the message would have to be using MIME also to decode the attachment. MIME is newer than UUENCODE and in many systems has replaced it. See also *Secure/Multipurpose Internet Mail Extensions (S/MIME)* and *UUENCODE.*

MX See *mail exchanger (MX) record.*

N

name resolution The DNS process of mapping a domain name to its IP address.

namespace Any bounded area in which a given name can be resolved.

nbtstat A command-line utility that is used to give statistics, view cache information, resolve NetBIOS names to IP addresses, and register with NetBIOS.

NetDiag A command-line utility that is used to troubleshoot and isolate network connectivity problems by performing a number of tests to determine the exact state of a server.

netstat A command-line utility that is used to display TCP/IP connection information and protocol statistics for a computer.

network load balancing (NLB) Provides horizontal scalability as well as high availability. Horizontal scaling is achieved by the servers sharing the load between them. If the application becomes oversubscribed, new servers can be built and added into the NLB web farm to spread the load out even more. High availability is achieved through the NLB web farm in that if a single (or even multiple) server fails, NLB will redistribute the load among the remaining servers.

Network News Transfer Protocol (NNTP) An Internet protocol used to transfer newsgroup information between newsgroup servers and clients (newsreaders) and between newsgroup servers.

NNTP See *Network News Transfer Protocol (NNTP).*

node In a Microsoft Management Console window, a node is any object that can be configured. In clustering, a node is one of the computers that is part of a cluster.

normal backup During this backup, all selected files are backed up, regardless of how their archive bit is set. After the backup, the archive bit is set to off for all files, indicating that those files have been backed up.

notification Defines the event that is triggered when a service or resource being watched by a server or link monitor fails. Notifications can send email and alerts and even run custom scripts.

nslookup A command-line utility that can be used to gather information about the DNS infrastructure inside and outside an organization and troubleshoot DNS-related problems.

O

object The representation, or abstraction, of an entity. As an object, it contains properties, also called *attributes*, that can be configured.

Object Linking and Embedding version 2 (OLE 2) The Microsoft protocol that specifies how programs can share objects and therefore create compound documents.

Offline Address Book (OAB) A copy stored on a client's computer of part or all of the server-based global address list (GAL). An OAB allows a client to address messages while not connected to their server.

offline backup A backup made while the Exchange services are stopped. When you perform an offline backup, users do not have access to their mailboxes while the backup takes place.

offline folder See *Offline Storage (OST) folder.*

Offline Storage (OST) folder Folders located on a client's computer that contain replicas of server-based folders. An OST allows a client to access and manipulate copies of server data while not connected to their server. When the client reconnects to their server, they can have their OST resynchronized with the master folders on the server.

OLE 2 See *Object Linking and Embedding version 2 (OLE 2).*

Open Shortest Path First (OSPF) A routing protocol developed for IP networks based on the shortest path first or link-state algorithm.

Organization The highest-level object in the Microsoft Exchange hierarchy.

organizational unit (OU) An Active Directory container into which objects can be grouped for permissions management.

Outlook Anywhere A new mode of connecting remote Outlook 2007 clients to an Exchange Server 2007 organization without requiring the use of a virtual private network (VPN) or Outlook Web Access (OWA). RPCs are passed over the HTTP connection and secured with SSL encryption. Basic authentication is used to authenticate the user and is also protected by the SSL. Outlook Anywhere was first introduced in Exchange Server 2003 as RPC over HTTP.

P

Outlook Web Access (OWA) A service that allows users to connect to Exchange Server and access mailboxes and public folders using a web browser.

OWA Light A scaled-down version of Outlook Web Access that was referred to as Basic in the Exchange Server 2003 version of OWA.

patch files Temporary logs that store transactions while a backup is taking place. Transactions in these logs are committed when the backup is finished.

pathping A new command that is a mix of both `ping` and `tracert`. The `pathping` command provides the ability to determine the packet loss along each link in the path and at each router in the path to the destination, which can be particularly helpful when troubleshooting problems where multiple routers and links are involved.

Performance Monitor See *Performance snap-in.*

Performance snap-in A utility used to log and chart the performance of various hardware and software components of a system. In various documentation, the Performance snap-in is also referred to as Performance Monitor, Performance tool, and System Monitor.

Performance tool See *Performance snap-in.*

perimeter network A network formed by using two firewalls to separate an internal network from the Internet and then placing certain servers, such as an Exchange front-end server, between the two firewalls. This is also referred to as a *demilitarized zone (DMZ).*

permission Provides specific authorization or denial to a user to perform an action on an object.

Personal Address Book (PAB) An address book created by a user and stored on that user's computer or a server.

Personal Store (PST) folder Folder created by a user and used for message storage instead of using their mailbox in the mailbox database. PSTs can be located on a user's computer or on a server, although they are not supported when accessed from a server over the network.

Pickup folder Used for outbound messages on some SMTP hosts. Exchange Server 2007 creates, but does not ordinarily use, this folder.

ping `ping` stands for Packet INternet Groper. The basic network connectivity troubleshooting tool that works by sending a series of ICMP Echo Request datagrams to a destination and waiting for the corresponding ICMP Echo Reply datagrams to come back. The return packets are then used to determine how many datagrams are getting through, the response time, and the time to live (TTL).

plain text Unencrypted data. Synonymous with *clear text.*

Point-to-Point Protocol (PPP) An Internet protocol used for the direct communication between two nodes. Commonly used by Internet users and their Internet service providers on the serial line point-to-point connection over a modem.

polling Process that queries a server-based mailbox for new mail.

POP3 See *Post Office Protocol version 3 (POP3).*

port number A numeric identifier assigned to an application. Transport protocols such as TCP and UDP use the port number to identify to which application to deliver a packet.

Post Office Protocol version 3 (POP3) An Internet protocol used for client retrieval of mail from a server-based mailbox.

postmaster mailbox The postmaster mailbox is required in every messaging infrastructure per RFC 2822 and receives non-delivery reports and delivery status notifications.

Primary Domain Controller (PDC) emulator An operations master role server that is responsible for authenticating non–Active Directory clients, such as Windows 95 or Windows 98 clients. The PDC emulator is responsible for processing password changes from these clients and is also the responsible server for time synchronization within the domain.

private folder See *mailbox*.

private key The half of a key pair that is known by only the pair's user and is used to decrypt data and to digitally sign messages.

property A characteristic of an object. Properties of a mailbox include display name and storage limits. The terms *property* and *attribute* are synonymous.

public database A database that holds public folders on an Exchange server. See also *database*.

public folder A folder stored in a public store on an Exchange server and accessible to multiple users.

public folder hierarchy The relative position of all the folders in a public folder tree.

public folder referral The process by which a client can locate a requested public folder outside their home Exchange server.

public folder replication The transferring of public folder data to replicas of that folder on other servers.

public folder tree A hierarchy of public folders associated with a particular public database.

public key The half of a key pair that is published for anyone to read and is used when encrypting data and verifying digital signatures.

public key infrastructure (PKI) A system of components working together to verify the identity of users who transfer data on a system and to encrypt that data if needed.

public-key encryption An encryption method that employs a key pair consisting of a public and a private key.

Q

queue folder A folder in which messages that have yet to be delivered are stored.

Queue Viewer A part of the Exchange System Manager that lets you view and manipulate the messages in a queue.

quorum disk The disk set that contains definitive cluster configuration data. All members of an MSCS cluster must have continuous, reliable access to the data that is contained on a quorum disk. Information contained on the quorum disk includes data about the nodes that are participating in the cluster, the applications and resources that are defined within the cluster, and the current status of each member, application, and resource.

R

random failover In this cluster operation mode, the clustered resource will be randomly failed over to an available cluster node.

recipient An object that can receive a message. Recipient objects include users, contacts, groups, and public folders.

recovery When it refers to Exchange databases, *recovery* means to replay transaction log files into a restored database. This action brings the database up-to-date. There are two distinct forms of recovery: soft recovery and hard recovery. *Soft recovery* occurs with a database that failed and has been repaired, or is just being remounted. A soft recovery is an automatic transaction log file replay process that occurs when a database is remounted after an unexpected failure. Soft recovery uses the log files that are currently in the log file location using the checkpoint file to determine which log files to start with during the sequentially replay process. A *hard recovery* occurs after a restore of a database. The hard recovery process plays the transaction log files into a restored database to bring the database back to a consistent state. The hard recovery process uses a `RESTORE.env` file that is generated during recovery to determine which transaction log files must be replayed from the temporary directory to which the backup was restored. The hard recovery process then continues to replay any additional transaction log files that it finds in the current transaction log file directory of the restored database.

recovery server A server separate from the organization that is used as a dummy server for recovering individual mailboxes or messages from a backup.

recovery storage group A feature first introduced in Exchange Server 2003 that provides a special storage group on a server that can be used for performing restorations without needing to use an alternative recovery forest or needing to take the database offline for an extended period of time.

regular expression A string or set of symbols used to describe or search for a set of strings. Regular expressions can be used in transport rules as a condition or exception. For example, you could use a regular expression to search message bodies for Social Security numbers and then perform an action on those messages if they had a Social Security number.

relative identity (RID) master An operations master role server that is responsible for maintaining the uniqueness of every object within its domain. When a new Active Directory object is created, it is assigned a unique security identifier (SID). The SID consists of a domain specific SID that is the same for all objects created in that domain and a relative identifier (RID), which is unique amongst all objects within that domain

remote delivery The delivery of a message to a recipient that does not reside on the same server as the sender.

remote domain An email domain outside your Exchange organization.

remote procedure call (RPC) A set of protocols for issuing instructions that can be sent over a network for execution. A client computer makes a request to a server computer, and the results are sent to the client computer. The computer issuing the request and the computer performing the request are separated remotely over a network. RPCs are a key ingredient in distributed processing and client/server computing. See also *local procedure call (LPC).*

replica A copy of a public folder located on an Exchange server.

replication The transferring of a copy of data to another location, such as another server or site. See also *directory replication* and *public folder replication.*

reserve log files Two transaction log files created by Exchange Server that are reserved for use when the server runs out of disk space.

resolving an address The process of determining where (on which physical server) an object with a particular address resides.

resource group Functions in a cluster that is not bound to a specific computer and can fail over to another node.

restore To return the original files that were previously stored in a backup to their location on a server. For Exchange, this generally means restoring a database backup to a recovery storage group.

rich-text format (RTF) A Microsoft format protocol that includes bolding, highlighting, italics, underlining, and many other format types.

role A group of permissions that define which activities a user or group can perform with regard to an object.

root CA Resides at the top of a certificate authority hierarchy; is trusted unconditionally by a client. All certificate chains terminate at a root CA. See also *certificate authority (CA).*

root domain The top domain in a domain tree.

routing group A collection of Exchange servers that have full-time, full-mesh, reliable connections between each and every server. Messages sent between any two servers within a routing group are delivered directly from the source server to the destination server.

routing group connector (RGC) The primary connector used to connect routing groups in an organization. The RGC uses SMTP as its default transport mechanism.

routing croup master A server that maintains data about all the servers running Exchange Server 2000/2003 in a routing group.

rule A set of instructions that define how a message is handled when it reaches a folder.

S

S/MIME See *Secure/Multipurpose Internet Mail Extensions (S/MIME).*

scalable The ability of a system to grow to handle greater traffic, volume, usage, and so on.

Schedule+ Free Busy public folder A system folder that contains calendaring and synchronization information for Exchange users.

schema The set of rules defining a directory's hierarchy, objects, attributes, and so on.

Schema master An operations master role server that controls all updates and changes that are made to the schema.

secret key A security key that can be used to encrypt data and that is known only by the sender and the recipients whom the sender informs.

Secure Sockets Layer (SSL) An Internet protocol that provides secure and authenticated TCP/IP connections. A client and server establish a "handshake" whereby they agree on a level of security they will use, such as authentication requirements and encryption. SSL can be used to encrypt sensitive data for transmission.

Secure/Multipurpose Internet Mail Extensions (S/MIME) An Internet protocol that enables mail messages to be digitally signed, encrypted, and decrypted.

security group A group defined in Active Directory that can be assigned permissions and has a SID. All members of the group gain the permissions given to the group.

server license Provides the legal right to install and operate Microsoft Exchange Server 2007 (or another server product) on a single-server machine.

service provider A MAPI program that provides messaging-oriented services to a client. There are three main types of service providers: address book, message store, and message transport.

signing The process of placing a digital signature on a message.

simple display name An alternate name for the mailbox that appears when, for some reason, the full display name cannot.

Simple Mail Transfer Protocol (SMTP) The Internet protocol used to transfer mail messages. It is has been the default transport protocol since Exchange 2000 Server.

Simple Network Management Protocol (SNMP) Internet protocol used to manage heterogeneous computers, operating systems, and applications. Because of its wide acceptance and applicability, SNMP is well suited for enterprise-wide management.

single copy cluster (SCC) This is a standard cluster much like previous server cluster implementations for Exchange. This implementation requires use of a shared disk implementation such as a SAN to host the quorum, the storage disks, and the transaction log disks.

single-instance storage Storing only one copy. A message that is sent to multiple recipients homed in the same storage group has only one copy (that is, instance) stored on that server. Each recipient is given a pointer to that copy of the message.

site A logical grouping of servers in previous versions of Exchange (prior to Exchange 2000 Server) that are connected by a full mesh (every server is directly connected to every other server) and communicate using high-bandwidth RPC. All servers in a site can authenticate one another either because they are homed in the same Windows domain or because of trust relationships configured between separate Windows domains. A site is also a group of Windows servers that are connected with full-time, reliable connections.

smart host An SMTP host designated to receive all outgoing SMTP mail. The smart host then forwards the mail to the relevant destination.

SMTP See *Simple Mail Transfer Protocol (SMTP).*

SMTP connector Using SMTP as its transport mechanism, the SMTP connector can be used to connect routing groups to one another and to connect Exchange to a foreign SMTP system.

SMTP virtual server A logical representation of the SMTP protocol on a physical server.

SNMP See *Simple Network Management Protocol (SNMP).*

spooling The process used by SMTP to temporarily store messages that cannot be delivered immediately.

stand-alone CA Used to issue certificates to users who are outside the enterprise and who do not require access to the Active Directory. See also *certificate authority (CA)* and *enterprise CA.*

Standard Edition The basic version of Exchange Server 2007 with support for up to five storage groups and five databases. Additionally, there is no support for CCR or SCC clustering in this edition.

standard permissions Permissions that are defined in a standard installation of Windows Server 2003. Extended permissions are created when Exchange Server 2007 is installed.

Storage Area Network (SAN) A SAN is a set of connected devices (such as disks and tapes) and servers that are connected to a common infrastructure such as Fibre Channel. The communication and data transfer channel for a given SAN environment is commonly called a *storage fabric.* The fabric of the SAN enables multiple servers to connect to a pool of storage devices that can include multiple arrays. In a SAN, any server can be configured to access any storage device or part of a storage device. In a SAN environment, management of the environment provides security for the storage units.

storage group A collection of databases (up to five) that all share a common set of transaction logs. Exchange 2007 allows for five storage groups, and the Enterprise Edition allows for 50 storage groups per server.

Store.exe The actual process that governs the use of stores on an Exchange server. Often referred to as the *Information Store service.*

store-and-forward A delivery method that does not require the sender and recipient to have simultaneous interaction. Instead, when a message is sent, it is transferred to the next appropriate location in the network, which temporarily stores it, makes a routing decision, and forwards the message to the next appropriate network location. This process occurs until the message is ultimately delivered to the intended recipient or an error condition causes the message to be returned to the sender.

subordinate CA A CA found underneath the root CA in the CA hierarchy and maybe even under other subordinate CAs. See also *certificate authority (CA)* and *root CA*.

subsystem A software component that, when loaded, extends the operating system by providing additional services. The MAPI program, `MAPI32.DLL`, is an example of a subsystem. `MAPI32.DLL` loads on top of the Windows 98 or Windows XP operating system and provides messaging services.

System Monitor See *Performance snap-in*.

system state backup A form of backup that includes the Windows registry, the IIS metabase, and the Active Directory (if run on a domain controller). Additionally, this may include the client access server configuration or cluster quorum for client access servers and clustered servers, respectively.

T

Task Manager Displays the programs and processes running on a computer. It also displays various performance information, such as CPU and memory usage.

telnet A text-based command-line tool that allows you to remotely communicate with a host.

template An object, such as a user or group that contains configuration information that is applicable to multiple users. Objects for each user can be easily created by copying the template and filling in individual information.

TLS encryption Transport Layer Security (TLS) encryption is a generic security protocol similar to Secure Sockets Layer encryption.

token The packet of security information a certificate authority sends to a client during advanced security setup. Information in the packet includes the client's public key and its expiration. A token is similar to a certificate.

top-level folders The folders found in the root level of a public folder tree.

tracert A command-line utility that uses ICMP packets to determine the path that an IP datagram takes to reach its final destination.

transaction log A file used to quickly write data. That data is later written to the relevant Exchange database file. It is quicker to write to a transaction log file because the writes are done sequentially (that is, one right after the other). Transaction log files can also be used to replay transactions from the log when rebuilding an Exchange database. All stores in a single storage group share the same set of transaction logs.

Triple Data Encryption Standard (3DES) A newer, more secure, variant of the DES standard that uses three 56-bit keys, one after another, to produce a 168-bit key.

Typical installation This option installs the Exchange Server software, the basic Messaging and Collaboration components, and the System Manager snap-in program. It does not include the additional connectors.

U

Unified Messaging server The Unified Messaging server role provides the following functionality to an Exchange Server 2007 organization:

- Fax reception and delivery to Exchange mailboxes
- Voice call answering and delivery of recorded voicemail file to Exchange mailboxes
- Voicemail access via a phone connection
- Message read back via a phone connection, including replying to the message or forwarding it to another recipient
- Calendar access via a phone connection, including meeting request acceptance
- Out-of-office messages in voicemail via a phone connection

uniform resource identifier (URI) A generic term for all types of addresses that refer to objects on the World Wide Web and private networks.

uniform resource locator (URL) An addressing method used to identify Internet servers and documents.

URL See *uniform resource locator (URL)*.

Usenet A network within the Internet that is composed of numerous servers containing information on a variety of topics. Each organized topic is called a *newsgroup*.

User object An object in Active Directory that is associated with a person on the network. Users can be mailbox-enabled or mail-enabled in Exchange Server 2007.

UUENCODE Stands for Unix-to- Unix Encode and is a protocol used to encode binary information within mail messages. UUENCODE is older than MIME. See also *Multipurpose Internet Mail Extensions (MIME)*.

V

virtual local area network (VLAN) A VLAN is an implementation where remote sites can be configured so that they appear to be on the same network segment.

virtual server A group of resources that contains an IP address resource and a network name resource. The network name is then published to the network so that others can attach to its name to access resources included within the group. Clients access the resources of a virtual server exactly like they would access the resources of a physical server. Whether the server is a virtual server or a physical server doesn't matter to client computers on the network. They don't know the difference, and they just don't care either.

volume shadow copy A new feature in the Windows Server 2003 Backup Utility to back up open files as if they were closed at the moment of the backup event.

W

W3svc The World Wide Web (WWW) publishing service of Internet Information Server (IIS).

Web The World Wide Web (WWW).

WebReady file types Certain file types, such as Microsoft Word documents and Adobe Acrobat PDF documents, that can be converted to HTML easily. You can configure OWA to display these file types as HTML documents, thus allowing access to them even on computers that may not have the original applications they were created in installed.

well-known port numbers Numbers that are commonly used as the TCP port numbers for popular applications, usually under 1,024.

Windows 2000 mixed domain functional level The domain functional level that allows Windows NT 4.0 backup domain controllers to exist and function within a Windows 2003 domain.

Windows 2000 native domain functional level The domain functional level that requires all domain controllers to be Windows 2000 Server or Windows Server 2003 and does not provide support for Windows NT 4.0 backup domain controllers.

Windows event log See *event log*.

Windows Internet Naming System (WINS) A name resolution service for resolving NetBIOS names on a Windows network.

Windows Server 2003 domain functional level The highest domain functional level in Windows 2003, which implements all the new features of Windows 2003 Active Directory.

Windows site A group of computers that exist on one or more IP subnets. Computers within a site must be connected by a fast, reliable network connection.

World Wide Web (WWW) The collection of computers on the Internet using protocols such as HTML and HTTP.

WWW See *World Wide Web (WWW).*

X.400 An International Telecommunications Union (ITU) standard for message exchange.

X.500 An International Telecommunications Union (ITU) standard for directory services.

X.509 certificate The most widely used format for certificates, X.509 certificates contain not only the public key but also information that identifies the user and the organization that issued the certificate.

Index

Note to the Reader: Throughout this index **boldfaced** page numbers indicate primary discussions of a topic. *Italicized* page numbers indicate illustrations.

A

A/C Privileged classification, 352
accepted domains
    creating, **160–163**, *160–163*
    defined, 606
access control entries (ACEs)
    defined, 606
    PFDAVAdmin for, 388
access control lists (ACLs)
    defined, 606
    PFAdmin for, 389
    PFDAVAdmin for, 388
    security lists in, 303
Account tab
    mail-enabled users, 292
    mailboxes, **281**, *282*
accounts
    mail-enabled. *See* mail-enabled users
    mailbox-enabled. *See* mailbox-enabled users
    service, **483–484**
ACEs (access control entries)
    defined, 606
    PFDAVAdmin for, 388
ACLs (access control lists)
    defined, 606
    PFAdmin for, 389
    PFDAVAdmin for, 388
    security lists in, 303
Action tab
    antispam, 220, *220*
    Sender Confidence, 227
    sender filtering, 225, *225*
    Sender ID, 226, *226*
    Sender Reputation, 227, *228*
actions, transport rules, 355
active/active clustering support, 6
Active Directory, **6–7**
    defined, 606
    deployment, **19**
    exam essentials, **20–21**
    Exchange Server dependence on, **15–18**
    for Exchange Server installation, **54–56**
        domain and forest functional levels, **56–57**, *57*
        domain preparation, **59–63**, *60–63*
        forest preparation, **57–59**, *58*
        organization changes, **63–64**
        verification, **94**, *95–96*
    logical components, **7–10**, *9–10*
    masters, **13–14**
    partitions, **12–13**, **17**
    physical components, **10–12**
    replication, **14–17**
    review questions, **22–27**
    site-based routing, 3
    summary, **19–20**
Active Directory Application Mode (ADAM)
    database, *565–566*
    for Edge Transport server, 36, 43, 98
    with EdgeSync, 209
    ports for, 105
Active Directory Topology service, 98, 578
active node computers in SCC, **508–512**, *509–512*
Active Remote Delivery Queue Length counter, 585
Active value for queued messages, 443
ActiveSync
    configuring, **414**
    mobile devices, **420–425**, *420–424*
    policies, **361–363**, *363*, **416–420**, *417–419*
    support, **415–416**, *415*
ActiveSync Internal Availability report, 593
ADAM (Active Directory Application Mode)
    database, *565–566*
    for Edge Transport server, 36, 43, 98
    with EdgeSync, 209
    ports for, 105
/AdamLdapPort option, 90
/AdamSslPort option, 90
Adapters and Bindings tab, 482, *482*
Add Address Space dialog box, 165
Add-AttachmentFilterEntry cmdlet, 229–230
Add-DistributionGroupMember cmdlet, 281
Add Edit Port Rule dialog box, 495, *495*
Add Exchange Administrator Wizard, 112–113, *112–113*
Add-ExchangeAdministrator cmdlet, 113
Add Nodes Wizard, 488, 515
Add-PublicFolderAdministrativePermission cmdlet, 380
Add-PublicFolderAdministrativePermission-User cmdlet, 381
Add-PublicFolderClientPermission cmdlet, 381
Add Users dialog box, 400
AddReplicaToPFRecursive.ps1 script, 381

Address and Phone tab
  contacts, 320
  mail-enabled users, 292
  mailboxes, **275**, *275*
address lists, **359–361**, *360*
Address Lists tab, 360
Address Space page, 165, **167**, *168*
address spaces
  defined, 606
  send connectors, **167**, *168*
/AddUmLanguagePack option, 89
AddUsersToPFRecursive.ps1 script, 381
administrative groups
  defined, 606
  support, 5
administrative rights
  defined, 606
  setting, 403
Administrative Rights tab, 403
Administrative roles, **109**
  configuring, **110–113**, *110–114*
  overview, **109–110**
Administrators group, 54–55, 62
Advanced Security Settings for User dialog box, 294, *294*
Advanced tab for distribution groups, 306, *308*
affinity, NLB, 495–496
age, message tracking logs, **453**
age limits
  defined, 606
  public folders, 386
Age Limits setting, 386
aliases
  defined, 606
  email, 291
  groups, 298, 300, 304
  mailboxes, 457–458
All Address Lists option, 187
All Contacts list, 359
All Groups list, 359
All Public Folders folder
  contents, 382–383
  defined, 606
All Rooms list, 359
All Users list, 359
Allow List dialog box, 181
Allow Nonprovisionable Devices setting, 361
Allow Simple Password policy, 361, 418
Allowed Addresses tab, 220–221, *221*
Alphanumeric Password Required policy, 361
Analyzing Configuration tool, 488
anonymous access, 606
Anonymous users, 176, 402
answer files, 234, *234*
/AnswerFile option, 90
Anti-spam tab, 218
Anti-spam Update service, 98, *579*
Antigen product, 234
Antimalware Engine, 237
antispam settings, **217**
  attachment filtering agents, **227–232**, *228*, *230–232*
  content filtering, **218–220**, *218–220*
  IP allow lists, **220–221**, *221*
  IP block lists, **222–223**, *222–223*
  new features, 4
  recipient filtering, **224**, *224*
  sender filtering, **224–225**
  Sender ID, **226**, *226*
  Sender Reputation, **226–227**, *227*
antivirus settings
  Forefront Security for Exchange Server, **242–243**, *242*
  new features, 4
API (application programming interface), 606
Application log, 581
application partitions, **13**
application programming interface (API), 606
Application Server dialog box, 46, *46*
Apply an Exchange ActiveSync Policy option, 419
Apply Security Policy page, 108, *108*
architecture, 606
archives, 606
attachment filtering agents, **227–232**, *228*, *230–232*
Attachment Removed classification, 352
Attachments Enabled policy, 361
attributes
  Active Directory objects, 7, 11
  CCR outages, **522–523**
  defined, 606
  distribution groups, 304, *304*
  mail-enabled users, 292
  public folders, **378–379**
Audit Policy page, 107
auditing, 606
Authenticated Users group, 62
authentication
  ActiveSync, 416
  defined, 607
  OWA, **185**, *186*
  SMTP connectors, **174**, *175*
Author role permissions, 402
Auto Accept Agent, 326
AutoDatabaseMountDial attribute, **522–523**
Autodiscover feature, **403–404**
  configuring, **406–410**, *407–409*
  internal vs. external, **404–406**, *404–406*
Automatically Process Meeting Requests and Cancellations option, 326
availability reports, **592–593**
Avg. Disk sec/Read counter, 584
Avg. Disk sec/Write counter, 584

B

- backfill, 607
- backticks (`) in cmdlets, 377
- backup domain controllers (BDCs), 14
- Backup tab, 546
- Backup utility, 545–547, *546*
- backups, 536
  - Client Access server, **563–564**
  - defined, 607
  - Edge Transport servers, **565–566**
  - Hub Transport servers, **564**
  - jobs, **545–547**, *545–546*
  - mailbox servers, **567**
  - overview, **541–544**
  - testing, **547–548**
- Bad Mail folder, 607
- -BadItemLimit option, 458
- BADMAIL value, 450
- Basic Authentication
  - defined, 607
  - receive connectors, 174
- Basic over Secure Sockets Layer (SSL) authentication, 607
- BDCs (backup domain controllers), 14
- Best Availability option
  - CCR scheduled outages, 522
  - CCR unscheduled outages, 524
- Bias setting, 243
- bin folder, 97
- Block List dialog box, 181
- block lists, 181, **222–223**, *222–223*
- Blocked Address tab, 222, *222*
- Blocked Recipients tab, 224, *224*
- Blocked Senders tab, 224–225, *225*
- bulk management
  - mailboxes
    - creating, **460–463**, *462–463*
    - moving, **459–460**
    - size, **464–465**, *464–465*
  - populating groups, **463**

C

- CA (continuous availability), 477, 609
- cache mode, 607
- calendars
  - mobile devices, 423
  - OWA, 187
- California SB 1386, 343
- CALs (client access licenses), **33**, 608
- CAs (certificate authorities), 607
- catalogs
  - Active Directory, **11**
  - partitions, **13**, 17
- categorizers, 607
- CCR. *See* cluster continuous replication (CCR)
- centralized models, 607
- certificate authorities (CAs), 607
- Certificate Request File Name page, 196–197
- certificate revocation lists (CRLs), 607
- certificate stores, 607
- Certificate Summary page, 410
- certificate templates, 608
- certificate trust lists (CTLs), 608
- certificates
  - defined, 607
  - installing, **192–197**, *193–197*
  - SSL, **410**
- challenge/response security, 608
- change numbers, 608
- Change Password option, 187
- checkpoint files
  - defined, 608
  - purpose, 125–126, 550
- checksums, 552
- child domains
  - Active Directory, 9
  - defined, 608
- .chk files, 125–126
- Choose Destination Location page, 238–239, *239*
- circular logging
  - defined, 608
  - overview, **133**
- classifications of messages, **351–353**, *352*
- Clean:Repair Document option, 243
- Clear-ActiveSyncDevice cmdlet, 425
- client access licenses (CALs), **33**, 608
- Client Access servers, **35–36**, **178**, 489
  - backing up and recovering, **563–564**
  - configuring
    - Outlook Anywhere, **190–191**, *190–191*
    - OWA. *See* Outlook Web Access (OWA)
    - process, **178–179**
    - SSL, **191–197**, *192–197*
  - defined, 608
  - requirements, **44–45**
- client connectivity, **403**
  - ActiveSync
    - configuring, **414**
    - mobile devices, **420–425**, *420–424*
    - policies, **416–420**, *417–419*
    - support, **415–416**, *415*
  - Autodiscover, **403–404**
    - configuring, **406–410**, *407–409*
    - internal vs. external, **404–406**, *404–406*
  - exam essentials, **427**
  - mobile devices, **420–425**, *420–424*
  - POP3 and IMAP4, **410–414**, *412*
  - review questions, **428–433**
  - summary, **426–427**
- client licenses, **33**, 608
- Client Permissions dialog box, **400–401**

Client Settings page
  databases, **142**, *142*
  SCC, 510
  for versions, 81, *81*
ClientAccess folder, 97
cloned configuration process, *565*
cloning, edge, **232–234**, *233–234*
Cluster Administrator, 485, 488
cluster continuous replication (CCR), 34, 478
  defined, 608
  file share witness, **515–516**
  installing, **519–521**, *519–521*
  limitations, **518–519**
  majority node sets, **513–515**
  outages
    scheduled, **521–523**
    unscheduled, **523–525**
  overview, **512–513**, *514*, **516**, *517*
  transport dumpster, **517–518**
Cluster Name and Domain page, 485, *485*
Cluster Parameters tab, 491–492, *492*
cluster resources, 608
cluster services, 608
Cluster Setting Selection page, 510
Cluster Settings page, *520*
clustering, 609
clusters
  defined, 608
  NLB, **491–493**, *492*
  server. *See* server clusters
cmdlet overview, **377**
/CMSDataPath option, 90
/CMSIPAddress option, 90
/CMSName option, 90
/CMSSharedStorage option, 90
command-line
  benefits, **114–115**
  Exchange Server installation from, **87–91**, *91*
committed transactions, 609
Company Confidential classification, 351–352
Company Internal classification, 352
compatibility
  Forefront Security for Exchange Server, 237
  SCC, **508**
Completion page
  contacts, 316
  distribution groups, 300
  mail-enabled users, 287–288
  mailbox-enabled users, 266–267
  resource mailboxes, 322
compliance
  defined, 609
  new features, 4
  requirements, **342–343**
Computer Management console, 580, 609
conditions
  dynamic distribution groups, 311, *311*, 313, *314*
  transport rules, 354
Conditions page, 311, *311*, 313, *314*
Configuration Action page, 101, *101*
configuration partitions, **12**, 17
Configure Data Collection page, 588, *588*
Confirm Port Configuration page, 106, *106*
Confirm Service Changes page, 104, *104*
Connect-Mailbox cmdlet, 286, 558
Connect Mailbox Wizard, 285–286, *286*, 557, *557*
Connect to Active Directory page, *590*, *590*
connecting disconnected mailboxes, **285–286**, *286*
connectivity checks, 49
connectors
  IMAP4 and POP3 clients, **413**
  SMTP, **163–164**
    deleting, **178**
    receive, **169–177**, *170–173*, *175–176*
    send, **163–169**, *165–169*
  support, *5*
Contact Information page, 316–317, *316*, **320–321**
contacts, 260, **314–315**
  creating
    Active Directory Users and Computers Console, **318–319**, *318*
    Exchange Management Console, **315–317**, *316*
    Exchange Management Shell, **317–318**
  defined, 609
  managing, **319**
  OWA, 187
  properties, **319–321**, *320–321*
Contacts option, 187
container objects, 609
content filtering, **218–220**, *218–220*
Content Filtering Properties dialog box, 218–219, *218–219*
contiguous namespaces, 16, 609continuous availability (CA), 477, 609
Contributor role permissions, 402
convergence
  defined, 609
  NLB, 490
  replication, 14
copy backups, 544, 609
copy database, **505–506**
copying database files, 552
Copying Files dialog box, 79
corrupt database recovery, **506**
counters, performance, **584–585**
CPU requirements
  Exchange Server, **38–39**
  LCR, 500
Create a New Certificate option, 195

Create a New Security Policy option, 101
Create Items permission, 401–402
Create New Folder dialog, 383, *383*
Create Subfolders permission, 401–402
Creating the Cluster page, *515*
Credential Service, 98, *579*
Critical Issues tab, *592*
CRLs (certificate revocation lists), 607
CTLs (certificate trust lists), 608
Custom Attributes dialog box
  distribution groups, 304, *304*
  mail-enabled users, 292
Custom Exchange Server Installation option, *509*, *519*
custom managed folders, 344–345
Custom Words tab, 218, *219*
Customer Information page, 235, *235*

D

DACLs (discretionary access control lists), 610
daily backups, 609
damaged database repair, **548–553**, *549*, *551–553*
Data Encryption Standard (DES), 609
data loss, avoiding, **538–539**
Database Management tab, 127, *127*
Database Recovery Management tool, *560*, *562*
databases, **124–125**, *125*, **136**
  creating, **136–139**, *137–139*
  defined, 609
  deleting, **146–147**, *147*
  guidelines, **148**
  LCR, **505–506**
  logs, 538
  mailbox, recovering, **559–562**
  mounting and dismounting, **145–146**, *146*
  portability, 539
  properties, **140–142**, *140–142*
  public folders, **375–376**, **380**
  queues, 446–447, *447*
  in recovery, 540
  repairing, **548–553**, *549*, *551–553*
  reports, **594–596**
Date Received field, 442
DAVEx component, 609
DCDiag utility
  for connectivity, **49–50**
  defined, 609
decentralized models, 610
decryption, 610
dedicated public folder servers, 610
default gateways, 481, 483
default global address list, 359
Default group, 401
default managed folders, 344
Default or Custom Managed Folder tab, 347
Default public store setting, 142
Default Transport Template, 241
Default user, 402
Default Web Site Properties dialog box
  OWA, **181–190**, *181–183*, *185–186*, *188*
  third-party SSL certificates, 193, *193*
DEFER value, 450
defragmenting databases, 551
Delayed or Immediate Request page, 195, *195*
Delete Items permission, 401–402
Deleted Items folder, **555**
deleted items retention, 142, 386, 539, 610
deleted mailboxes, **283–286**, *283–286*
  recovering, **556–558**, *556–558*
  retention, 539
DeleteSourceMailbox option, 458
deleting
  attachments, 243
  databases, **146–147**, *147*
  SMTP connectors, **178**
  storage groups, **147–148**
DELIVER status, 450–451
Delivery Options dialog box, 278, *279*
Delivery Type field, **439**
Dell OpenManage monitor, 589
deployment
  Active Directory, **19**
  in large organizations, **65**
DES (Data Encryption Standard), 609
Device Encryption Enabled setting, 361
diagnostics tests, **49–50**, *50*
dial-tone recovery, 539, 560–561, 610
differential backups, 544, 610
digital signatures, 610
Direct File Access Settings dialog box, 188–189, *188*
directories, 610
directory replication, 610
directory rights, 403, 610
Directory Rights tab, 403
Directory Security tab, 193, *193*, 197, 410
directory services requirements, **42–43**
Disable-DistributionGroup cmdlet, 303
Disable Local Continuous Replication option, 502
Disable-Mailbox cmdlet, 273, 324
Disable-MailContact cmdlet, 319
Disable-MailPublicFolder cmdlet, 379
Disable-MailUser cmdlet, 290
Disable-StorageGroupCopy cmdlet, 503
disabling and Disable option
  contacts, 319
  distribution groups, 303
  LCR, **502–503**

mail-enabled users, 290
mailbox-enabled users, 273
message tracking, **452**
message tracking logs, **453**
resource mailboxes, 324
SharePoint and file server integration, **182–183**, *182–183*

disaster recovery
avoiding data loss, **538–539**
backups. *See* backups
damaged databases, **548–553**, *549*, *551–553*
defined, 610
exam essentials, **567–568**
messaging data, **553–562**, *554*, *556–558*
overview, **536–537**
reactions in, **539–540**
review questions, **569–575**
summary, **567**

Disaster Recovery mode, 610
DisconnectDate setting, 558
disconnected mailboxes, **283–286**, *283–286*
discovery, 610
discretionary access control lists (DACLs), 610
disk hardware
SCC requirements, 508
server clusters, **480**, **484**

Dismount-Database cmdlet, 145, *506*
dismounting
databases, **145–146**, *146*
defined, 610

display filters, 144, *144*
distribution groups, **296**
creating
Active Directory Users and Computers Console, **302–303**, *302*
Exchange Management Console, **297–299**, *297–298*
Exchange Management Shell, **300**, *301*
defined, 610
dynamic, **309–313**
mail-enabling, **299–300**, *299*, *301*
modifying, **303–304**
properties, **304–309**, *304–308*

distribution lists, 295
DMZs, **210–211**
DNS (Domain Name Service), 8, **16**
dcdiag for, 50
defined, 611
round-robin, **497**
server clusters, 482–483

DNSConnectorDelivery value, 439
Do Not Change the Startup Mode of the Service option, 104
Do Not Permanently Delete Items Until This Database Has Been Backed Up option, *554*, *556*
Do Not Send Delivery Reports option, 307
Documents page, 183, *184*
Domain Admins group, 54
domain controllers
Active Directory, **10–11**
defined, 611
diagnostics tests, **49–50**, *50*

domain forests
Active Directory, **10**, *10*
functional levels, **56–57**, *57*
preparation, **57–59**, *58*
Windows Server 2003, **16**

domain local groups, **296**
Domain Name Service (DNS), 8, **16**
dcdiag for, 50
defined, 611
round-robin, **497**
server clusters, 482–483

domain naming masters, 13
domain partitions, **12**, 17
domain trees
Active Directory, **9**, *9*
defined, 611

/DomainController option, 88
DomainPrep command, 56, 62
domains
Active Directory, **8**
defined, 611
functional levels, **56–57**, *57*
Hub Transport servers, **156–163**, *157–163*
mobile devices, 421, *421*
preparation, **59–63**, *60–63*
SCC, 507

/DoNotStartTransport option, 88
dsadd user command, 270, 460
DSN value, 450
Dynamic Distribution Group Preview dialog box, 313, *314*
dynamic distribution groups, **309**
creating, **310–312**, *310–312*
defined, 611
managing, **312–313**
properties, **313**, *313–314*

E

E-mail Address Policy tab, 358
E-Mail Addresses tab
contacts, 320–321, *321*
distribution groups, 306, *307*
mail-enabled users, 292
mailboxes, **282**, *283*

E-mail Signature option, 187
E00.log file, *550*
E007FFFFFFF.log file, *550*
E00res00001.jrs file, *550*

EAS (Exchange ActiveSync)
  configuring, **414**
  mobile devices, **420–425**, *420–424*
  policies, **361–363**, *363*, **416–420**, *417–419*
  support, **415–416**, *415*
EDB (rich-text) files, 124, 126, 550
edge cloning, **232–234**, *233–234*
edge subscription files, **212–213**, *212–213*
Edge Transport server, **36**, **208**, *209*
  antispam settings. *See* antispam settings
  backing up and recovering, **565–566**
  defined, 611
  edge cloning, **232–234**, *233–234*
  EdgeSync. *See* EdgeSync service
  NLB, 489
  requirements, 43
EdgeSync service, 98, 579
  configuring, **209–210**
  edge subscription files, **212–213**, *212–213*
  firewall ports, **210–211**
  internal SMTP servers, **211–212**, *212*
  process, **214–216**, *214–217*
EdgeTransport.exe.config file, 447
Edit Items permission, 401–402
editions, **30–32**
Editor role permissions, 402
EHLO command, 611
email
  address-generation policies, **356–359**, *358*
  contacts, 320–321, *321*
  defined, 611
  groups. *See* mail-enabled groups
  mailboxes. *See* mailboxes
  mobile devices, 423
  users. *See* mail-enabled users; mailbox-enabled users
EMC (Exchange Management Console)
  for configuration, 84, *84*
  defined, 611
  new features, 3
  for public folders, **377**
EMS (Exchange Management Shell)
  new features, 3
  for public folders, **377**
  for storage group paths, 135
Enable Anti-Spam Updates page, 238, *238*
Enable-DistributionGroup cmdlet, 300, 302
Enable Domain Security (Mutual Auth TLS) option, 168
Enable Local Continuous Replication for This Storage Group option, 501
Enable-Mailbox cmdlet, 269–270, 324, 461
Enable-MailContact cmdlet, 318
Enable-MailPublicFolder cmdlet, 379
Enable-MailUser cmdlet, 289
Enable Outlook Anywhere Wizard, 190, *190*, 407, *407*
Enable-OutlookAnywhere cmdlet, 407
Enable Storage Group Local Continuous Replication Wizard, 500
Enable-StorageGroupCopy cmdlet, 503
Enable Unified Messaging option, 324
/EnableErrorReporting option, 90
/EnableLegacyOutlook option, 89
enabling
  LCR, **500**
  message tracking, **452**
  message tracking logs, **453**
  NLB, **491**, *491*
  POP3 and IMAP4 client services, **411–412**, *412*
  storage group replication, 500–501
encryption, 611
Engine Updates Required page, 237–238, *238*
Engines page, 237, *237*
Enter Product Key dialog box, 86, *86*
Enterprise Admins group, 54
enterprise CAs, 611
Enterprise Edition, 31, 611
EOO.chk file, 550
Error Reporting page
  CCR, 519
  installation setting, 80, *80*
  SCC, 509
ESE (Extensible Storage Engine)
  databases, 436, **549–550**
  defined, 612
  instances, 125
ESEUtil.exe (Exchange Server Database Utility), **550–552**
ethical walls, 611
EU Data Protection Act, 343
event log, 611
Event Viewer
  for Exchange Server installation verification, **92**, *92*
  working with, **580–581**, *581*
EventID field, 450
ExBPA (Exchange Best Practices Analyzer), 87, 552, 589–590
exceptions and Exceptions tab
  antispam, **219**, *219*
  IP block lists, 223, *223*
  transport rules, 354
Exchange 5.5 support, 5
Exchange ActiveSync (EAS)
  configuring, **414**
  mobile devices, **420–425**, *420–424*
  policies, **361–363**, *363*, **416–420**, *417–419*
  support, **415–416**, *415*
Exchange ActiveSync Integration option, 187

Exchange ActiveSync Mailbox Policy tab, 362
Exchange ActiveSync Properties dialog box, 419, *419*
Exchange ActiveSync tab, 416
Exchange Advanced tab, 398, *399*
Exchange Best Practices Analyzer (ExBPA), 87, 552, 589–590
Exchange Database Recovery Management, 552–553
Exchange Database Troubleshooting Assistant, 552–553
Exchange Install Domain Servers group, 62
Exchange Management Console (EMC)
  for configuration, 84, *84*
  defined, 611
  new features, 3
  for public folders, **377**
Exchange Management Shell (EMS)
  new features, 3
  for public folders, **377**
  for storage group paths, 135
Exchange Organization Administrators group, 55, 62, 109
Exchange Organization dialog box, 81, *81*
Exchange Recipient Administrators group, 55, 62, 110
Exchange Server 2007, **30**
  and Active Directory, **15–18**, **54–56**
    domain and forest functional levels, **56–57**, *57*
    domain preparation, **59–63**, *60–63*
    forest preparation, **57–59**, *58*
    organization changes, **63–64**
  installation, **30**, **76**
    exam essentials, **115–116**
    GUI-based, **77–84**, *78–83*
    post-installation configuration, **84–87**, *85–86*
    review questions, **117–122**
    roles, **76–77**, **109–113**, *110–114*
    Security Configuration Wizard, **99–108**, *100–108*
    summary, **115**
    unattended installations, **87–91**, *91*
    verification. *See* verification
  new features, **2–4**
  preparation
    directory services and network requirements, **42–43**
    editions, **30–32**
    exam essentials, **66–67**
    hardware requirements, **38–41**, *42*
    licensing issues, **32–33**
    name resolution, **48–49**, *49*
    network and domain controller diagnostics tests, **49–50**, *50*
    review questions, **68–74**
    roles, **34–37**
    SCW, **48**
    software requirements, **43–44**
    storage, **50–54**, *51*
    summary, **66**
    Windows services and components, **45–48**, *46–47*
  removed and deemphasized features, **5–6**
Exchange Server 2007 Setup dialog box, 79–83, *79–83*
Exchange Server Administrators group, 55, 110, 112
Exchange Server authentication, 174
Exchange Server Database Utility (ESEUtil.exe), **550–552**
Exchange Servers group, 55, 62
Exchange servers permission group, 177
Exchange users permission group, 176
Exchange View-Only Administrators group, 55, 110
Exchange2003Interop group, 55
ExchangeOAB folder, 97
ExchangeSetup.log file, 93–94, *93*, *95*
ExchangeSetup.msilog file, 93, *94*
Existing User option, 286
EXPAND value, 450
expanding distribution groups, 612
Expansion Server option, 306
Expiration Time field, 442
Export-CSV cmdlet, 465
Export-Message cmdlet, 445
ExportEdgeConfig command, 233
ExportEdgeConfig.ps1 script, 565–566
extended permissions, 612
Extensible Storage Engine (ESE)
  databases, 436, **549–550**
  defined, 612
  instances, 125
extensions, registering, 100, *100*
external Autodiscover, **404–406**, *404–406*
External DNS Lookups tab, **151**, *152*
Externally Secured authentication, 174
ExTRA tool, 552

F

FAIL value, 450
failback, 612
failover, 612
fault-tolerant components, 480
Favor Certainty option, 243
Favor Performance option, 243
Favorites folder, 382
features
  new, **2–4**
  removed and replaced, **5–6**

fiber switches, 479
Fibre Channel, **51**
File Deletion Text dialog box, 241, *241*
File Distribution Service, 98, *579*
file dumps, 552
file server access in OWA, **180–183**, *180–183*
file share witness (FSW), **515–516**, 612
Filter Settings page, 310–311, *310*
Filter tab, 313, *313*
filters
  antispam settings
    agents, **227–232**, *228*, *230–232*
    content, **218–220**, *218–220*
    recipient, **224**, *224*
    sender, **224–225**
  display, 144, *144*
  dynamic distribution groups, 310–311, *310*, 313, *313*
  quarantine views, 248
Finalize Installation Using the Exchange Management Console option, 83
firewalls
  defined, 612
  port configuration, **210–211**
First Storage Group, 127
folder-based applications, 612
Folder Contact permission, 401–402
Folder Owner permission, 401–402
Folder Visible permission, 401–402
folders
  installation structure, **96–97**, *96*
  managed, **343–345**
    assistant, **350–351**, *350*
    creating, **345–346**, *345*
    mailbox policies, 343, **346**, **348–349**, *348–349*
  public. *See* public folders
ForEach-Object cmdlet, 462
Forefront Security for Exchange Server, **234**
  installing, **235–239**, *235–239*
  settings, **240–241**, *240*
    Antivirus, **242–243**, *242*
    General Options, **245**, *245*
    Incidents, **248**, *248*
    Notification, **246–247**, *247*
    Operate, **246**, *246*
    Quarantine, **248**, *249*
    Report, **246–248**, *247–248*
    Scan Job, **241**, *241–242*
    Scanner Updates, **243–245**, *244*
foreign systems, 612
/ForeignForestFQDN option, 89
forest root domains, 10, 612
ForestPrep command, 56
forests
  Active Directory, **10**, *10*
  functional levels, **56–57**, *57*
  preparation, **57–59**, *58*
  Windows Server 2003, **16**
forms registry, 612
FQDNs (fully qualified domain names), 613
free/busy applications, 612
From Address field, 443
FSW (file share witness), **515–516**, 612
full backups, 543
full-text indexing, 613
fully qualified domain names (FQDNs), 613
function calls, 613

G

GAL (global address list)
  contents, 359
  defined, 613
general-purpose trees, 613
General tab and settings
  accepted domains, **160–162**, *160*, *163*
  ActiveSync, 416, *417*
  antispam, 218, *218*
  contacts, 319, *320*
  databases, **140–141**, *140*
  distribution groups, 304, *304*
  Forefront Security for Exchange Server, **245**, *245*
  Hub Transport servers, **151**, *151*
  mail-enabled users, 291, *291*
  mailboxes, **273–274**, *274*
  Outlook Anywhere, 191
  OWA, 181, **183**, *184*
  public folders, 385, *385*, **398**, *398*
  receive connectors, **173**, *173*
  resource mailboxes, 324
  send connectors, **167**, *167*
geoclustering, **512–513**, *514*
Geographical Information page, 196, *196*
Get-ActiveSyncDeviceStatistics cmdlet, 425
Get-AttachmentFilterListConfig cmdlet, 228–230, 232
Get-AutodiscoverVirtual Directory cmdlet, 406
Get-ClusteredMailboxServerStatus cmdlet, 522
Get-ExchangeAdministrator cmdlet, 111
Get-ImapSettings cmdlet, 412
Get-Mailbox cmdlet, 420, 458, 464–465, 596, 598–599, *599*
Get-MailboxDatabase cmdlet, 594
Get-MailboxStatistics cmdlet, 284, 558, 599
Get-MailPublicFolder cmdlet, 379
Get-Message cmdlet, 444–445
Get-MessageTrackingLog cmdlet, 448–449
Get-OABVirtualDirectory cmdlet, 408
Get-OutlookAnywhere cmdlet, 408
Get-PopSettings cmdlet, 412

Get-PublicFolder cmdlet, 378
Get-PublicFolderAdministrativePermission cmdlet, 381
Get-PublicFolderClientPermission cmdlet, 381
Get-PublicFolderDatabase cmdlet, 380, *595–596*
Get-PublicFolderStatistics cmdlet, 378, 397
Get-Queue cmdlet, 441, *596*
Get-ReceiveConnector cmdlet, 413
Get-Service cmdlet, **582–583**, *582*
Get-SetupLog.ps1 script, 94
Get-StorageGroupCopyStatus cmdlet, 504–505
Get-TransportAgent cmdlet, 227
Get-TransportConfig cmdlet, 517, *565*
Get-TransportServer cmdlet, 156
Get-User cmdlet, 459, 463
Get-WebServicesVirtualDirectory cmdlet, 409
global address list (GAL)
  contents, 359
  defined, 613
global catalogs
  Active Directory, **11**
  defined, 613
  partitions, **13**, 17
global groups, **296**
Good Availability option
  CCR scheduled outages, 522
  CCR unscheduled outages, 524
Group Information page, 298, *298*, 300, 304–305, *305*
groups, 260
  Active Directory, **54–55**
  defined, 613
  distribution. *See* distribution groups
  mail-enabled. *See* mail-enabled groups
  populating, **463**
  removing, 113
  storage. *See* storage and storage groups
groupware, 613
GUI-based installations, **77–84**, *78–83*

H

HA. *See* high availability (HA)
Handling Unspecified Services page, 104, *104*
handoffs, SCC, 512
hard disk space requirements, 38
hardware
  for avoiding data loss, 538
  monitoring, **589**
  requirements, **38–41**, *42*
  server clusters, **479–480**
hardware compatibility list, 479
HBAs (host bus adapters), 479, 613
Health Insurance Portability and Accountability Act (HIPAA), 343
health reports, **589–592**, *590–592*
heartbeat networks, 479
heartbeats, 613
HELO command, 613
Hide Group from Exchange Address Lists option, 307
hierarchies
  defined, 613
  public folders, **389–390**
high availability (HA)
  cluster continuous replication. *See* cluster continuous replication (CCR)
  defined, 613
  exam essentials, **525–526**
  local continuous replication. *See* local continuous replication (LCR)
  network load balancing. *See* network load balancing (NLB)
  new features, 4
  overview, **476–478**
  review questions, **527–534**
  server clustering. *See* server clusters
  single copy cluster
    installing, **508–512**, *509–512*
    overview, **506–507**, *507*
    requirements, **507–508**
  summary, **525**
HIPAA (Health Insurance Portability and Accountability Act), 343
host bus adapters (HBAs), 479, 613
hosts, NLB, **493**, *494*, 496
HTML (HyperText Markup Language), 614
HTTP (HyperText Transfer Protocol), 614
Hub Transport server, 18, **34–35**, **148–149**
  backing up and recovering, **564**
  defined, 614
  domains, **156–163**, *157–163*
  message routing, **149**
  postmaster mailbox, **154–156**, *154–156*
  queues, **437**
  requirements, 44
  settings, **150–153**, *150–153*
  SMTP connectors, **163–164**
    deleting, **178**
    receive, **169–177**, *170–173*, *175–176*
    send, **163–169**, *165–169*
  transport rules, **354–355**
    address lists, **359–361**, *360*
    creating, **355–356**
    email address-generation policies, **356–359**, *358*
HyperText Markup Language (HTML), 614
HyperText Transfer Protocol (HTTP), 614

I

IBM Director, 589
IFS (installable file system), 388
IGMP (Internet Group Management Protocol), **492–493**
IIS (Internet Information Services), 615
IIS Metabase
- backing up, 563
- defined, 614

IMAP4 (Internet Message Access Protocol version 4), 98, 579
- access to public folders, 6
- Client Access server settings, 563
- clients, **410–411**
  - configuring, **413–414**
  - mailboxes, **412–413**
  - receiver connectors, **413**
  - server, **412**
  - services, **411–412**, *412*
- defined, 615

IMF (intelligent message filter), 217
Import-CSV cmdlet, 268, 462
Import-ExchangeCertificate cmdlet, 410
ImportEdgeConfig command, 234
ImportEdgeConfig.ps1 script, 565–566
Inbox, 614
Inbox repair tool, 614
Incidents area, **248**, *248*
incremental backups, 544, 614
information rights management (IRM), 351
Information Store Integrity Checker (ISInteg.exe), **552–553**, *552–553*
Information Store service, 98, 579
infrastructure masters, 13–14, 614
inheritance, 614
installable file system (IFS), 388
installation
- CCR, **519–521**, *519–521*
- Exchange Server. *See* Exchange Server 2007
- Forefront Security for Exchange Server, **235–239**, *235–239*
- SCC, **508–512**, *509–512*
- SCW, **48**
- server clustering, **478–479**

Installation Location page, 235–236, *236*
Installation Type page
- Forefront Security for Exchange Server, 236, *236*
- roles, 80, *80*

installer package (MSI file), 614
installer transform (MST file), 614
Integrated Authentication
- defined, 615
- receive connectors, 174

integrity, database, 551
intelligent message filter (IMF), 217
internal Autodiscover, **404–406**, *404–406*
Internal DNS Lookups tab, **152**, *152*
internal SMTP servers, **211–212**, *212*
InternalSMTPServers list, 213
Internet Group Management Protocol (IGMP), NLB, **492–493**
Internet Information Services (IIS), 615
Internet Information Services (IIS) dialog box, 46, *46*
Internet Information Services (IIS) page, 107
Internet Message Access Protocol. *See* IMAP4 (Internet Message Access Protocol version 4)
Internet Message ID field, 443
Internet SCSI (iSCSI) storage, **52**, 480
intersite replication, 14
Introduction page
- CCR, 519
- contacts, 317
- distribution groups, 299–300
- LCR, 500
- postmaster mailbox, 155, *155*
- SCC, 509

IP addresses
- NLB, 493, 495
- server clusters, 481–483, 486

IP Allow List Providers Properties dialog box, 220, *221*
IP allow lists, **220–221**, *221*
IP Block List Properties dialog box, 222–223, *222–223*
IP block lists, **222–223**, *222–223*
ipconfig utility, 615
IRM (information rights management), 351
iSCSI (Internet SCSI) storage, **52**, 480
ISInteg.exe (Information Store Integrity Checker), **552–553**, *552–553*

J

JET (Joint Engine Technology) database, 549
jobs, backup
- creating, modifying, and performing, **545–546**, *545–546*
- monitoring and validating, **547**

Joint Engine Technology (JET) database, 549
Journal folder, 187
journaling, 140
.jrs files, 126
Junk E-mail Filtering option, 187

K

/kbname option, 100
KCCEvent checks, 50
Kerberos authentication, 615
key pairs, 615
keys, 615

L

large organizations, deployment in, **65**
Last Error field, 440, 443
Last Retry Time field, 440
latency, replication, 15
LCR. *See* local continuous replication (LCR)
LDAP (Lightweight Directory Access Protocol), 615
leaf objects, 615
Legacy Exchange servers permission group, 177
legacy streaming backups, **541**
/LegacyRoutingServer option, 89
licensing and License Agreement page
  Exchange Server, **32–33**, 79, *79*, 84
  Forefront Security for Exchange Server, 235
Lightweight Directory Access Protocol (LDAP), 615
Limits tab
  databases, **141–142**, *141*
  Hub Transport servers role, **153**, *153*
  mailboxes, 283, *283*
  public folders, **386–387**, *387*
local continuous replication (LCR), 34, 478, **497–498**, *498*
  copy database, **505–506**
  defined, 615
  disabling, **502–503**
  enabling, **500**
  existing storage groups, **500–502**
  preparing for, **499–500**
  seeding, **503–504**
  testing, **505**
Local Continuous Replication tab, *505*
Local delivery rate counter, 585
Local Network Settings page, 171–172, *171*
local procedure call (LPC), 615
lockbox process, 615
log file replay process, 616
.log files, 125–126, 550
log shipping, 497
Logging folder, 97
logical components in Active Directory, **7–10**, *9–10*
logical unit numbers (LUNs)
  configuration and design, **52–53**
  defined, 616
  server clusters, 480
LogicalDisk counters, 584
logs and log files, 125–126, 550
  for avoiding data loss, 538
  circular, **133**
  ESE database, 550
  Exchange Server installation verification, **93–94**, *93–94*
  message tracking, **452–453**
loosely consistent replication, 14
Lossless option
  CCR scheduled outages, **522**
  CCR unscheduled outages, **524–525**
Lotus Notes connector support, 5
LPC (local procedure call), 615
LUNs (logical unit numbers)
  configuration and design, **52–53**
  defined, 616
  server clusters, 480

M

MAC addresses
  NLB, **492–493**
  switch flooding, 496
Mail and Directory Management (MADMAN) MIB, 616
mail attributes, **378–379**
mail-enabled contacts. *See* contacts
mail-enabled groups, **295**
  creating
    Active Directory Users and Computers Console, **302–303**, *302*
    Exchange Management Console, **297–299**, *297–298*
    Exchange Management Shell, **300**, *301*
  distribution. *See* distribution groups
  mail-enabling, **299–300**, *299*, *301*
  modifying, **303–304**
  properties, **304–309**, *304–308*
  scope, **296–297**
  types, **295–296**
mail-enabled users, **260–261**
  creating
    Exchange Management Console, **287–288**
    Exchange Management Shell, **288–289**, *289*
  defined, 616
  managing, **290–291**, *290*
  properties, **291–293**, *291*
  Send As permissions, **293–295**, *294*
mail exchanger (MX) records, 616
Mail Flow Settings tab
  contacts, **321**
  distribution groups, **307–309**, *308*
  mail-enabled users, **293**
  mailboxes, **278–280**, *278*

Mail.que file, 446
Mail Settings page, 287–288
Mail Submission service, 98, 149, *579*
Mailbox Assistants service, 98, *579*
Mailbox Database.edb file, 124
mailbox databases
  defined, 616
  recovering, **559–562**
Mailbox delivery queue, 437
mailbox-enabled users, **260–261**
  creating, **263–266**, *263–265*
  defined, 616
  enabling, **266–267**, *266*
  mailbox properties
    Account, **281**, *282*
    Address and Phone, **275**, *275*
    E-Mail Addresses, **282**, *283*
    General, **273–274**, *274*
    Mail Flow Settings, **278–280**, *278*
    Mailbox Features, **280**, *281*
    Mailbox Settings, **276–277**, *276*
    Member Of, **281**, *282*
    Organization, **276**, *276*
    User Information, **274**, *275*
  managing, **272–273**, *273*
Mailbox Features tab, **280**, *281*, 419
Mailbox folder, 97
Mailbox Server Role Storage Requirements Calculator, 41, *42*
Mailbox servers, 18, **34**
  backing up and recovering, **567**
  databases, **136**
    configuring, **140–142**, *140–142*
    creating, **136–139**, *137–139*
    deleting, **146–147**, *147*
    mounting and dismounting, **145–146**, *146*
  defined, 616
  storage and storage groups, **127**
    creating, **127–131**, *127–132*
    deleting, **147–148**
    paths, **134–136**, *134–136*
    properties, **131–134**, *132*
    structure, **124–127**, *125*
    viewing, **143–145**, *143–145*
Mailbox Service Availability report, 593
Mailbox Settings page, **276–277**, *276*
  disconnected mailboxes, 286, *286*
  mailbox-enabled users, 265–267, *265*
  managed folders, 349
  postmaster mailbox, 156
  resource mailboxes, 322
mailboxes
  aliases, 457–458
  defined, 616
  deleted, **283–286**, *283–286*
    recovering, **556–558**, *556–558*
    retention, 539
  moving, **453–454**
    bulk management, **459–460**
    Exchange Management Console, **454–456**, *454–456*
    Exchange Management Shell, **456–459**, *457–458*
  POP3 and IMAP4 clients, **412–413**
  reports, **596–600**, *597*
  requirements, 44
  resource, **321–322**
    creating, **322–324**, *323*
    managing, **324**
    properties, **324–326**, *325–327*
    working with, **328**
  SCC, 507
  size, **464–465**, *464–465*
Mailflow Local Service Availability report, 593
Mailflow Remote Service Availability report, 593
Maintain Per-User Read and Unread Information for This Folder option, 385
majority node set (MNS)
  clusters, 616
  quorums, **513–515**
Manage Mobile Device Wizard, 425
managed content settings, 343, **346–348**, *347*
managed folders, **343–345**
  assistant, **350–351**, *350*
  creating, **345–346**, *345*
  mailbox policies, 343, **346**, **348–349**, *348–349*
management information base (MIB), *589*, 616
Managing Queues value, 439
MAPI (Messaging Application Programming Interface), 617
MAPI clients, 617
MAPI subsystems, 617
MapiDelivery value, 439
masters, Active Directory, **13–14**
Matching User option, 286
MaxDumpsterSizePerStorageGroup setting, 517
MaxDumpsterTime setting, 517
Maximum Attachment Size setting, 362
Maximum Certainty option, 243
Maximum Concurrent Outbound Connections setting, 153
Maximum Concurrent Outbound Connections per Domain setting, 153
Maximum Failed Password Attempts setting, 362
Maximum Inactivity Time Lock setting, 362
Maximum Number of Recipients to Display link, 315
Maximum Performance option, 243
Maximum Time Since Submission (Days) setting, 153
Member Of tab
  contacts, 320
  distribution groups, 306, *306*
  mail-enabled users, 292
  mailboxes, **281**, *282*

Members tab, 305, *305*
Memory counters, 584
memory requirements
  Exchange Server, **38–41**
  LCR, 500
message compliance, **342–343**
Message Count value, 440
Message Delivery Restrictions dialog box
  contacts, 321
  distribution groups, 309
  mail-enabled users, 293
  mail flow, 280, *280*
Message Format tab
  accepted domains, 160, *161*
  remote domains, 160
message queues
  databases, 564
  reports, **594–596**
Message Size Restrictions dialog box
  contacts, 321
  distribution groups, 309
  mail-enabled users, 293
  mail flow, 278–280
Message Source Name field, 443
message state information, 617
message tracking, **448**, *448*
  configuring, **451–453**, *451*
  disabling or enabling, **452**
  logs, **452–453**, 564
  process, **448–451**, *449–450*
messages
  classifications, **351–353**, *352*
  content settings, **346–348**, *347*
  flow, **17–18**
  queues. *See* queues
  recovery, **553–562**, *554*, *556–558*
  routing, **149**
Messages Received/sec counter, 585
Messages Sent/sec counter, 585
Messaging and Security Feature Pack (MSFP), **414**, *415*
Messaging Application Programming Interface (MAPI), 617
messaging records management (MRM), **343–344**
Messaging Records Management option, 276, 350
MIB (management information base), 589, 616
Microsoft Clustering Service (MSCS), 617
Microsoft Exchange System Objects container, 62–63, *63*
Microsoft Management Console (MMC), 617
Microsoft Office Outlook 2007, 617
Microsoft Office SharePoint Server (MOSS), 180, 425
Microsoft Operations Manager (MOM), 499
  availability reports, 592–593
  benefits, 599
Microsoft Search Service, 617
migration
  defined, 617
  organization changes for, **63–64**
MIME (Multipurpose Internet Mail Extensions), 618
Minimum Password Length setting, 362
MMC (Microsoft Management Console), 617
MNS (majority node set)
  clusters, 616
  quorums, **513–515**
mobile devices
  configuring, **420–425**, *420–424*
  policies, **361–363**, *363*
/mode option, 88
Modify the Current Certificate Assignment page, 194, *194*
Modify the Maximum Number of Recipients to Display link, 262
MOM (Microsoft Operations Manager), 499
  availability reports, 592–593
  benefits, 599
monitoring
  backups jobs, **547**
  exam essentials, **600**
  hardware, **589**
  performance, **583–585**, *583–584*
  Performance Troubleshooter for, **586–589**, *586–588*
  review questions, **601–603**
  server services, **578–583**, *580–582*
  summary, **600**
Monitoring service, 99, 579
MOSS (Microsoft Office SharePoint Server), 180, 425
Mount-Database cmdlet, 146, 562
Mount This Database option, 137, 376
mounting
  databases, **145–146**, *146*
  defined, 617
Move-ClusteredMailboxServer cmdlet, 512, 523
Move-Mailbox cmdlet, 456–459, 560
Move Mailbox option
  mail-enabled users, 291
  mailbox-enabled user, 273
  resource mailboxes, 324
Move Mailbox Wizard, 454, *454*, 460
Move Options page, 455, *455*
Move Schedule page, 455–456, *455*
Move Storage Group Path link, 134
Move Storage Group Path Wizard, 134, *134*
move-StorageGroupPath cmdlet, 135–136
MoveAllReplicas.ps1 script, 381
moving mailboxes, **453–454**
  bulk management, **459–460**
  Exchange Management Console, **454–456**, *454–456*
  Exchange Management Shell, **456–459**, *457–458*

MRM (messaging records management), **343–344**
MSCS (Microsoft Clustering Service), 617
MSExchange Store Interface counters, *585*
MSExchangeIS counters, *585*
MSExchangeSyncAppPool pool, 416
MSExchangeTransport SmtpReceive counters, *585*
MSFP (Messaging and Security Feature Pack), **414**, *415*
MSI file (installer package), 614
msilog file, 93, *94*
MST file (installer transform), 614
multicast support in NLB, **492–493**
multimaster replication model, 617
multipathing
  defined, 617
  server cluster configuration, 480
Multiple Users Are Complaining of Delays While Using Outlook option, 587
Multipurpose Internet Mail Extensions (MIME), 618
MX (mail exchanger) records, 616

N

Name and Security Settings page, 195, *195*
name resolution, **48–49**, *49*, 618
names
  certificates, 195, *195*
  databases, 140
  organizations, 83
  remote domains, 158
  SMTP domains, 159
  storage groups, 129
namespaces, 16, 618
nbtstat utility, 618
netdiag tool, **49–50**, 618
NetLogons checks, 49
netstat utility, 618
network load balancing (NLB), 477, **489–490**, *489*
  cluster parameters, **491–493**, *492*
  defined, 618
  DNS round-robin, **497**
  enabling, **491**, *491*
  host parameters, **493**, *494*
  host TCP/IP properties, 496
  port rules, **493–495**, *494–495*
  switch flooding, **496–497**
Network News Transfer Protocol (NNTP), 5, 618
Network Security page, 105, *105*
Network Settings page, 165–166, *165*
Network tab
  receive connectors, **174**, *175*
  send connectors, **167–168**, *168*
networks
  diagnostics tests, **49–50**, *50*
  Exchange Server requirements, **42–43**
  SCC requirements, 508
  server clusters, 479, 482, *482*
Neutral option, 243
New Accepted Domain Wizard, 161–162, *161*
new-AcceptedDomain cmdlet, 162
New ActiveSync Policy Wizard, 362–363, *363*
New-ActiveSyncMaiboxPolicy cmdlet, 363
New-ActiveSyncPolicy cmdlet, 418
New-ActiveSyncVirtualDirectory cmdlet, 416
New Address List Wizard, 360, *360*
New-AddressList cmdlet, 361
New Cluster Wizard, 514
New Content Setting Wizard, 347
New Custom Managed Folder Wizard, 345, *345*
New Distribution Group Wizard, 298–299, *298*
new-DistributionGroup cmdlet, 300
New Dynamic Distribution Group Wizard, 310–311, *310–311*
new-DynamicDistributionGroup cmdlet, 312
New Edge Subscription Wizard, 210, 214–215, *214–215*
New-EdgeSubscription cmdlet, 212, 215
New Email Address Policy Wizard, 358, *358*
New-EmailAddressPolicy cmdlet, 359
New Exchange ActiveSync Mailbox Policy, 362
New-ExchangeCertificate cmdlet, 409–410
new features, **2–4**
New Group option, 298
New Mail Contact Wizard, 316–317, *316*
New Mail User Wizard, 287–288
New-Mailbox cmdlet, 267–268, 323, 462
New Mailbox Database Wizard, 137, *137*
New Mailbox page, 266–267, 322
New Mailbox Wizard
  mailbox-enabled users, 263–266, *263–265*
  postmaster mailbox, 155, *155*
  resource mailboxes, 322
New-MailboxDatabase cmdlet, 562
New-MailContact cmdlet, 317
new-MailUser cmdlet, 288
New Managed Content Settings Wizard, 347, *347*
New Managed Folder Mailbox Policy Wizard, 348, *348*
New Managed Folder Wizard, 345
New-ManagedContentSettings cmdlet, 348
New-ManagedFolder cmdlet, 346
New-ManagedFolderMailboxPolicy cmdlet, 349
New-MessageClassification cmdlet, 353
New Object - Contact dialog box, 318, *318*
New Object - Group dialog box, 302, *302*
New Object - User dialog box, 271, *271*
New Public Folder Database Wizard, 376
New-PublicFolder cmdlet, 378

New-PublicFolderDatabase cmdlet, 380
new-ReceiveConnector cmdlet, 172
New Remote Domain Wizard, 158, *158*
new-RemoteDomain cmdlet, 158
new-SendConnector cmdlet, 166
New Server Cluster Wizard, 484–487, *484–487*
New SMTP Receive Connector Wizard, 171–172, *171–172*
New SMTP Send Connector Wizard, 165, *165*
New Storage Group link, 128, *128*
New Storage Group Wizard, 129–130, *129–130*, 501
New-StorageGroup cmdlet, 502, 561
New Transport Rule Wizard, 356, *356*
New-TransportRule cmdlet, 356
New User option
  mail-enabled users, 287
  mailbox-enabled users, 264
/NewCms option, 89
/NewProvisionedServer option, 89
Next Hop Domain field, **439**
Next Retry Time value, 440
NLB. *See* network load balancing (NLB)
NNTP (Network News Transfer Protocol), 5, 618
nodes, 618
non-MAPI clients, 179
Nonediting Author role permissions, 402
nonprovisionable devices, 418
NonSmtpGatewayDelivery value, 439
normal backups, 618
/NoSelfSignedCertificates option, 90
Notes option, 187
notifications
  defined, 618
  Forefront Security for Exchange Server, **246–247**, *247*
Notify Sender When Message Is Delayed More Than (Hours) setting, 153
nouns in cmdlets, 377
Novell GroupWise connector, 5
nslookup utility, 49, *49*, 618

O

OABs (Offline Address Books), 87
  for address lists, 359–360
  configuring, **408**, *409*
  defined, 619
Object Linking and Embedding version 2 (OLE 2), 619
objects
  Active Directory, 7
  defined, 619
Obtain Product Key dialog box, 85, *85*
Offline Address Books (OABs), 87
  for address lists, 359–360
  configuring, **408**, *409*
  defined, 619
Offline address list setting, 142
offline backups, 619
Offline Storage (OST) folder, 619
OLE 2 (Object Linking and Embedding version 2), 619
Open Ports and Approve Applications page, 105, *105*
Open Shortest Path First (OSPF) protocol, 619
Operate area, **246**, *246*
operating systems
  requirements, 38
  server clusters, **481**
operations masters, 13
optical drive requirements, 38
Organization Information page, 195–196, *195*
organization management, **436**
  bulk management, **460–465**, *462–465*
  exam essentials, **467**
  message tracking, **448**, *448*
    configuring, **451–453**, *451*
    disabling or enabling, **452**
    logs, **452–453**, *564*
    process, **448–451**, *449–450*
  for migration, **63–64**
  moving mailboxes, **453–454**
    bulk management, **459–460**
    Exchange Management Console, **454–456**, *454–456*
    Exchange Management Shell, **456–459**, *457–458*
  queues. *See* queues
  review questions, **468–474**
  summary, **466–467**
Organization object, 619
Organization tab
  contacts, 320
  mail-enabled users, 292
  mailboxes, **276**, *276*
organizational units (OUs), **7–8**, 619
/OrganizationName option, 88
OSPF (Open Shortest Path First) protocol, 619
OST (Offline Storage) folder, 619
OUs (organizational units), **7–8**, 619
outages, CCR
  scheduled, **521–523**
  unscheduled, **523–525**
Outbound Connection Failure Retry Interval (Minutes) setting, 153
Outlook
  Autodiscover with, 405–406, *406*
  deleted items in, *555*
  public folders with, **382–384**, *383–384*

Outlook Anywhere
configuring, **190–191**, *190–191*, 407–408, *407–408*
defined, 619
Outlook Anywhere tab, 191, *191*
Outlook Web Access (OWA), **179**
Authentication settings, **185**, *186*
defined, 619
deleted items in, 555
General settings, 183, *185*
mobile devices, 424, *424*
Private Computer File Access settings, 189
Public Computer File Access settings, **187–189**, *188–189*
Remote File Servers settings, 190
for resource mailboxes, **326**, *327*
Segmentation settings, **185–187**, *186*
for SharePoint and file server access, **180–183**, *180–184*
Outlook Web Access External Service Availability report, 593
Outlook Web Access Internal Service Availability report, 593
outsourced dial tone, 540
OWA. *See* Outlook Web Access (OWA)
OWA Light, 619
Owner role permissions, 402

P

PAB (Personal Address Book), 620
Pages/sec counter, 584
partitions, Active Directory, **12–13**, **17**
Partner Mail classification, 352
Partners permission group, 177
passive node computers, **508–512**, *509–512*
Password Enabled setting, 361
Password Expiration setting, 361
Password History setting, 362
password page
ActiveSync, 418, *418*
users, 272, *272*
Password Recovery setting, 362
passwords
ActiveSync, 361–362, 416, 418, *418*
mailboxes, 463
mobile devices, 421, *421*
server clusters, 483
users, 268–269, *268*, 272, *272*
patch files, 619
Path field, 385
pathping command, 620
paths
public folders, 385
storage groups, **134–136**, *134–136*
PDC (Primary Domain Controller) emulators
defined, 621
masters, **14**
Pending Certificate Request page, 197, *197*
PendingRemove value, 443
PendingSuspend value, 443
Perform a Remote Wipe to Clear Mobile Device Data option, 425
Performance console, 583
Performance Details tab, 589
Performance Monitor, **583–585**, *583–584*, 620
Performance Snap-in tool, 620
Performance Summary tab, 589
Performance Troubleshooter, **586–589**, *586–588*
perimeter networks, 620
Permission Entry dialog box, 294
Permission Groups tab, **176–177**, *176*
permissions
defined, 620
mail-enabled users, **293–295**, *294*
public folders, **380–381**, **399–403**, *400*
receive connectors, **176–177**, *176*
Permissions tab, **399–403**, *400*
Personal Address Book (PAB), 620
Personal Store (PST) folder, 620
PFAdmin tool, 389
PFDAVAdmin (Public Folder DAV Administration) tool, **387–388**
PFInfo tool, 389
PFMigrate.wsf tool, 389
physical components in Active Directory, **10–12**
Pickup folder, 620
ping tool, 620
PKI (public key infrastructure), 621
plain text, 620
Point-to-Point Protocol (PPP), 620
Poison message queue, 437
POISONMESSAGE value, 450
policies
ActiveSync, **416–420**, *417–419*
email address-generation, **356–359**, *358*
exam essentials, **364**
managed folder mailbox, **346**, **348–349**, *348–349*
mobile device, **361–363**, *363*
review questions, **365–371**
summary, **364**
Policy Refresh Interval setting, 362
polling, 620
pools, RID, 14
POP3 (Post Office Protocol version 3) protocol, 99, 579
Client Access server settings, 563
clients, **410–411**
configuring, **413–414**
mailboxes, **412–413**
receiver connectors, **413**

server, **412**
services, **411–412**, *412*
defined, 620
populating groups, **463**
port flooding, 497
port numbers, 620
port rules in NLB, **493–495**, *494–495*
portability, database, *539*
post-installation configuration, **84–87**, *85–86*
Post Office Protocol. *See* POP3 (Post Office Protocol version 3) protocol
postmaster mailboxes
defined, 621
Hub Transport servers, **154–156**, *154–156*
PowerShell
benefits, **114–115**
Exchange Server installation verification, **91**, *92*
PPP (Point-to-Point Protocol), 620
Premium Client option, 187
/PrepareAD command, *55–56*, *59–61*, *61*
/PrepareDomain command, *55–56*, *59*, **62–63**, *65*
/PrepareLegacyExchangePermissions command, **63–65**
/PrepareSchema command, **55–59**
Primary Domain Controller (PDC) emulators
defined, 621
masters, **14**
priorities
public folder replication, 396
server clusters, 482, *482*
Private Computer File Access tab, 183, *183*, 189–190
private keys, 621
private networks, TCP/IP configuration for, **482–483**
Process the Pending Request option, 197
Processing Security Configuration Database page, 101
Processor counters, *585*
processor requirements, **38–39**
% Processor Time counter, *585*
Product Key, 85–86
Progress page
CCR, *520*
Exchange Server installation, 82, *82*
SCC, *510*
properties
accepted domains, **160–162**, *160*
ActiveSync, 418–420, *418–419*
contacts, **319–321**, *320–321*
databases, **140–142**, *140–142*
defined, 621
distribution groups, **304–309**, *304–308*
dynamic distribution groups, **313**, *313–314*
Hub Transport servers, **150–153**, *150–153*
IP allow lists, **220–221**, *221*
mail-enabled users, **291–293**, *291*
mailboxes, 144, *145*
Account, **281**, *282*
Address and Phone, **275**, *275*
E-Mail Addresses, **282**, *283*
General, **273–274**, *274*
Mail Flow Settings, **278–280**, *278*
Mailbox Features, **280**, *281*
Mailbox Settings, **276–277**, *276*
Member Of, **281**, *282*
Organization, **276**, *276*
resource, **324–326**, *325–327*
User Information, **274**, *275*
Outlook Anywhere, **191**, *191*
OWA, **181–190**, *181–183*, *185–186*, *188*
public folders, 383–387, *384–387*
Advanced, 398, *399*
General, **398**, *398*
Permissions, **399–403**, *400*
replication, **394–398**, *394–396*
queues, **445–447**, *446–447*
send connectors, **167–169**, *167–169*
storage groups, **131–134**, *132*
Properties task for queued messages, 444
Proposed Cluster Configuration page, 487, *487*, *515*
Providers tab, 220, *221*, 223, *223*
PST (Personal Store) folder, 620
Public Computer File Access tab, 182, *182*, **187–189**, *188*
public databases, 621
Public folder, 97
Public Folder DAV Administration (PFDAVAdmin) tool, **387–388**
Public Folder Migration Tool, 389
public folders, 260, **374–375**
complicated tasks, **381–382**
databases, **375–376**, **380**
defined, 621
exam essentials, **427**
general tasks, **377**
hierarchy, **389–390**, 621
mail attributes, **378–379**
management options, **376–377**
managing, **392**, *393*
with Outlook, **382–384**, *383–384*
permissions, **380–381**
properties, **397–398**
Advanced, 398, *399*
General, **398**, *398*
Permissions, **399–403**, *400*
Public Folder DAV Administration tool, **387–388**
referrals, 621
replicating, **390–391**, *391*, **394–397**, *394–396*, 621
review questions, **428–433**
specific folder tasks, **377–378**
summary, **426–427**

support, *6*
System Manager for, **384–387**, *385–387*, **392**, *393*
Public Folders list, 359
public-key encryption, 621
public key infrastructure (PKI), 621
public keys, 621
public networks, TCP/IP configuration for, **481–482**
Publishing Author role permissions, 402
Publishing Editor role permissions, 402
purging mailboxes, 284
push email, 414

Q

Quarantine area, **248**, *249*
Quarantine Security Settings page, 236–237, *237*
queue folders, 621
Queue ID field, 443
Queue Viewer Options dialog box, 445, *446*
Queue Viewer tool, **438–440**, *438*, *440*, 621
queues, **436**
managing, **437–442**, *438*, *440–442*
message management, **442–445**, *443–445*
overview, **436–437**
properties, **445–447**, *446–447*
reports, **594–596**
quorum disks, 622

R

RAID Levels, **53–54**
Raise Domain Functional Level dialog box, 57, *57*
random failover, 622
Read Items permission, 401–402
Readiness Checks page
CCR, 520, *520*
Exchange Server installation, 82, *82*
SCC, 510, *510*
Ready value, 443
receive connectors
POP3 and IMAP4 clients, **413**
SMTP, 163, **169–177**, *170–173*, *175–176*
RECEIVE value, 450
recipient filtering, **224**, *224*
Recipient Filtering Properties dialog box, 224, *224*
Recipient Update Service (RUS)
in migration, **63–64**
support, 5, 356–357
recipients, **260–261**
defined, 622
exam essentials, **329**
mail contacts. *See* contacts
mail-enabled groups. *See* mail-enabled groups
mail-enabled users. *See* mail-enabled users
mailbox-enabled users. *See* mailbox-enabled users
resource mailboxes. *See* resource mailboxes
review questions, **330–339**
summary, **328–329**
record management, **342–343**
/RecoverCms option, 89
RecoverServer option, 539
recovery. *See* disaster recovery
recovery servers, 622
recovery storage groups (RSGs), *560*, 622
REDIRECT value, 450
redundant components
for avoiding data loss, 538
server clusters, 480
registry settings
Client Access server, 563
Hub Transport servers, 564
message classifications, 353
server roles, 100, *100*, 106, *106*
Registry Settings page, 106, *106*
regular expressions, 622
Reject option, 231
relative identifier (RID) masters, **14**, 622
Reminders and Notifications option, 187
remote delivery, 437, 623
remote domains
creating, **157–160**, *157–159*
defined, 623
Remote File Servers tab, 181, *181*
Remote Network Settings page, 172, *172*
remote procedure calls (RPCs), 623
Remove-AttachmentFilterEntry cmdlet, 230
Remove-DistributionGroup cmdlet, 304
Remove-DynamicDistributionGroup cmdlet, 313
Remove-ExchangeAdministrator cmdlet, 113
Remove-Mailbox cmdlet, 284, 324
remove-mailboxesdatabase cmdlet, 146
Remove-MailContact cmdlet, 319
Remove-MailUser cmdlet, 291
Remove-Message cmdlet, 442, 444
Remove Messages (with NDR) task, 441
Remove Messages (Without Sending NDR) task, 441
Remove-PublicFolder cmdlet, 378
Remove-PublicFolderAdministrativePermission cmdlet, 381
Remove-PublicFolderClientPermission cmdlet, 381
Remove-PublicFolderDatabase cmdlet, 380
remove-StorageGroup cmdlet, 147
Remove (with NDR) task, 443
Remove (Without Sending NDR) task, 444
/RemoveCms option, 89
/RemoveProvisionedServer option, 89

RemoveReplicaFromPFRecursive.ps1 cmdlet, 381–382
/RemoveUm LanguagePack option, 89
removing and Remove option
- contacts, 319
- distribution groups, 304
- mail-enabled users, 291
- mailbox-enabled users, 273
- resource mailboxes, 324
- roles, **198**
- users and groups, 113

repairing databases, **548–553**, *548*, *551–553*
ReplaceReplicaOnPFRecursive.ps1 cmdlet, 382
ReplaceUserPermissionOnPFRecursive.ps1 cmdlet, 382
ReplaceUserWithUserOnPFRecursive.ps1 cmdlet, 382
replaying transaction log files, 551
replicas, 623
replication
- Active Directory, **14–17**
- CCR. *See* cluster continuous replication (CCR)
- dcdiag for, 49
- defined, 623
- LCR. *See* local continuous replication (LCR)
- public folders, **390–391**, *391*, **394–397**, *394–396*

Replication Service, 99, *579*
Replication Status dialog box, 396, *396*
Replication tab, 385, *386*, 395, *395*
reports
- availability, **592–593**
- database and message queue, **594–596**
- Forefront Security for Exchange Server, **246–248**, *247–248*
- health, **589–592**, *590–592*
- mailbox and user usage, **596–600**, *597*

Request File Summary page, 197
reserved log files, 550, 623
RESOLVE value, 450
resolving addresses, 623
Resource Custom Properties field, 325
resource groups, 623
Resource Information tab, **325–326**, *325*
resource mailboxes, **321–322**
- creating, **322–324**, *323*
- managing, **324**
- properties, **324–326**, *325–327*
- working with, **328**

Resource Settings option, 326
Restart Exchange Transport Service page, 239, *239*
Restore-StorageGroupCopy cmdlet, 505–506
restoring
- Client Access server, **563–564**
- database files, 552
- defined, 623
- Edge Transport servers, **565–566**
- Hub Transport servers, **564**
- mailbox databases, **559–562**
- mailbox servers, **567**

resume-generating events (RGEs), 537
Resume Local Continuous Replication option, 504
Resume-Message cmdlet, 444
Resume-PublicFolderReplication cmdlet, 378
Resume-Queue cmdlet, 441
Resume task, 441, 443
Retry-Queue cmdlet, 442
Retry Remote Delivery Queue Length counter, 585
Retry task, 441, 443
Reviewer role permissions, 402
RGCs (routing group connectors), 623
RGEs (resume-generating events), 537
rich-text (EDB) files, 124, 126, 550, 623
RID (relative identifier) masters, **14**, 622
RIDManager checks, 49
Rights Management Service (RMS) Exchange Agents, **351**
risk management and identification process, 476
Role-Based Service Configuration page, 101
roles
- Active Directory, **13–14**
- adding and removing, **198**
- Administrative, **109**
  - configuring, **110–113**, *110–114*
  - overview, **109–110**
- Client Access server. *See* Client Access servers
- defined, 623
- exam essentials, **199**
- Exchange Server, **34–37**
- extensions for, 100, *100*
- Hub Transport server. *See* Hub Transport server
- installing, **76–77**
- Mailbox server. *See* Mailbox servers
- permissions, **402**
- review questions, **200–205**
- selecting, 102, *102*
- summary, **198**

/roles option, 88
Room Mailbox option, 322
root CAs, 623
root domains, 9–10, **59–61**, *60–61*, 623
round-robin DNS, **497**
routing group connectors (RGCs), 623
routing group masters, 623
routing groups, 5, 623
RPC Averaged Latency counter, 585
RPC Latency average (msec) counter, 585
RPC Requests counter, 585
RPCs (remote procedure calls), 623
RSGs (recovery storage groups), 560, 622
RTF (rich-text format), 623
rules
- defined, 623
- exam essentials, **364**
- firewall ports, **210–211**

port, **493–495**, *494–495*
review questions, **365–371**
summary, **364**
transport, **354–355**
address lists, **359–361**, *360*
creating, **355–356**, *356*
email address-generation policies, **356–359**, *358*
Run Job area, 246, *246*
Run Update-StorageGroupCopy cmdlet, 503
RUS (Recipient Update Service)
in migration, **63–64**
support, 5, *356–357*

S

S/MIME (Secure/Multipurpose Internet Mail Extensions), 624
SANs (storage area networks), 480, 625
Sarbanes-Oxley (SOX) Act, 343
SAS (Serial-attached SCSI) disks, **51**
SATA (Serial ATA) interface, **51–52**
Save Security Policy page, 107
scalability, 624
Scan Job section, **241**, *241–242*
Scanner Updates area, **243–245**, *244*
SCC (single copy cluster), 478
defined, 624
installing, **508–512**, *509–512*
overview, **506–507**, *507*
requirements, **507–508**
Schedule+ Free Busy public folders, 624
schedules
CFR outages, **521–523**
database routines, 141
managed folders assistant, 350, *350*
moving mailboxes, 455, *455*
tape rotation, 543
Schema Admins group, 54
schema masters, 13, 624
schemas
Active Directory, **12**, **55–59**
defined, 624
partitions, **12–13**, 17
SCL field, 443
SCL (spam confidence level) value, 218
scope in mail-enabled groups, **296–297**
SCPs (service connection points), 404
Scripts folder, 97
SCSI devices, 480
SCW (Security Configuration Wizard), **48**, **99–108**, *100–108*
scwcmd register, 100
Search Folders option, 187
Search Indexer service, 99, 579
Search service, 99, 579
Second Storage Group, 131
secret keys, 624
Secure Mode in Forefront Security for Exchange Server, 237
Secure/Multipurpose Internet Mail Extensions (S/MIME), 624
Secure Sockets Layer (SSL)
configuring, **191–197**, *192–197*, **409–410**
defined, 624
security, **208**
Edge Transport server. *See* Edge Transport server
exam essentials, **250**
Forefront Security for Exchange Server. *See* Forefront Security for Exchange Server
review questions, **251–258**
Security Configuration Wizard, **99–108**, *100–108*
summary, **250**
Security Configuration Wizard (SCW), **48**, **99–108**, *100–108*
security groups
defined, 624
mail-enabled, 303
working with, **295**
security identifiers (SIDs), 14
Security Policy File Name page, 107, *107*
Security tab, 294, *294*
seeding LCR, **503–504**
Segmentation tab, **185–187**, *186*
Select a Best Practices Scan to View page, *592*, *592*
Select a Public Store dialog box, 395, *395*
Select Additional Services page, 103, *103*
Select Administration and Other Options page, 103, *103*
Select Client Features page, 102, *102*
Select Computers page, 515
Select Contact dialog box, 317
Select Group dialog box, 299–300, *299*
Select-Object cmdlet, 595
Select Organizational Unit dialog box
contacts, 316
mail-enabled users, 287
mailbox-enabled users, 265, *265*
resource mailboxes, 322
Select Program Folder page, 239, *239*
Select Resource Custom Property dialog box, 326, *326*
Select Server page, 101
Select Server Roles page, 102, *102*
Select User dialog box
mail-enabled users, 288
mailbox-enabled users, 266–267, *266*
Select User, Computer, or Group dialog box, 294
self-signed SSL certificates, 192
Send As permissions, **293–295**, *294*
send connectors, **163–169**, *165–169*
Send Delivery Reports to Group Manager option, 307

Send Delivery Reports to Message Originator option, 307
Send Out-of-Office Messages to Originator option, 307
SEND value, 450
Sender Confidence tab, 227, *227*
sender filtering, **224–227**, *226–227*
Sender Filtering Properties dialog box, 224–225, *225*
Sender ID Properties dialog box, 226, *226*
sender reputation level (SRL), 227
Sender Reputation Properties dialog box, 226–227, *227*
Serial ATA (SATA) interface, **51–52**
Serial-attached SCSI (SAS) disks, **51**
Server Certificate page, 194–195, *194–195*
server clusters
  CCR. *See* cluster continuous replication (CCR)
  disk configuration, **484**
  hardware, **479–480**
  installing, **478–479**
  operating systems, **481**
  service accounts, **483–484**
  service configuration, **484–488**, *484–488*
  single copy clusters, **506–512**, *507*, *509–512*
  TCP/IP configuration, **481–483**
Server Configuration folder, 137
Server Configuration node, 85, *85*
Server Role Selection page
  CCR, 520
  SCC, 510
/ServerAdmin option, 89
servers
  adding and removing, **198**
  Client Access. *See* Client Access servers
  Edge Transport. *See* Edge Transport server
  Hub Transport. *See* Hub Transport server
  licenses, **33**, 624
  Mailbox. *See* Mailbox servers
  new features, 3
  POP3 and IMAP4 clients, **412**
  SMTP, **211–212**, *212*, 625
Service Availability Summary report, 593
service connection points (SCPs), 404
Service Host service, 99, 579
service providers, 624
services
  directory, **42–43**
  monitoring, **578–583**, *580–582*
  POP3 and IMAP4 clients, **411–412**, *412*
  server clusters, **483–484**
  verifying, **97–99**, *98*
Services console, **580**, *580*
Services node, 94
Set-ActiveSyncVirtualDirectory cmdlet, 416
Set-AttachmentFilterListConfig cmdlet, 231–232
Set-CASMailbox cmdlet, 412–413, 420
Set-Mailbox cmdlet, 350
Set-MailboxCalendarSettings cmdlet, 326
Set-MailboxDatabase cmdlet, 562
Set-MailboxServer cmdlet, 351, 452
Set-MailPublicFolder cmdlet, 379
Set-OABVirtualDirectory cmdlet, 408
Set Paths page, 500
Set-PublicFolder cmdlet, 379
Set-PublicFolderDatabase cmdlet, 380
Set-ReceiveConnector cmdlet, 280
Set-ResourceConfig cmdlet, 325
Set-SendConnector cmdlet, 280
Set-Service msExchangeIMAP4 cmdlet, 411
Set-Service msExchangePOP3 cmdlet, 411
Set-TransportConfig cmdlet, 211, 279, 518, 565
Set-TransportServer cmdlet, 156, 452–453
Set-WebServicesVirtualDirectory cmdlet, 409
setup.com command, 87–89
Setup folder, 97
setup log files, **93–94**, *93–94*
SharePoint
  configuring, **180–182**, *180–181*
  disabling, **182–183**, *182–183*
  Microsoft Office SharePoint Server, 180, 425
sharing content and information. *See* public folders
SIDs (security identifiers), 14
signing, 187, 624
SilentDelete option, 231
SIM (Systems Insight Manager), 589
Simple Display Name setting, 306
simple display names, 306, 624
Simple Mail Transfer Protocol (SMTP)
  connectors, **163–164**
    defined, 625
    deleting, **178**
    receive, **169–177**, *170–173*, *175–176*
    send, **163–169**, *165–169*
  defined, 624
  domains, 158–159
  mail-enabled users, 287–288
  servers
    EdgeSync, **211–212**, *212*
    virtual, 625
Simple Network Management Protocol (SNMP), 589, 624
single copy cluster (SCC), 478
  defined, 624
  installing, **508–512**, *509–512*
  overview, **506–507**, *507*
  requirements, **507–508**
single-instance storage, 625
site link object replication, 15
sites, 625
64-bit features, 3

size
  mailbox, **464–465**, *464*
  message tracking logs, **452–453**
  queued messages, 443
Size (KB) field, 443
Skip:Detect Only option, 243
smart hosts, 625
SmartHostConnectorDelivery value, 439
SMTP. *See* Simple Mail Transfer Protocol (SMTP)
SMTP Address dialog box, 287–288
SmtpRelaytoRemoteAdSite value, 439
SmtpRelaytoTiRg value, 439
SmtpRelayWithinAdSite value, 439
SmtpRelayWithinAdSitetoEdge value, 439
SNMP (Simple Network Management Protocol), *589*, 624
software
  requirements, **43–44**
  SCC, 508
Source IP field, 443
Source Server page, 166, **169**, *169*
SOX (Sarbanes-Oxley) Act, 343
spam confidence level (SCL) value, 218
special characters in organization names, 83
Speech Engine service, *99*, *579*
Spelling Checker option, 187
spooling, *625*
SRL (sender reputation level), 227
SSL (Secure Sockets Layer)
  configuring, **191–197**, *192–197*, **409–410**
  defined, 624
stand-alone CAs, *625*
Standard Edition, **30**, *625*
standard permissions, 625
Start a New Best Practices Scan page, *591*, *591*
Start Copying Files page, 239
Start-EdgeSynchronization cmdlet, 215
Start-Service cmdlet, 411–412
Status field, 440, 443
storage and storage groups, **124–127**
  configuring, **50–54**, *51*
  creating, **127–131**, *127–132*
  databases, **124–125**, *125*
  defined, *625*
  deleting, **147–148**
  guidelines, **148**
  LCR, **500–502**
  memory requirements, **40–41**, *42*
  paths, **134–136**, *134–136*
  properties, **131–134**, *132*
  public folders. *See* public folders
  viewing, **143–145**, *143–145*
storage area networks (SANs), 480, *625*
Storage Limits setting, 386
Storage Quotas dialog box, 276, *276*
store-and-forward method, 626
Store.exe process, 625
stories, *565*
streaming backups
  legacy, **541**
  support for, 6
streaming database support, *5*
Strip option, 231
Subject field, 443
Submission queue, 437
SUBMIT value, 450
subnet masks, 481, 483
subordinate CAs, 626
subsystems, 626
support agreements, 538
Suspend Local Continuous Replication option, 504
Suspend-Message cmdlet, 444
Suspend-PublicFolderReplication cmdlet, 378
Suspend-Queue cmdlet, 441
Suspend-StorageGroupCopy cmdlet, 503
Suspend task, 441, 443
Suspended value, 443
switch flooding, **496–497**
synchronization event log entries, 215, *216*
System Attendant service, *99*, *579*
System log, 581
System Manager, **384–387**, *385–387*, **392**, *393*
system state backups, 626
Systems Insight Manager (SIM), 589

T

Tag Text dialog box, 241, *242*
tape rotation schedules, 543
/TargetDir option, 88
Task Manager, 626
Tasks option, 187
TCP/IP configuration
  Network Load Balancing, 496
  server clusters, **481–483**
telnet tool, 626
templates
  defined, 626
  Forefront Security for Exchange Server, 241–242
temporary database, 550
testing
  backups, **547–548**
  LCR, **505**
Theme Selection option, 187
third-party dial tones, 561
third-party SSL certificates, **192–197**, *193–197*
Third Storage Group, 131
This Object Only from the Apply Onto list, 294
TLS (Transport Layer Security)
  encryption, 626
  receive connectors, 174
  send connectors, 168
Tmp.edb file, 126, 446, 550

tokens, 626
top-level folders, 626
topology checking, 50
Topology service, 98, *578*
tracert utility, 626
transaction logs, 125–126
  for avoiding data loss, 538
  defined, 627
  ESE database, 550
TRANSFER value, 450
Transient Failure Retry Attempts setting, 153
Transient Failure Retry Interval (Seconds) setting, 153
transitive trust relationships, 9
transport dumpster, **517–518**
Transport Layer Security (TLS)
  encryption, 626
  receive connectors, 174
  send connectors, 168
Transport Log Search service, 99, *579*
transport rules, **354–355**
  address lists, **359–361**, *360*
  creating, **355–356**, *356*
  email address-generation policies, **356–359**, *358*
Transport Rules tab, *355–356*
Transport service, 99, *579*
TransportRoles folder, 97
Triple Data Encryption Standard (3DES), 627
Trn.chk file, 446
Trn.log file, 446
Trnres00001.jrs file, 446
Trntmp.log file, 446
trust relationships, 9
two-node MNS clusters, **514–515**
two of three rule, 480
two-way trust relationships, 9
Typical installation, 80, 627

U

unattended installations, **87–91**, *91*
UNC File Access setting, 362
Undefined value, 439
unicast support in NLB, **492**
Unified Messaging Integration option, 187
Unified Messaging Local Fax Service Availability report, 593
Unified Messaging Local Voice Service Availability report, 593
Unified Messaging Remote Voice Service Availability report, 593
Unified Messaging server and service, 99, *579*
  defined, 627
  functions, **36–37**
  Hub Transport servers for, 18
  new features, 3
  OWA, 187
  requirements, 44
UnifiedMessaging folder, 97
uniform resource identifiers (URIs), 627
uniform resource locators (URLs), 627
universal groups, **296**
Unreachable queue, 437, 439
unscheduled CCR outages, **523–525**
Update-EmailAdressPolicy cmdlet, 357
Update-PublicFolder cmdlet, 379
Update-PublicFolderHierarchy cmdlet, 378
Update-StorageGroupCopy cmdlet, *503–504*
/UpdatesDir option, 88
URIs (uniform resource identifiers), 627
URLs (uniform resource locators), 627
Usenet network, 627
user behavior in memory recommendations, **41**
User Information page
  mail-enabled users, 287, 292
  mailbox-enabled users, 264, *264*
  mailboxes, **274**, *275*
  postmaster mailbox, 155, *155*
  resource mailboxes, 322
User Mailbox option, 266
User Type page
  contacts, 317
  mail-enabled users, 288
  mailbox-enabled users, 264, *264*, 266
  mailboxes, 286
  postmaster mailbox, 155
  resource mailboxes, 322
usernames for mobile devices, 421, *421*
users and user accounts, **260–262**
  anonymous, 176, 402
  creating
    Active Directory Users and Computers, **270–272**, *271–272*
    Exchange Management Console, **262–266**, *262–265*
    Exchange Management Shell, **267–269**, *268–269*
  defined, 627
  deleted, **283–286**, *283–286*
  mail-enabled. *See* mail-enabled users
  mailbox-enabled. *See* mailbox-enabled users
  mailboxes. *See* mailboxes
  removing, 113
  usage reports, **596–600**, *597*
UUENCODE protocol, 627

validating backups jobs, **547**
verbs in cmdlets, 377
verification
    Exchange Server installation
        Active Directory, **94**, *95–96*
        Event Viewer, **92**, *92*
        folder structure, **96–97**, *96*
        PowerShell, **91**, *92*
        services, **97–99**, *98*
        setup log files, **93–94**, *93–94*
    public folder replication, **396–397**, *396*
versions
    Exchange Server, **31–32**, **44–45**
    MSFP information, 414, *415*
View Best Practices Report page, 591, *591*
View Messages task, 441
virtual directories, 406
virtual local area networks (VLANs), 513, 628
virtual servers, 628
Virus Administrators notifications, 247
Virus Recipients (external) notifications, 247
Virus Recipients (internal) notifications, 247
virus scanning API (VSAPI), 6
Virus Sender (external) notifications, 247
Virus Sender (internal) notifications, 247
VLANs (virtual local area networks), 513, 628
volume configuration and design, **52–53**
Volume Shadow Copy Service (VSS), 513, **542**, 628
VSAPI (virus scanning API), 6

W

W3svc service, 628
WAN link replication, 15
Web, 628
web.config file, 563
web pages for Client Access server, 563
Web Server Certificate Wizard, 194, *194*
web service configuration, **409**
WebDAV extension support, 6
WebReady Document Viewing Settings dialog box, 189, *189*
WebReady file types, 189, *189*, 628
well-known port numbers, 628
Windows 2000 mixed domain functional level, 8, 628
Windows 2000 native domain functional level, 8, 628
Windows Components dialog box, 46–47, *47*
Windows Internet Name Service (WINS), 16
    defined, 628
    server clusters, **482–483**
Windows Server 2003 domain functional level, 8, 628
Windows Server 2003 interim domain functional level, 8
Windows Server 2003 sites, **11–12**
Windows Server Catalog, 479
Windows services and components for Exchange Server, **45–48**, *46–47*
Windows sites, **11–12**, 628
WINS (Windows Internet Name Service), 16
    defined, 628
    server clusters, **482–483**
wiping mobile devices, **425**
working log files, 550
World Wide Web (WWW), 629
WSS File Access setting, 362

X.400 message transfer agent, 5
X.400 standard, 629
X.500 standard, 629
X.509 certificates, 629
XML files, 233–234, *233–234*

Your Site's Common Name page, 196, *196*

Wiley Publishing, Inc.
End-User License Agreement

READ THIS. You should carefully read these terms and conditions before opening the software packet(s) included with this book "Book". This is a license agreement "Agreement" between you and Wiley Publishing, Inc. "WPI". By opening the accompanying software packet(s), you acknowledge that you have read and accept the following terms and conditions. If you do not agree and do not want to be bound by such terms and conditions, promptly return the Book and the unopened software packet(s) to the place you obtained them for a full refund.

1. License Grant. WPI grants to you (either an individual or entity) a nonexclusive license to use one copy of the enclosed software program(s) (collectively, the "Software," solely for your own personal or business purposes on a single computer (whether a standard computer or a workstation component of a multi-user network). The Software is in use on a computer when it is loaded into temporary memory (RAM) or installed into permanent memory (hard disk, CD-ROM, or other storage device). WPI reserves all rights not expressly granted herein.

2. Ownership. WPI is the owner of all right, title, and interest, including copyright, in and to the compilation of the Software recorded on the physical packet included with this Book "Software Media". Copyright to the individual programs recorded on the Software Media is owned by the author or other authorized copyright owner of each program. Ownership of the Software and all proprietary rights relating thereto remain with WPI and its licensers.

3. Restrictions On Use and Transfer.

(a) You may only (i) make one copy of the Software for backup or archival purposes, or (ii) transfer the Software to a single hard disk, provided that you keep the original for backup or archival purposes. You may not (i) rent or lease the Software, (ii) copy or reproduce the Software through a LAN or other network system or through any computer subscriber system or bulletin-board system, or (iii) modify, adapt, or create derivative works based on the Software.

(b) You may not reverse engineer, decompile, or disassemble the Software. You may transfer the Software and user documentation on a permanent basis, provided that the transferee agrees to accept the terms and conditions of this Agreement and you retain no copies. If the Software is an update or has been updated, any transfer must include the most recent update and all prior versions.

4. Restrictions on Use of Individual Programs. You must follow the individual requirements and restrictions detailed for each individual program in the About the CD-ROM appendix of this Book or on the Software Media. These limitations are also contained in the individual license agreements recorded on the Software Media. These limitations may include a requirement that after using the program for a specified period of time, the user must pay a registration fee or discontinue use. By opening the Software packet(s), you will be agreeing to abide by the licenses and restrictions for these individual programs that are detailed in the About the CD-ROM appendix and/or on the Software Media. None of the material on this Software Media or listed in this Book may ever be redistributed, in original or modified form, for commercial purposes.

5. Limited Warranty.

(a) WPI warrants that the Software and Software Media are free from defects in materials and workmanship under normal use for a period of sixty (60) days from the date of purchase of this Book. If WPI receives notification within the warranty period of defects in materials or workmanship, WPI will replace the defective Software Media.

(b) WPI AND THE AUTHOR(S) OF THE BOOK DISCLAIM ALL OTHER WARRANTIES, EXPRESS OR IMPLIED, INCLUDING WITHOUT LIMITATION IMPLIED WARRANTIES OF MERCHANTABILITY AND FITNESS FOR A PARTICULAR PURPOSE, WITH RESPECT TO THE SOFTWARE, THE PROGRAMS, THE SOURCE CODE CONTAINED THEREIN, AND/OR THE TECHNIQUES DESCRIBED IN THIS BOOK. WPI DOES NOT WARRANT THAT THE FUNCTIONS CONTAINED IN THE SOFTWARE WILL MEET YOUR REQUIREMENTS OR THAT THE OPERATION OF THE SOFTWARE WILL BE ERROR FREE.

(c) This limited warranty gives you specific legal rights, and you may have other rights that vary from jurisdiction to jurisdiction.

6. Remedies.

(a) WPI's entire liability and your exclusive remedy for defects in materials and workmanship shall be limited to replacement of the Software Media, which may be returned to WPI with a copy of your receipt at the following address: Software Media Fulfillment Department, Attn.: *MCTS: Microsoft Exchange Server 2007 Configuration Study Guide*, Wiley Publishing, Inc., 10475 Crosspoint Blvd., Indianapolis, IN 46256, or call 1-800-762-2974. Please allow four to six weeks for delivery. This Limited Warranty is void if failure of the Software Media has resulted from accident, abuse, or misapplication. Any replacement Software Media will be warranted for the remainder of the original warranty period or thirty (30) days, whichever is longer.

(b) In no event shall WPI or the author be liable for any damages whatsoever (including without limitation damages for loss of business profits, business interruption, loss of business information, or any other pecuniary loss) arising from the use of or inability to use the Book or the Software, even if WPI has been advised of the possibility of such damages.

(c) Because some jurisdictions do not allow the exclusion or limitation of liability for consequential or incidental damages, the above limitation or exclusion may not apply to you.

7. U.S. Government Restricted Rights. Use, duplication, or disclosure of the Software for or on behalf of the United States of America, its agencies and/or instrumentalities "U.S. Government" is subject to restrictions as stated in paragraph (c)(1)(ii) of the Rights in Technical Data and Computer Software clause of DFARS 252.227-7013, or subparagraphs (c) (1) and (2) of the Commercial Computer Software - Restricted Rights clause at FAR 52.227-19, and in similar clauses in the NASA FAR supplement, as applicable.

8. General. This Agreement constitutes the entire understanding of the parties and revokes and supersedes all prior agreements, oral or written, between them and may not be modified or amended except in a writing signed by both parties hereto that specifically refers to this Agreement. This Agreement shall take precedence over any other documents that may be in conflict herewith. If any one or more provisions contained in this Agreement are held by any court or tribunal to be invalid, illegal, or otherwise unenforceable, each and every other provision shall remain in full force and effect.

The Absolute Best MCTS: Microsoft Exchange Serv 2007 Book/CD Package on the Market!

Get ready for the new MCTS: Microsoft Exchange Server 2007, Configuration exam (70-236) with the most comprehensive and challenging sample tests anywhere!

The Sybex Test Engine features:

- All the review questions, as covered in each chapter of the book
- Challenging questions representative of those you'll find on the real exam
- Two full length bonus exams available only on the CD
- An Assessment Test to narrow your focus to certain objective groups

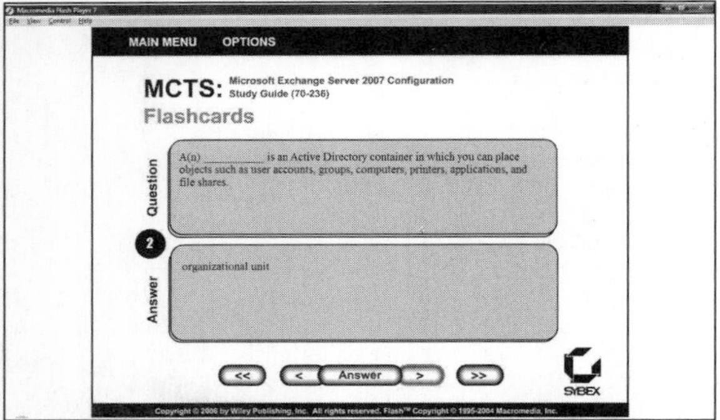

Search through the complete book in PDF!

- Access the entire *MCTS: Microsoft Exchange Server 2007 Configuration Study Guide,* complete with figures and tables, in electronic format.
- Search the *MCTS: Microsoft Exchange Server 2007 Configuration Study Guide* chapters to find information on any topic in seconds.

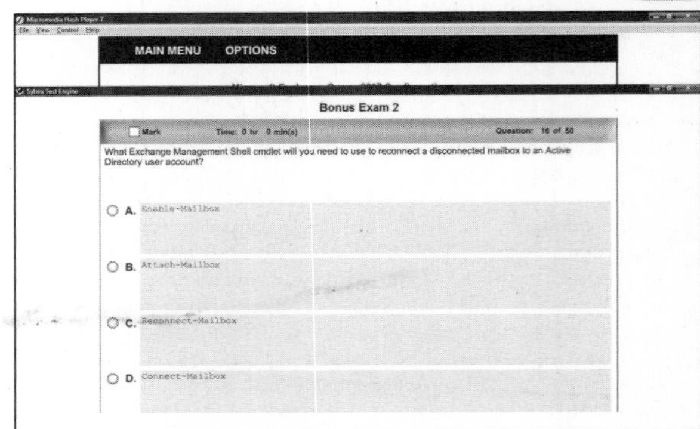

Use the Electronic Flashcards for PCs or Palm devices to jog your memory and prep last-minute for the exam!

- Reinforce your understanding of key concepts with these hardcore flashcard-style questions.
- Download the Flashcards to your Palm device and go on the road. Now you can study for the MCTS: Microsoft Exchange Server 2007, Configuration exam any time, anywhere.

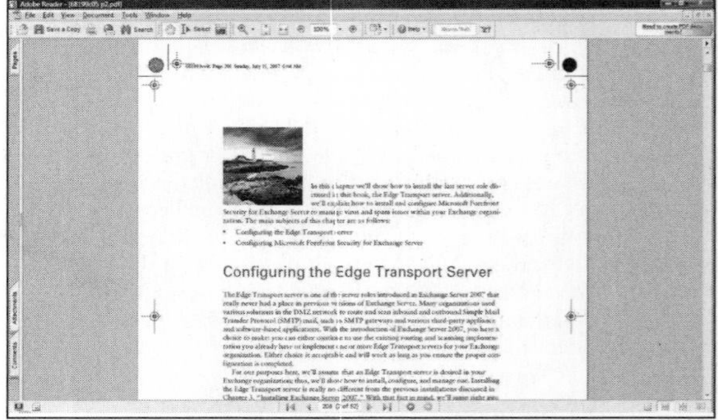